The CONNECTICUT RIVER FROM THE AIR

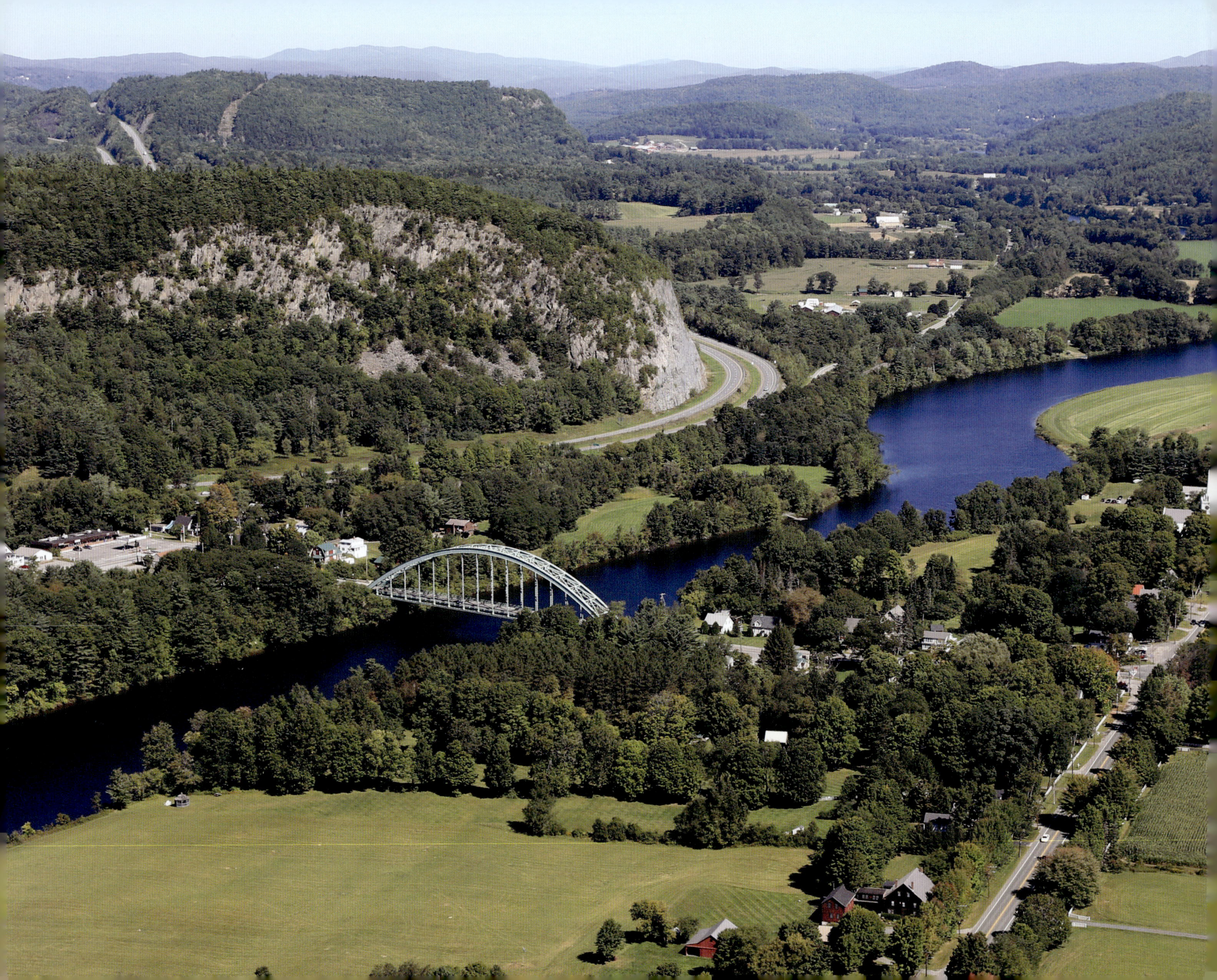

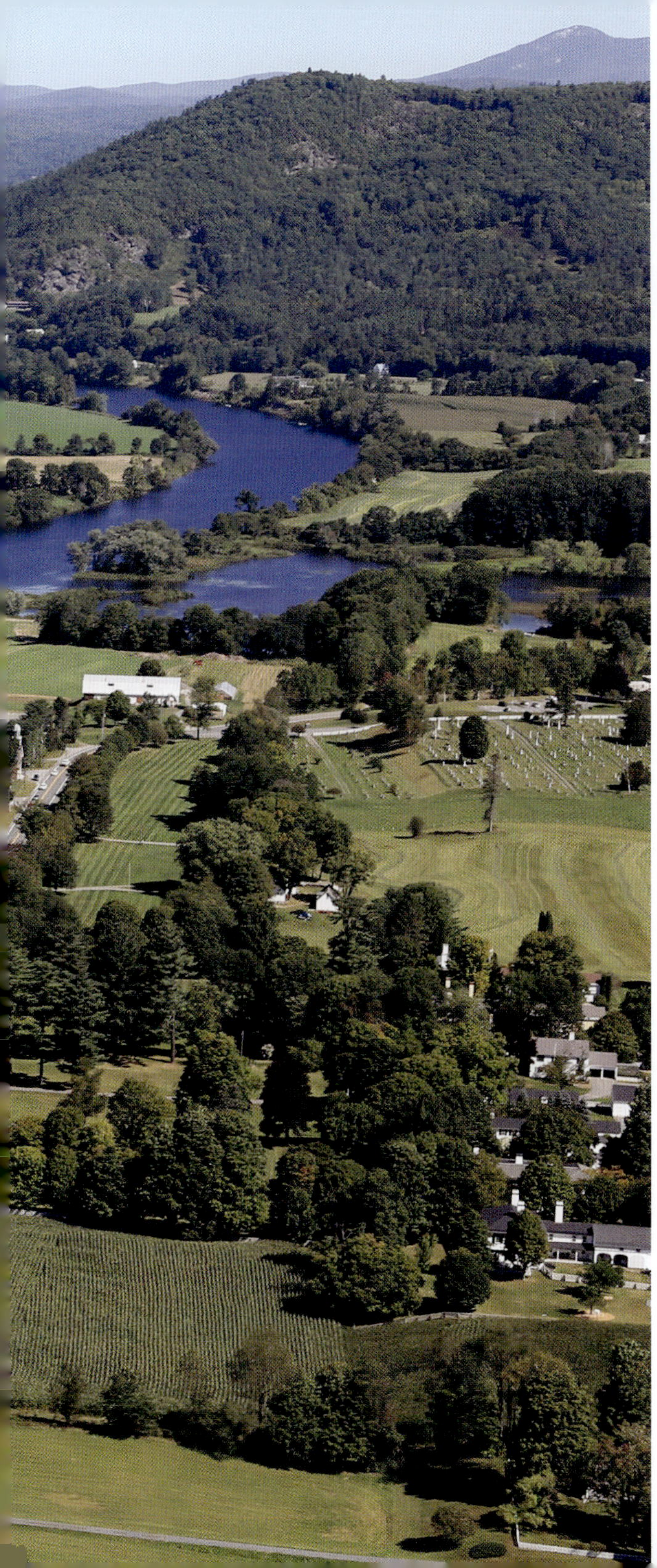

The CONNECTICUT RIVER FROM THE AIR

AN INTIMATE PERSPECTIVE OF NEW ENGLAND'S HISTORIC WATERWAY

JERRY ROBERTS | *Photography by Tom Walsh*

Globe Pequot

GUILFORD, CONNECTICUT

Globe Pequot

An imprint of The Rowman & Littlefield Publishing Group, Inc.
4501 Forbes Blvd., Ste. 200
Lanham, MD 20706
www.rowman.com

Distributed by NATIONAL BOOK NETWORK

All vintage images courtesy of the Connecticut River Museum unless otherwise noted.
Design by Nancy Freeborn

British Library Cataloguing in Publication Information Available

Library of Congress Cataloging-in-Publication Data Available

ISBN 978-1-4930-2772-9 (hardcover)
978-1-4930-2773-6 (e-book)

∞™ The paper used in this publication meets the minimum requirements of American National Standard for Information Sciences—Permanence of Paper for Printed Library Materials, ANSI/NISO Z39.48-1992.

Printed in the United States

MAJOR REGIONS *of the* RIVER

INTRODUCTION, ix

The Connecticut River can be divided into four distinct regions, from the deeply wooded forests near the Canadian border, through the fertile Upper and Middle Valleys, and down into the tidelands where the ocean's cycles influence the river's ecosystems.

ACKNOWLEDGMENTS, 236

ABOUT THE AUTHORS & PHOTOGRAPHER, 238

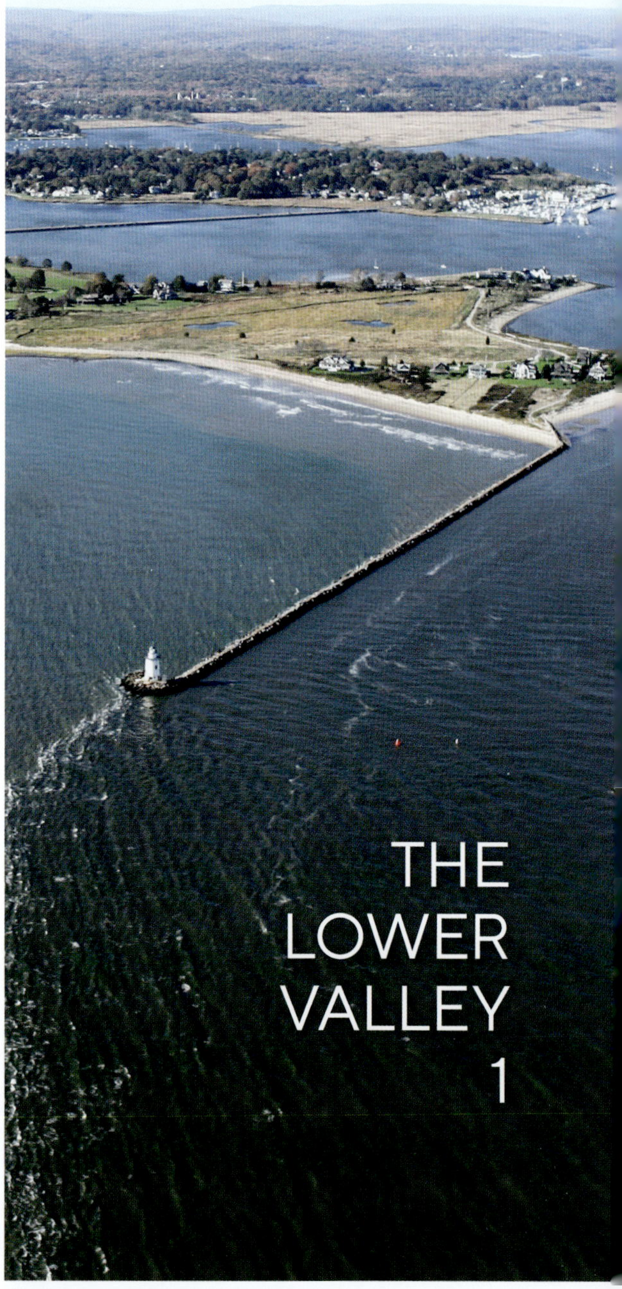

THE LOWER VALLEY 1

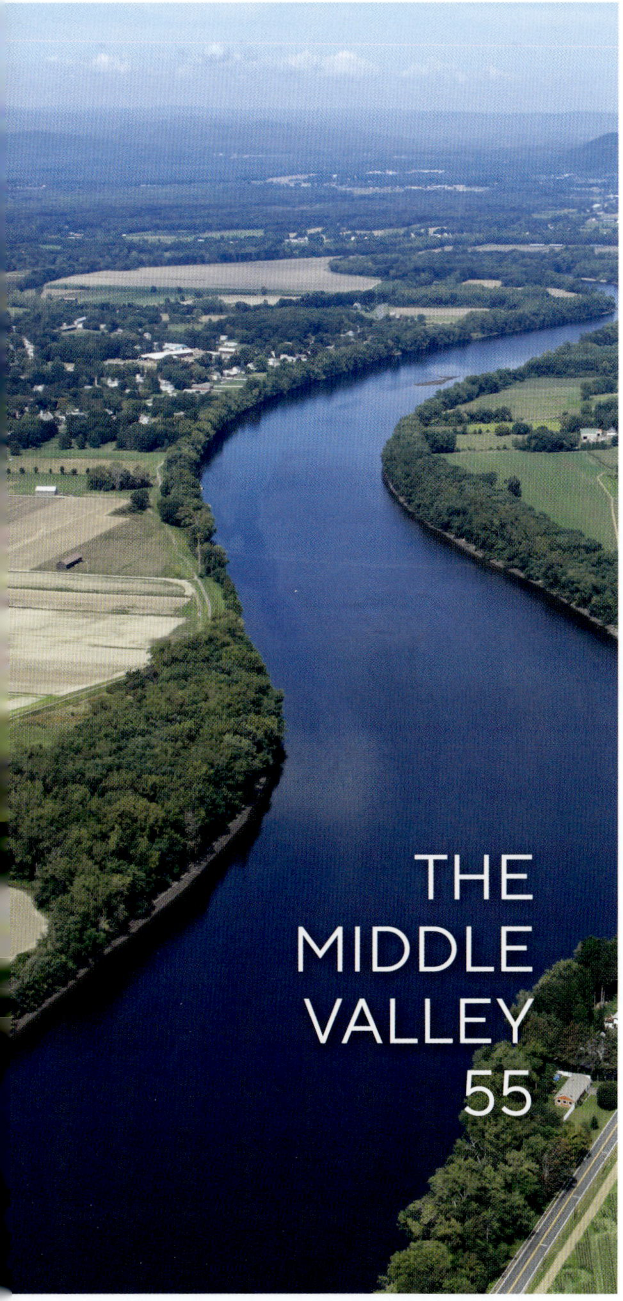

THE MIDDLE VALLEY 55

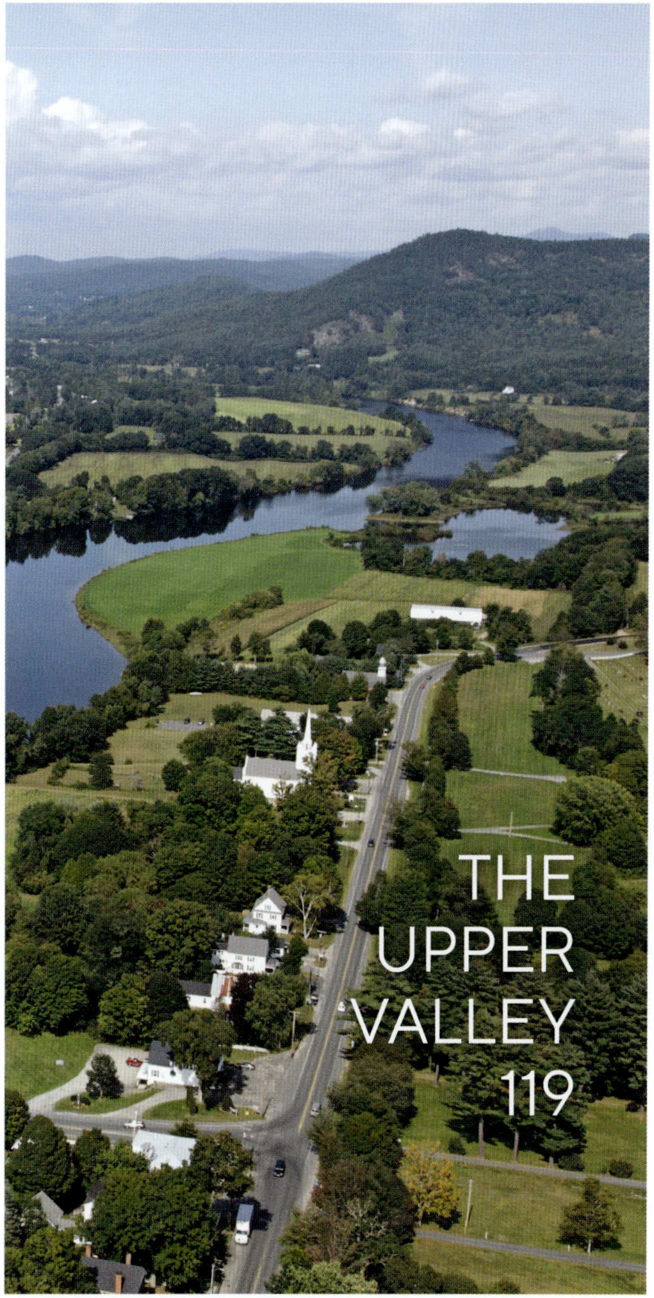

THE UPPER VALLEY 119

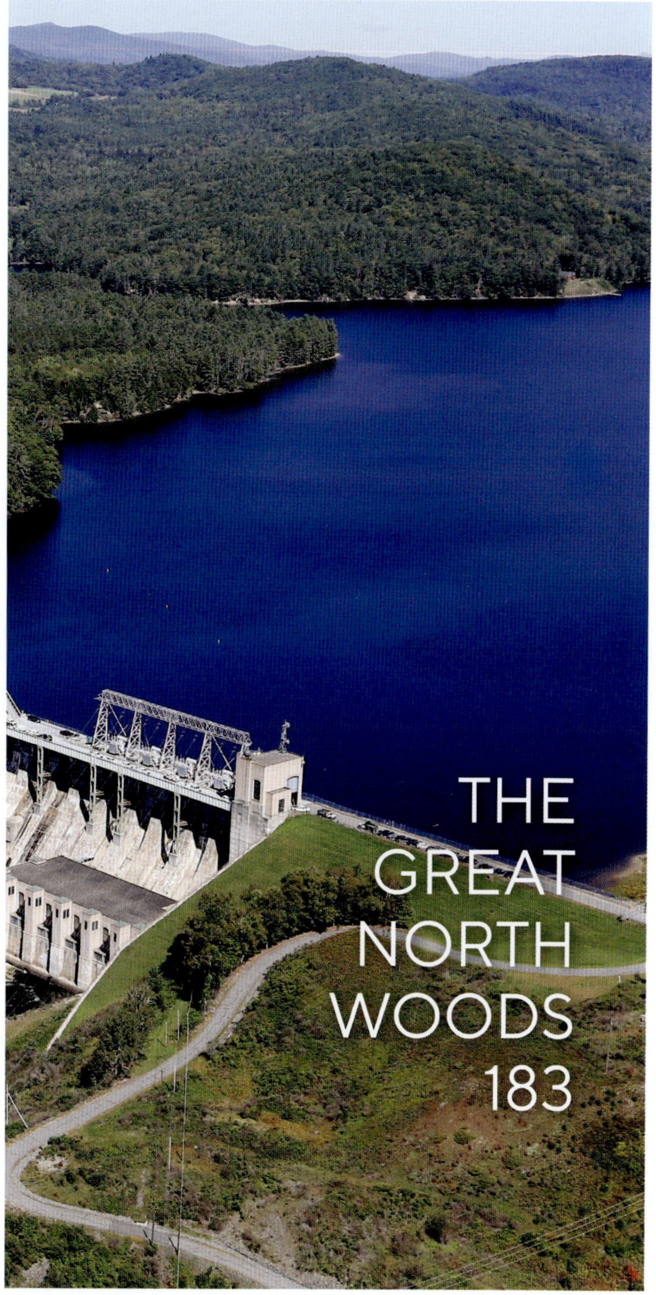

THE GREAT NORTH WOODS 183

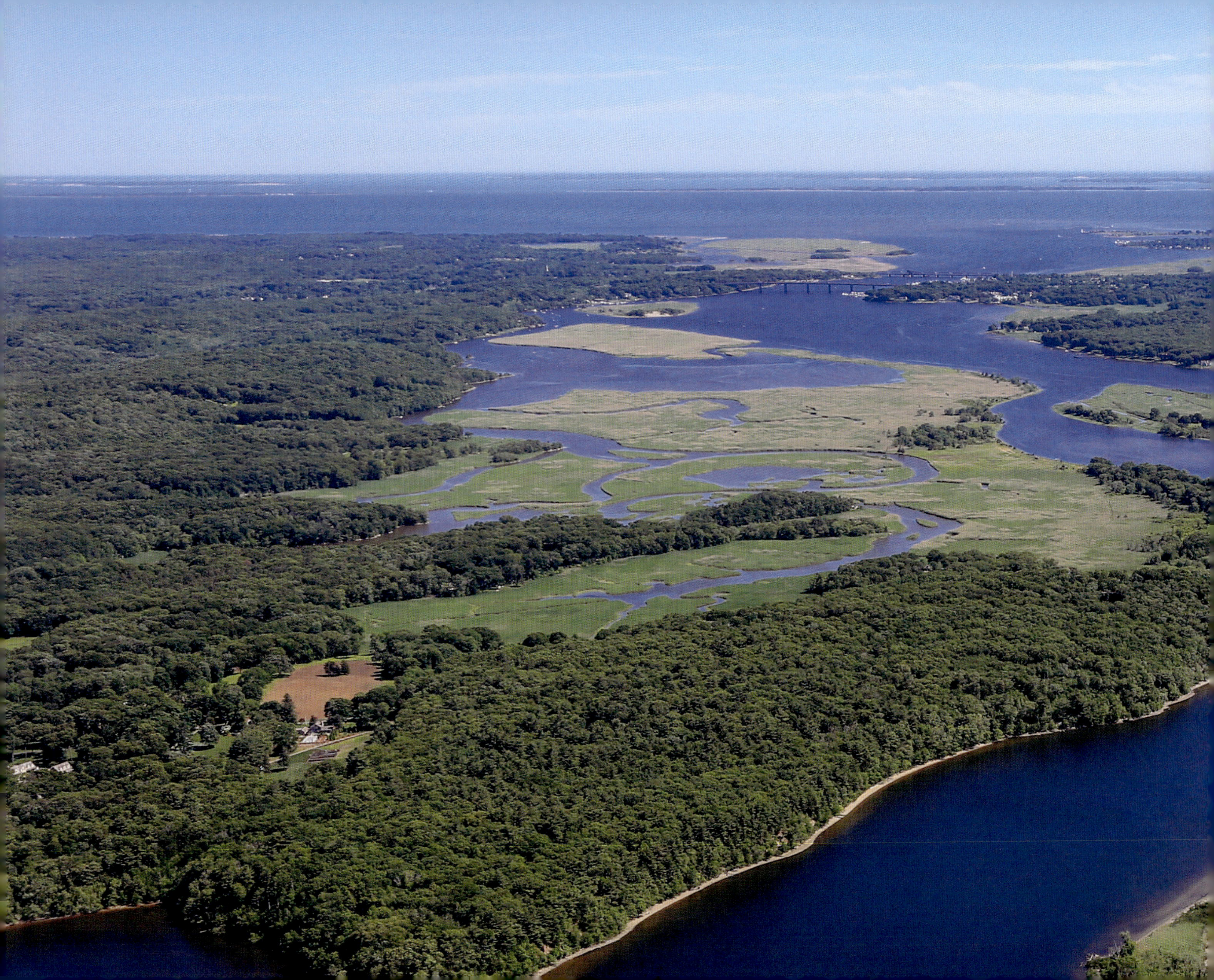

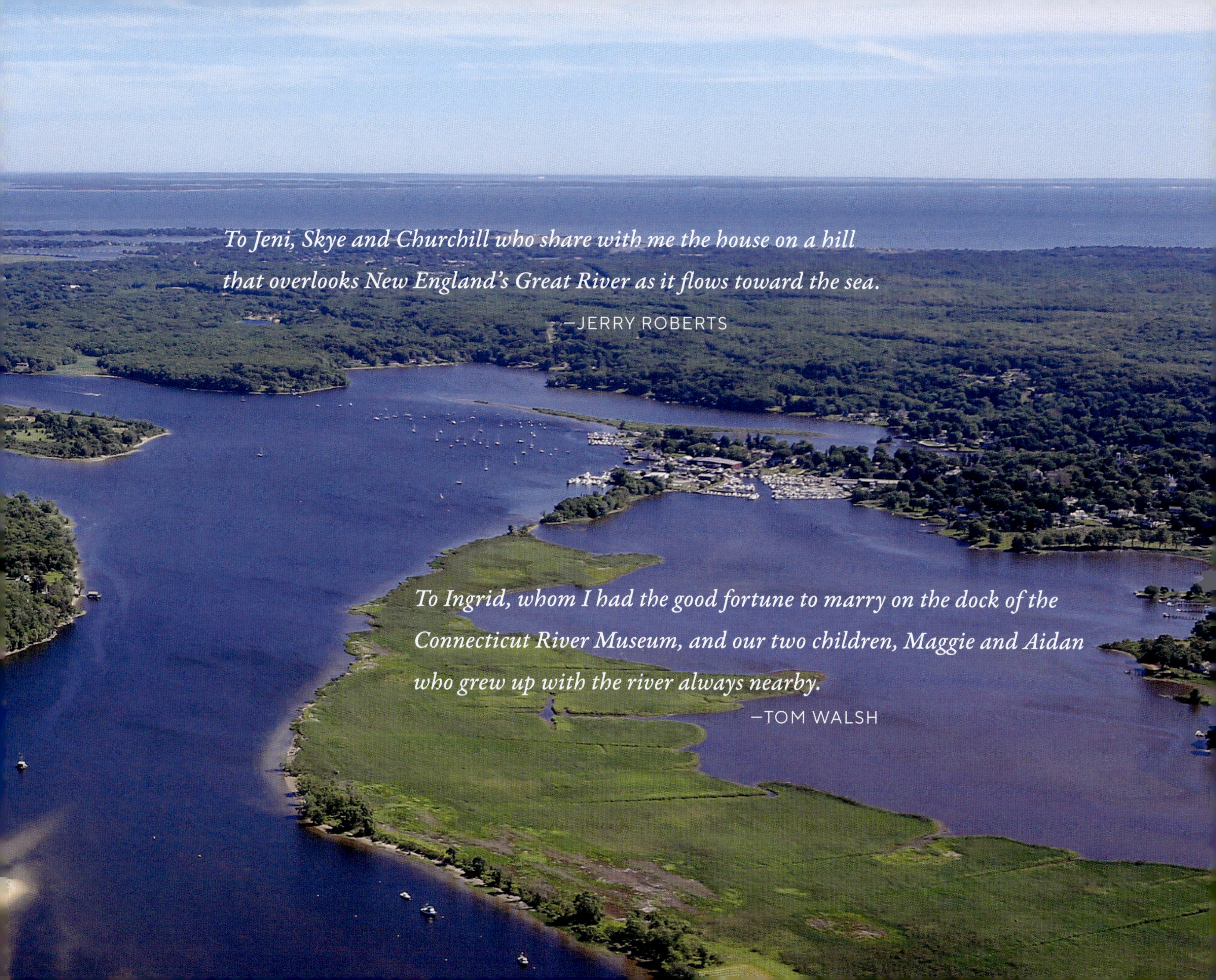

To Jeni, Skye and Churchill who share with me the house on a hill that overlooks New England's Great River as it flows toward the sea.

—JERRY ROBERTS

To Ingrid, whom I had the good fortune to marry on the dock of the Connecticut River Museum, and our two children, Maggie and Aidan who grew up with the river always nearby.

—TOM WALSH

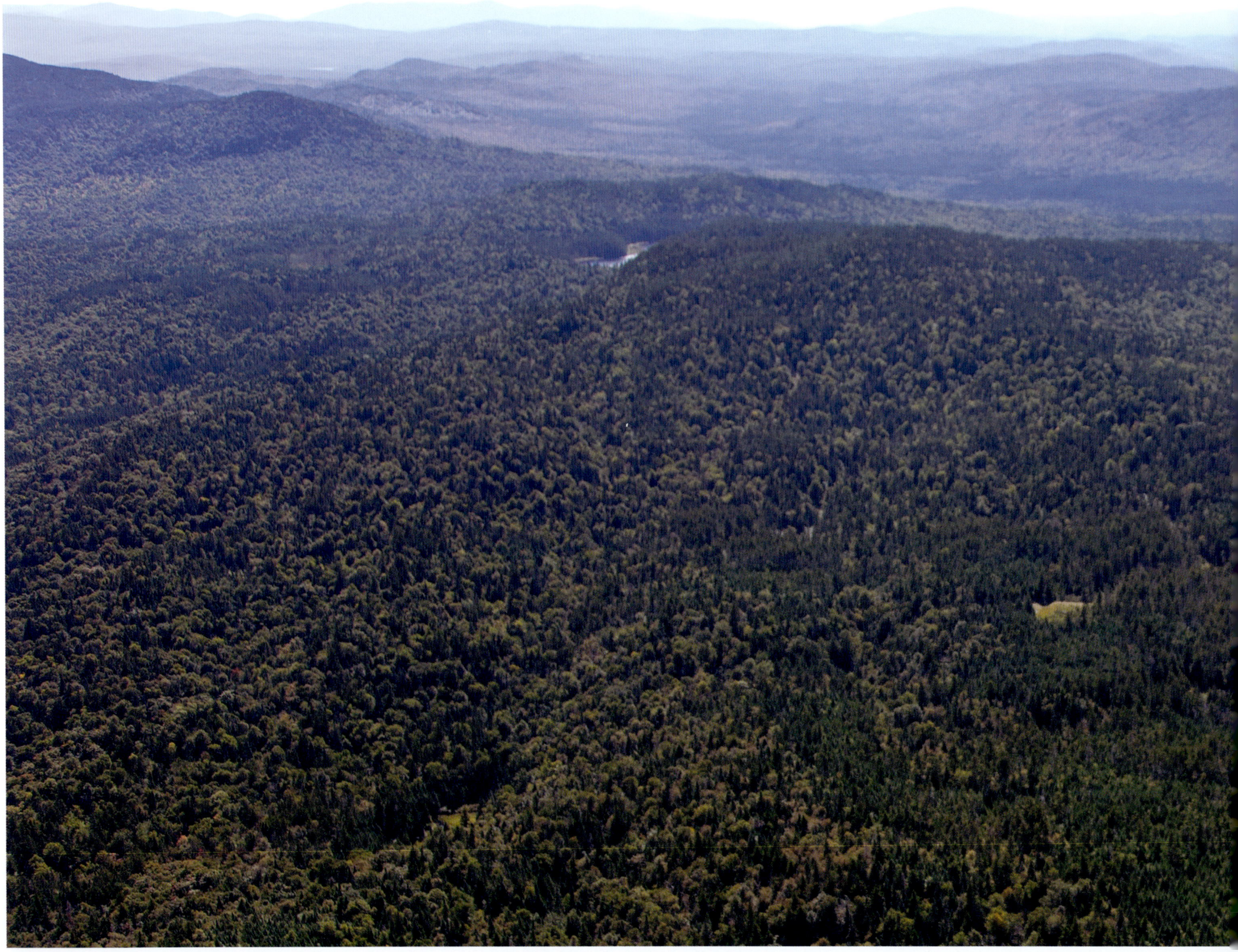

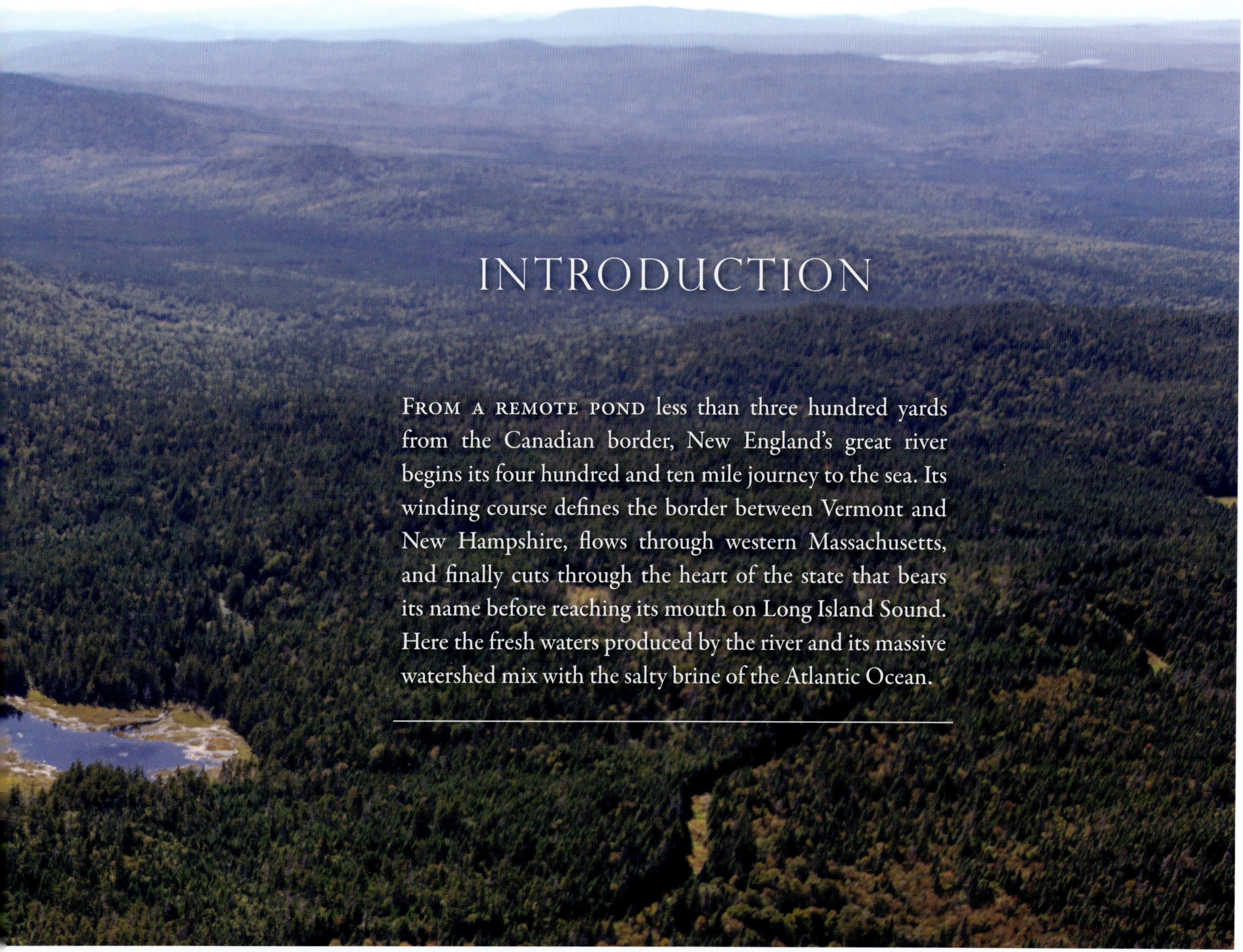

INTRODUCTION

FROM A REMOTE POND less than three hundred yards from the Canadian border, New England's great river begins its four hundred and ten mile journey to the sea. Its winding course defines the border between Vermont and New Hampshire, flows through western Massachusetts, and finally cuts through the heart of the state that bears its name before reaching its mouth on Long Island Sound. Here the fresh waters produced by the river and its massive watershed mix with the salty brine of the Atlantic Ocean.

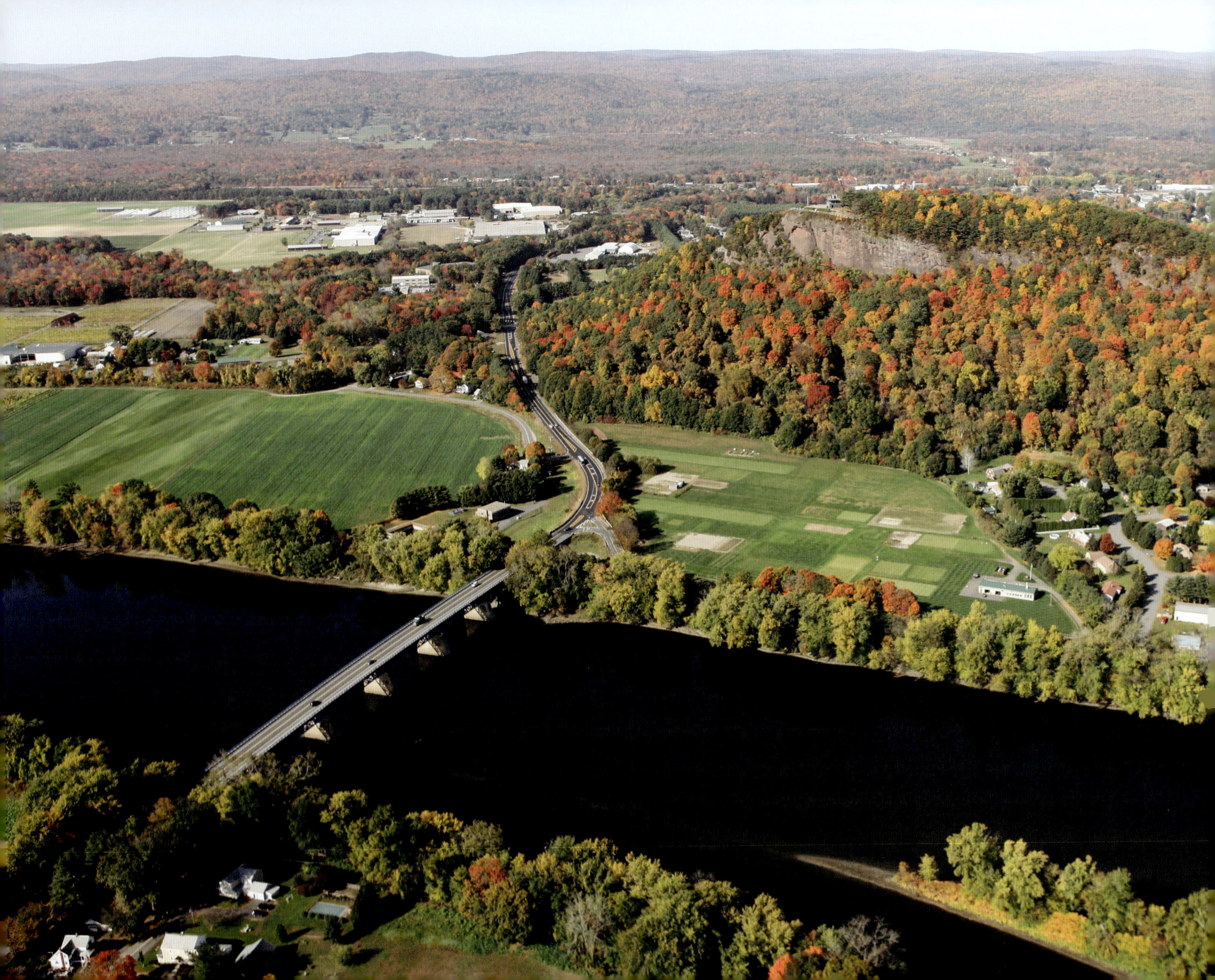

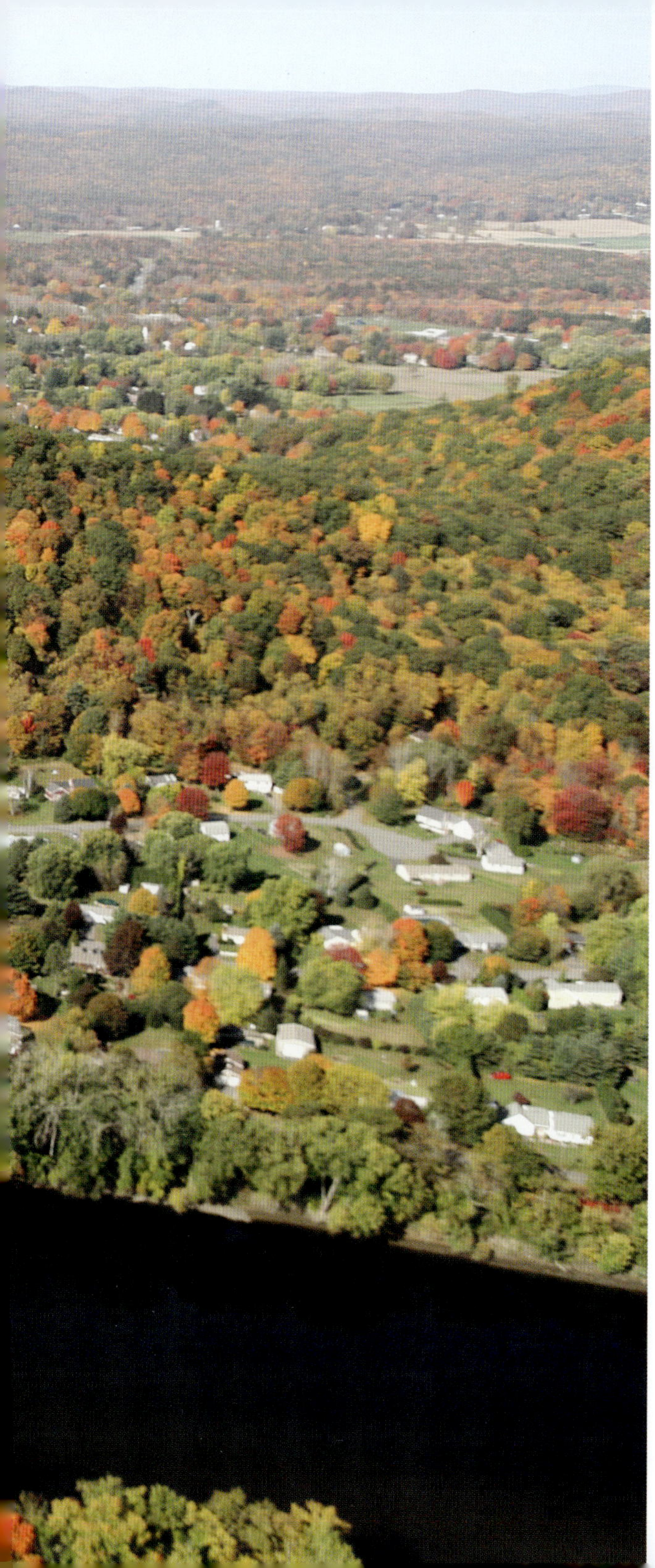

The word Connecticut is a colonial bastardization of the Native American word Quonehtacut, or Quinatucquet, meaning *long tidal river*. Before Dutch explorer Adrian Block became the first European to venture up its course in 1614, the Connecticut had provided both sustenance and mobility to the Native peoples who had already lived along its banks for thousands of years. It is a waterway steeped in history and flowing with natural beauty and environmental diversity.

The River has played an important role in the settlement of colonial America and the growth of the United States. Before there were roads, it was the river that allowed the first Europeans to make their way inland from the sea. It linked the communities that sprang up along its course and, in a very real sense, served as a gateway into the heart of what would become New England.

The swift current of the river and its tributaries would eventually help power the mills and factories of the industrial revolution while its majesty and energy has inspired artists, entrepreneurs, industrialists, and environmental activists alike. It has been celebrated and cherished, used and abused, and choked with pollution. By the mid 20th Century it teetered on the brink of ecological disaster. Katherine Hepburn, who lived at the mouth of the river, once referred to it as "the world's most beautiful open sewer." But with the environmental movement of the 1960s, culminating in the Clean Water Act in 1972, the great river began to make a remarkable comeback and is now considered one of the cleanest major waterways in America. In 1997 it was named as one of only fourteen American Heritage Rivers, and in 2012 it became the first river to be designated as a National Blueway noted for its diverse ecosystems.

Along many stretches, the river appears locked in time and looks much as it might have to its original inhabitants and early explorers. Despite the reversal of its ecological fate however, ongoing threats remain. Areas that were once farmlands or wooded enclaves continue to be encroached upon by development and urbanization. Combined sewage outflow and agricul-

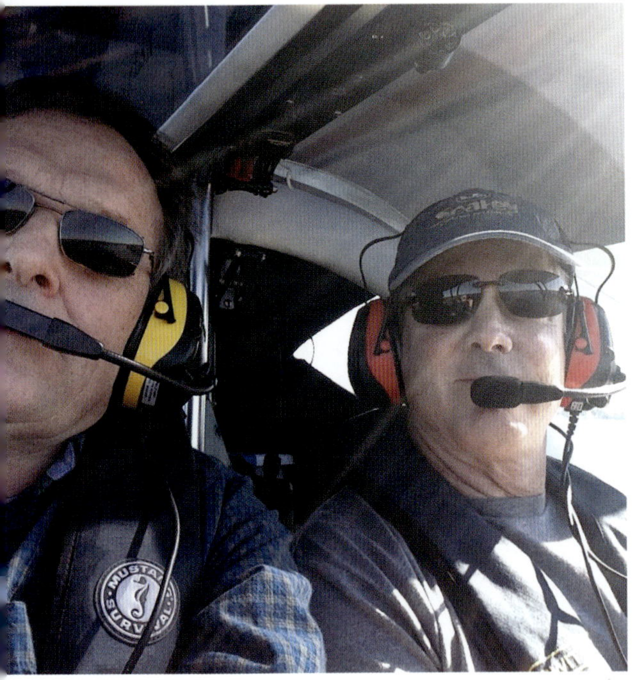

Jerry and Tom over the river.

tural run-off continue to leach into the river. Yet the Connecticut remains one of the most beautiful rivers in the developed world, especially considering that it flows through the heart of one the nation's most populated areas, halfway between New York and Boston.

THE VIEW FROM ABOVE

From the cockpit of a canoe or kayak, a sailing vessel or powerboat, the river can appear two dimensional with its vast miles of forests and hills, interspersed with towns and cities, masking the interior just beyond its banks. But from the air the Connecticut River is revealed to full scope and scale as it cuts its way through both changing landscapes and changing times. It is only from the air that many hidden treasures, amazing vistas, vast woodlands, and productive farmlands can be fully appreciated... and the advance of urban sprawl recognized.

I came to the river in 2006 after living in Manhattan, an island city on another great river, to serve as executive director of the Connecticut River Museum in Essex. Six miles up from the river's mouth, the museum chronicles the history and environmental majesty of this great waterway. One of my Manhattan fantasies was to live in a small New England village and walk down to the docks with a cup of coffee and shoot the breeze with local sailors and fisherman. Essex, a twenty-first century Brigadoon, first settled in 1648, is certainly the place to do it. While I have, in fact, met plenty of New England Yankees and characters straight out of Central Casting, one of the most interesting locals I bumped into turned out to be an unexpected catch.

Tom Walsh is not a sailor or a fisherman. He is a pilot. Not just a guy who flies airplanes on the weekend, although he does plenty of that, Tom was a fighter pilot in the United States Marine Corps and now flies large airliners internationally out of JFK. As if that isn't enough, in his "off-time" he flies his own small aircraft and runs a one-man aerial photography company. Armed only with a hand held, gyro stabilized, high resolution camera Tom has photographed thousands of sites all over New England and beyond for hundreds of clients from individuals to municipalities. He routinely sees the world from a very different perspective than most of us. Looking out the window of an airliner flying six miles above the earth is one thing, but soaring above the landscape down low in a small aircraft is quite another experience altogether.

In 2009 I asked Tom if I could use a handful of his stock images to create an exhibit at the River Museum. He in turn suggested that he could provide an even more comprehensive selection of images if

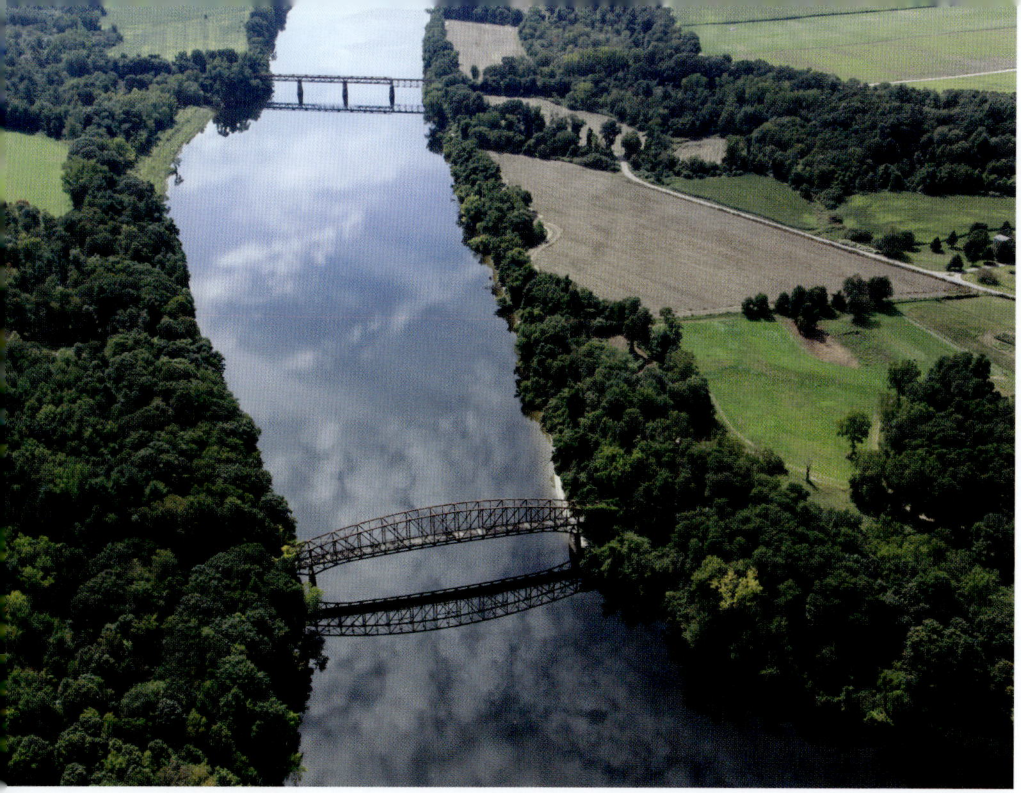

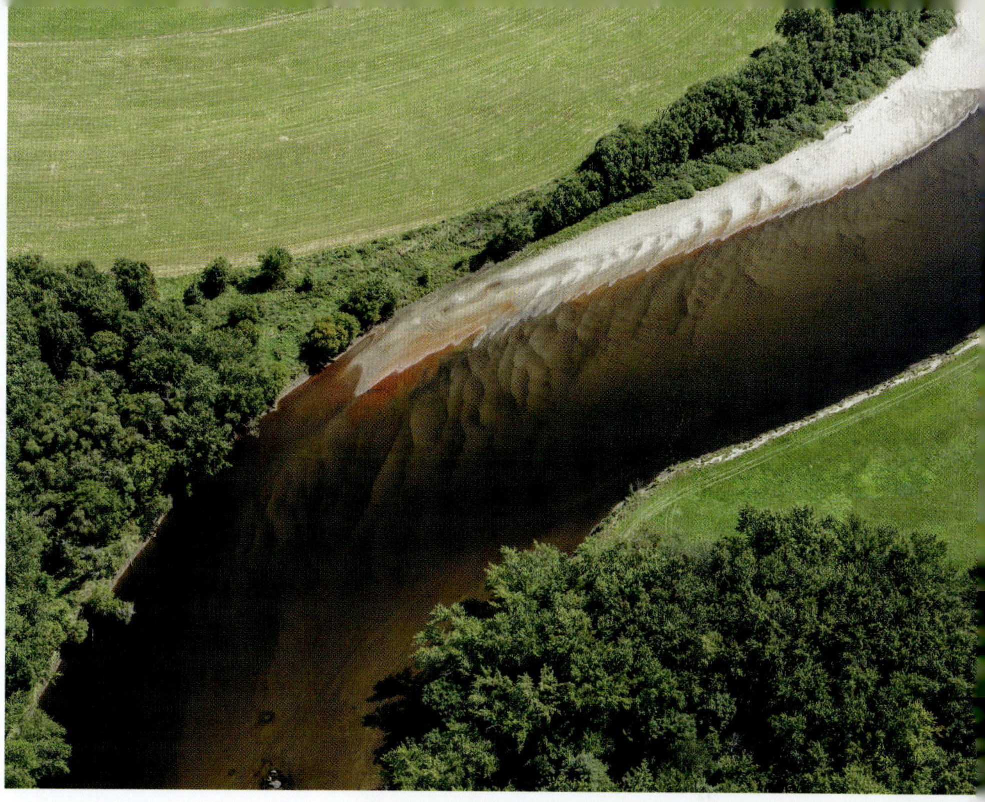

we would just cover the fuel costs for another flight or two. In fact, he ended up flying all the way to the river's source at the Canadian border and all the way back again the next day, just to make sure we had enough material for the exhibit. The resulting images were astounding and the exhibit was a big success. The project represented the most comprehensive documentation of the river from the air since one carried out in 1934 by the US Geological Survey. Those images were shot in black and white and from such a high altitude that, while capturing the big picture, lacked the intimacy found when flying a few hundred feet above the landscape. Tom's images capture every bend and twist, every bridge, village, dam and city, and even the patterns sculpted into the river bottom by its ever-flowing waters.

With the exhibit installed, I then asked Tom to take some aerial photos for a War of 1812 battle site archaeology project I was coordinating along the river. This led to several more photographic expeditions to support other projects I was working on. Through all of this we began kicking around the obvious idea of a book. When I took over the New England Air Museum in 2015, the idea of chronicling the region's great river from the air became a no-brainer. The time had come.

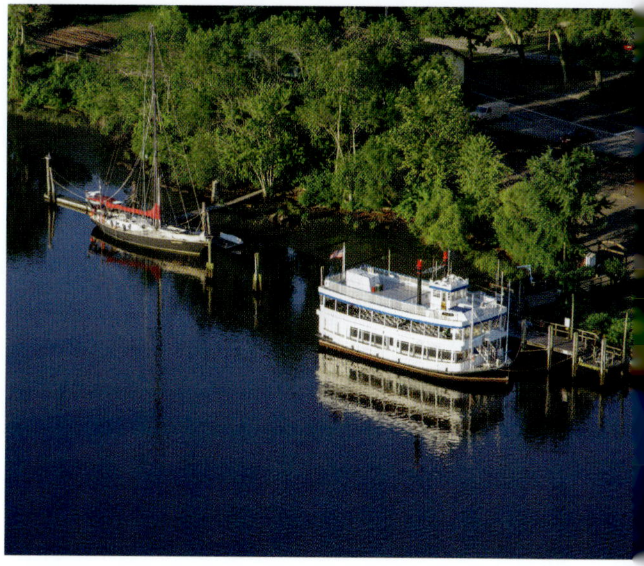

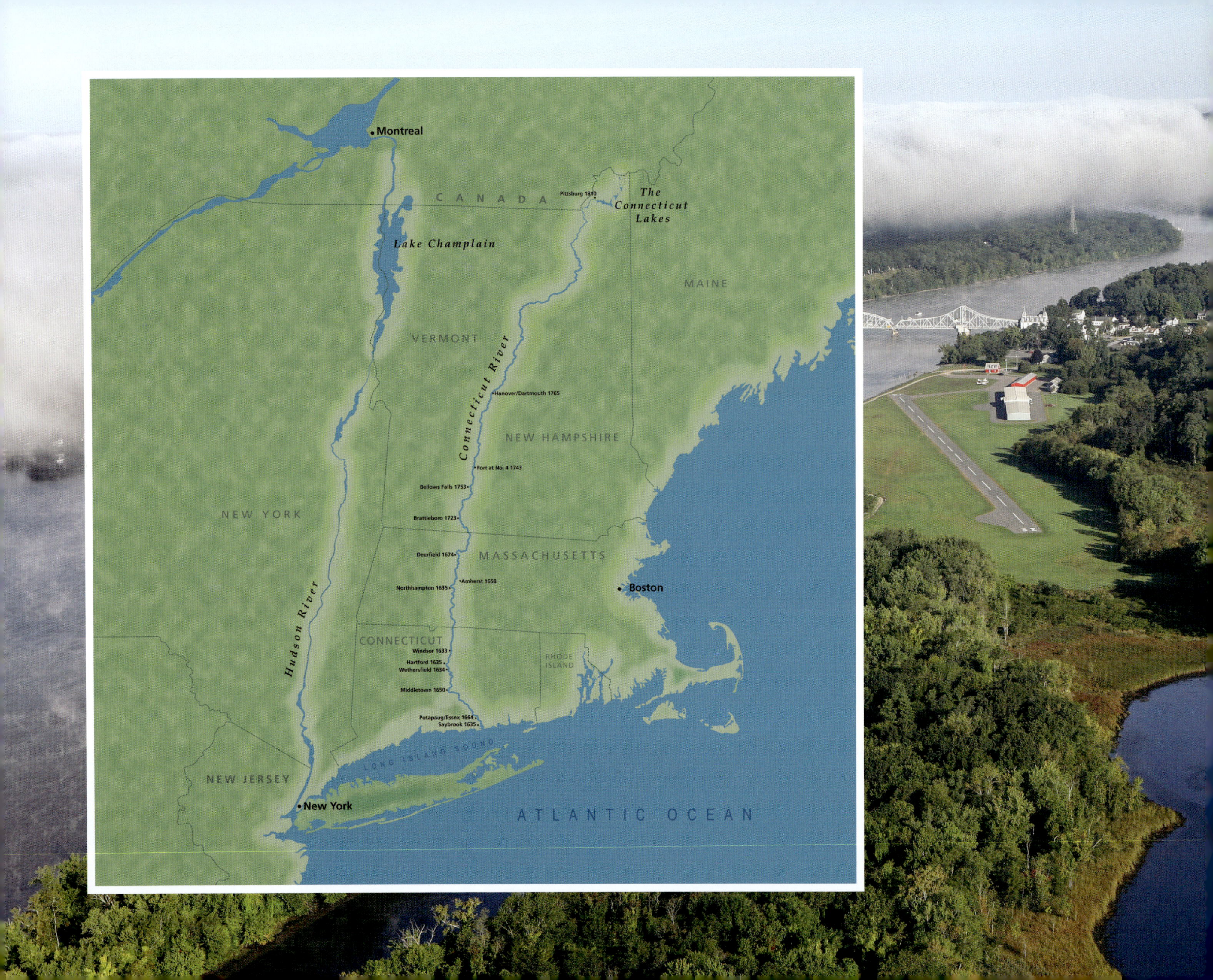
Montreal
CANADA
Pittsburg 1810
The Connecticut Lakes
Lake Champlain
MAINE
VERMONT
Connecticut River
Hanover/Dartmouth 1765
NEW HAMPSHIRE
Fort at No. 4 1743
Bellows Falls 1753
Brattleboro 1723
NEW YORK
Deerfield 1674
MASSACHUSETTS
Amherst 1658
Northhampton 1635
Boston
Hudson River
CONNECTICUT
Windsor 1633
Hartford 1635
Wethersfield 1634
RHODE ISLAND
Middletown 1650
Potapaug/Essex 1664
Saybrook 1635
LONG ISLAND SOUND
NEW JERSEY
New York
ATLANTIC OCEAN

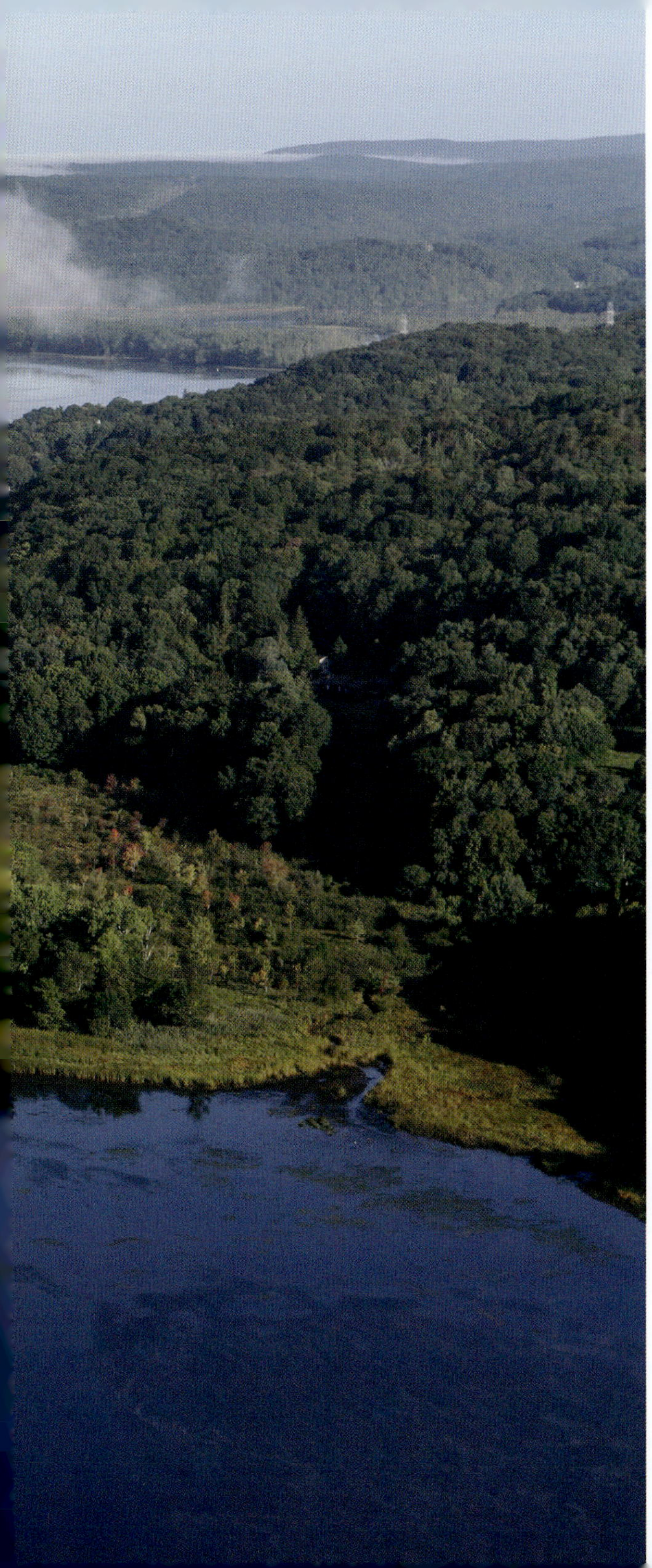

WHERE TO START?

When deciding how to lay out this aerial adventure above the longest river in New England there were two obvious choices. First, we could follow the water from its source to its mouth with the story growing in velocity and volume along with the river. Having been brought up reading Holling C. Holling's *Paddle to the Sea*, this was very appealing. I even imagined following a theoretical drop of water as it made its way from that little pond in the distant North past forests, under bridges, over dams, in between towns, villages and eventually cities before it reached the sea. I wondered how this journey might affect that drop and how different it would be by the time it reached the Sound.

The other option was to begin at the river's mouth and make our way north, much like Adrian Block and those who followed, as well as Tom's initial flight for the exhibit. This would allow us to begin with the familiar populated and urbanized areas near the coast and then venture inland in the spirit of 19th Century explorers searching for the source of the Nile.

In one direction the river and its story grows as it flows toward the sea. In the other we begin with the more well-traveled parts of the river and move north to explore the remote towns, farmlands, forests and hillsides hundreds of miles from the Connecticut coast.

There was a third option as well. That was to follow an historical timeline, visiting towns and villages in the order of their establishment. Looking at the settlement dates of each town generally leads from south to north, but the progression was not always geographically linear. There was a lot of leap-frogging by the Dutch and the English, and even competing groups of English settlers, each trying to control trade with the Native peoples by getting higher up the river. This was most often accomplished by water but sometimes by overland routes from the Massachusetts coast. Geography and geology also offered challenges to settlement patterns.

In the end we decided to begin, like most explorers, at the river's broad mouth and work our way upstream. To that end, unless otherwise noted, all of the images in this book look to the north towards the river's source. Of course, if *you* prefer to start at the other end you can simply turn to the last page and make your way downstream along with that theoretical drop of water. Regardless of where you begin, this is a voyage worth taking, an adventure worth having. From the air you will see more than any mariner or terrestrial explorer ever imagined, and we promise you won't even get your feet wet. So adjust your seat backs to the upright position, buckle that belt, and hold onto your hat... we're flying low and slow with the windows open. See you at the other end!

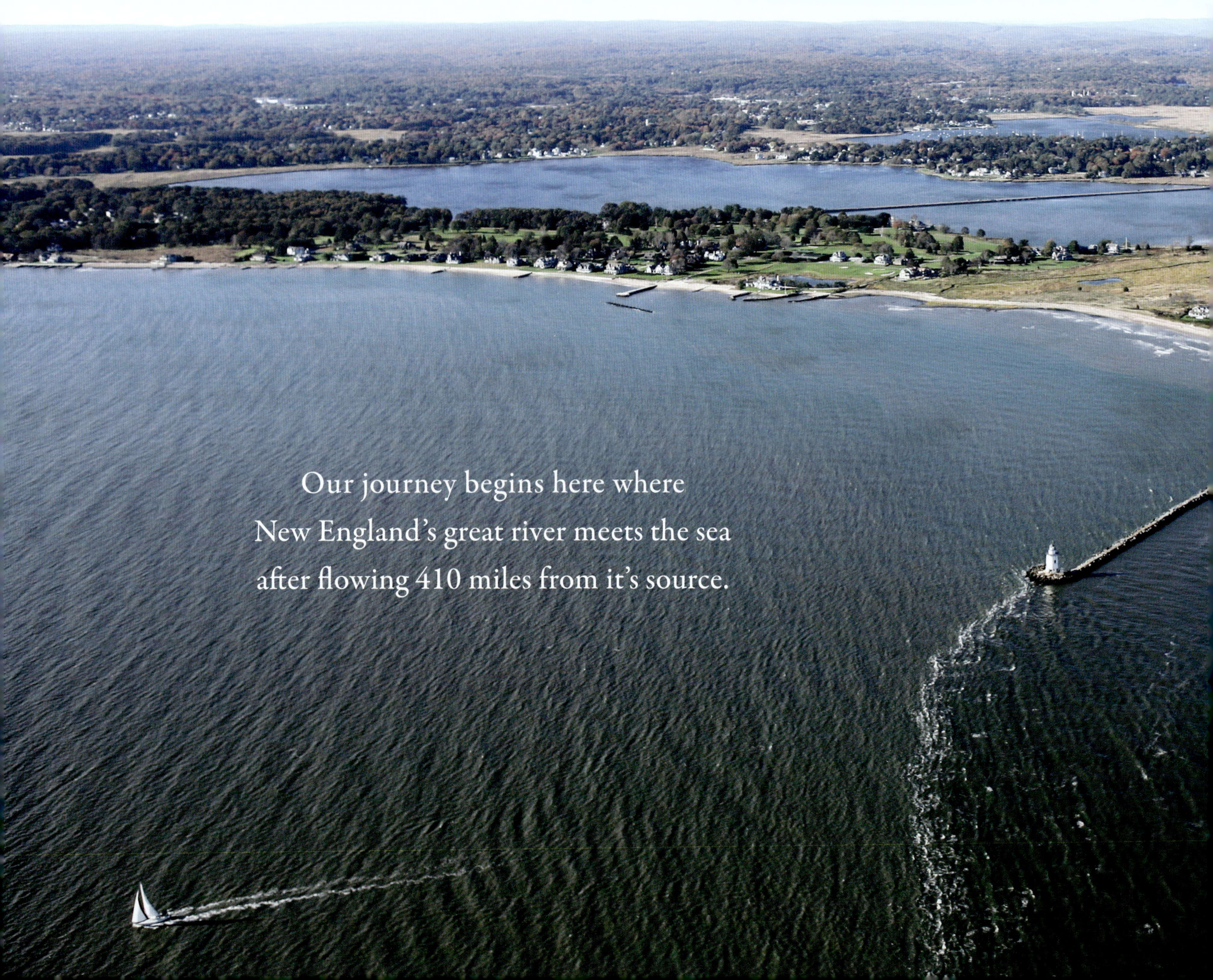

Our journey begins here where
New England's great river meets the sea
after flowing 410 miles from it's source.

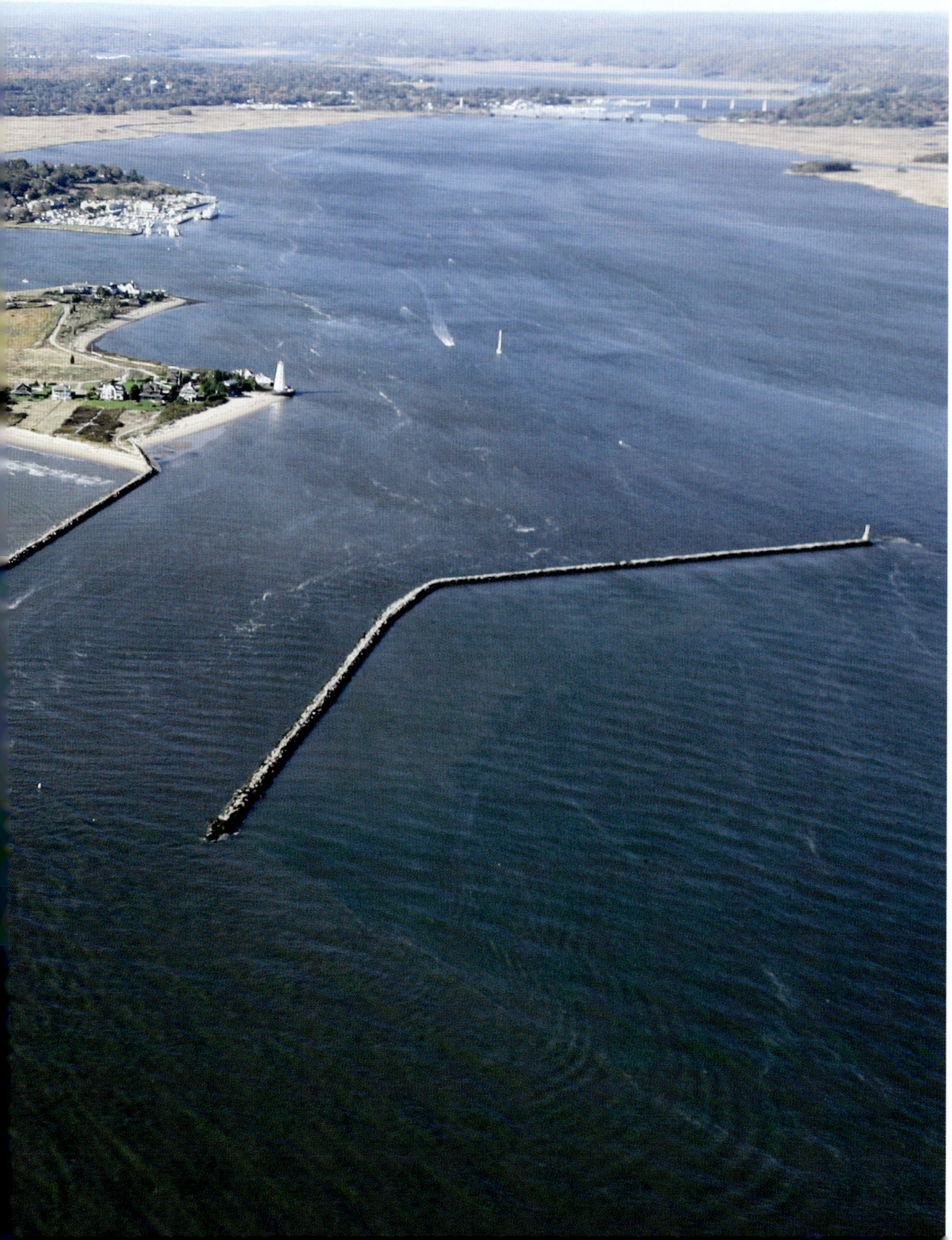

THE FIRST HUNDRED MILES

Long Island Sound to Holyoke, Massachusetts

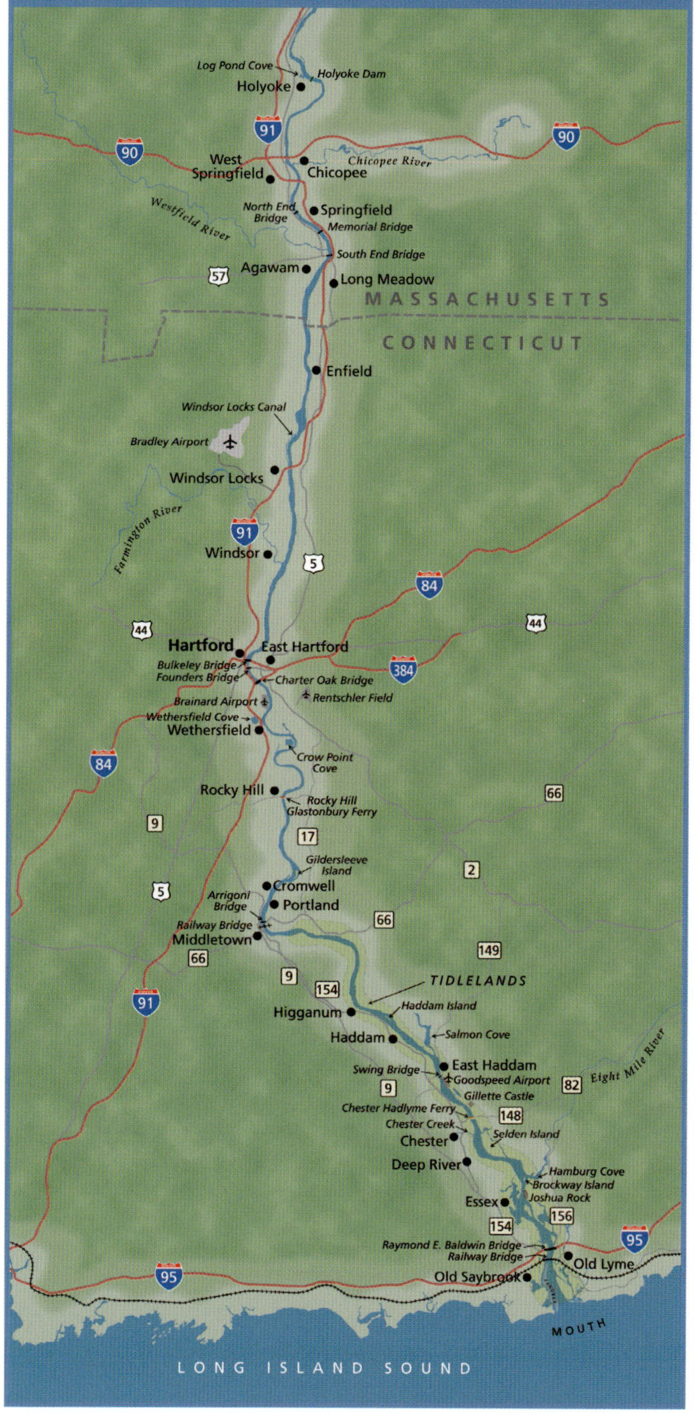

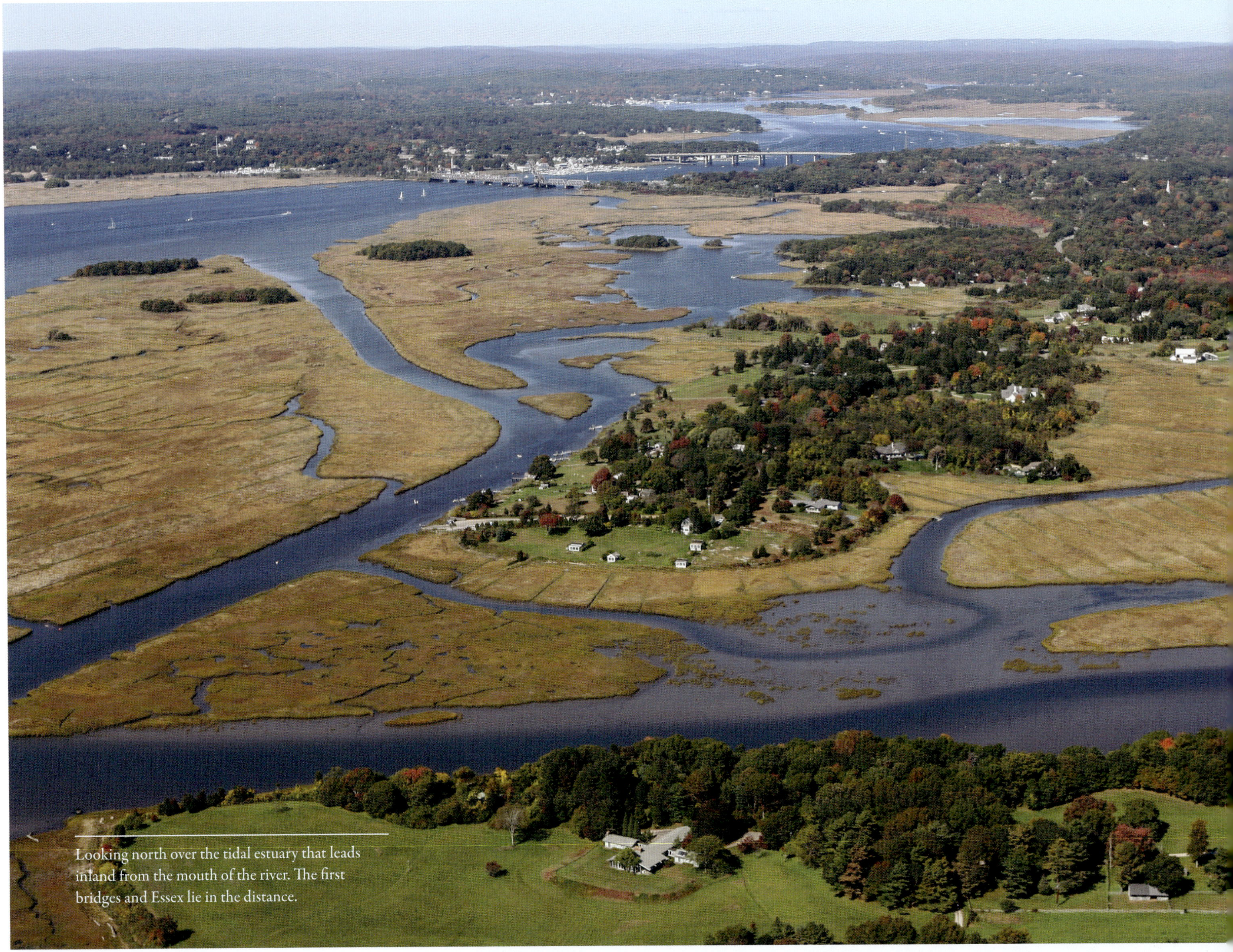

Looking north over the tidal estuary that leads inland from the mouth of the river. The first bridges and Essex lie in the distance.

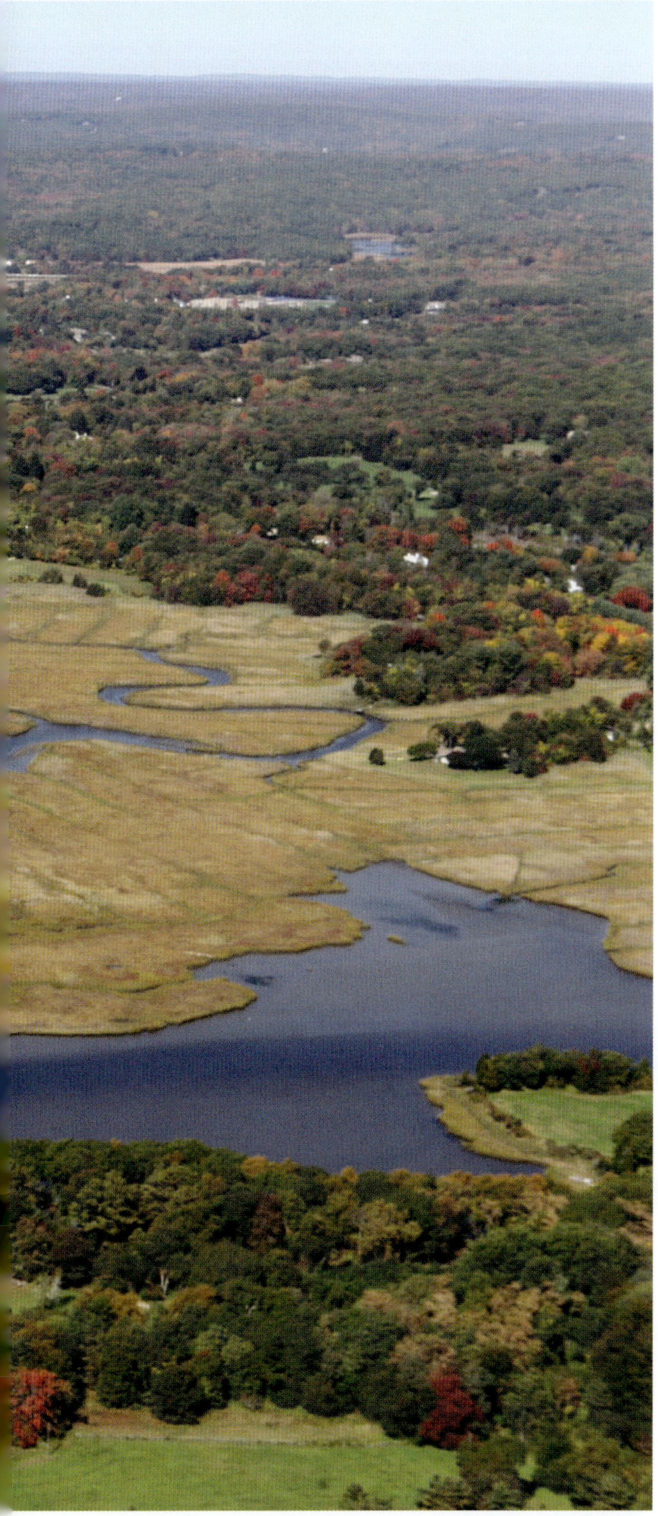

THE LOWER VALLEY

Also known as the Tidelands this lower thirty mile stretch of river runs from Middletown, Connecticut down to Long Island Sound. Here at its mouth tidal wetlands form a unique and environmentally important ecosystem. Although saltwater does not reach further north than Essex, six miles upriver, the rise and fall of the ocean's tide extends as far north as Hartford. This stretch of the river was dominated by shipbuilding and maritime trade, which connected river ports to markets along the Eastern seaboard, across the Atlantic to the West Indies, and beyond.

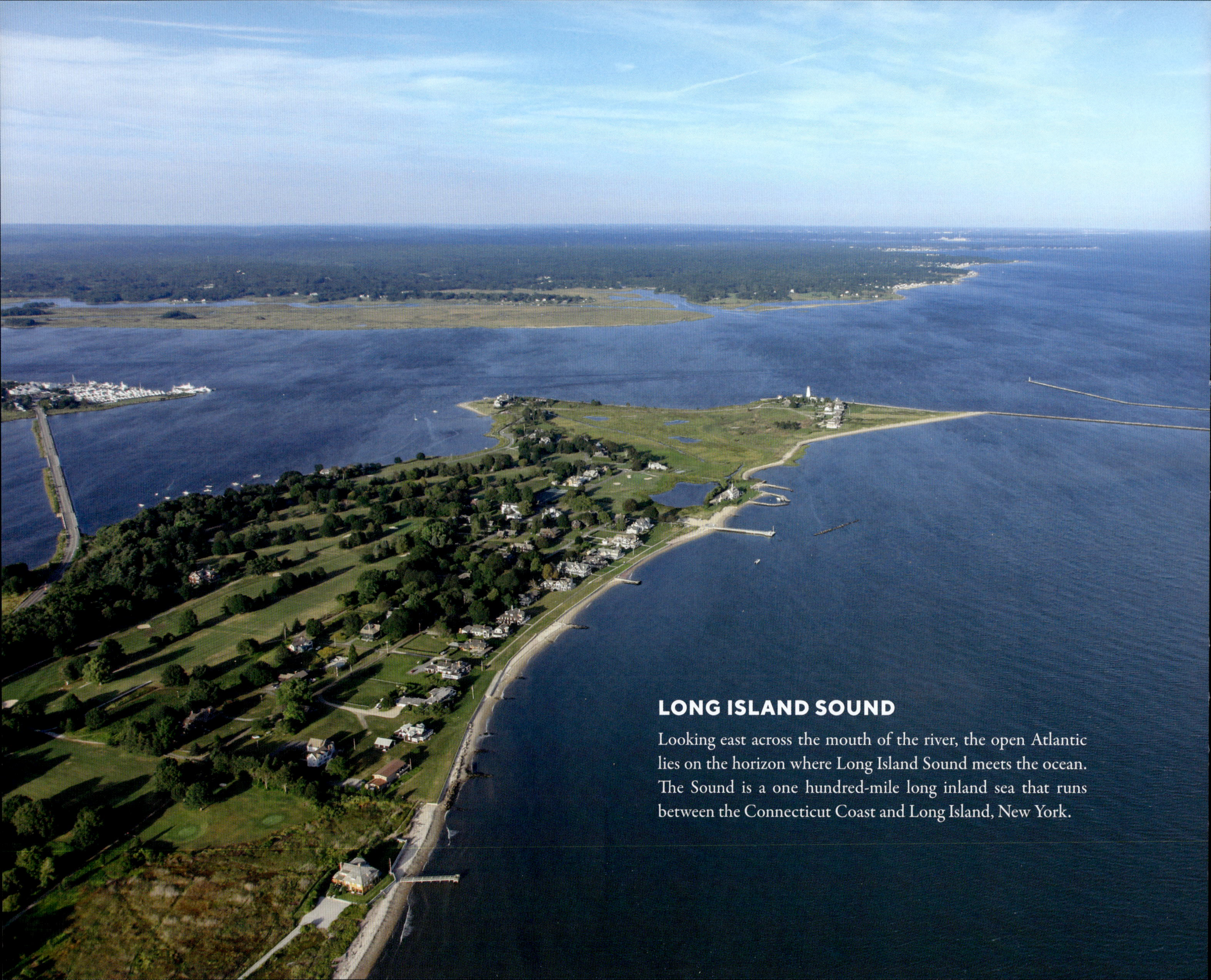

LONG ISLAND SOUND

Looking east across the mouth of the river, the open Atlantic lies on the horizon where Long Island Sound meets the ocean. The Sound is a one hundred-mile long inland sea that runs between the Connecticut Coast and Long Island, New York.

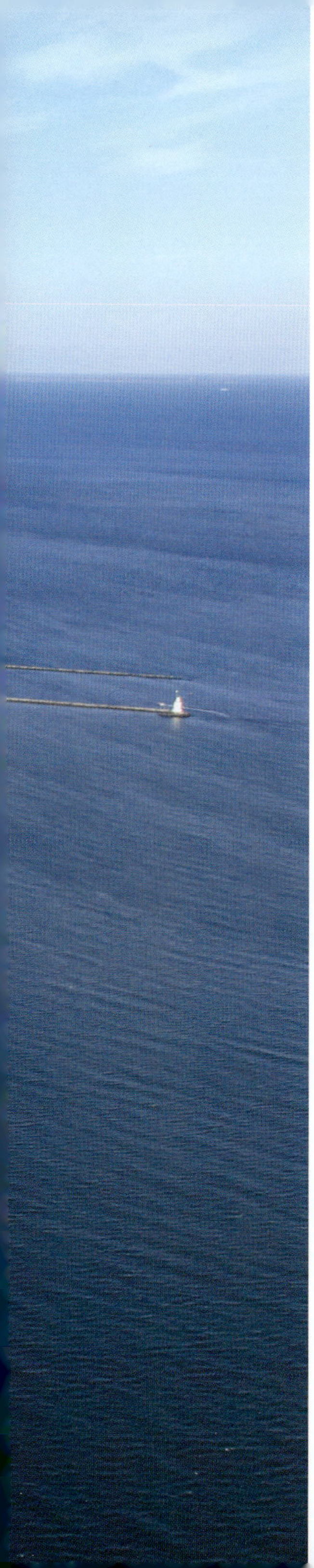

THE MOUTH

Looking north into the river's mouth, a plume of fresh water pours through the jetties that mark the dredged entry channel.

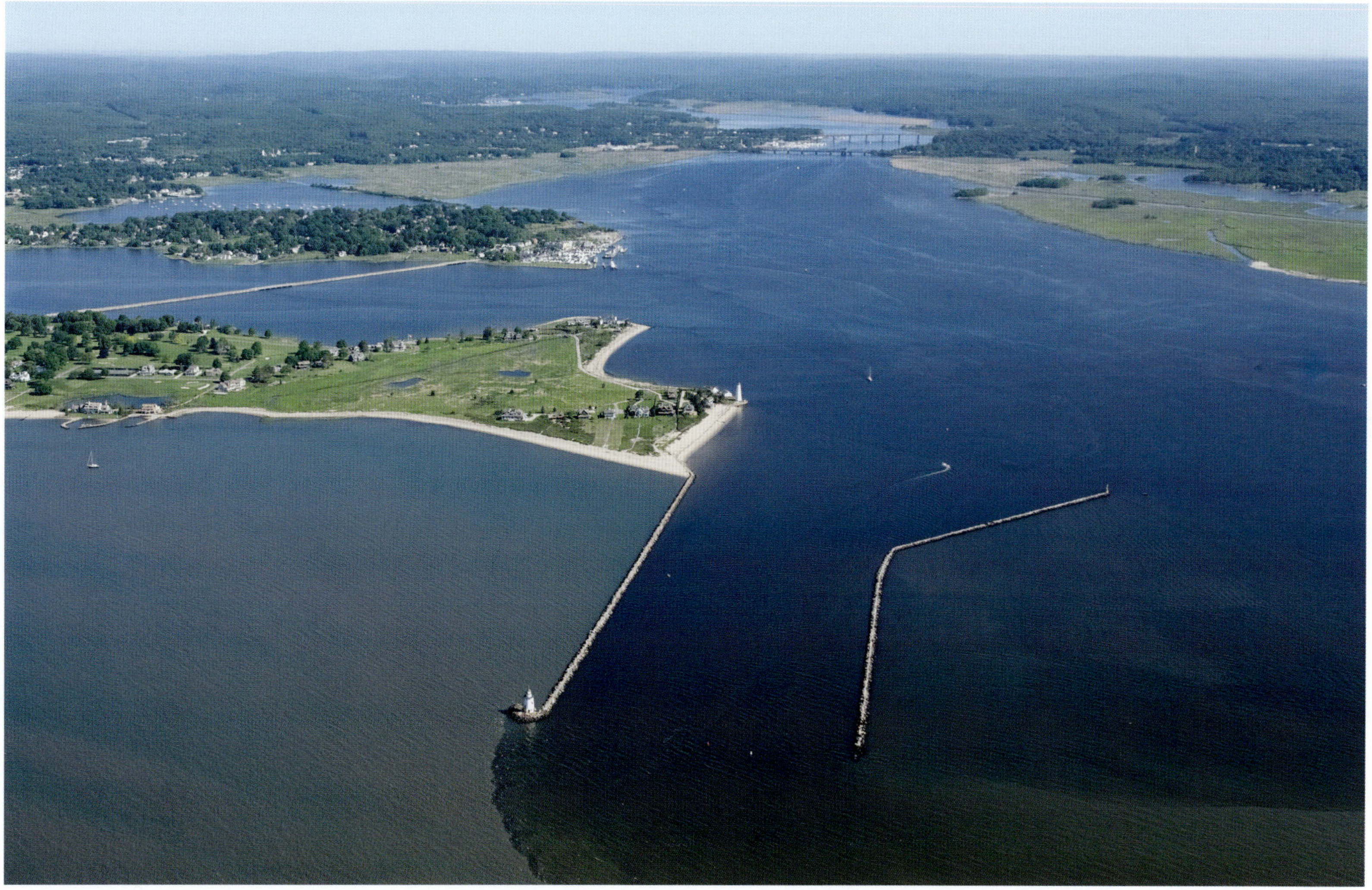

(above) In the foreground, just beyond the outer lighthouse, lies Fenwick, which is connected to Saybrook Point by a diagonal causeway. In the distance, to the north, the first bridges span the river. To the east is Great Island with Old Lyme beyond it on the mainland.

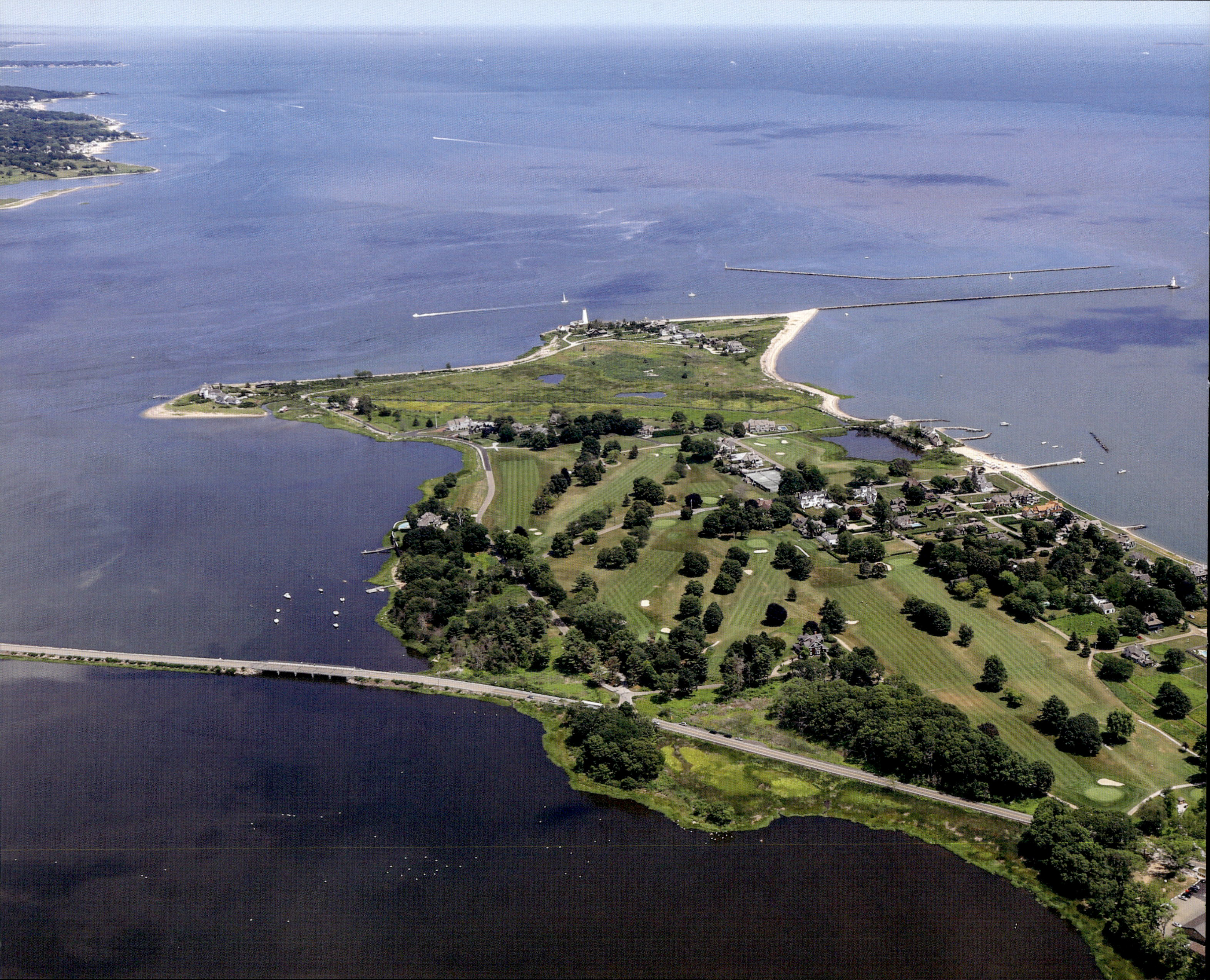

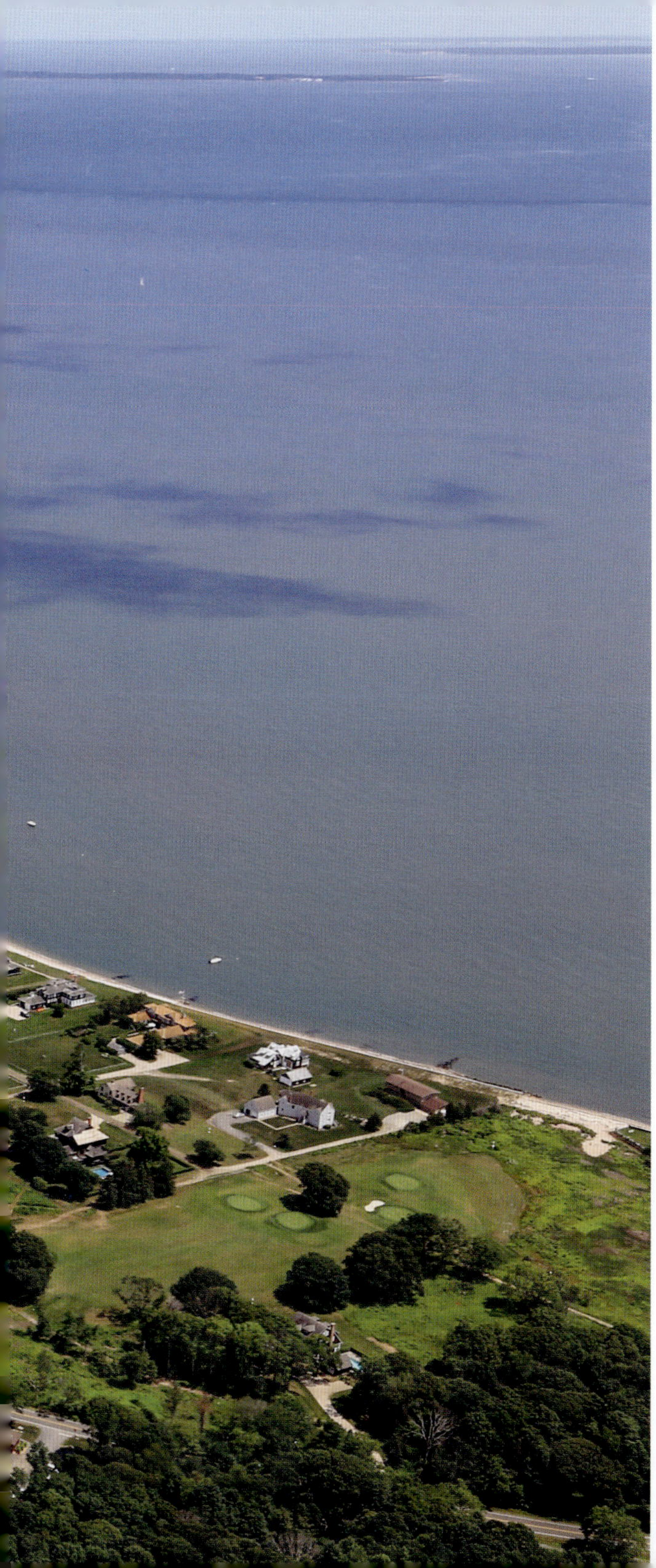

THE SAYBROOK BAR

The Connecticut River is unique in that it is one of the few waterways in the developed world without a major industrial port city at its mouth. Unlike the Hudson River with New York Harbor, the Charles with Boston, the Quinnipiac with New Haven, and the Thames with New London, the Connecticut's interface with the sea remains surprisingly natural and serene. Here tidal wetlands form an ecosystem that is home to a wide variety of plant life, fishes, and birds including eagles, osprey, and great blue herons. The reason for this anomaly among rivers is the great Saybrook Bar, a massive sand barrier that until the establishment of a dredged channel in the mid-1800s prevented all but relatively small coastal vessels from passing upriver. There was no deep-water anchorage or natural harbor where ocean-going ships could encourage the evolution of a major port city.

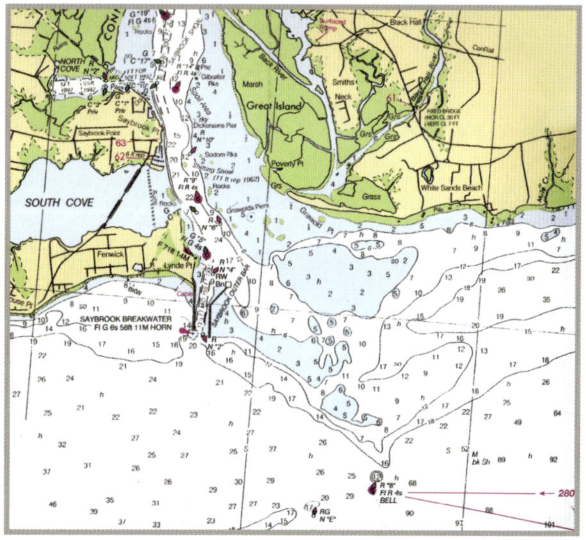

The Connecticut River is a long and relatively shallow river, carrying sediment picked up along its winding course. At its mouth, twice a day, this down-flow is dramatically slowed or stopped dead in its tracks by the incoming Atlantic tide. This tidal roadblock forces the river to drop its sediment, creating the massive sand bar that stretches across the river's mouth and well out into the Sound. Although the mouth is a mile wide and apparently easily navigable by any size vessel, there is only about eight to ten feet of water at low tide in most places. Ironically, while over 4,000 ships have been built in ports farther up the river, the larger ones could only be brought out with their masts and ballast removed and only at moon high tides. It was a deterrent to industrial growth, but it is what has allowed New England's greatest river to remain relatively unspoiled.

Looking southeast into the Sound, the shallows of the Saybrook Bar are visible, dappled with cloud shadows.

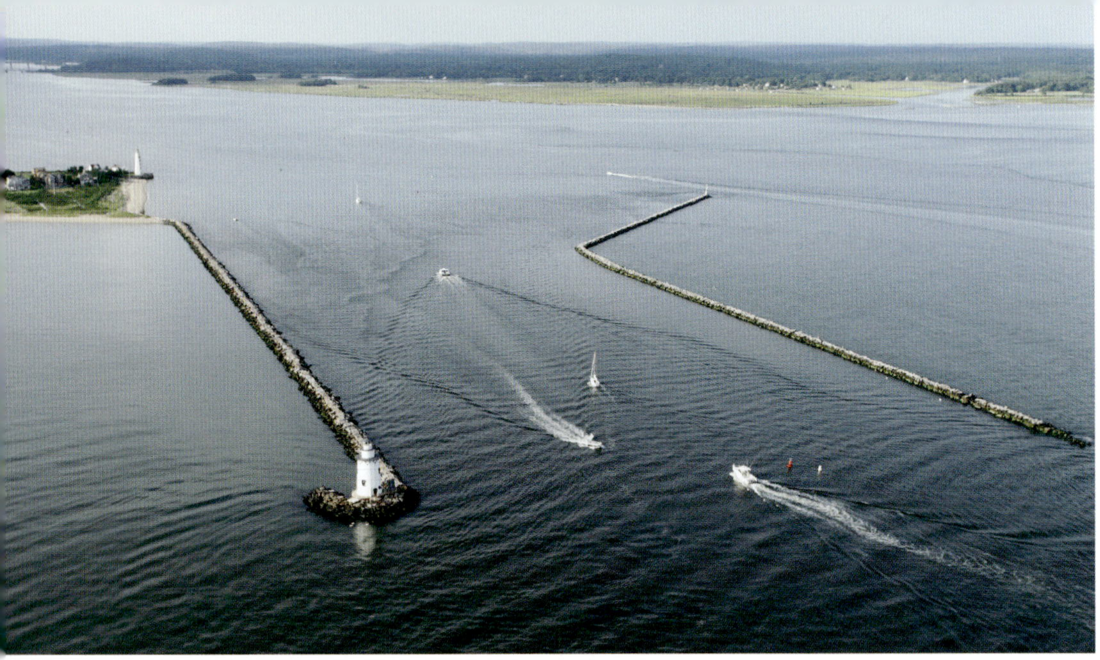

(above) Old Saybrook's Outer Light, built in 1886, marks the entrance to the river's channel.

(below) Lynde Point Light, also known as the Saybrook Inner Light, was built on Fenwick in 1838. This octagonal brownstone tower is the third lighthouse to be located here to guide vessels into the river. The first tower, made of wood, was built in 1803.

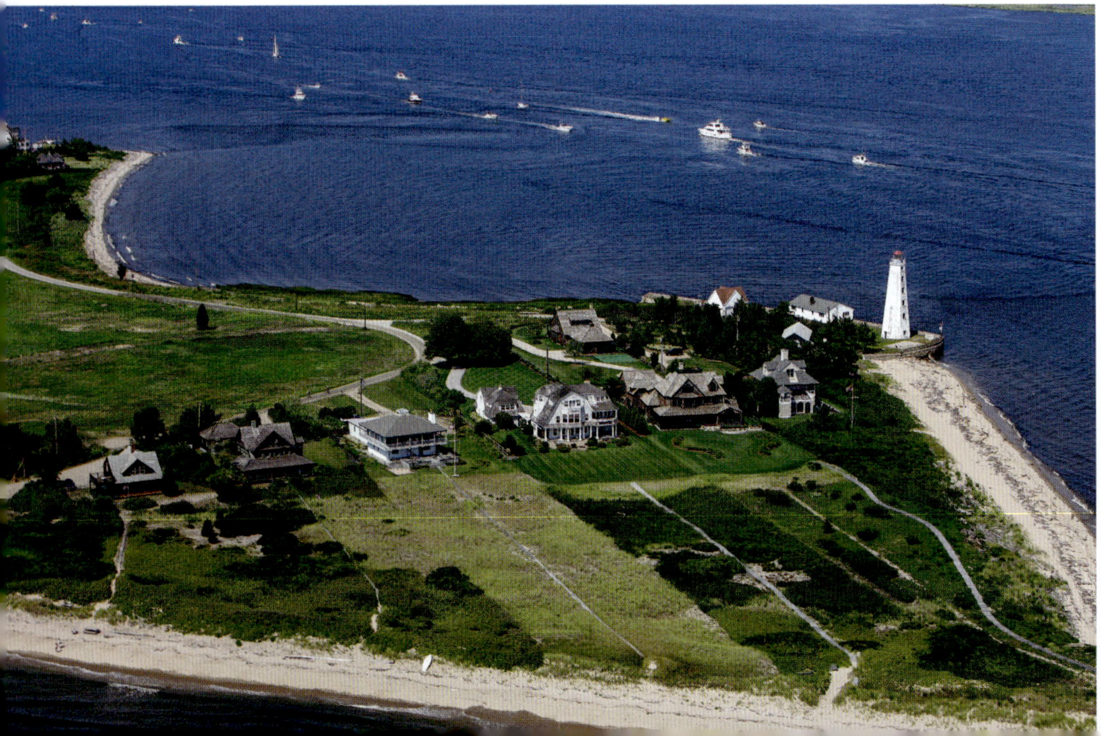

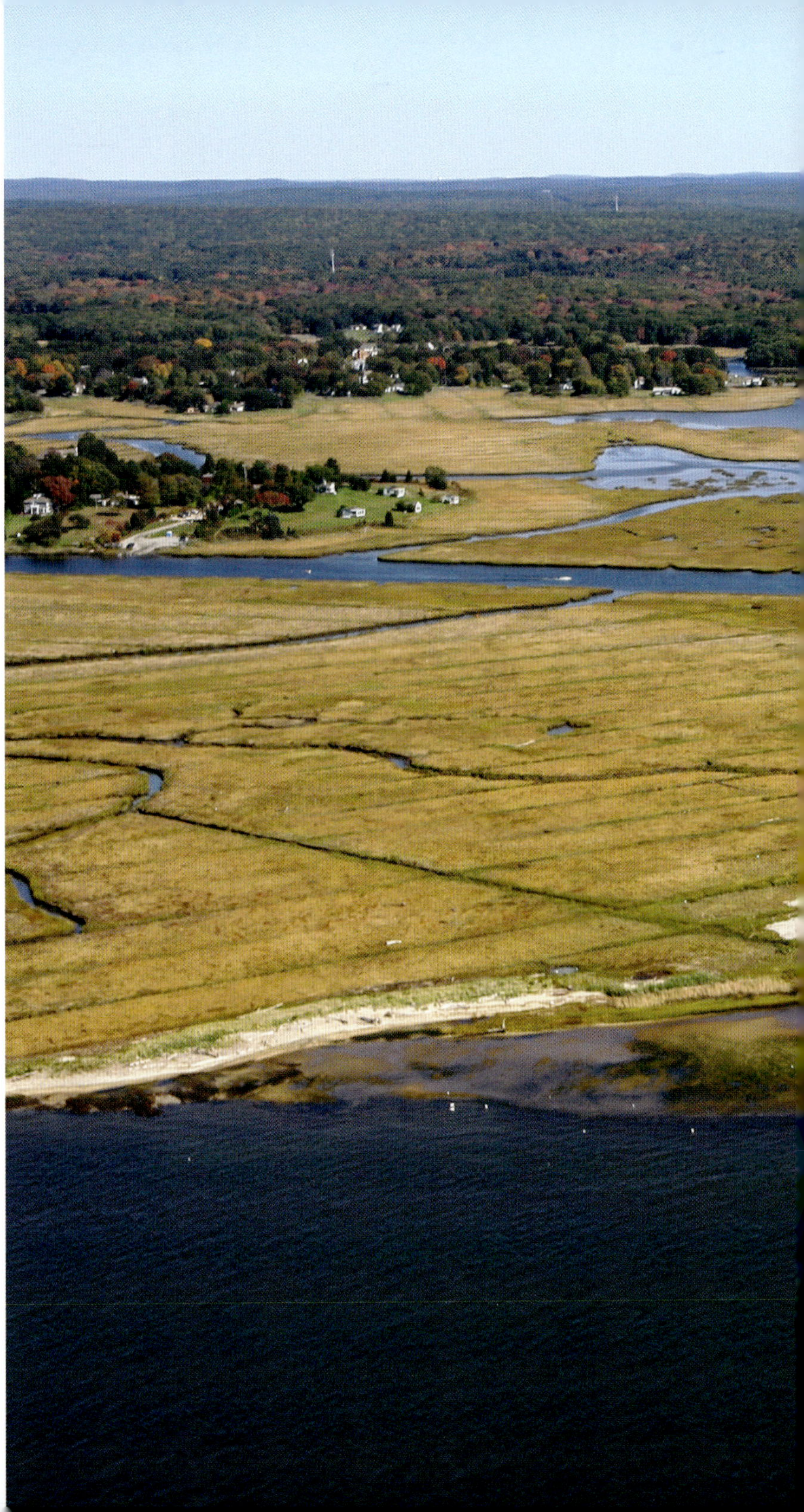

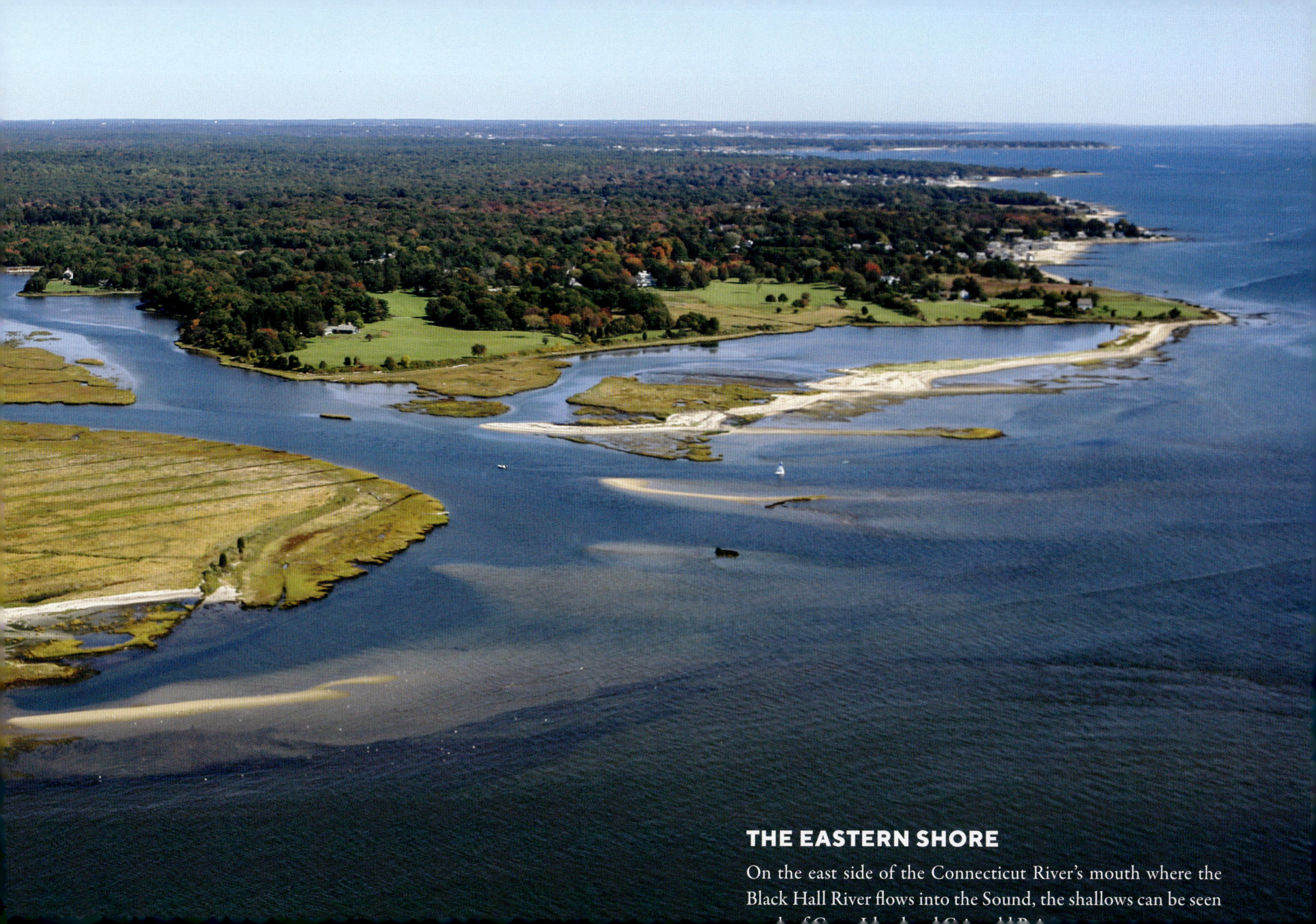

THE EASTERN SHORE

On the east side of the Connecticut River's mouth where the Black Hall River flows into the Sound, the shallows can be seen

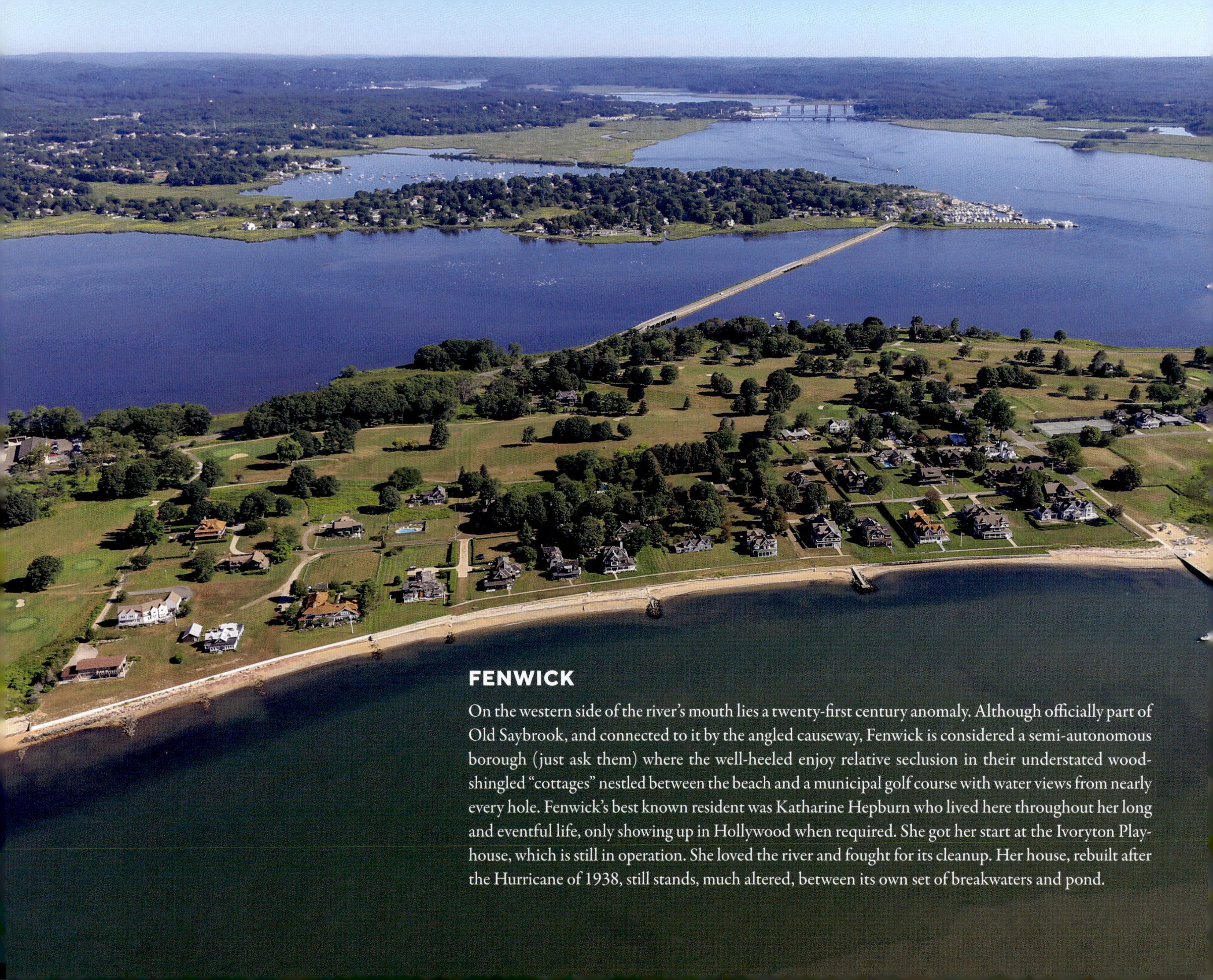

FENWICK

On the western side of the river's mouth lies a twenty-first century anomaly. Although officially part of Old Saybrook, and connected to it by the angled causeway, Fenwick is considered a semi-autonomous borough (just ask them) where the well-heeled enjoy relative seclusion in their understated wood-shingled "cottages" nestled between the beach and a municipal golf course with water views from nearly every hole. Fenwick's best known resident was Katharine Hepburn who lived here throughout her long and eventful life, only showing up in Hollywood when required. She got her start at the Ivoryton Playhouse, which is still in operation. She loved the river and fought for its cleanup. Her house, rebuilt after the Hurricane of 1938, still stands, much altered, between its own set of breakwaters and pond.

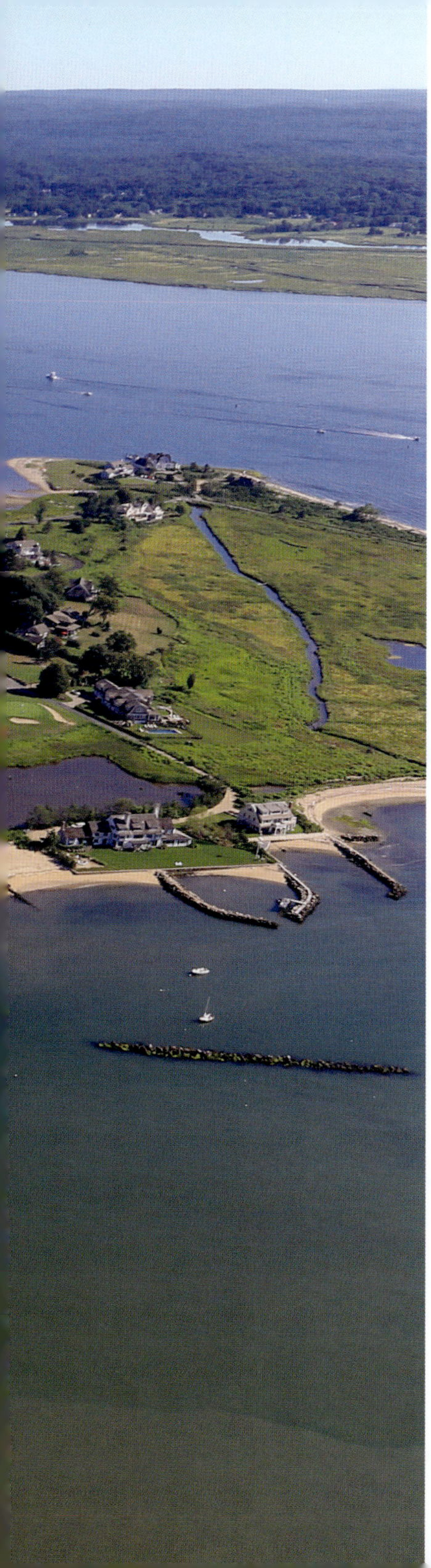

SAYBROOK POINT

(top right) Looking east over Saybrook Point to the mouth of the river, with Fenwick on the right. To the left is North Cove with its fleet of moored boats behind the remnants of the old railroad causeway. To the right, the outer leg of the causeway connects Saybrook point to Fenwick by road. By 1872 these two causeways formed one continuous arch, traversed by the railway that connected Fenwick, Saybrook, and Hartford.

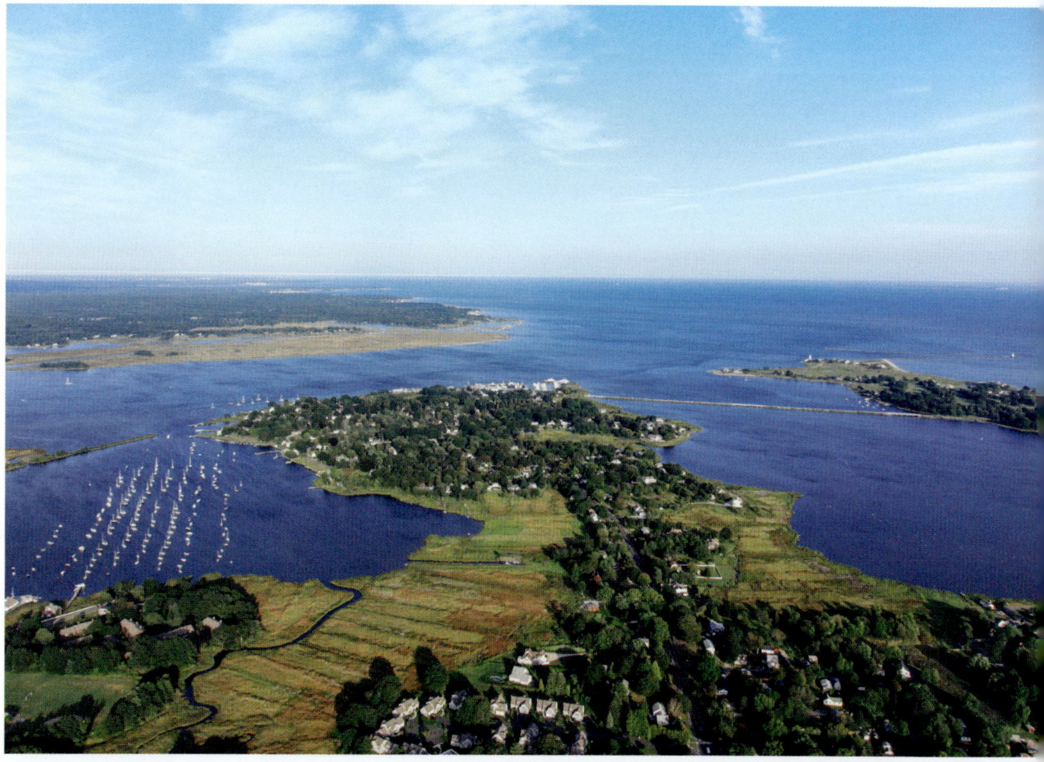

(bottom right) Looking south over Saybrook Point, with Fenwick beyond, the remains of the original colonial settlement can still be seen behind the abandoned parking lot just this side of the marina. These wetlands and the small inlet and pond that remain were the site of a cove where small vessels could be anchored beneath the wooden palisaded fort that stood on the hillside from about 1635 to 1647. When the causeway brought the railroad across the point in the early 1870s, the area was completely altered and filled. Recent archeology however has un-earthed bits and pieces of this important colonial bridgehead at the mouth of the river. A gap in the old causeway now allows small craft to enter North Cove.

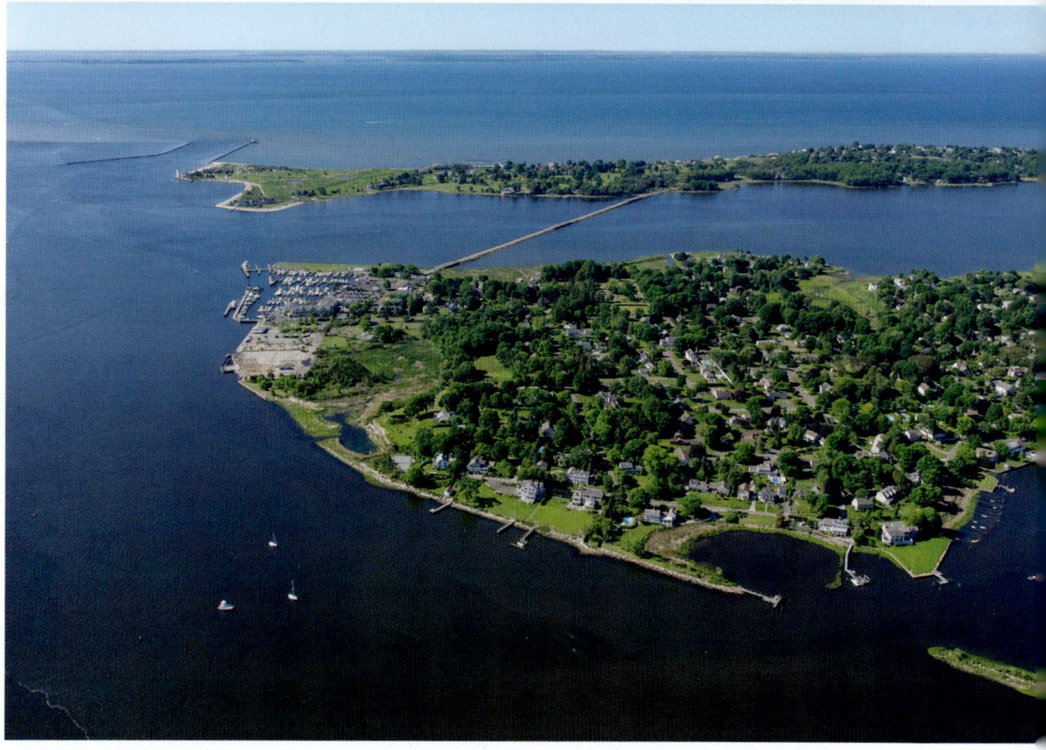

SAYBROOK COLONY

In 1631 the Earl of Warwick issued a Royal patent authorizing a group of English gentry to establish a colony at the mouth of the Connecticut River. In 1635 Captain Lion Gardiner was commissioned to build a fort on what is now Saybrook Point. In 1637 this fort withstood a bloody siege during the Pequot War and was the launching point for English counterattacks. The Saybrook Colony expanded to include the land now comprising Old Saybrook, parts of Westbrook, Killingworth, Essex, Deep River, and Chester on the western side of the river, and Lyme, Old Lyme, and parts of East Lyme on the eastern side. In 1644 the colony merged with the larger Connecticut Colony, which had been established in Hartford.

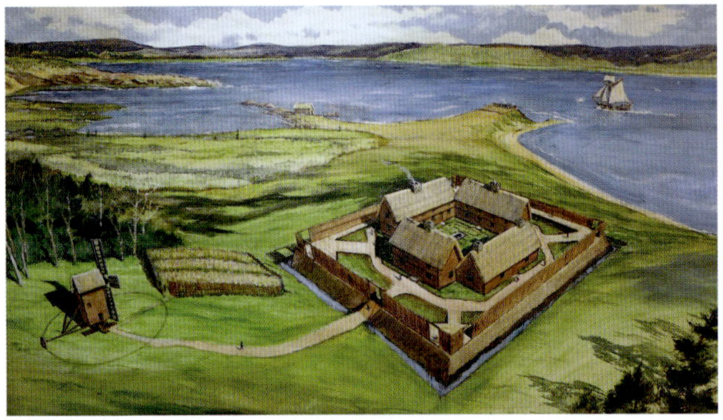

(above) A depiction of Fort Fenwick at Saybrook Point, circa 1640. This was the first fortified settlement in Connecticut and played a significant role in the Pequot War. When the British raided Essex in 1814 they stormed a gun battery depicted here on the mound protruding into the river. *Painting by Roger Epply, courtesy of Old Saybrook Town Hall.*

OLD SAYBROOK

Looking westward from Saybrook Point, with the coast of Long Island Sound beyond, the modern town of Old Saybrook lies to the right, just above the moored boats in North Cove. It features everything from antique shops and restaurants to the Katharine Hepburn Cultural Arts Center.

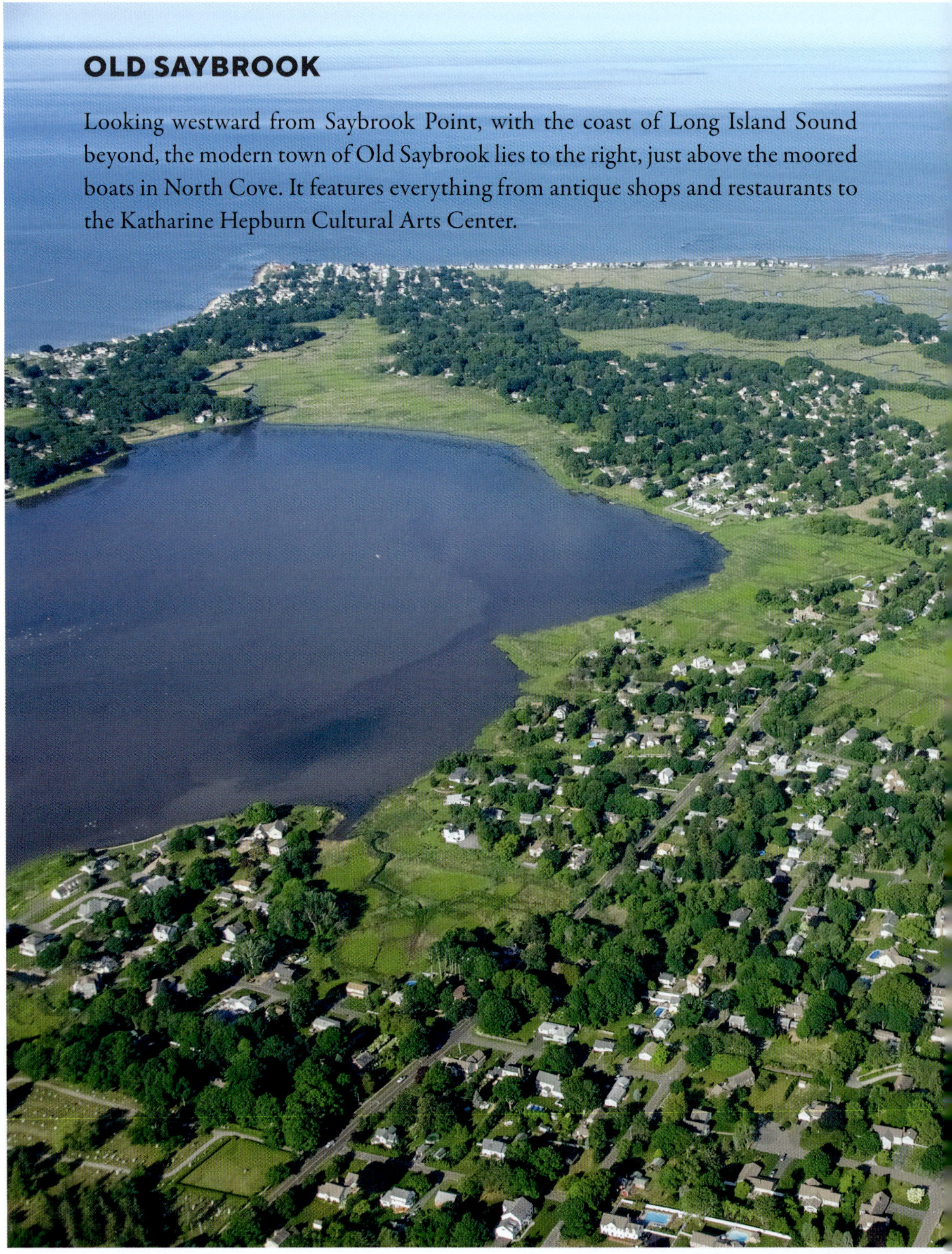

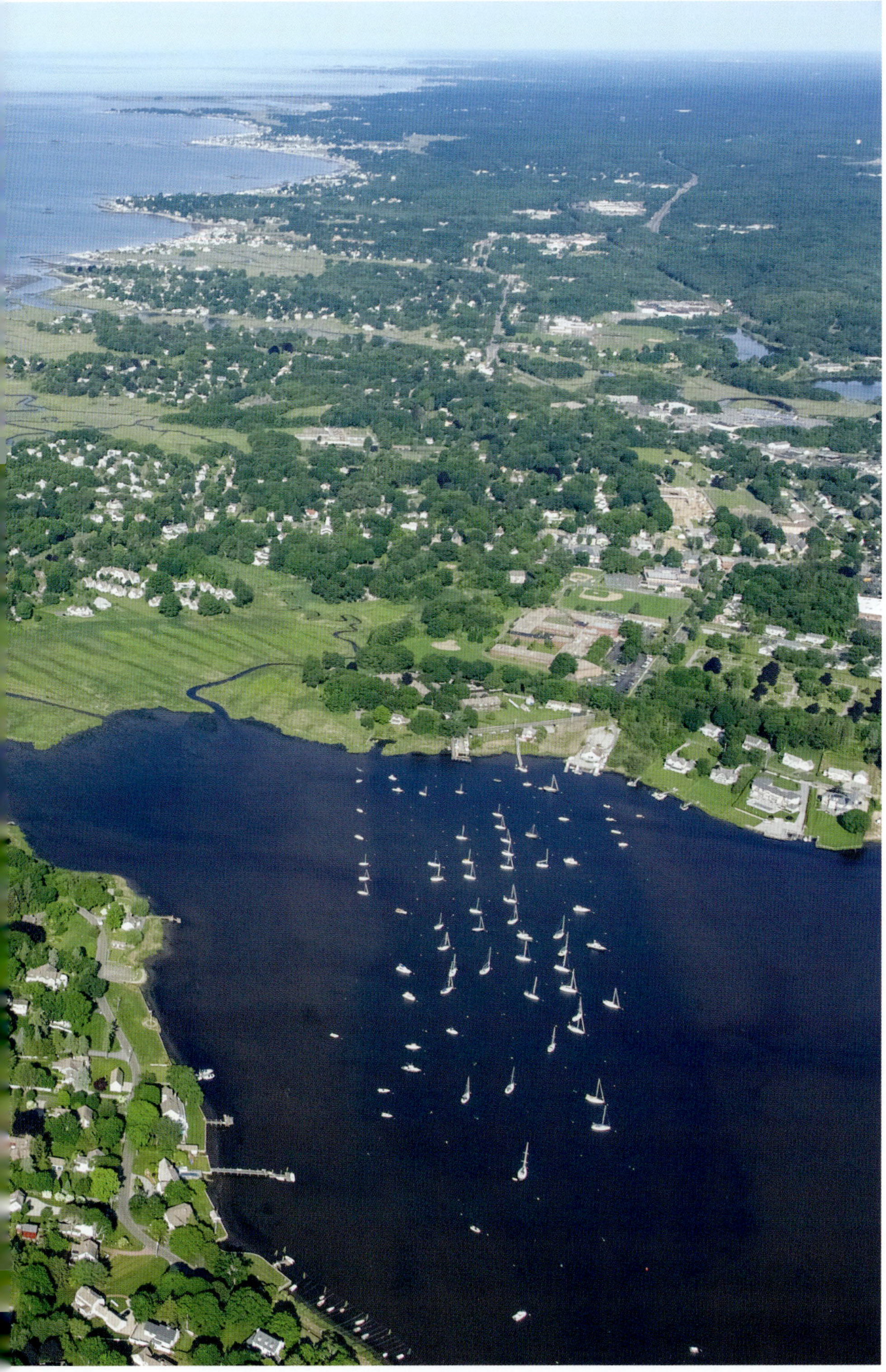

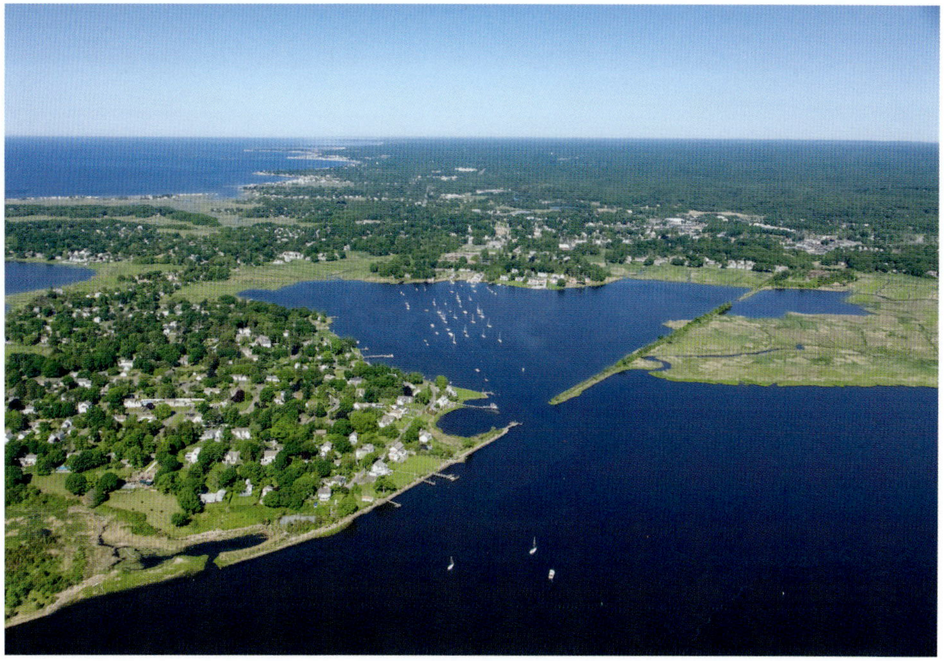

(above) Another view of Old Saybrook across North Cove. With Saybrook Point to the left, access to North Cove is through a gap in the old railroad causeway.

(below) At the tip of the causeway a dark shape in the water has a story to tell.

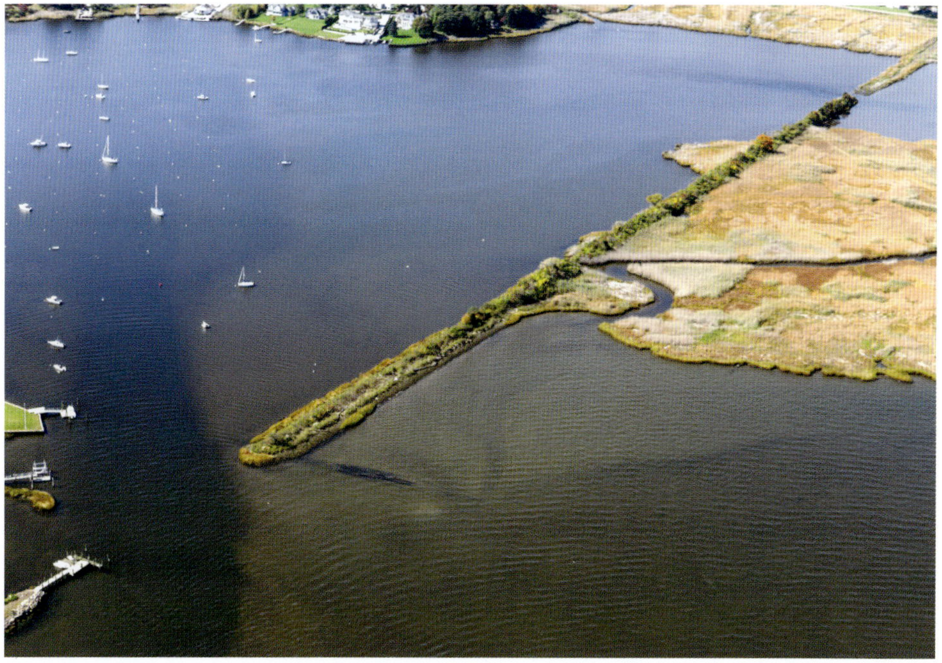

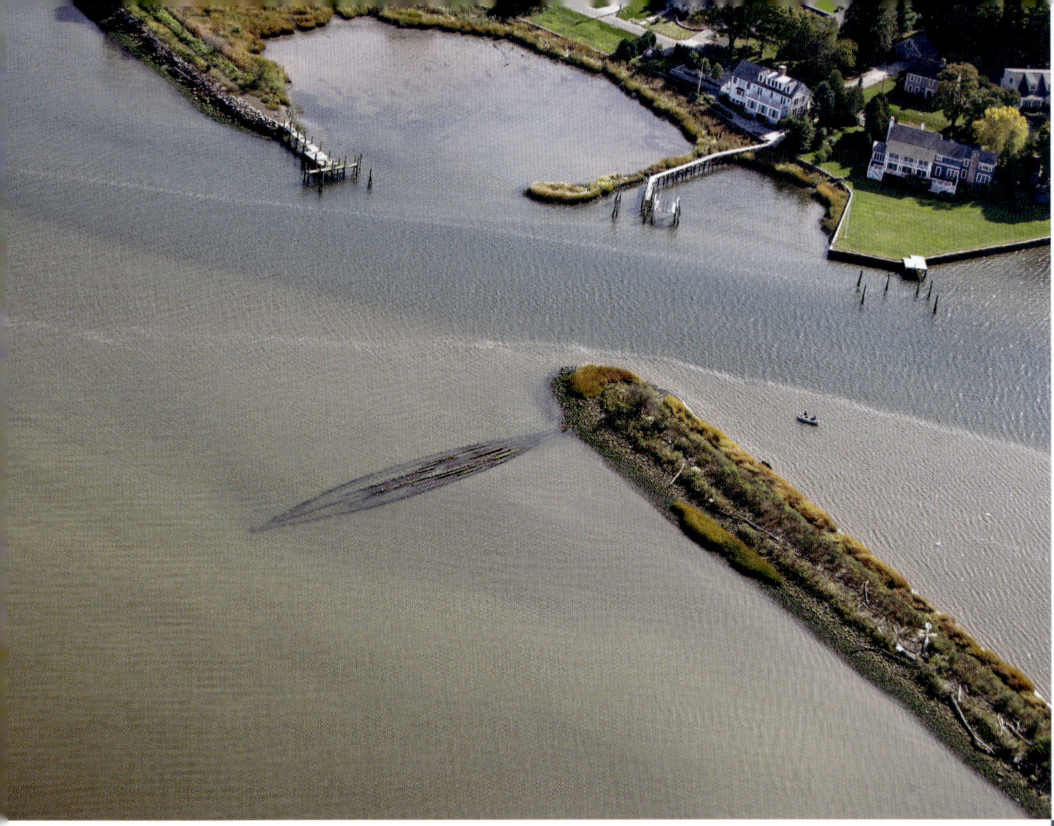

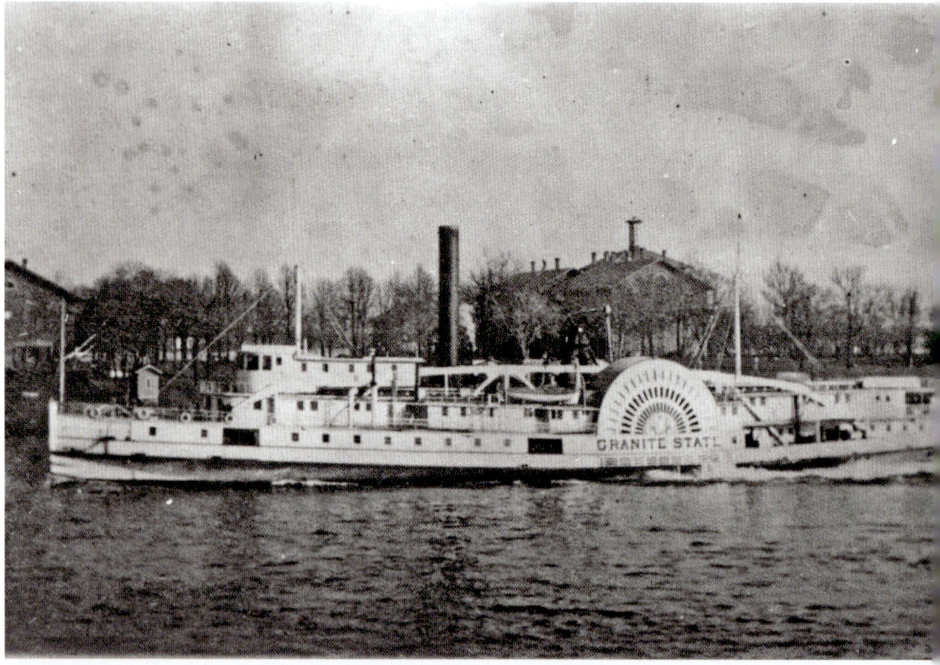

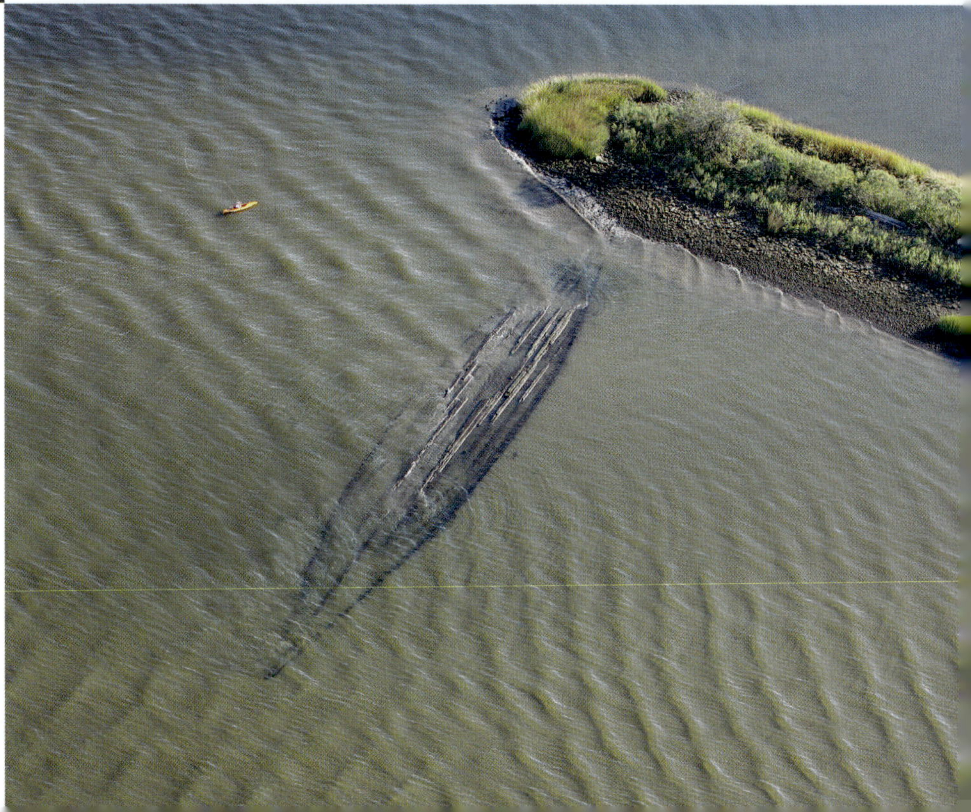

(clockwise, from top left) Here the remnants of hull timbers from the steamboat *Granite State* lay nosed up against the old railroad causeway. The 300-foot steamboat once served as an excursion vessel on the Hudson River and also plied the waters of Long Island Sound and the Connecticut River. It caught fire and was beached farther up the river in 1883. Its burned hull was later towed downstream to Saybrook where its bones now rest in shallow water, occasionally breaking the surface at low tides.

The steamboat, *Granite State*

A fly-fishing kayaker casts his line just off the wreck.

OLD LYME

Settled along the Lieutenant River on the eastern side of the Connecticut River, Lyme was originally part of Saybrook Colony but separated in 1665. First known as East Saybrook and then Lyme, it eventually split into the three towns now called Old Lyme, Lyme, and East Lyme. Until the first bridge connecting the Lymes to Saybrook was built in 1911, only a ferry joined the two sides of the river. Even after bridges spanned the mouth of the river, Old Lyme remained, as it does today, a community unto itself with its own identity on the "quiet" side of the river. Talk of a new high speed rail corridor poses a potential threat to the area's bucolic tranquility.

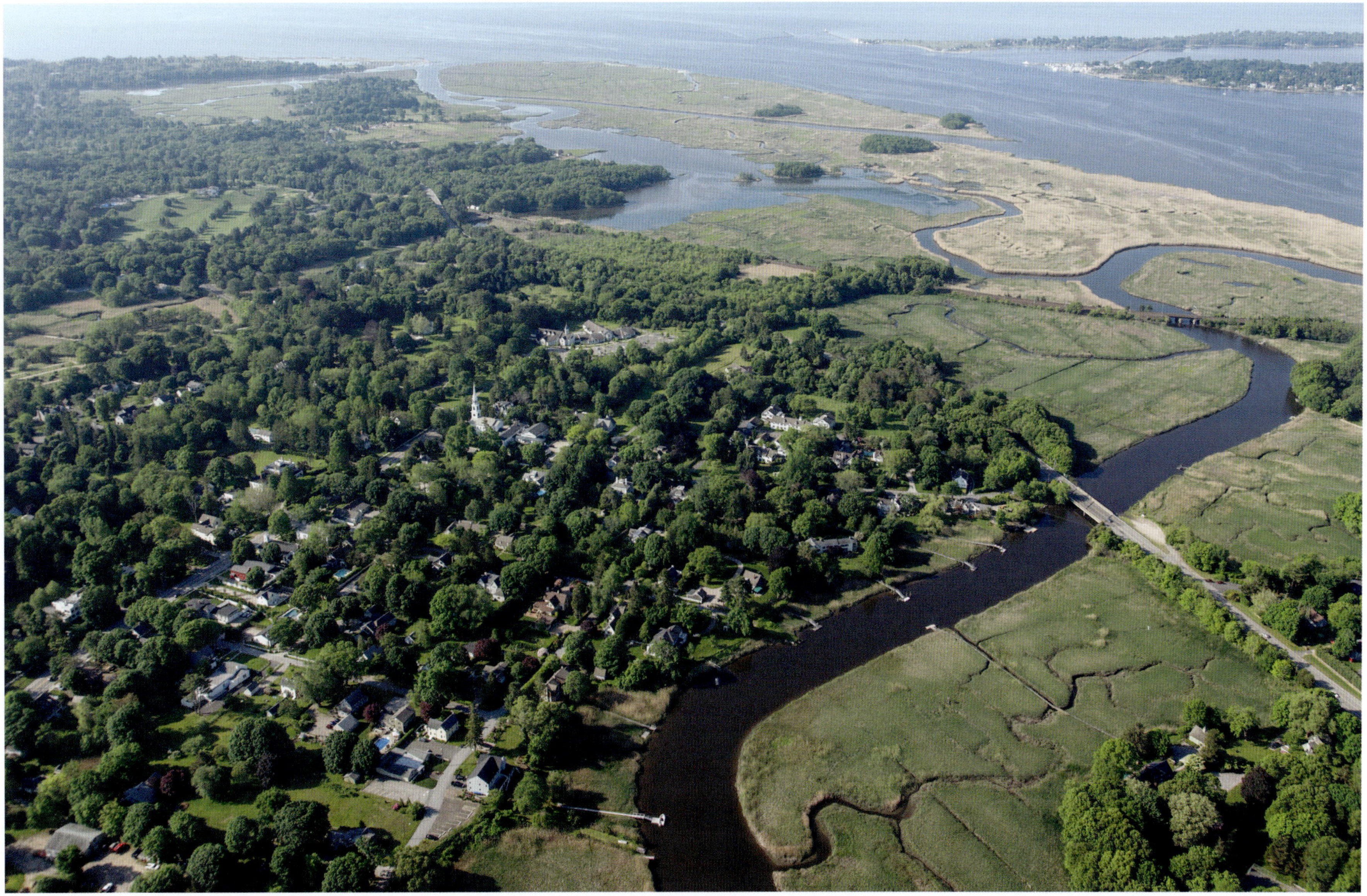

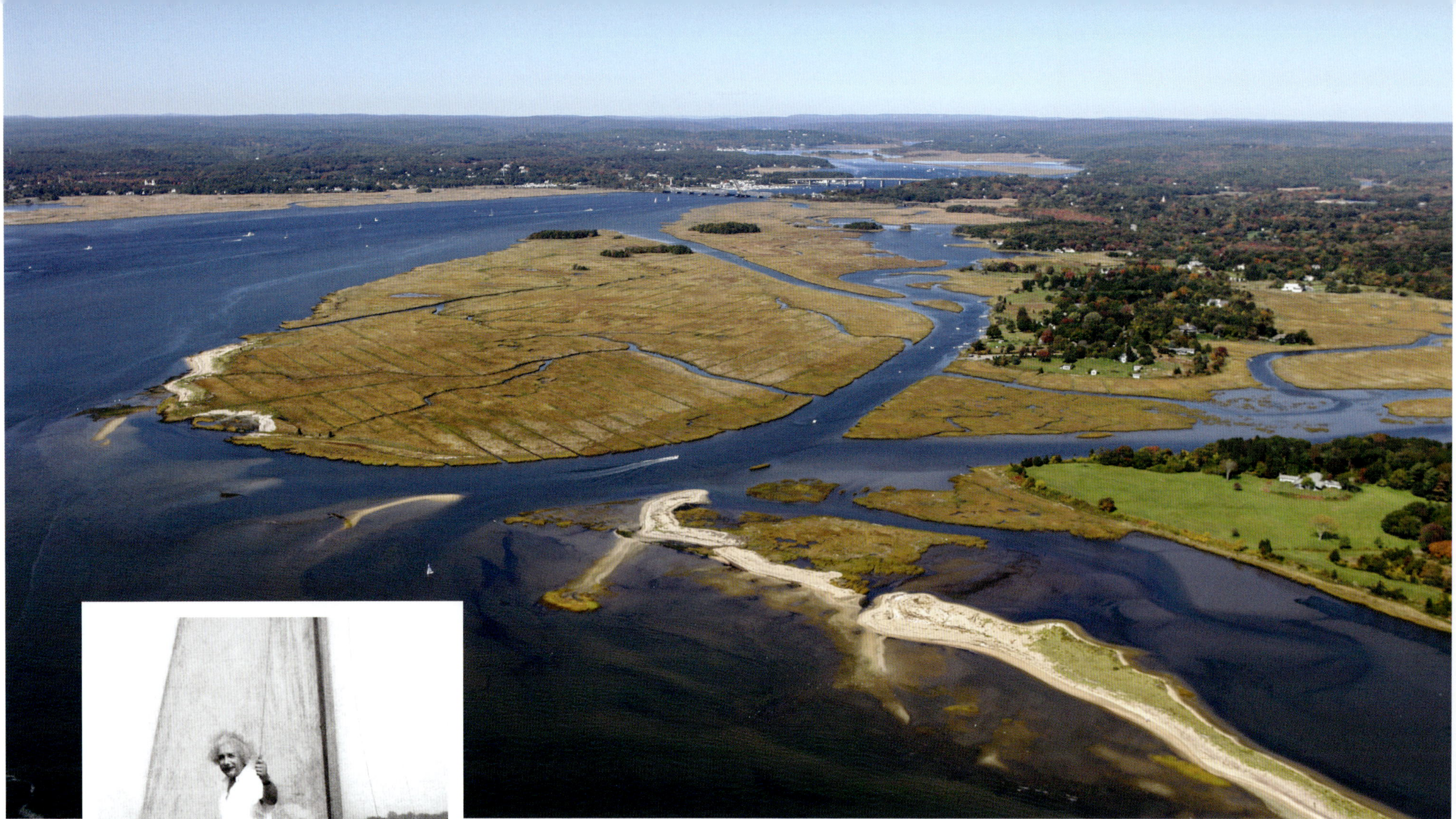

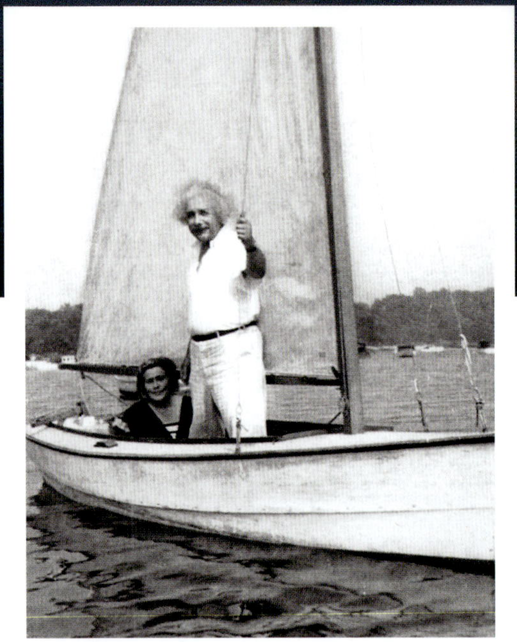

Due to the shoals at its mouth and shifting sands within its course, it is said that any mariner who claims they have never gone aground in the Connecticut River is a liar. Albert Einstein spent a fair amount of time messing about in small boats along this coast and it is said by locals that although he discovered relativity only once, he discovered the Great Saybrook Bar over and over again!

The sand shoals off Griswold Point and Great Island mark the eastern side of the river at its mouth. Their changing shapes are evidence that the interface between the river and the sea are still fluid. The river deposits material and storms erode or reshape this mini barrier island.

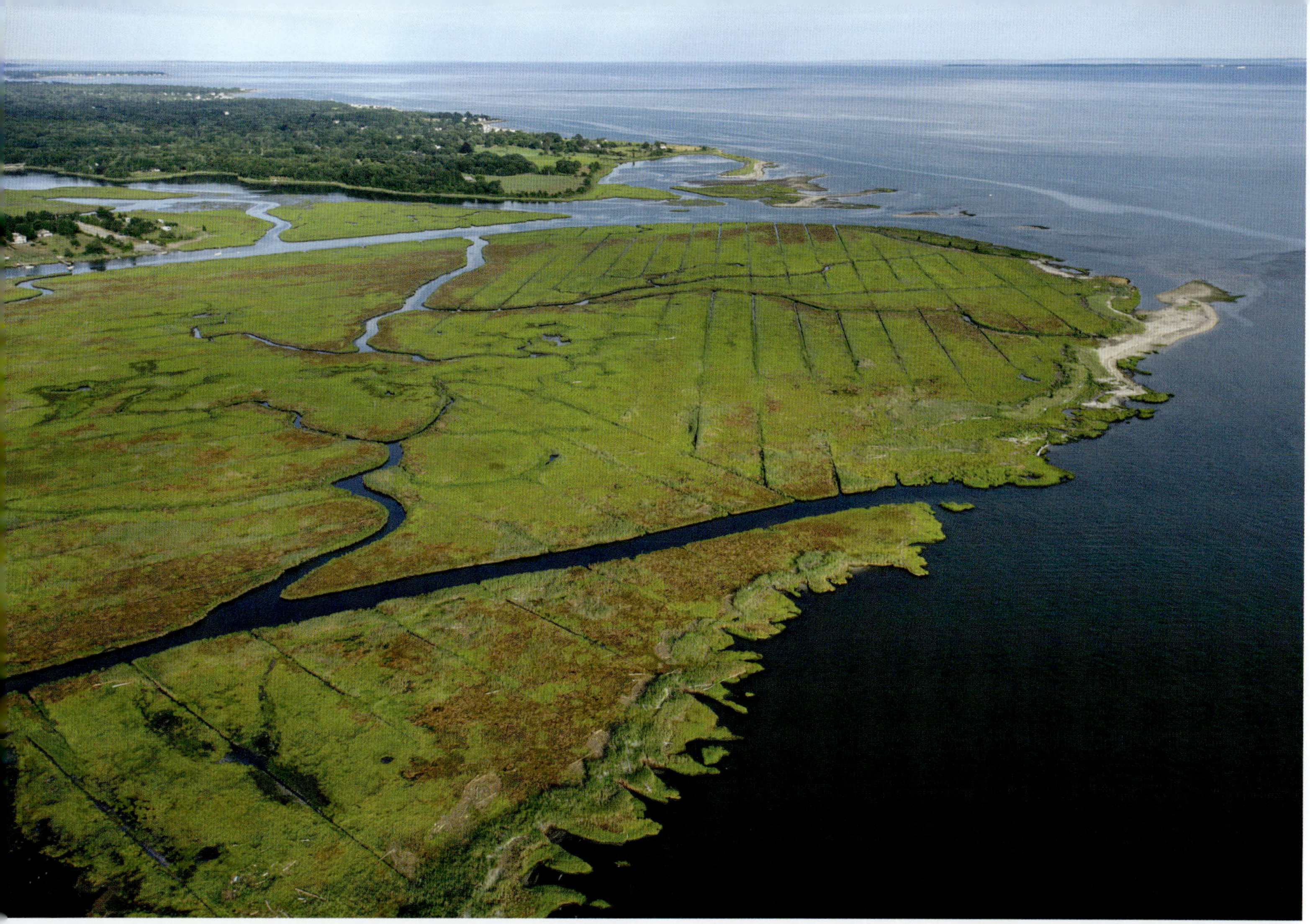

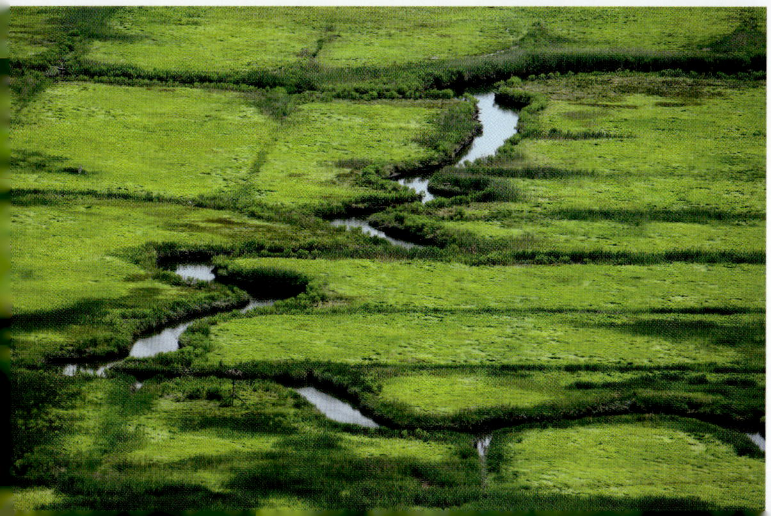

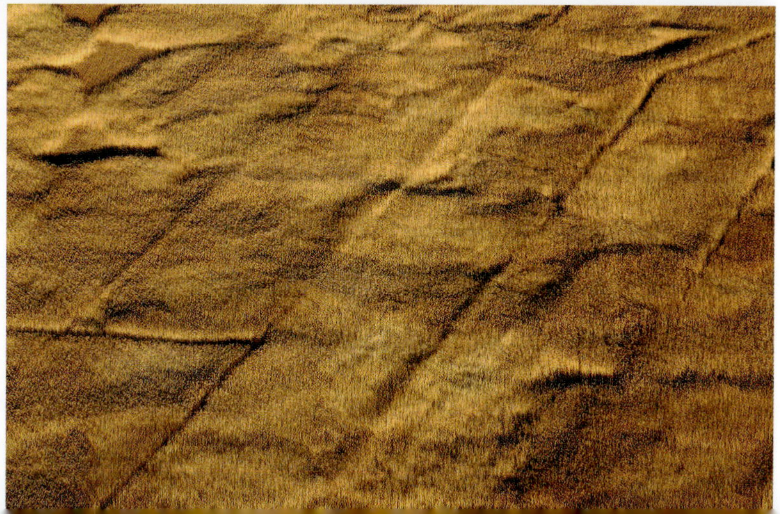

In the 1930s drainage trenches were dug through the marshes of Great Island for mosquito control, leaving quilt-like patterns across the island's wetlands. Now out of favor, efforts to manage the natural tidal wetlands have switched to an attempt to control invasive species like phragmites, which are choking out native saltwater grasses.

THE FLIGHTS

If flown non-stop at a moderate cruising speed of 80 miles per hour, the journey from Sound to source would take about five hours. In fact, this photographic expedition covers eight years of flights from 2009 to 2016. While most of the images are from the more recent flights, we wanted to include some earlier images that show changes that have occurred just in this short span of time. Selecting 300 images out of the thousands Tom has taken was quite a challenge. More recent images were automatically imbedded with GPS mapping data, but identifying obscure areas from the earlier flights required hours of comparing images to Google Earth maps in order to locate each bend and twist, bridge and town so that the years of flights could be arranged into one continuous south-to-north adventure. In fact I strongly recommend following along on Google Earth as you make your way through this collection. It will allow you to scroll your way upstream and identify exactly where particular images were taken and how it interfaces with its surroundings. It is also a good way to fill in the miles between some of the pages. Like me, you may find a place or two that you will want to visit in person.

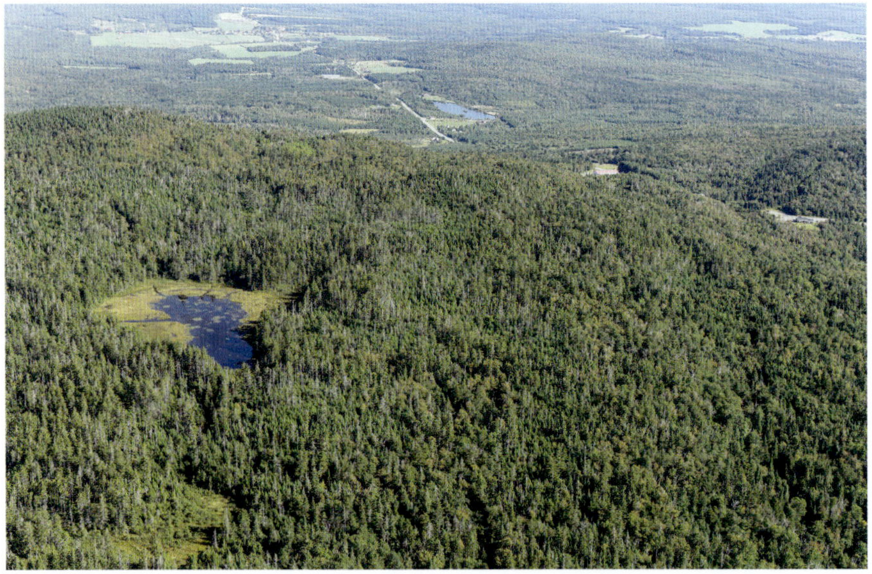

The Fourth Connecticut Lake, 407 miles to the north.

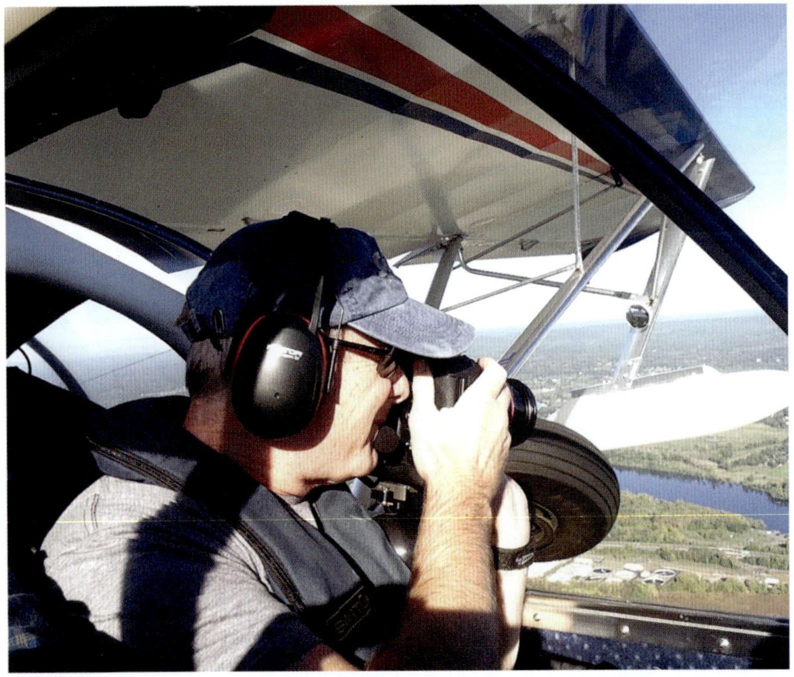

Tom does almost all of his work flying solo, trimming his aircraft to remain stable as he shoots out the open window with well-practiced expediency and precision. On a handful of occasions I have been lucky enough to join him, enabling me to point out some needed shots and angles... but mostly to experience this amazing perspective. My first aerial adventure with Tom was in the 1946 Piper Cub he owned at the time. I sat in the front seat of the narrow cockpit while he piloted the tiny aircraft, itself a piece of aviation history, from the second seat, directly behind me. For most of his commercial work these days Tom uses his four seat Cessna Cardinal but also flies a small Searey amphibian. This high tech morphing of aircraft wings with an engine mounted on a pylon above what is, in essence, a speedboat hull is a modern day adventure machine. It allows an incredibly intimate experience with the river and its surrounding landscape.

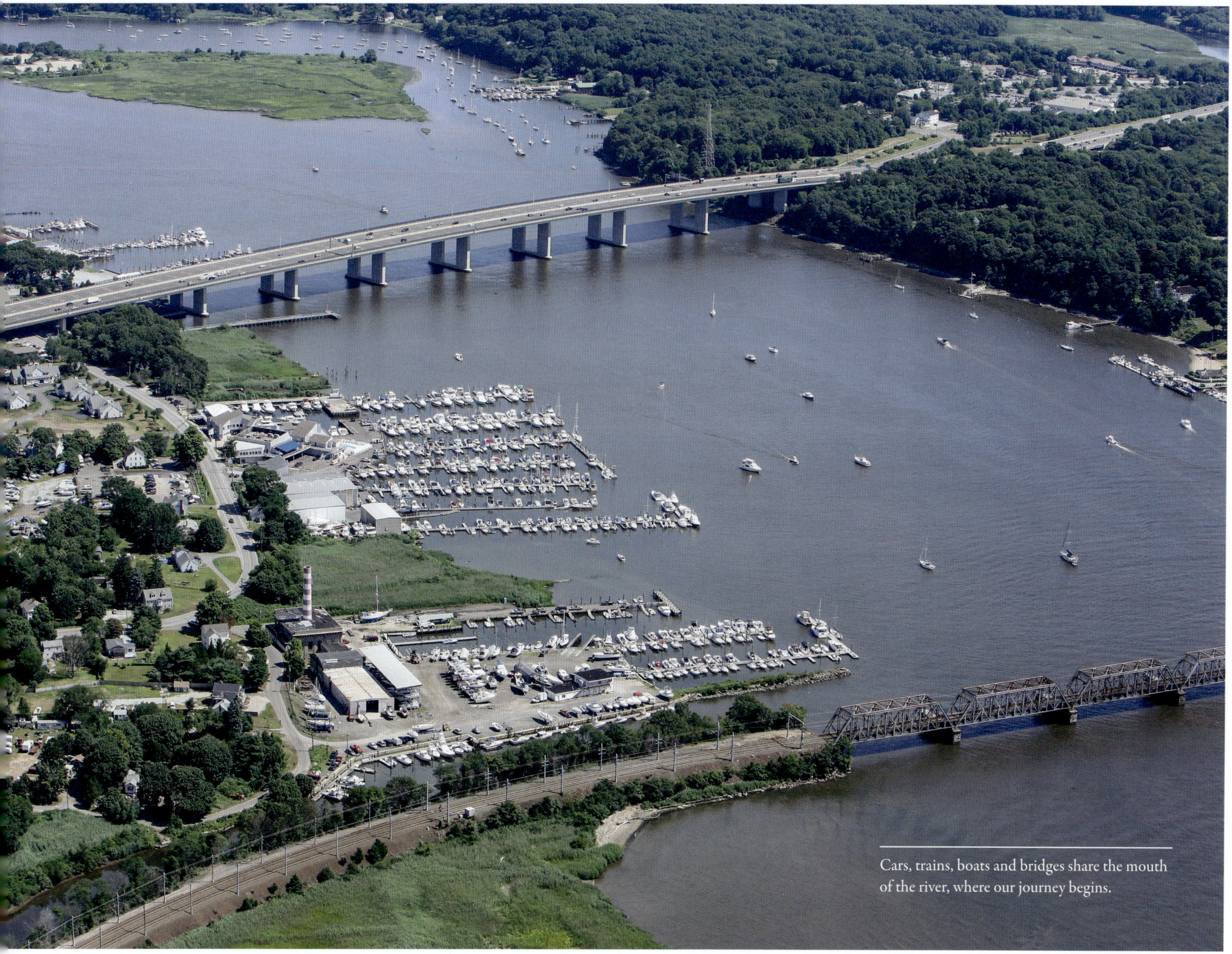

Cars, trains, boats and bridges share the mouth of the river, where our journey begins.

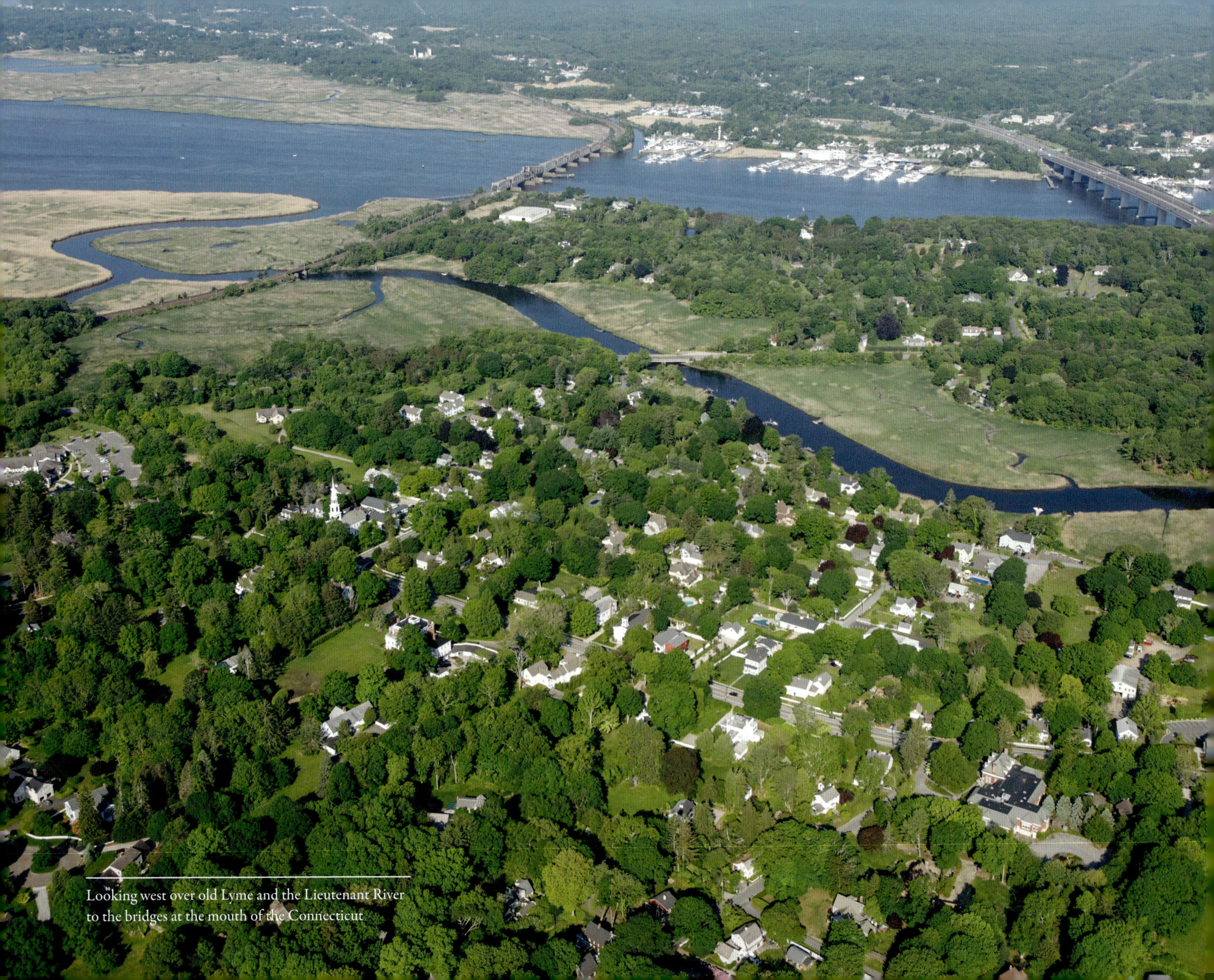

Looking west over old Lyme and the Lieutenant River to the bridges at the mouth of the Connecticut

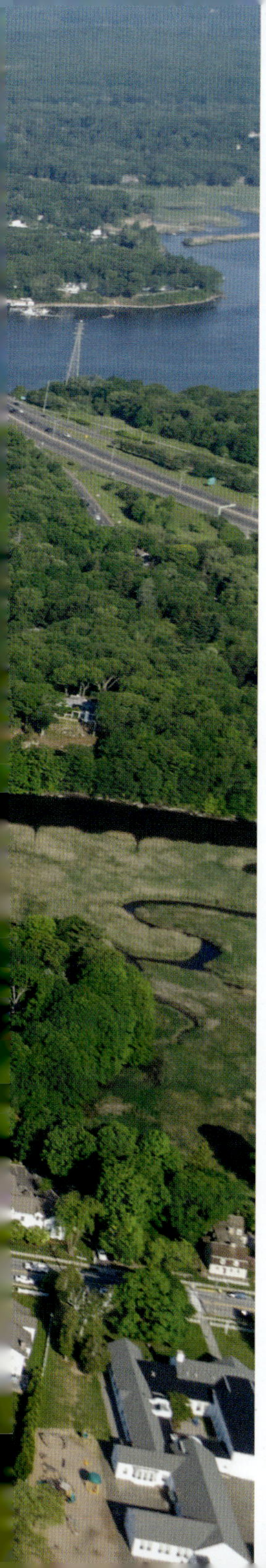

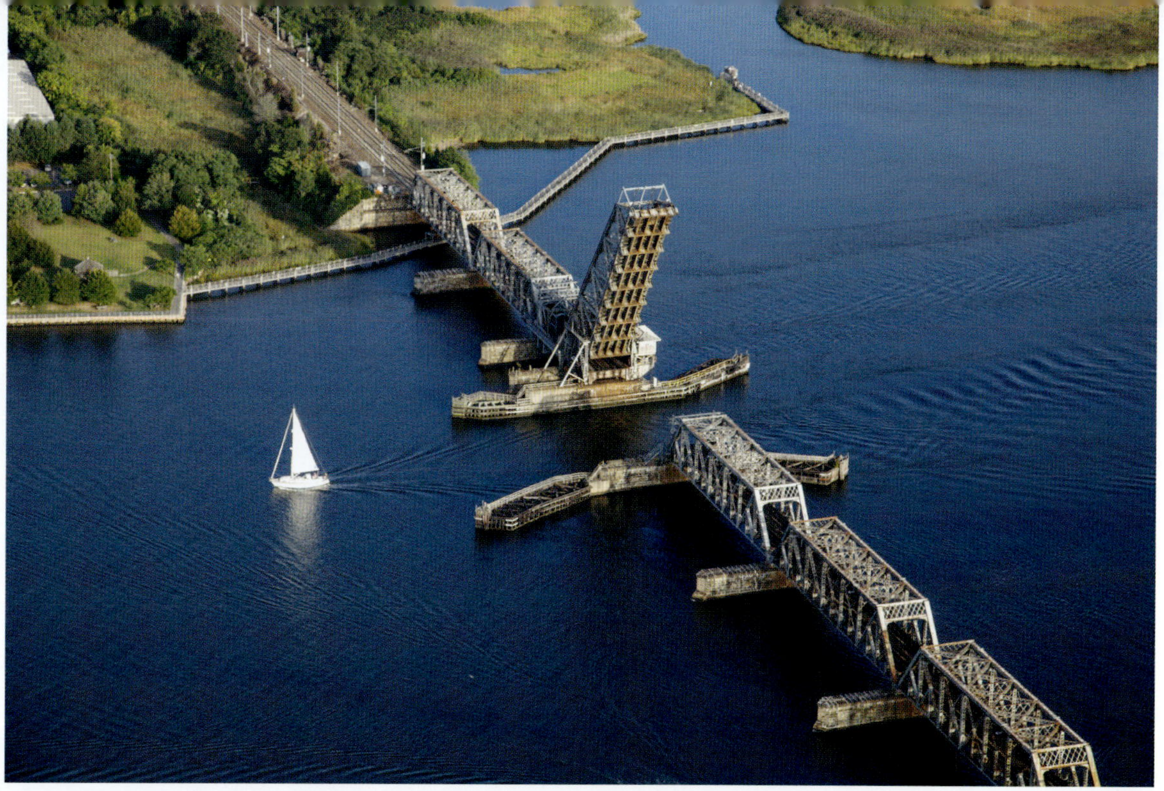

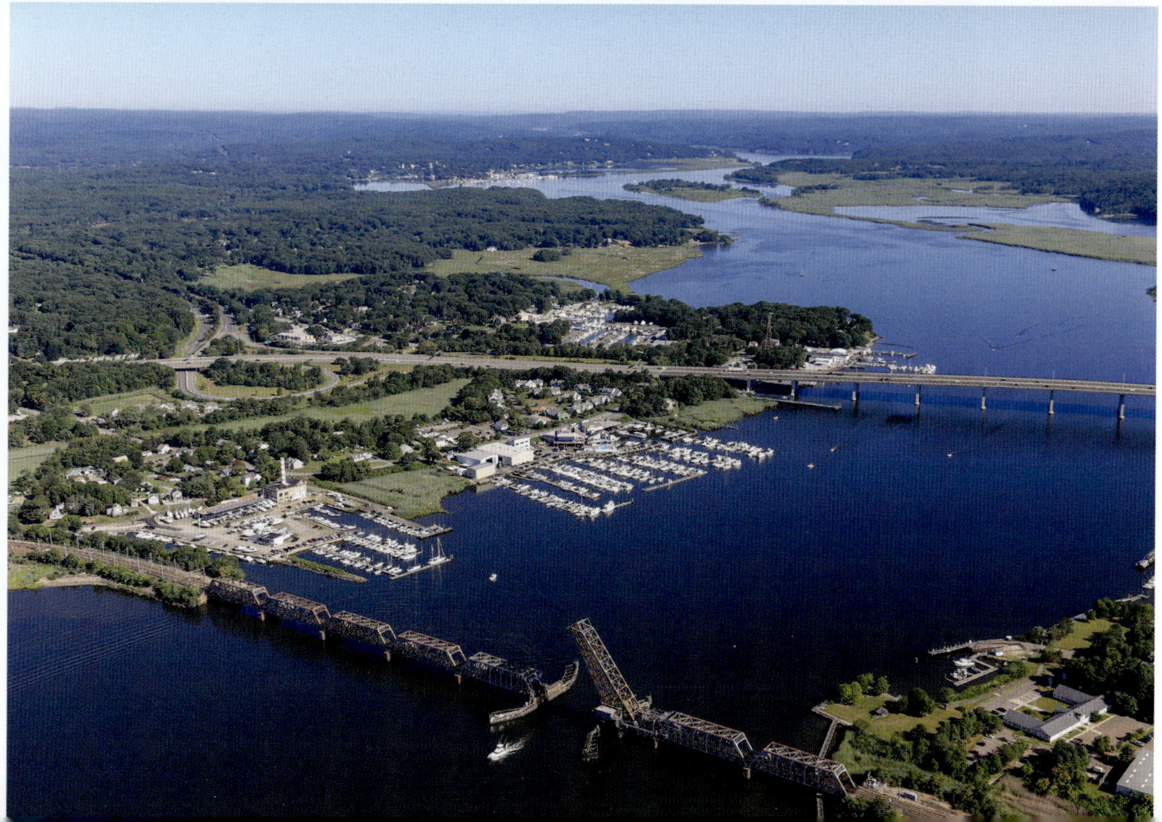

RIVER CROSSINGS

While the river serves as a nautical gateway into the heart of New England, it has long been an obstacle to east-west land travel from one riverbank to another. Ferries were a solution, but bridges were the answer to safe, dependable, cross-river transportation. The first bridge was built near Bellows Falls, Vermont, in 1784. Since then, bridges of all shapes and sizes have spanned the river, from quaint wooden or iron structures to modern steel and concrete multi-lane arteries. Today, more than eighty bridges, and two ferries, are still in service along the river's 410-mile course.

(top left) Sailboat enters the river through the Old Lyme Railway Bridge

(bottom left) Looking northwest over the Old Lyme Railway Bridge and the Baldwin Bridge which carries Interstate 95 across the river

RIVER FACTS

The source of the Connecticut River lies 2,670 feet above sea level. This vertical drop along its 410-mile course, combined with its many tributaries and a watershed that encompasses more than 11,000 square miles, drives tremendous amounts of water toward the sea. In fact seventy percent of the fresh water that enters Long Island Sound flows into it from the Connecticut River.

The river's average flow rate of 19,600 cubic feet per second is hard to comprehend, so try this. If you were to stand on the docks of Essex and look across the river, you would see the same amount of water flow downstream every hour (on an annual average) as cascades over Niagara Falls every thirteen to fourteen minutes. Over the past three centuries this incredible natural power has been harnessed to drive mills and factories and even generate electricity, but it has also proven to be a destructive force. During spring floods it has repeatedly overflowed its banks, carried away dams and bridges, and reshaped its own course during its relentless drive to the sea.

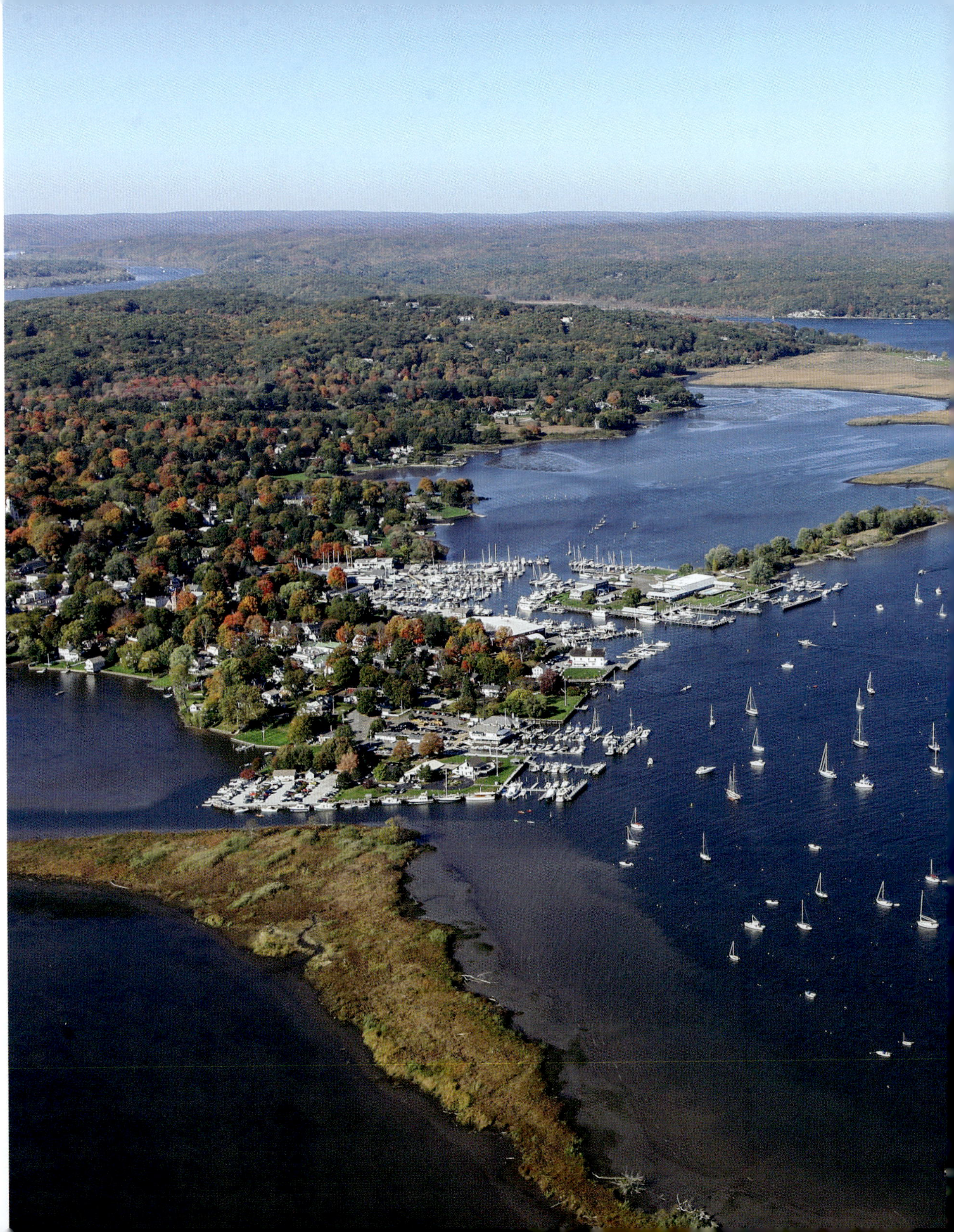

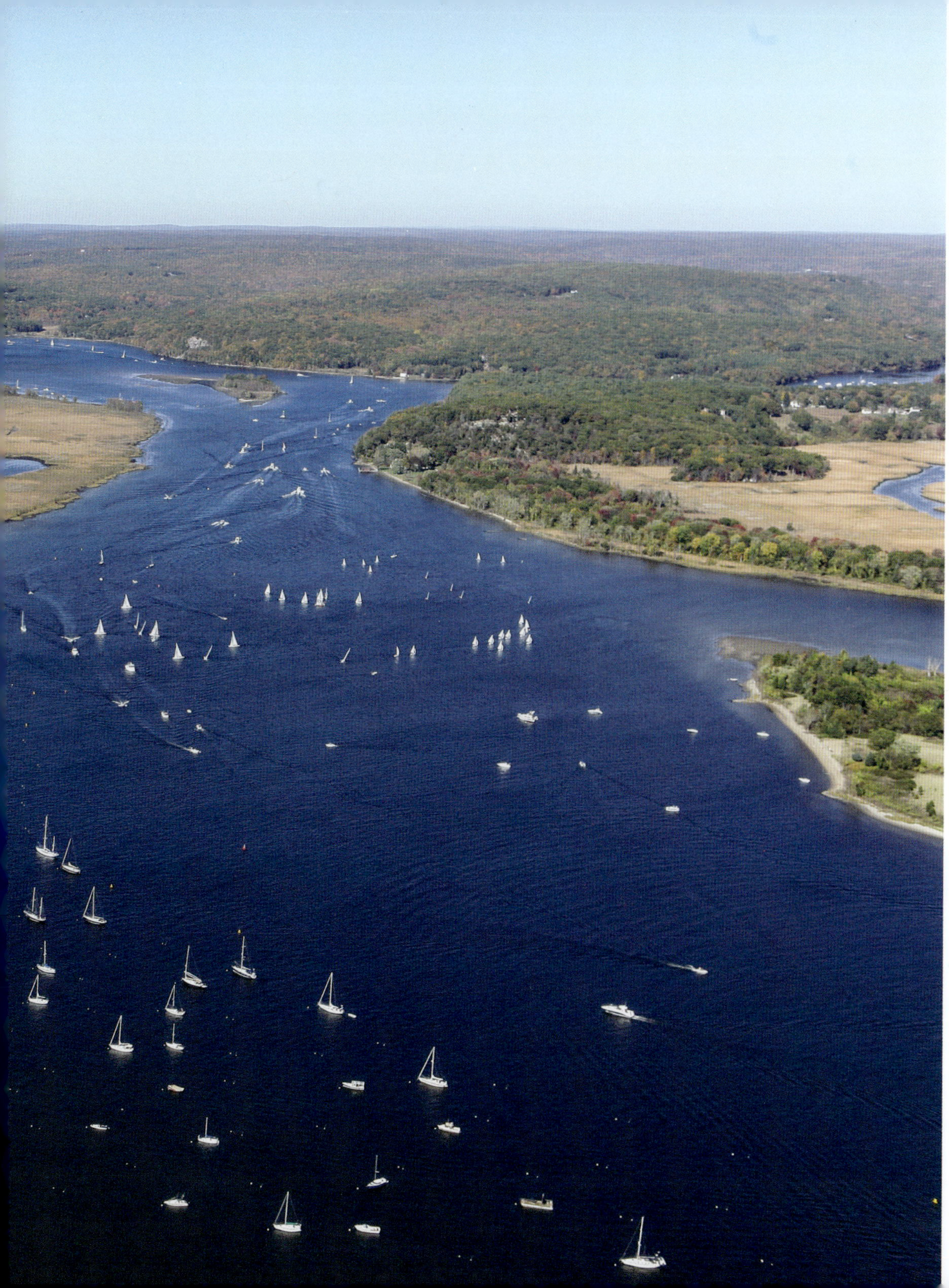

ESSEX, CT

The town of Essex is actually made up of three distinct villages, Centerbrook, Ivoryton, and the original village of Essex situated on a peninsula jutting out into a bend in the river six miles upstream from its mouth. First settled in 1648, it can appear to be frozen in time. Its Main Street, lined with the former homes of ship builders and sea captains, reminds visitors that the town was once a colonial river port involved in ship-building and maritime trade. Here alone, 600 vessels were built, including the Revolutionary War frigate *Oliver Cromwell*.

In nearby Westbrook, Bushnell's *Turtle*, the world's first combat submarine and a true example of Yankee ingenuity at its best, was also built for use during the Revolutionary War. During the War of 1812, a British raiding force burned twenty-seven ships here, including several newly built American privateers. It was the largest single maritime loss of the war. Today the ghosts of the past coexist peacefully with the marinas and yacht clubs that dominate the picturesque harbor.

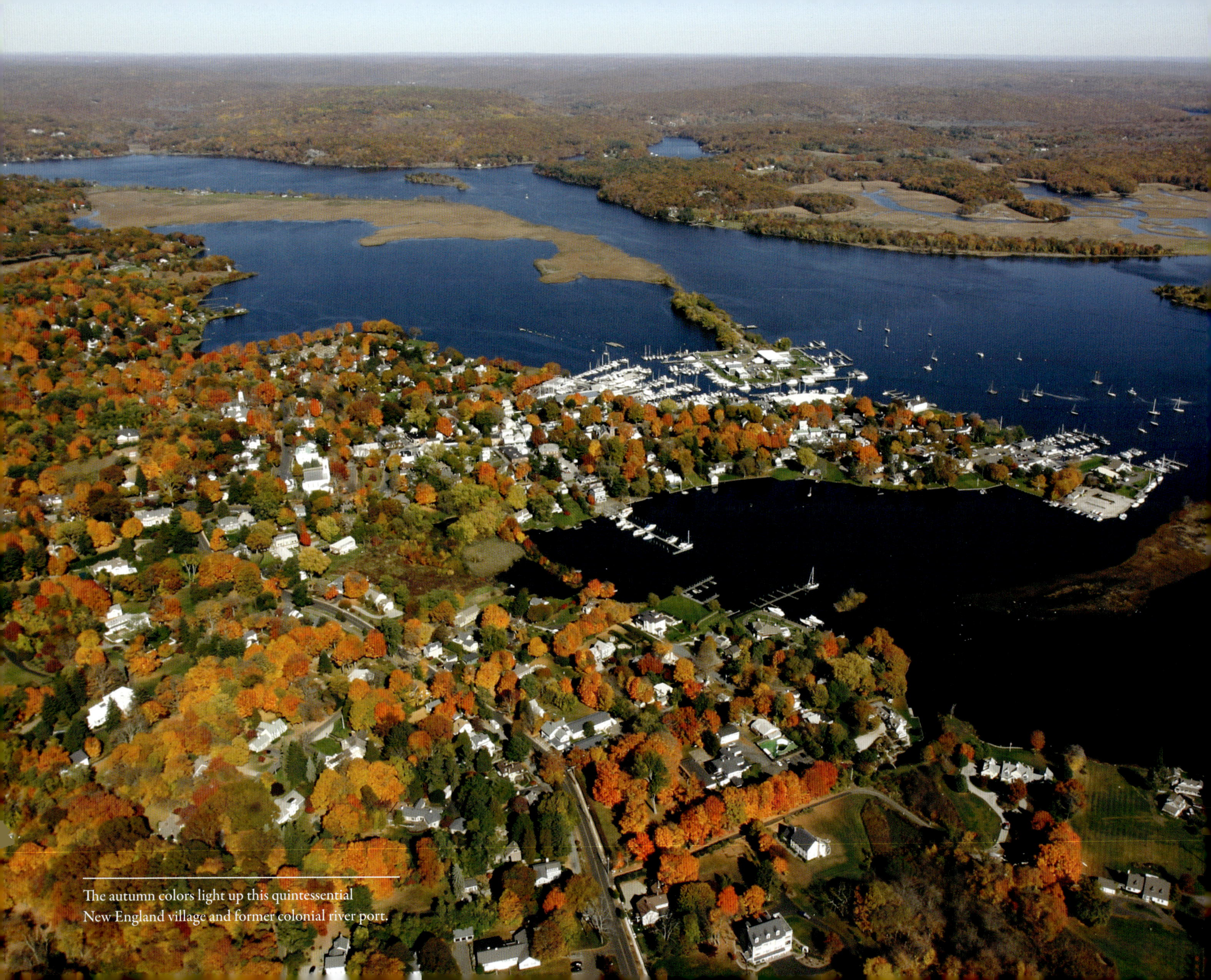

The autumn colors light up this quintessential New England village and former colonial river port.

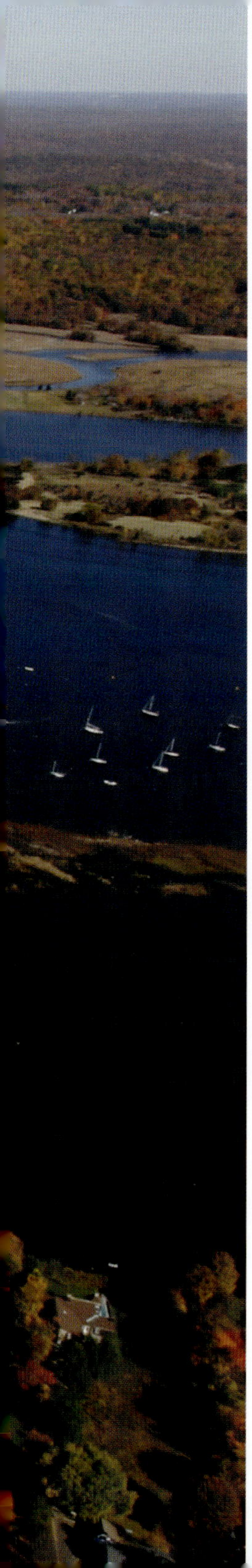

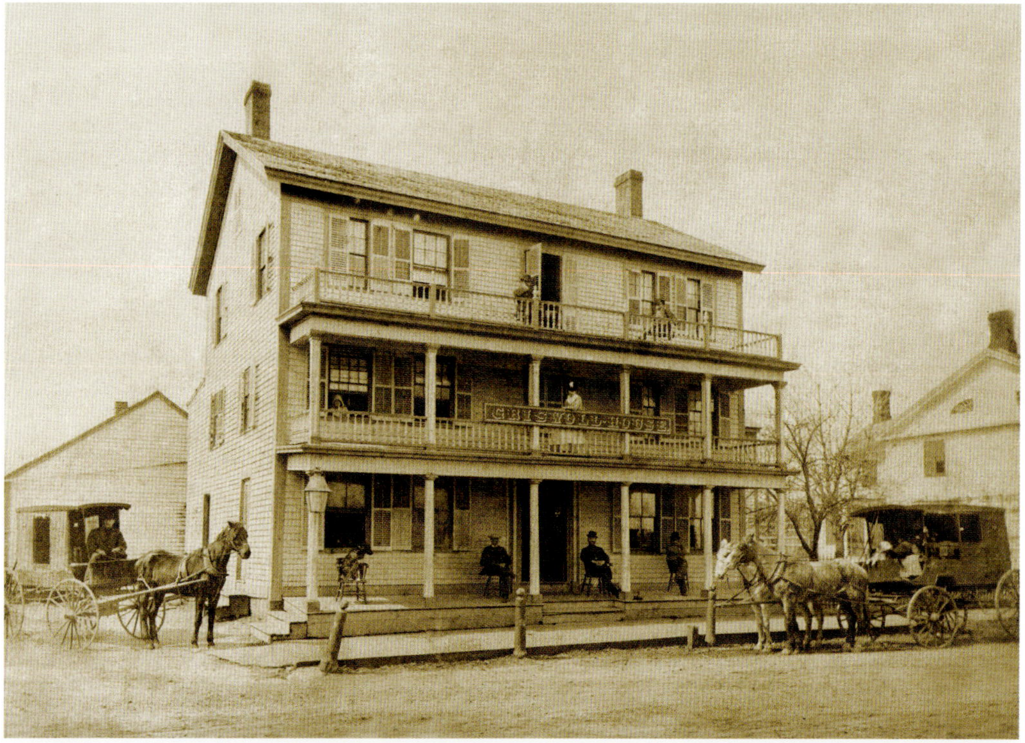

(clockwise from top left) Halfway up Main Street in Essex stands the iconic Griswold Inn, which has been in operation, in one form or another, for well over 200 years while its taproom pre-dates the Revolution. This is the inn as it appeared in 1865. *Courtesy of the Paul Foundation.*

The British Raid on Essex by Kip Soldwedel, *courtesy Connecticut River Museum.*

On the waterfront, the Connecticut River Museum, which occupies the 1878 Steamboat Dock and warehouse, celebrates the great river and its history. From 1824 to 1931 large passenger steamboats, also carrying freight, connected river towns such as Hartford, Middletown, and Essex to New York City via overnight service through the Sound.

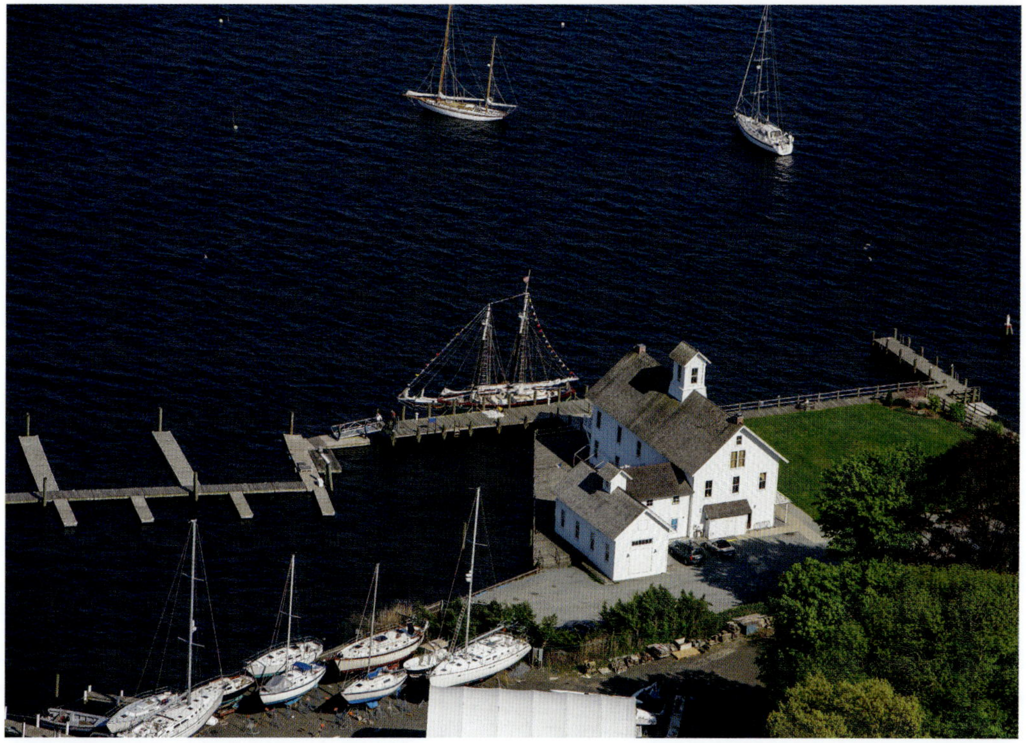

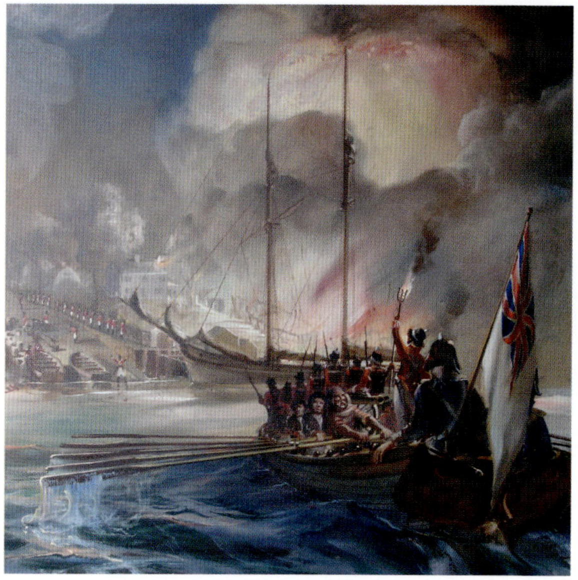

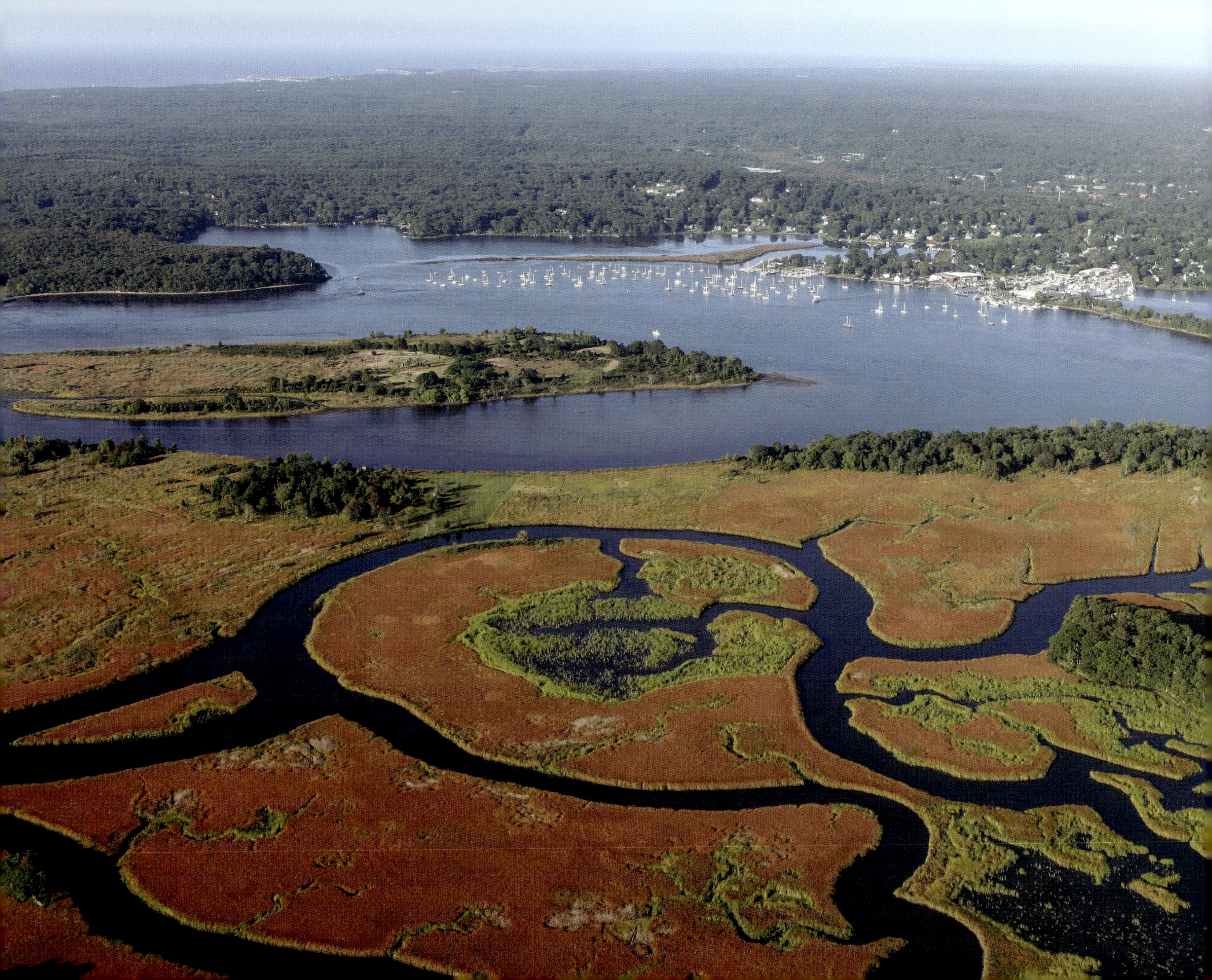

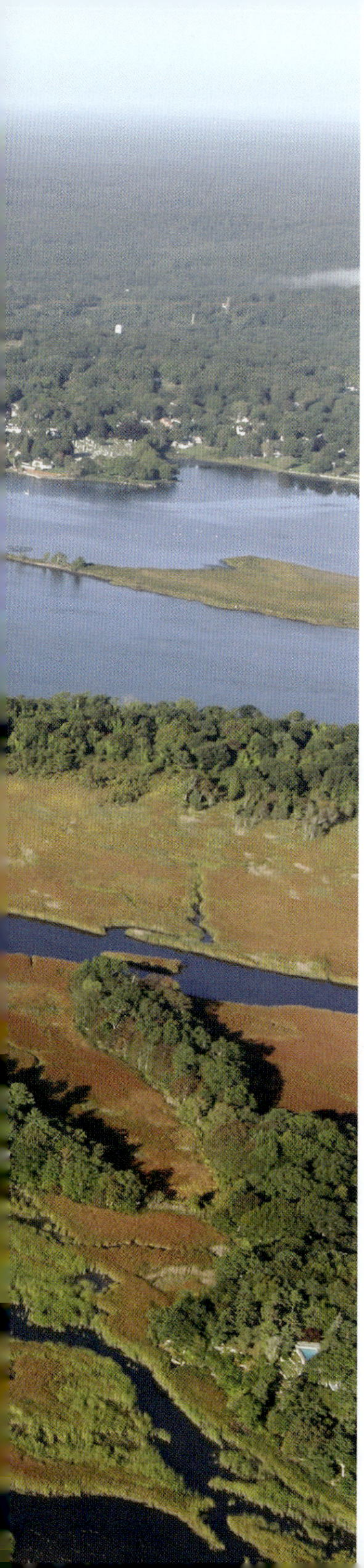

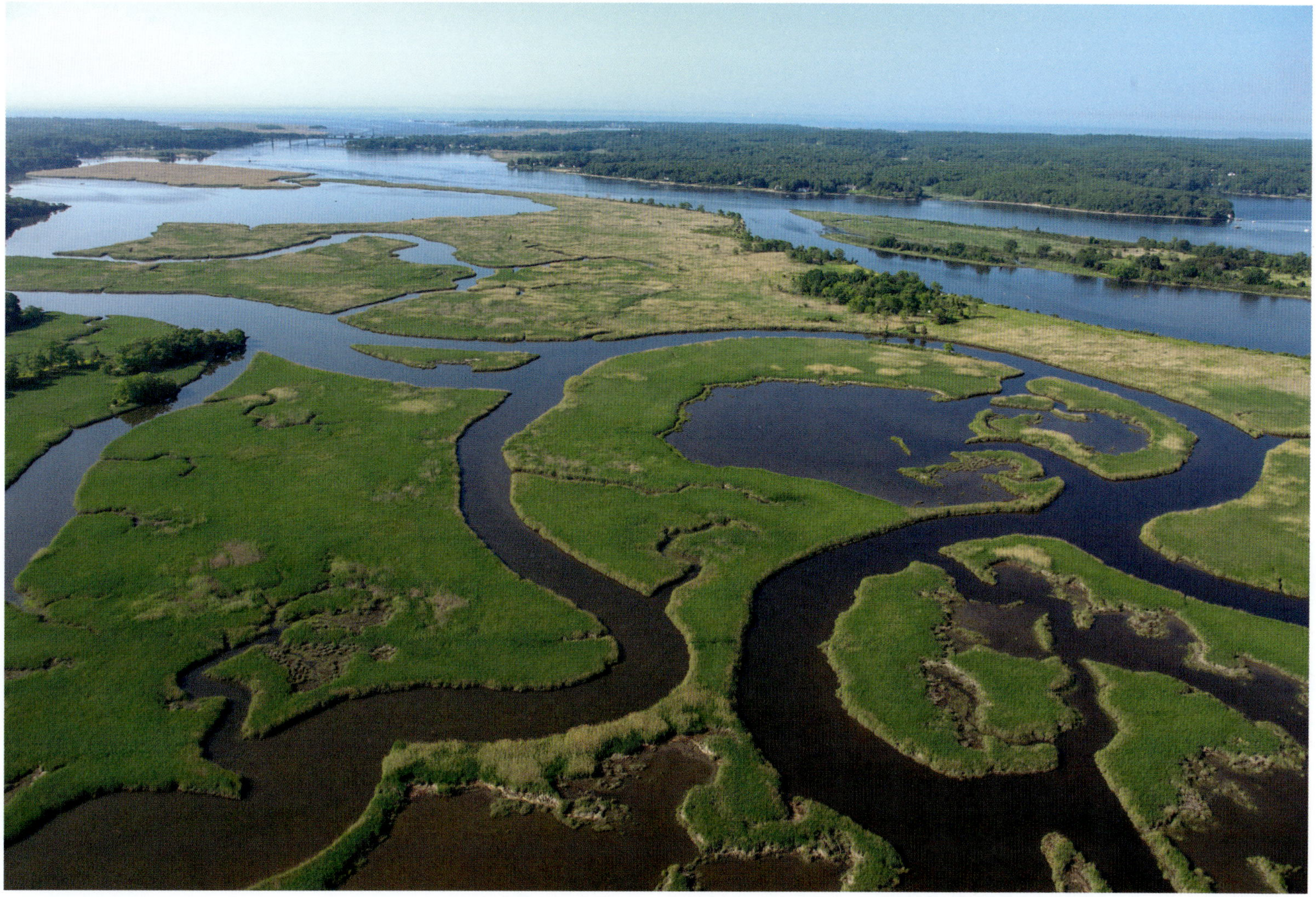

Lords Cove is located directly across the river from Essex, behind Nott Island. Swirling tides interacting with the cove's own tributary and the river's down-flow have formed a unique maze of marshy twists and turns and mini-oxbows. Only recognizable from the air, this area is seldom seen even by those who live nearby or traverse the river's main channel by boat.

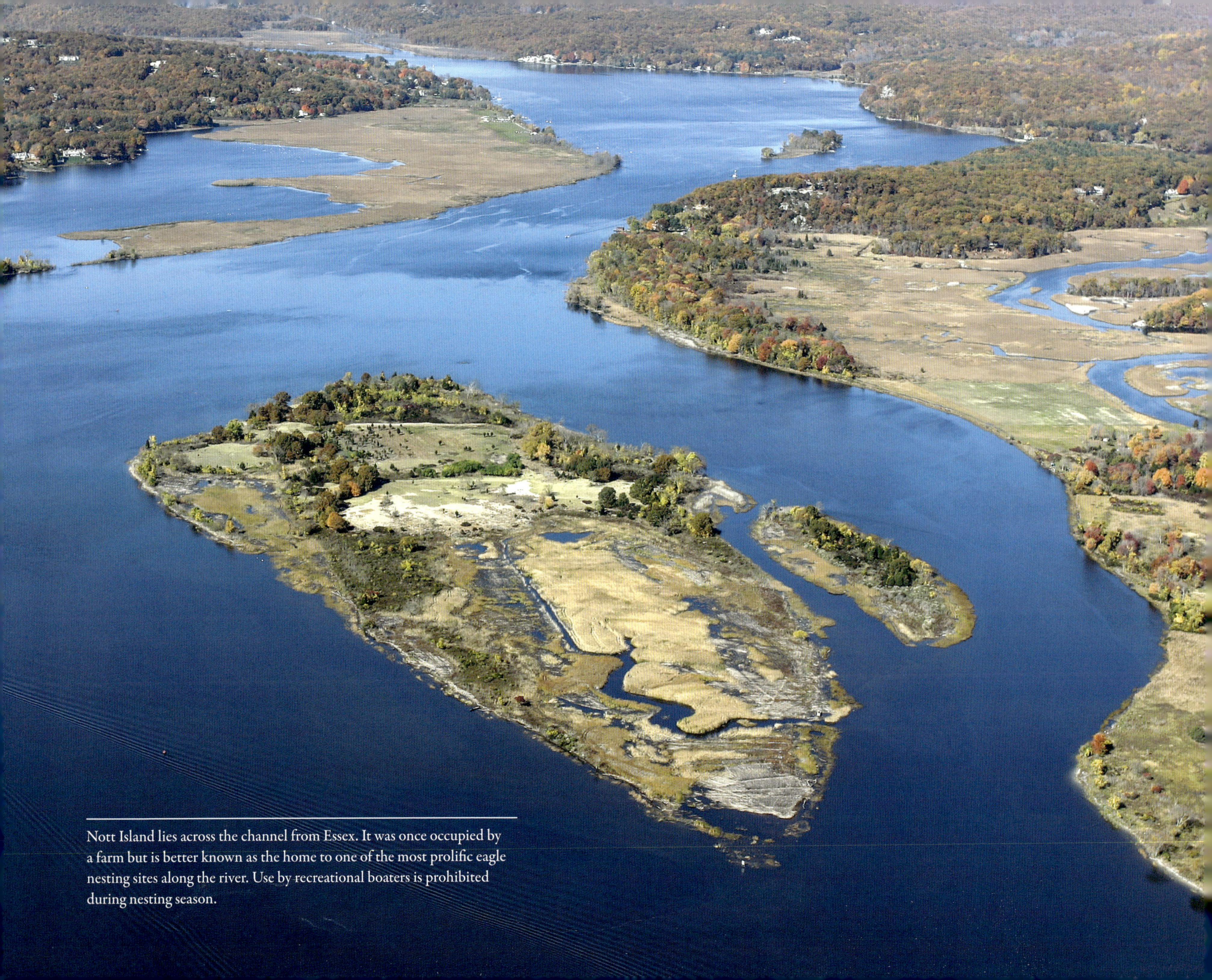

Nott Island lies across the channel from Essex. It was once occupied by a farm but is better known as the home to one of the most prolific eagle nesting sites along the river. Use by recreational boaters is prohibited during nesting season.

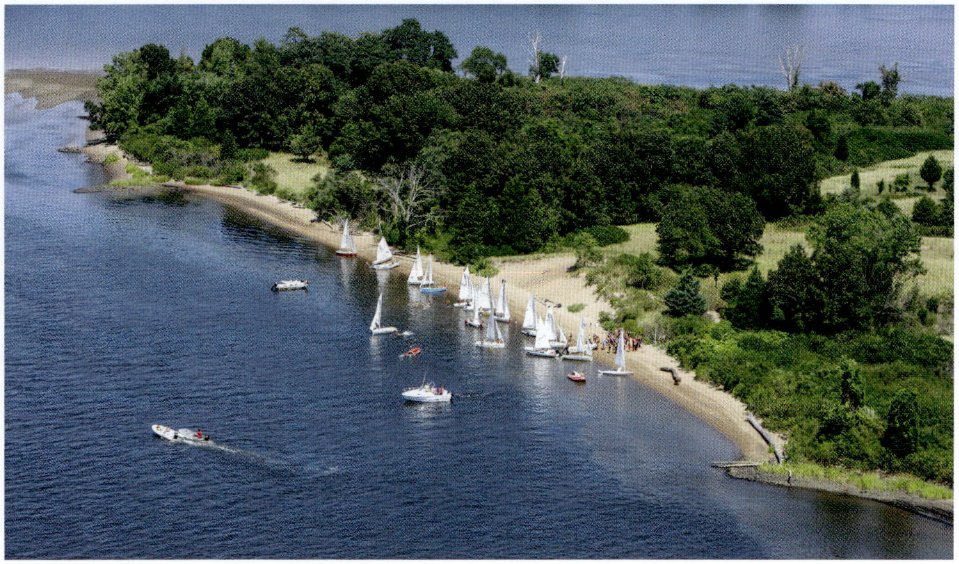

Students and instructors from Pettipaug Yacht Club, which runs an excellent youth sailing program, have hauled up on Nott Island to stretch their legs. Essex is still very much a boating community with four yacht clubs and several marinas. The Essex Yacht Club has been hosting the annual off-season frostbite series since 1933.

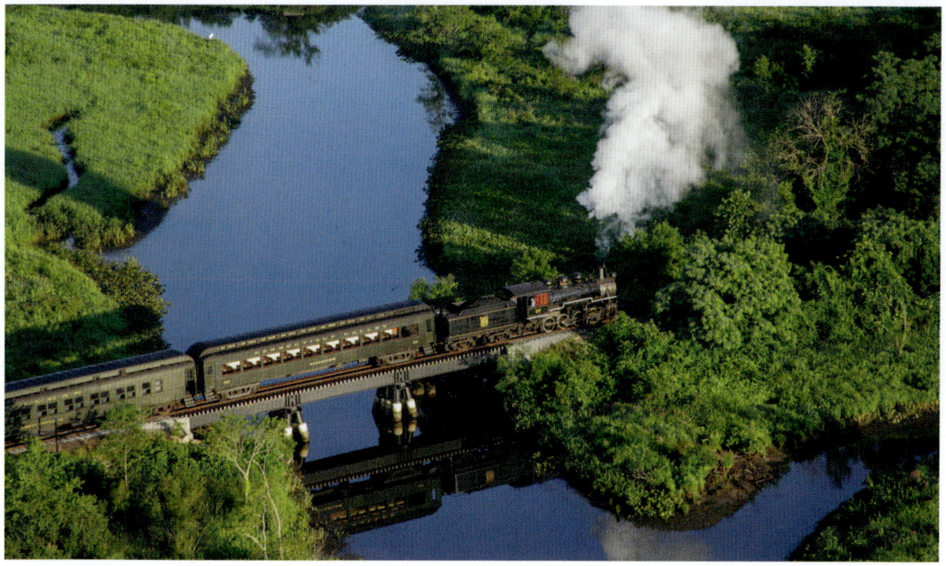

The Essex Steam Train crosses Deep River heading north along tracks that once connected Fenwick and Old Saybrook to Hartford, the vintage trains have become one of Connecticut's major attractions. Boarding in Essex, passengers transfer to the paddle-wheeler *Becky Thatcher* at Deep River landing to continue their adventure up the river.

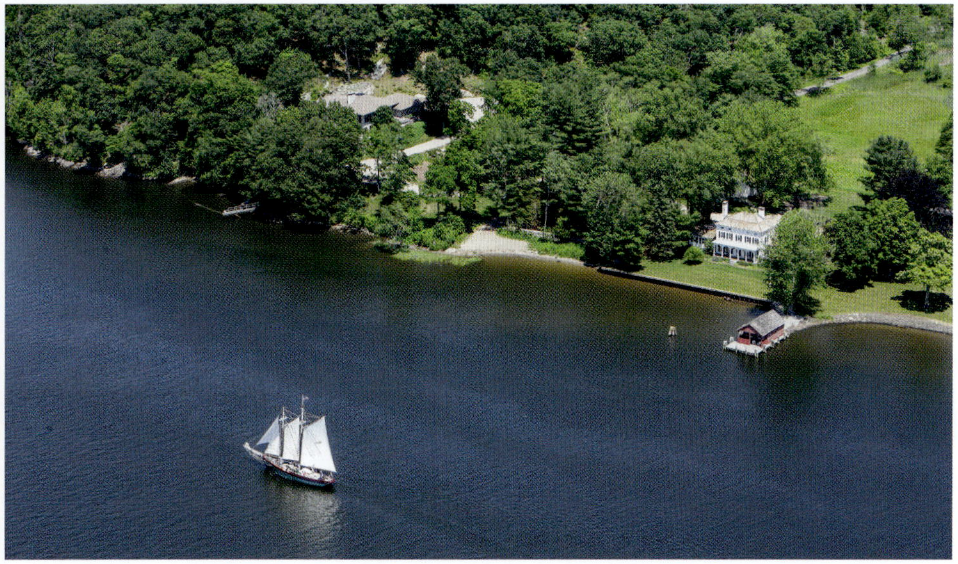

The historic Schooner *Mary E* sails past the old Ely's ferry landing on the east side of the river. Foundation stones of the inn and tavern that once accommodated travelers on this important colonial stage route can still be found just to the left of the beach.

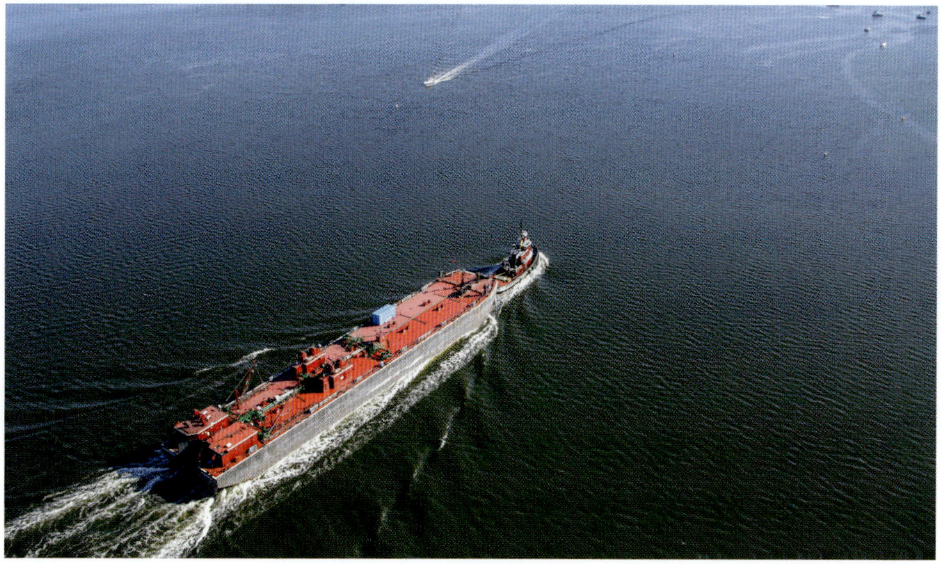

Now a rare sight on the river, a tug and fuel barge approach Nott Island from the north heading toward the Sound. Not so long ago the river was busy with commercial traffic, but today only a handful of excursion vessels share the river with recreational boaters.

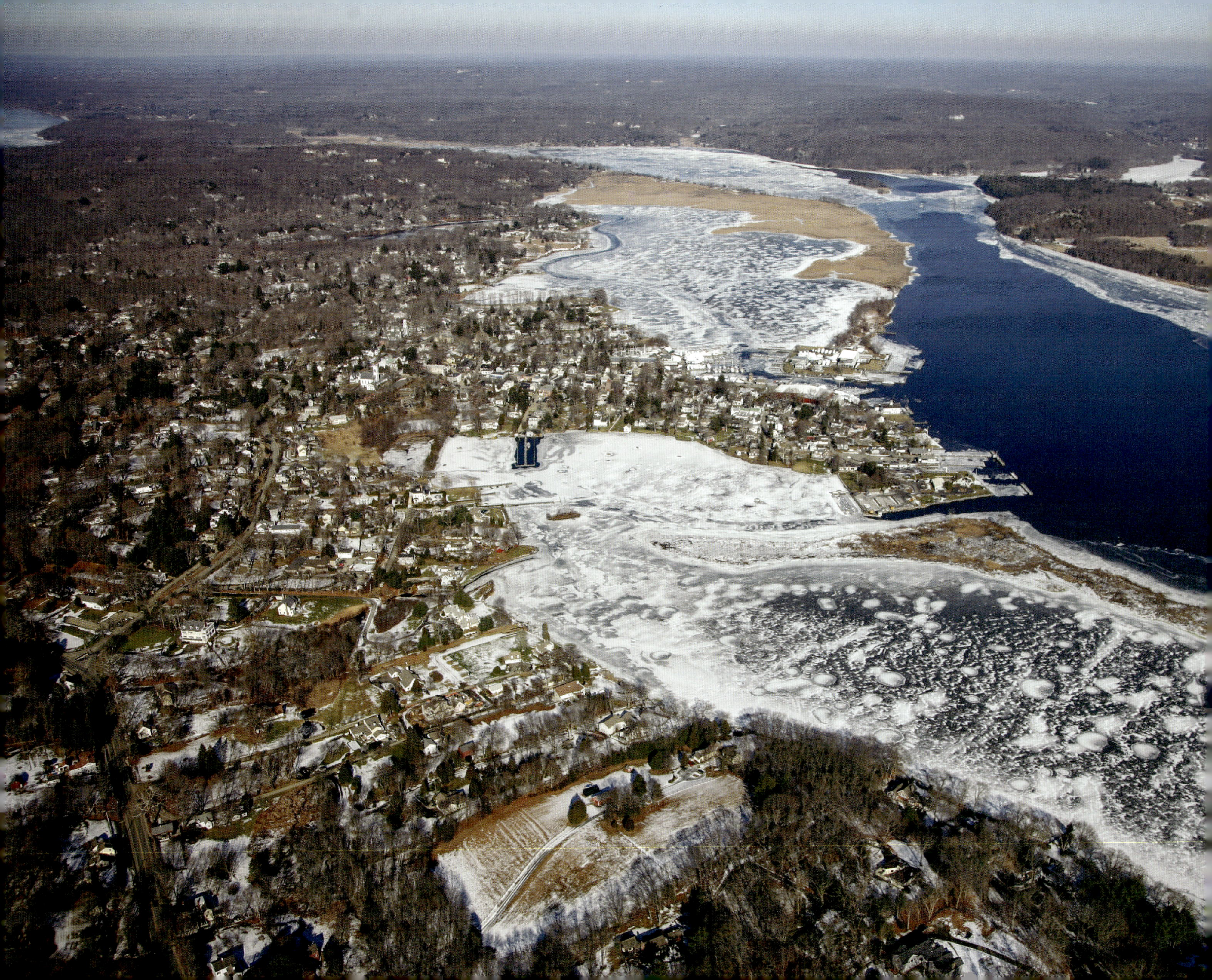

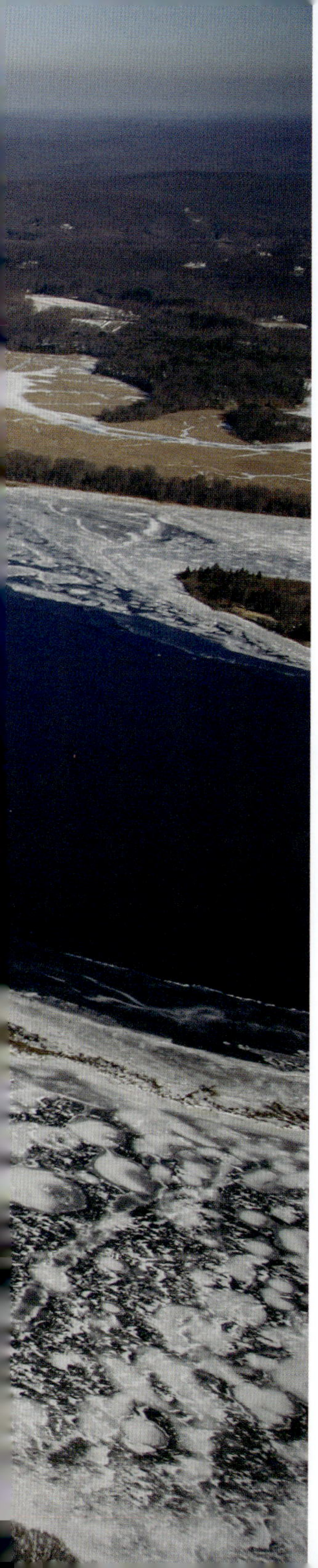

(left) Although Essex and its north and south coves are frozen in, the river itself normally remains open here. This is because the incoming ocean tides bring saltwater this far up the river. For this reason, large numbers of bald eagles, which need open water to fish, congregate here. While there are always several pairs of nesting eagles in the area, the open water attracts dozens more during the winter season, which in turn makes Essex a great attraction to eagle watchers!

(top right) Ice flows past Essex.

(bottom right) A tug pulls a barge laden with lumber up the river just north of Essex.

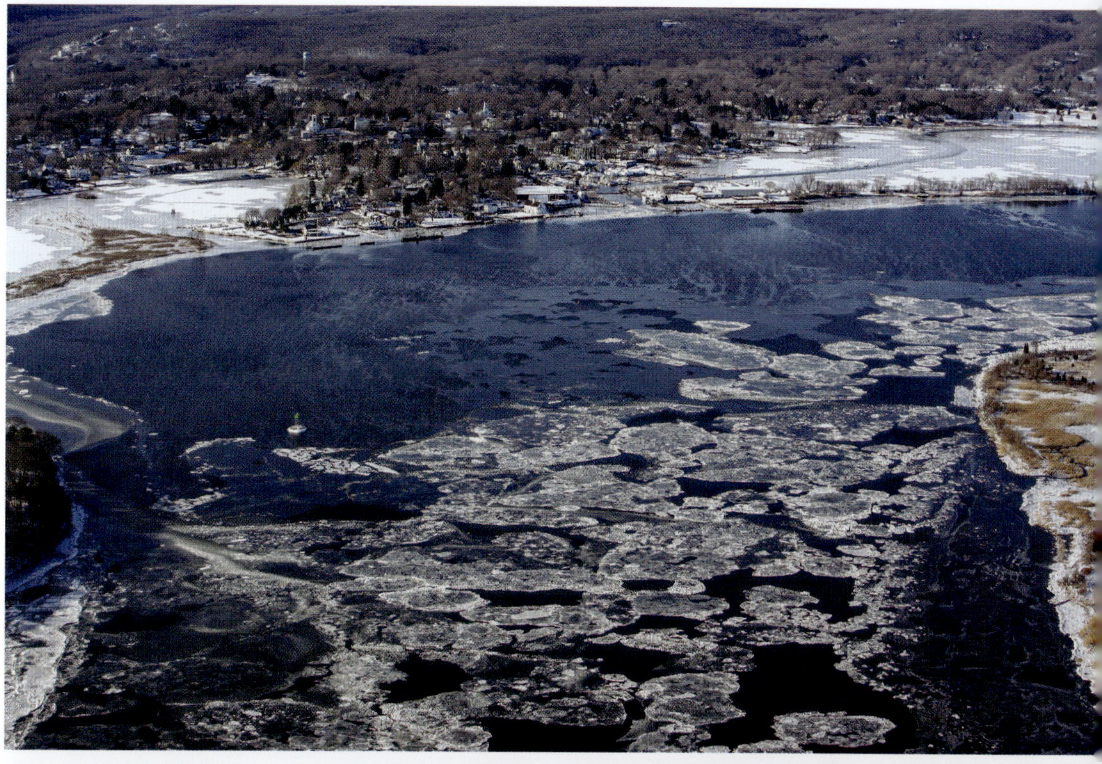

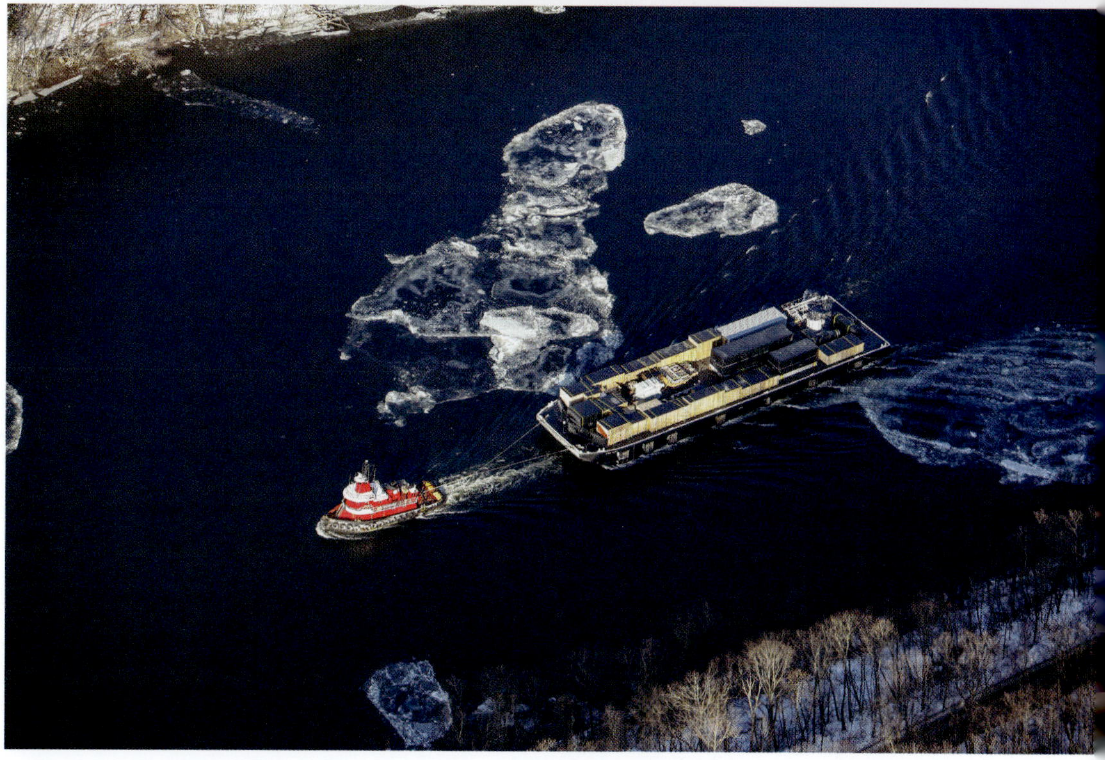

HAMBURG COVE

This enchanted cove, where the Eight Mile River joins the Connecticut, has long been a favorite anchorage for boaters and is cherished for its scenic beauty and tranquility. The small village with its marinas and churchyard was settled as part of Lyme and has always been strongly connected to maritime trade. Its broad outer cove is protected from wind and waves from all directions and is still considered the perfect "hurricane hole" providing shelter from the nor'easters that frequently wreak havoc on the New England coast. When the barometer starts to fall, boaters in the know head for the cove to hunker down. If you haven't figured it out yet, the Eight Mile River got its name, not for being eight miles long, but because it joins the Connecticut River eight miles upstream from Long Island Sound. Creative people, those colonials!

(below) From the air it is easy to understand why locals say that anyone who has not gone aground in Hamburg Cove is a liar!

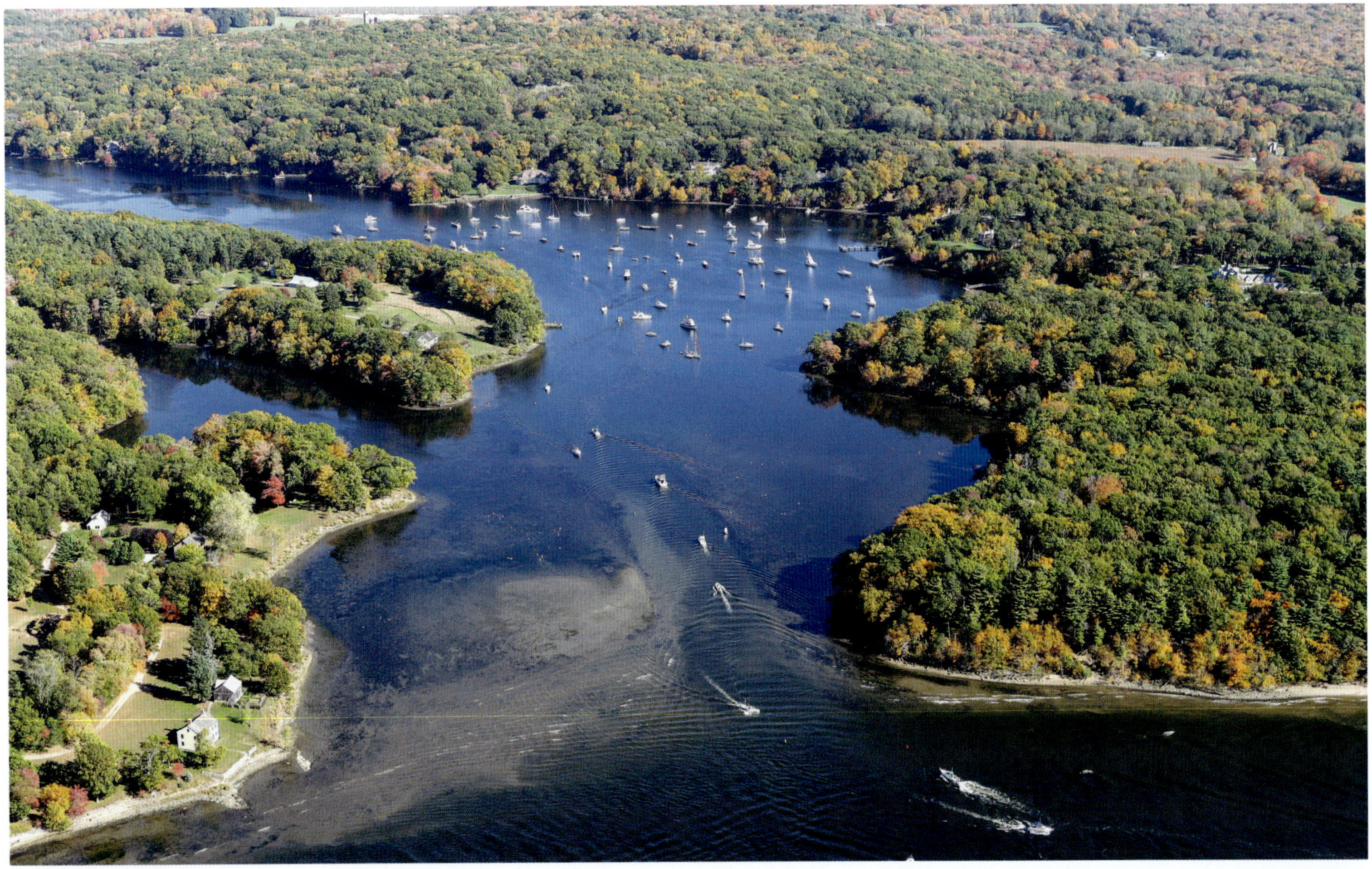

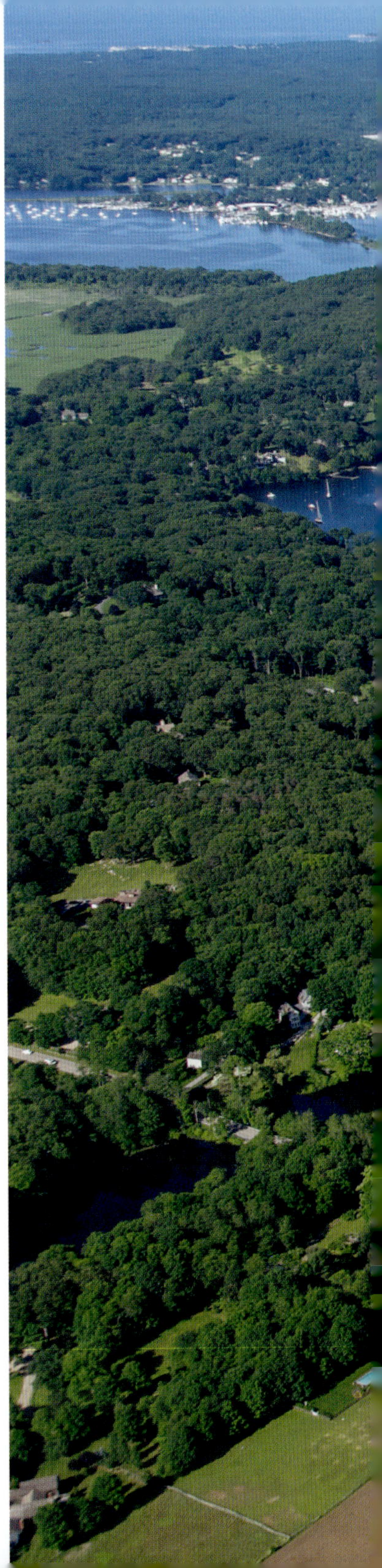

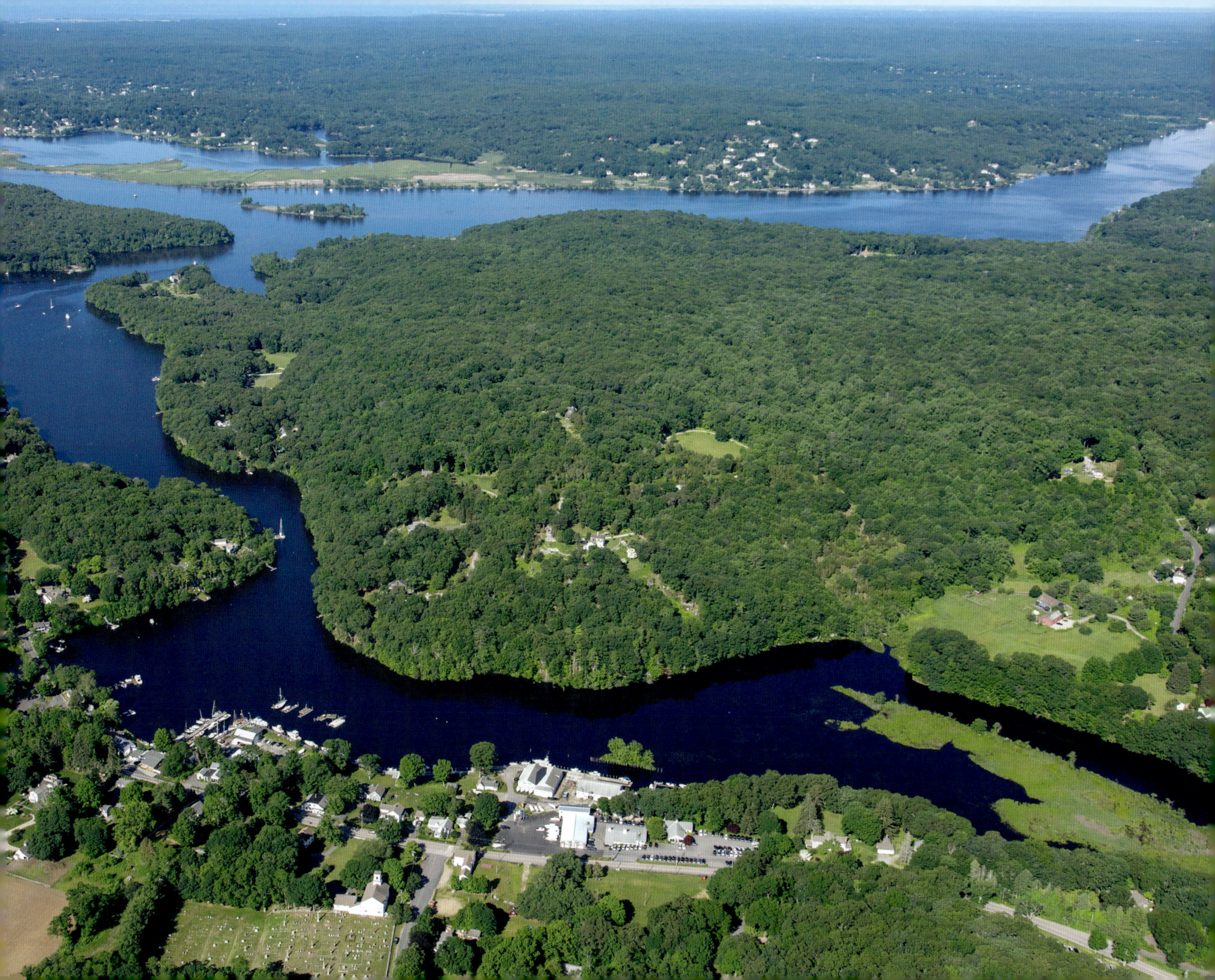

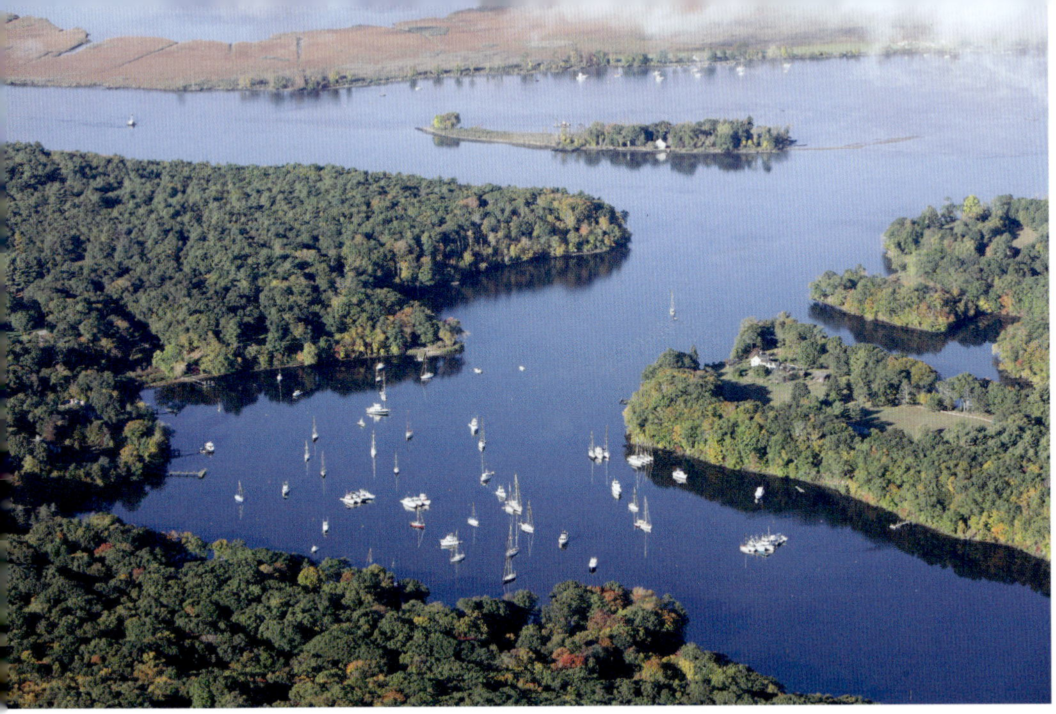

(above) Looking across the outer cove to Brockway Island it is hard to imagine a more tranquil scene.

(below) Looking very much like a secluded inlet in Maine, it is clear why Hamburg Cove has been a favorite destination for generations of boaters.

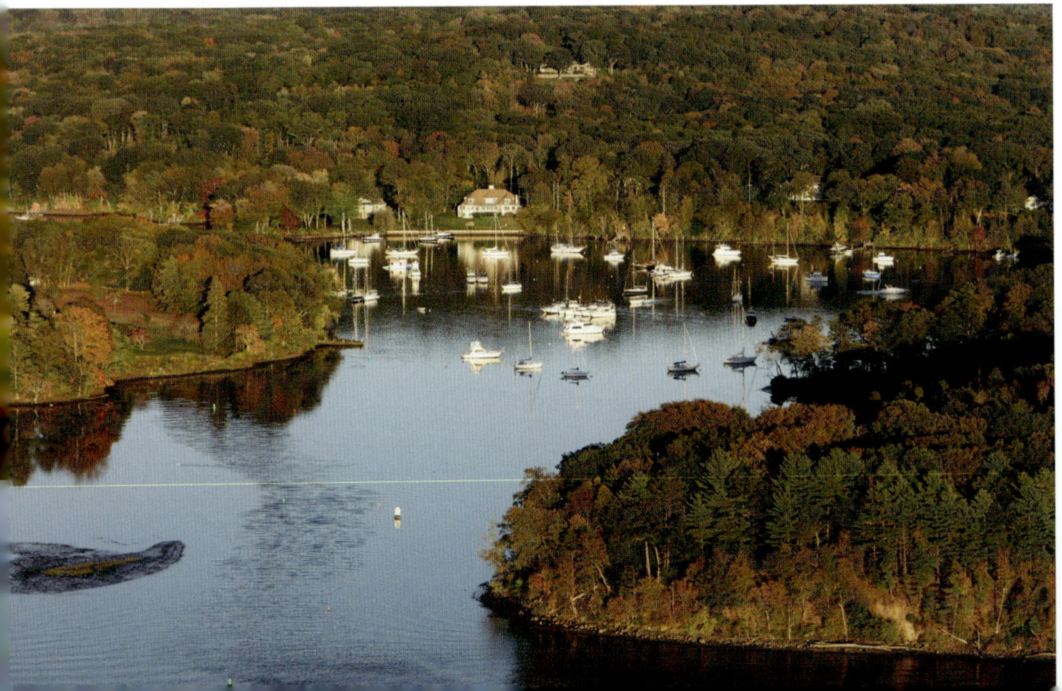

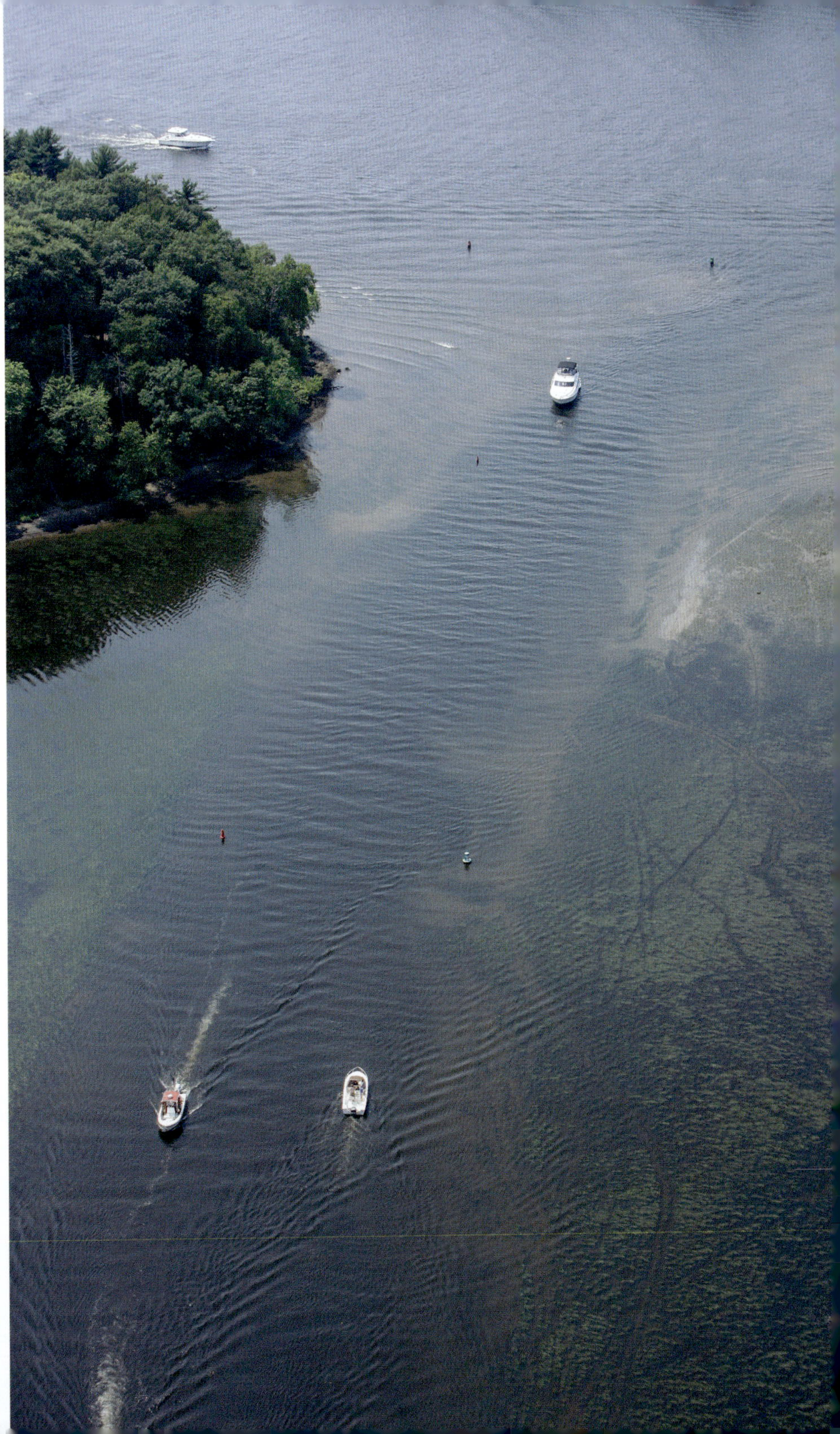

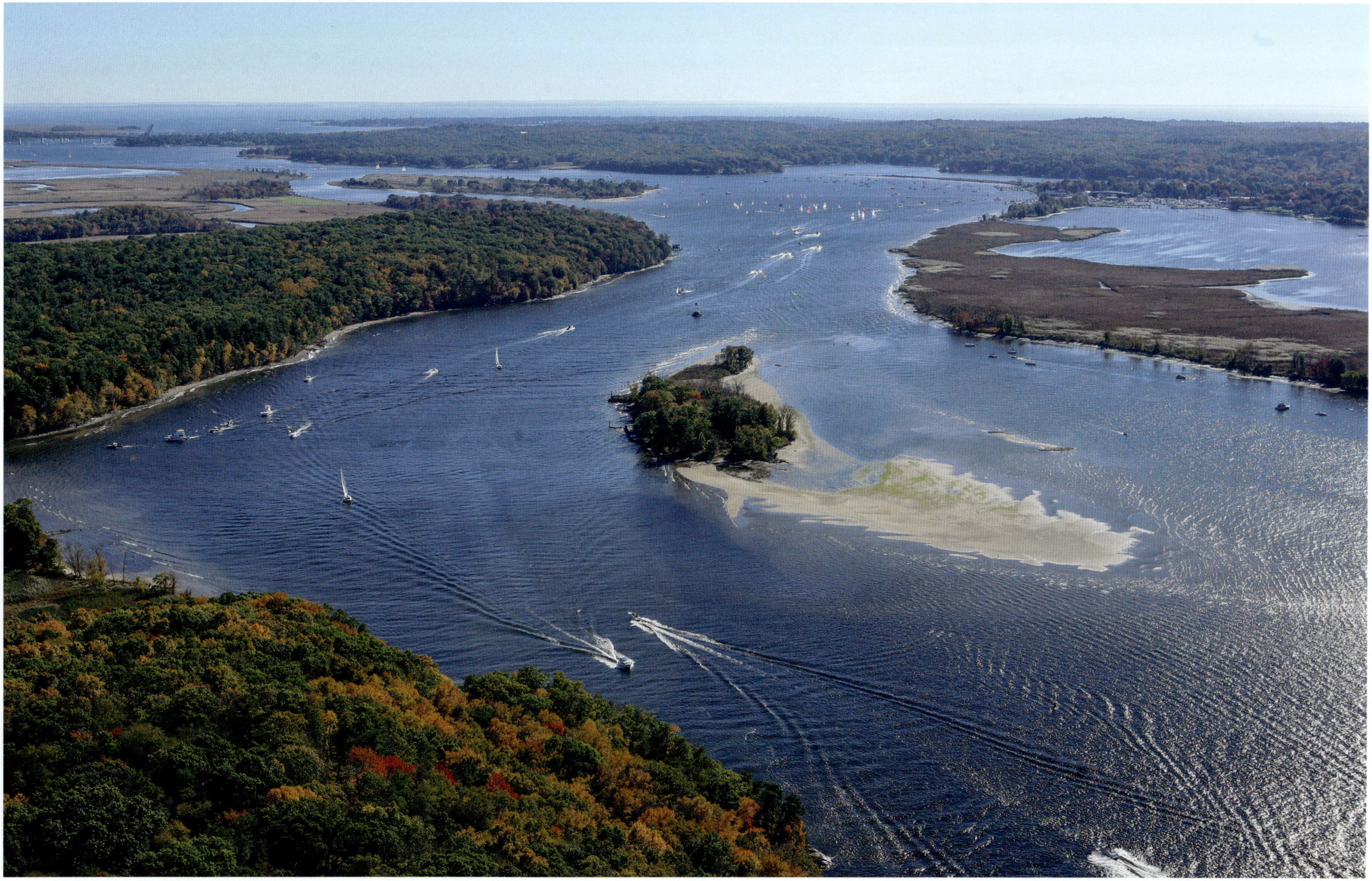

(above) Once bustling with commercial traffic the river is now heavily used by recreational boaters coming and going to and from the Sound, which lies in the distance to the south.

(left) Furrows carved into the bottom outside the marked channel illustrate just how unforgiving the entry into Hamburg Cove can be.

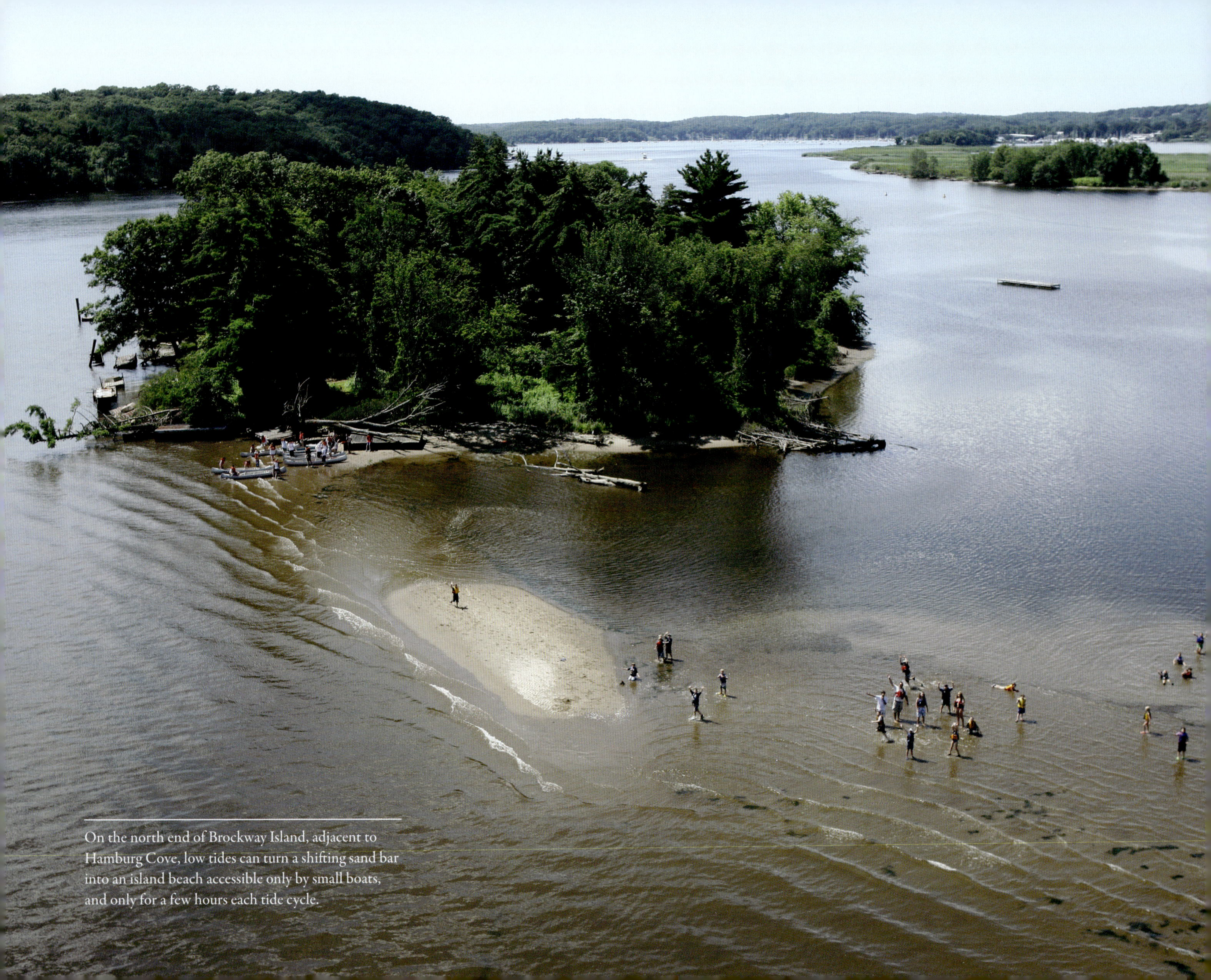

On the north end of Brockway Island, adjacent to Hamburg Cove, low tides can turn a shifting sand bar into an island beach accessible only by small boats, and only for a few hours each tide cycle.

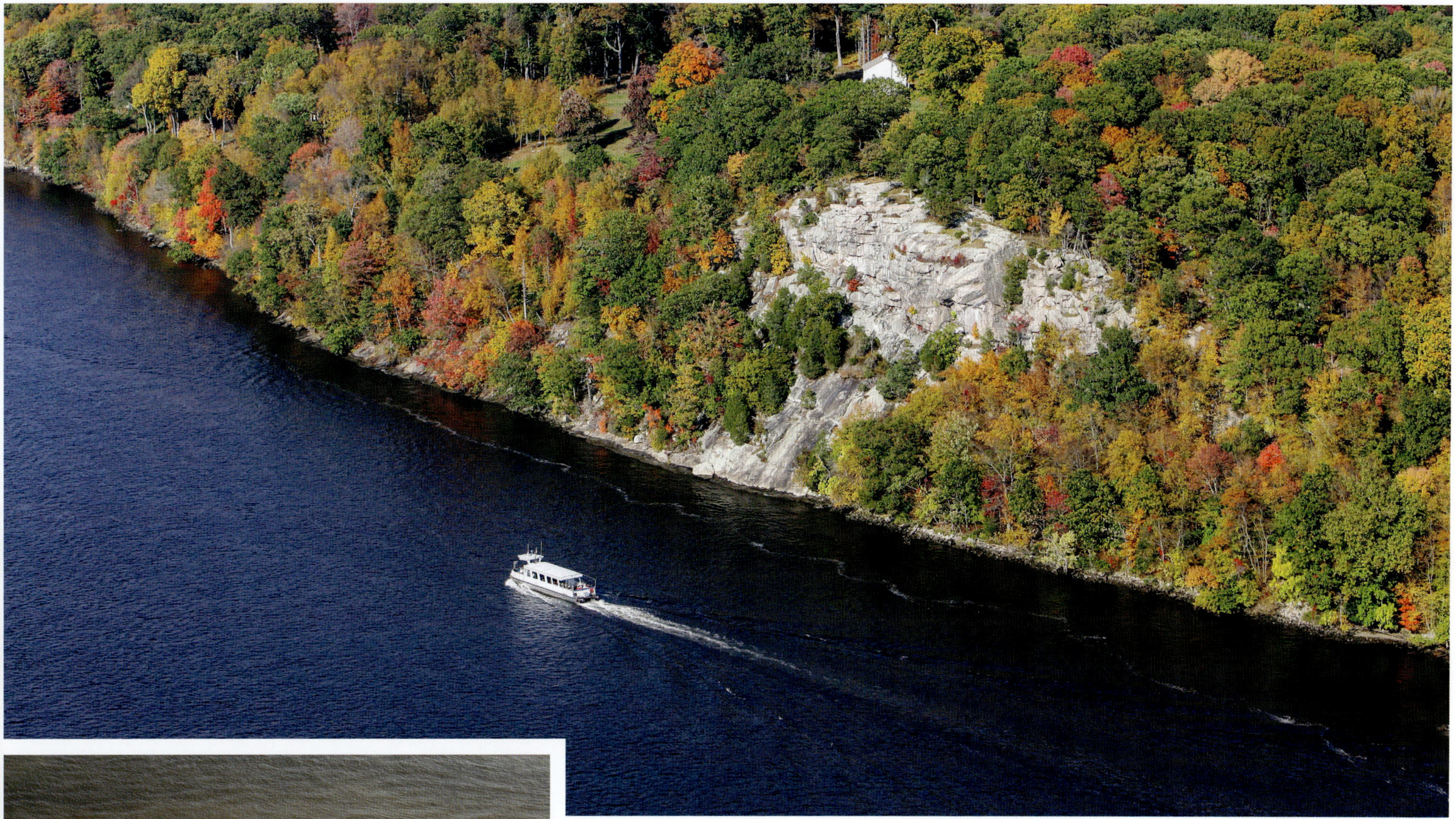

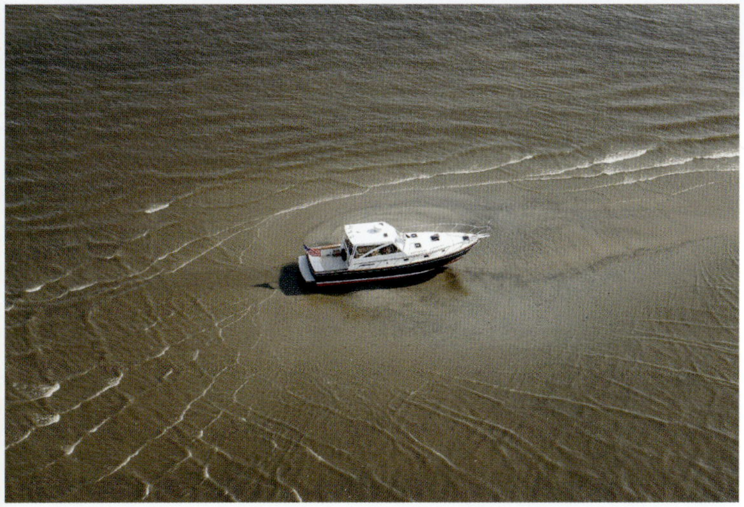

(above) The eco-tour boat *RiverQuest* passes below Joshua Rock on the eastern bank of the river just north of Hamburg Cove. Local legend says that this dramatic outcropping was a favorite perch of Chief Attawanhood, the third son of the great Mohegan Sachem, Uncas. Attawanhood, who adopted the Christian name Joshua, apparently liked to sit atop the rock gazing down upon his people as they fished. Composed of the same granite-like Gneiss as found just up the river on Selden Island, it too was quarried for paving stones and building blocks.

(left) The river is deceptively wide but sandbars and even a few rocks are always ready to remind boaters that nautical charts and tide tables are still relevant. Local knowledge helps!

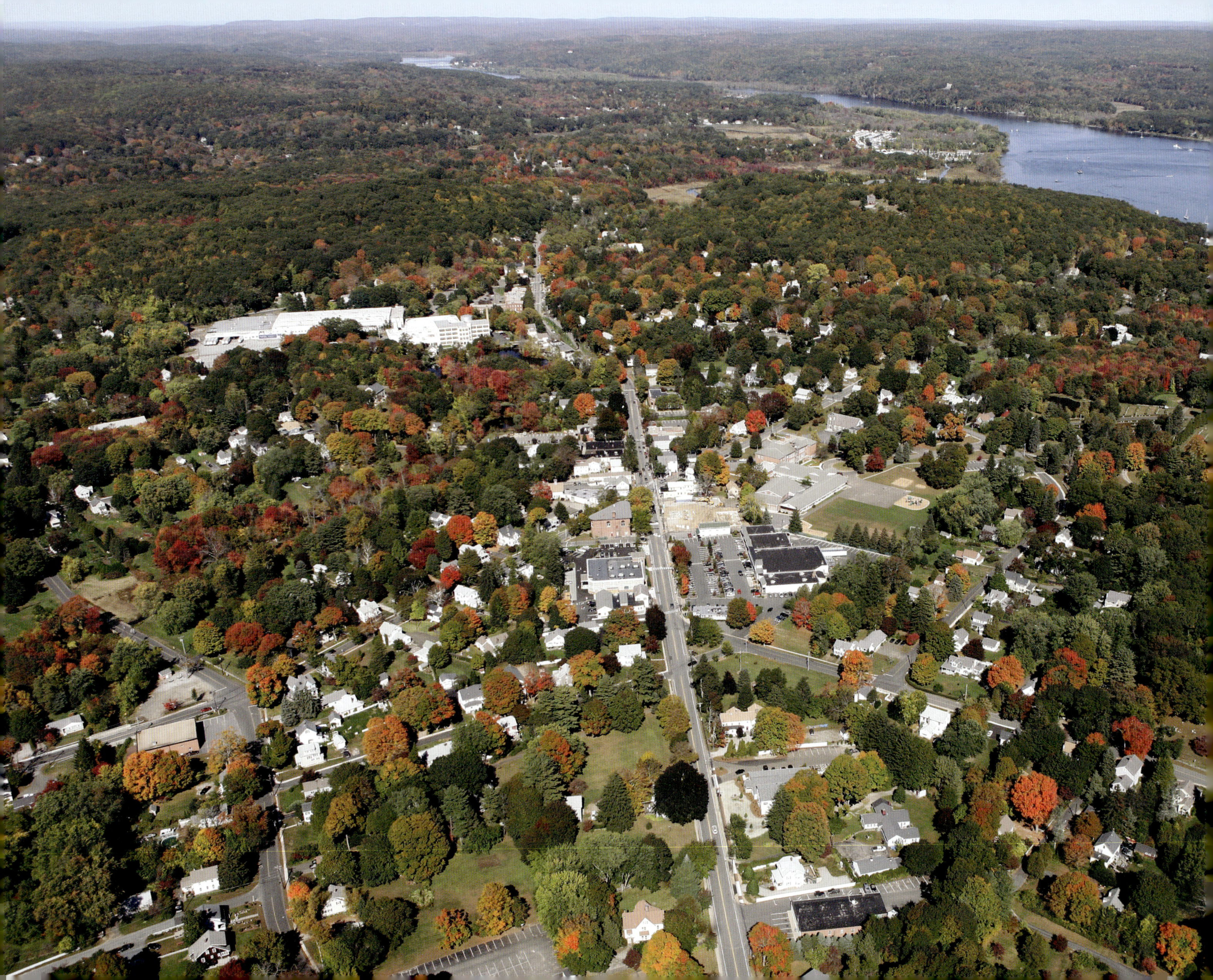

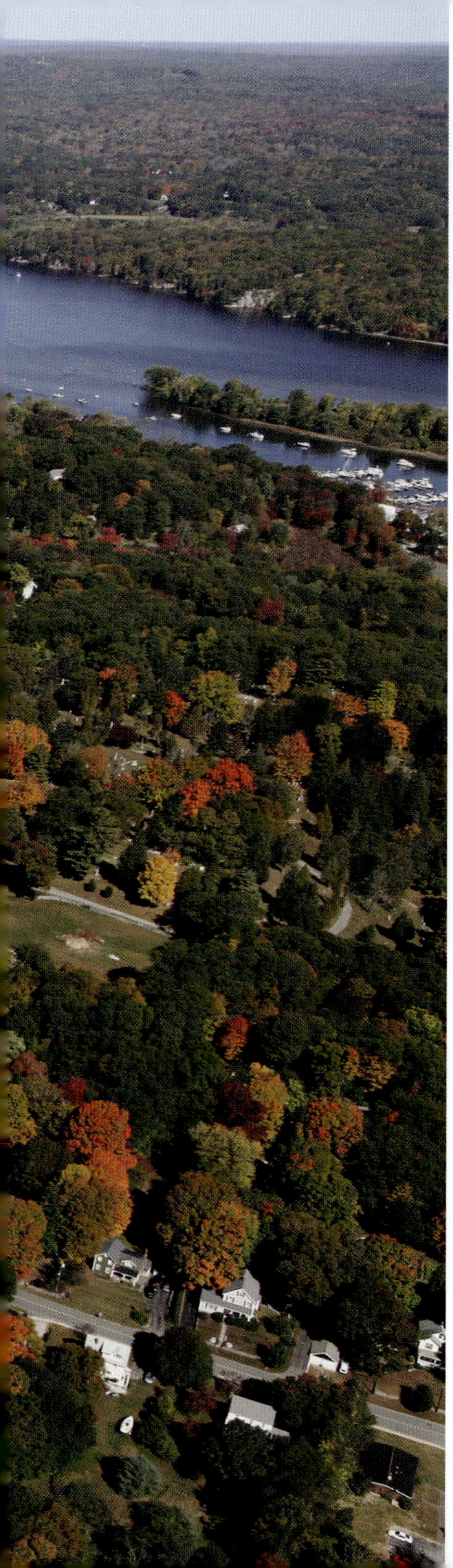

DEEP RIVER, CT

Deep River was originally part of Saybrook Colony settled in 1635. Most people believe the name comes from a deep spot in the Connecticut River but in fact the town sits astride the Deep River, which is a tributary to the Connecticut. It was a shipbuilding town and later, along with Ivoryton in Essex, became a center for the manufacturing of ivory products, most notably piano keys and keyboard actions. The old Pratt & Reed piano works, now a condominium, still dominates the center of town. During the Second World War, the company produced troop-carrying gliders to be used in airborne assaults such as D-Day. Over 970 troop transports and 250 training gliders were produced here.

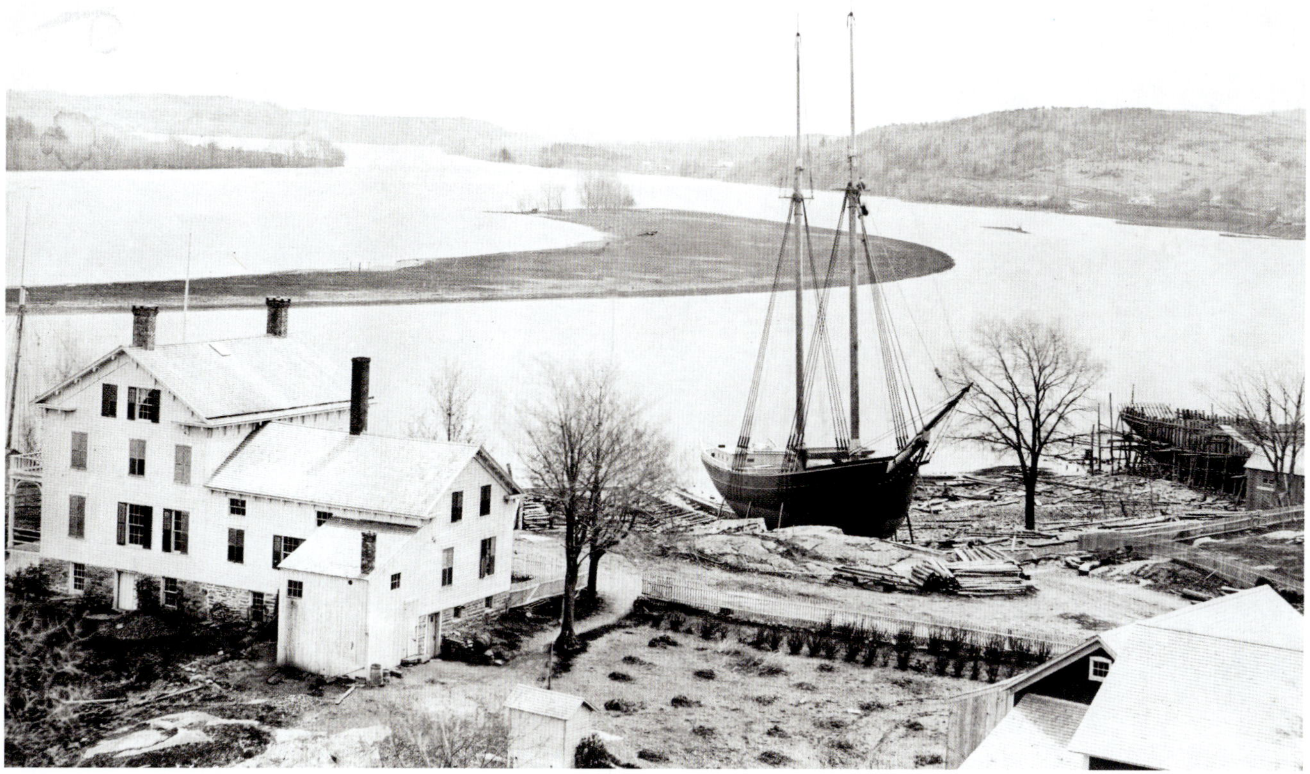

(above) Looking south over Deep River Landing, with Estuation Island in the distance, a schooner is being built in the late 1800s. The house is still there but the area is now dominated by a town park, a marina, and a stop for the Essex Steam train and riverboat.

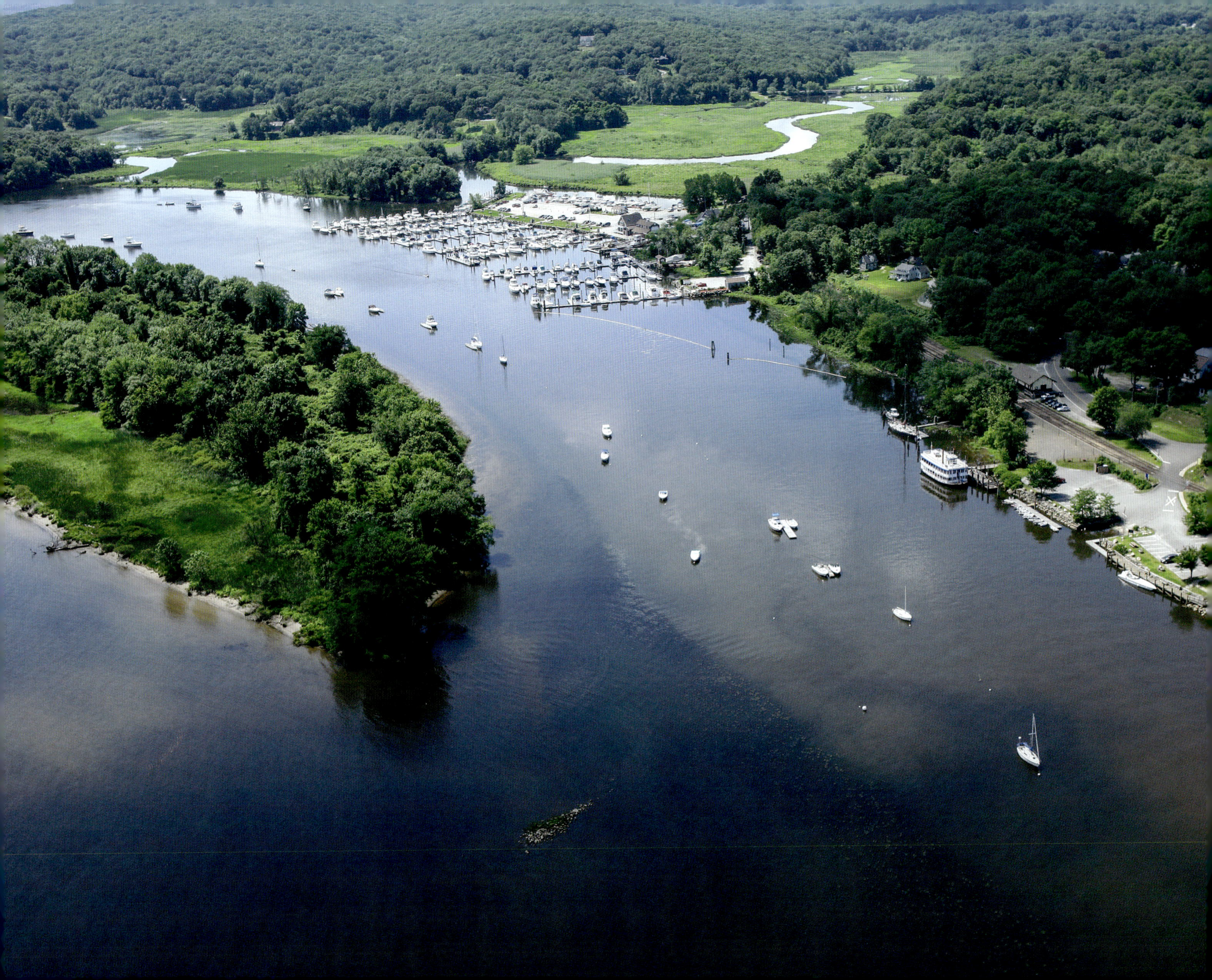

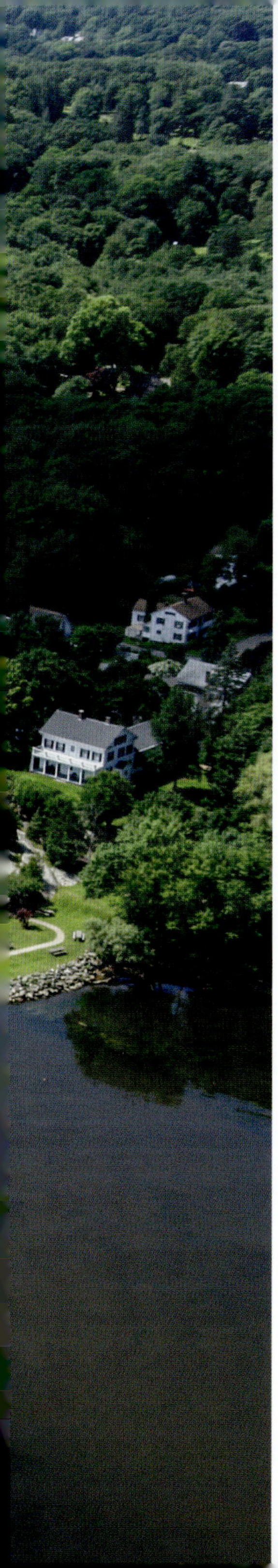

(left) Today, Deep River landing, where schooners were once built and launched, features a waterfront park, a boat launch, a marina, and is the home port of the paddle-wheeler *Becky Thatcher*, which is part of the Essex Steam Train experience.

(top right) Looking northeast over Pratt Cove, Deep River Landing, and the crescent-shaped Eustasia Island. Beyond this lies Selden Island, the largest island on the entire river.

(bottom right) The Essex Steam Train heads north after a stop at Deep River Landing.

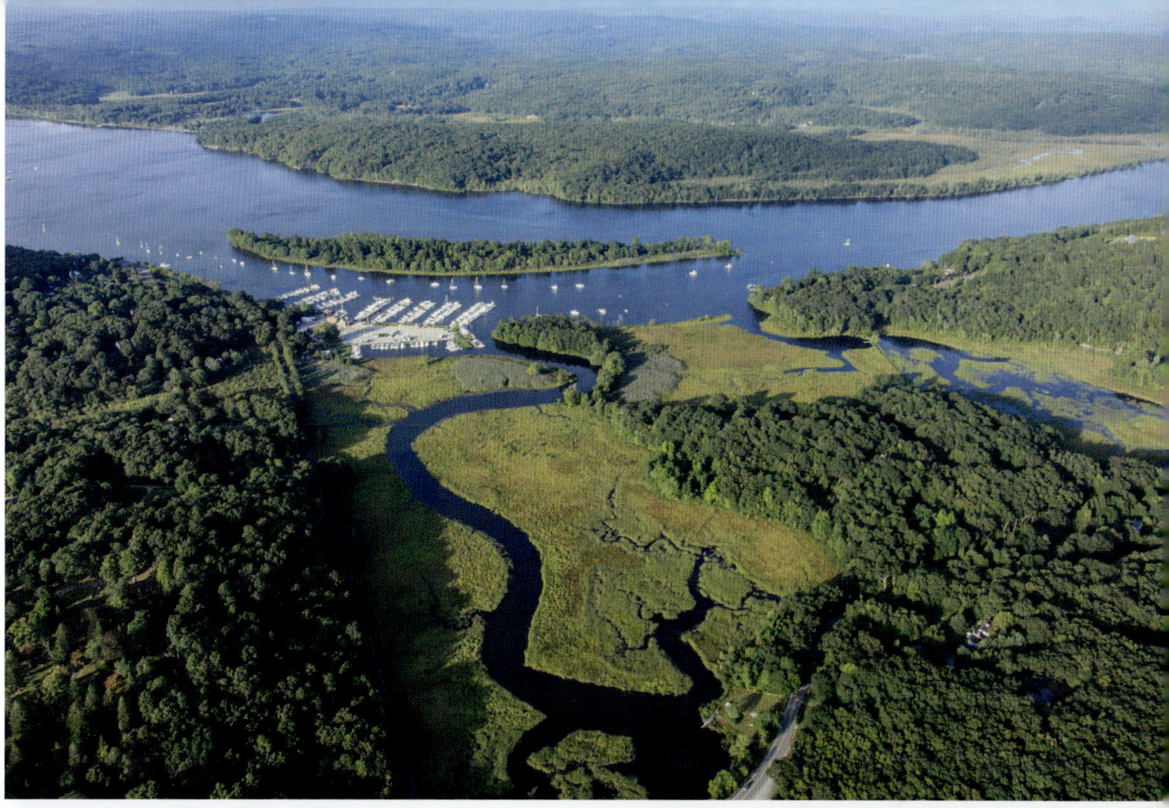

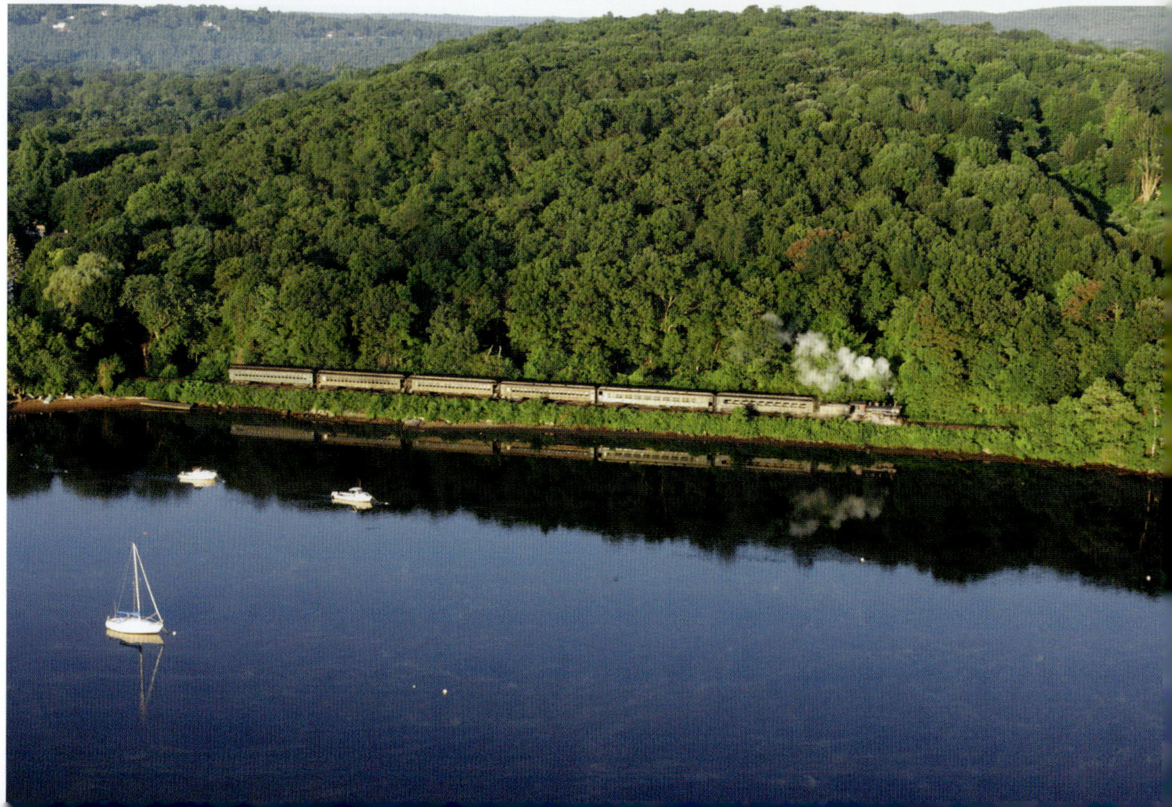

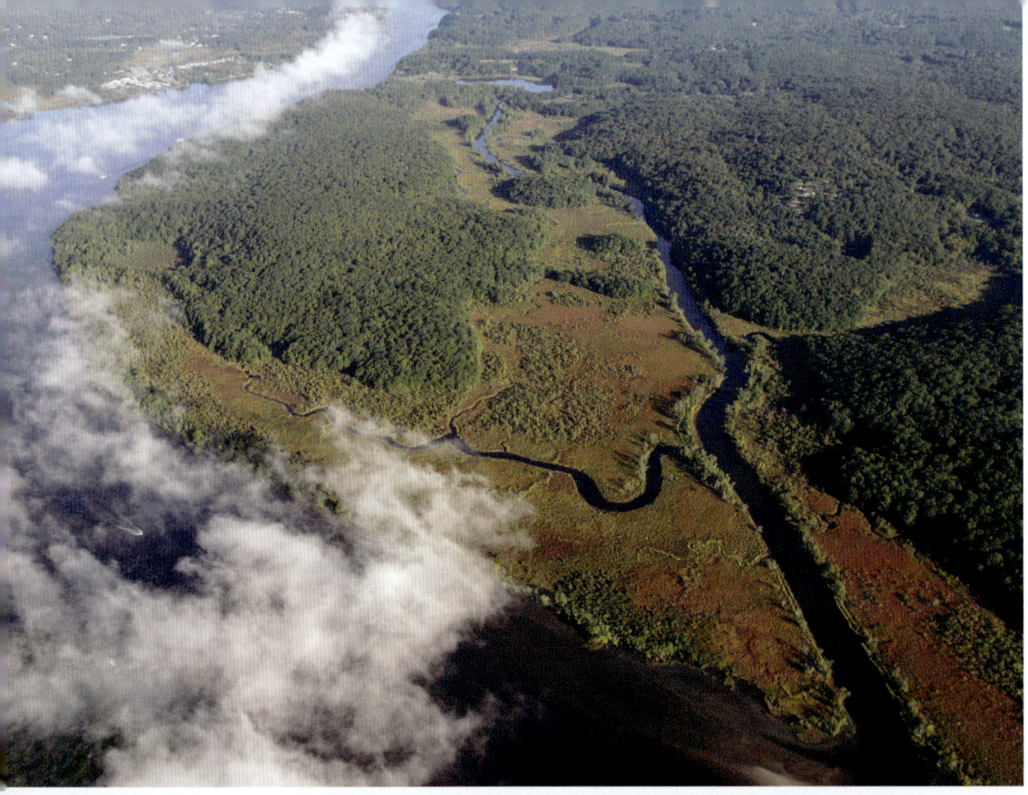

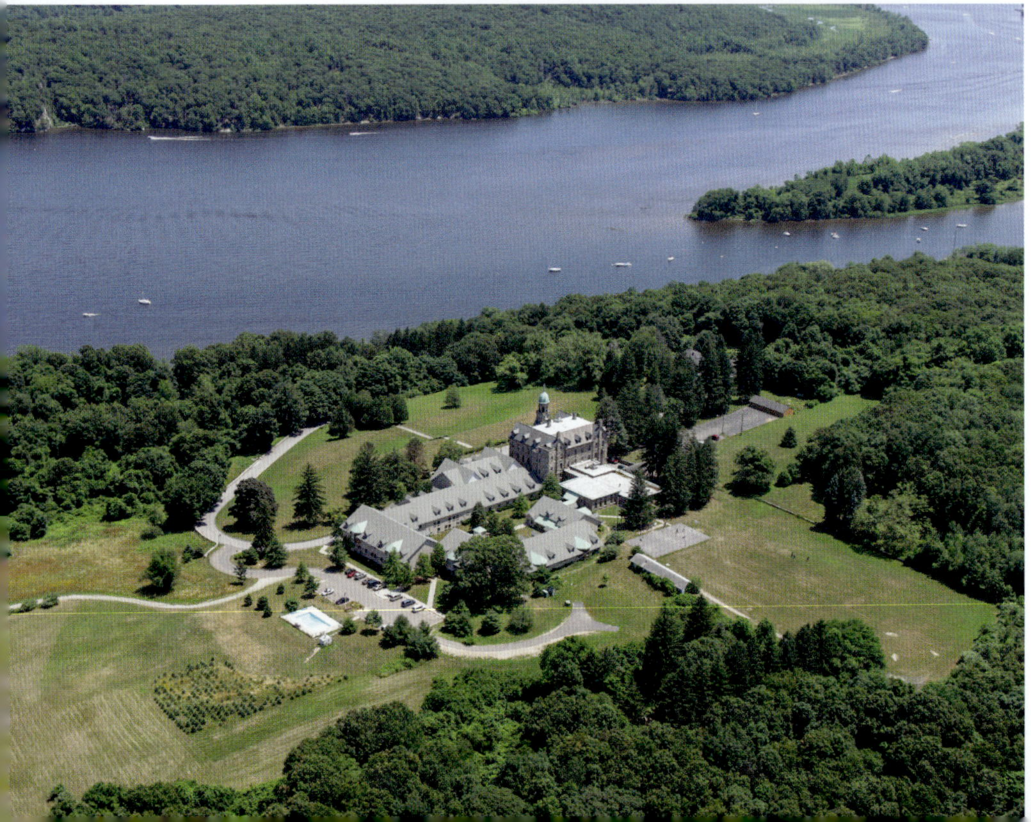

SELDEN ISLAND

Selden is the largest island on the Connecticut River and was once the site of intensive quarrying of the granite-like gneiss that forms much of the island's central ridge. From the 1890s through 1911, up to 600 men, largely immigrants, lived and worked on the island seasonally, producing paving stones, curbstone, and building blocks. The cut stone was transported down the river out into the Sound to destinations along the Eastern Seaboard. The pavers and curbstones were used on the streets of New York, Philadelphia, and many other cities and towns. Today Selden Island is a state park accessible only by kayaks, canoes, and small powerboats. Limited overnight camping at a handful of prepared sites is available by permit only. The remnants of the quarries are long overgrown, but cut stone can still be seen at some of the landing sites.

Originally known as Selden Neck, the island was once connected to the mainland at its northern end before flooding allowed Selden Creek to flow all the way along the island's eastern side.

(left) Just north of Deep River Landing and directly across the Connecticut River from Selden Island is the Academy at Mount St. John's. Built in 1907, it has served as an orphanage and a residential school for at-risk boys. It now operates as a vocational day school for boys and young men with learning and behavioral challenges. Looking a bit reminiscent of Hogwarts Academy, St. John's also offers a co-ed summer day camp program called Magic at the Castle.

(right) Looking south over Selden Creek with the main course of the river and Deep River's Eustasia Island on the western bank.

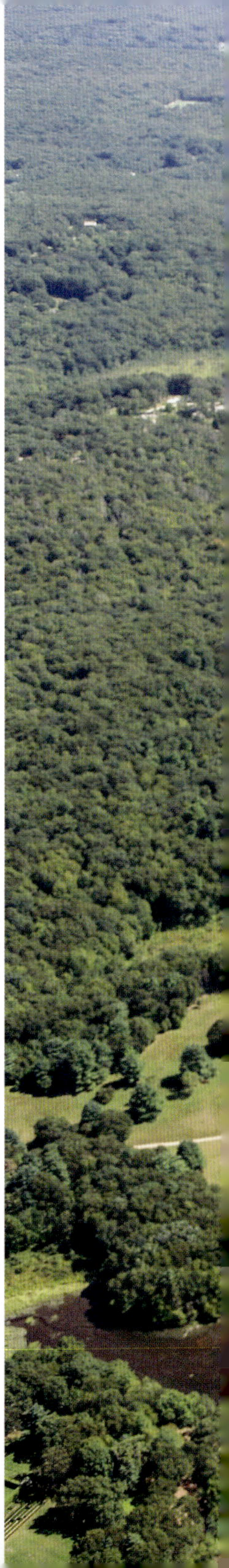

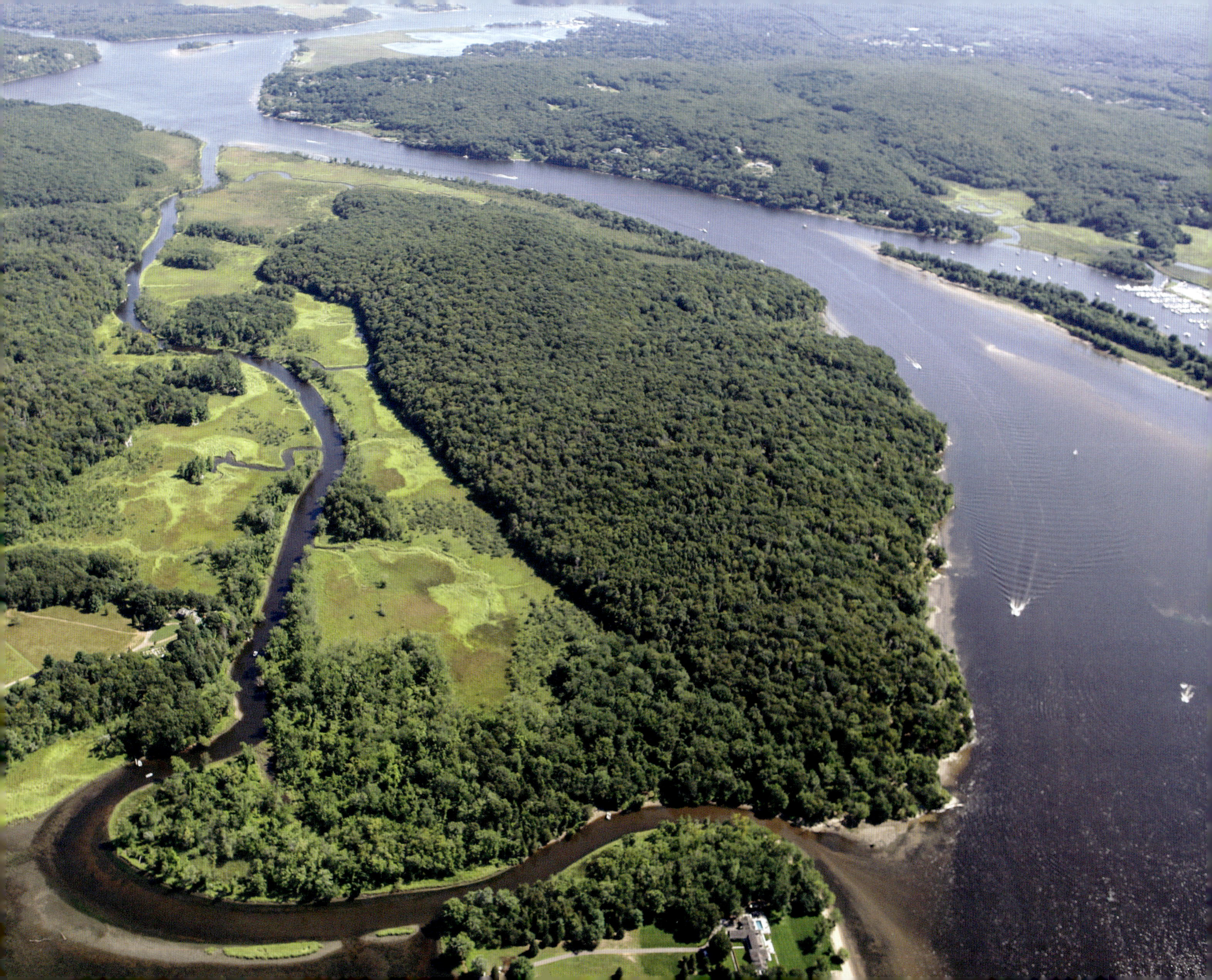

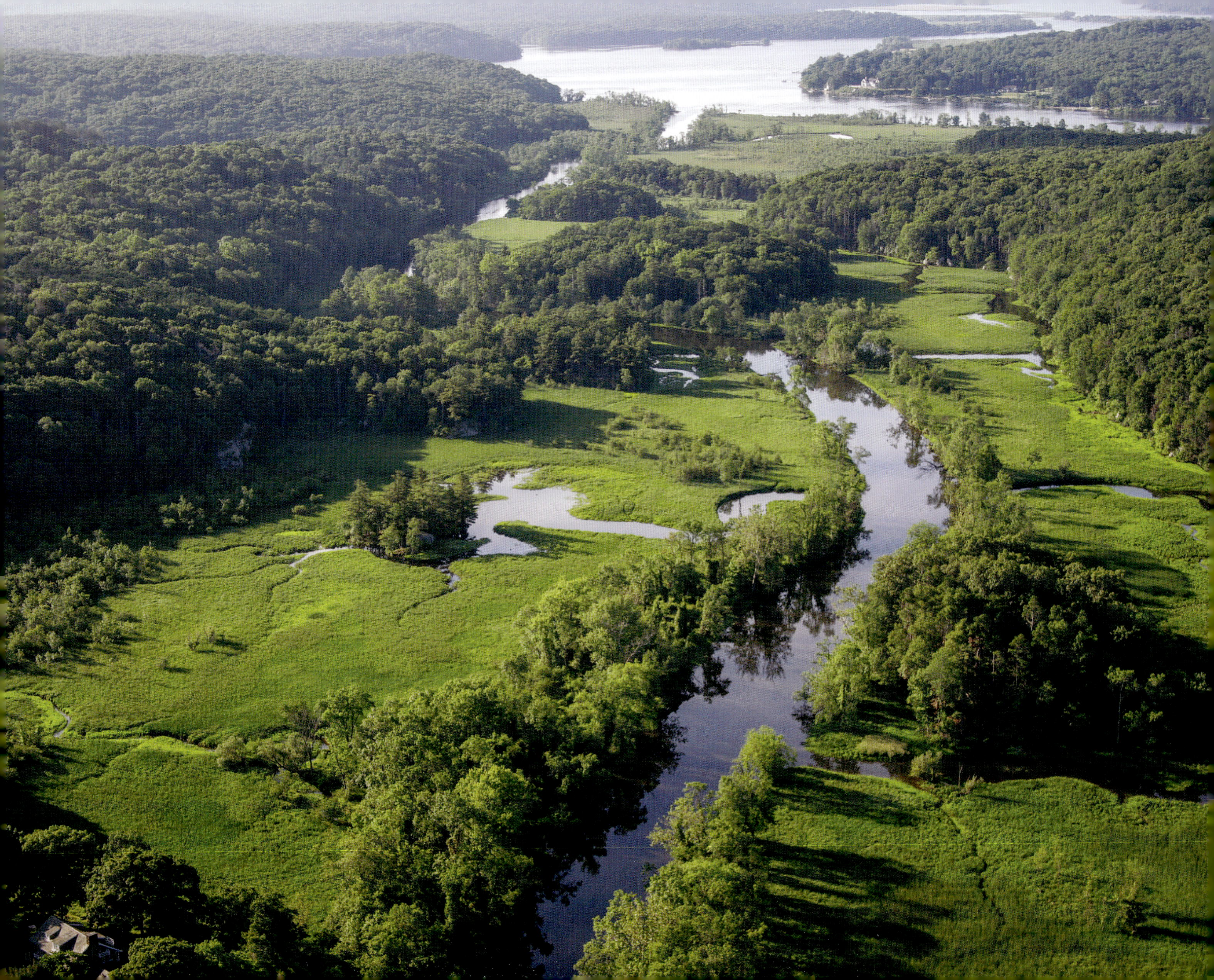

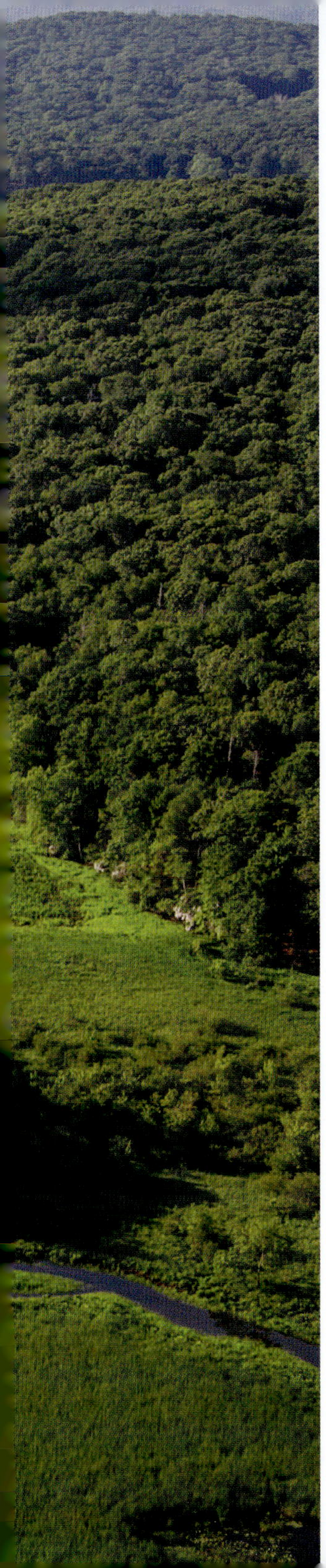

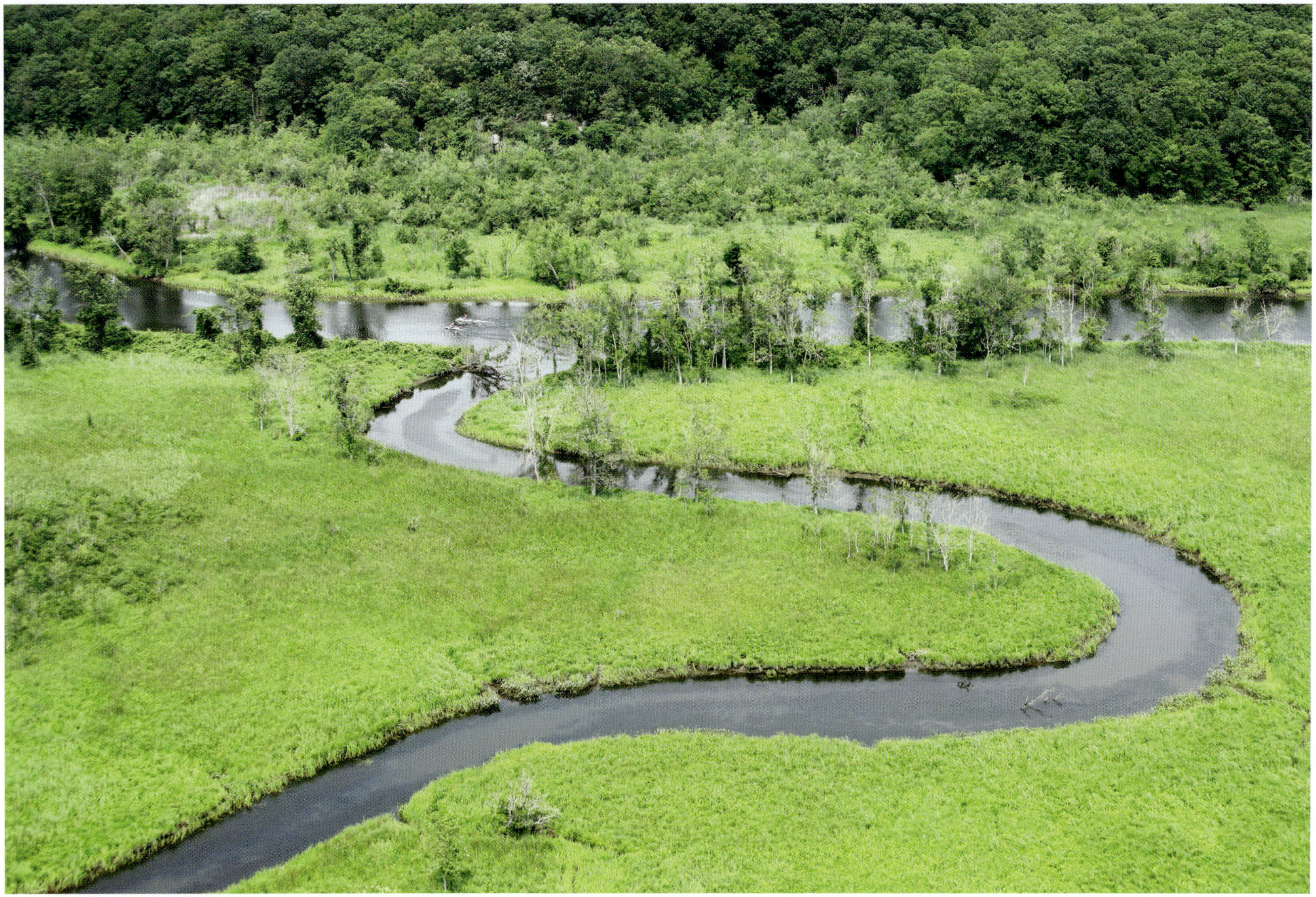

(above) A rivulet meanders through the southern end of Selden Island.

(left) Looking south, Selden Creek resembles a hidden Irish glen.

CHESTER, CT

First settled in 1692, Chester was also originally part of Saybrook Colony. Although today it is shut off from the river by Route 154 and railway tracks, Chester Creek was once navigable and the town was involved in the maritime trade and shipbuilding supported by its sawmills and lumberyards. Waterpower from the creek and dams also supported gristmills, tanneries, and forges. The ferry that connects Chester to Hadlyme on the eastern side of the river has been in operation since 1796. It is one of the last two operational ferries on the Connecticut. Today the village is known for its quaint center through which the creek still flows under the main street where restaurants, art galleries, and antiques shops make it a perfect place to stroll and soak up an authentic small town New England vibe.

(right) Beneath Gillette Castle the historic Chester–Hadlyme ferry approaches its landing on the east side of the river. Originally established in 1769, it is the second oldest continually operated ferry crossing in the United States. The oldest connects Rocky Hill and Glastonbury, about twenty-five miles upstream.

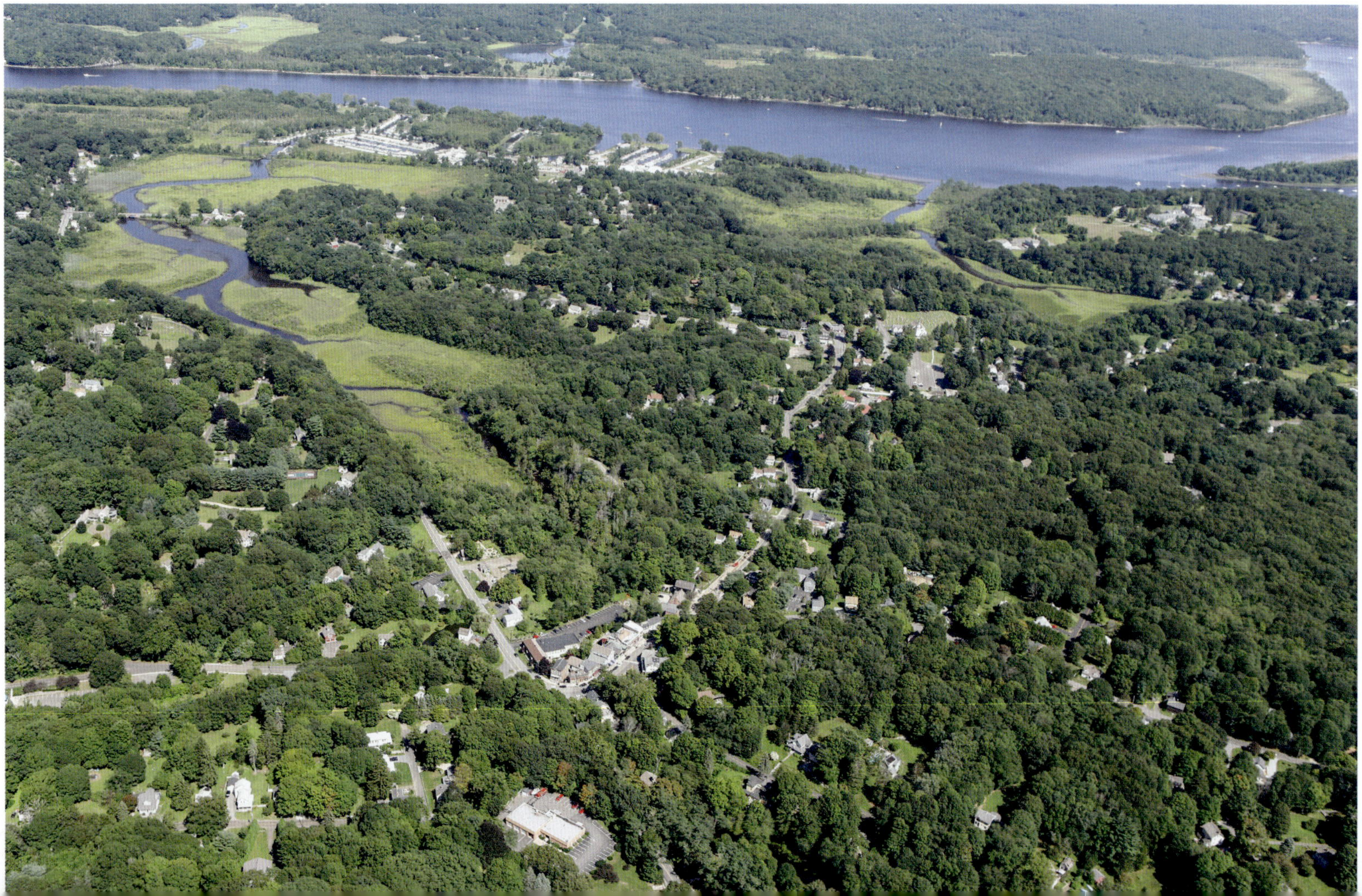

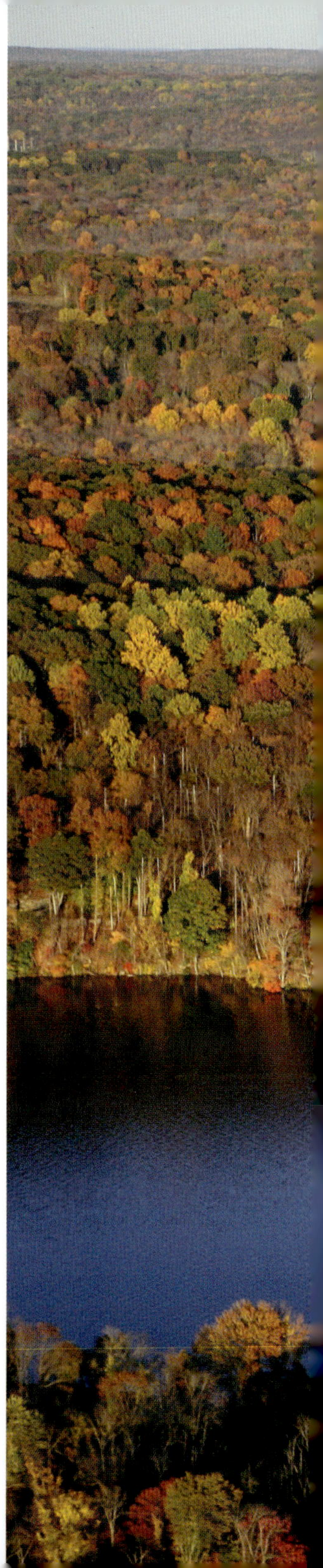

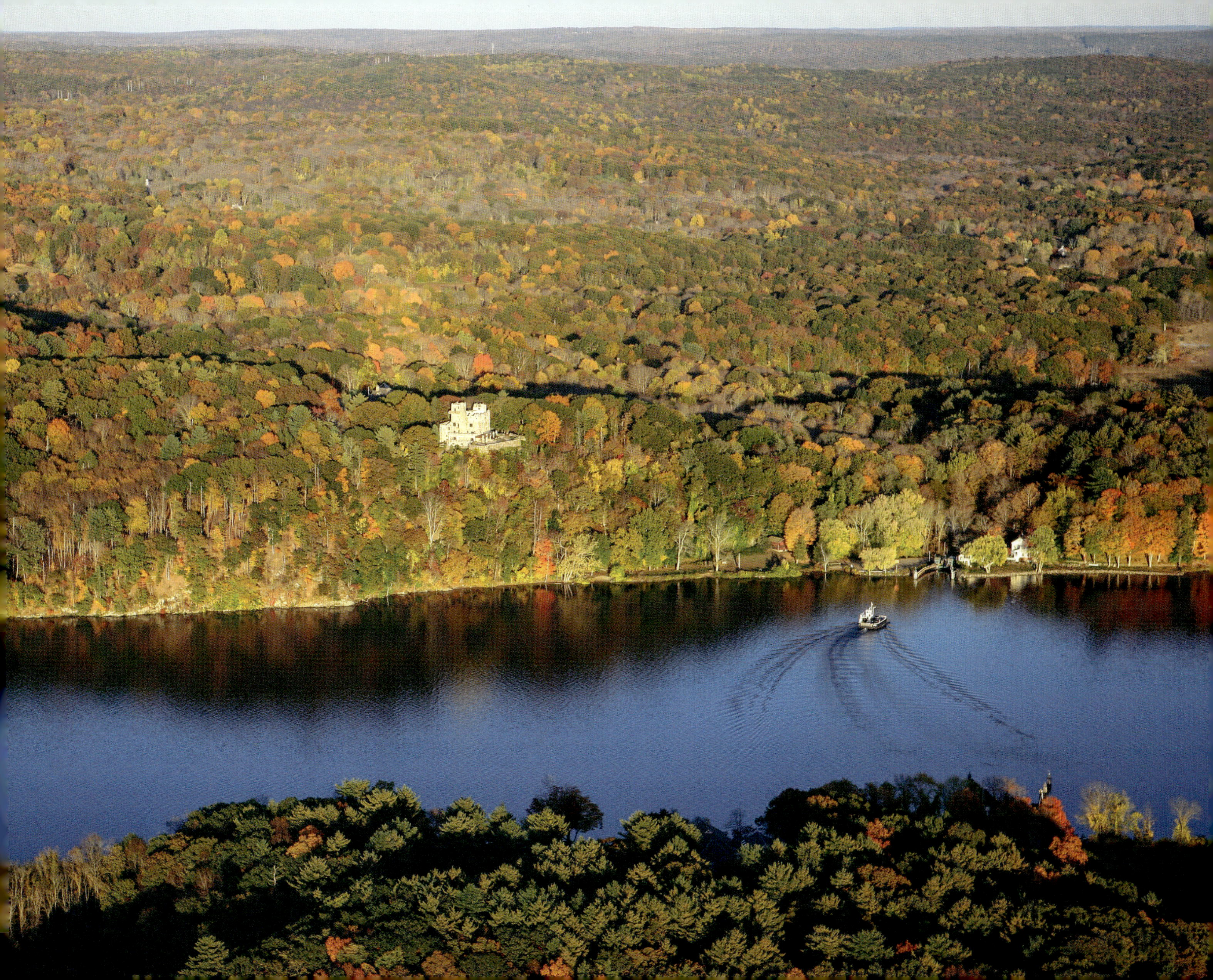

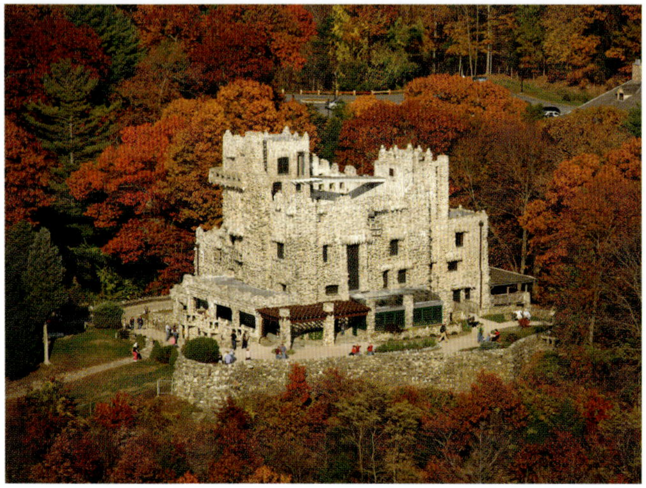

GILLETTE CASTLE

Legendary actor and playwright William Gillette built this iconic faux castle from 1914 to 1919 on the southern-most of a chain of hills along the river known as the Seven Sisters. A member of one of Connecticut's oldest families, Gillette brought Sir Arthur Conan Doyle's Sherlock Holmes to life on stage in New York and London and became one of the most famous actors and playwrights of his time. Built to entertain guests, which included fellow actors, and in some cases, actual royalty, the castle featured quirky wood and stone details and hidden passageways while the 122-acre grounds included seven miles of small-gauge railway. The celebrated actor himself played engineer as guests rode in open cars through tunnels and woodlands, and over precipitous wooden trestles overlooking the river. Left to the state by Gillette, the castle and grounds are now a much-loved state park with the former rail lines now serving as a hiking trail still passing through its tunnel.

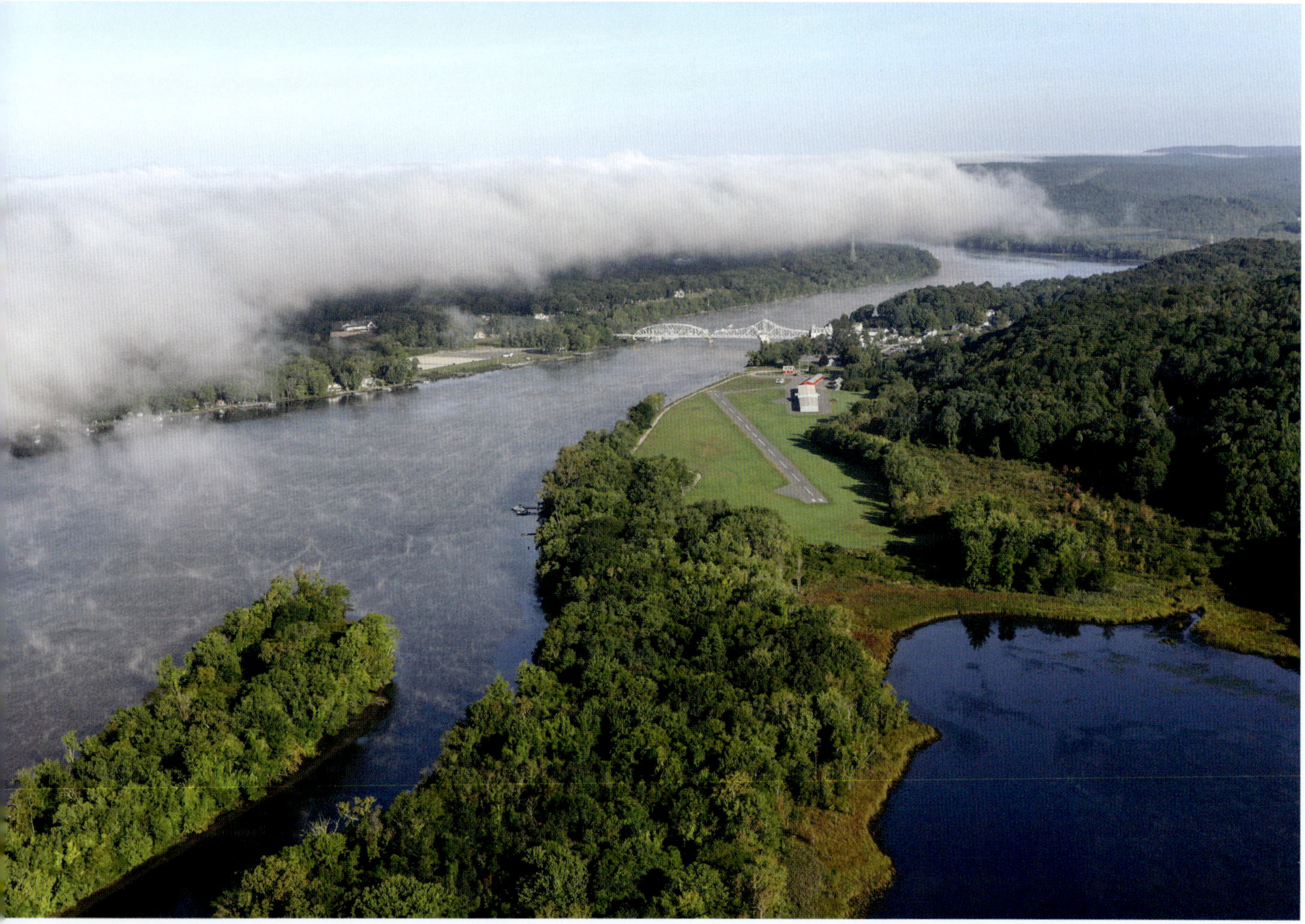

Approaching tiny Goodspeed Airport, which is wedged between the river and wooded hillsides of East Haddam. With the lofty spans of the East Haddam Bridge less than 1,800 feet off the end of the runway, and beset by frequent cross-winds, flying in and out of this airport can be a thrilling experience. This is Tom's summer base of operations; perfectly situated for exploring the river. In addition to its 2,120-foot-long runway, the airport features a ramp for small seaplanes and amphibians.

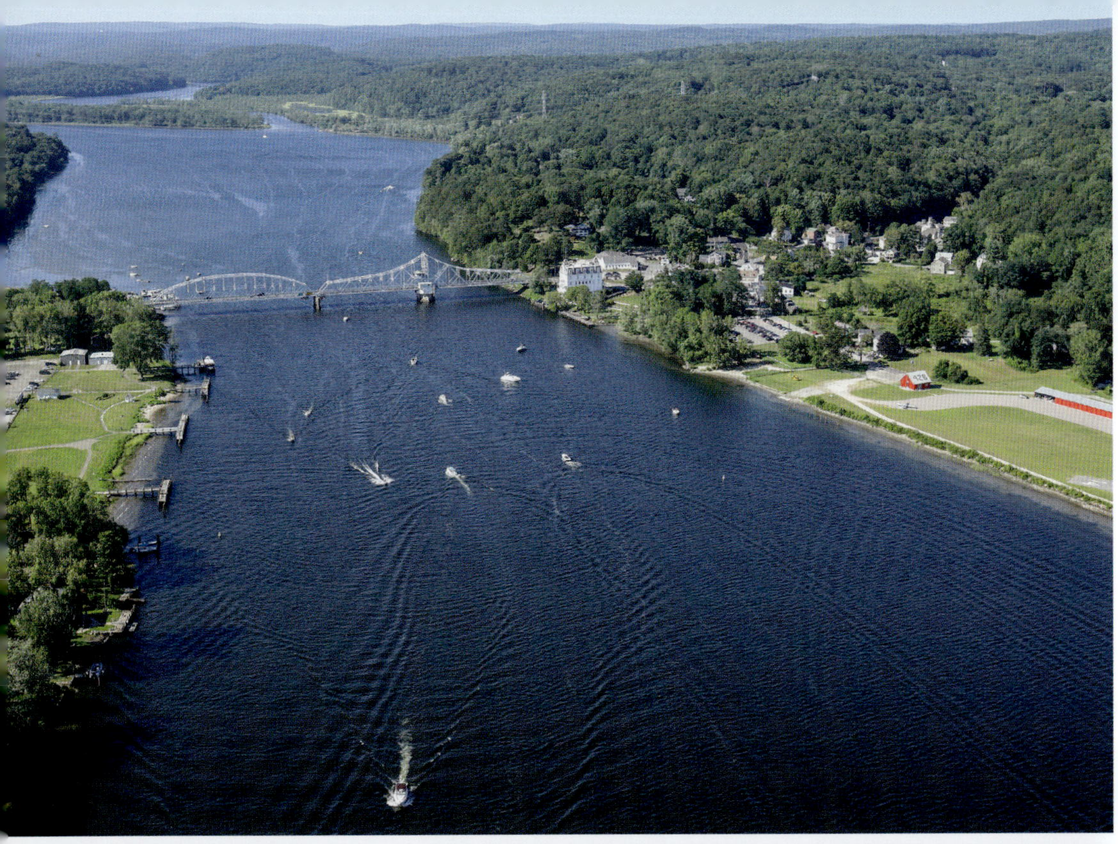

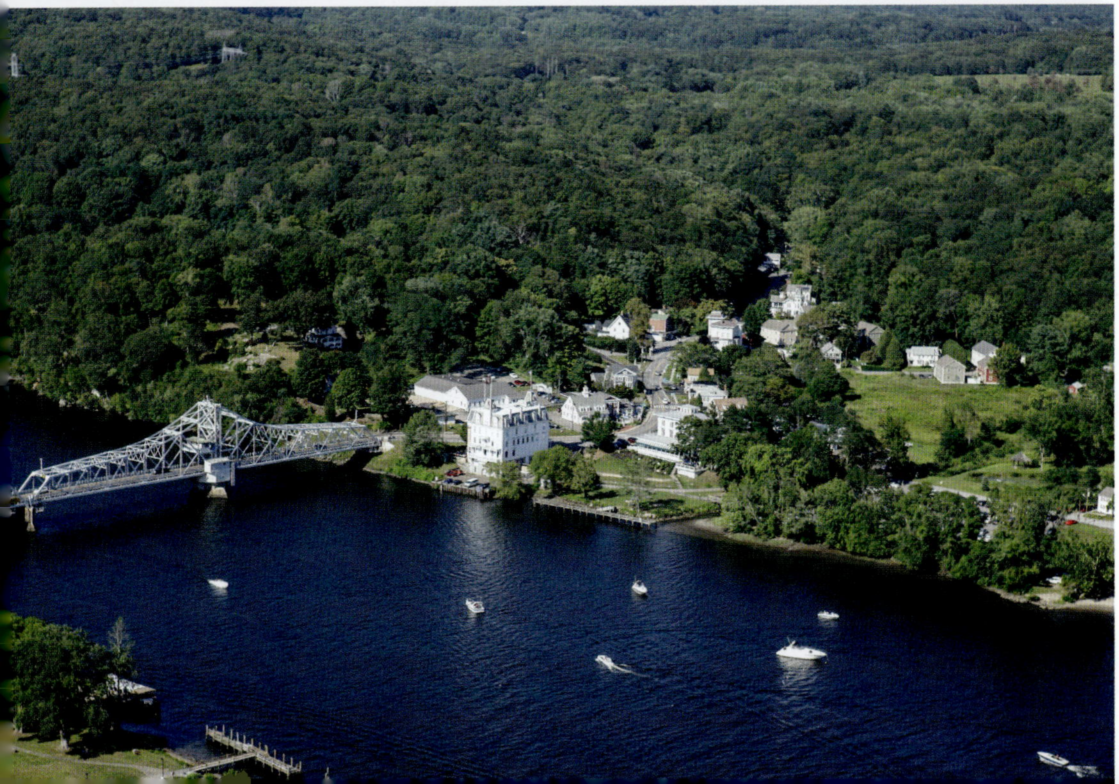

EAST HADDAM SWING BRIDGE

Opened in 1913, the East Haddam Swing Bridge, more commonly referred to as the Goodspeed Bridge, is made up of two large steel truss spans and a smaller approach span on the west side of the river. The 326-foot arched western span is fixed and rests on two stone and masonry pillars, while the 456-foot eastern span pivots on a central pillar to allow river traffic to pass. The East Haddam Swing Bridge is said to have the longest pivoting span in the world.

GOODSPEED OPERA HOUSE

Created in 1877 by William Goodspeed, the Goodspeed Opera House in East Haddam, operated for many years as a theater until it fell on hard times after his death. Following decades of sometimes dubious adaptive re-use, it was reopened as a musical theater in 1963. It has been extremely successful and critically renowned for its world-class productions including over seventy premieres, many of which were then exported to Broadway. The adjacent Gelston House was opened as an inn in 1853 and still provides accommodations in addition to its topnotch restaurant overlooking the river.

Where the opera house's parking lot now stands, the Goodspeed Shipyard produced vessels of all kinds between 1835 and 1872. These included barges, schooners, brigs, barks, full rigged ships, and both side-wheel- and propeller-driven steamboats. Their most important contract was the construction of a large turreted gunboat for the Union Navy during the Civil War. Shipyards across the river in Higganum were also quite active and built several Nantucket whalers. Altogether, the four yards in this area produced more than 400 vessels.

TOM'S PERSPECTIVE

Flying low and slow over the Connecticut River and capturing the images for this book is in stark contrast to my 40-year career in the air. As a fighter pilot in the Marine Corps, I flew the supersonic F-4 Phantom and in the reserves I flew the nimble little A-4 Skyhawk. It was very exciting to be a young Marine pilot, accelerating with after-burners or learning to land on the deck of an aircraft carrier. It was great to be able to get this incredible experience while serving my country. But there was not much time for sightseeing. Over the past 30 years, as a commercial airline pilot, things have not been quite so hectic, but from 30,000 feet or more the view is not very intimate. It wasn't until I purchased a vintage 1946 Piper Cub that I was able to get back to my roots, experiencing flight much as I had as a teenager taking lessons while still in high school.

The Cub opened a whole new world of exploration and freedom. But with a young family I couldn't justify owning an aircraft unless it could pay for itself. So in 2004 I founded Shoreline Aerial Photography. It has allowed me to photograph countless sights throughout New England and beyond for a wide range of clients. Meanwhile, as a Senior International Captain flying around the world for a major airline there is still profound satisfaction every time I safely transport hundreds of passengers and crew, along with over half a million pounds of airplane, to destinations around the globe. I am fortunate that I have been able to earn my livelihood in the air both with the airlines and my own company.

I love to fly, I love to photograph, and I love history. All of these things came together when I met Jerry Roberts, then the new executive director of the Connecticut River Museum where I was a member. In fact my wife and I were married on the museum's docks and my kids learned to swim and sail in the river. No matter where I travel, the Connecticut River remains an important part of my life. When Jerry asked if he could use some of my images for an exhibit about the River from the air, I jumped at the chance. I offered to fly to the river's source, 410 miles to the north, to take images of every town, bridge, bend and oxbow. I was also able to get Jerry up in the modern version of the Cub that I was flying at the time. This gave him a look at the river from my perspective, while he was able to point out many historic locations I had not been aware of while flying right over them. The exhibit was a big success and I was glad to contribute all of the images to the museum where many are still on display. I have also made additional flights for other historic projects Jerry has worked on.

We had kicked around the idea of a book over the years, but when he became executive director of the New England Air Museum, the time was right. By this point, in addition to the Cessna Cardinal that I use for most of my work, I had replaced the Cub with a Searey amphibious aircraft, a flying boat hull with retractable wheels. It's still low and slow and can enjoy an unparalleled view with the engine behind me and two sliding canopies that can be opened in flight! I used this airplane to take most of the newer images you will see in this book.

A brief word about my photography. I'm not a classically trained or technical photographer. Although I have been told I have a good eye, I rely on top quality camera gear for much of what I do. To me, nature and sometimes man is the artist and I do my best to capture it. I shoot with a hand held gyro stabilized digital camara.

Since I'm flying the airplane as well as taking the pictures, I have but brief moments to capture the images. It's only later when I see the pictures on a computer screen that I get to truly appreciate what I've captured. Every time I look at the images, I usually find some new detail that I wasn't even trying to capture! Jerry and I have both found this to be the case while working on this book and we hope you experience the same feeling of discovery.

Finally, I want to tell you that I have two firm rules with my aerial photography. I never shoot through a window or canopy. There is never anything but air between my camera and the scene. Secondly, I don't edit things out or add things in to change the photographs. Aside from minor cropping and color and brightness corrections, what you will see is what my camera saw. Enjoy your time in the air!

—Tom Walsh

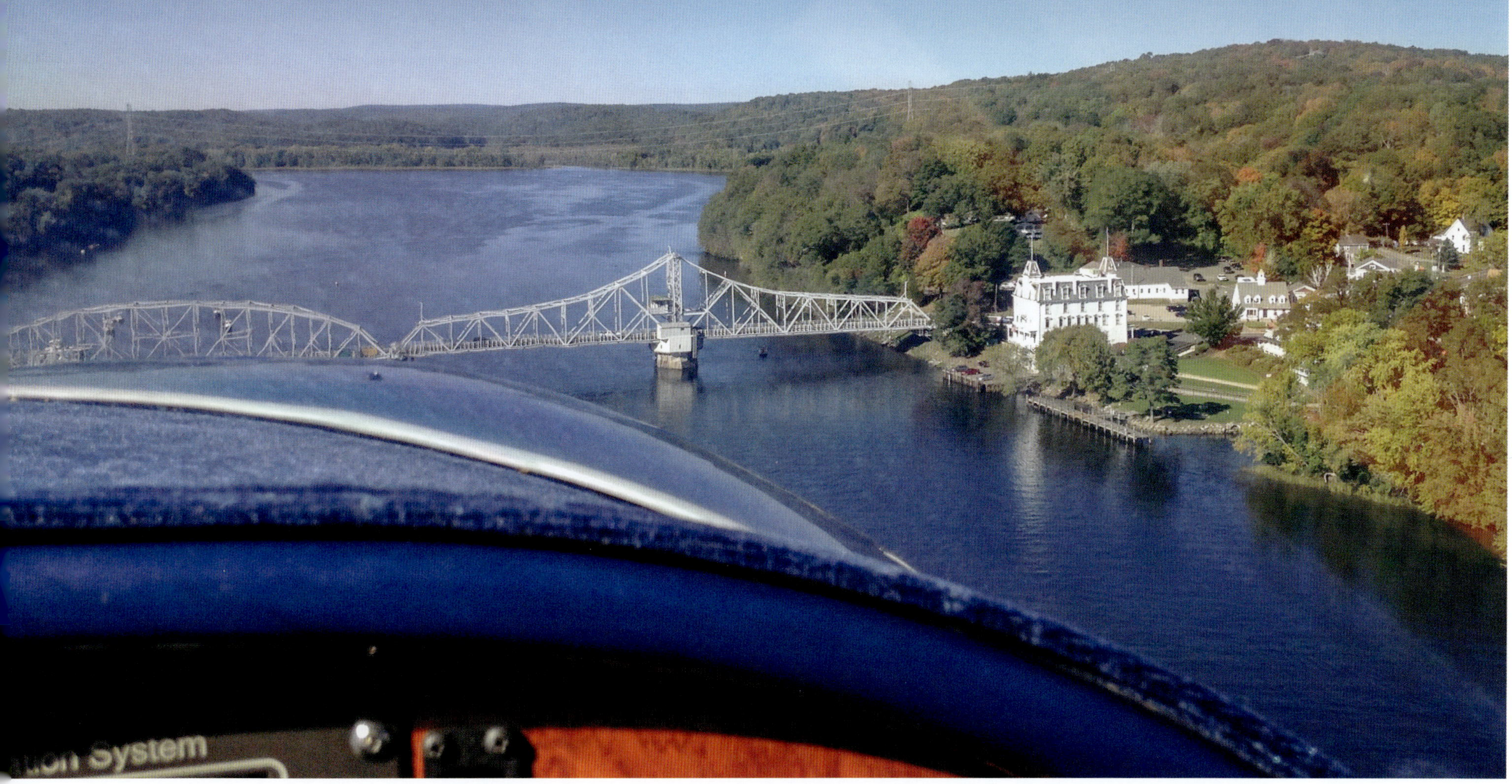

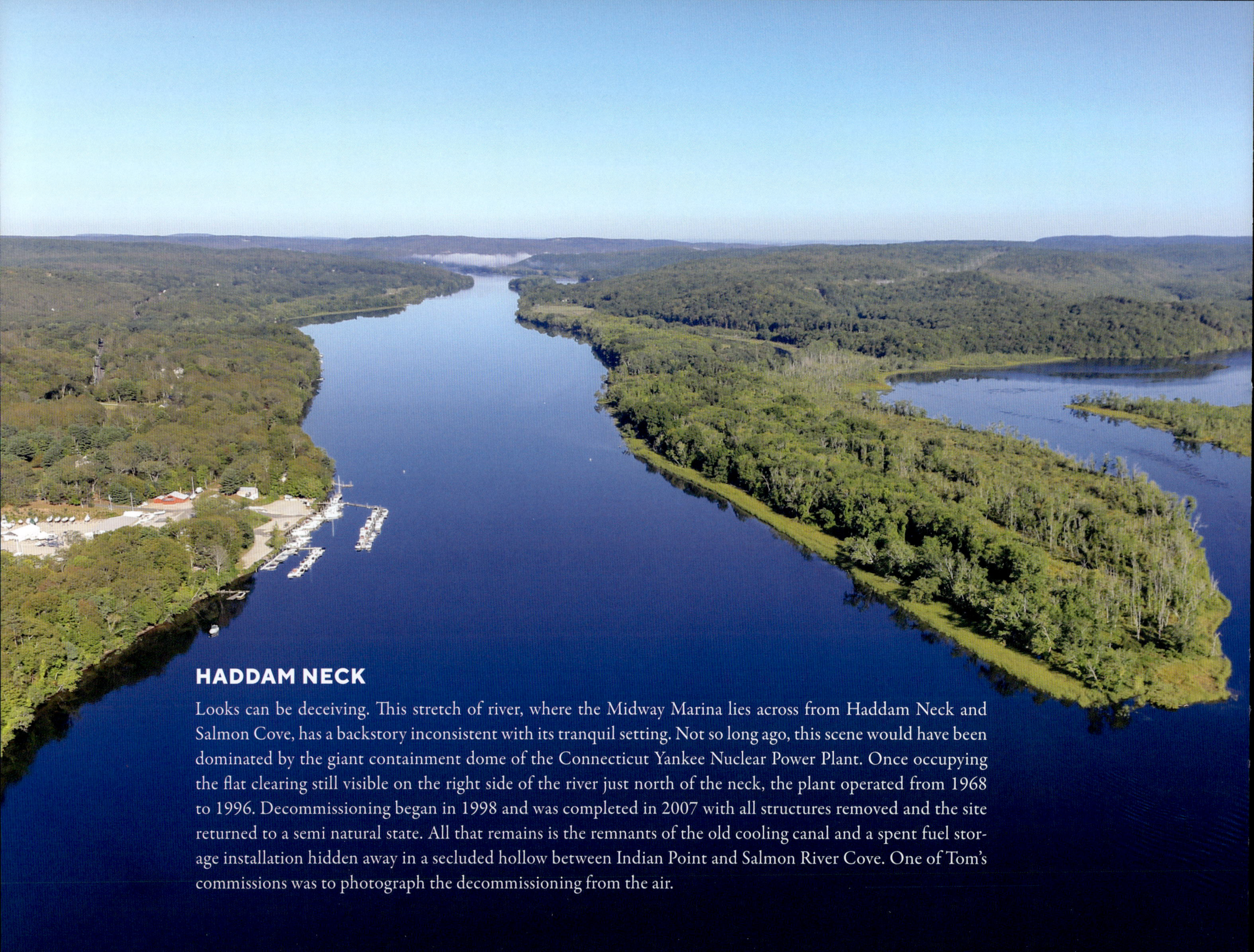

HADDAM NECK

Looks can be deceiving. This stretch of river, where the Midway Marina lies across from Haddam Neck and Salmon Cove, has a backstory inconsistent with its tranquil setting. Not so long ago, this scene would have been dominated by the giant containment dome of the Connecticut Yankee Nuclear Power Plant. Once occupying the flat clearing still visible on the right side of the river just north of the neck, the plant operated from 1968 to 1996. Decommissioning began in 1998 and was completed in 2007 with all structures removed and the site returned to a semi natural state. All that remains is the remnants of the old cooling canal and a spent fuel storage installation hidden away in a secluded hollow between Indian Point and Salmon River Cove. One of Tom's commissions was to photograph the decommissioning from the air.

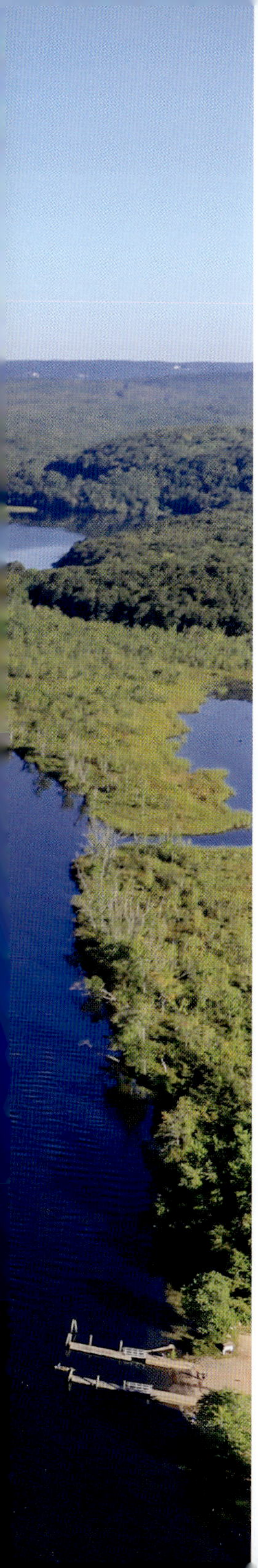

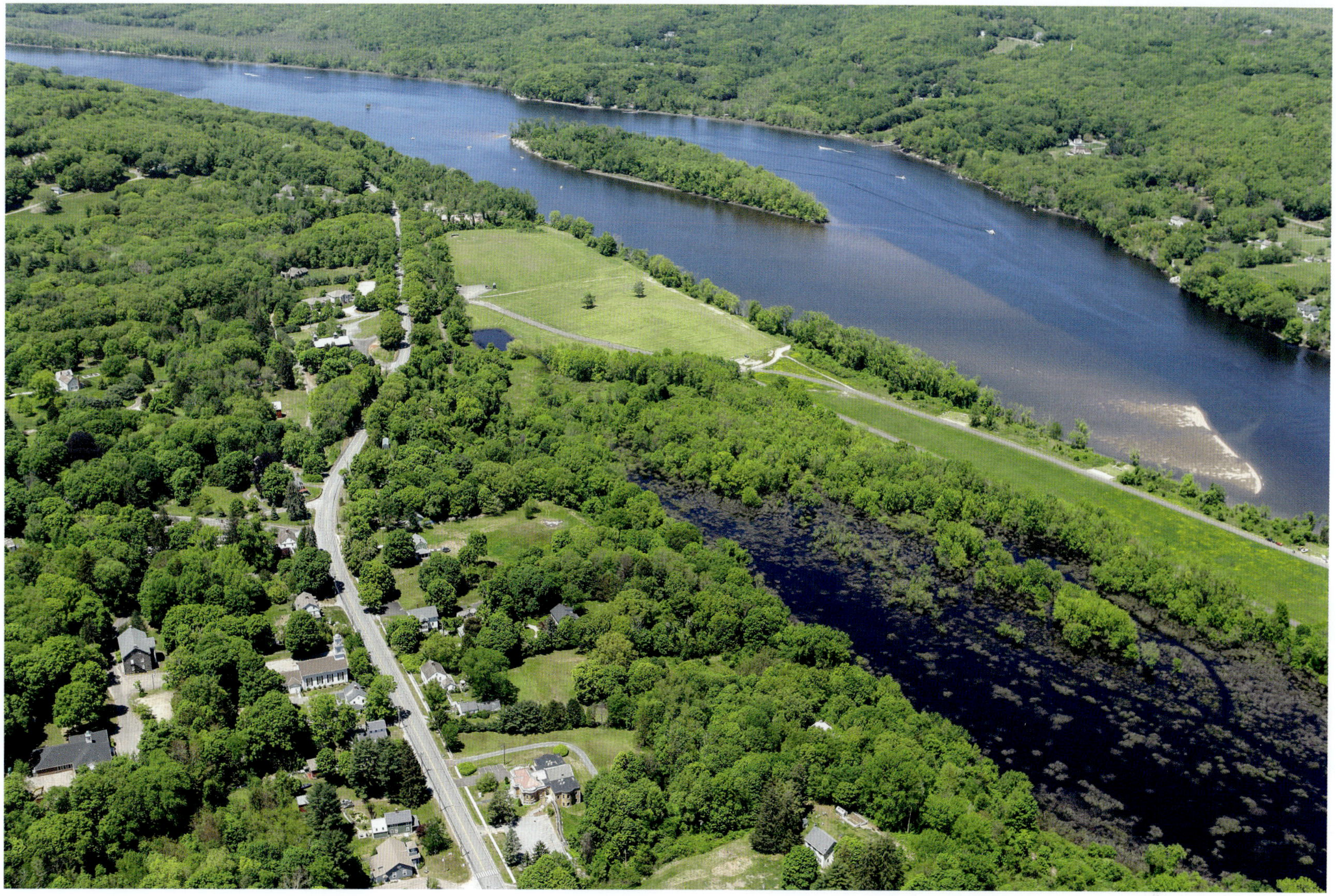

HADDAM MEADOW

Haddam Meadow State Park (with Haddam Island in the river nearby) is part of a flood plain where hay and grain grew abundantly and was used as a grazing common after the harvest. It was later an important trans-shipping point where local steamboats exchanged cargos bound to and from New York. Still later, passenger trains stopped here on their way to and from Saybrook and Hartford. It now offers a boat launch, hiking, picnicking, and open space for recreation.

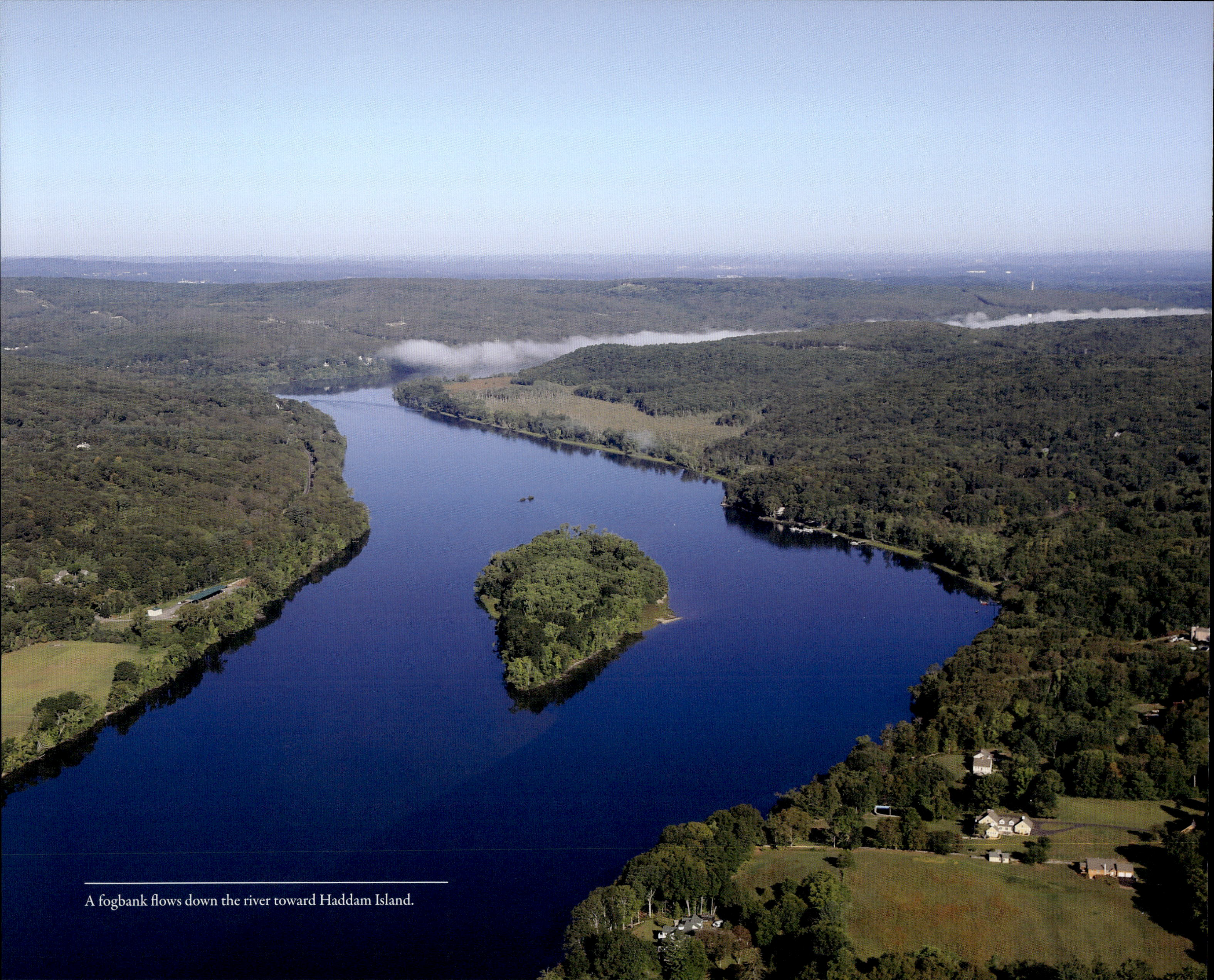

A fogbank flows down the river toward Haddam Island.

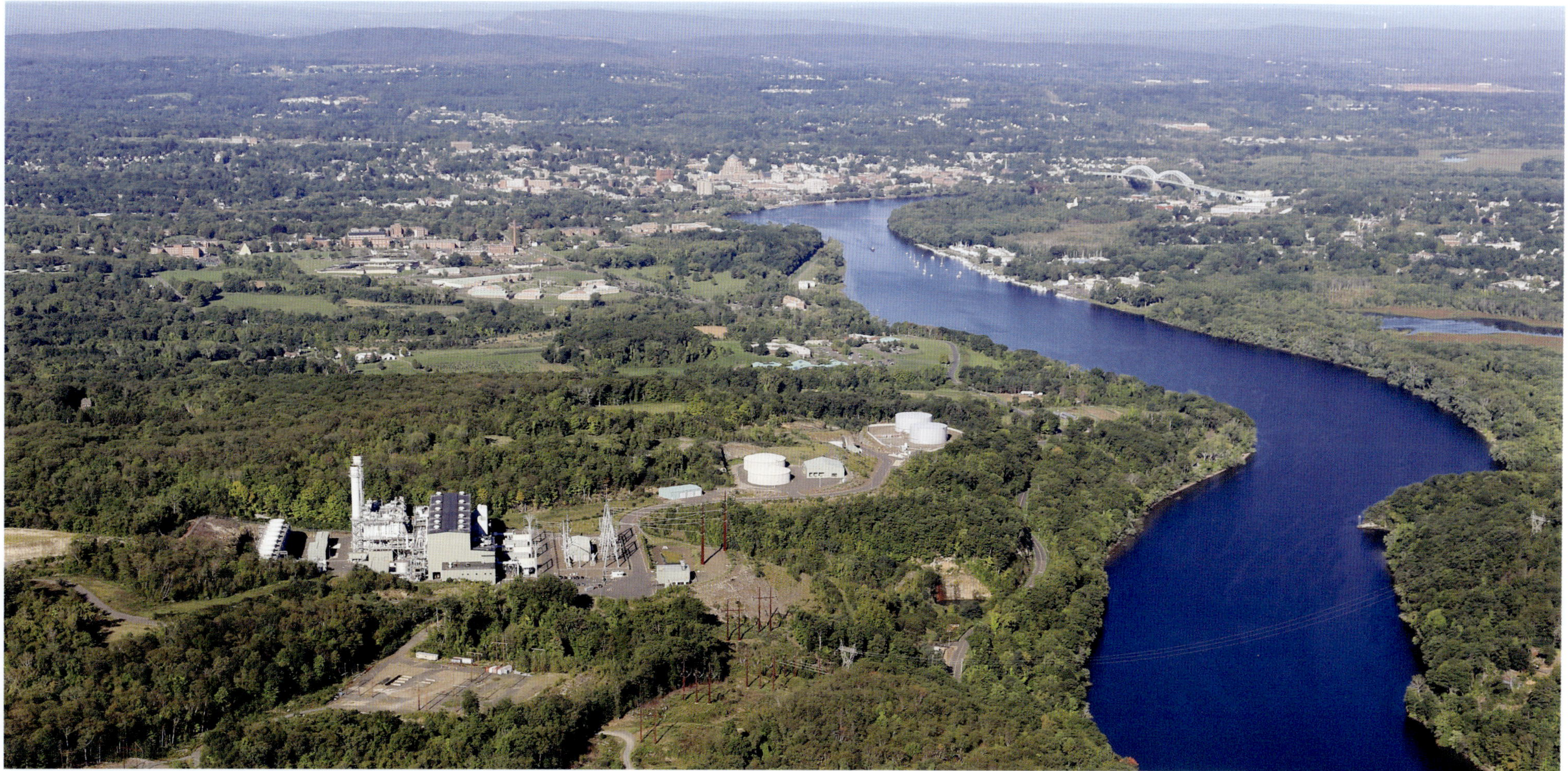

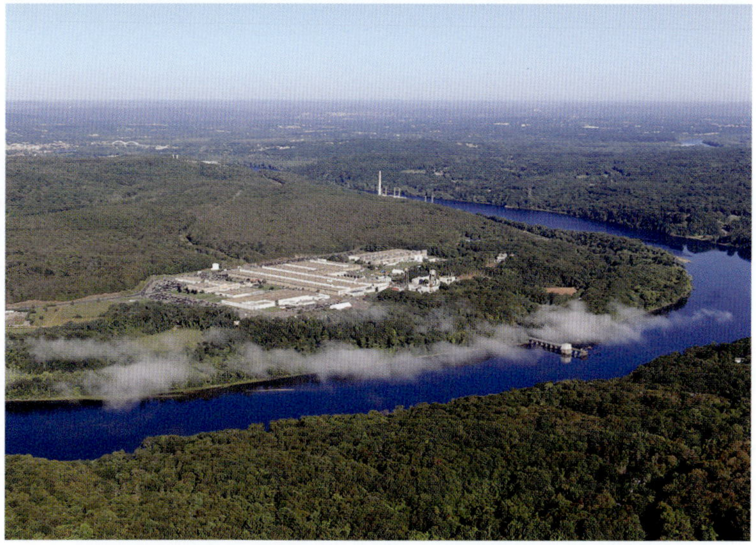

(left) Situated along the western side of the river just below Middletown, jet engines for both military and commercial aircraft have been built at this Pratt & Whitney plant, with 3,000 employees, since 1966. Before that, from 1957 to 1965, the U.S. Government operated it as a research facility. Pratt & Whitney, a division of UTC, was founded in 1925. Pratt's global headquarters and engineering facilities are located farther up the river in East Hartford at Rentschler Field.

(above) Also on the western side of the river as we approach Middletown is the site of Kleen Energy Systems power plant. In 2010 the plant was rocked by a deadly explosion just months away from going on line. Rebuilt in 2011, it now feeds up 620 megawatts of electricity into the New England power grid.

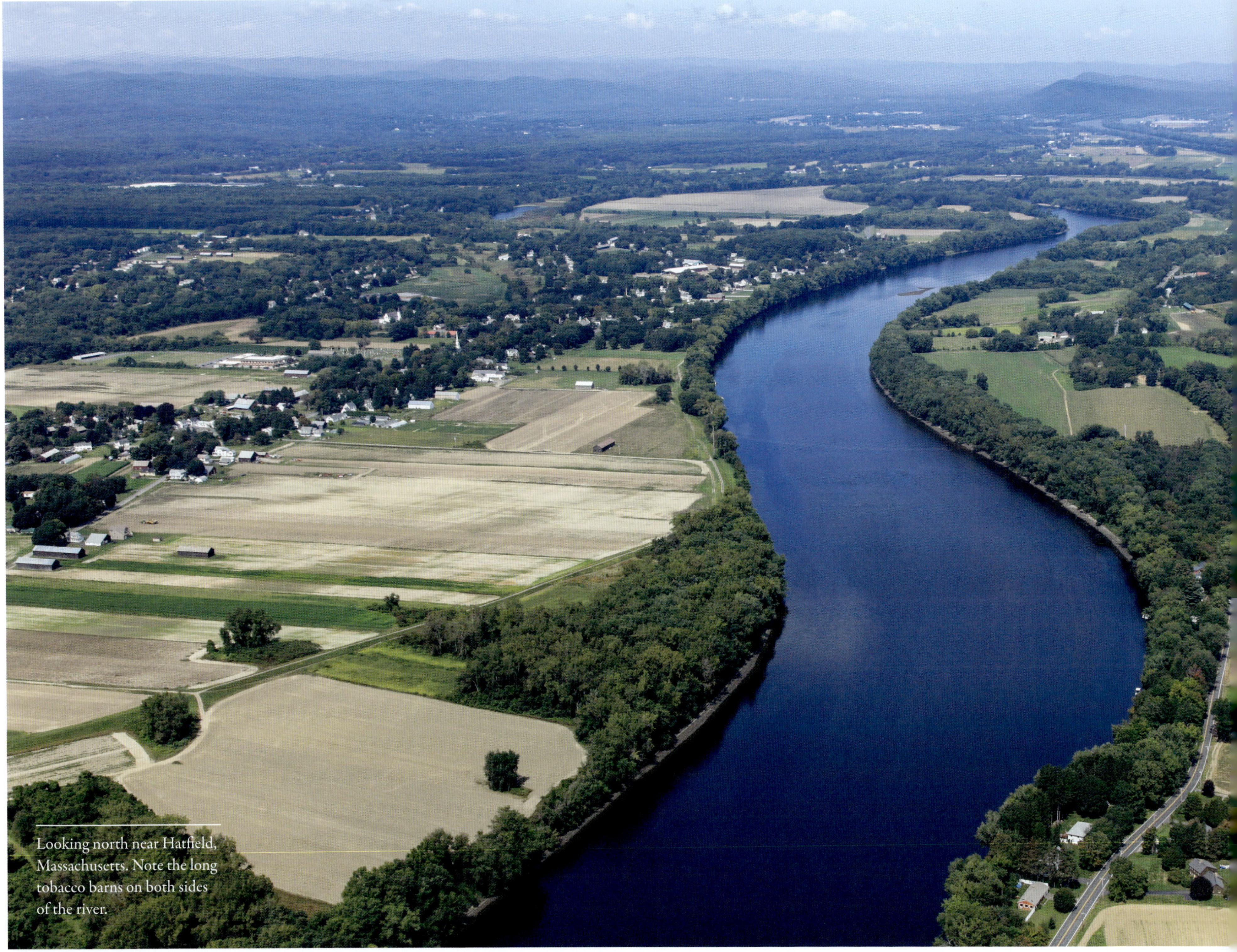

Looking north near Hatfield, Massachusetts. Note the long tobacco barns on both sides of the river.

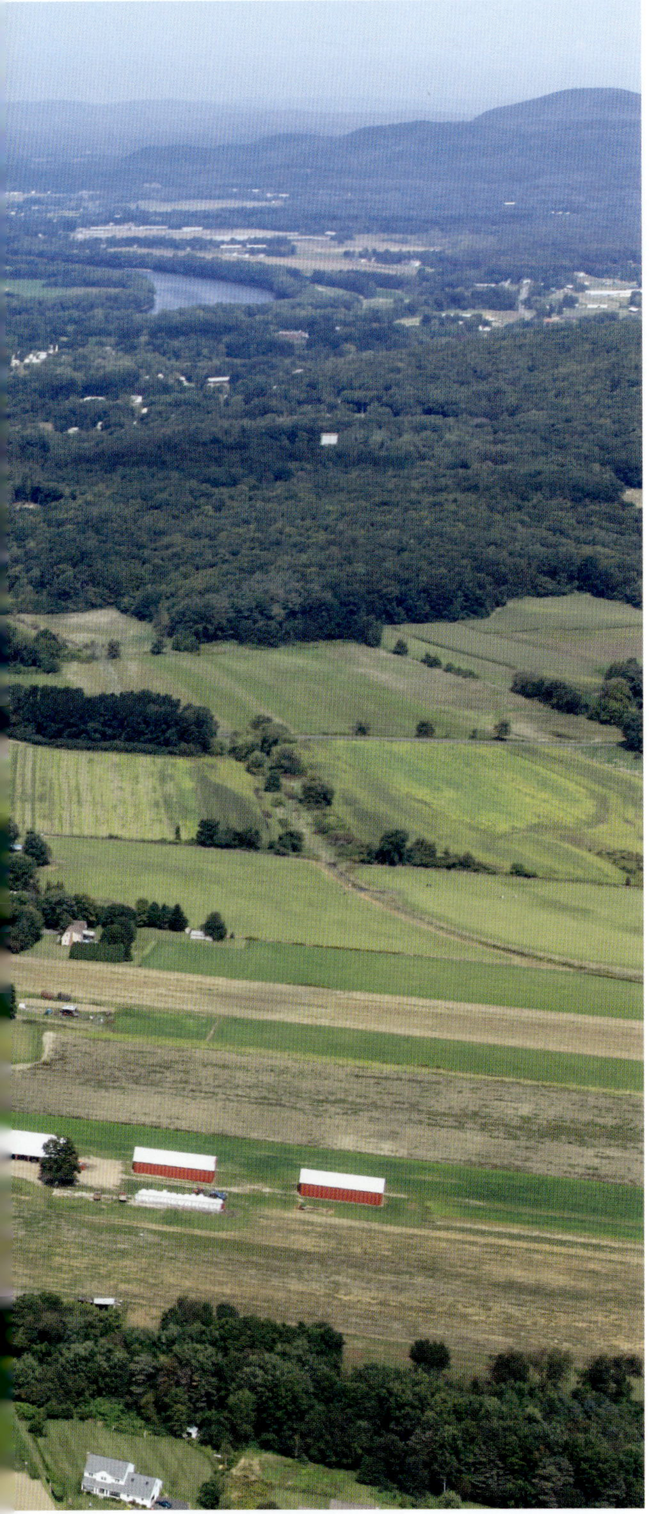

THE MIDDLE VALLEY

Also called the Central Valley, this stretch begins at the northern border of Massachusetts and runs 100 miles down to Middletown, Connecticut. The lower portion is sometimes called Tobacco Valley for the prized shade grown tobacco that is still an important regional crop here. The northern portion running through Massachusetts is known as Pioneer Valley. The fertile soil left by ancient Lake Hitchcock, and the ready transportation and water power supplied by the Connecticut and its tributaries, attracted early settlers and helped power the Industrial Revolution.

MIDDLETOWN, CT

Middletown is located at a sweeping bend in the river where its southerly flow is abruptly diverted to the southeast by the Metacomet Range, a geological formation made up of a series of hard, trap-rock ridges that shape the river's course as far north as Greenfield, Massachusetts. At Middletown, this prevented the river from flowing straight down to New Haven and instead diverted it through softer ground along its present course to the Sound.

Settlers first arrived in what is now Middletown in 1650. Its name references the fact that it is located halfway between Saybrook and Windsor, both of which were prominent settlements during colonial times. Middletown became a bustling river port engaged in maritime trade and shipbuilding. By the mid-1800s it was the largest and most populous city in Connecticut. With the decline of its maritime economy in the early nineteenth century, precision manufacturing, including firearms, typewriters, and marine instruments and hardware, became more important. When the New Haven to Hartford railway lines bypassed Middletown, manufacturing suffered. Today the city is better known as the home of Wesleyan University, founded in 1831, and medical facilities such as Middlesex Hospital.

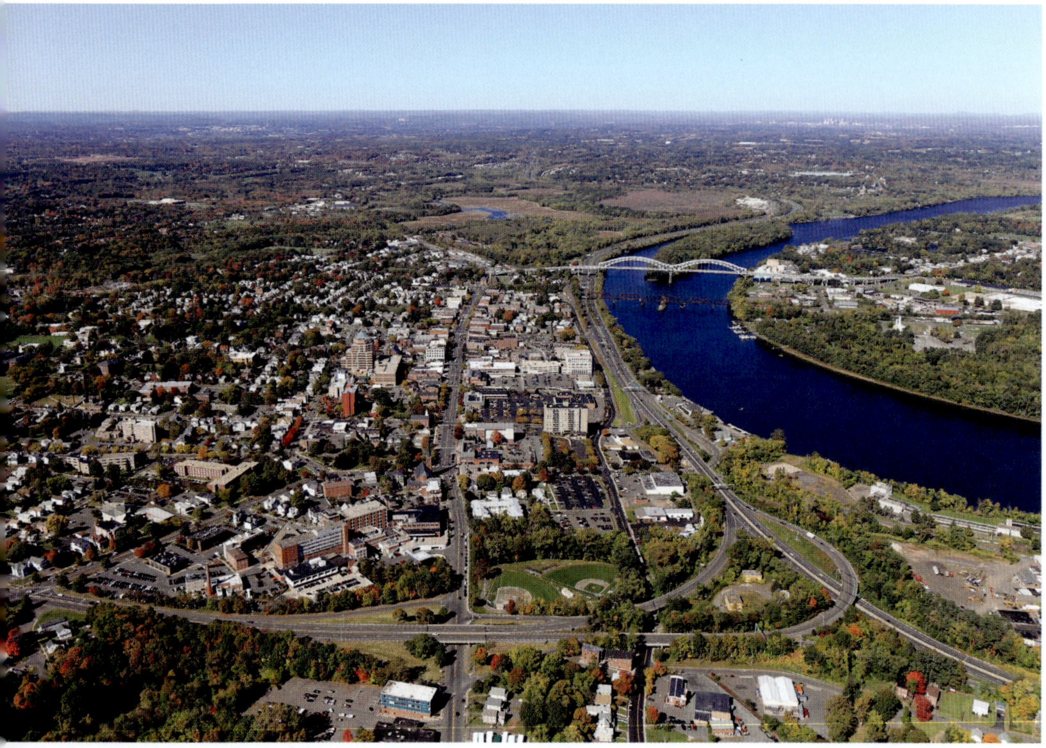

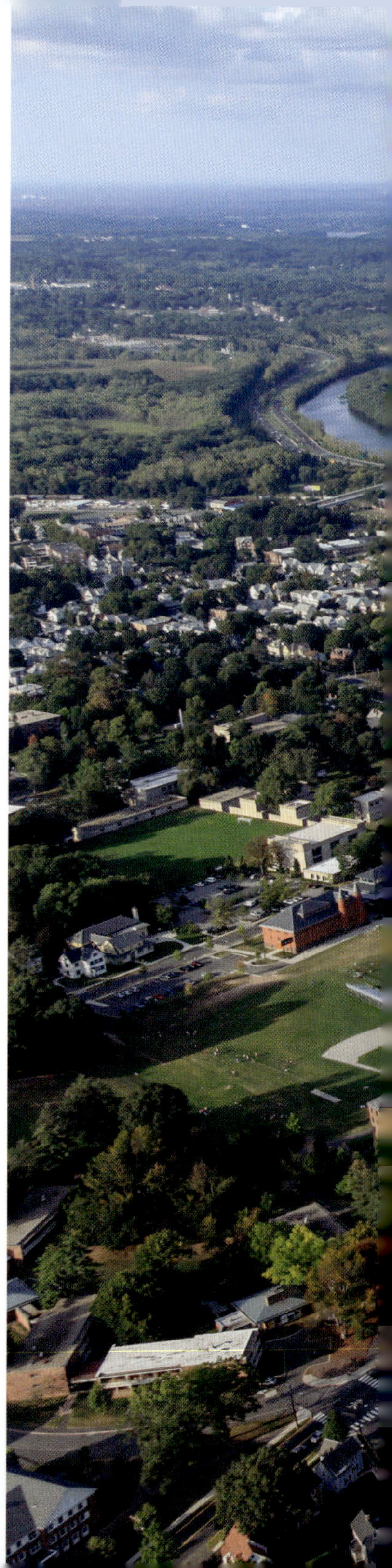

(left) Looking north, directly up Main Street it is clear how the modern city has long ago turned its focus away from the river where wharves and maritime commerce once lined the waterfront. CT Route 9, built in 1964, underscores Middletown's detachment from its maritime past. More recently a pedestrian underpass has allowed citizens to enjoy a riverside park, which is also home to Wesleyan University's crew team, the Mattabesett Canoe Club, and *Lady Katherine* river cruises.

(right) Looking northeast, the sprawling city of Middletown is formed around the river's dramatic curve to the southeast. In the foreground, the campus of Wesleyan University overlooks this once formidable port town.

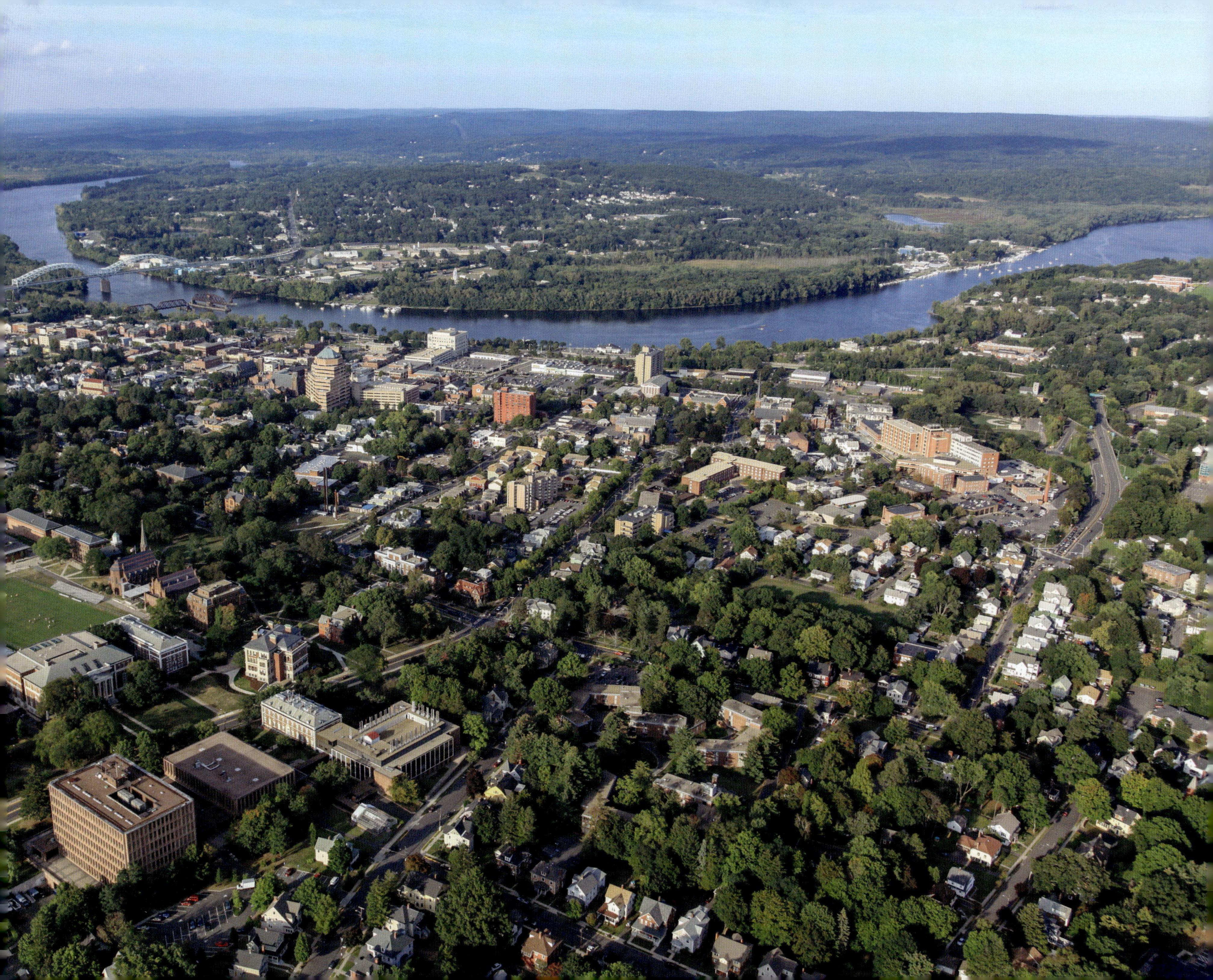

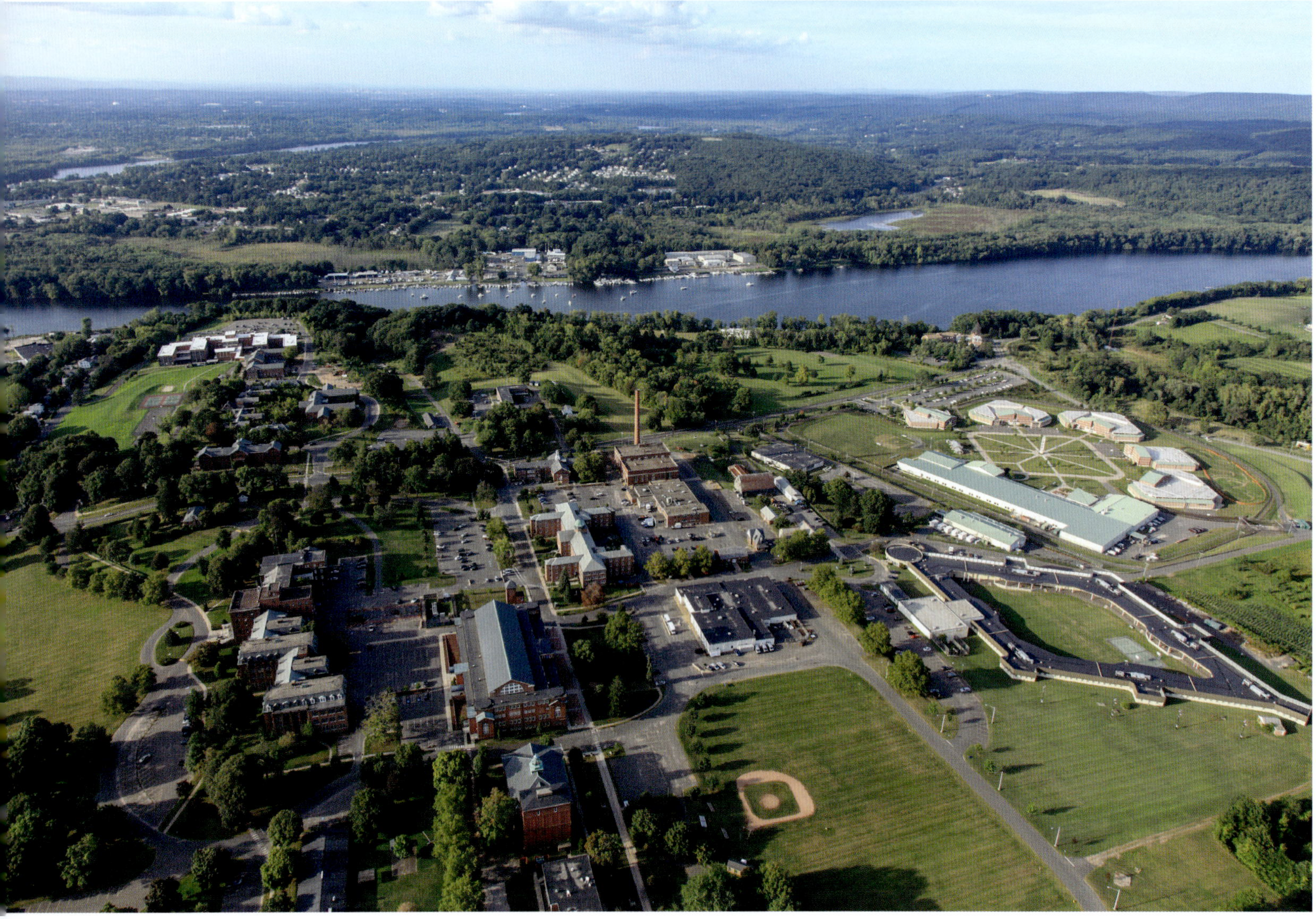

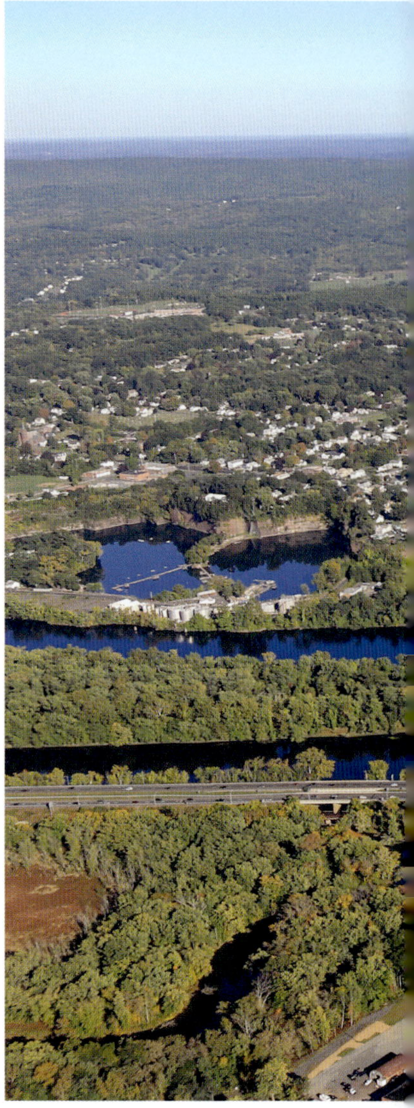

Looking directly north toward the river, this campus of forty red brick buildings at the eastern end of Middletown is the Rocky Hill Veterans Home and Hospital. In 1940 it became the state's primary facility to house and care for veterans, mostly from the First World War but it also included men from many earlier conflicts including the Indian and Spanish American Wars and even one from the Civil War. Today the facility continues to serve veterans with chronic health issues.

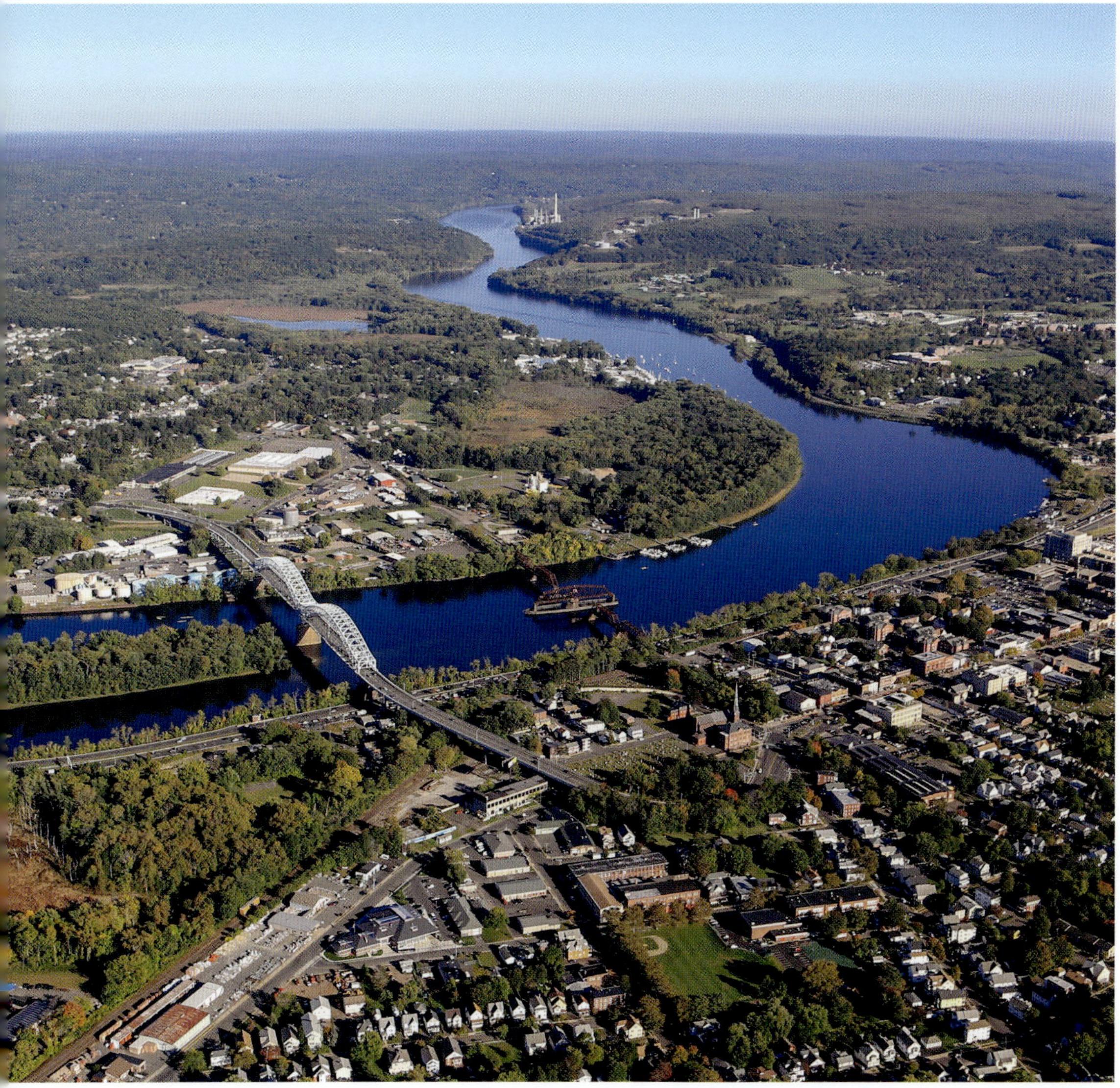

Looking east down the river after its abrupt turn at Middletown, the brownstone quarries of Portland are just across the river on the left, with the Arrigoni Bridge and Wilcox Island in the center.

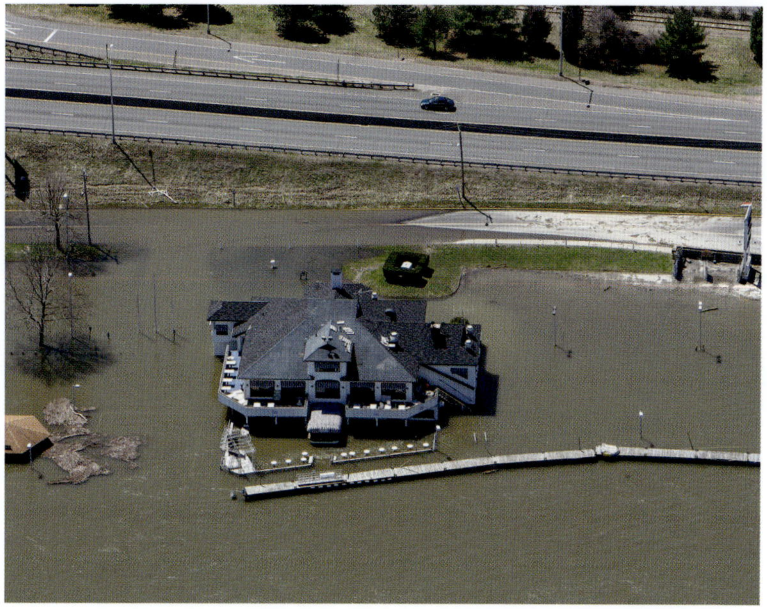

(above) Located in a flood plain, Middletown has been impacted by the river overflowing its banks throughout its existence. Here the Canoe Club and the adjacent River Side Park are surrounded by high water during a spring freshet. The club's floating docks mark the normal location of the riverbank. The historic building was once the home of the Middletown Yacht Club, but now serves as a restaurant and event facility.

FRESHET

During the spring freshet, as snow and frozen earth along the river's course and watershed melt, the downflow can even overpower the incoming ocean tide. In the best of times the freshet brings annual flooding to the lower river, a natural occurrence that actually helps re-nourish the soil along the floodplain. But when heavy winter snows combine with an early spring thaw, and heavy rainfall, as happened in March of 1936, the resulting floods can be incredibly destructive and even deadly.

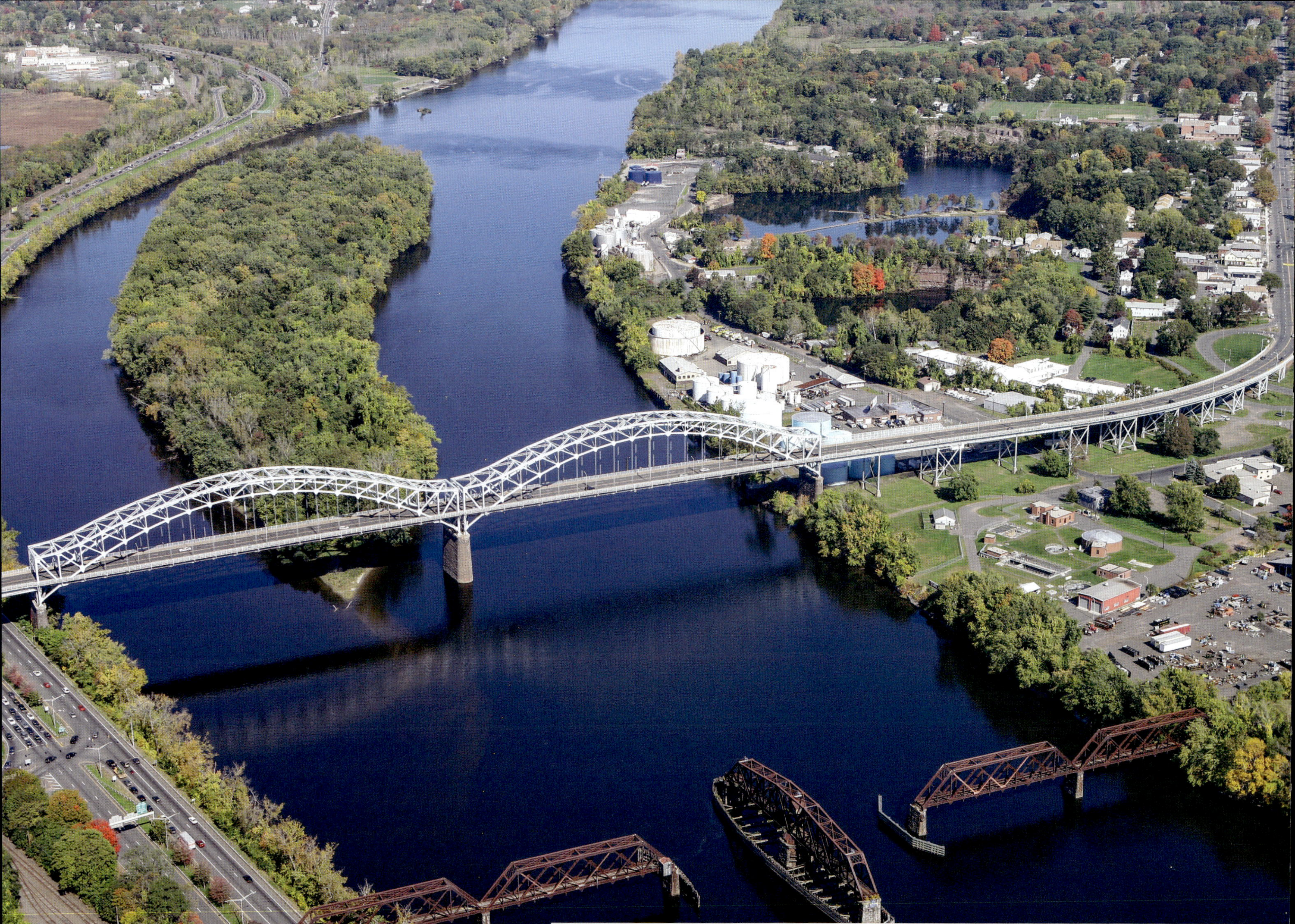

Two bridges span the river between Middletown and Portland. The seldom-used railway bridge uses a pivoting span to allow river traffic to pass while the 1938 Arrigoni Bridge employs two distinctive steel arches with the roadbed suspended below from cables to carry its roadway high above the river and Wilcox Island.

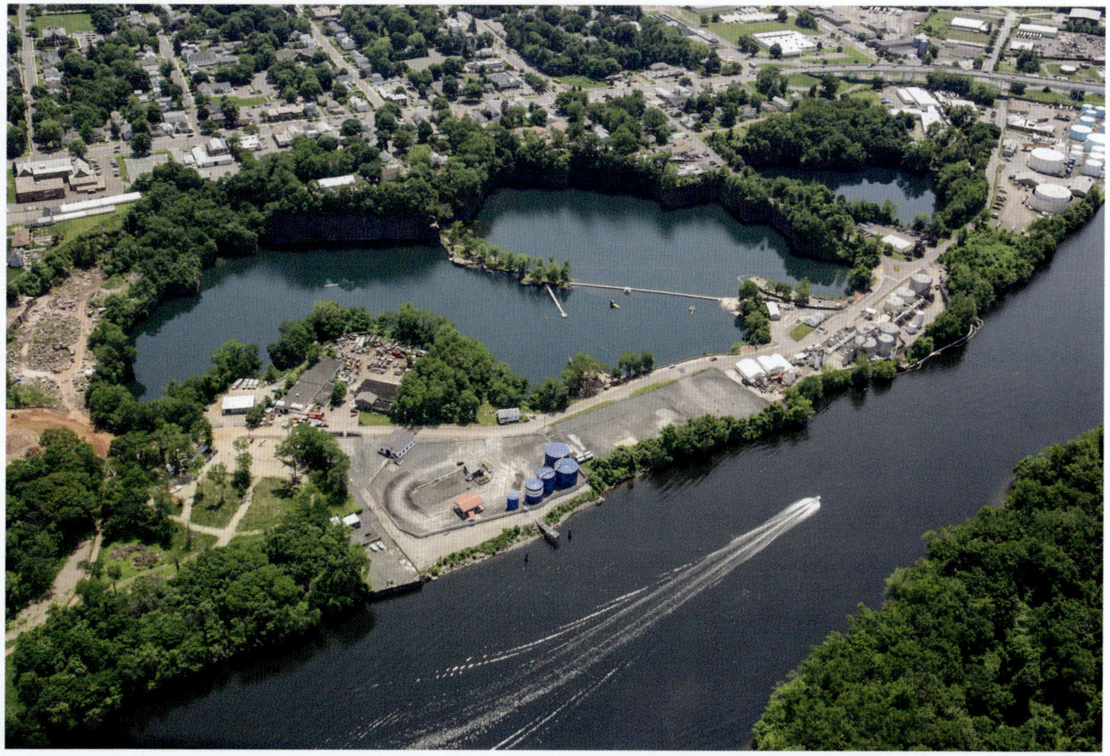

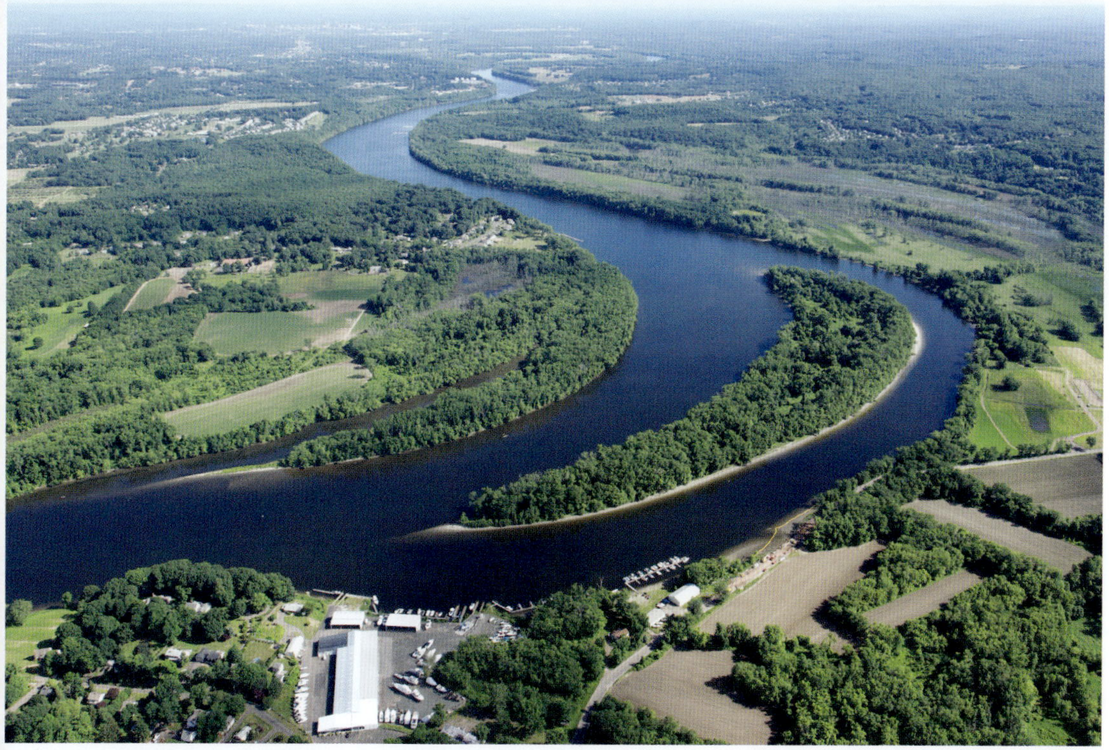

PORTLAND, CT

The famous brownstone apartment buildings of New York, as well as buildings in cities as far away as San Francisco, were made of Portland brownstone quarried across the river from Middletown and transported by ships and boats. Commercial operations began in the late 1700s and stretched through the mid-1930s. Today the flooded quarries, once abandoned and dangerous, are a public attraction featuring kayaking, zip lining, and scuba diving.

Although known today mostly for its brownstone quarries, Portland, which was named Chatham from 1767 until 1841, was also one of the most prolific shipbuilding centers along the river creating a wide variety of vessels from the mid-1700s through the early 1930s. The name most associated with Portland shipbuilding was the Gildersleeve family. They turned out more vessels than all of the other Portland yards combined, including the twenty-four-gun frigate, *Connecticut* built during the Revolution; a large heavily armed steam- and sail-powered gun boat built for the Union Navy during the Civil War, schooners and steamboats built to transport brownstone from the quarries; and the largest two vessels ever built on the river, a pair of huge steam-powered cargo ships, built during the First World War.

GILDERSLEEVE ISLAND

Shown in the photo on the left, just north of Portland the modern marina adjacent to Gildersleeve Island marks the site of one of the most prolific shipbuilding dynasties on the river.

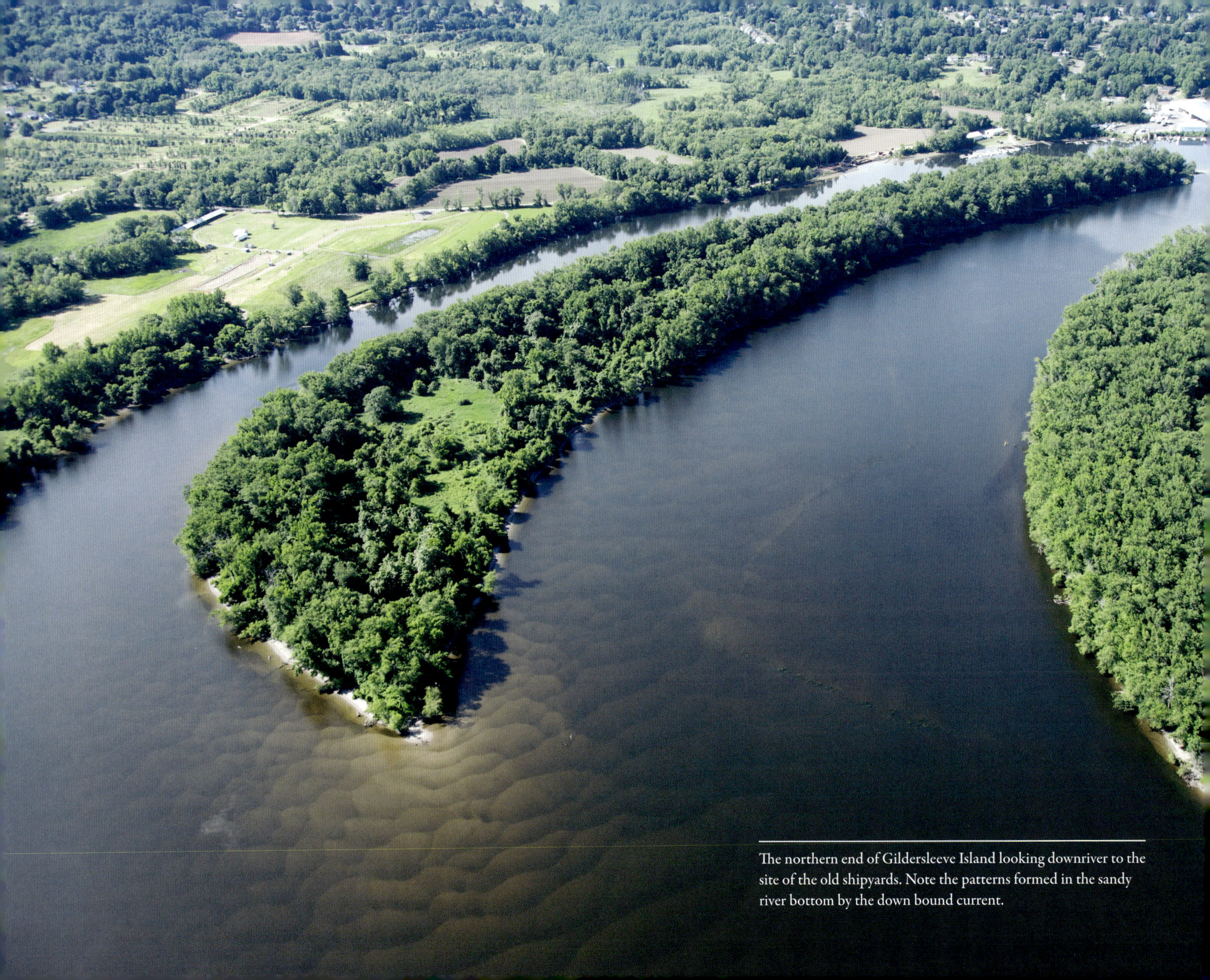

The northern end of Gildersleeve Island looking downriver to the site of the old shipyards. Note the patterns formed in the sandy river bottom by the down bound current.

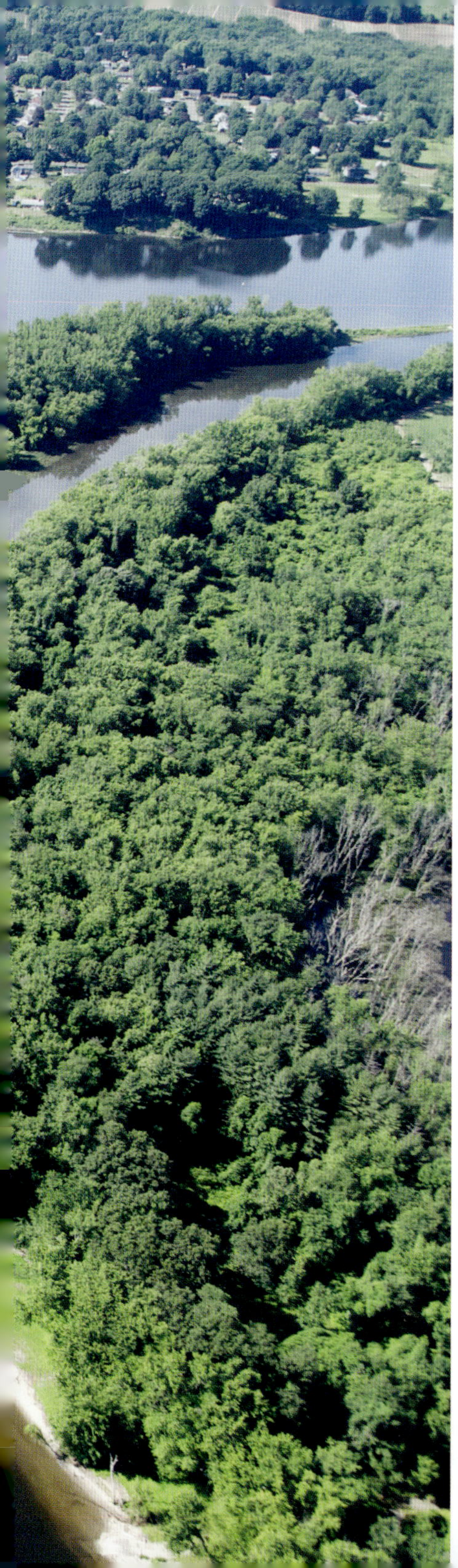

ROCKY HILL–GLASTONBURY FERRY

Established in 1655, the Rocky Hill–Glastonbury Ferry is the oldest continuously operated ferry site in the United States and, along with the Chester–Hadlyme Ferry, is one of the only two remaining in operation on the Connecticut River. The original ferries were poled across the river. The present ferry carries three cars on a barge propelled by the small towboat, *Cumberland*, alongside. Note the Wesleyan University crew team and their chase boat training nearby. The old foundry complex in the foreground, with a significant history of its own, has since been demolished.

See page 70 for map detailing the next twenty-five miles from Rocky Hill to Windsor Locks.

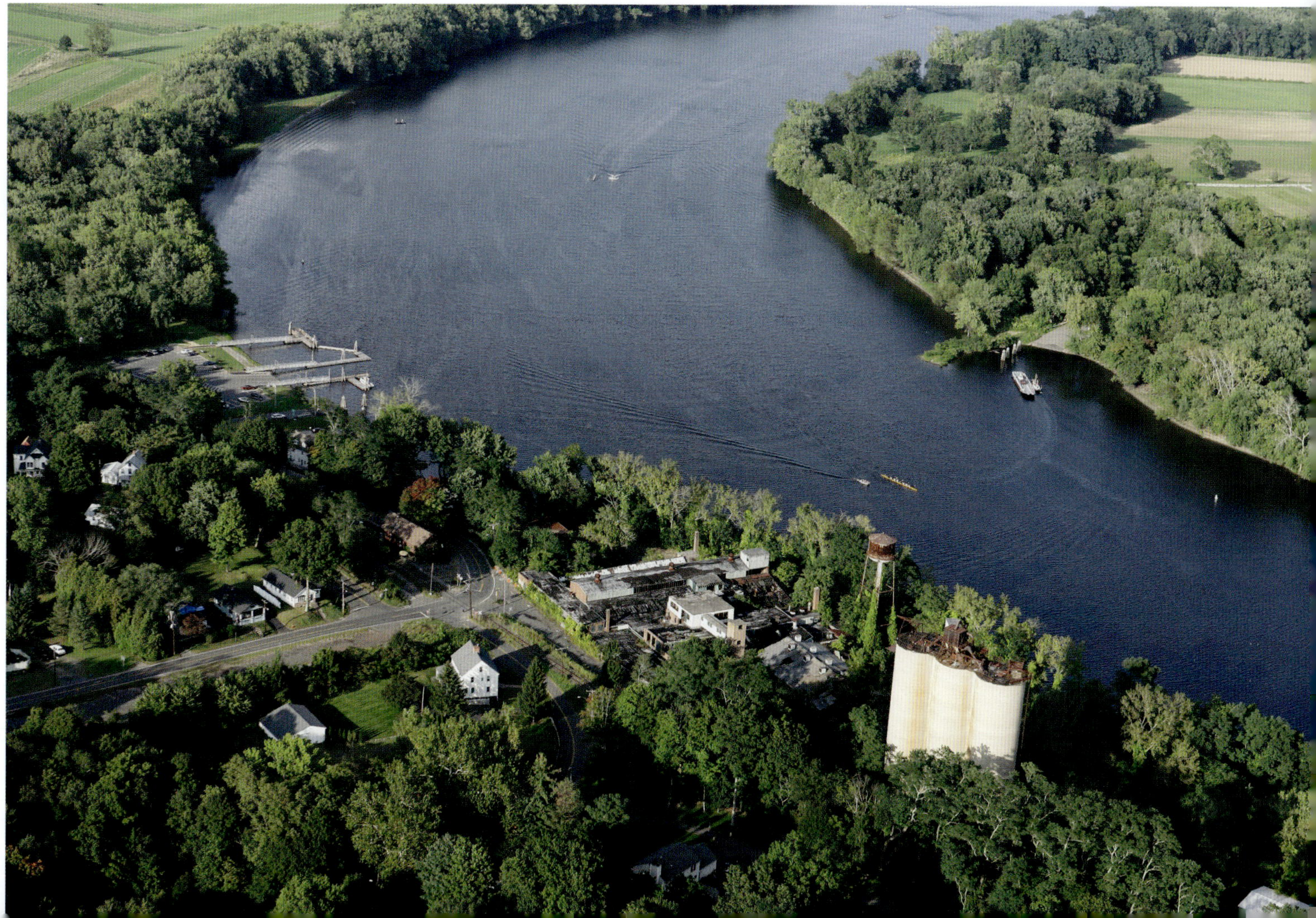

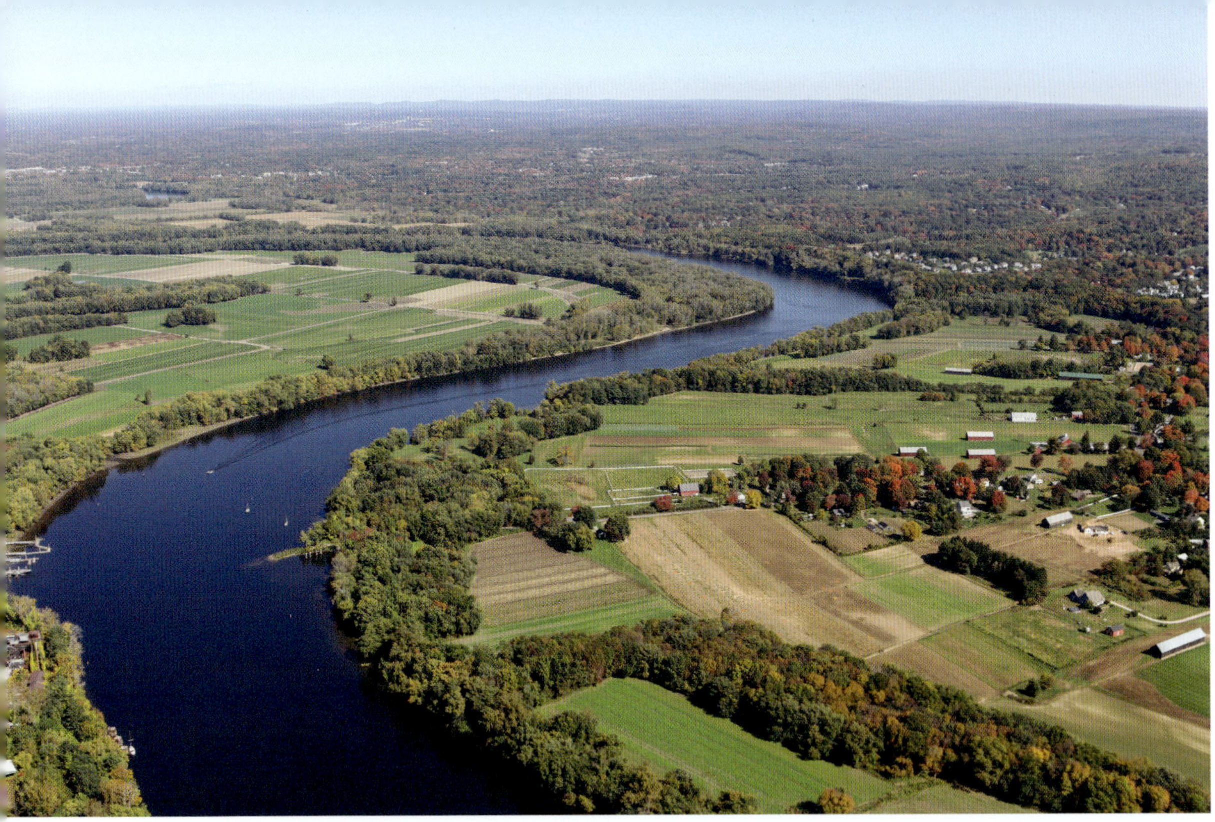

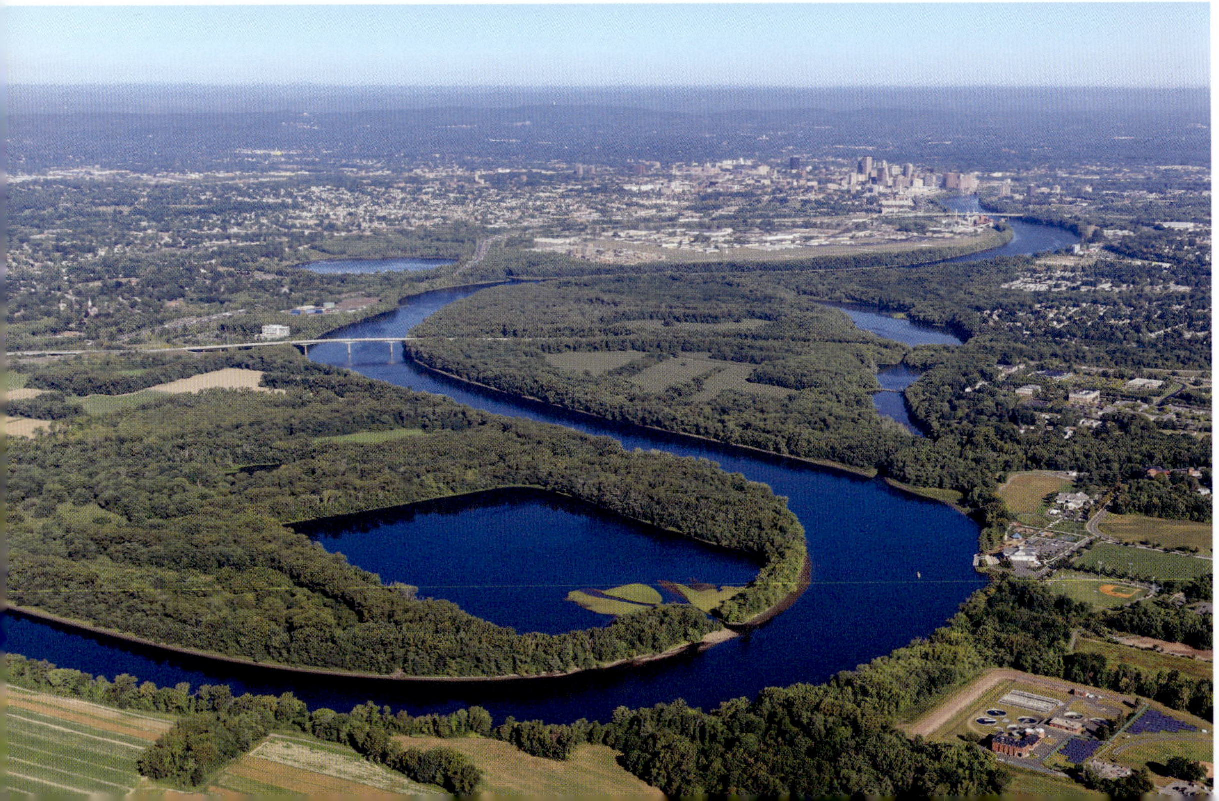

(top left, and right) As the river winds south from Hartford, the rich farmland, some of it still producing Connecticut shade-grown tobacco, is indicative of the fertile soil created within this broad flood plain.

(bottom left) In a bend in the river, just south of Hartford, Crow Point cove was created as soil was excavated for the construction of Interstate 91 and the reinforcement of the riverbank that maintains the river's modern configuration as it flows past Wethersfield and Hartford.

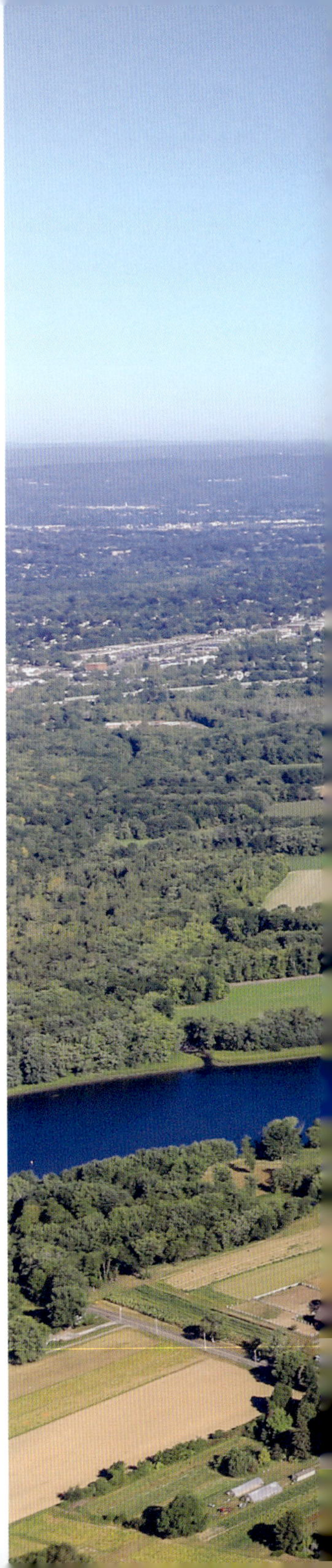

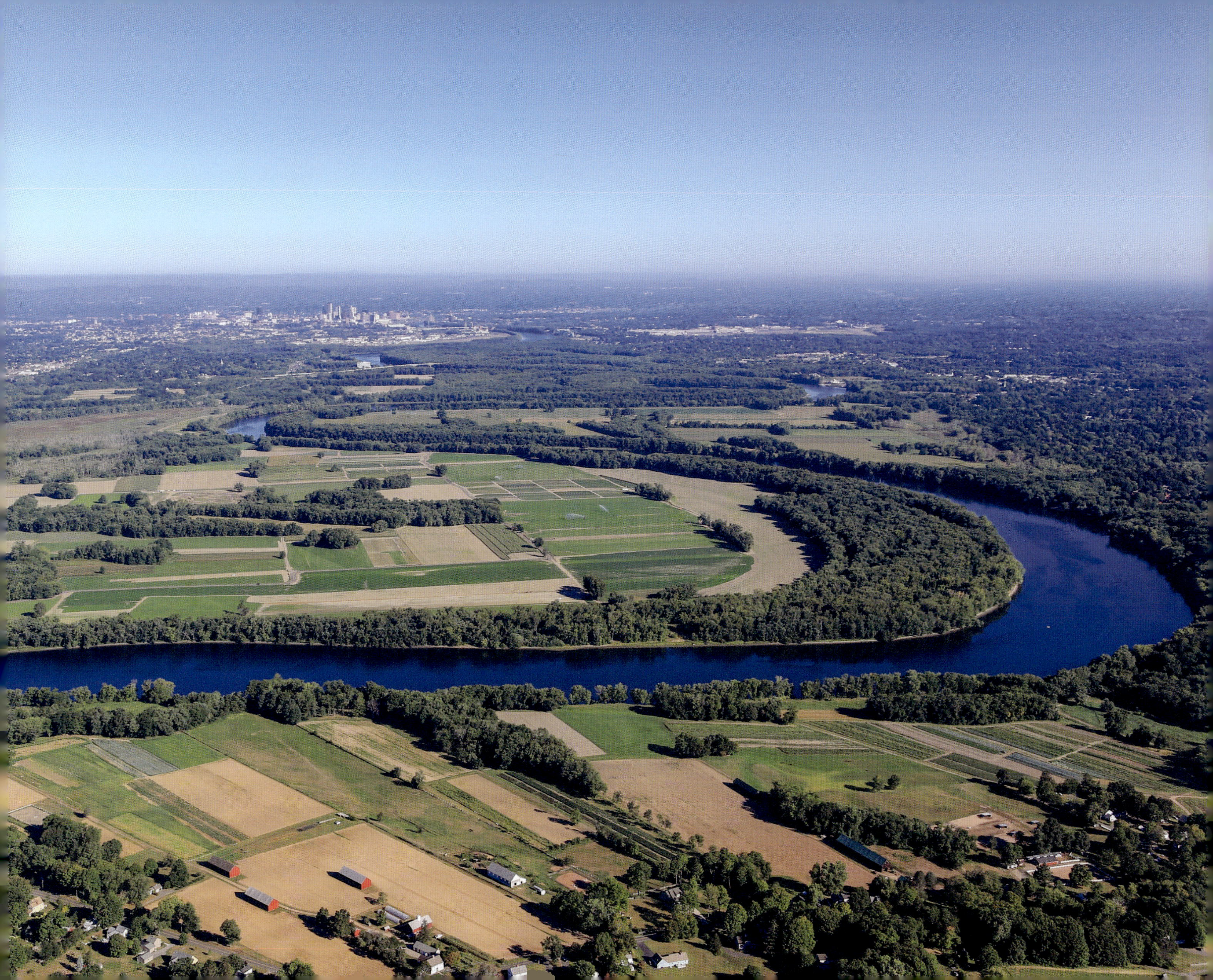

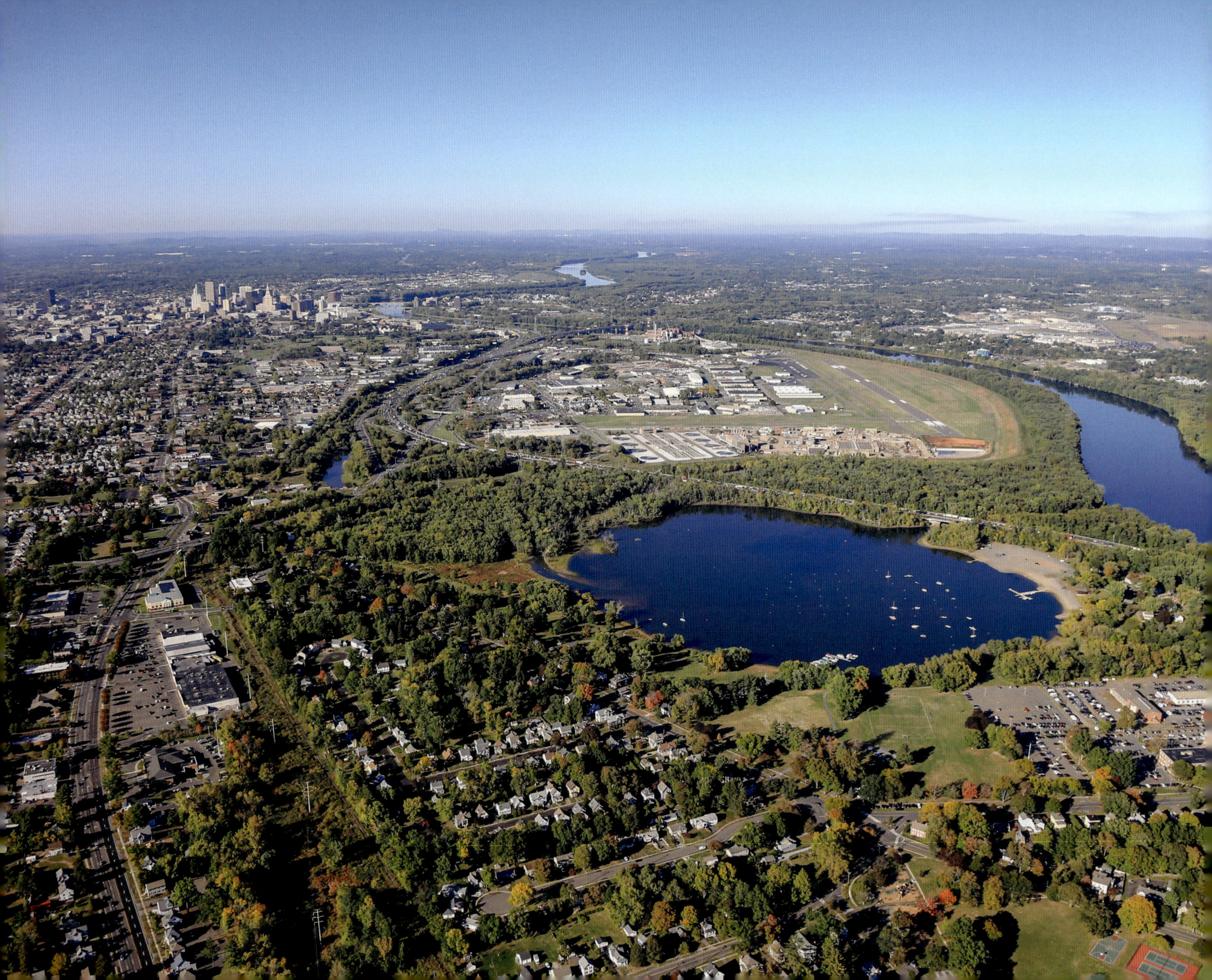

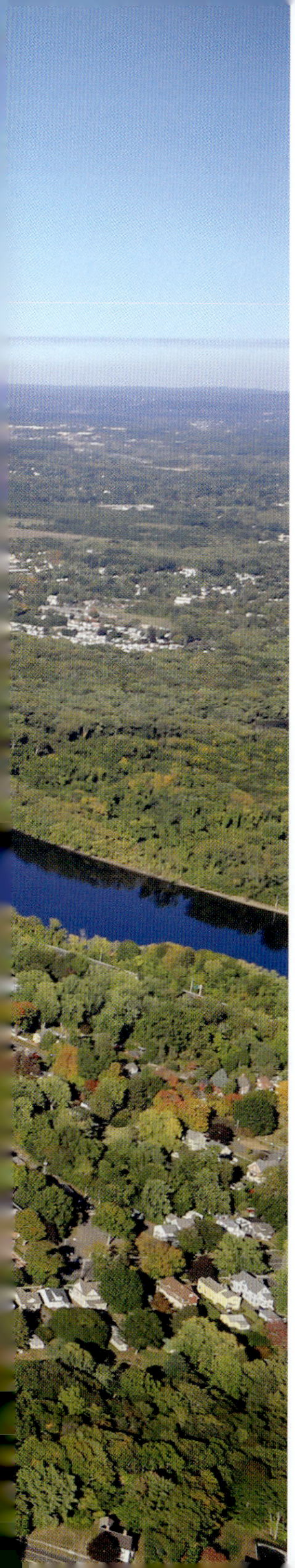

WETHERSFIELD, CT

Originally settled in 1634 in a sharp bend in the river, Wethersfield is one of the oldest English settlements in Connecticut. In fact, it claims to be the first. Here in 1649, the sloop, *Tryal,* the first ocean-going vessel to be constructed on the river, began trading with the West Indies. In about 1700, annual flooding dramatically changed the course of the river, bypassing the bend and turning it into the cove we see today. This isolation of the original port from the river was underscored in the 1960s when Interstate 91 and a dyke system to maintain the river's modern course, cut off the mouth of the cove and the historic district from the river altogether. Today, only a small channel passes under the highway allowing small boats to transit between the cove and the river. Ironically, as Interstate 91 arcs down from Hartford to the left of Brainard Airport, it traces the original course of the river that once connected Wethersfield to the sea.

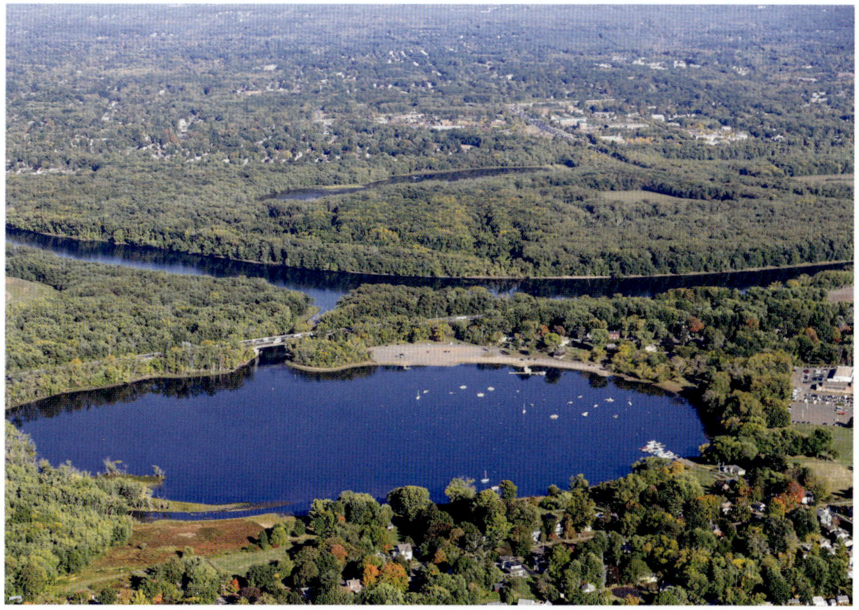

WETHERSFIELD OR WINDSOR?

Although these two towns are fifteen miles apart, one south of Hartford, and the other to the north, Wethersfield and Windsor are inextricably linked by a battle for the bragging rights of which was settled first.

Who did come first?

As you drive into most New England towns you are likely to encounter signs that say, "settled in," "established in," "incorporated in," or "founded in." What does it all mean? Does it really matter? In Windsor, and Wethersfield, Connecticut, it certainly does. By 1635 there were several English settlements along the Connecticut River. But which was in fact first? Windsor has had English boots on the ground since the arrival, by ship, of William Holmes and a group of men from Plymouth who established a trading outpost near the mouth of the Farmington River in 1633.This was the vanguard of what would eventually become Windsor. In 1635 a larger group of settlers from the Massachusetts Bay Colony arrived and would eventually squeeze out the original group from Plymouth. Meanwhile in 1634 John Oldham and another group from Massachusetts Bay settled what was to become Wethersfield. Wethersfield fans contend that Oldham's settlers arrived a year before the permanent settlers arrived in Windsor. But what do they say about the Holmes party who reached the Farmington River in 1633? Depending on semantics and one's point of view there is still plenty of room for the bragging rights rivalry to live on . . . and it will.

HARTFORD-BRAINARD AIRPORT

In 1921 a cow pasture between Wethersfield Cove and Hartford was transformed into what is said to be America's first municipal airport. For more than twenty years Brainard Field was Hartford's primary airport, serving corporate, commercial, military, and private aviation needs until Bradley became the state's main commercial airport after the Second World War. Although Brainard saw military service before and during the war, its location hemmed in by the river made it too small to support the larger military and civil aircraft that evolved during and after the war. Brainard is still one of the busiest airports in the region, supporting corporate and private aviation, a flight school, an aviation technical school, and a Civil Air Patrol squadron.

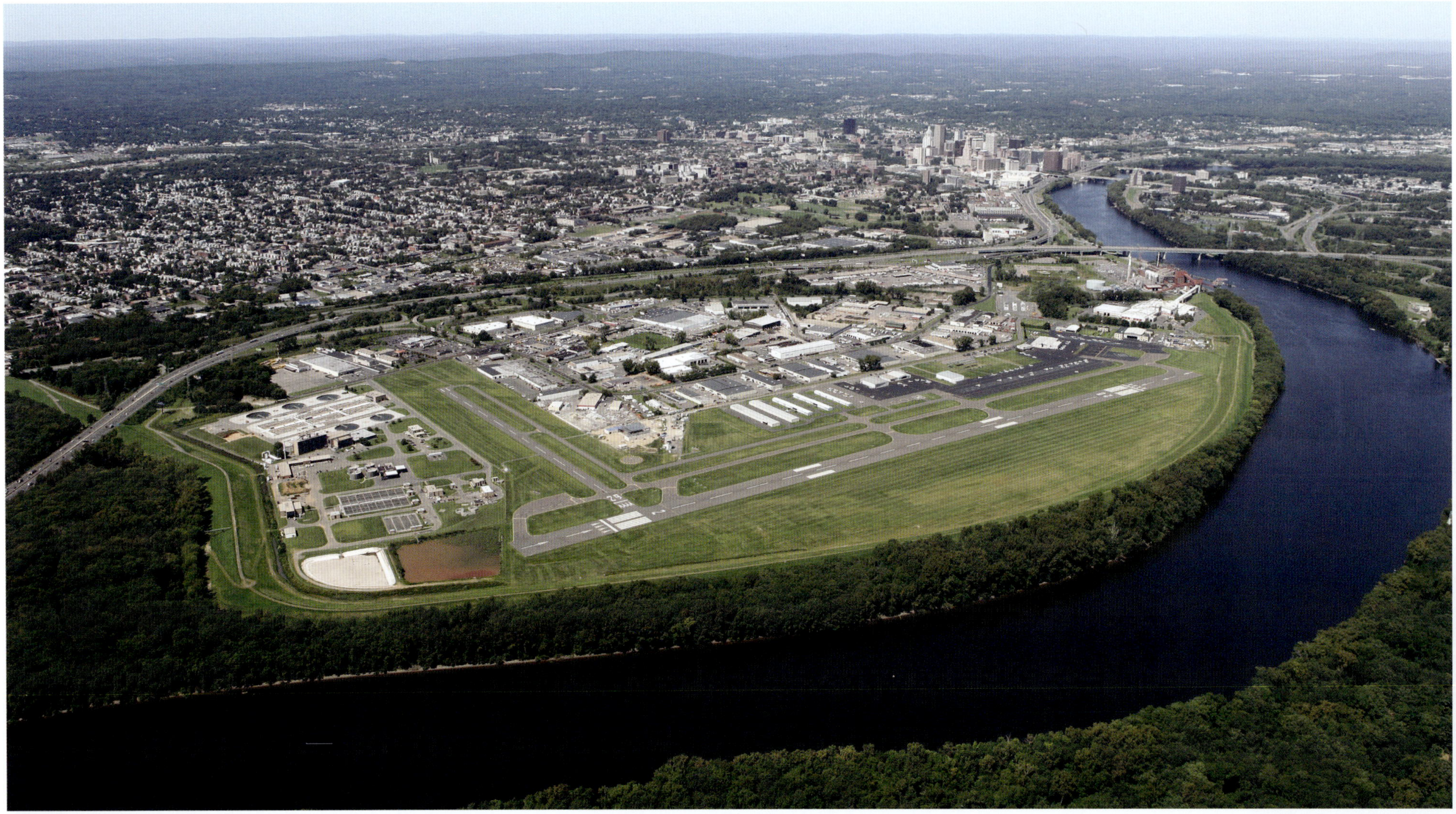

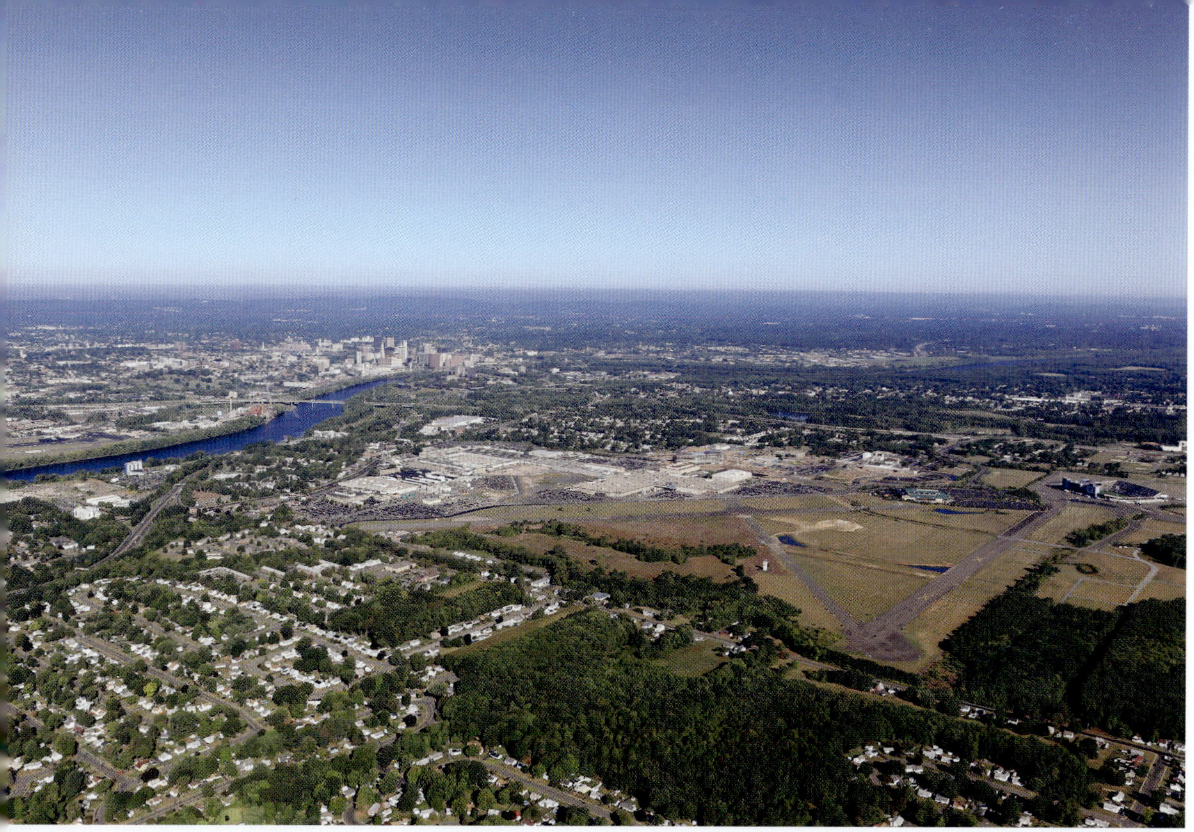

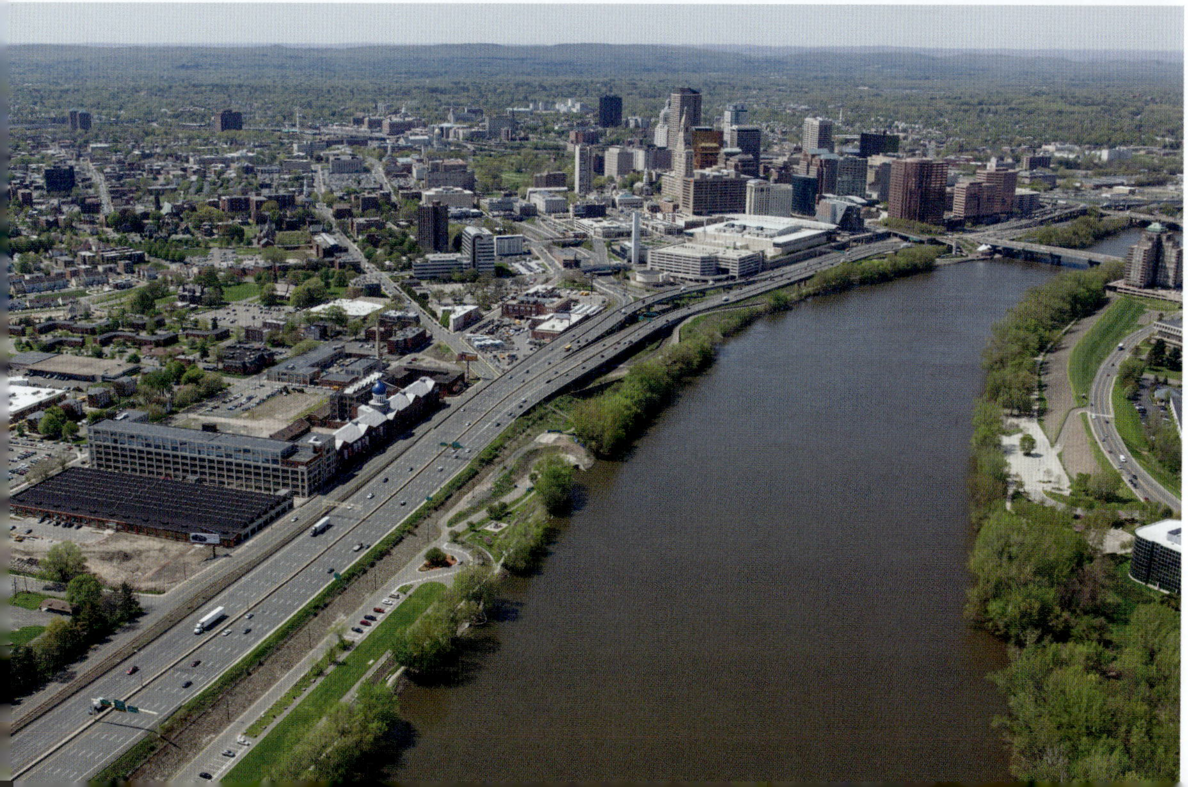

RENTSCHLER FIELD

Located almost directly across the river from Brainard, Rentschler Field (top left) served as Pratt & Whitney's private airport from 1933 to its decommissioning in 1999. During the Second World War, in addition to Pratt's aircraft engine development, production and testing, a squadron of the 57th Fighter Group was deployed here to aid in the defense of Hartford. Founded by Fred Rentschler in 1925, Pratt is one of the three largest manufacturers of aircraft engines in the world. Engines, including the pioneering Wasp series, and many turbojets were manufactured in the large buildings west of the runways before engine production was shifted to Middletown in 1966. Pratt's corporate headquarters, engineering, and parts manufacturing facilities remain here. A new engineering complex has just been completed here, guaranteeing Pratt's commitment to this historic location just across the river from Hartford.

(bottom left) The Colt Armory complex with its distinctive, blue "onion dome" overlooks Interstate 91 and the river just south of Hartford. It was once the heart of Samuel Colt's empire that turned out small arms for the U.S. military and civilian use from 1855 to 1994. Today the complex is on the National Register of Historic Places and is being redeveloped as live-work space with both residential and commercial lofts. In a unique public-private partnership, the National Park Service is developing part of the complex into the Coltsville National Historical Park to preserve the legacy of the armory.

HARTFORD AREA

Cromwell to Windsor Locks

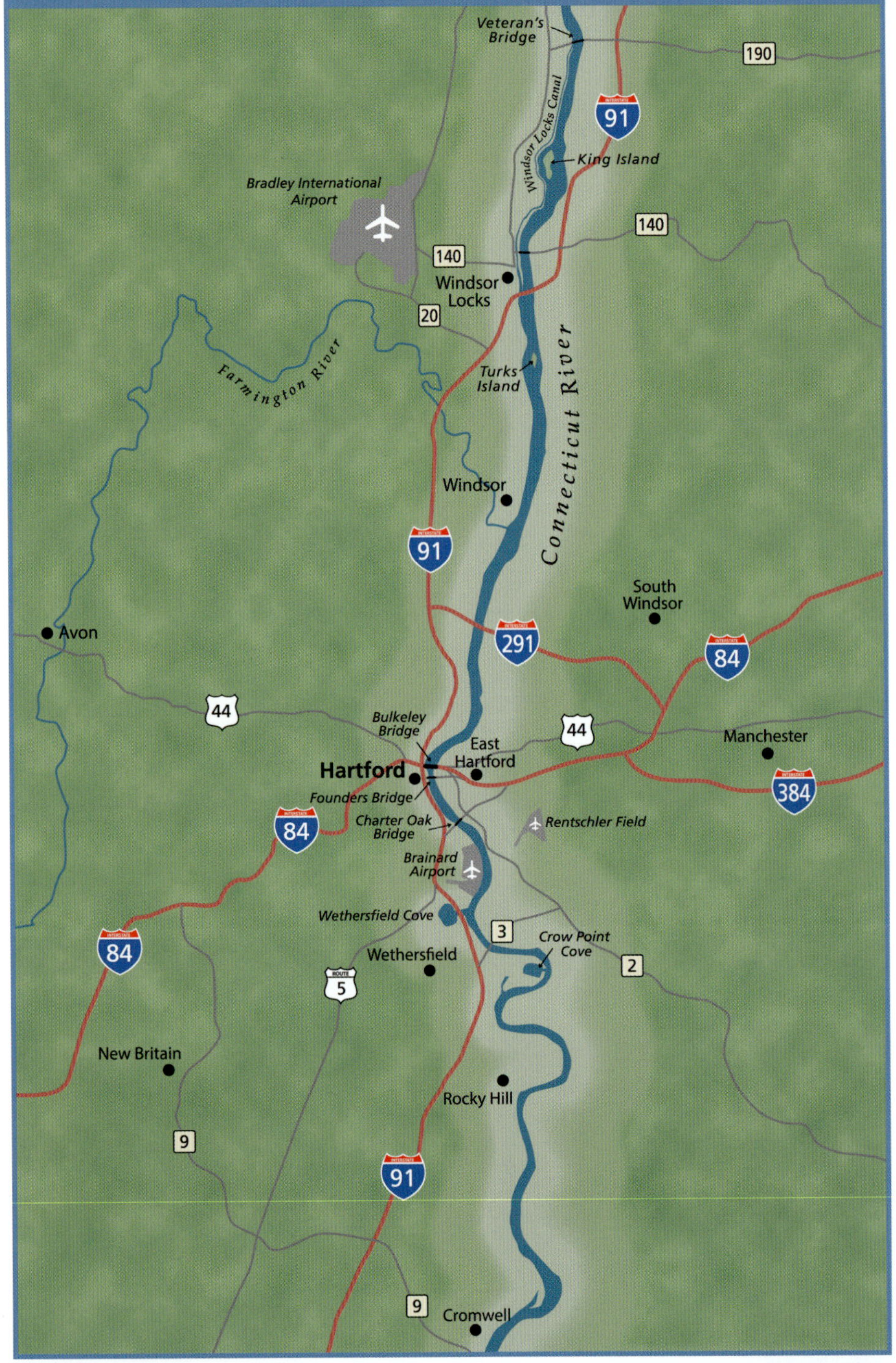

HARTFORD, CT

Hartford, Connecticut's capital, was one of the earliest settlements in Connecticut. Although the area was reached by Adriaen Block in 1614, it was not until 1633 that the Dutch established a fur trading post here called the House of Good Hope. Leapfrogged by the English in 1633, who established an outpost at Windsor farther up the river, Hartford soon had its own English community as the Dutch left the area. Once a shipping and shipbuilding center, Hartford was linked to New York by overnight steamboat service from the mid-1800s through 1931. It became better known as home to the nation's major insurance companies, Colt Firearms, and Pratt & Whitney aircraft engines. Hartford was dramatically cut off from its maritime heritage in the 1960s by Interstate 91 making it virtually impossible to reach the river by foot or car from the city. In recent years, through the Riverfront Recapture project, Hartford has reestablished a recreational connection to the river that once drove its economy.

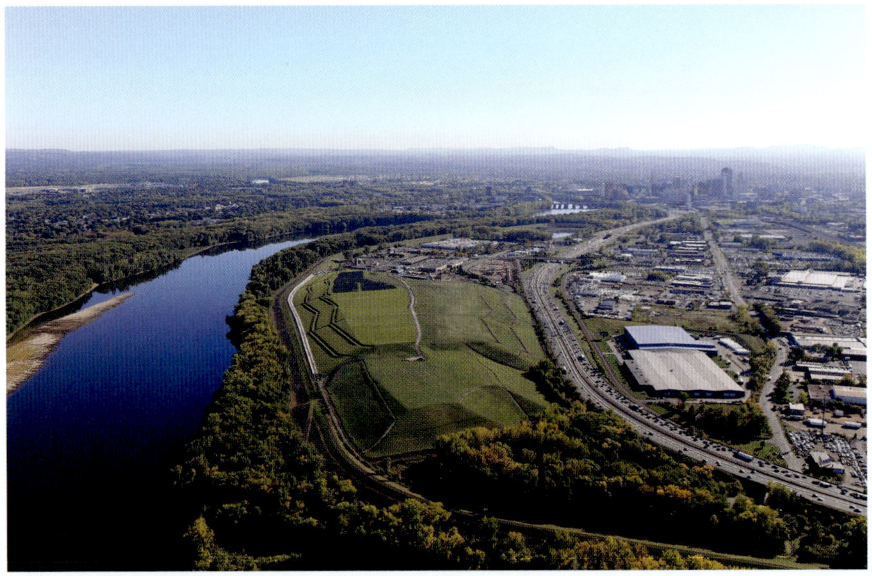

Just north of Hartford (looking south), a giant mound covers what was once the city's primary garbage dump. It is known locally as "Mount Trashmore."

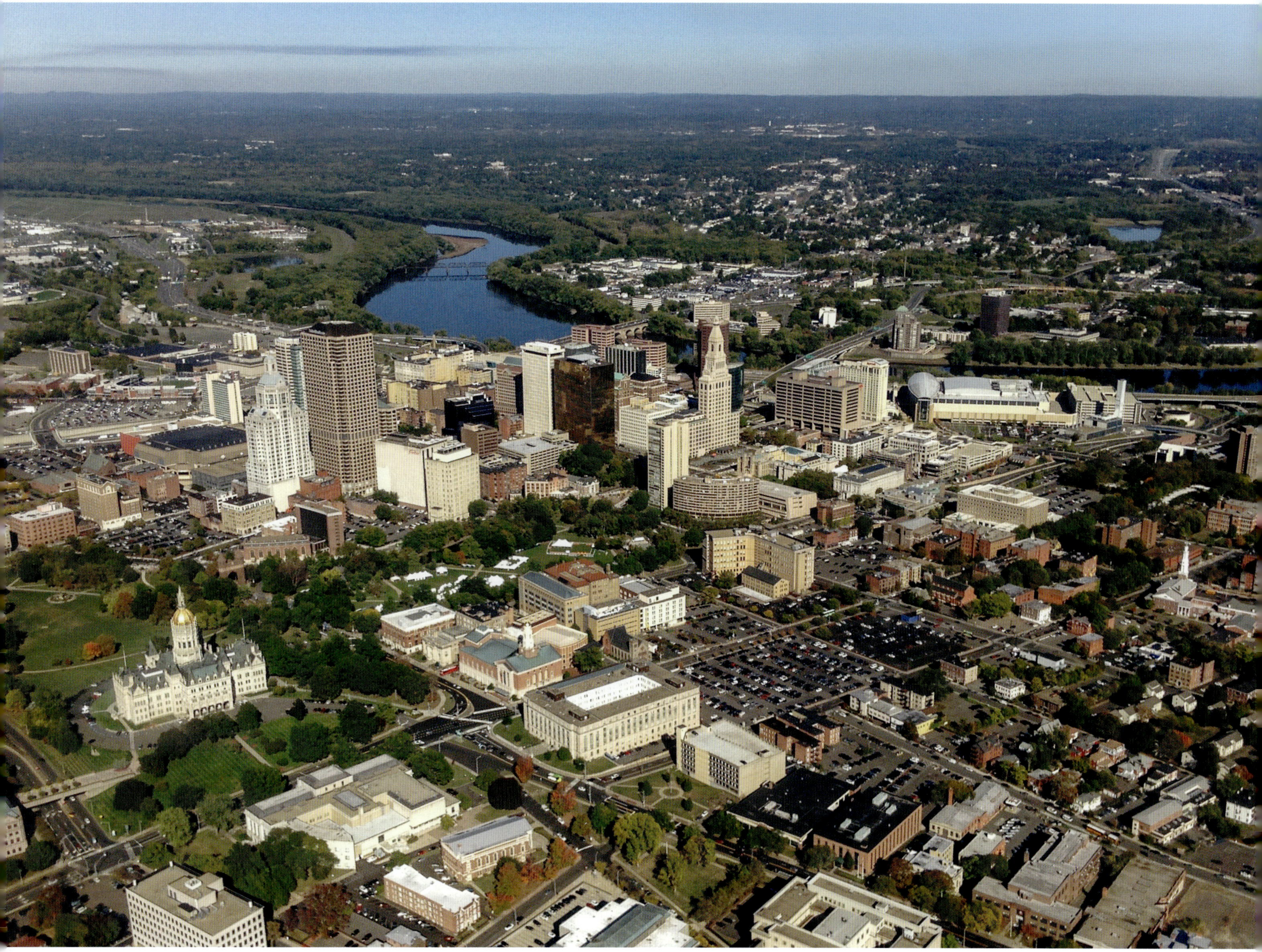

BIRD'S-EYE VIEWS

Before aircraft offered lofty vistas, Nineteenth Century panoramic maps, also known as Bird's-Eye Views, depicted communities from elevated perspectives, allowing people to gaze down upon their towns and cities. Bird's-Eye Views were immensely popular from the 1870s through the 1920s because they showcased a town's best assets: factories, public and domestic architecture, parks, roads, and other natural and manmade landmarks. *Bird's-Eye Views* captured these communities and froze them in time. Today we are able to compare these utopian visions with modern aerial photographs and to see what has changed, and what remains the same. High altitude black and white images taken during the comprehensive 1934 US Geological Survey also offer an import visual benchmark of the river.

Tom often flies from tiny Goodspeed Airport, a few miles north of Essex, wedged in between the River, the wooded hillsides, and the historic East Haddam Swing Bridge. Flights in a Searey Amphipian begin with donning inflatable life jackets as if we are going sailing, and then climbing up and over the hull into the snug side-by-side cockpit. Each side has a sliding canopy section that allows for pilot and passenger to sit with an elbow on the side just like riding in a convertible through the countryside. With its retractable landing gear this amazing airplane can taxi in and out of the water, morphing from boat to flying machine at will. When flying low, sometimes just above the surface of the water it is surreal exchanging waves with people fishing along the riverbank.

Once airborne, as we climb up over the treetops and bridges, the broader view of the surrounding countryside is truly magic. Houses and roads along the course of the river look like toy villages punctuated by country lanes and railroad tracks. The vintage Essex steam train chugs along as if this were all some miniature HO layout complete with puffs of white smoke and the magic sound of a steam whistle. Flying over the river and its tranquil banks is one thing, but when Tom took us over Hartford, and Bradley International Airport so I could get a bird's eye look at the New England Air Museum, I began to fully appreciate his skill as a pilot as he calmly talked to the control tower. Here we were in our sparrow-like amphibian orbiting above the runways as sleek jets came and went to destinations near and far. It was all pretty extraordinary to me, but just another day in the air for Tom.

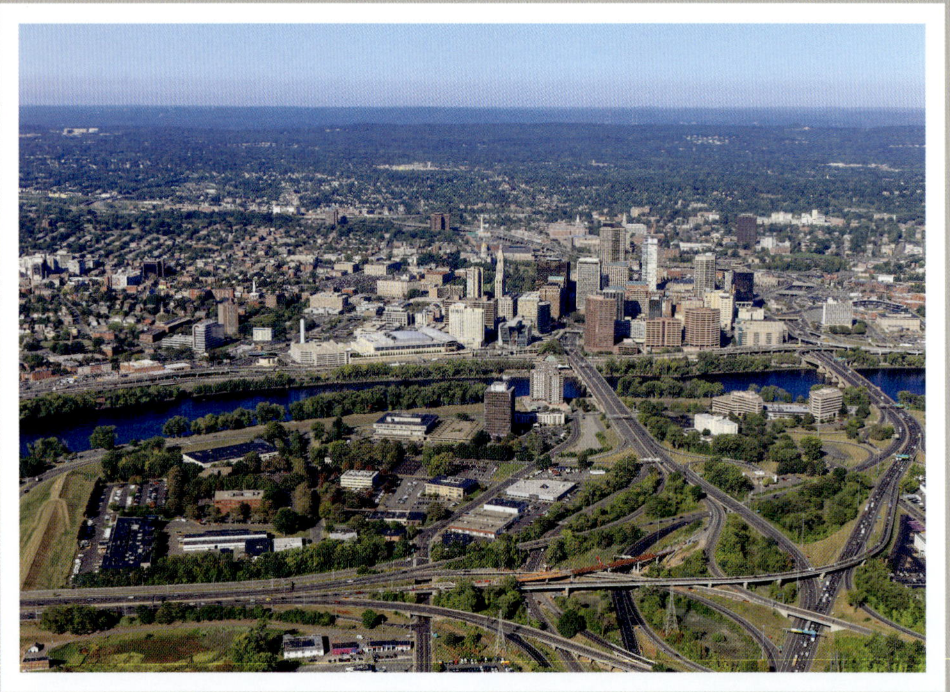

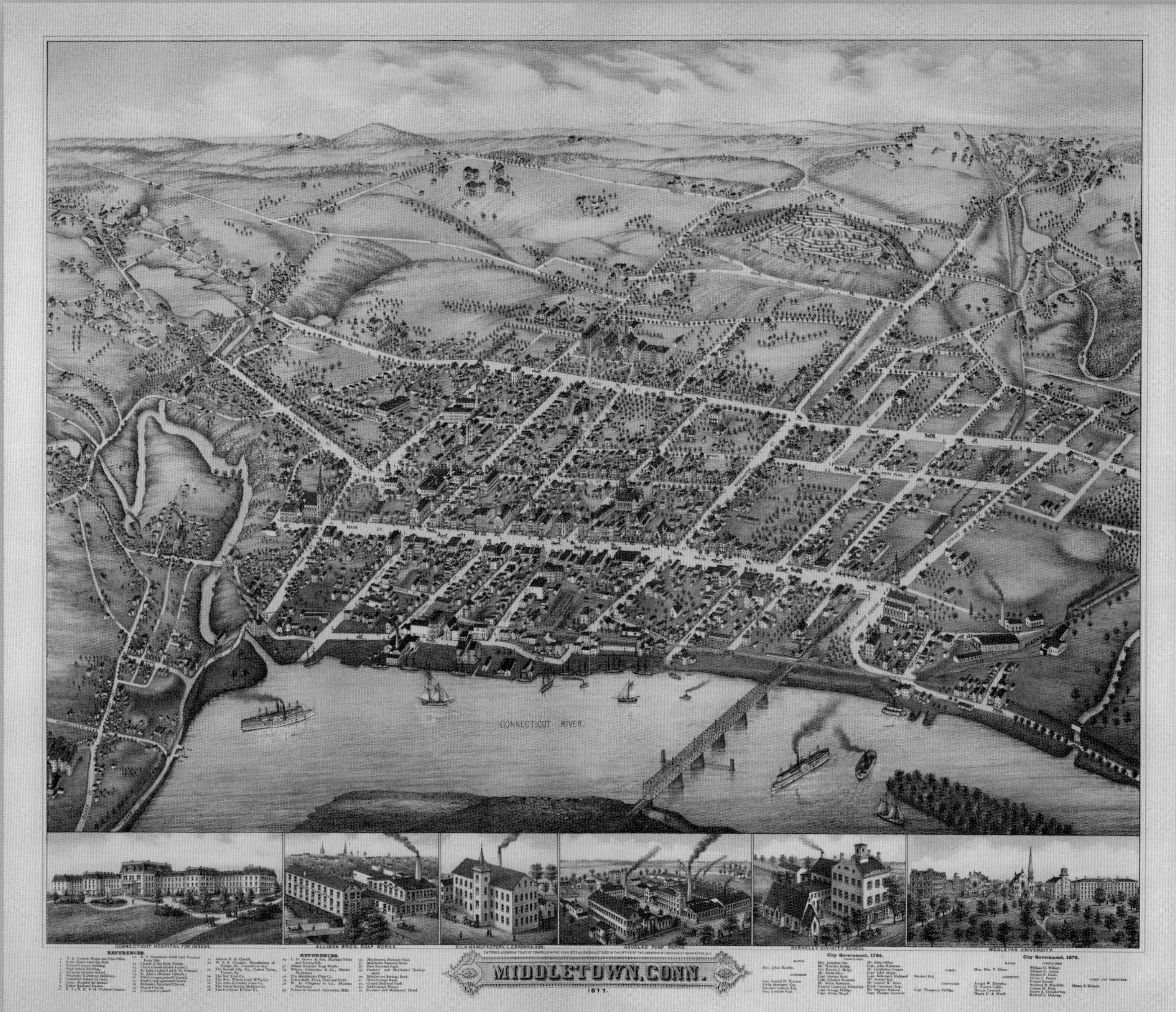

CONNECTICUT RIVER
CONNECTICUT HOSPITAL FOR INSANE.
ALLISON BRO'S. SOAP WORKS.
SILK MANUFACTORY, L. D. BROWN & SON.
DOUGLAS PUMP WORKS.
BERKELEY DIVINITY SCHOOL.
WESLEYAN UNIVERSITY.
REFERENCES.
MIDDLETOWN, CONN.
1877.
City Government, 1784.
City Government, 1876.

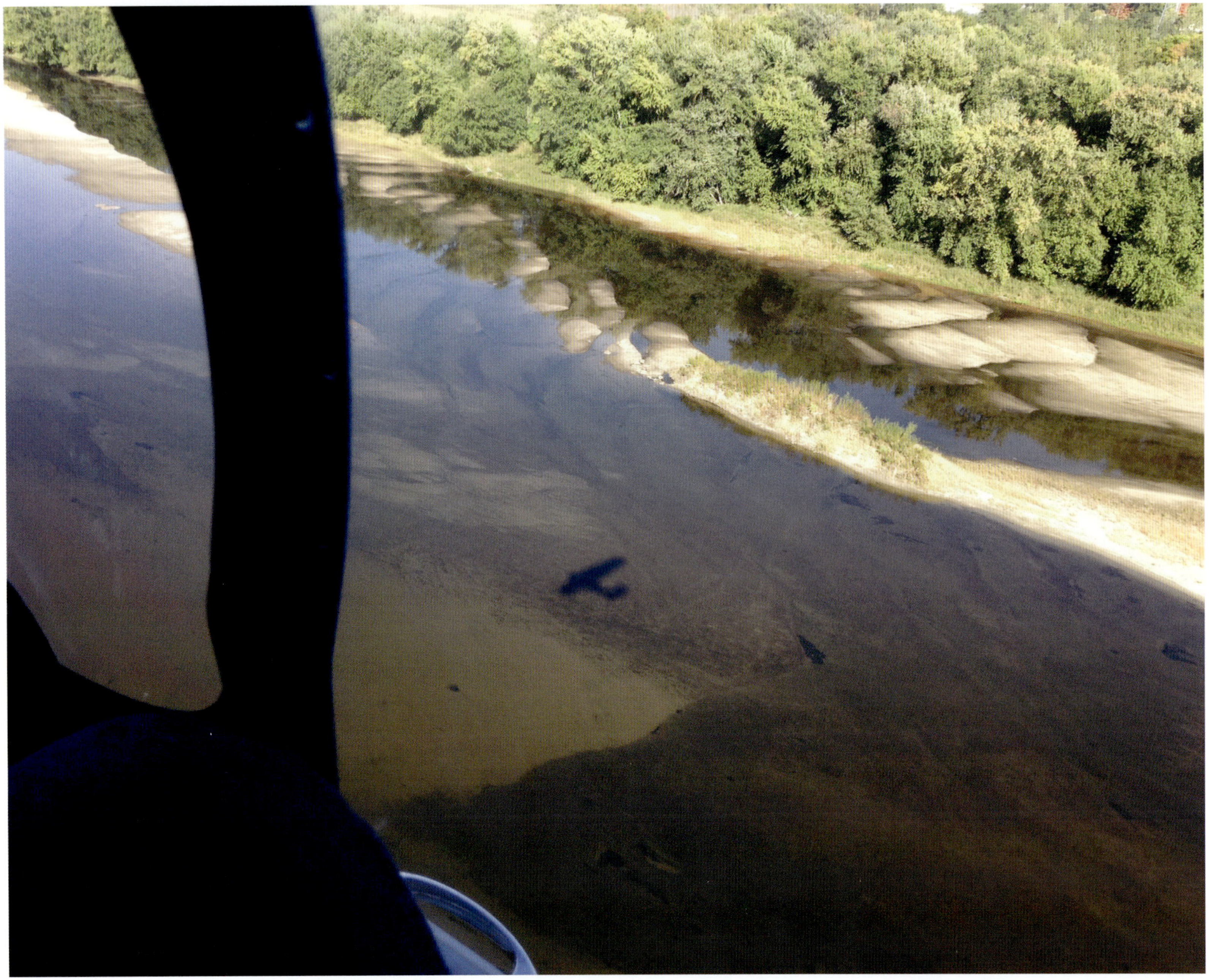

Continuing north from Hartford, our aircraft casts a shadow on the sculpted river bottom near the Farmington River's confluence with the Connecticut.

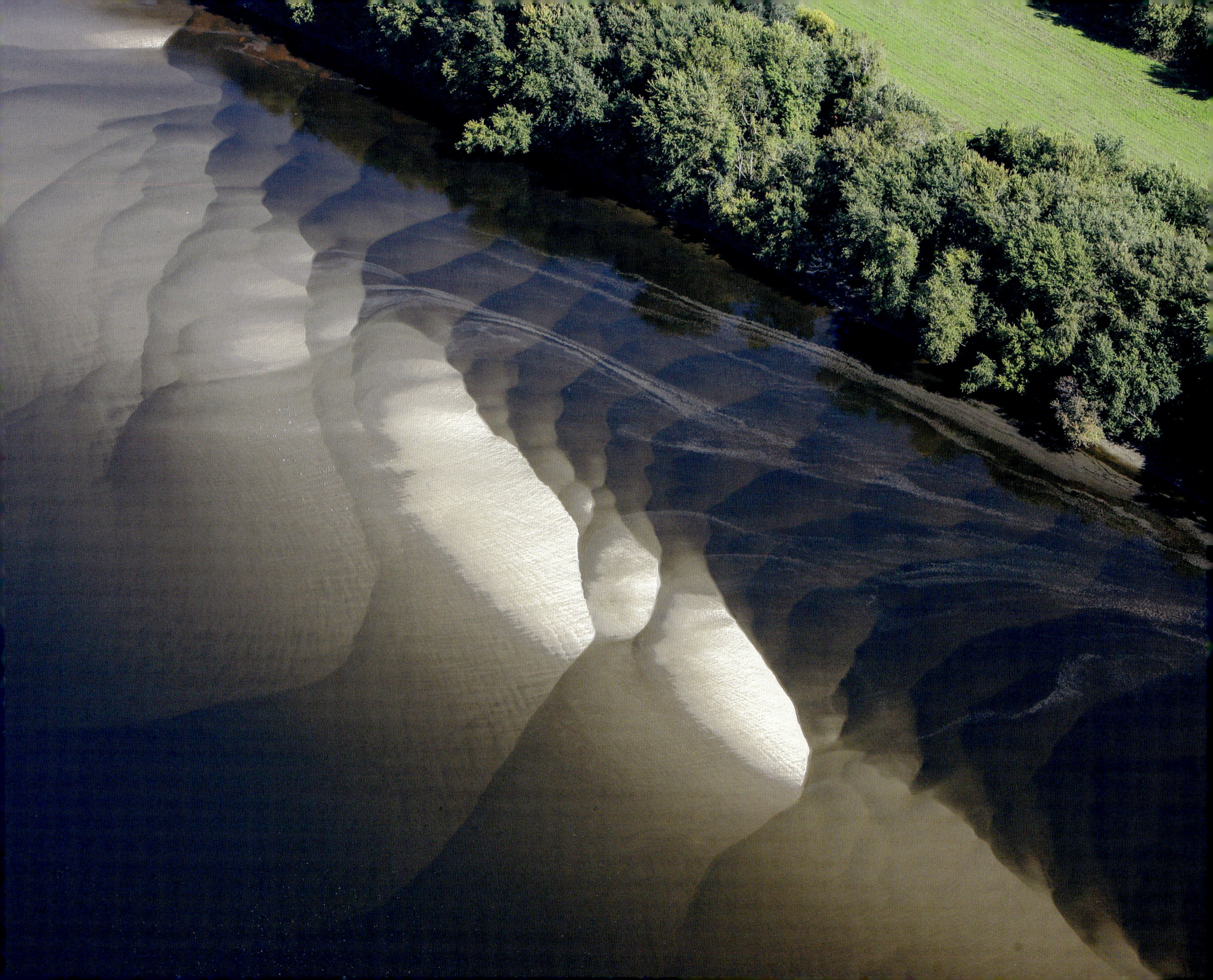

WINDSOR, CT

It was here in 1633 that Captain William Holmes and a small group of men from Plymouth, Massachusetts, arrived after defiantly sailing past the Dutch outpost in Hartford. They set up a prefabricated frame house and established what would become the first English settlement in Connecticut. The town of Windsor, which can be seen here, was established just up the Farmington River. The local Podunk Indians, who were looking for an ally to counter the growing influence of the Pequot and their Dutch trading partners, had invited the Holmes expedition here.

(below and right) Five miles north of Hartford, the Farmington River joins the Connecticut. This stretch of river offers a clear view of patterns formed by the down-bound current in the shallow river bottom.

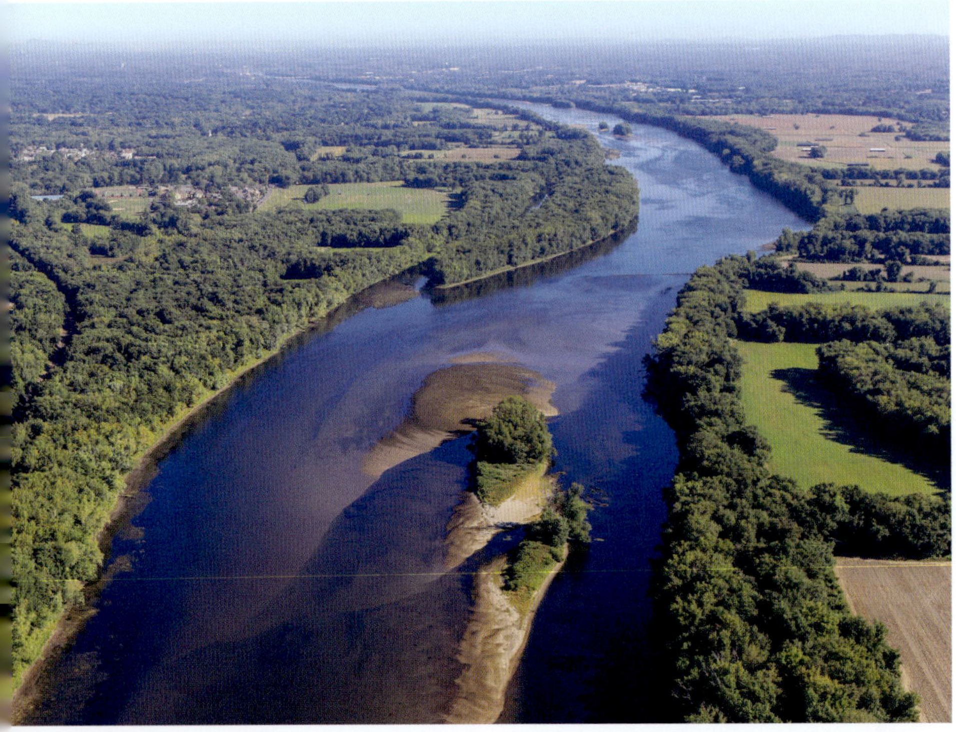

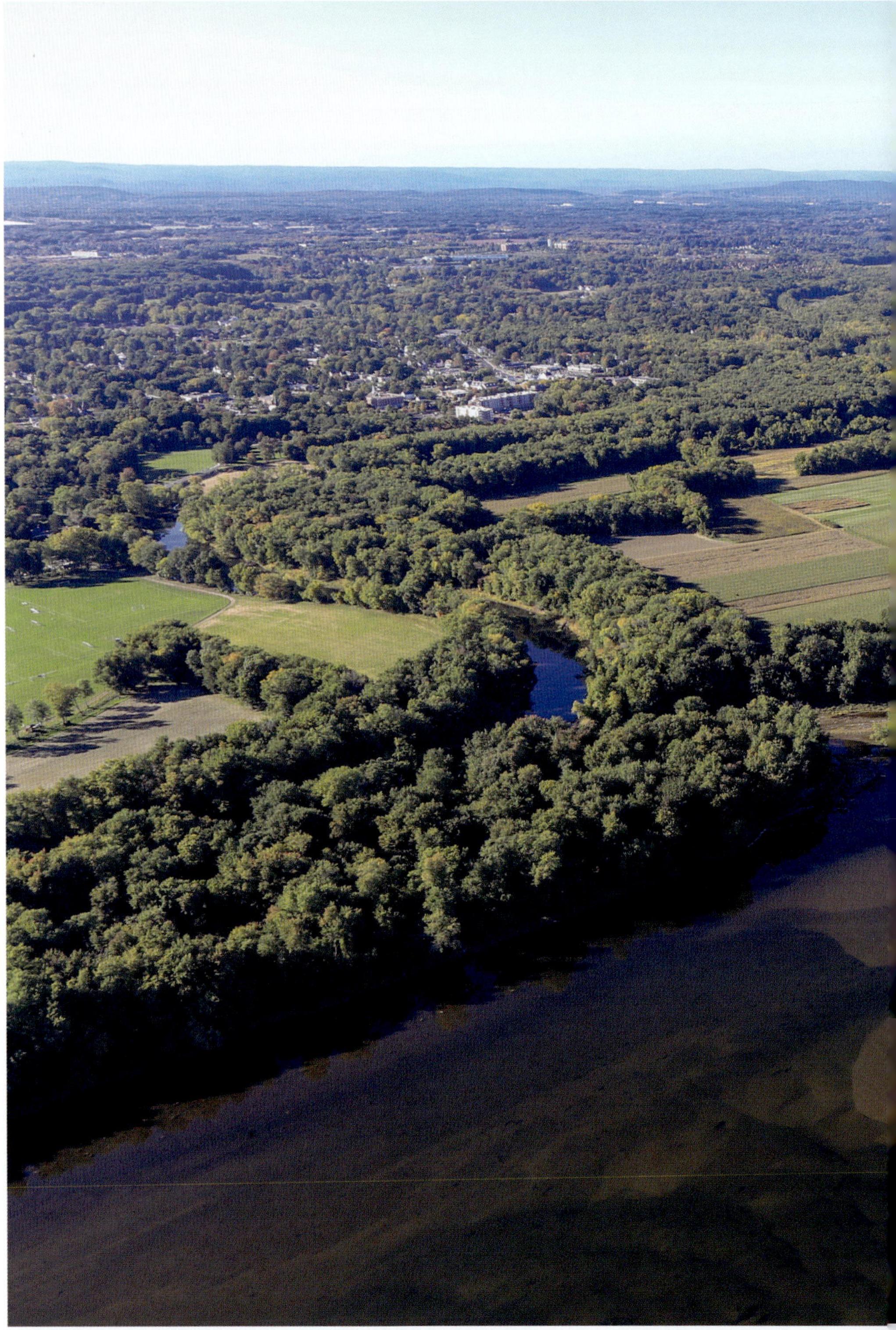

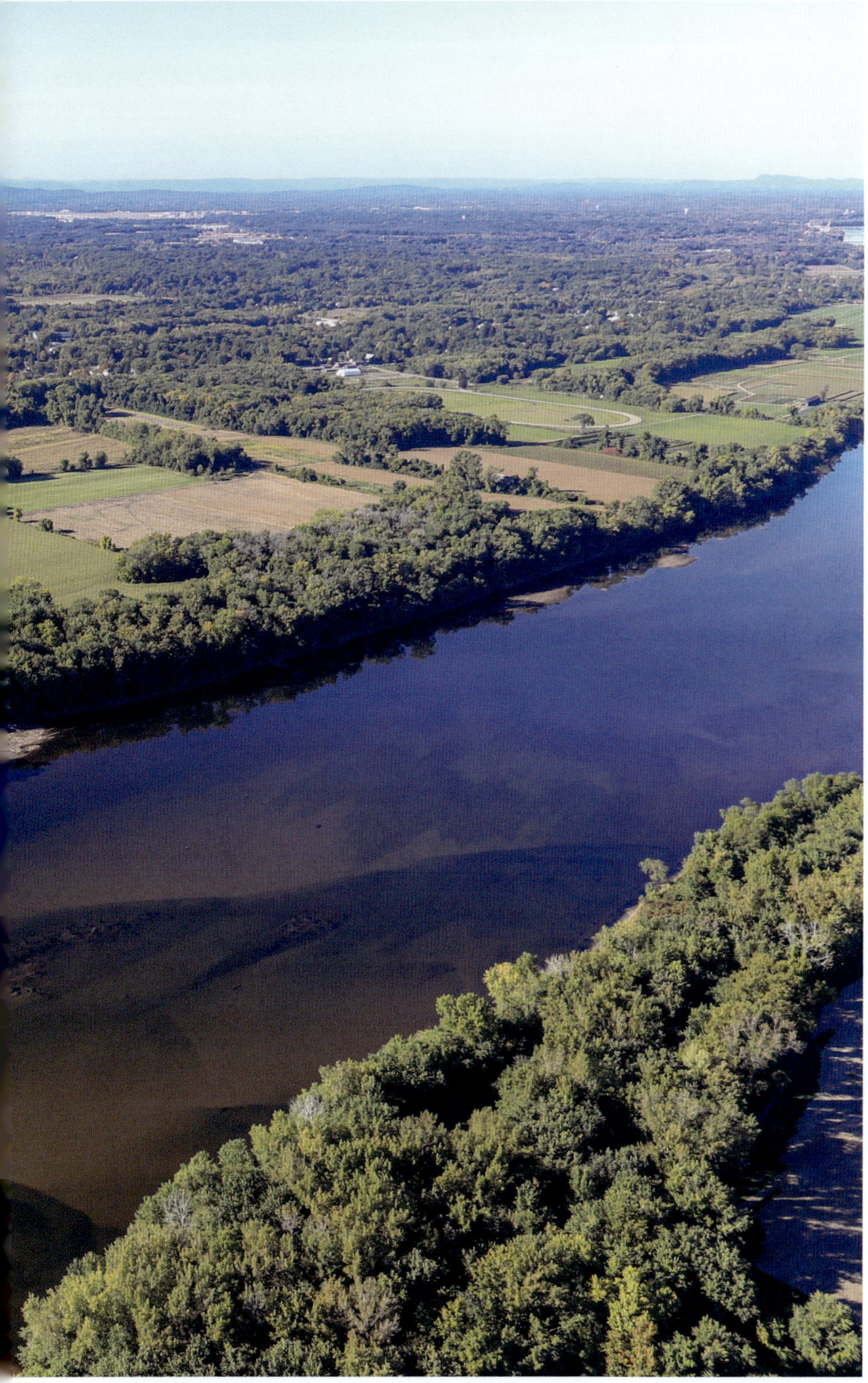

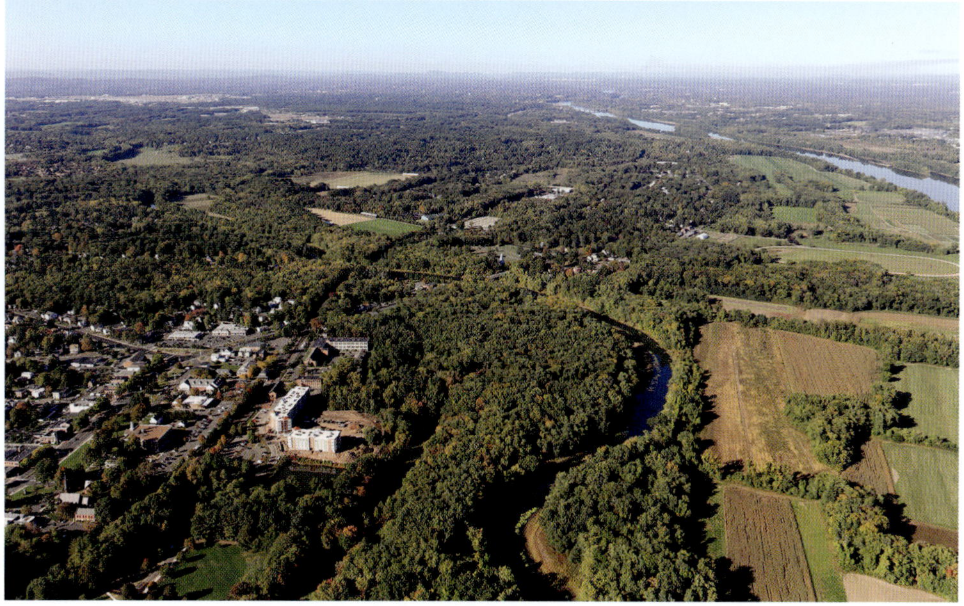

(above) Modern Windsor is located on the southwest side of the Farmington River. The early palisaded cluster of dwellings was just across the Palisado Avenue Bridge.

(below) The site of Windsor's original palisade and burial ground looking east over the Farmington Bridge. The Connecticut River parallels the horizon hidden behind the double tree line between the cleared fields on either side of the river.

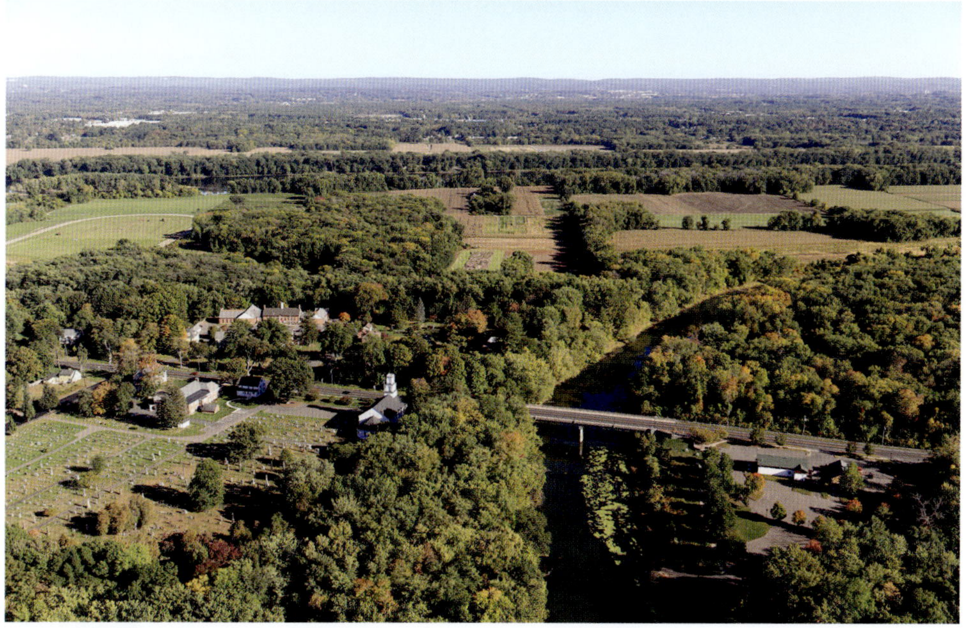

BRADLEY INTERNATIONAL AIRPORT

In 1940, as the Battle of Britain raged across the Atlantic, it was felt that if war should come to this side of the Atlantic Hartford might be vulnerable to enemy air attacks due to its insurance industry and small arms and aircraft engine manufacturing. The state purchased 1,600 acres of tobacco fields outside of Windsor Locks and, in just five months, the Army Corps of Engineers transformed it into a major air base.

Throughout the war, bomber, fighter, and transport squadrons trained here along with replacement pilots before being dispatched to combat zones overseas. It was named for Eugene Bradley, the first pilot killed here during training—just three days after the base became operational on August 18, 1941. Commercial flights began after the war in 1947. Today, several major airlines and air freight companies operate out of Bradley, which is also shared by the Army National Guard and the Connecticut Air National Guard, better known as the Flying Yankees.

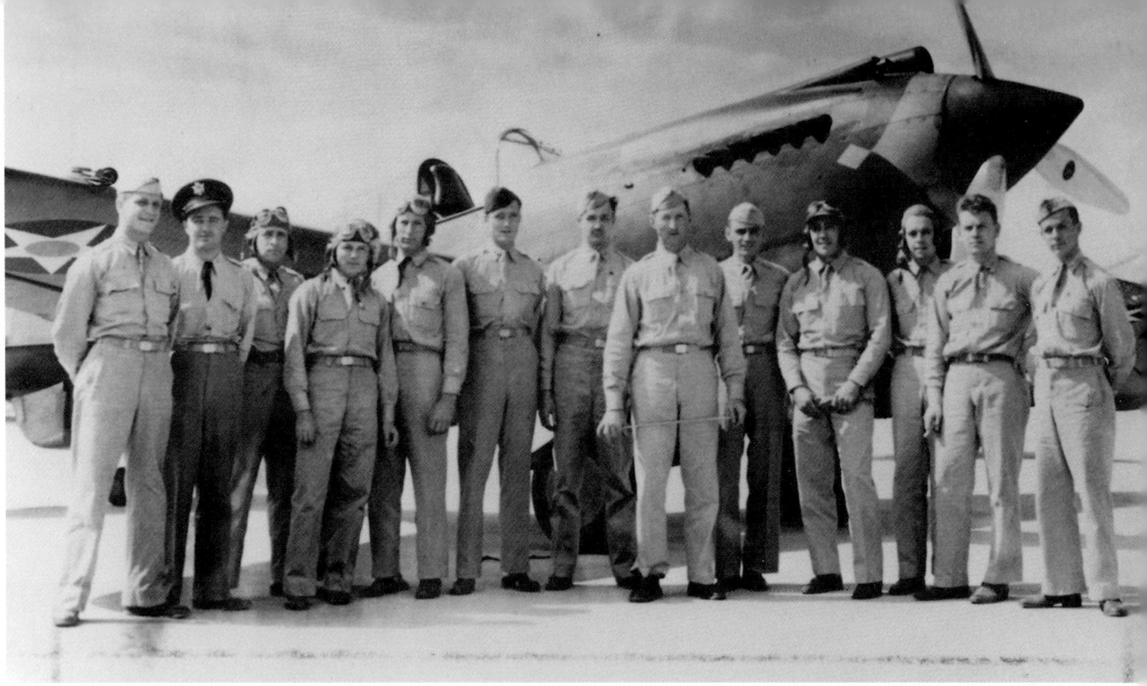

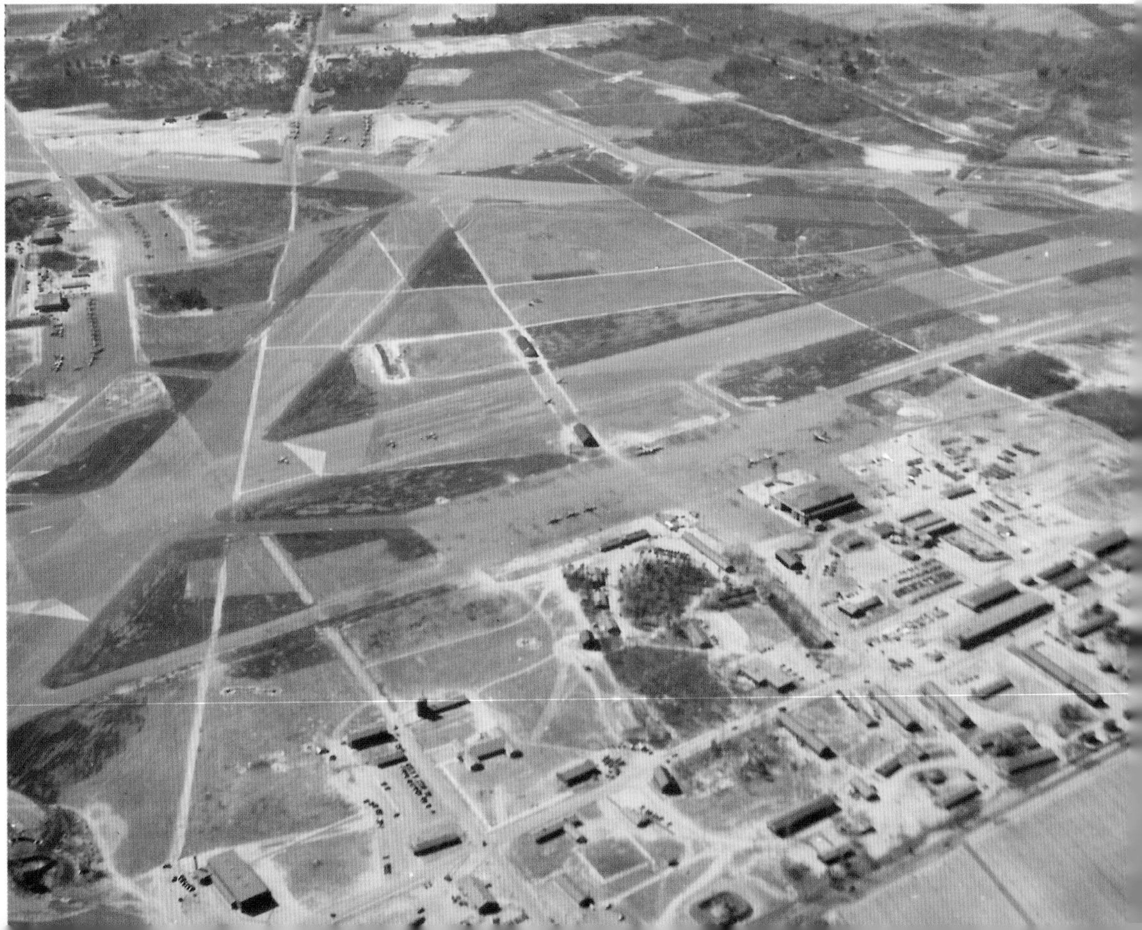

(right) Aerial photo of Bradley Field during the Second World War, camouflaged to blend in with surrounding farmlands.

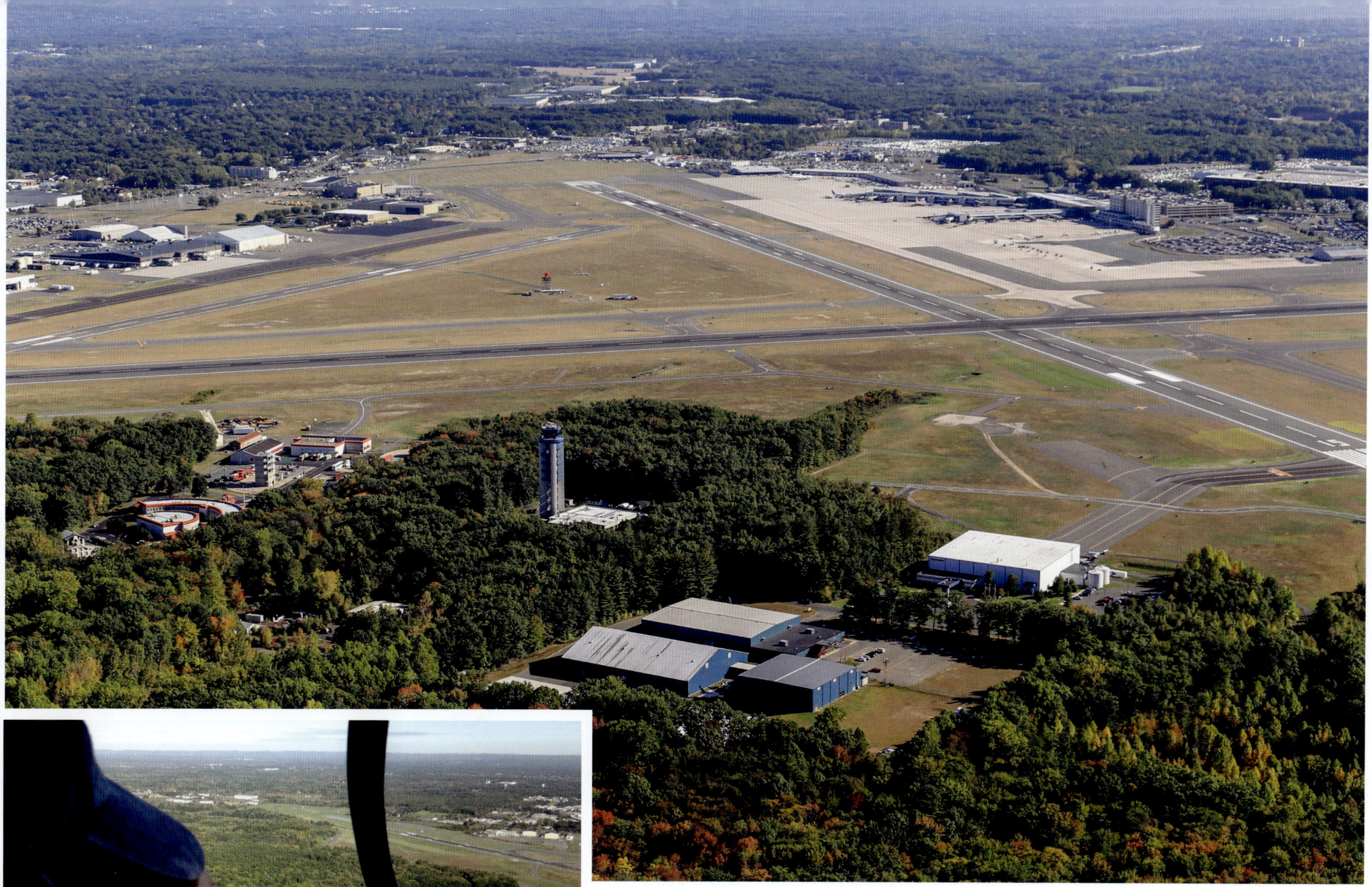

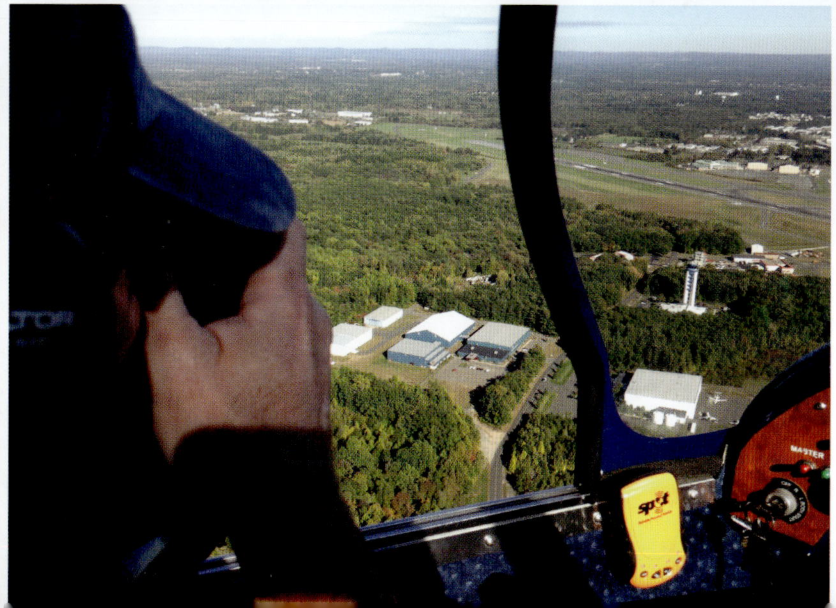

(left) Tom snaps a shot of the flight tower and the New England Air Museum hangars at Bradley International Airport near Windsor Locks.

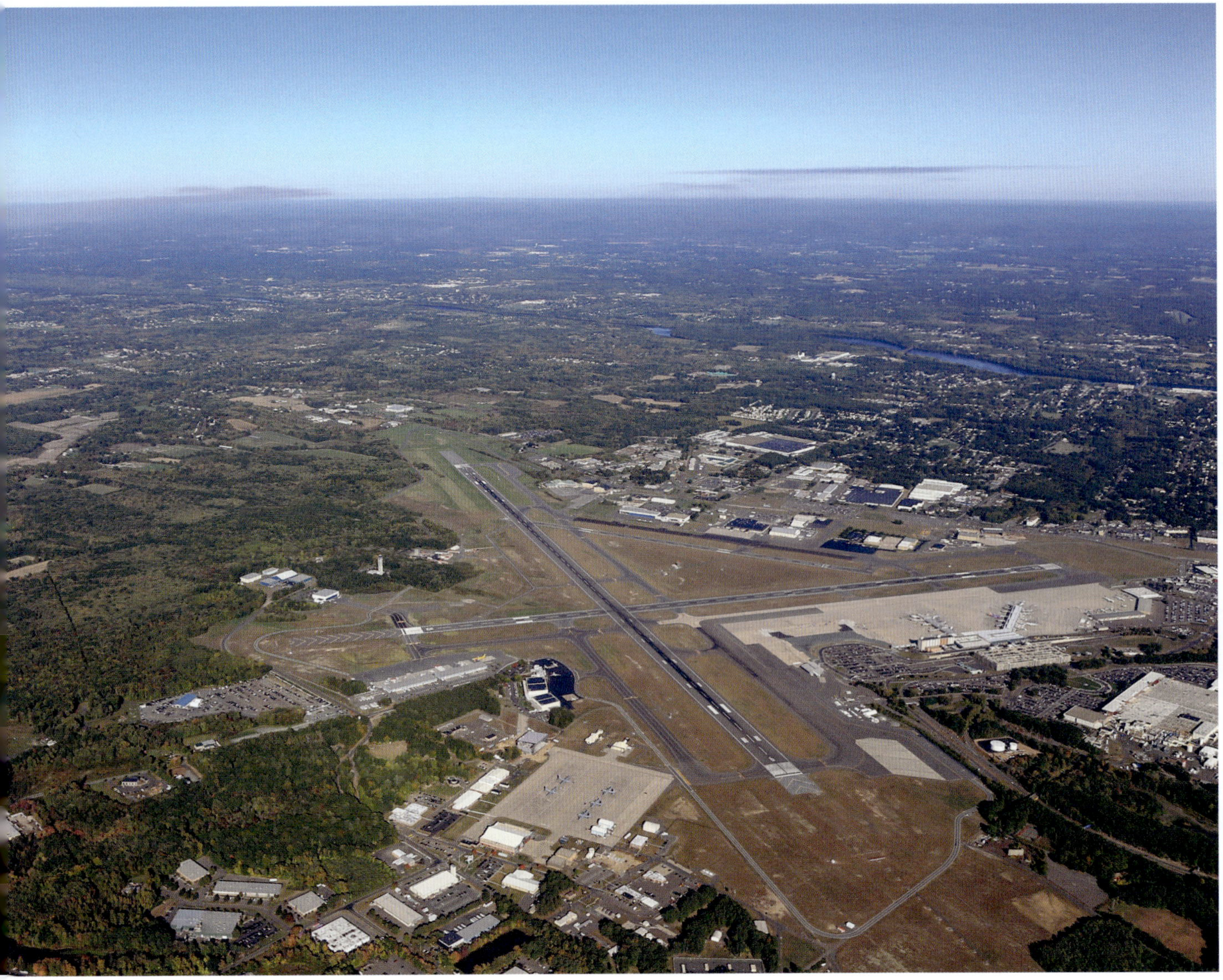

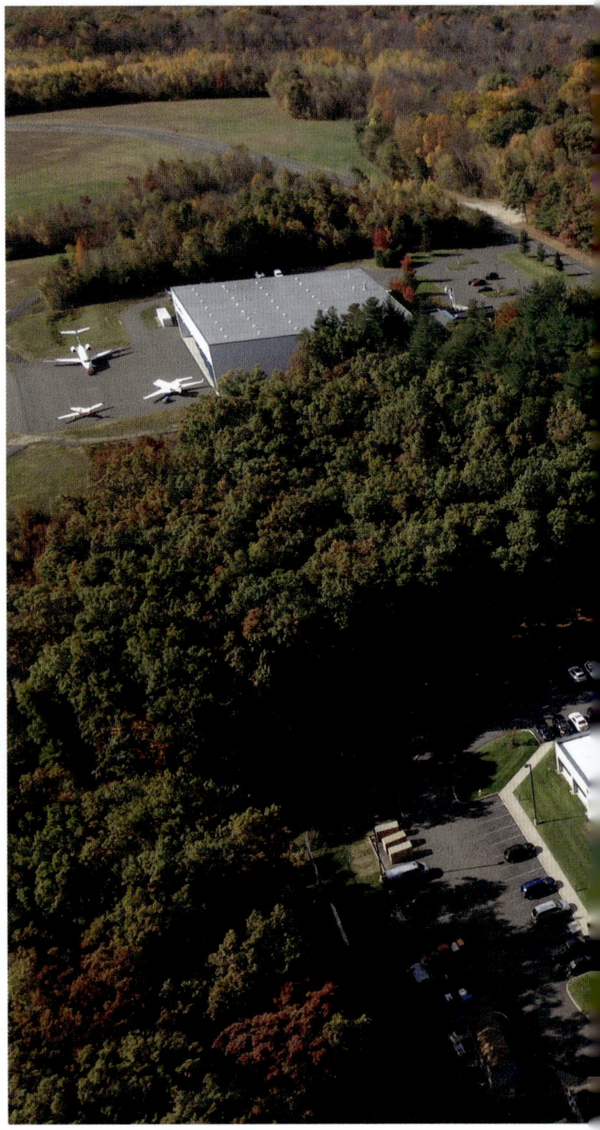

In order to capture the airport's proximity to the river, we had to climb to 4,000 feet. In the foreground is the Connecticut Air National Guard base with C-130 transports on the apron. During the Second World War, the base also included a POW camp for German prisoners. Just to the north, across the end of Runway 15, are the flight tower and six hangars of the New England Air Museum. The passenger terminal is to the right of the runway marked with an II .

Located next to Bradley's flight tower the New England Air Museum preserves and celebrates Connecticut's unique aerospace heritage—from pioneering balloons and early flying machines through the jet age and beyond.

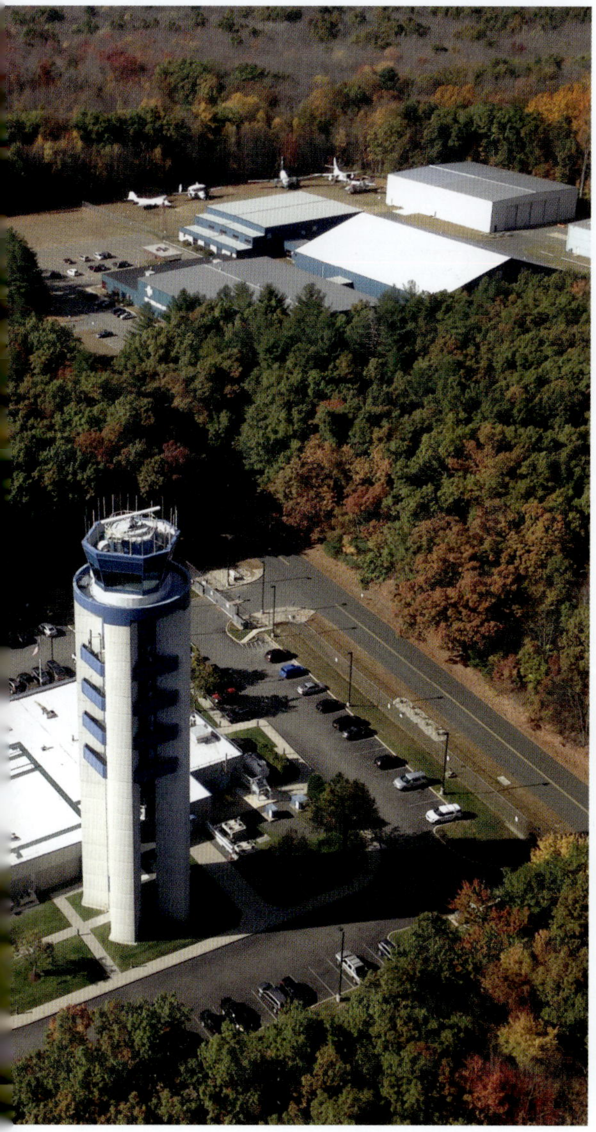

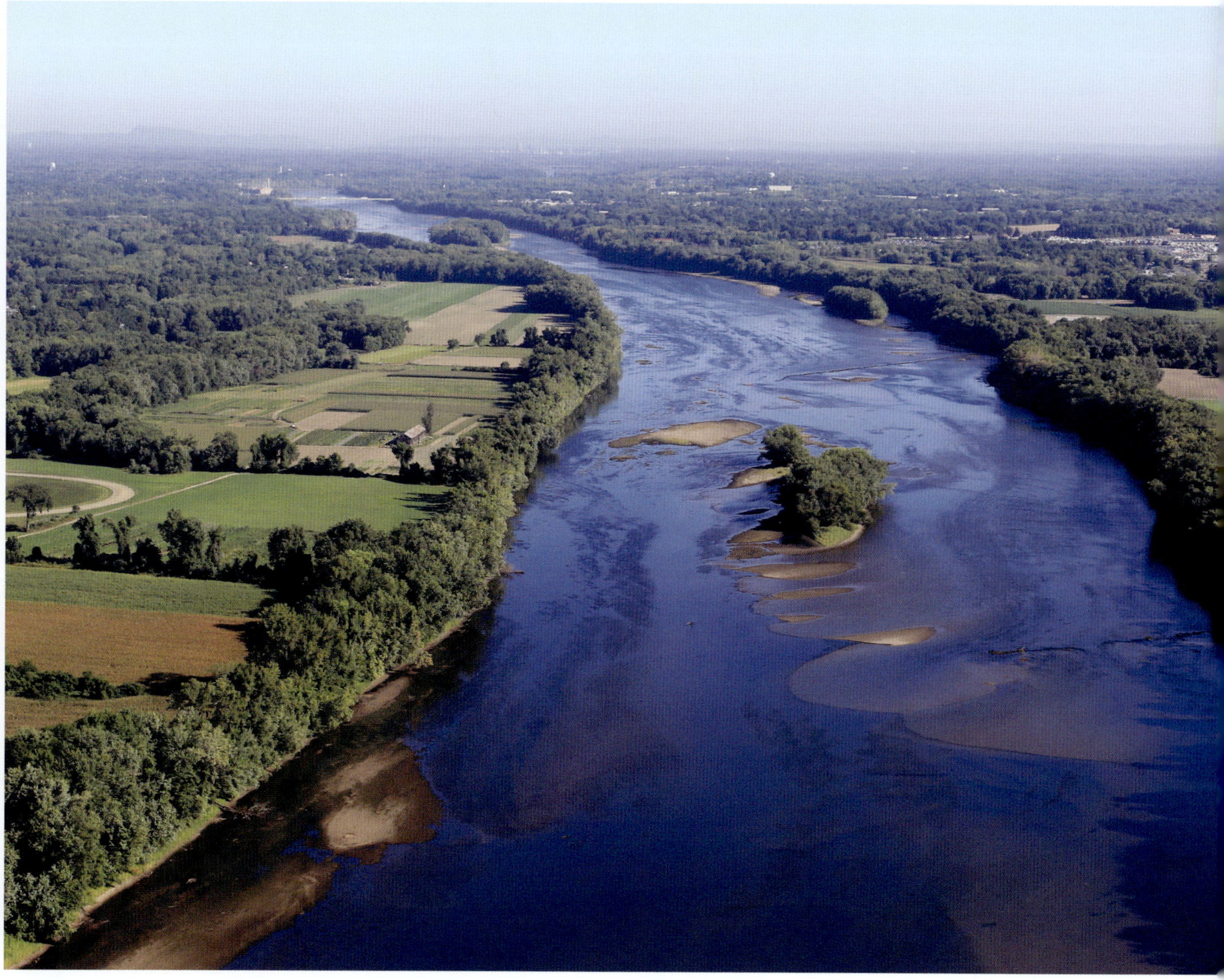

Back on the river traveling north between Windsor on the left and East Windsor on the right.

WINDSOR LOCKS & THE ENFIELD RAPIDS

Upstream of the Farmington River's junction with the Connecticut, shallows, shifting sand bars, and the Enfield Rapids provided a major obstacle to waterborne commerce traveling farther north. The only options were to unload the cargo at Warehouse Point and either have hauled it overland by oxen, or load it onto flat-bottomed scows to be laboriously poled over the rapids. In the early 1820s business interests in New Haven believed this obstacle offered an opportunity to make that city the main port of entry into the heart of New England and they began developing the 80-mile-long Farmington Canal. It would run all the way from New Haven on Long Island Sound and join the Connecticut River at North Hampton, Massachusetts, twenty miles above Hartford.

In response, shipping interests in Hartford created the five-and-a-quarter-mile-long Windsor Locks Canal. Construction began in 1827. The canal would enable vessels up to ninety feet long to climb the thirty-two-foot vertical rise and bypass the rapids. After it was completed in 1829 several mills and factories sprang up along the canal. The Farmington Canal opened in 1828 but, plagued by fluctuating water levels and competition with the railroads, it was never successful. The Windsor Locks Canal did much better but it, too, eventually became obsolete as a means of transportation. A big difference between the two canals and their longevity however, is that while the Farmington was a "ditch" canal with earthen banks, the Windsor Locks system was lined with brick in anticipation of steam-powered vessels. After it was no longer needed for commercial transportation the canal provided waterpower to twenty small factories along its length, including the Dexter paper mill built in 1876. Founded in 1767, Dexter was the oldest company listed on the New York Stock exchange before it was sold to the Ahlstrom Corporation in 2000. The locks remained in operation into the 1970s when the diagonal wood and stone dam that forced the river to flow into the canal failed. Although the locks have been inoperable since then, the waterway still supplies the Ahlstrom Corporation, which is still making paper products in the old Dexter plant. A hiking trail along the old towpath provides recreation and visual access to this once important industrial waterway.

(right) Approaching Turks Island with the Route 140 bridge and Windsor Locks in the distance. Note the diagonal structure in the foreground. These were built to channel the current to the deeper side of the river to help prevent shoaling.

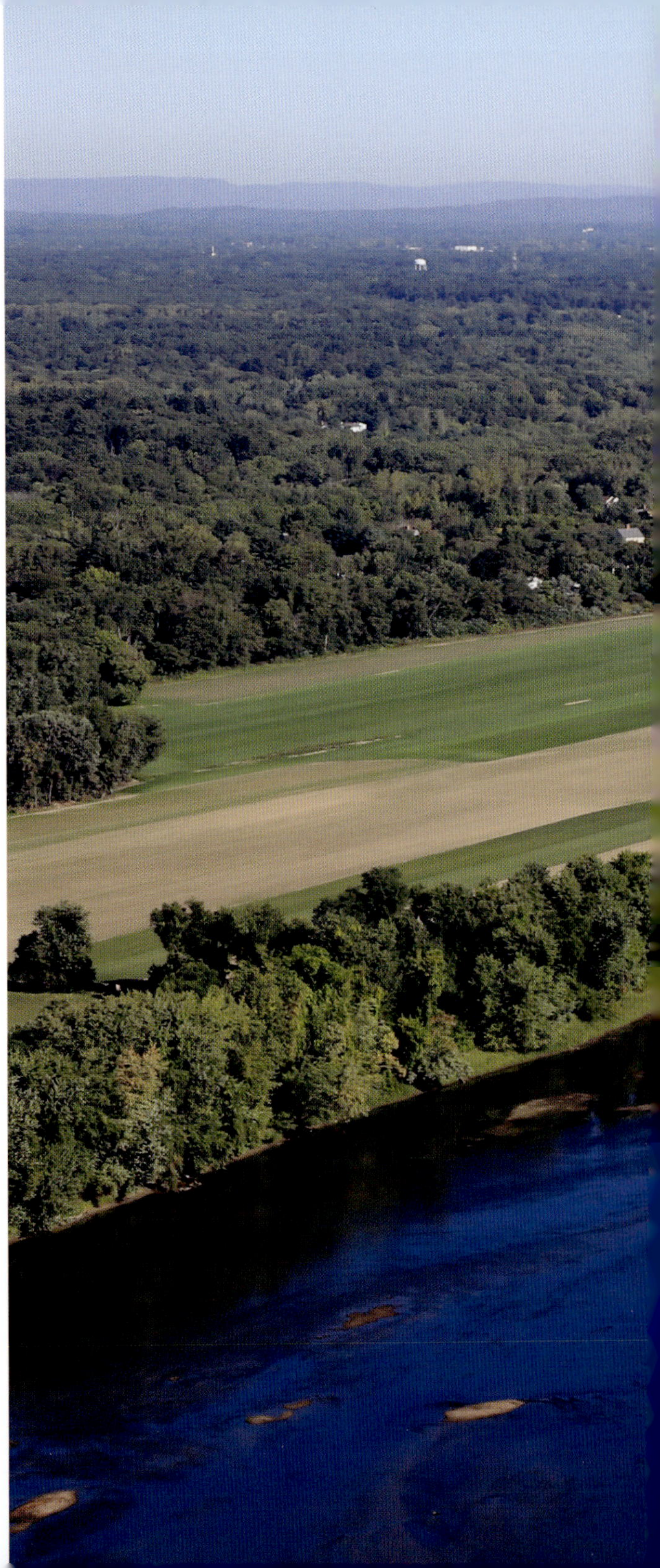

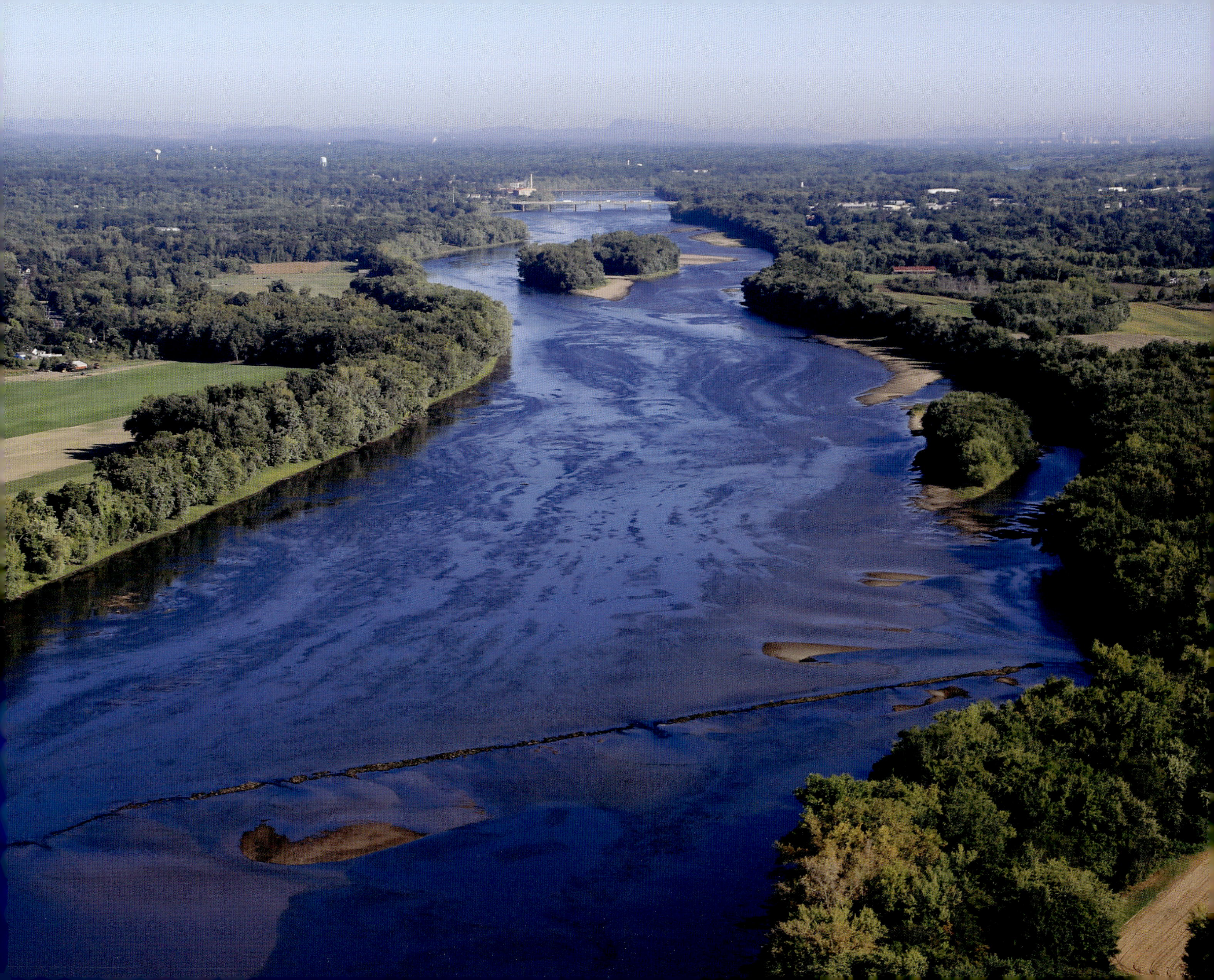

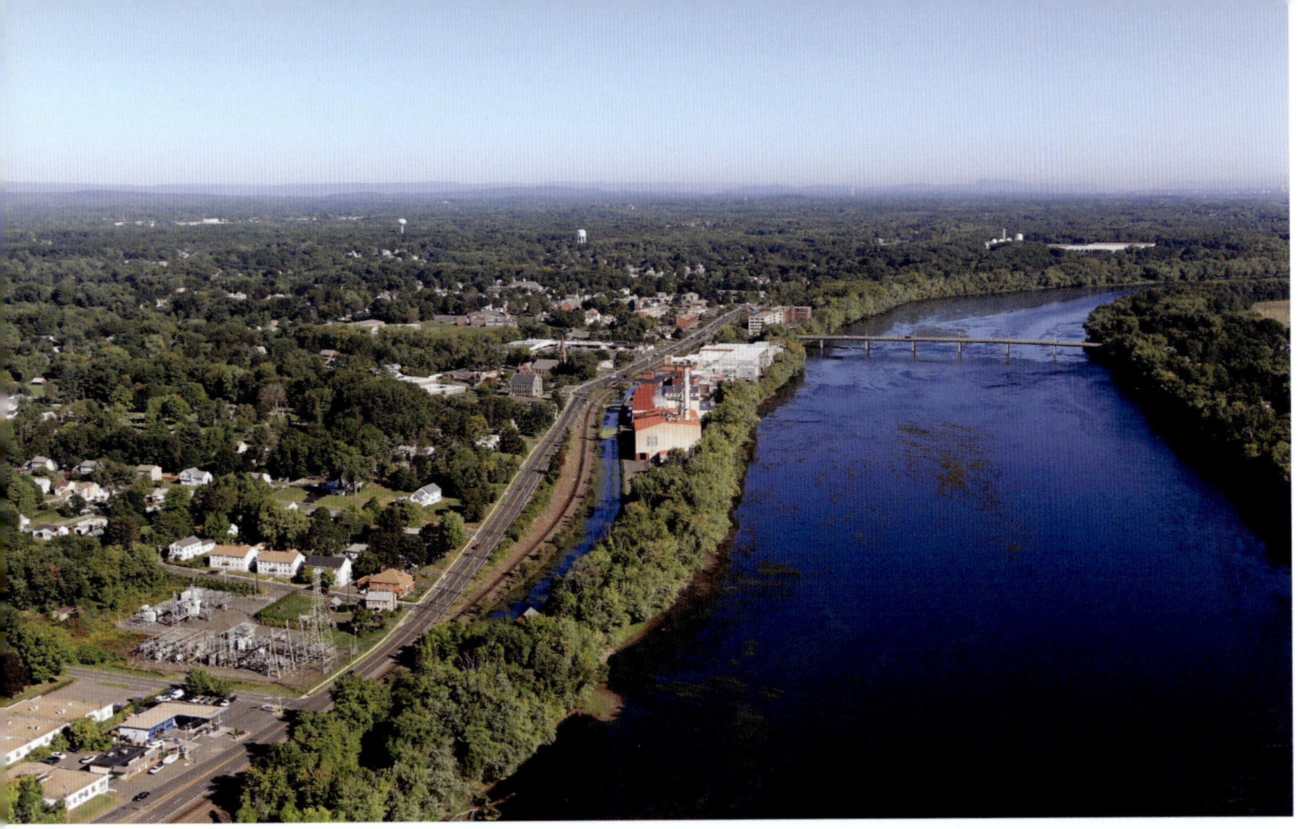

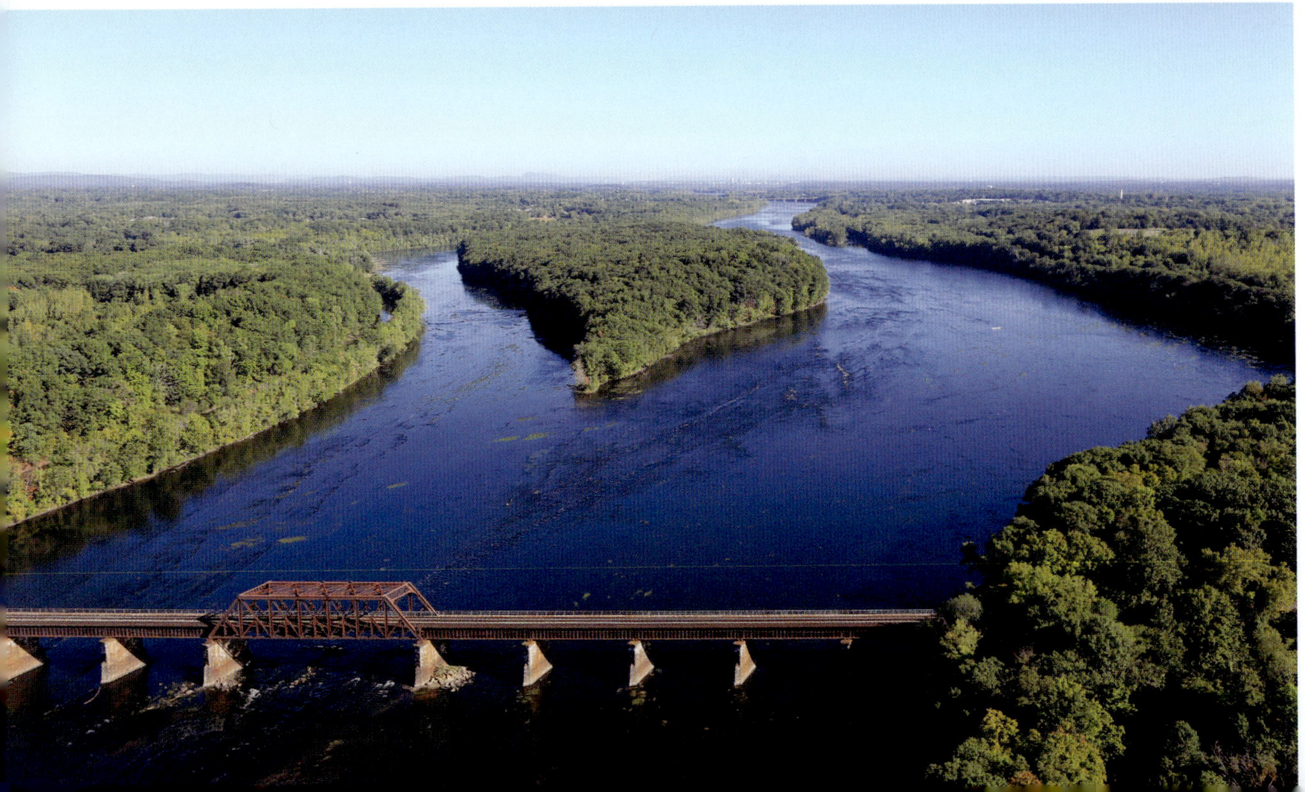

(top left) Looking north toward the bridge that carries CT Route 140 across the river the canal and the old Dexter paper mill are on the left.

(bottom left) King Island divides the river just beyond the railway bridge at Warehouse Point where vessels were unloaded and cargo transported around the Enfield Rapids before the canal was built.

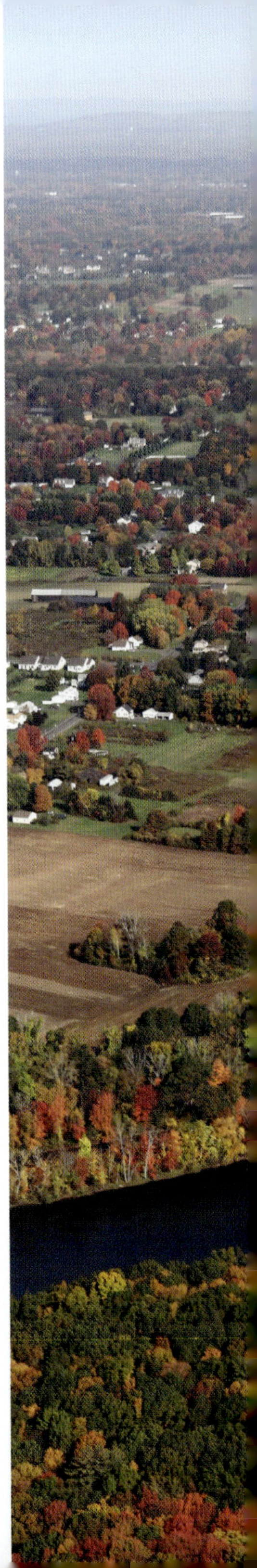

(right) Autumn colors punctuate the river and canal looking north over King Island. Springfield, Massachusetts, can just be seen in the distance.

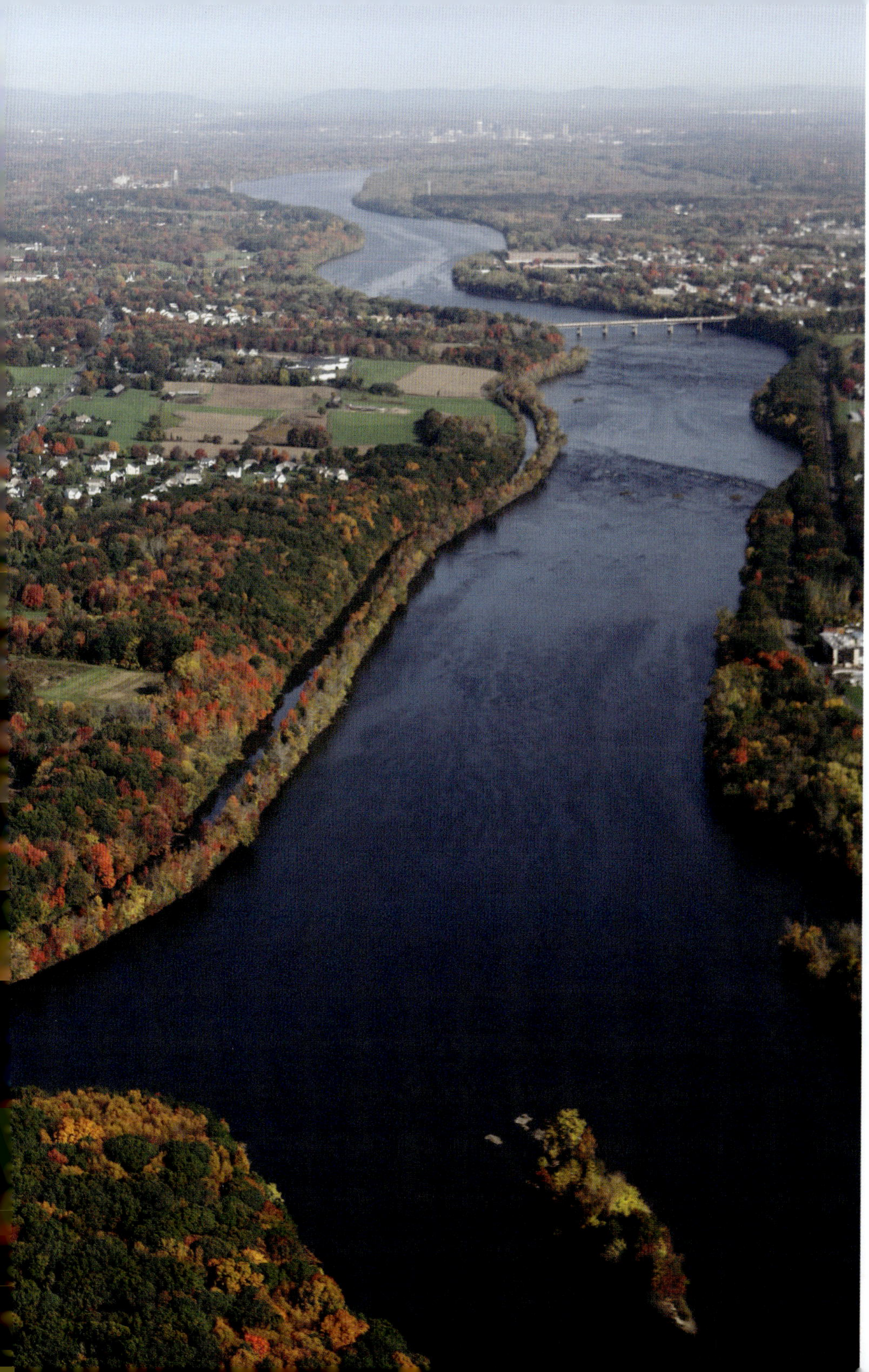

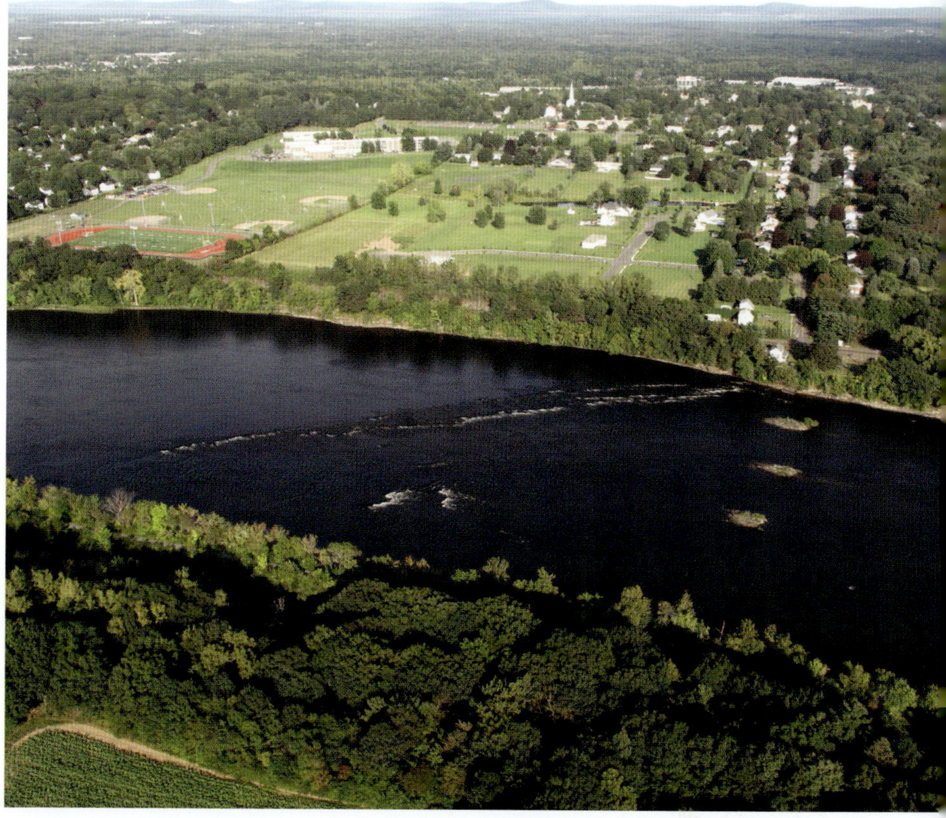

(above) Looking east across the river toward the sprawling campus of Enfield High School, one can see the crumbled piers that are all that is left of the covered wooden bridge that once connected Suffield on the western side to Enfield on the east. Built in the 1820s, it was partially swept away by a flood in 1900. A worker who was on the bridge at the time actually rode downstream on the wreckage and was rescued by a rope lowered from Warehouse Point Bridge. Ironically, over a century later, the roads that once led to the crossing are still called Bridge Street on the western side and Bridge Lane on the other.

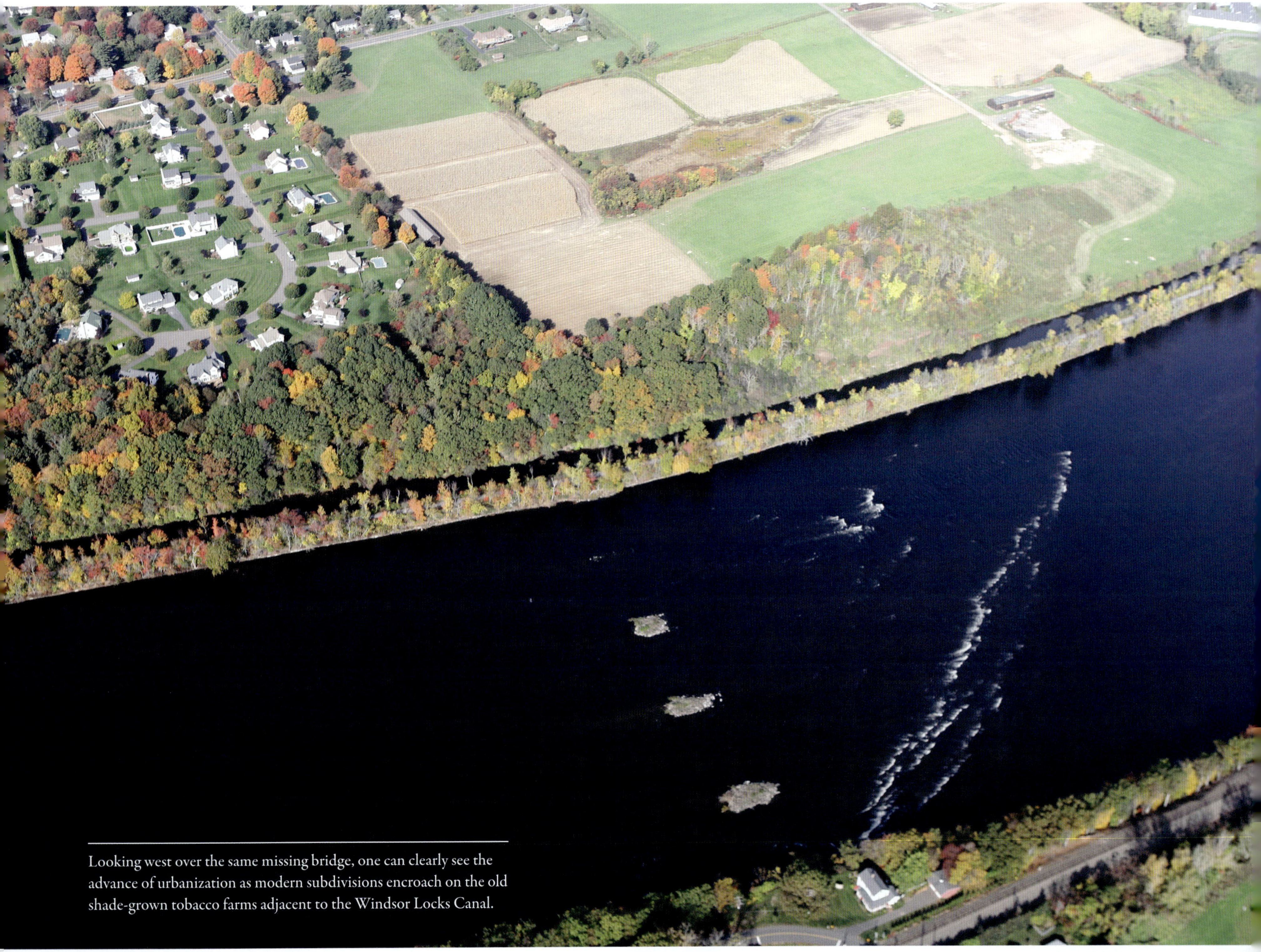

Looking west over the same missing bridge, one can clearly see the advance of urbanization as modern subdivisions encroach on the old shade-grown tobacco farms adjacent to the Windsor Locks Canal.

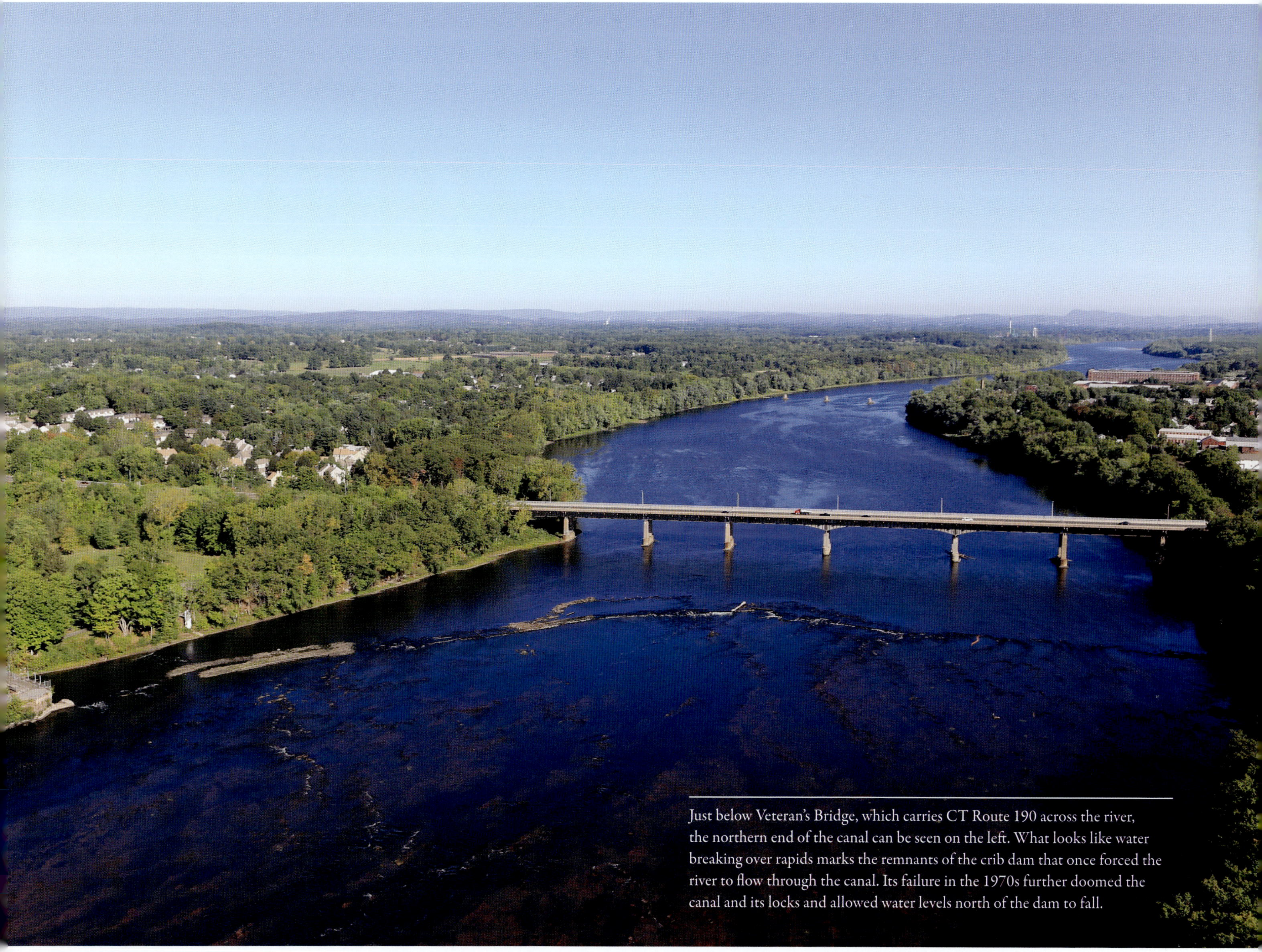

Just below Veteran's Bridge, which carries CT Route 190 across the river, the northern end of the canal can be seen on the left. What looks like water breaking over rapids marks the remnants of the crib dam that once forced the river to flow through the canal. Its failure in the 1970s further doomed the canal and its locks and allowed water levels north of the dam to fall.

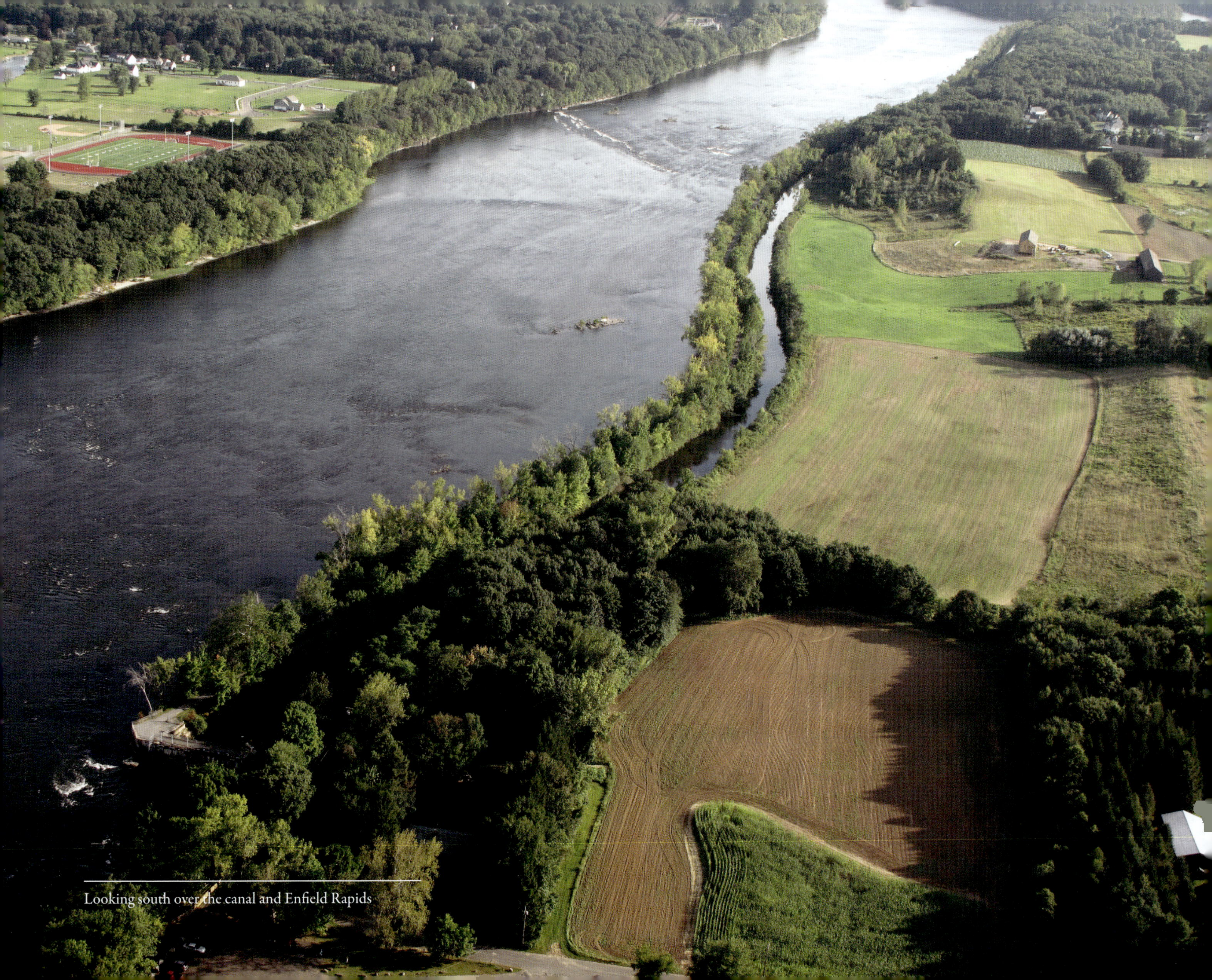

Looking south over the canal and Enfield Rapids

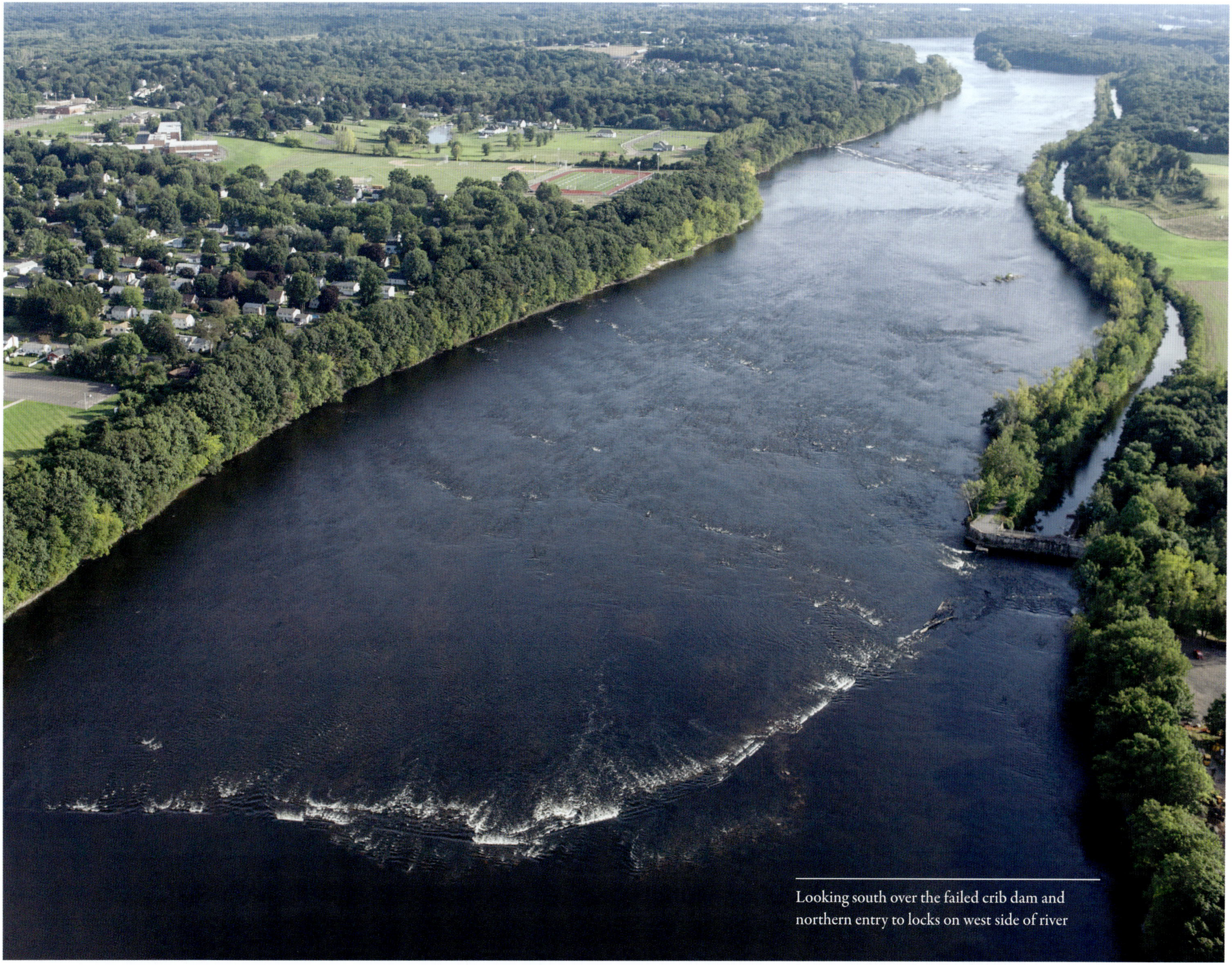

Looking south over the failed crib dam and northern entry to locks on west side of river

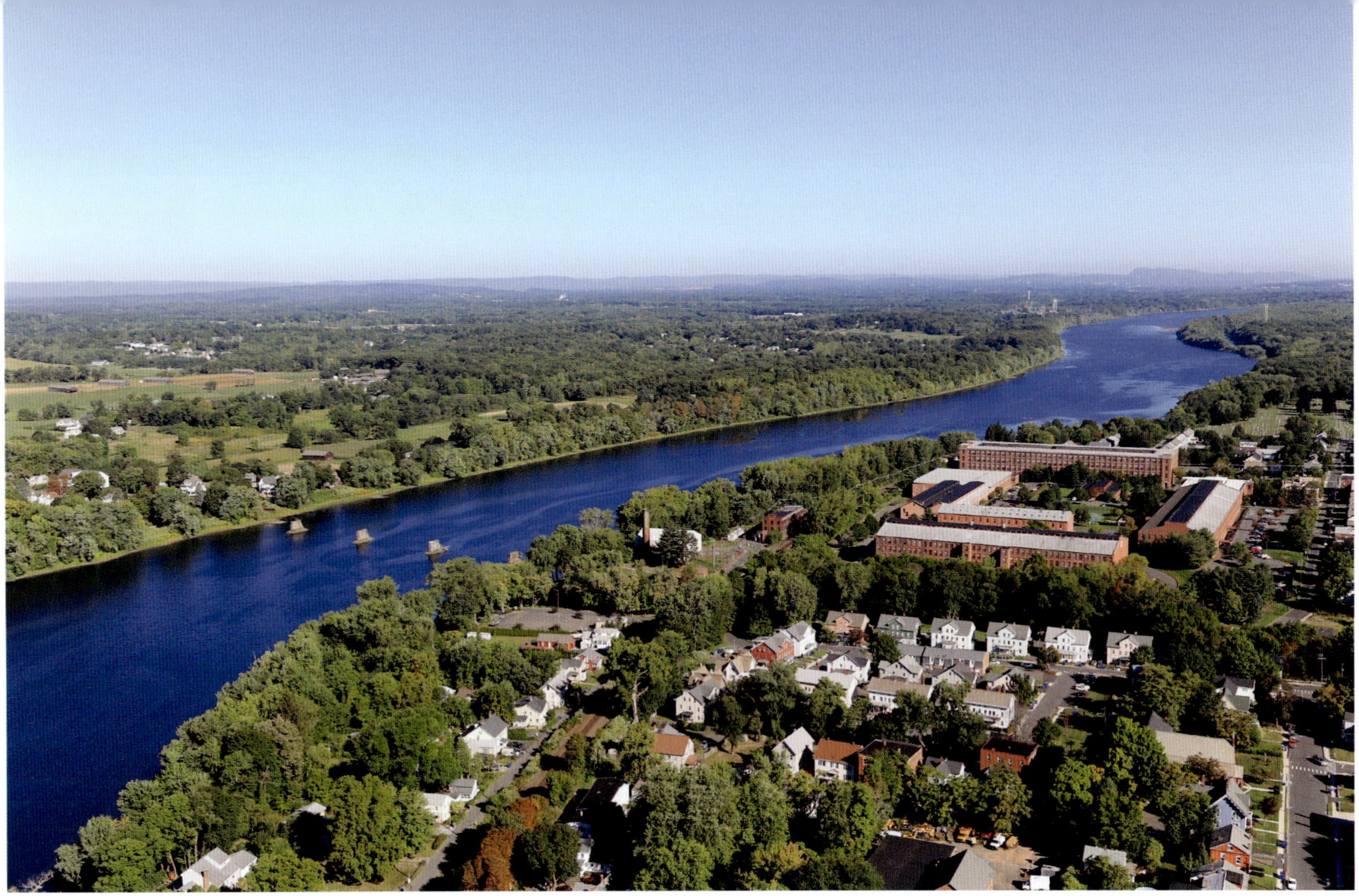

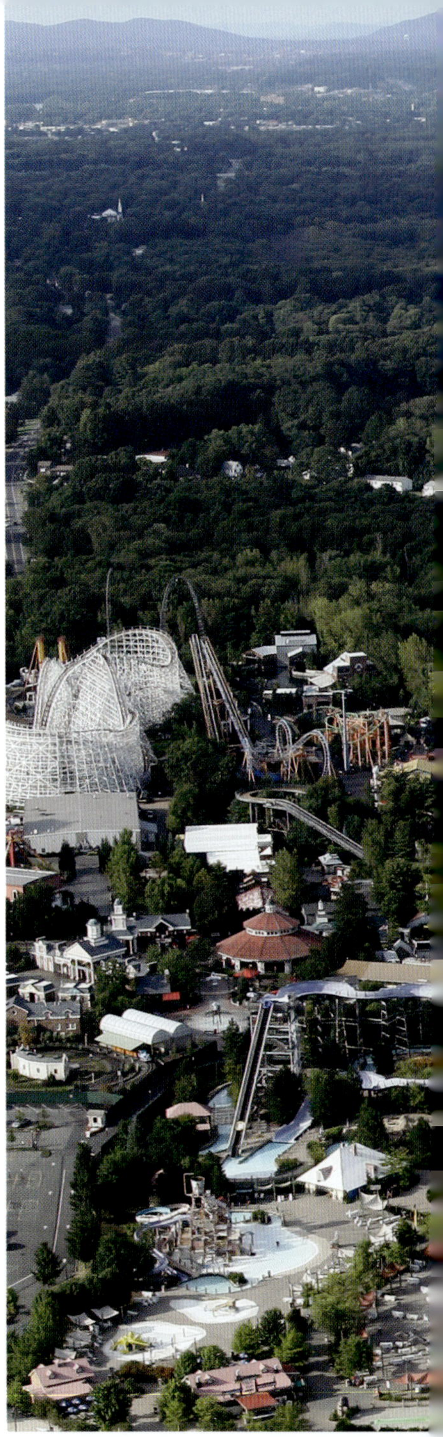

(above) Just above Veterans Bridge are the pilings of the old Suffield–Thompsonville iron truss bridge that was built here in 1889. It was closed after Veterans Bridge opened in 1966. The five iron spans of the old bridge were removed but the pilings remain. The large red brick industrial buildings were part of the massive Bigelow-Sanford carpet manufacturing complex whose legacy reaches back to 1846. By 1948 the carpet mills employed more than 9,000 workers. When operations finally ended in 1971, it was a tremendous blow to Enfield, which had become a company town. The buildings that remain now support mixed income apartments.

(right) The Six Flags New England amusement park lies just over the Massachusetts border with Springfield five miles to the north. The park opened in 1840 as a family picnic area called Gallops Grove. It was owned by the Springfield Street Railway Company, which provided a trolley service to the park. By the early 1900s it featured a carousel along with a few other rides. Its name was changed to Riverside Grove and then Riverside Park. In 1910 the park got its first rollercoaster but closed during the Great Depression. It reopened in 1940 and Riverside Park Speedway was added in 1948. The park was sold in 1999 and became Six Flags New England. There is no longer a raceway at the park.

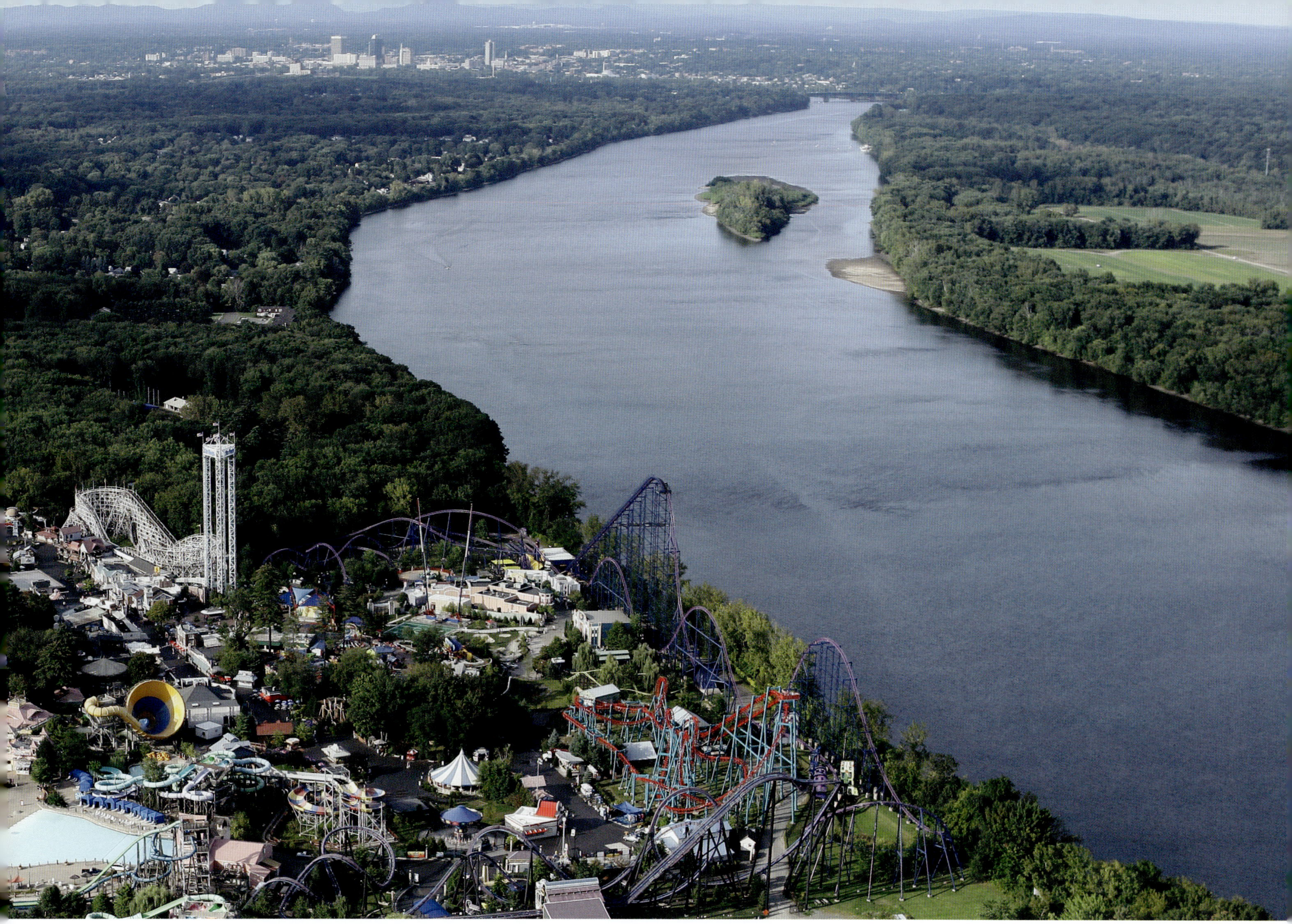

SPRINGFIELD, MA

As we cross into Massachusetts, we reach Springfield, this state's largest city on the Connecticut River. Once known for its industries and entrepreneurs, it has produced cars, including license-built Rolls Royces, Indian Motorcycles, train cars, racing aircraft, and myriad other products. Today it boasts a campus of four world-class museums, including a sculpture garden and new museum dedicated to Dr. Seuss who called Springfield home. Amongst other attractions are the Basketball Hall of Fame and one of the most attractive bridges on the river.

(clockwise, starting this page) Downtown Springfield and the Memorial Bridge.

Memorial Bridge was built in 1922 and dedicated to "those who died as pioneers, and soldiers in the Revolutionary, Civil and Foreign Wars."

Looking south with Springfield's two iconic bridges reflecting in the mirror-like river.

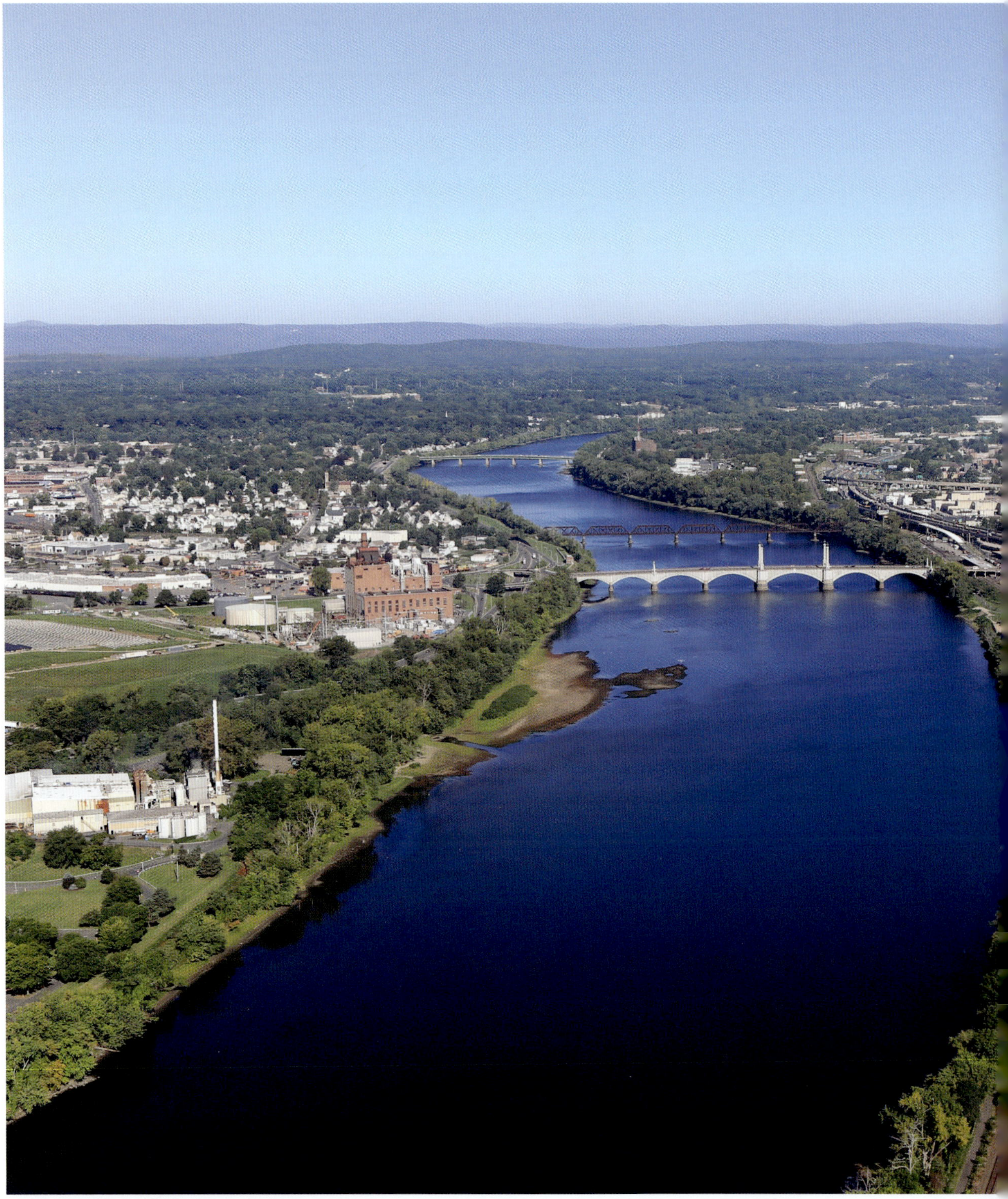

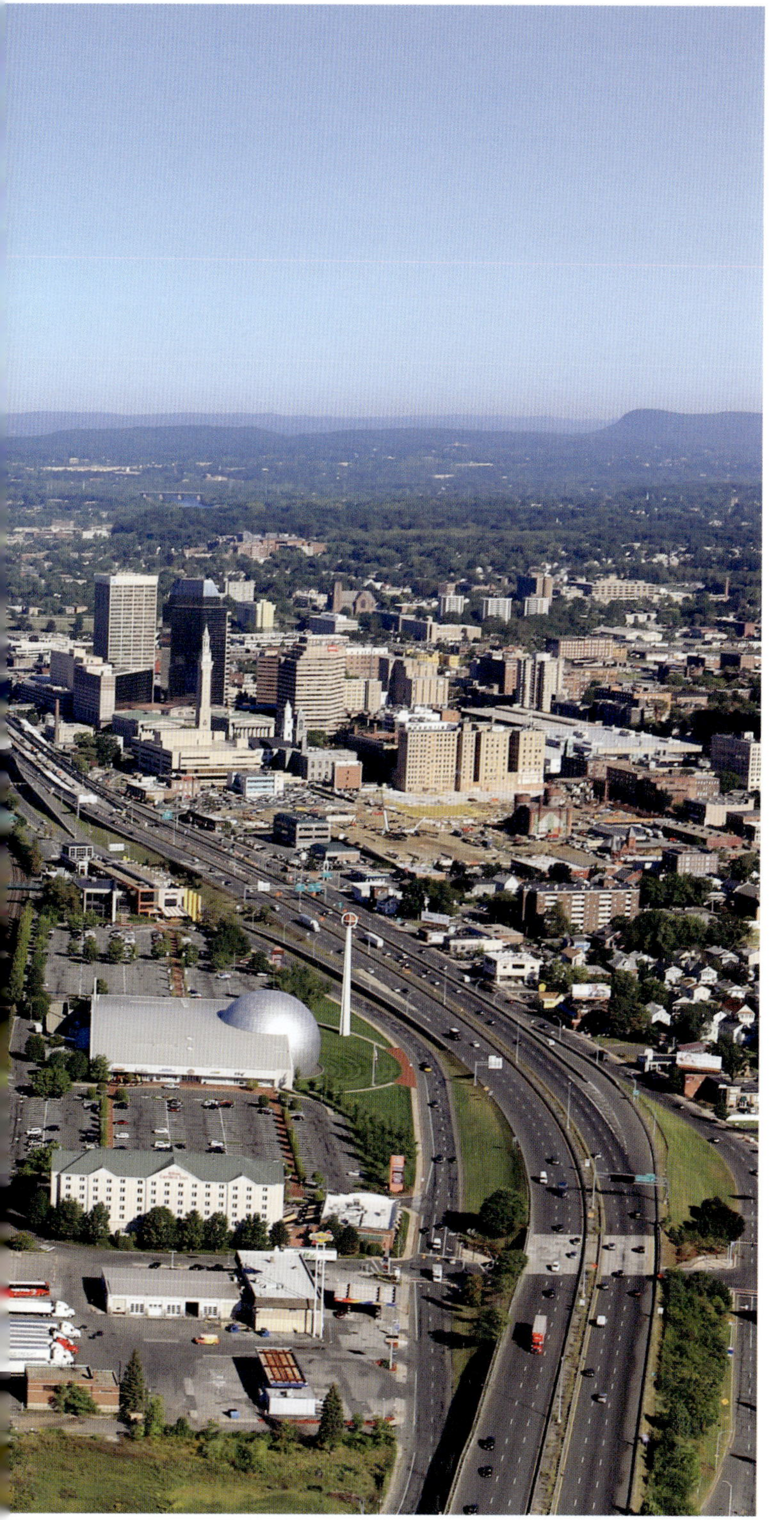

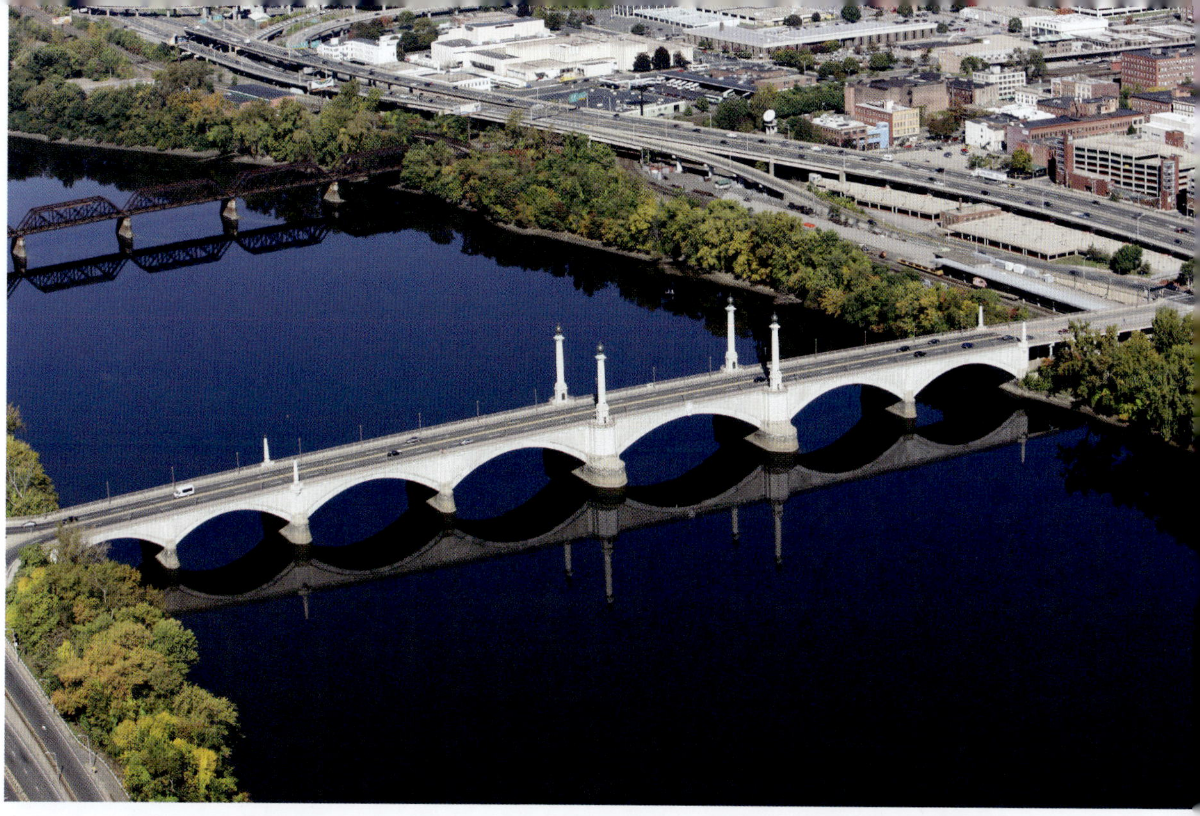

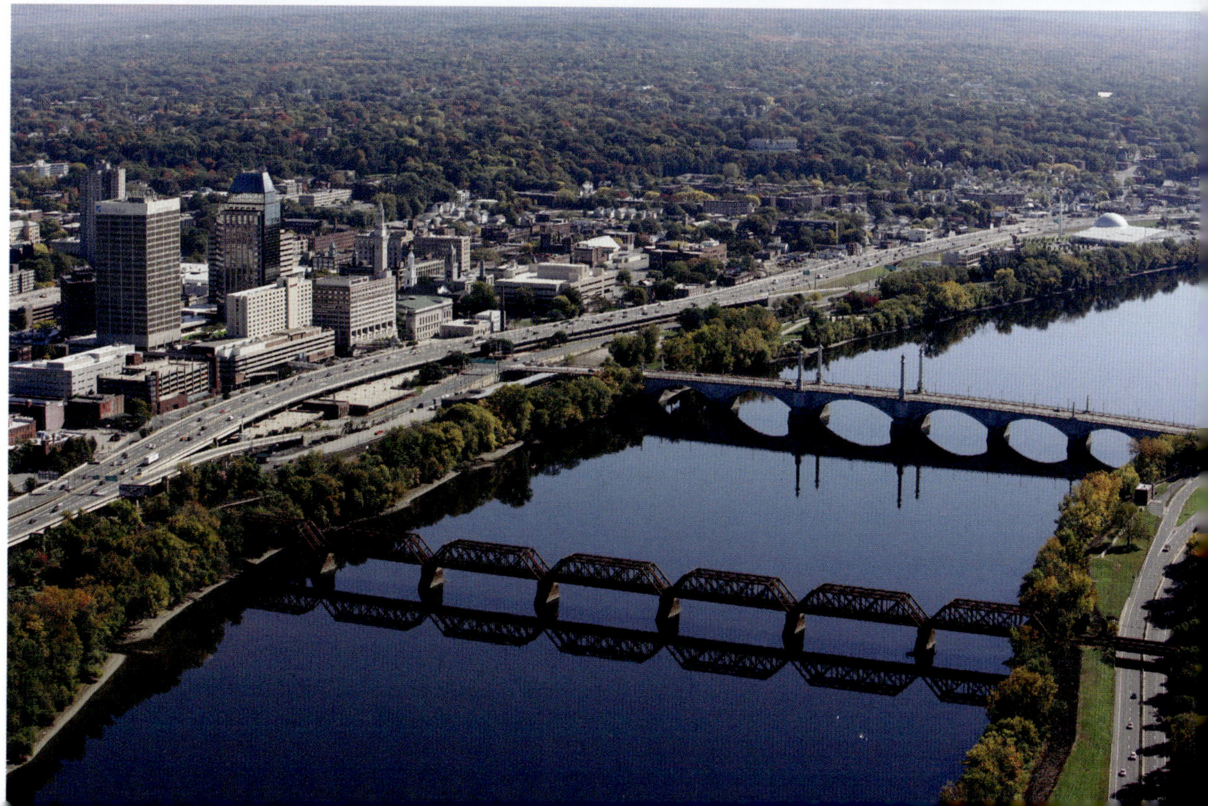

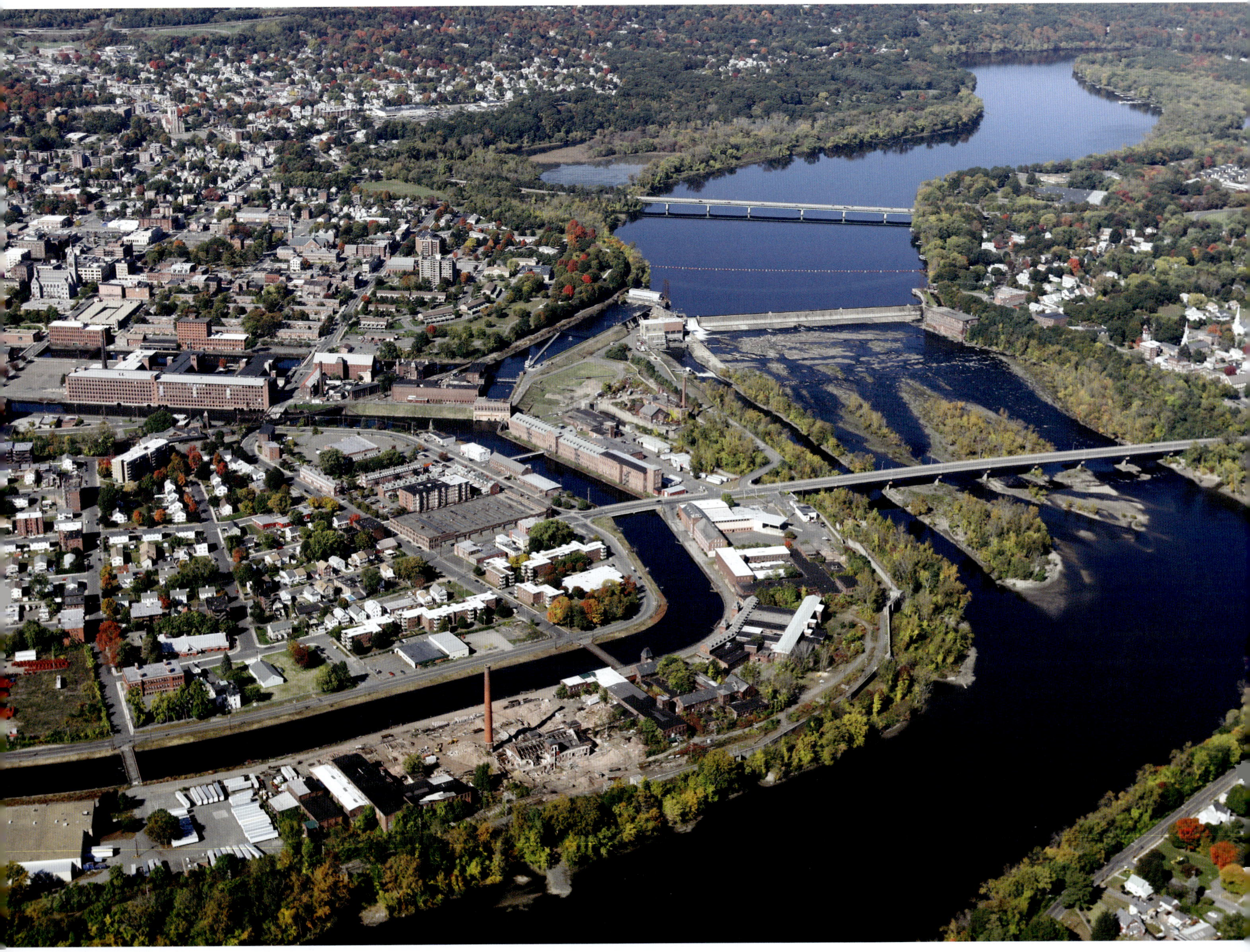

HOLYOKE, MA

Built in a bend in the river where a fifty-seven-foot drop in elevation offered maximum potential for the harnessing of waterpower, Holyoke holds the distinction of being the first planned industrial city in the nation. In 1847, investors began construction of a dam and a three-level power-canal system here, bypassing the natural course of the river to drive dozens of mills and factories. The present granite dam was built in 1900. Interconnected with roads, train tracks, and bridges, the labyrinth of water-powered industry produced textiles and paper. At its height of operations Holyoke supported twenty-five paper mills, earning it the title, "paper city of the world." Although the mills and factories are long closed, the canals are still used to generate electrical power. While some buildings have fallen into disrepair or have been demolished, most of the complex remains intact and continues to evolve through adaptive re-use. Revitalization efforts, including canal walking paths, have preserved the flavor of this icon of the industrial revolution as Holyoke seeks to find its place in the modern world.

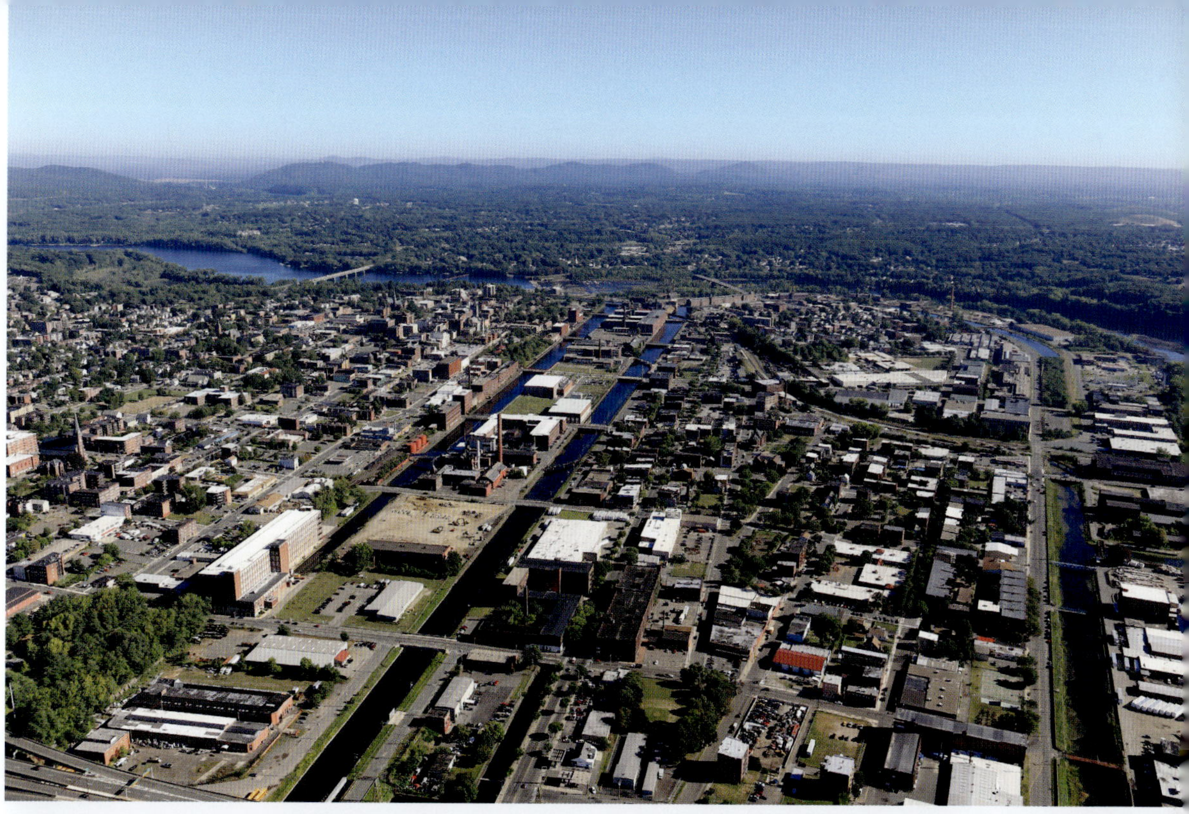

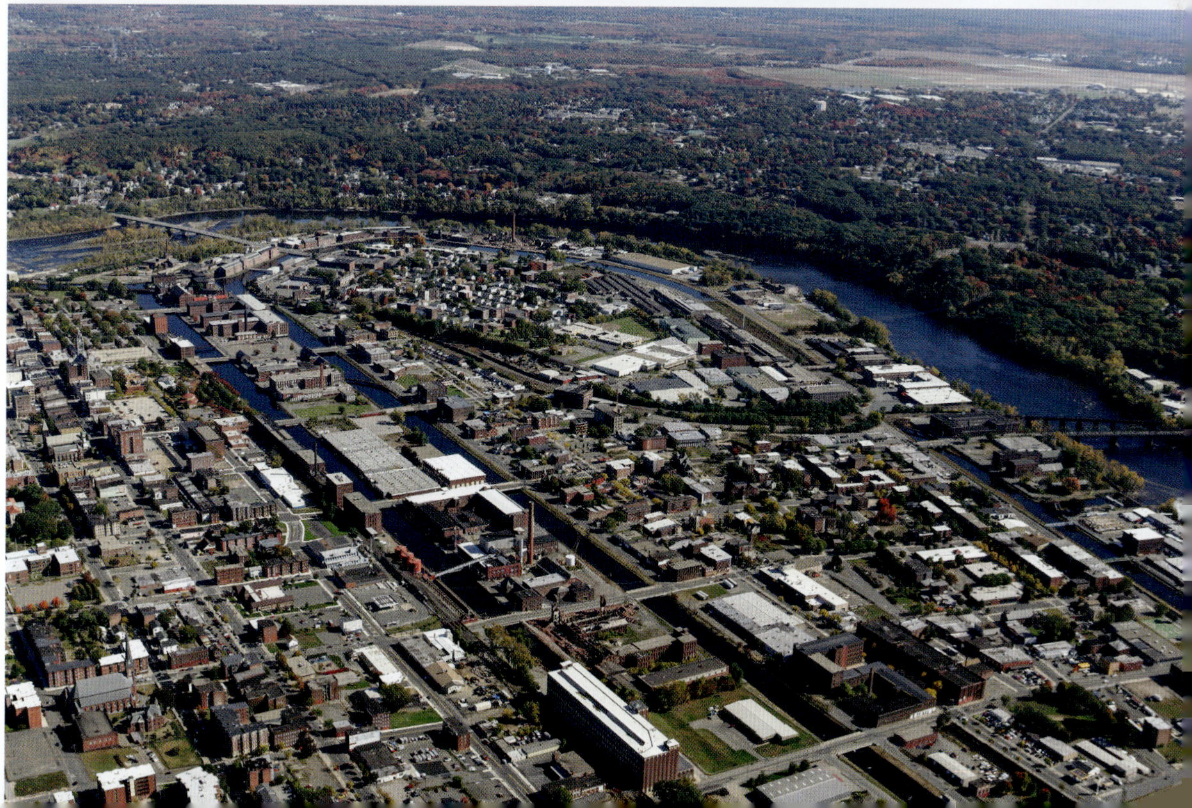

(top right) As the river sweeps down from the northwest it is diverted into three levels of canals.

(bottom right) Looking to the southeast, one can see Westover Air Force Base just beyond Holyoke's complex system of canals and the great sweep of the river's natural course.

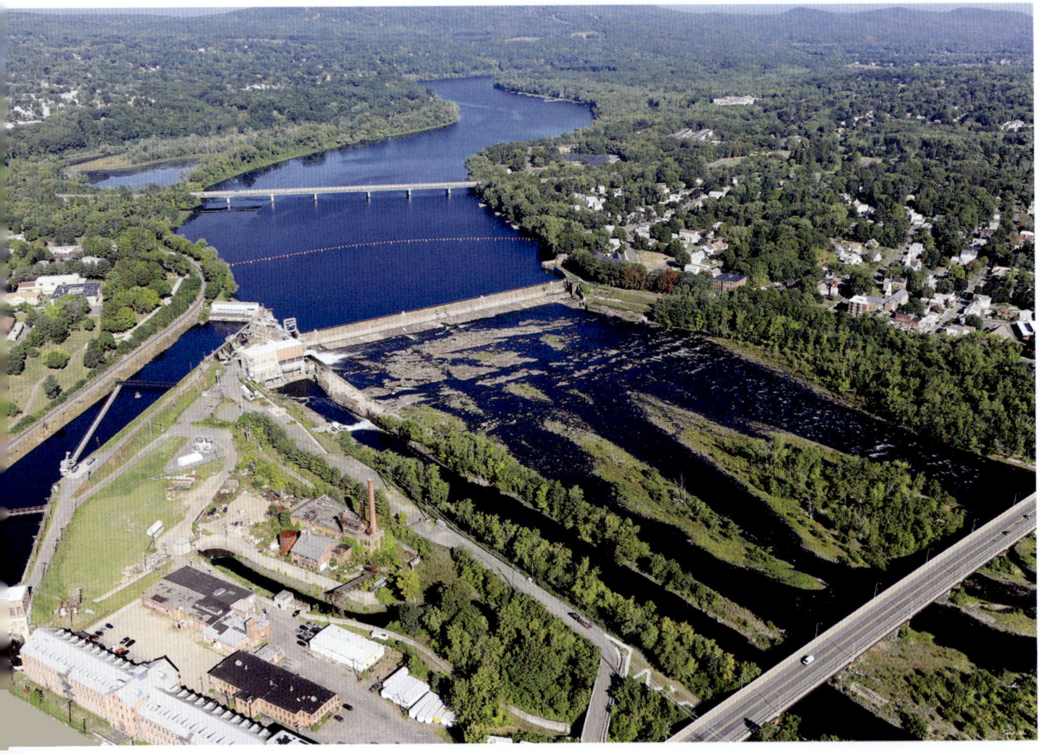

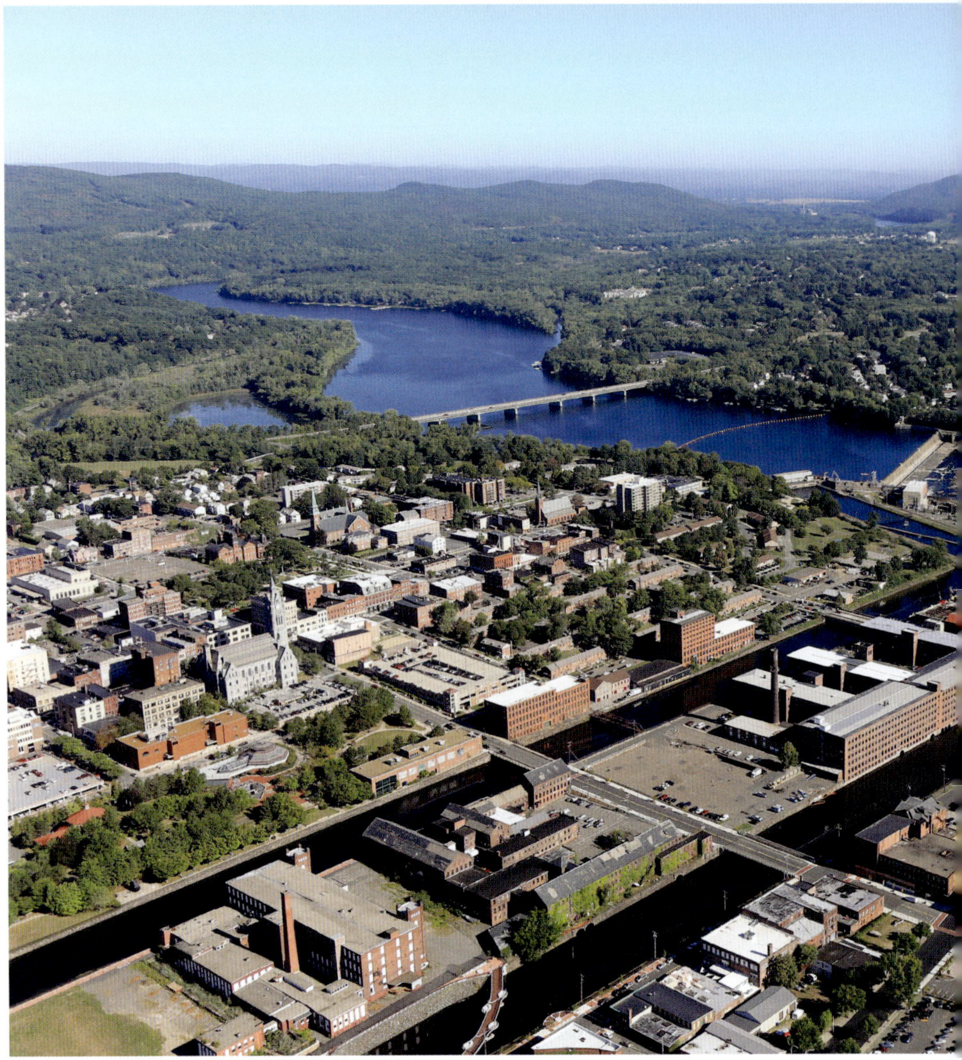

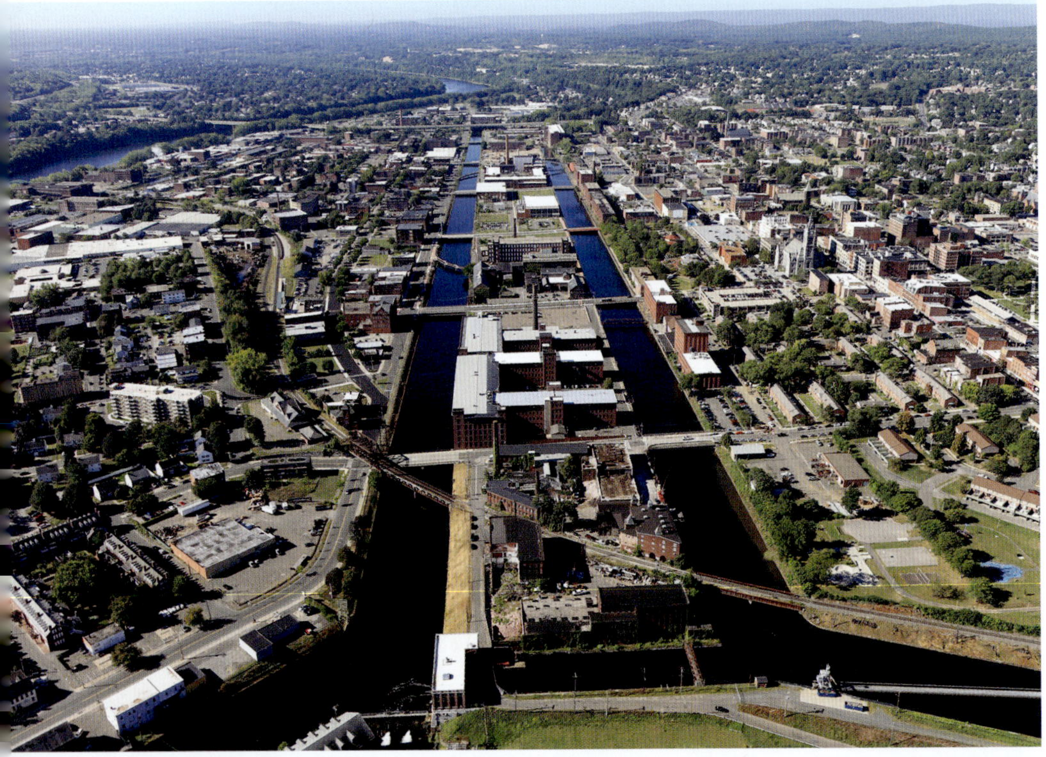

(top left) At the northern end of the complex, the Holyoke Dam diverts much of the river's natural flow into the canal system that drove dozens of mills and factories here at the height of the industrial revolution.

(top right) Looking north, the city of Holyoke, which supported the vast workforce employed here, lies just above the network of canals.

(bottom left) Looking southwest straight down two of the canals with the river to the left and the city to the right.

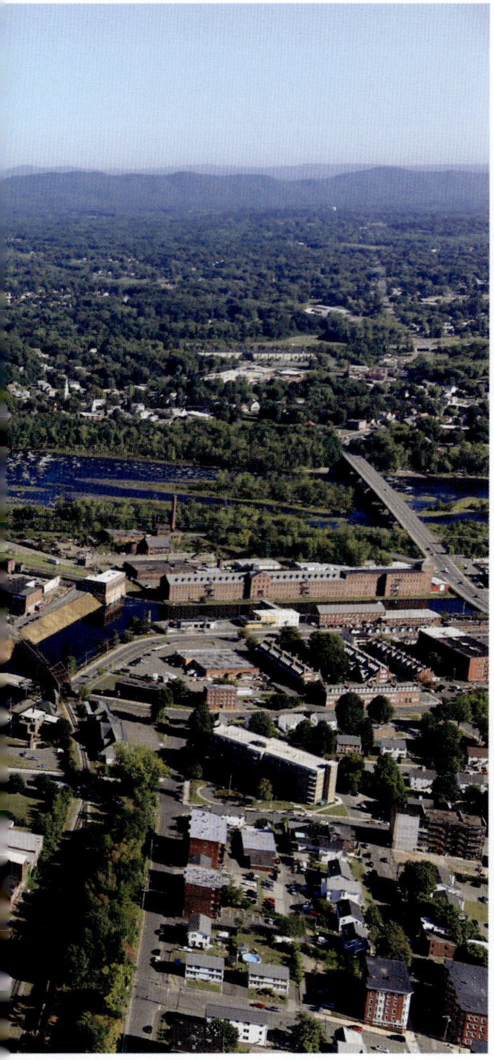

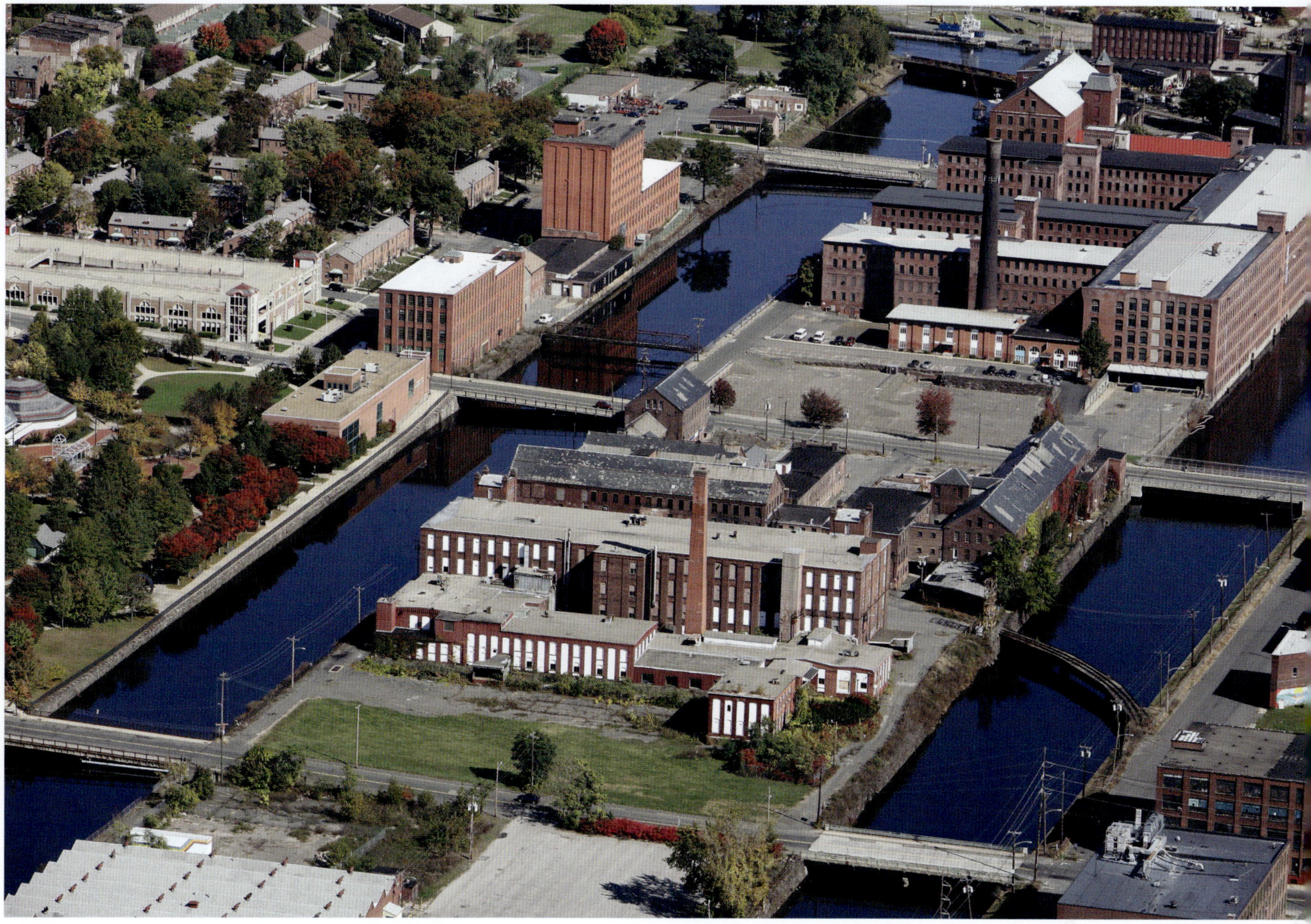

(above) Detail of mills and factories between canals

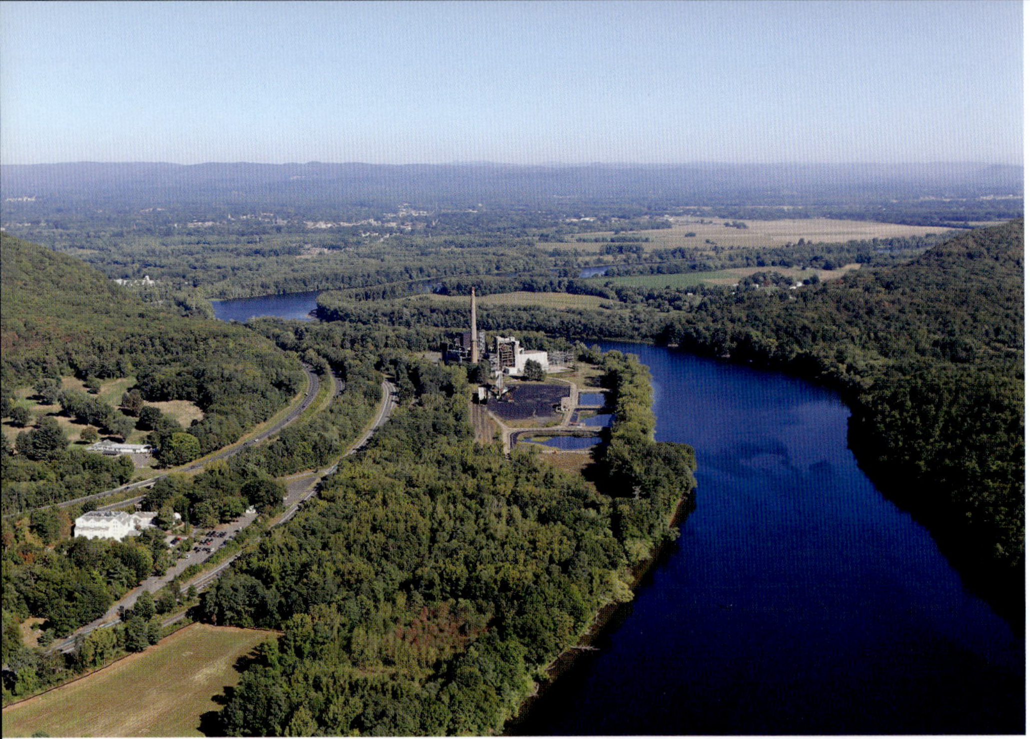

MOUNT TOM OXBOW

Of the hundreds of oxbows along the Connecticut River, the one adjacent to Northampton's Mount Tom, is no doubt the best known (right). It is one of the most painted and photographed places on the river, immortalized in Thomas Cole's 1836 work. Looking due west across the Connecticut from above Mount Holyoke on the eastern side, it is easy to see how the river was diverted sharply eastward by Mount Tom, which lay right in its course. The oxbow formed as the river tried, but failed, to find a westerly route around the imposing mountain, part of the Holyoke Range. Motorists driving here on Interstate 91 or Mount Tom Road (Route 5) would never know they are crossing the most iconic oxbow on the Connecticut River.

(left) The coal-fired Mount Tom Station generated electricity from 1960 to 2014.
(below) Another perspective from a lower altitude.

OXBOWS

Oxbows are another unique feature of the river that can only be appreciated from the air. Named from the curved U-shaped, wooden hoops that form the bottom part of the yokes used to harness oxen to plows, they have been formed as the river's current cuts serpentine paths through softer areas of sediment along its banks. When the thin neck of an oxbow erodes through, the flow creates a straighter course bypassing the old bend in the river. Eventually the currents establish new banks and the old oxbow is cut off from the river altogether. Some survive as crescent shaped ponds while others are totally filled in with silt and become dry land with the only telltale of their former existence being vegetation and trees marking the old course. The best known Oxbow is at Northampton, Massachusetts. In 1836 Thomas Cole, founder of the Hudson River School, painted a dramatic scene of the Oxbow after a thunderstorm. It is on permanent display in the Metropolitan Museum of Art in New York. In the northern stretches of the river, the number of existing, and bypassed, oxbows is truly staggering.

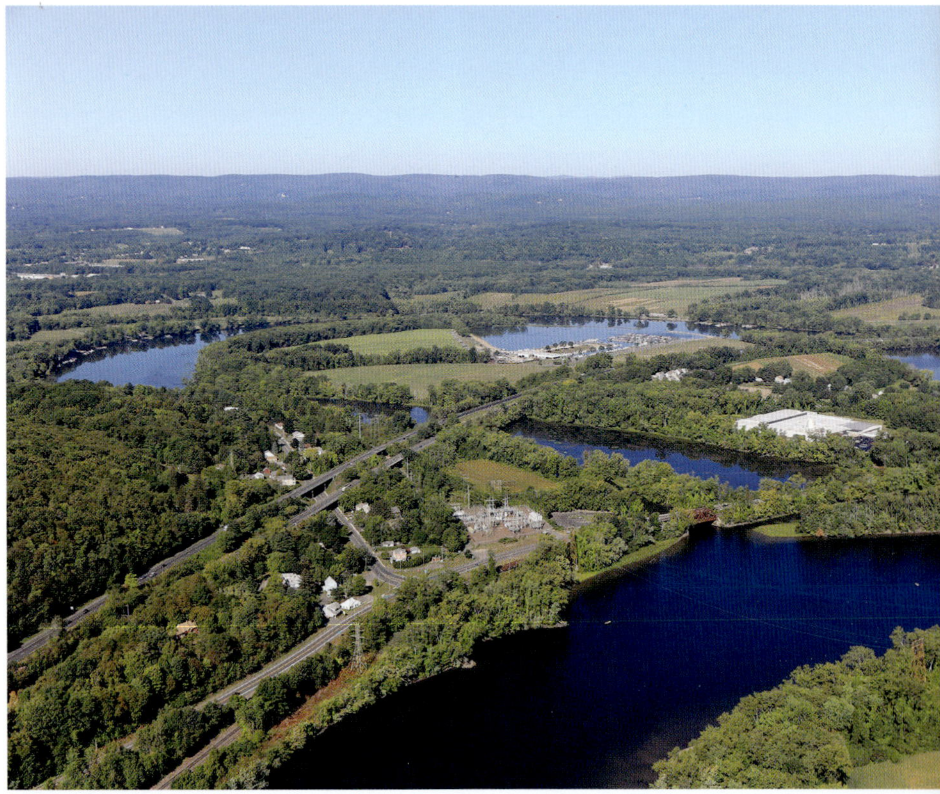

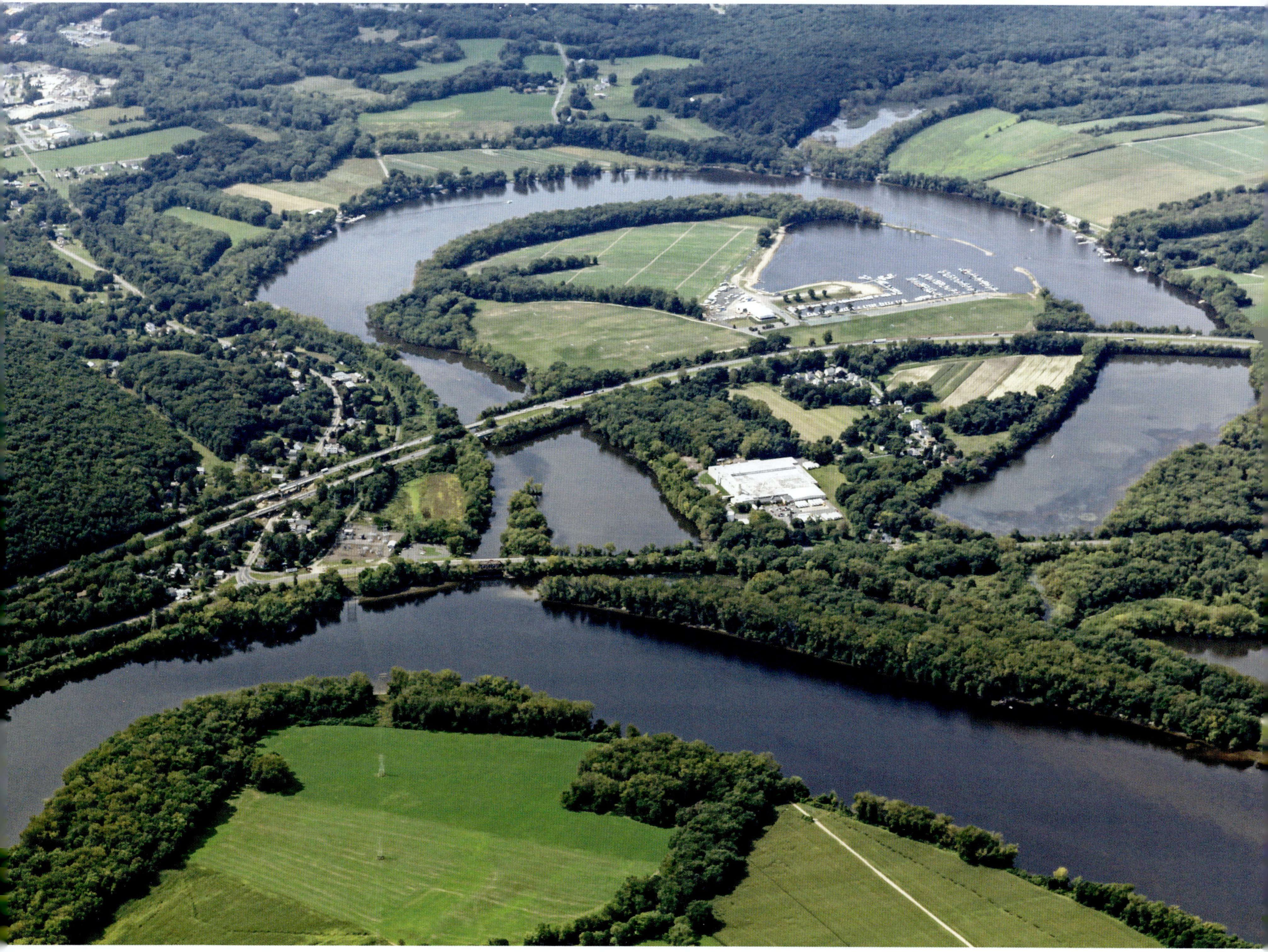

THE NEXT HUNDRED MILES

Hadley, MA to Charleston, NH

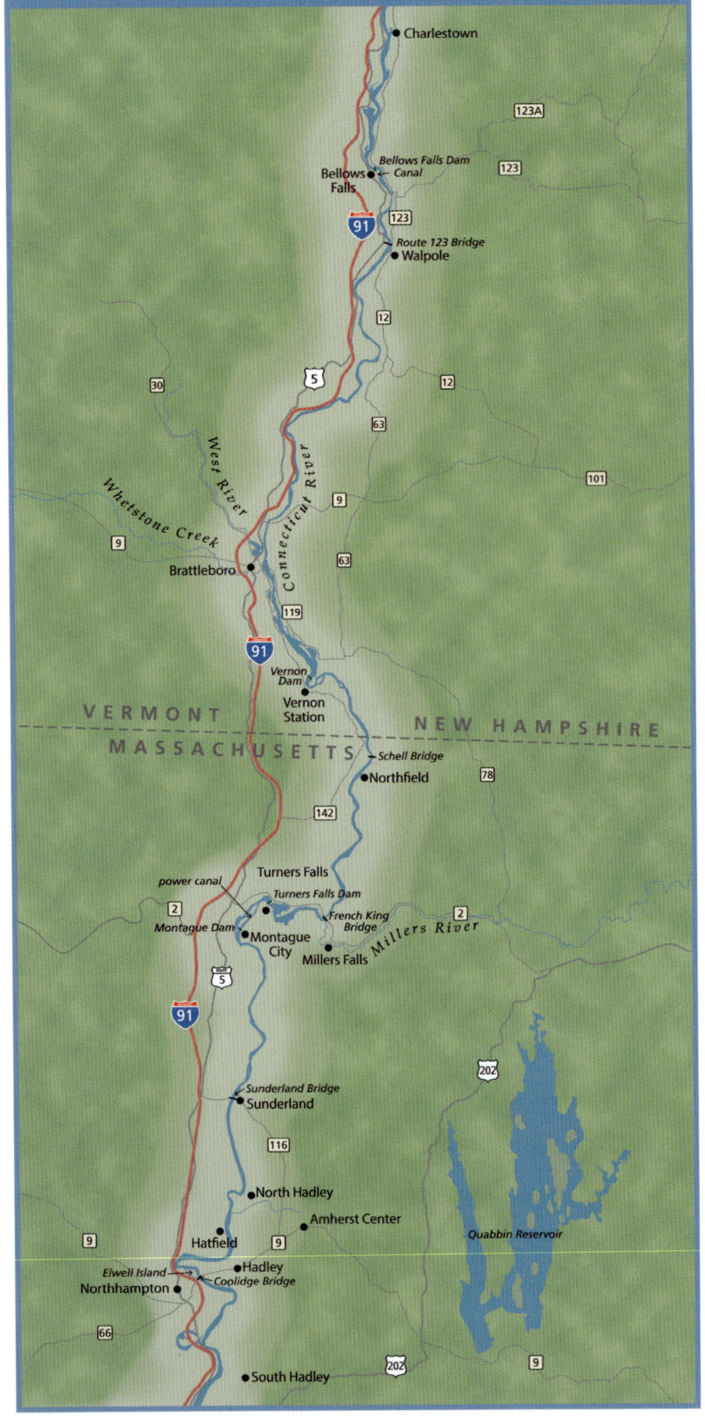

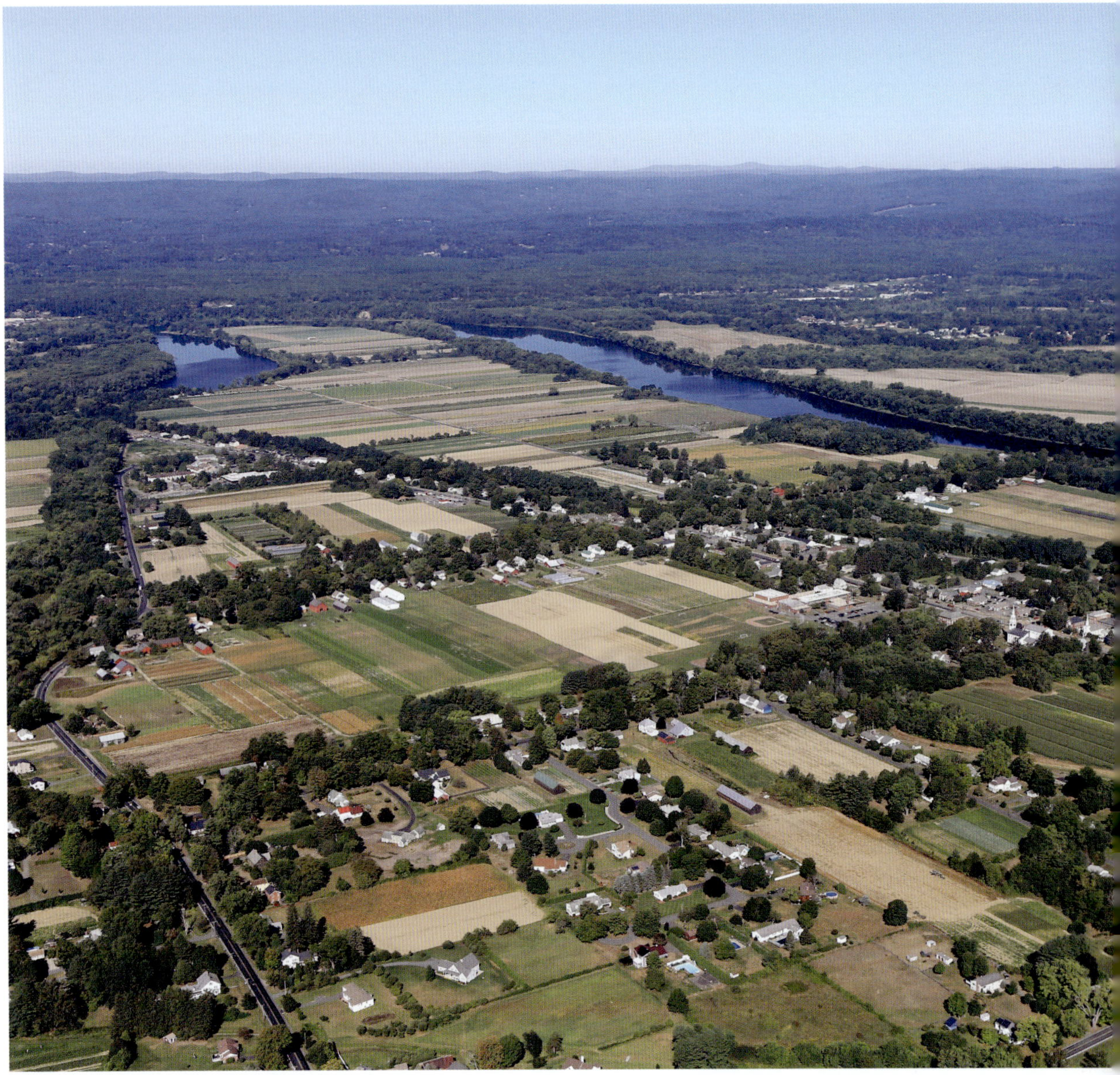

Looking west over Hadley, which sits at the base of a sharp peninsula-like bend in the river. Agriculture thrives in this flat and fertile landscape. Note the handful of shade-grown tobacco barns in the foreground and across the river in Hatfield.

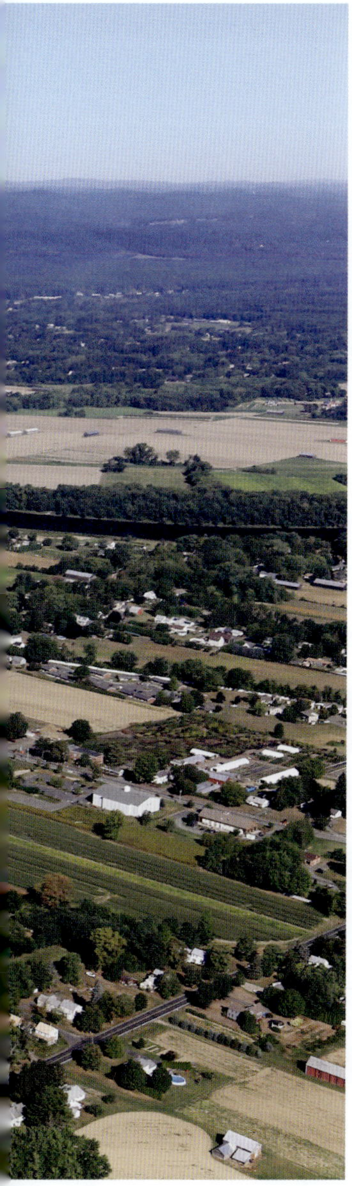

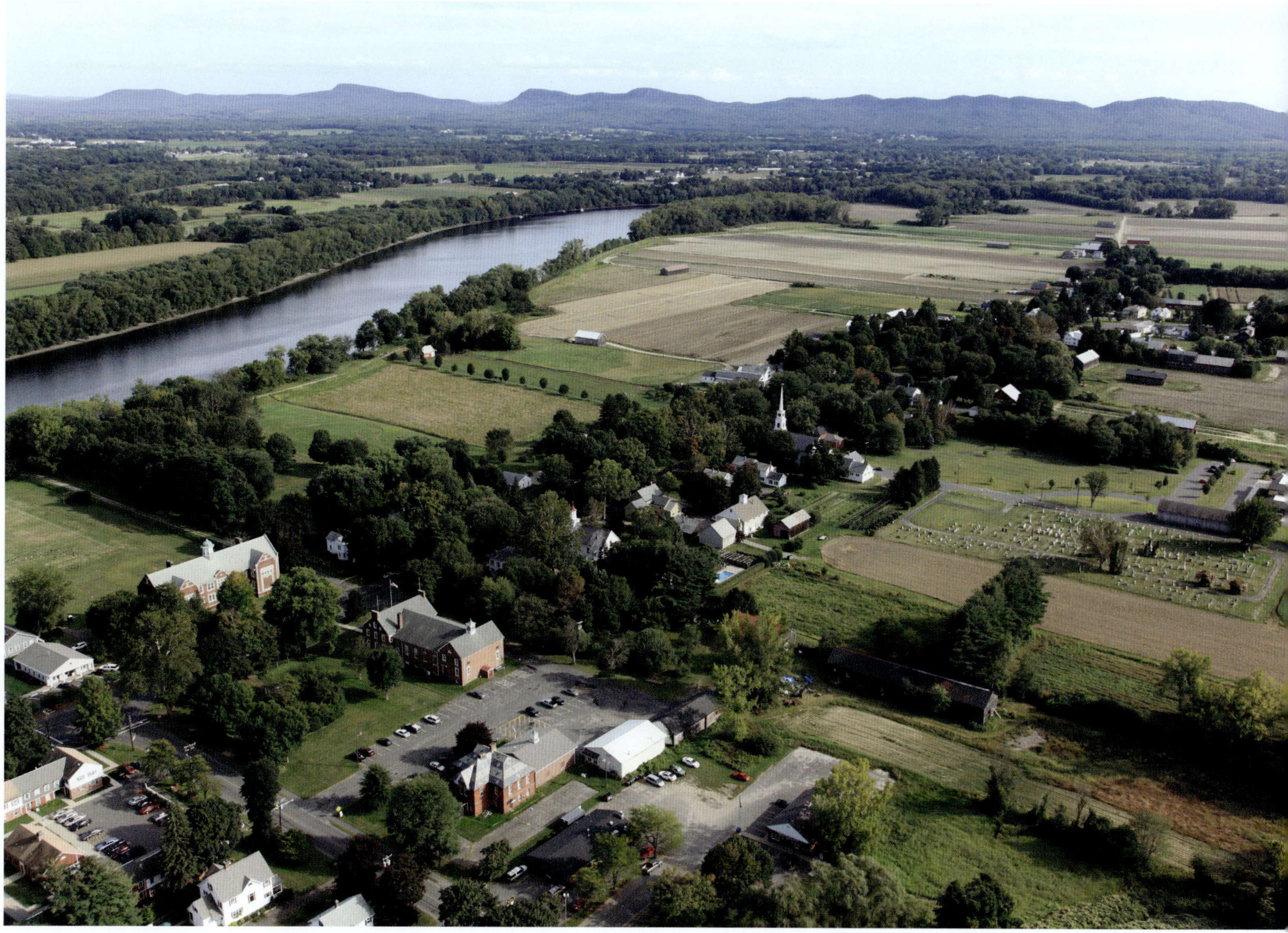

Looking to the southeast over the picturesque town of Hatfield.

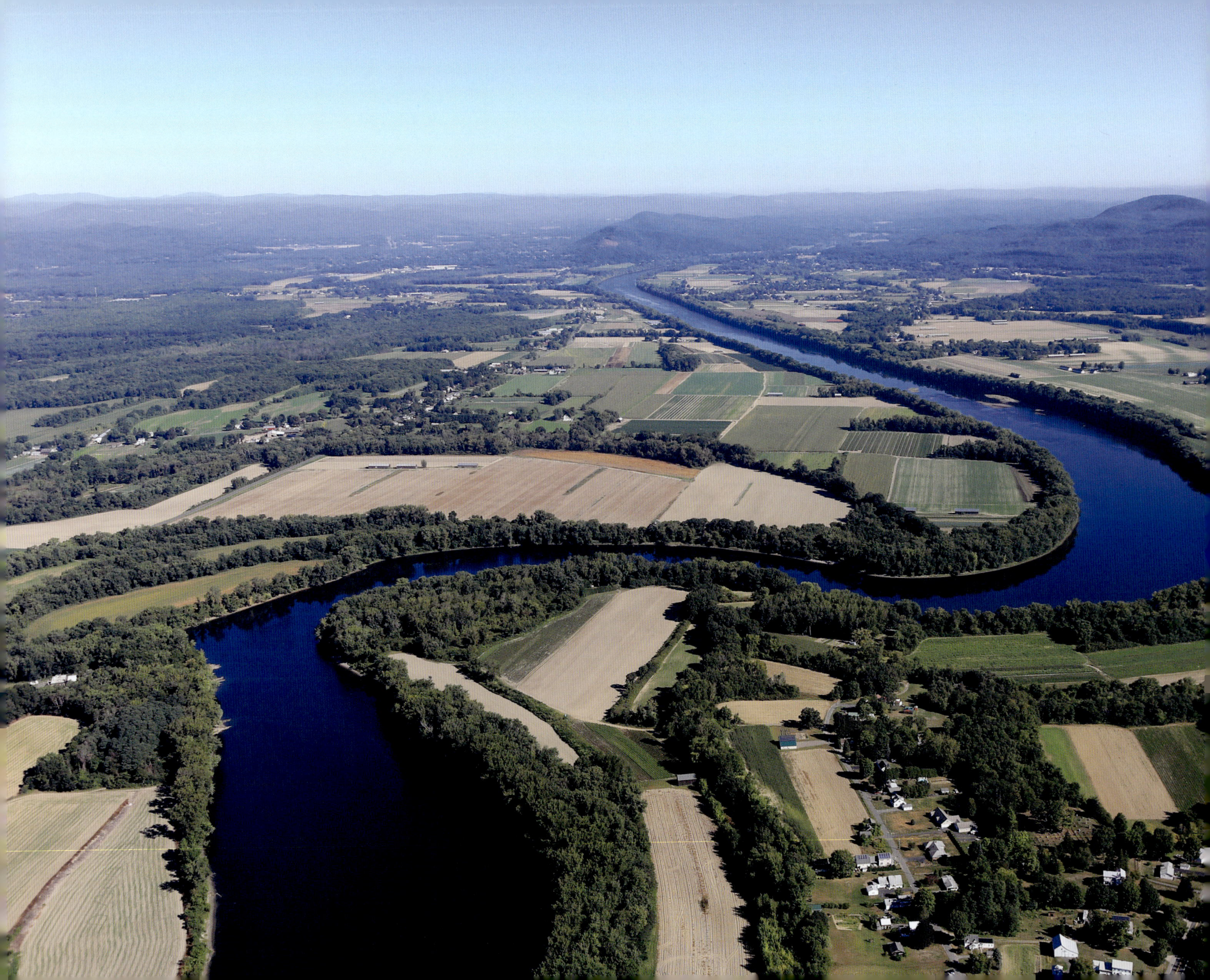

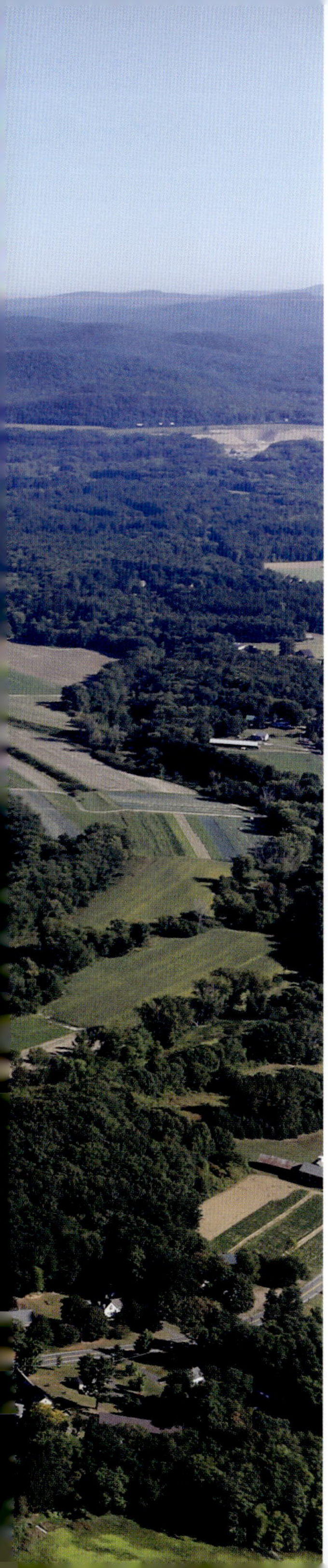

(left) Opposing peninsulas define an S-turn in the river near North Hadley.

(top right) Crops follow a sweeping bend in the river.

(bottom right) Heading upriver toward Sunderland, autumn colors accentuate farmlands and tobacco barns.

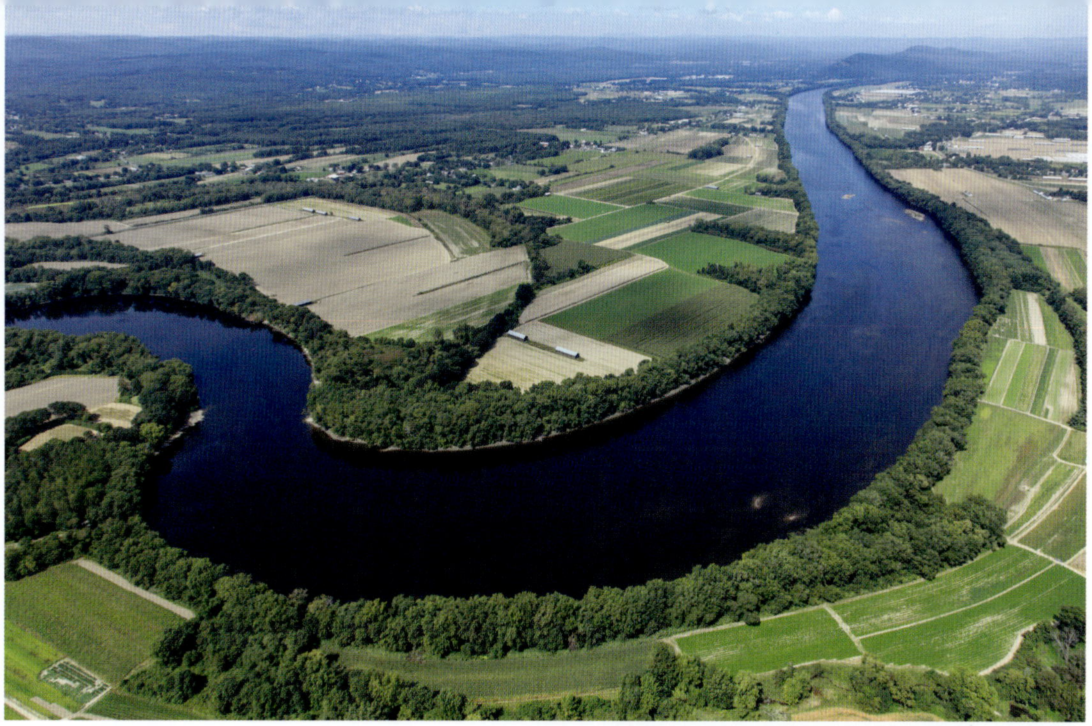

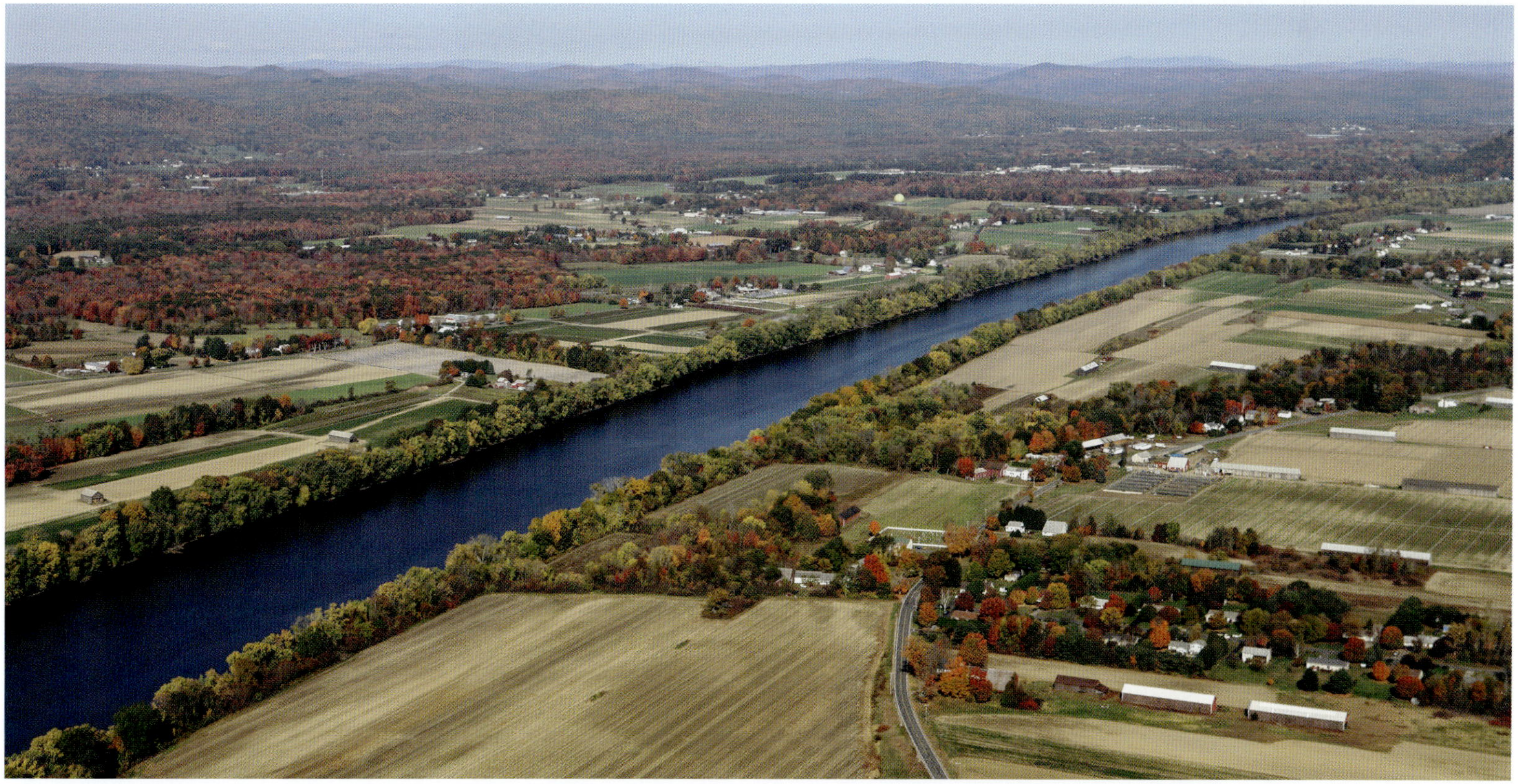

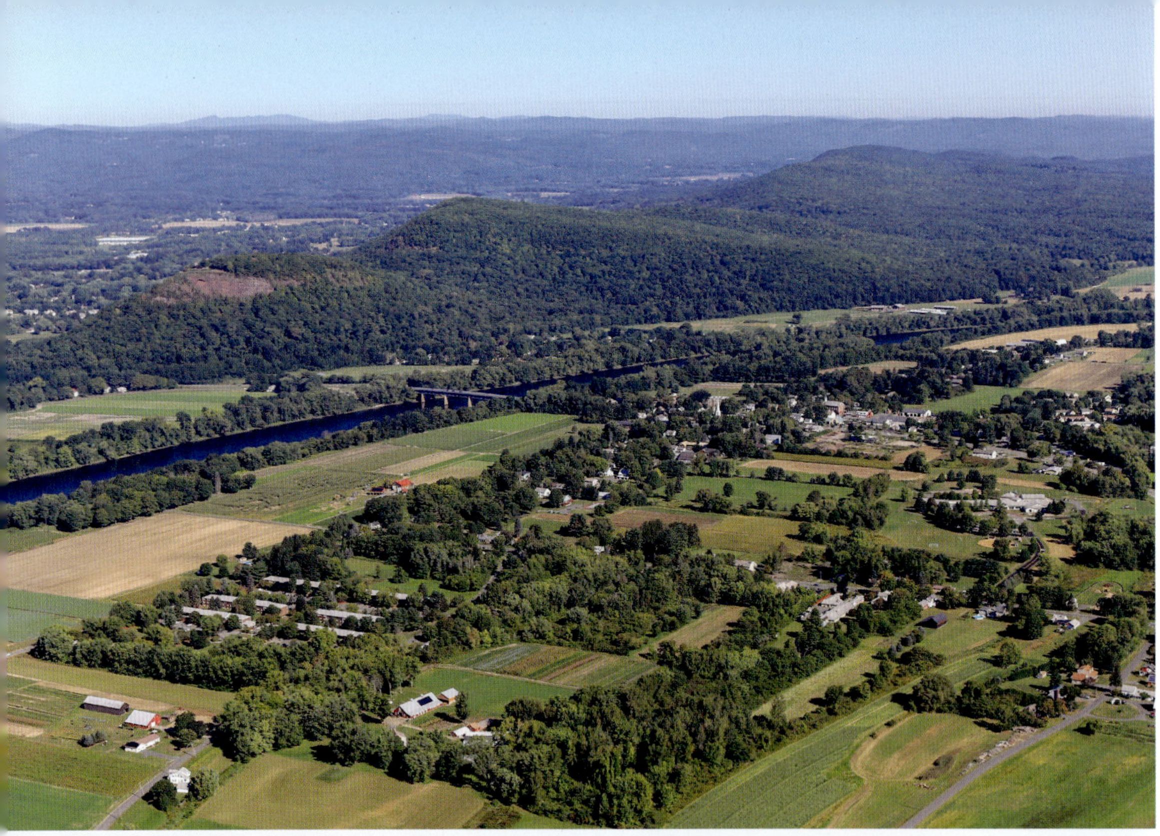

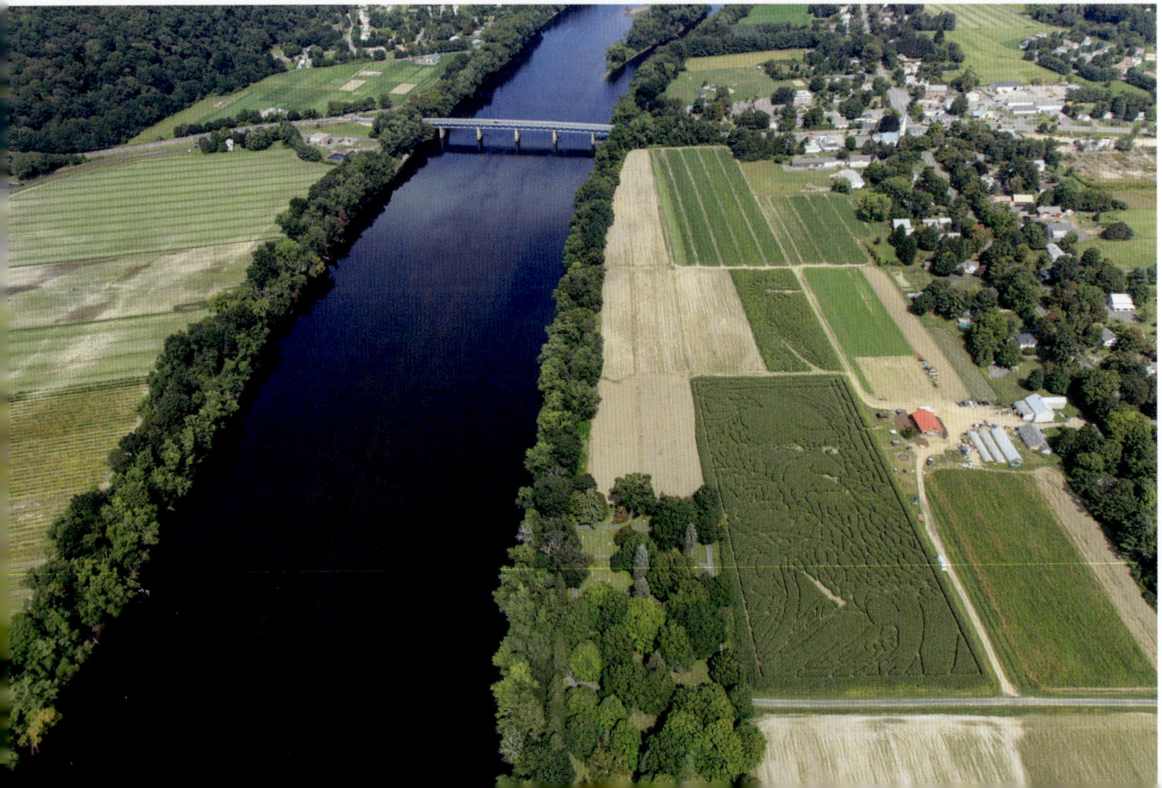

SUNDERLAND, MA

For ten generations, Warner's Farm in Sunderland, Massachusetts, has been growing a wide variety of crops on 150 acres of land next to the river. Keeping up with modern times, the owners have created a new annual tradition using GPS and a grid system to produce living works of art in their eight-acre corn maze. Although more than 8,000 people explore the intricate creations each year, they are clearly best appreciated from the air.

(left top) Approaching Sunderland with Sugarloaf Mountain looming just across the river

(left bottom) A stoic Charles Darwin ponders the corn maze just below the town of Sunderland, Massachusetts.

(right) Looking west over the Odyssey's Cyclops as it's one eye stares up from the Warner's Farm maze.

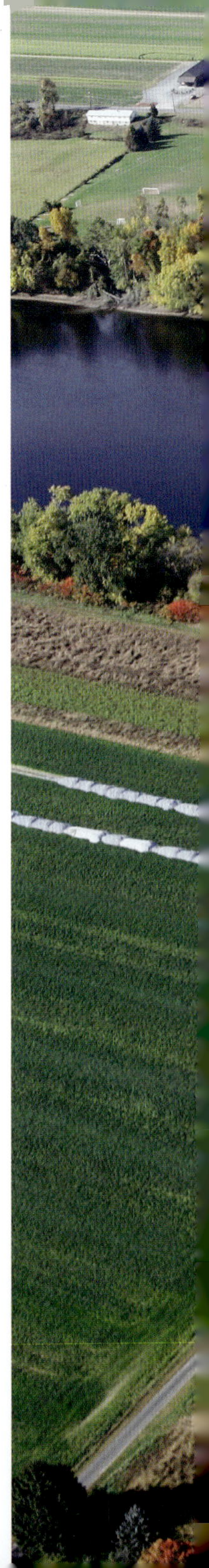

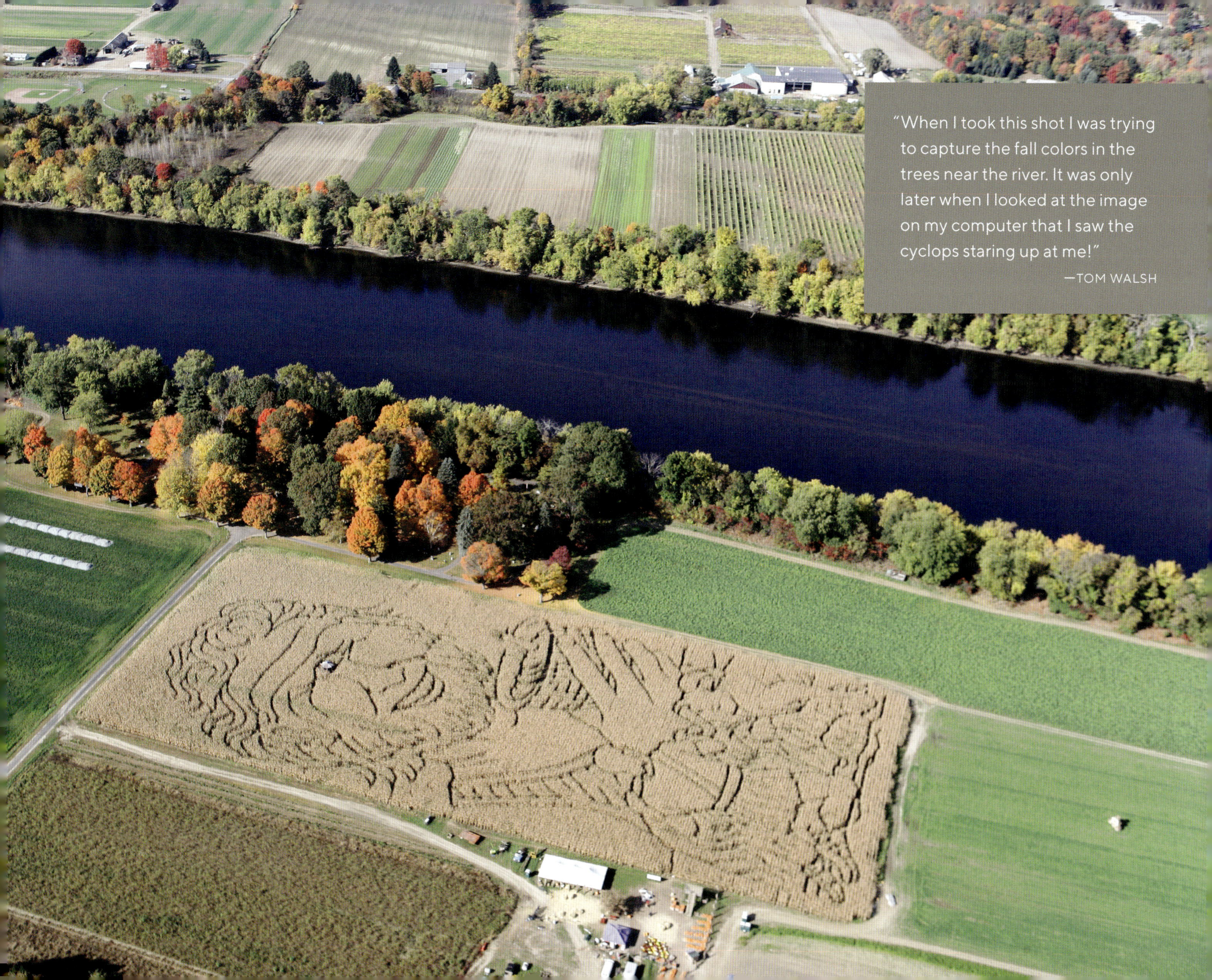

"When I took this shot I was trying to capture the fall colors in the trees near the river. It was only later when I looked at the image on my computer that I saw the cyclops staring up at me!"

—TOM WALSH

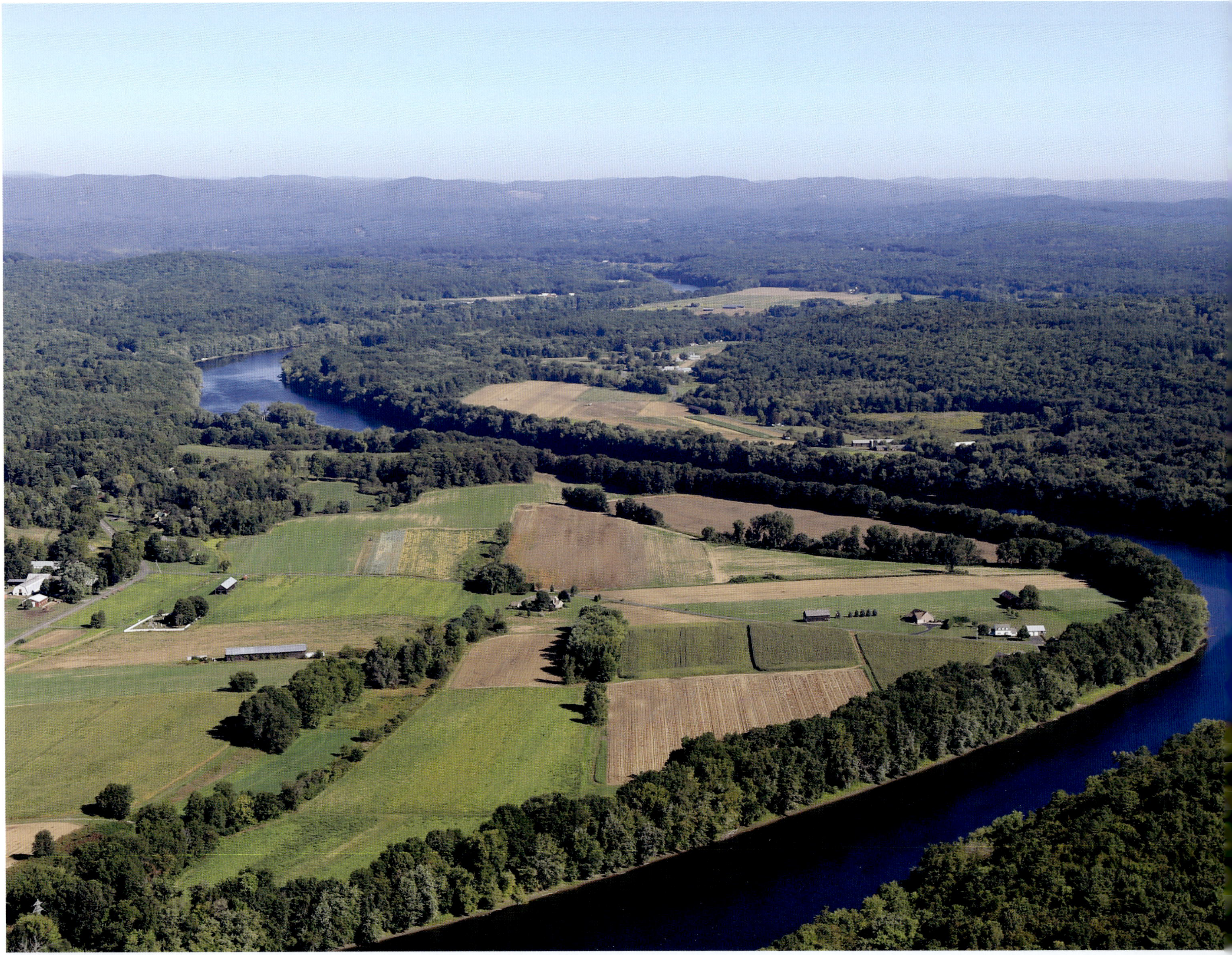

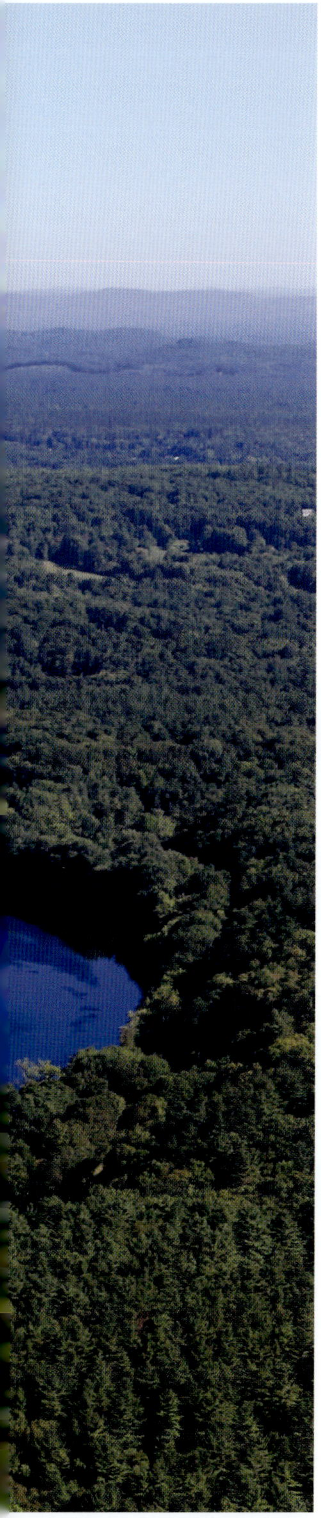

(left and topr right) Winding north toward Turners Falls between Deerfield and Montague. In 1704, during Queen Anne's War, about 300 French troops along with their Pocumtuc allies raided the English settlement at Deerfield, killing 47 and taking 112 captives.

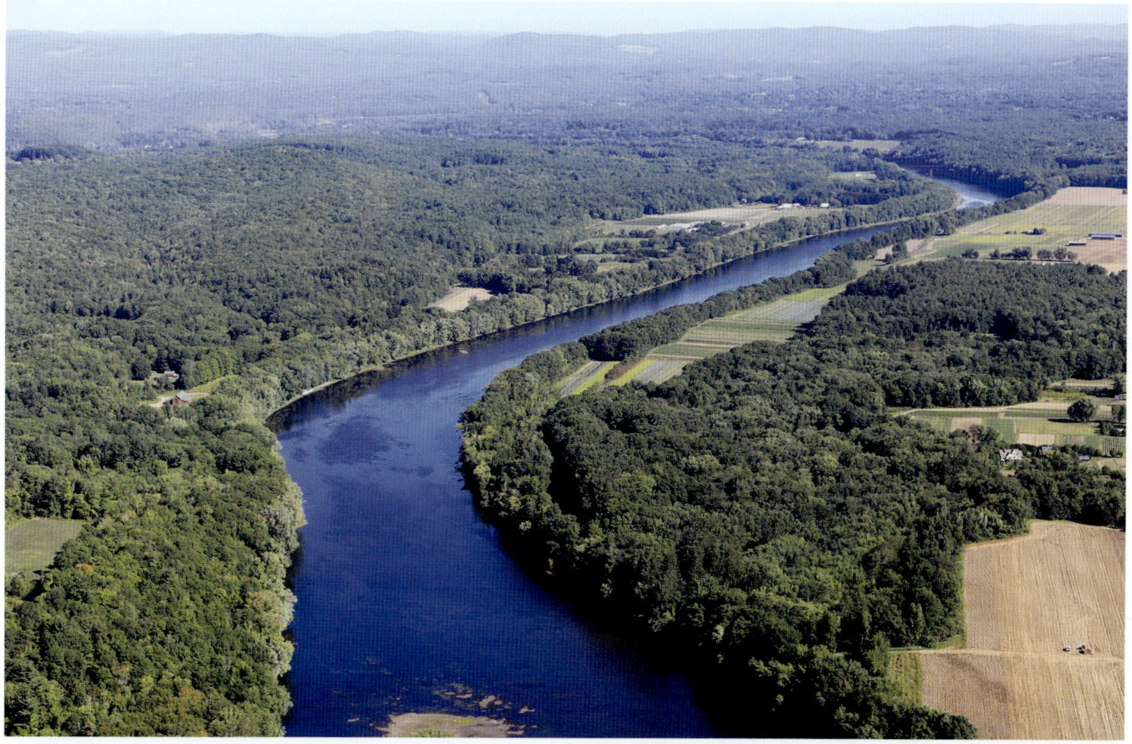

(bottom) The railway bridge and train yards, just south of Turners Falls, underscore the pivotal role railroads have played in cities, towns, and villages along the entire Connecticut River.

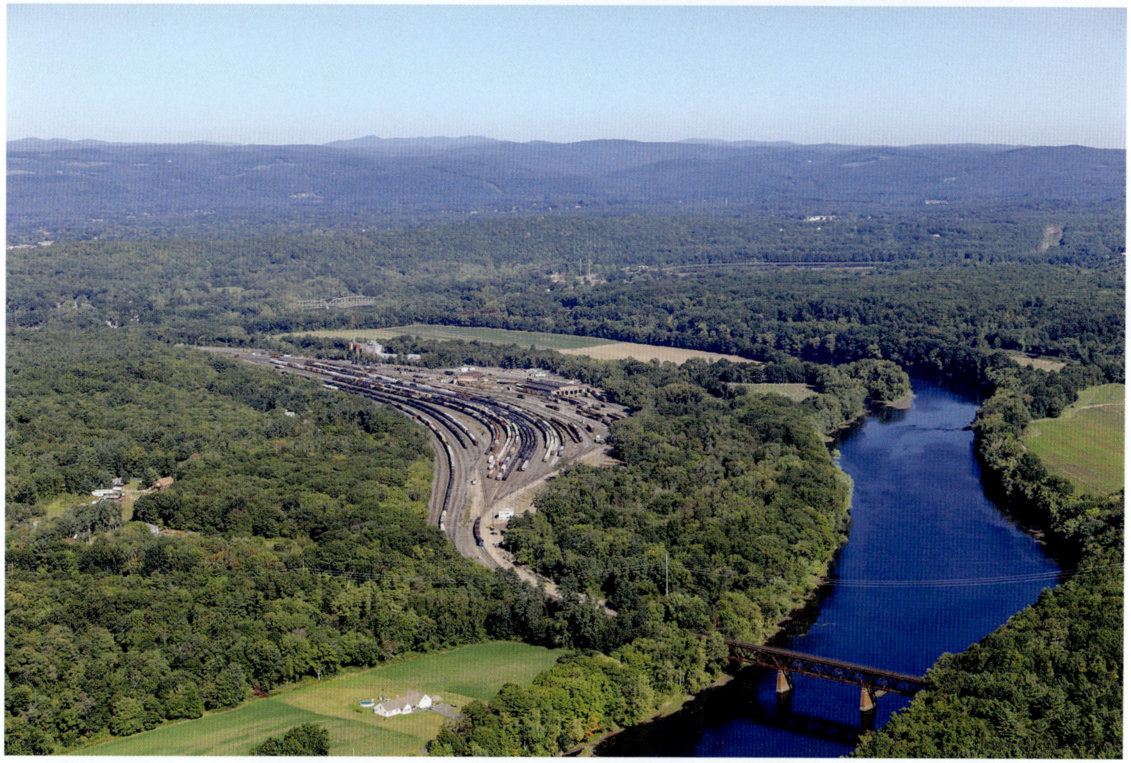

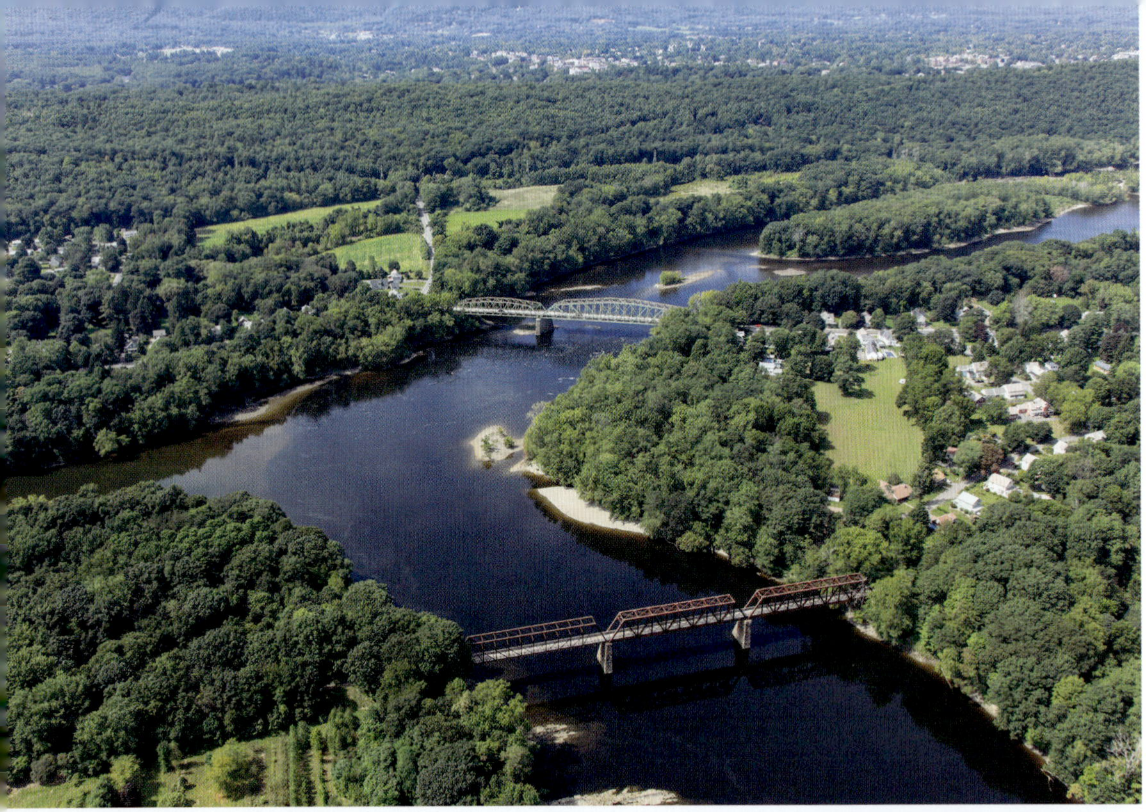

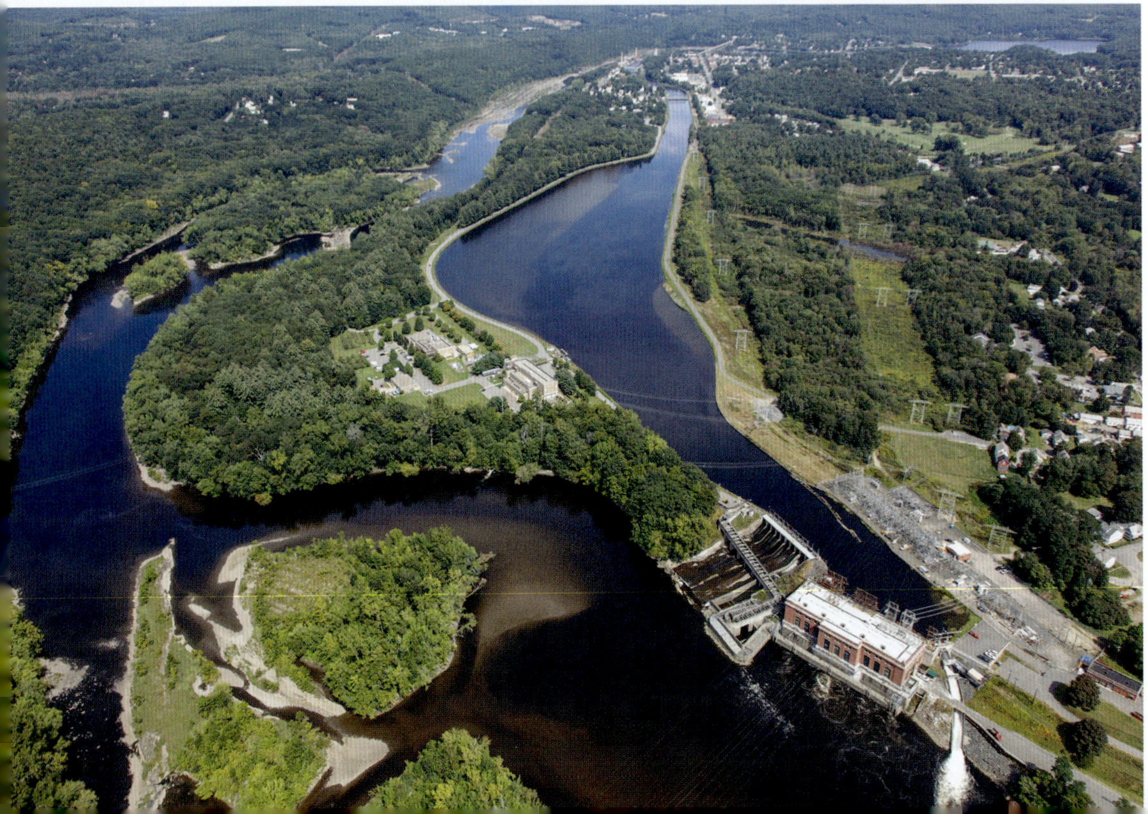

TURNERS FALLS, MA

Turners Falls was named for Captain William Turner who played a significant role in the King Philip's War. He led a raid in 1676, now known as the Turners Falls massacre, on a nearby Peskeompscut encampment. This devastating war represented the last significant Native American resistance to the English settlement and domination of New England.

Founded in 1868, Turners Falls was a planned industrial community designed to take advantage of the water power that could be generated by the river's forty foot drop in elevation here. An earlier dam built in 1798 was part of a lock and canal system used to bypass the falls. The 1868 dam and power canal were built to drive paper mills and other factories, which soon lined the canal as the town grew to support the work force.

Turners Falls was also a lumber town and the terminus of great log drives that brought timber downstream from forests near the Canadian border to feed lumber and paper mills along the river. Local taverns often filled with rivermen celebrating the end of another long hard drive. It was dangerous work and apparently they sometimes celebrated with significant exuberance. The danger of log driving was not always limited to the men on the river. In 1909, logging baron George Van Dyke met an untimely end when his chauffer-driven car accidently backed over the edge of a seventy-five-foot embankment while supervising a log drive at the falls.

(top left) Here the Deerfield River joins the Connecticut between the Keystone railway bridge (1880) and the Montague City Road Bridge with Greenfield in the distance.

(bottom left) Located about two miles downstream from Turners Falls, the Montague Dam and Hydroelectric power plant mark the southern end of the extended nineteenth-century power canal that drove paper mills and other factories in this area throughout the industrial revolution and beyond.

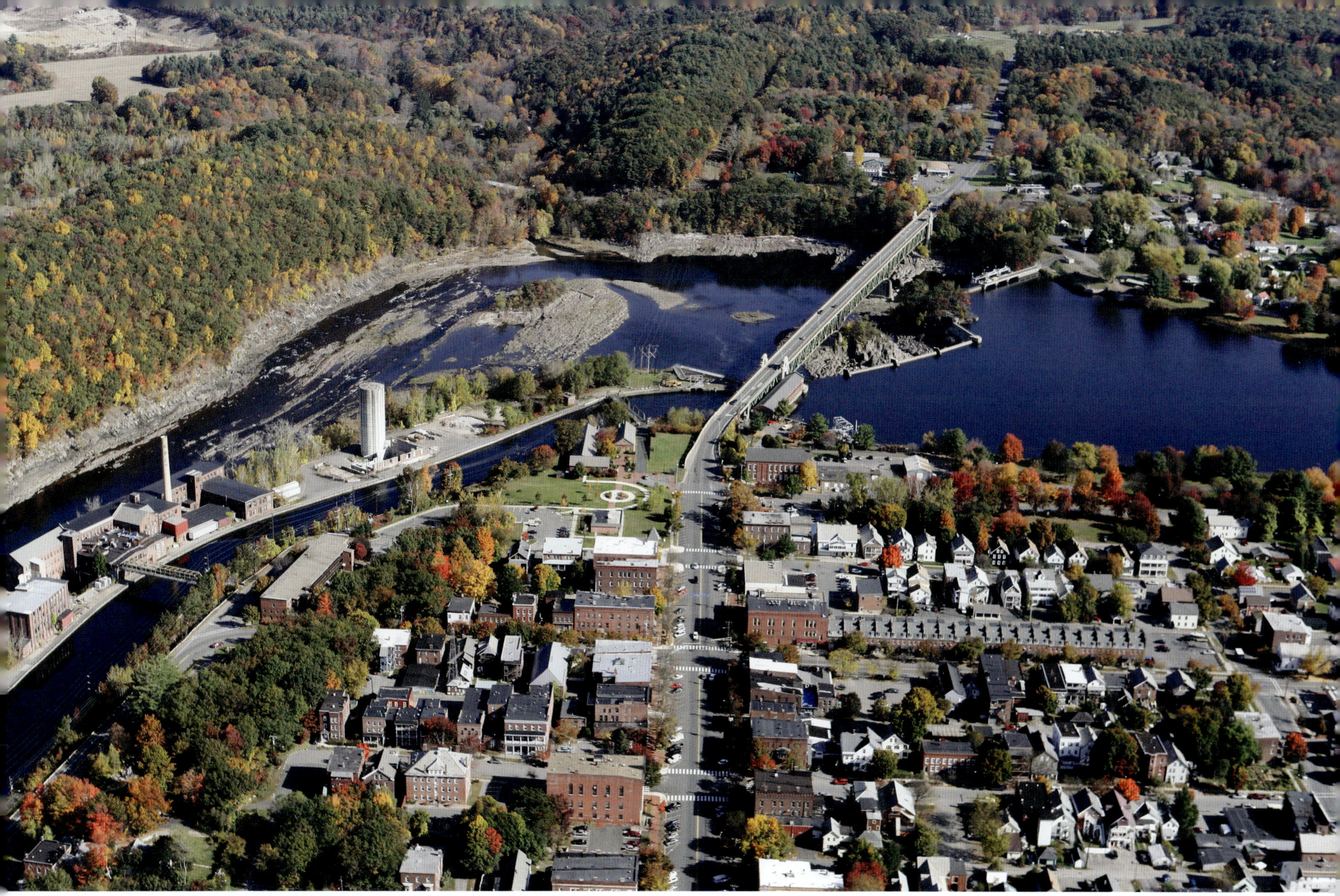

(above) Here at the northern end of the complex, the Turners Falls dam directs much of the river's flow into the power canal, which drove mills and factories and still helps generate electricity.

FORMATION

The formation of what is now the Connecticut River began about 250 million years ago as the supercontinent Pangea drifted apart. An incomplete tear, known as the Eastern Border Fault, in what would become the eastern seaboard of North America would eventually evolve into the Connecticut River Valley. During the last ice age, 60 to 20 thousand years ago, glaciers descended across what is now New England. When they eventually ground to a halt, just beyond the Connecticut coast, the sandy debris at their leading edge became Long Island.

When the ice finally melted, about 15,000 years ago, several super-lakes were created, one of which would eventually become Long Island Sound. Further inland, a 200-mile headwater formed behind a dam of glacial debris at what is now Rocky Hill, Connecticut. Stretching all the way north to the Passumpsic River in Vermont, ancient Lake Hitchcock covered what would become the central river valley. When the glacial debris breached, about 12,000 years ago, the Connecticut River, as we now know it, began to flow into Long Island Sound, and the Atlantic Ocean, just 12 miles beyond the river's mouth.

(right) Evidence of the river's formation can be found in the stone quarries of Selden Island and Portland, Connecticut, the sedimentary farmlands of the Middle and Lower Valleys, (far right, top to bottom) and the gorge spanned by the French King Bridge here in Massachusetts. The gorge is part of the Eastern Border Fault, the great rift that formed as the supercontinent Pangea tore apart. This rift became the Connecticut River Valley.

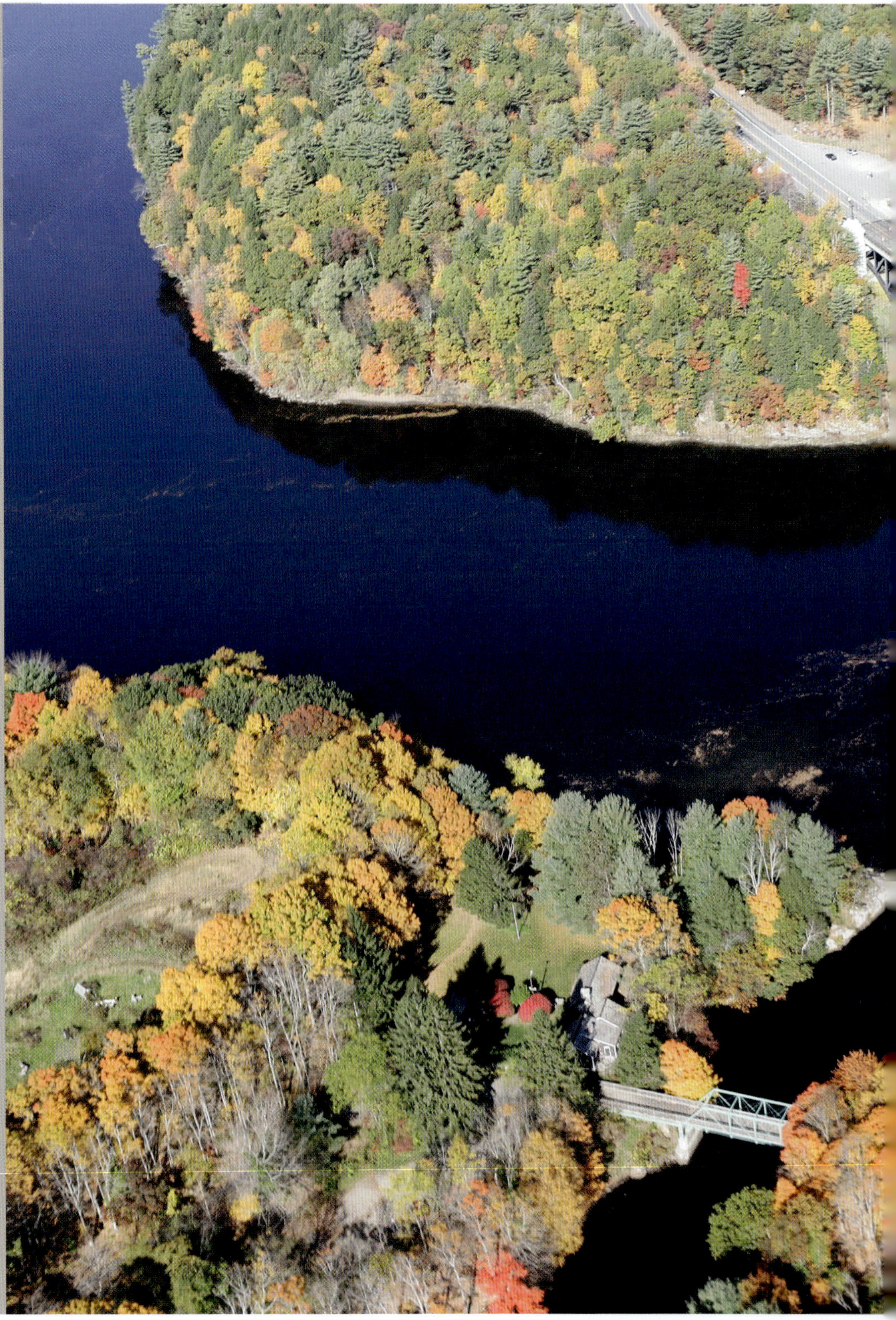

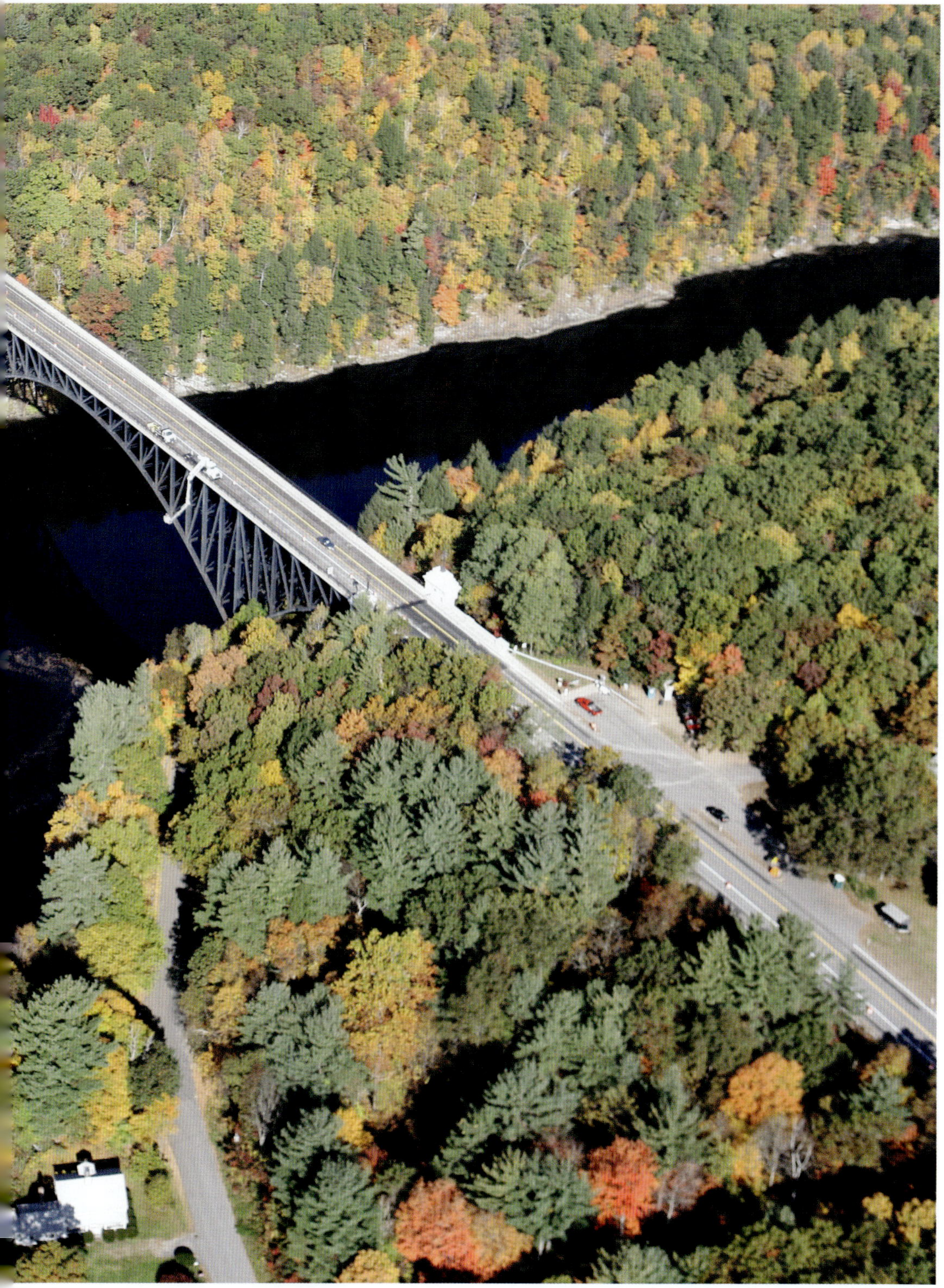
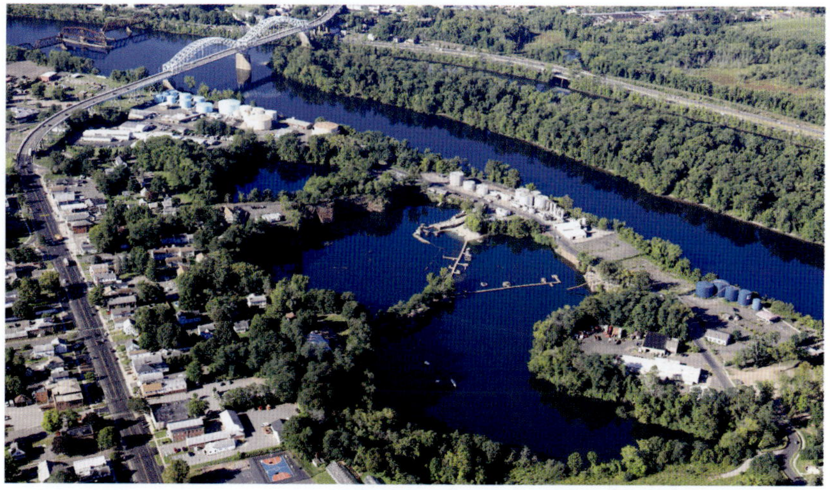
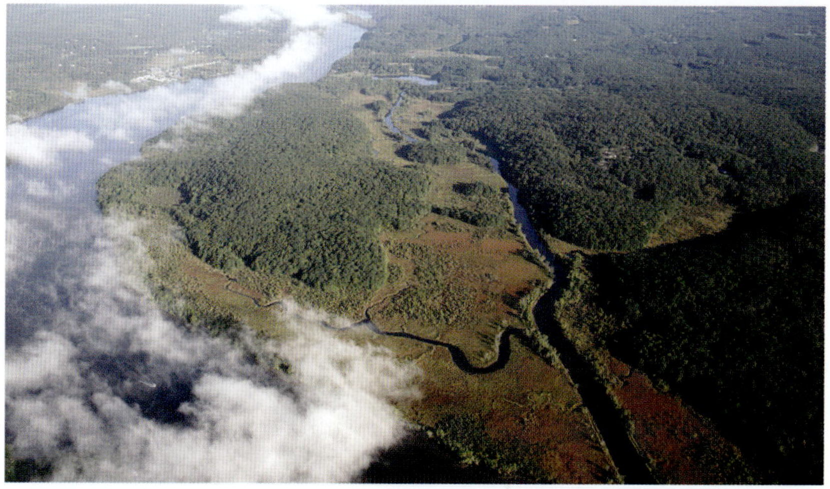
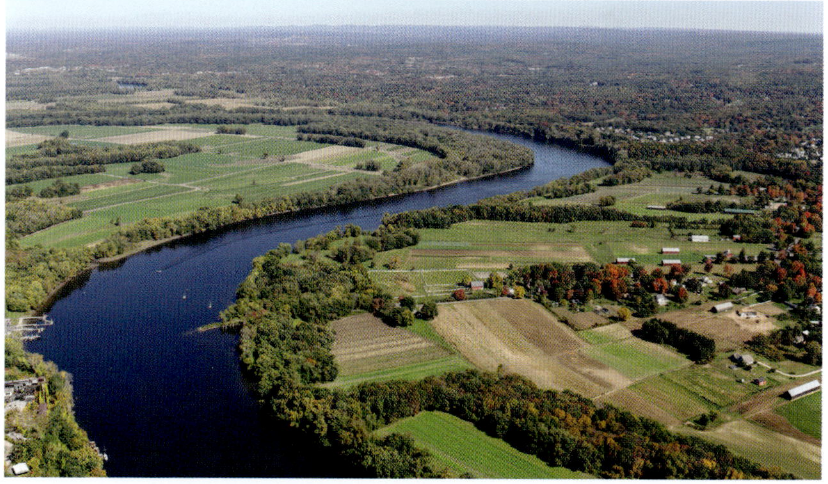

FRENCH KING BRIDGE

Built in 1932, the French King Bridge carries MA Route 2 across the gorge where Millers River joins the Connecticut near the town of Millers Falls. Shortly after it was completed it was named the most beautiful steel bridge in the nation.

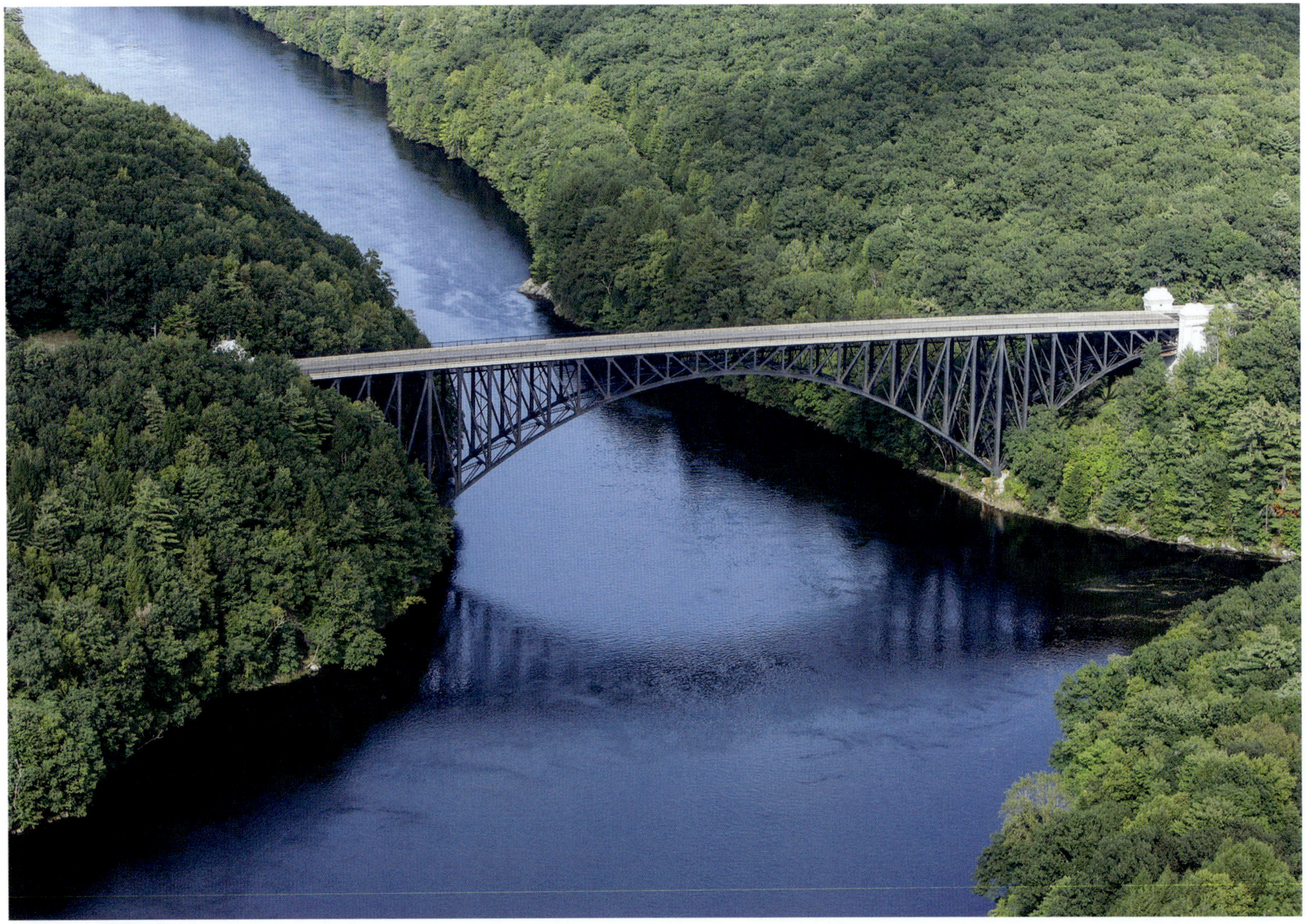

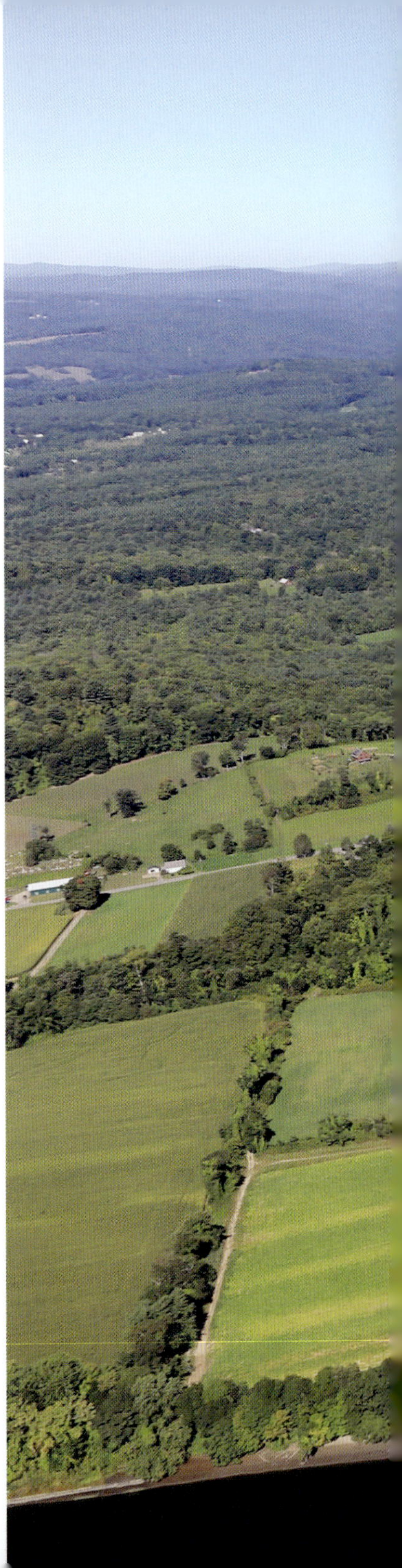

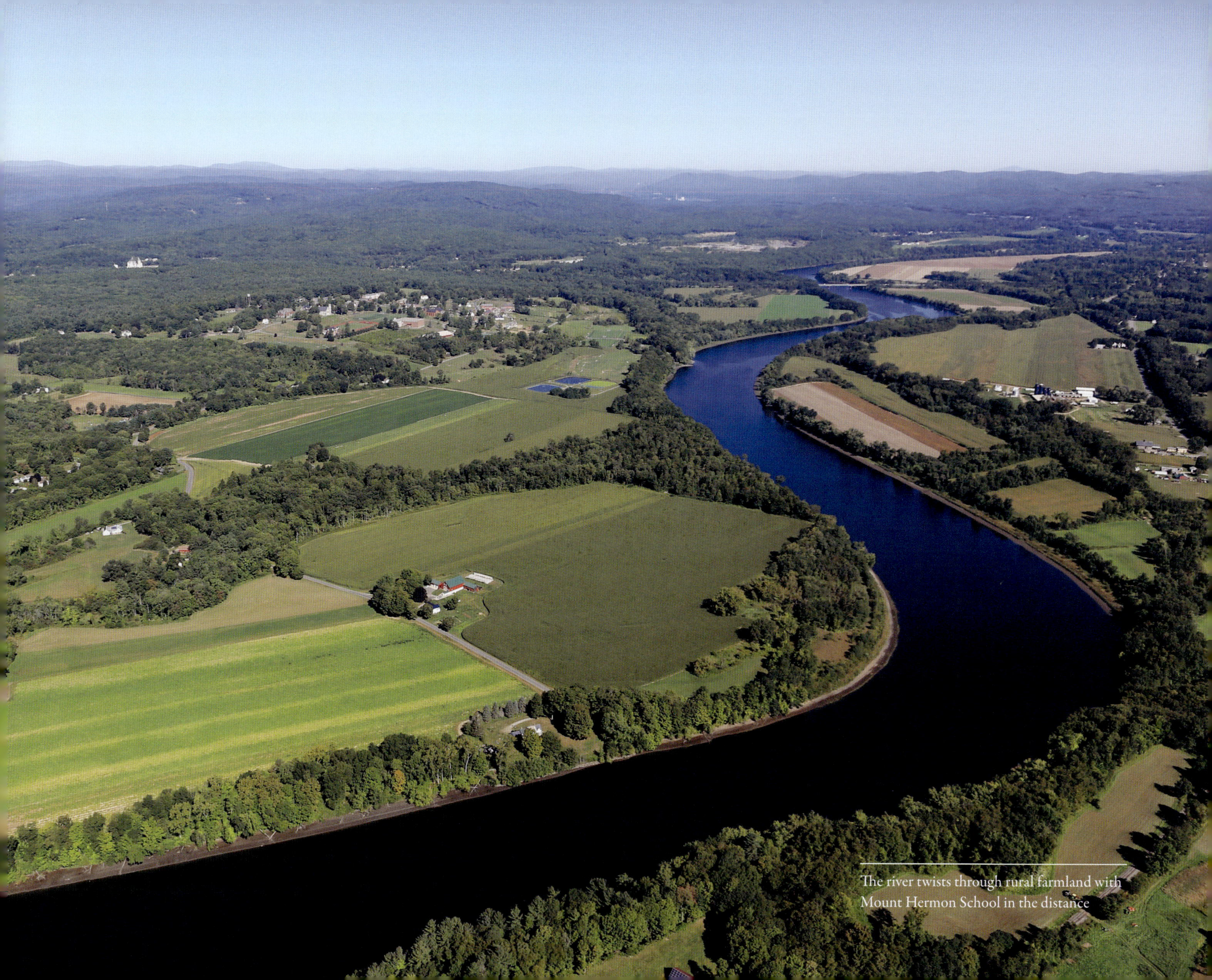

The river twists through rural farmland with Mount Hermon School in the distance

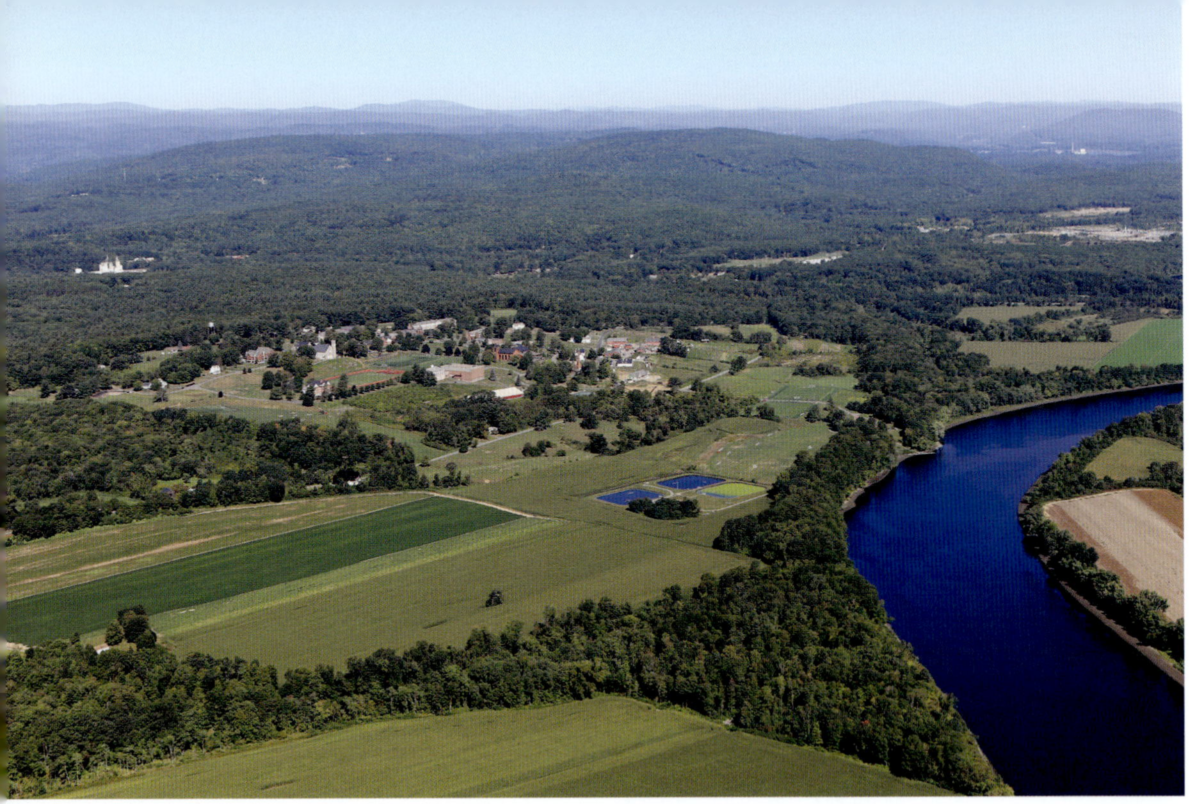

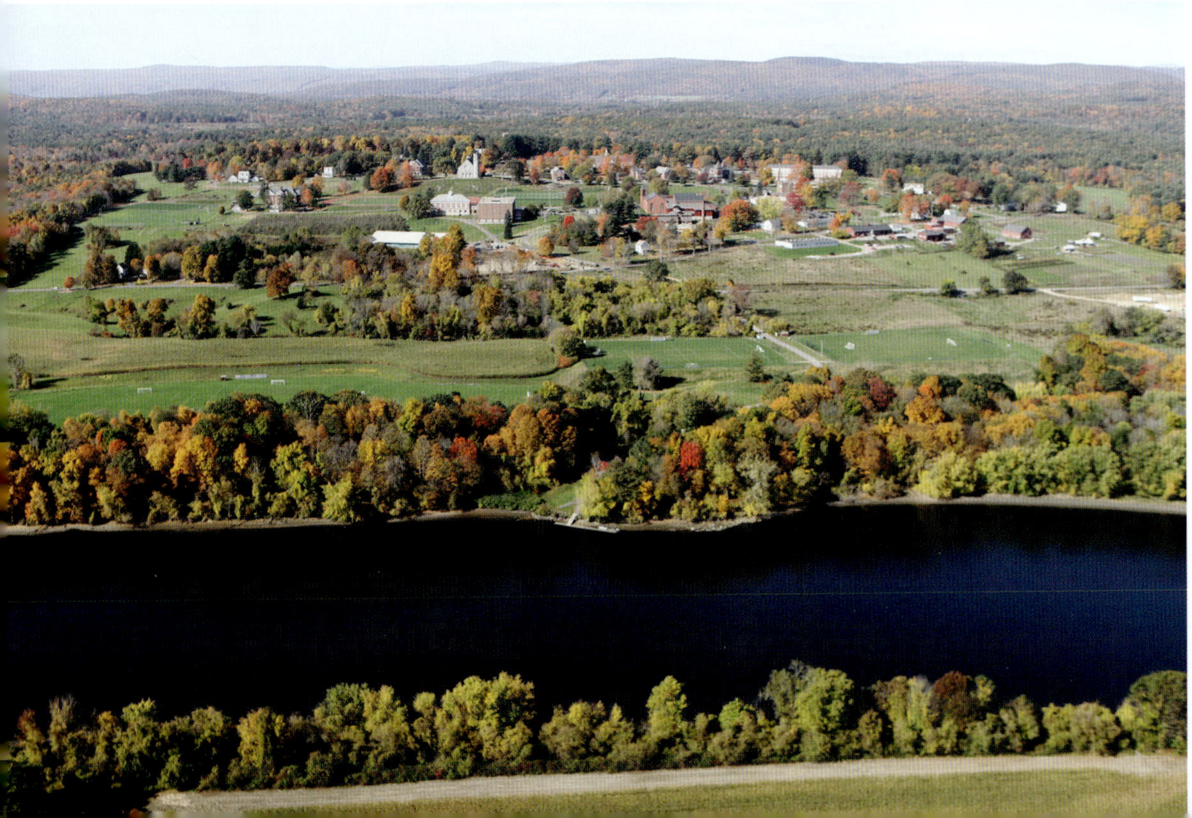

(top and bottom left) Northfield Mount Hermon School was originally founded in 1879 as the Northfield Seminary for Young Ladies. The Mount Hermon School for Boys was founded nearby in 1881. Both schools were established by a leading nineteenth-century evangelist to provide education for students with limited financial resources. The schools stressed bible study and manual labor to build Christian values and welcomed students form all races and ethnicities including Native Americans and former enslaved people. The two schools merged and consolidated in 1971. Today the school has more than 650 students, most of whom board on campus. Over fifty countries and thirty-four states are represented in the student body of this now highly selective college preparatory school.

(right) Approaching Northfield, a classic railway bridge spans the river on the left while the iconic Schell Bridge is reflected on the water just up river.

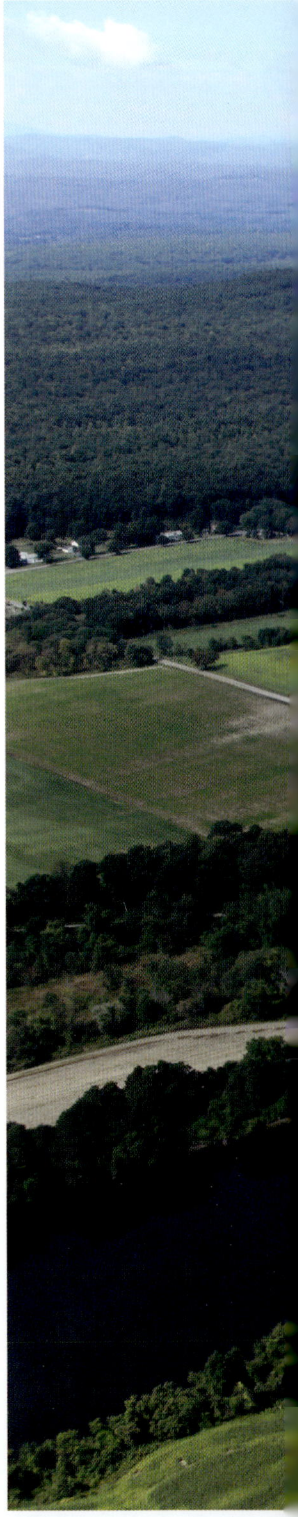

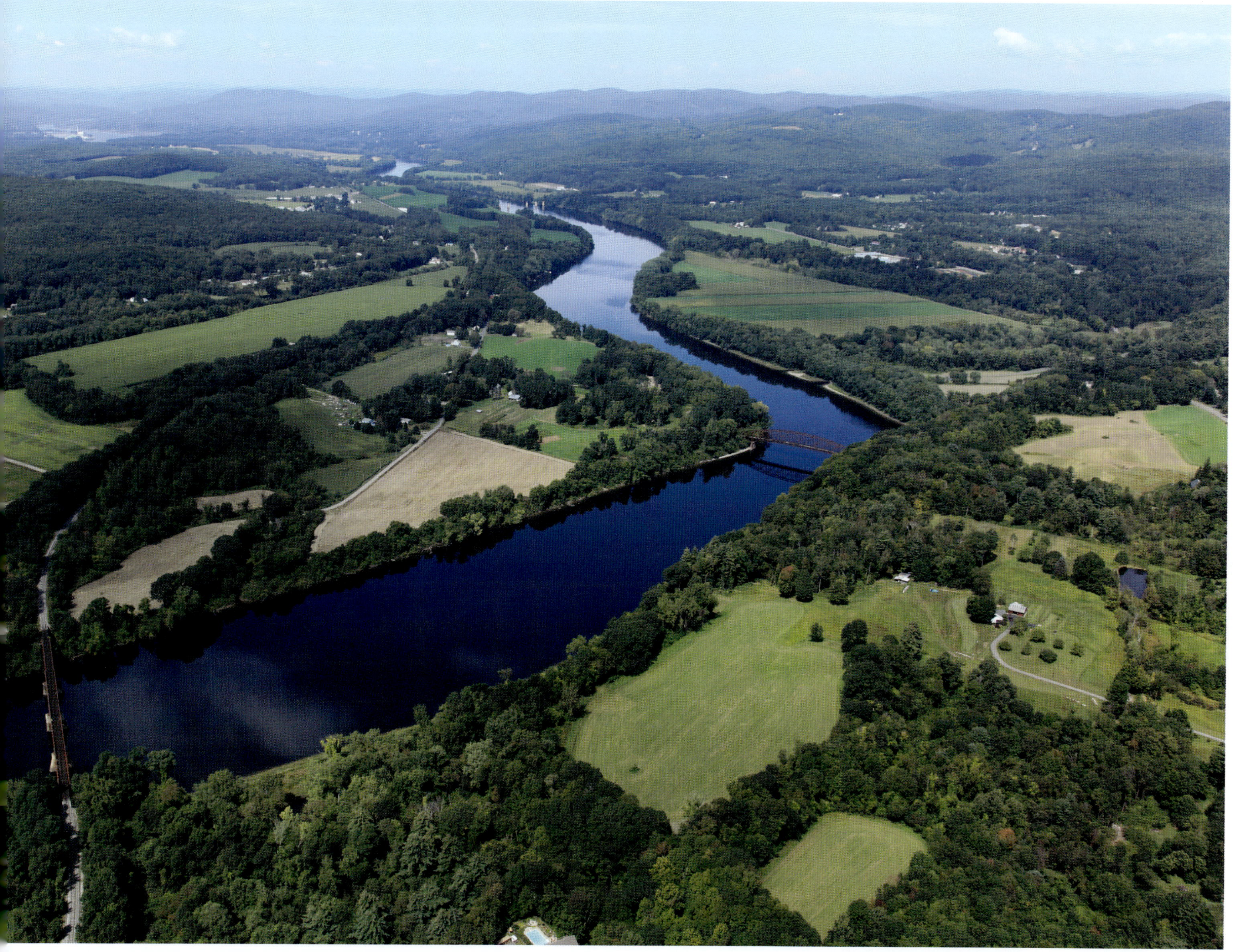

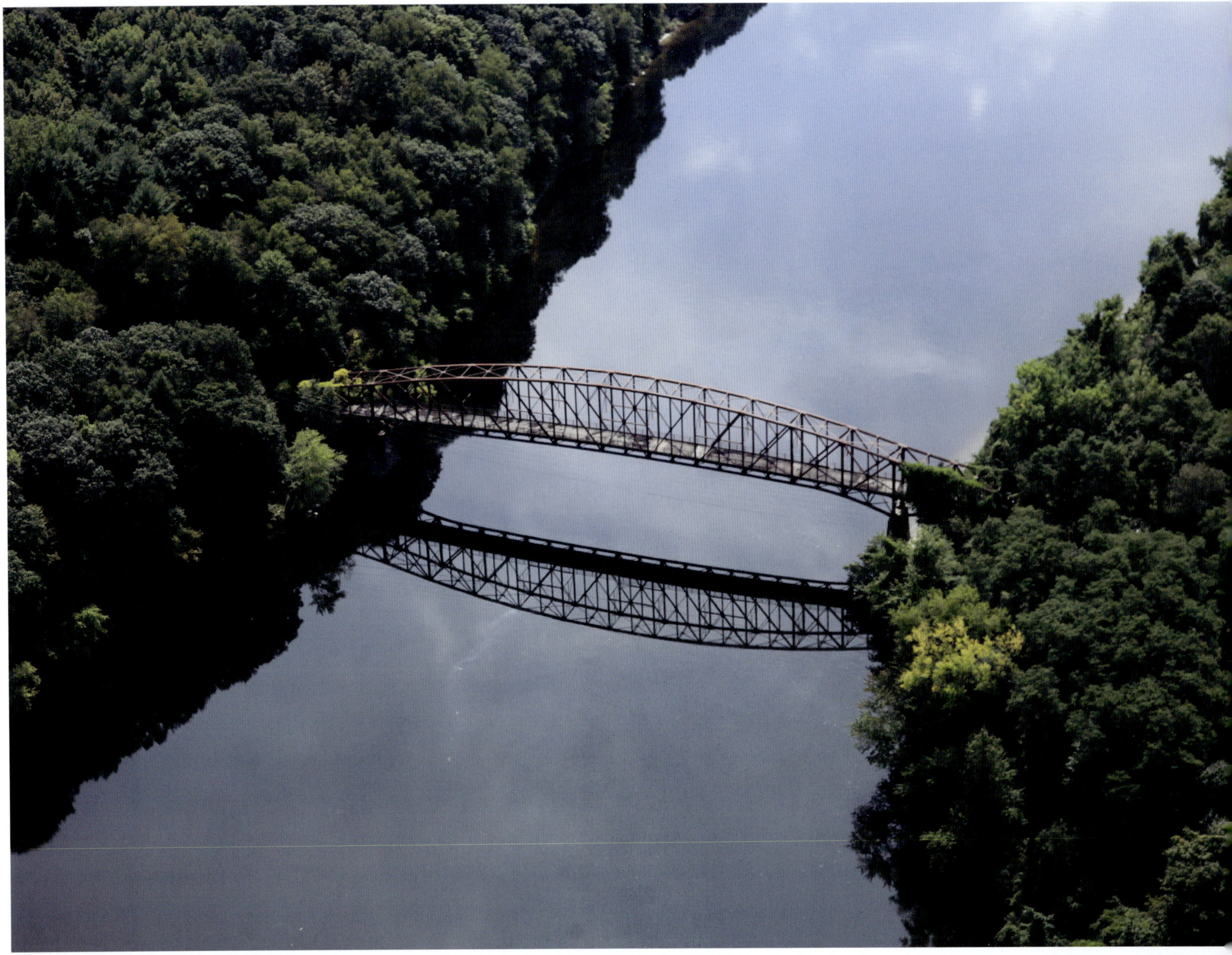

SCHELL BRIDGE

The Schell Bridge was built in 1903 to connect the two sides of Northfield, Massachusetts, a town divided by the river. It is considered one of the most attractive bridges on the river despite being closed in 1985 when it was deemed to be structurally unsound. Although there have been determined efforts over several decades to save the much-loved bridge, demolition now seems inevitable as the cost to repair it is estimated to greatly exceed the cost of replacement. How long will one of New England's most beautiful bridges continue to span the river? All I can say is that as this book goes to press, it is still there. You might want to check for yourself to see if it's still there.

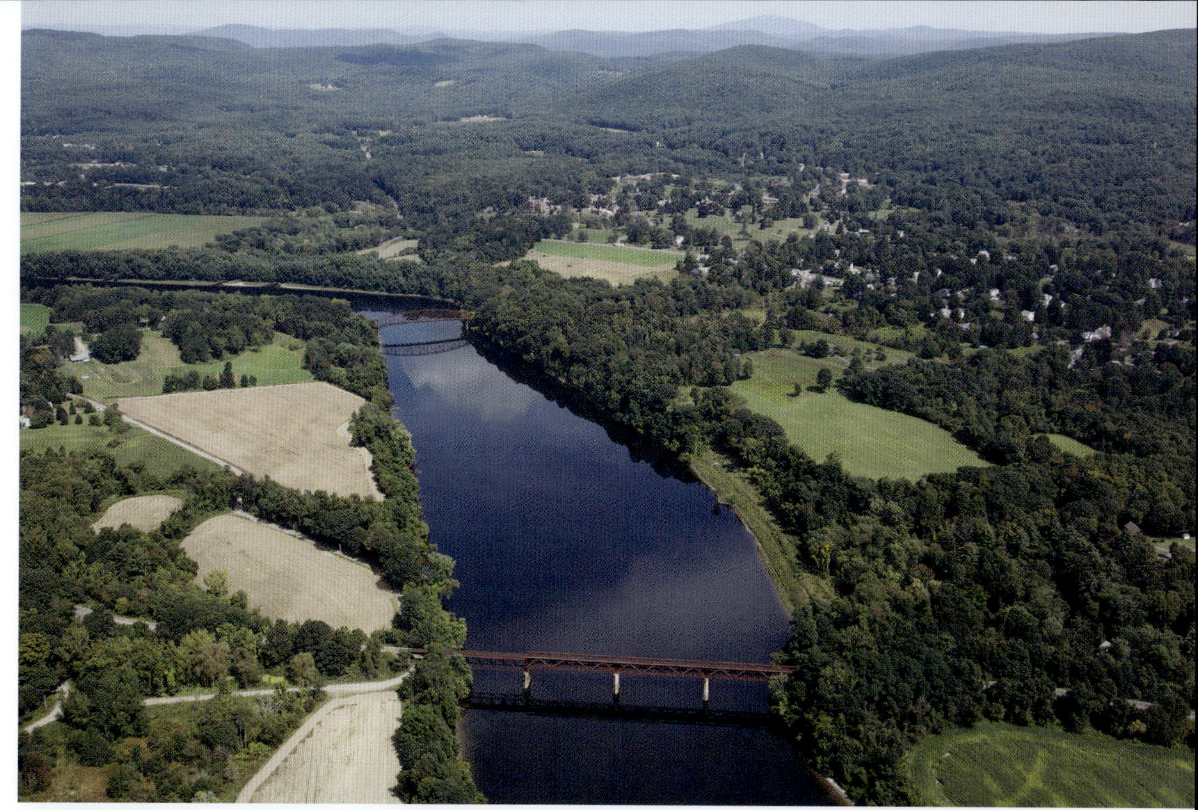

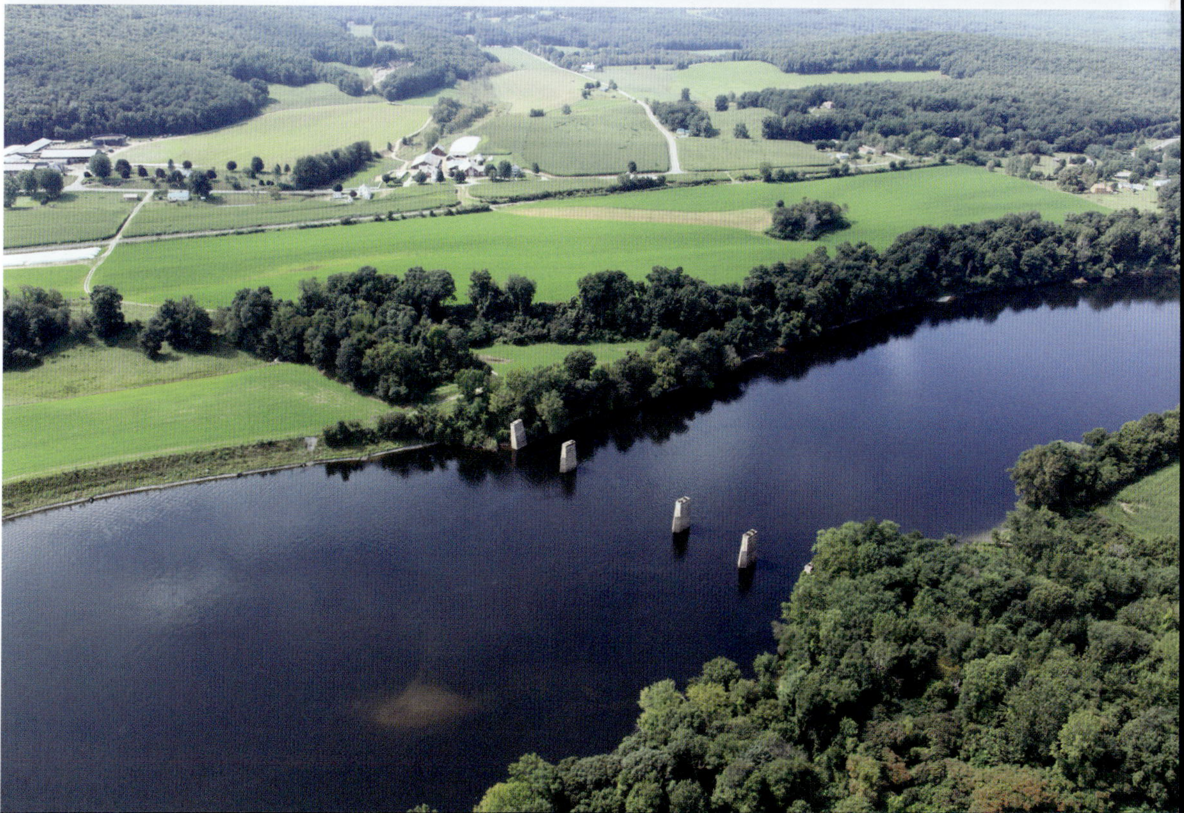

(top right) So close but so far, Northfield remains cut off from the west side of the river despite the bridge that once made the crossing so easy. The nearest crossing is more than two miles to the south.

(bottom right) Less than two miles up the river from the endangered Schell Bridge, this set of five pylons are all that are left of another lost bridge.

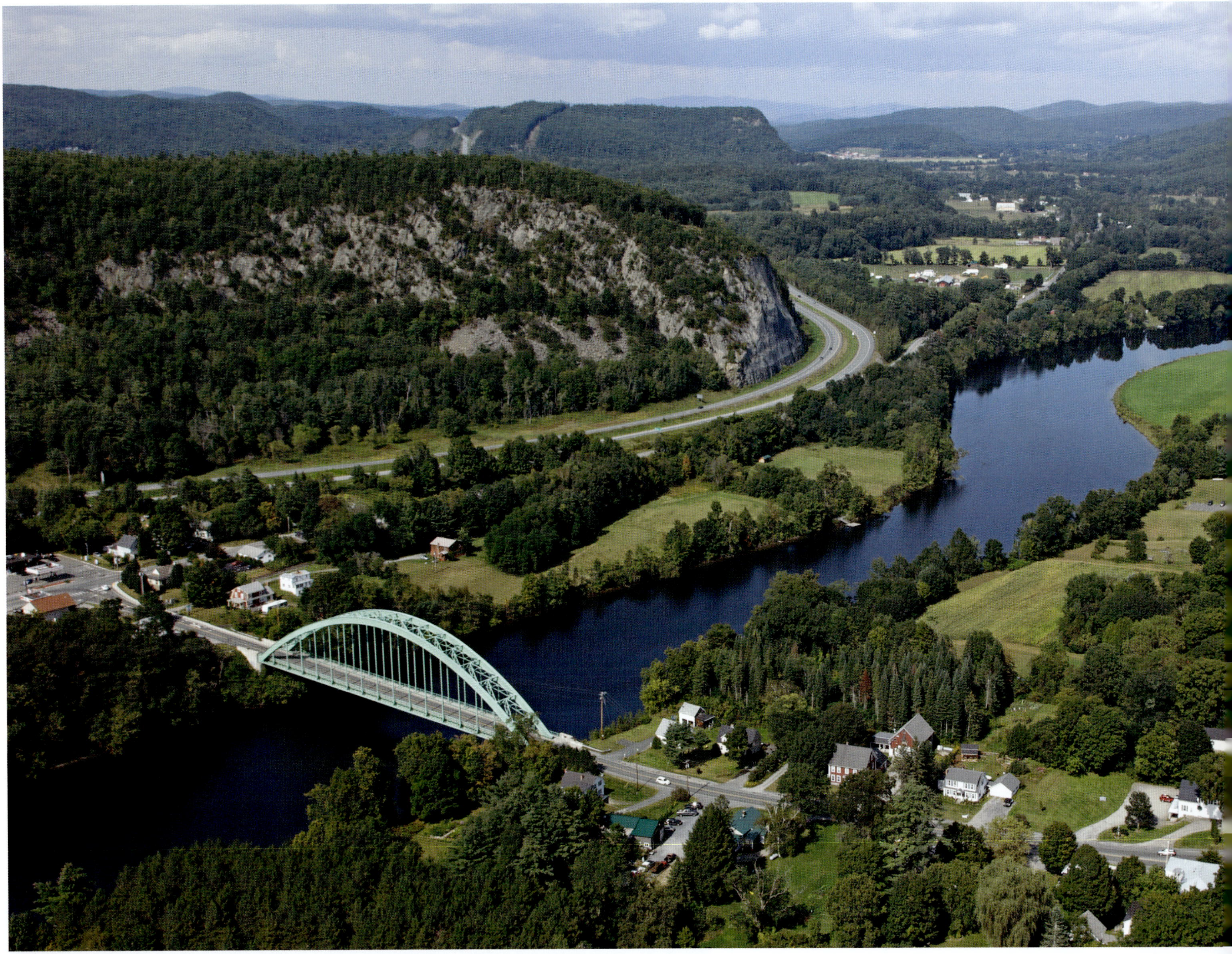

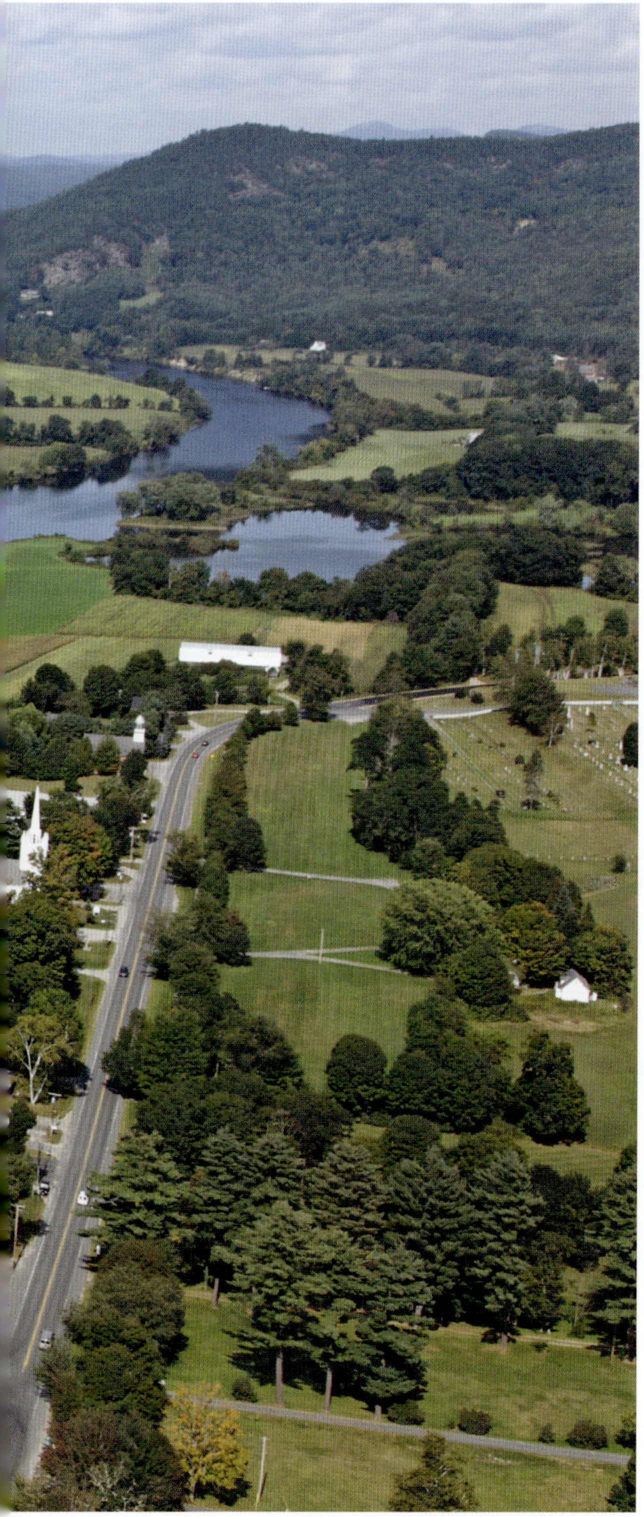

THE UPPER VALLEY

From the Passumpsic River, 150 miles upstream, down to northern Massachusetts, this stretch defines the borders between Vermont and New Hampshire. During colonial times it was the frontier between English and French controlled regions. Not until after the French and Indian War did large scale settlement take hold. Along its course, the river has powered small mill towns and large industrial cities. Several of the river's largest dams can be found here as well as a number of classic covered bridges and quaint farming communities.

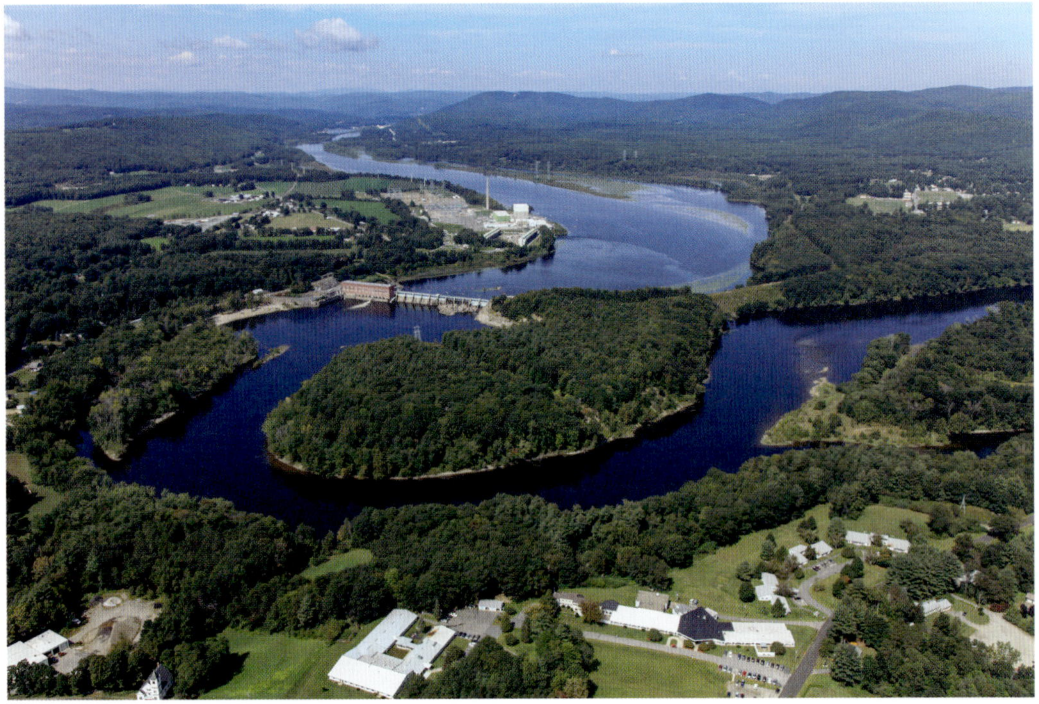

The dam and hydroelectric power plant, built within the oxbow at Vernon, Vermont, have been generating electricity since 1909. In sight, just upstream, the Vermont Yankee Nuclear Power plant began splitting atoms for energy in 1972. By 1988 it was producing more than 30 percent of the electricity used in the state. However, with its reactors cooled by the river's waters, it was also the largest producer of thermal pollution on the Connecticut River. After decades of controversy and protests over safety and environmental concerns, the operators called it quits for economic reasons. It was shut down in 2014 and the long process of decommissioning began. Meanwhile, the traditional power station, upgraded in 2008 to a 34-megawatt capacity, continues to churn out electricity as it has for well over a century.

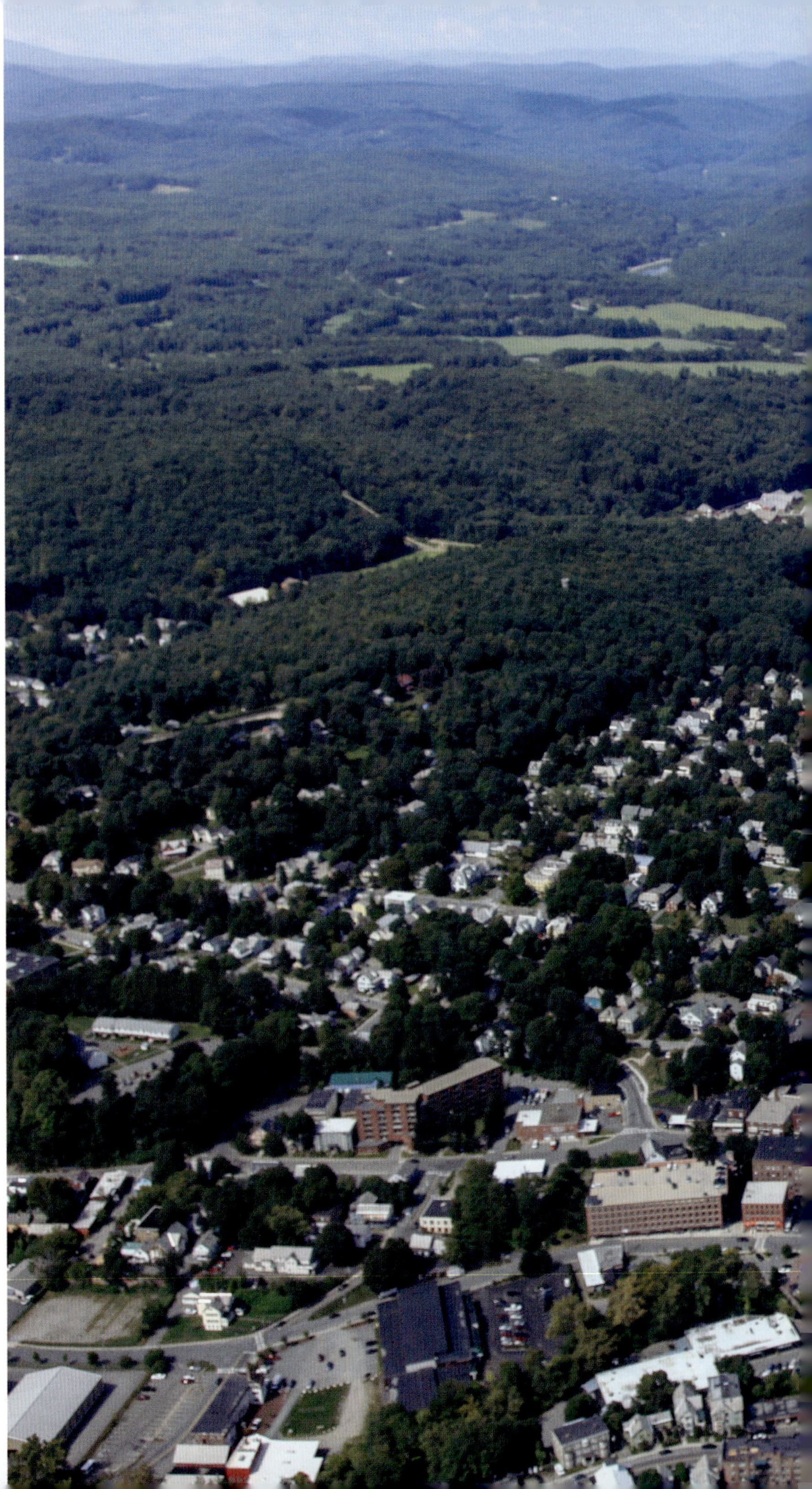

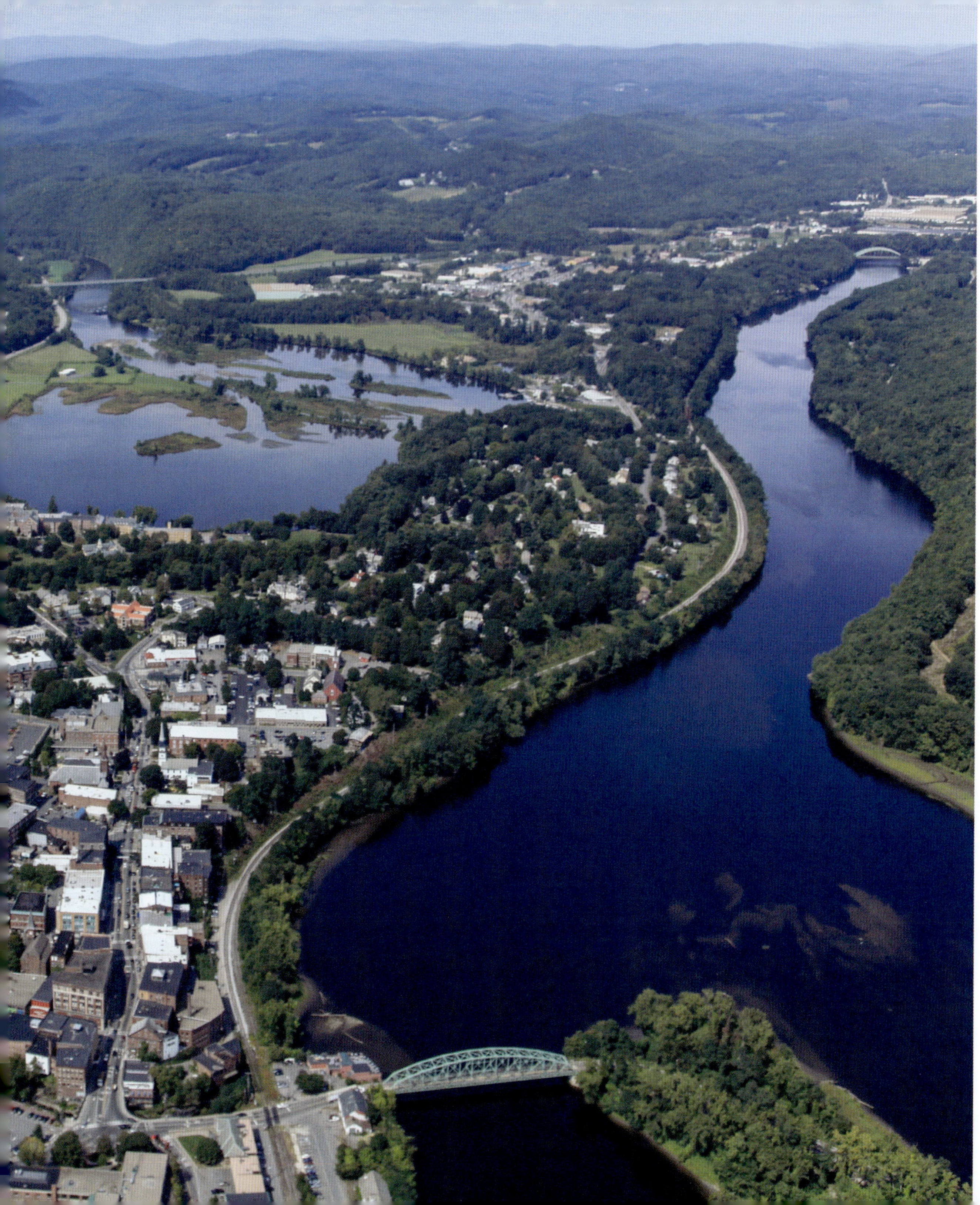

BRATTLEBORO, VT

First settled in 1724 as an English outpost called Fort Dummer, Brattleboro became a prosperous water-powered mill town and manufacturing center, situated on Whetstone Creek just downstream from where the West River flows into the Connecticut. Products included paper, paper making machinery, and printing. Melodeon reed organs were also produced here, and for over a century Brattleboro was home to the Estey Organ Company, the largest producer of organs in the United States. The railroad made it an important transportation hub and the town was also a major producer of lumber. In 1892 British author Rudyard Kipling made Brattleboro his home after marrying a local woman. It was here that he wrote *The Jungle Book*!

Approaching Brattleboro

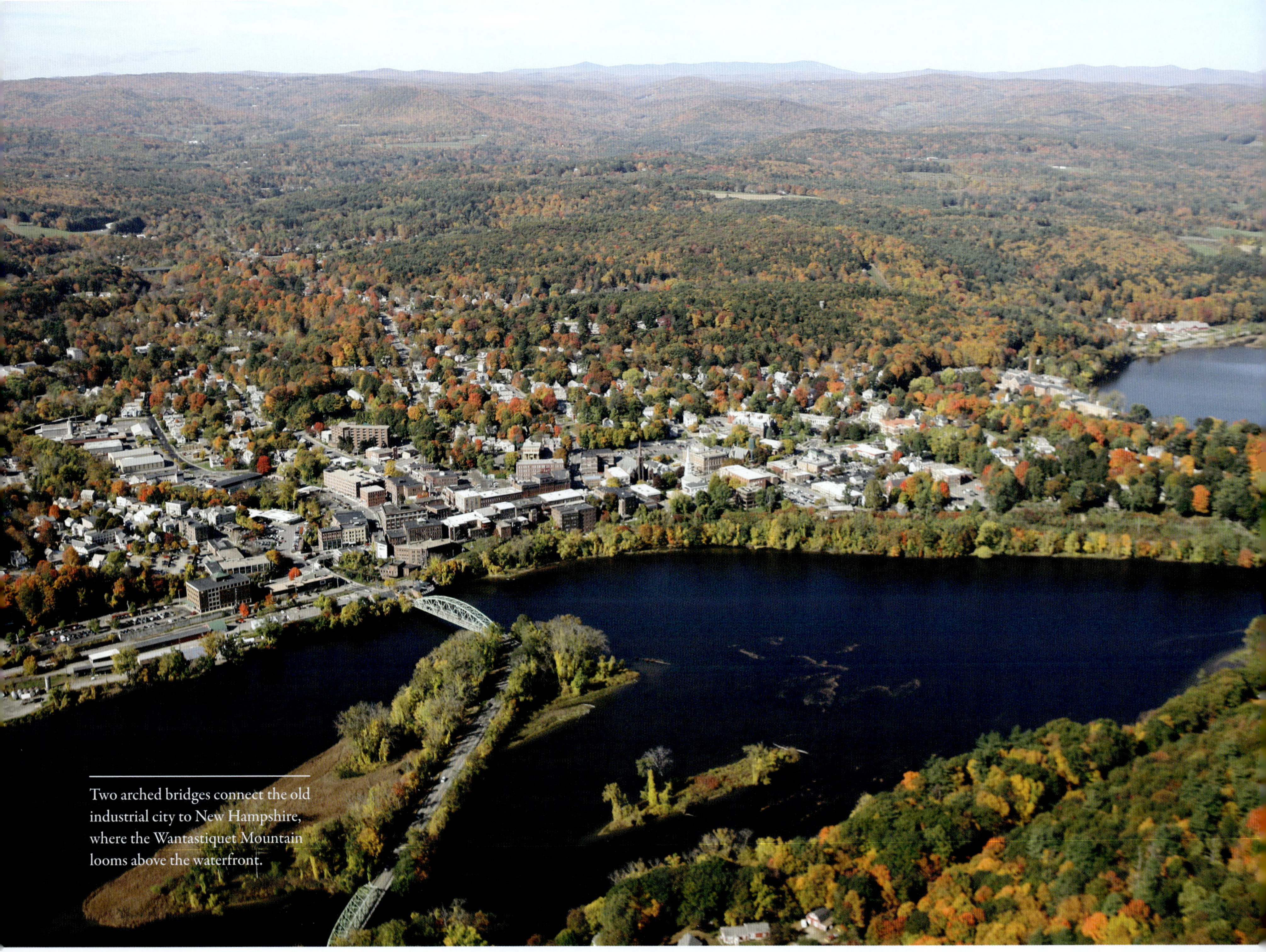

Two arched bridges connect the old industrial city to New Hampshire, where the Wantastiquet Mountain looms above the waterfront.

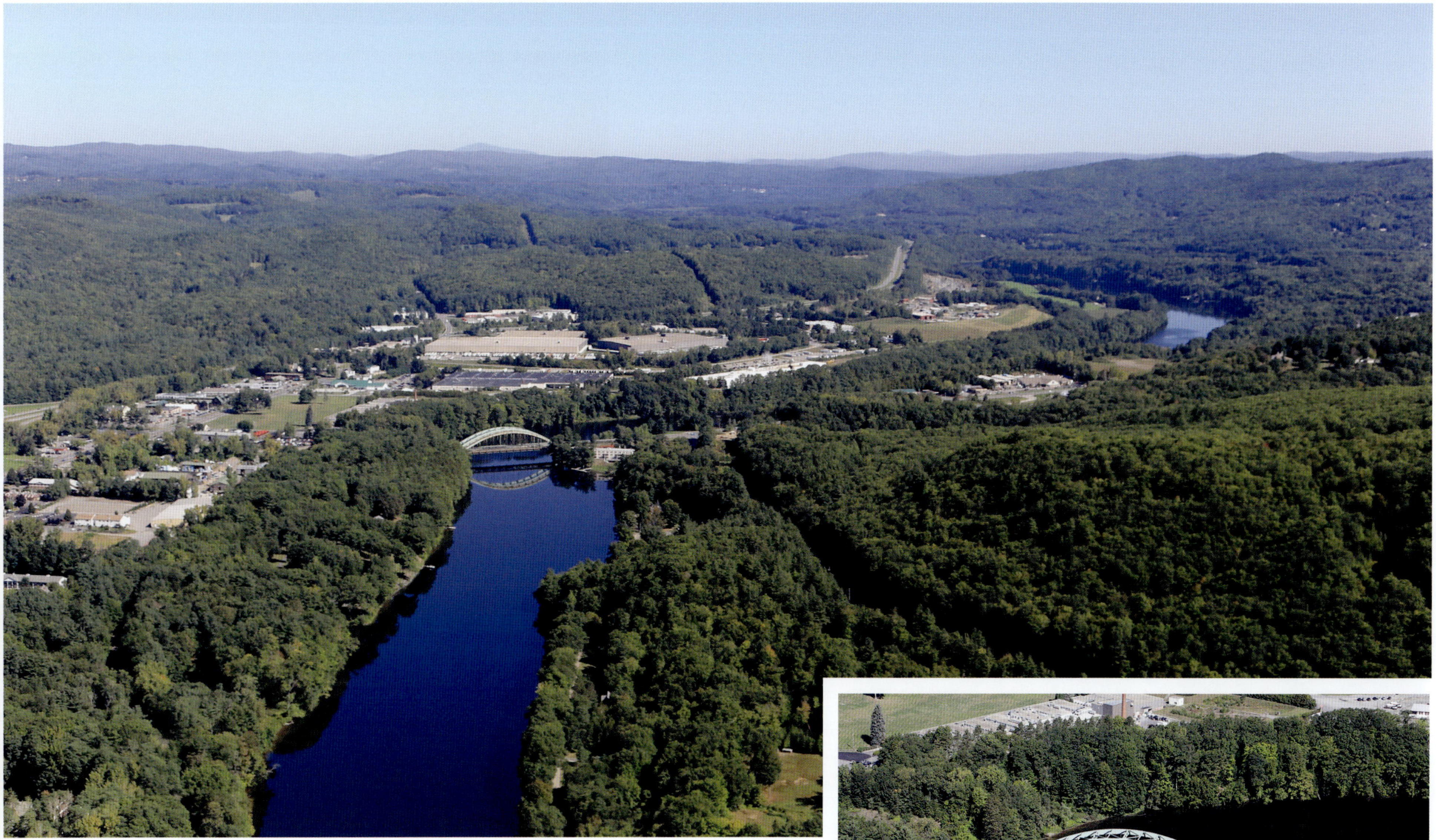

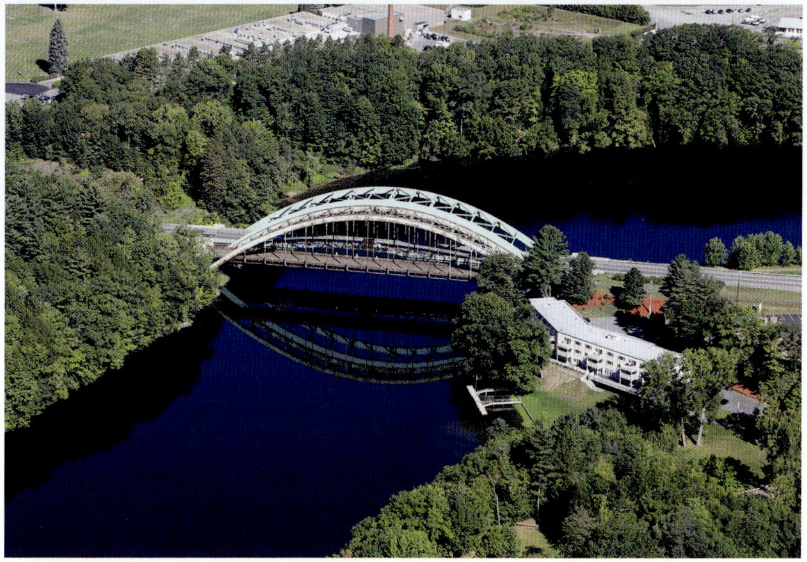

(above and right inset) Just up the river from Brattleboro, where Route 9 crosses the Connecticut, what looks like one bridge is actually two. The old 1936 bridge is now part of a river-walking path. A modern bridge that allowed for a wider roadway was built next to it in 2003 and was designed to match the graceful arched span of the original.

WALPOLE, NH

The town of Walpole was first settled in 1734 as the third in a line of colonial forts established along the river. It is named for Sir Robert Walpole, the first prime minister of Great Britain. Three miles up the river, North Walpole sits across the river from Bellows Falls.

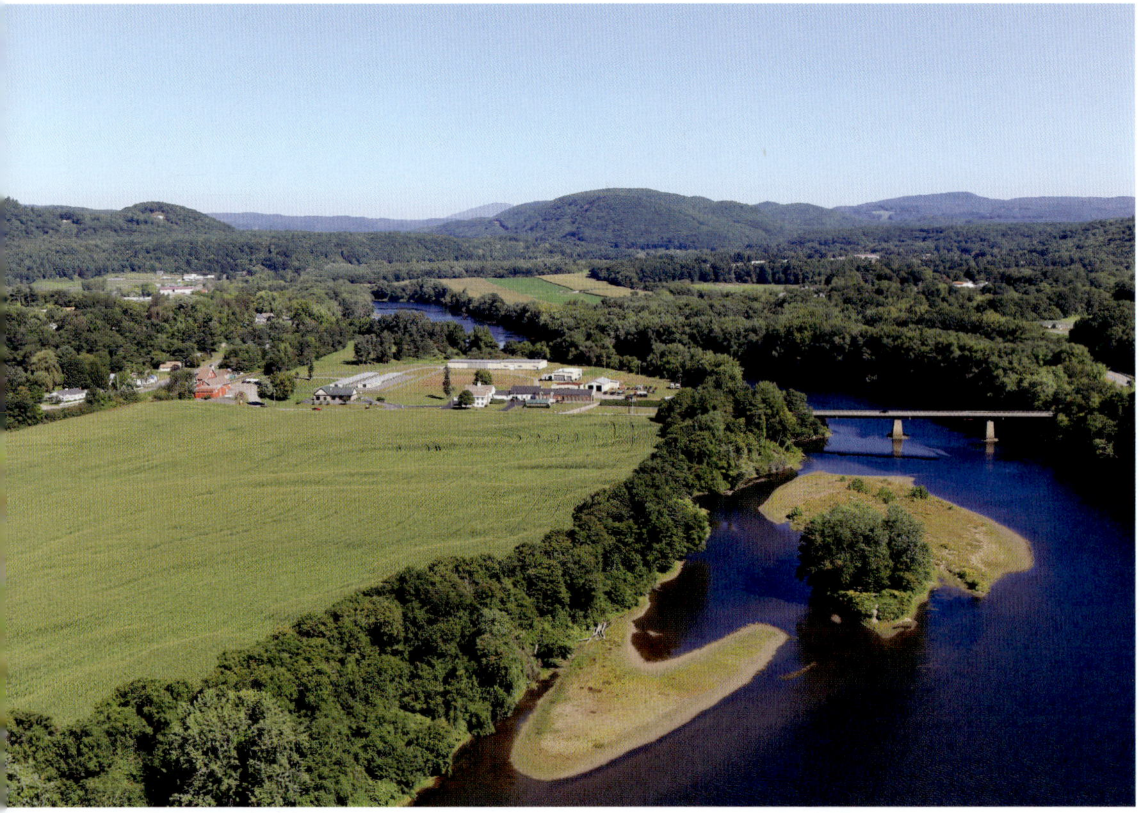

(above) Where the Route 123 Bridge crosses the river between Westminster, Vermont, and Walpole, New Hampshire, a sand-spit and a tiny island form a sheltered cove just outside the river's main channel.

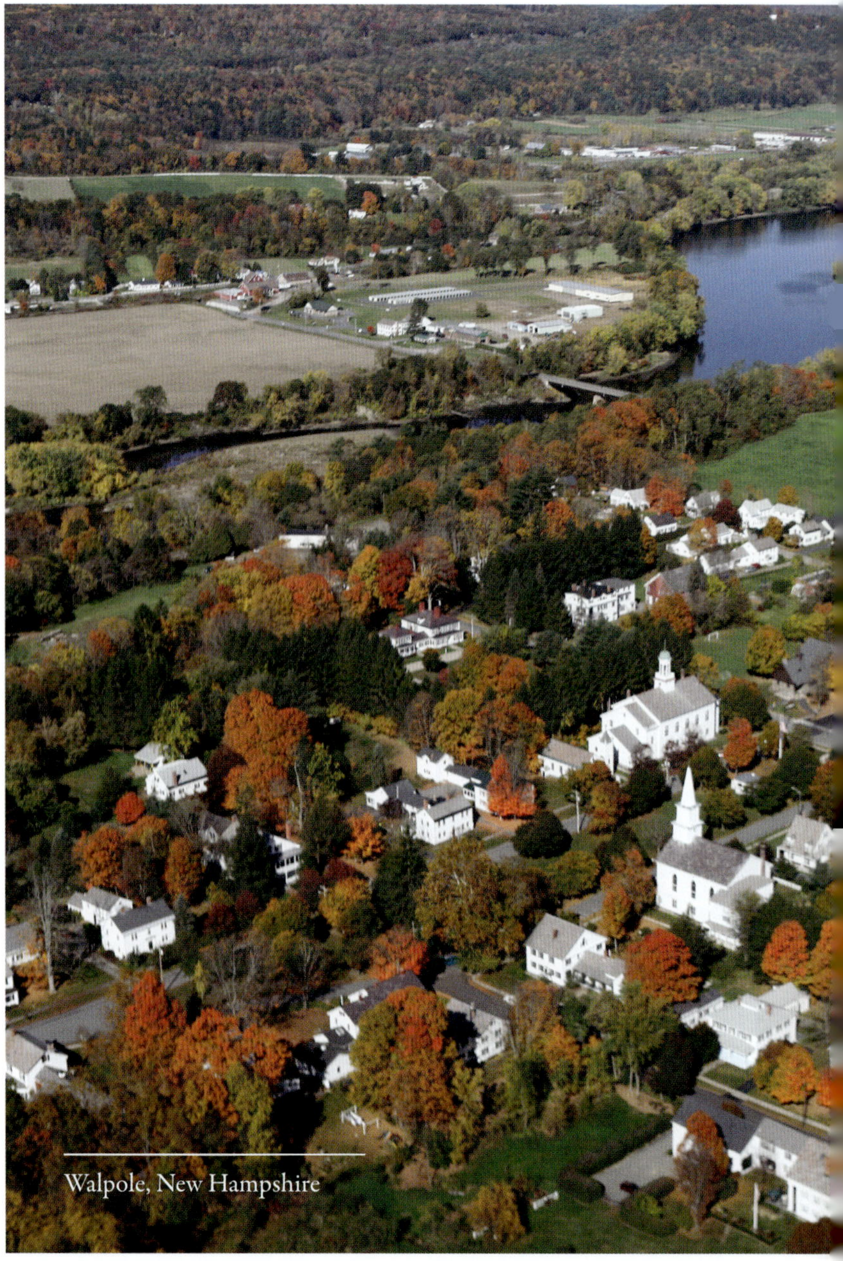

Walpole, New Hampshire

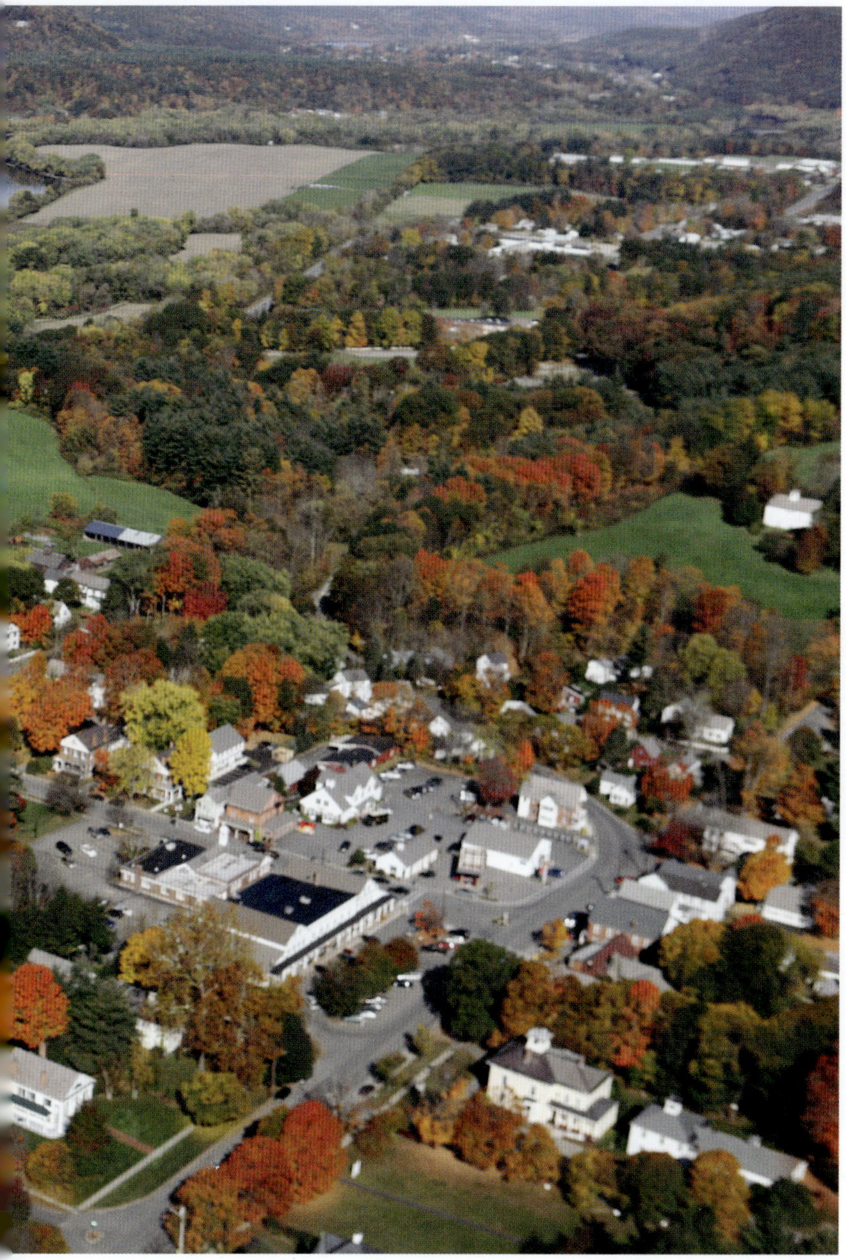

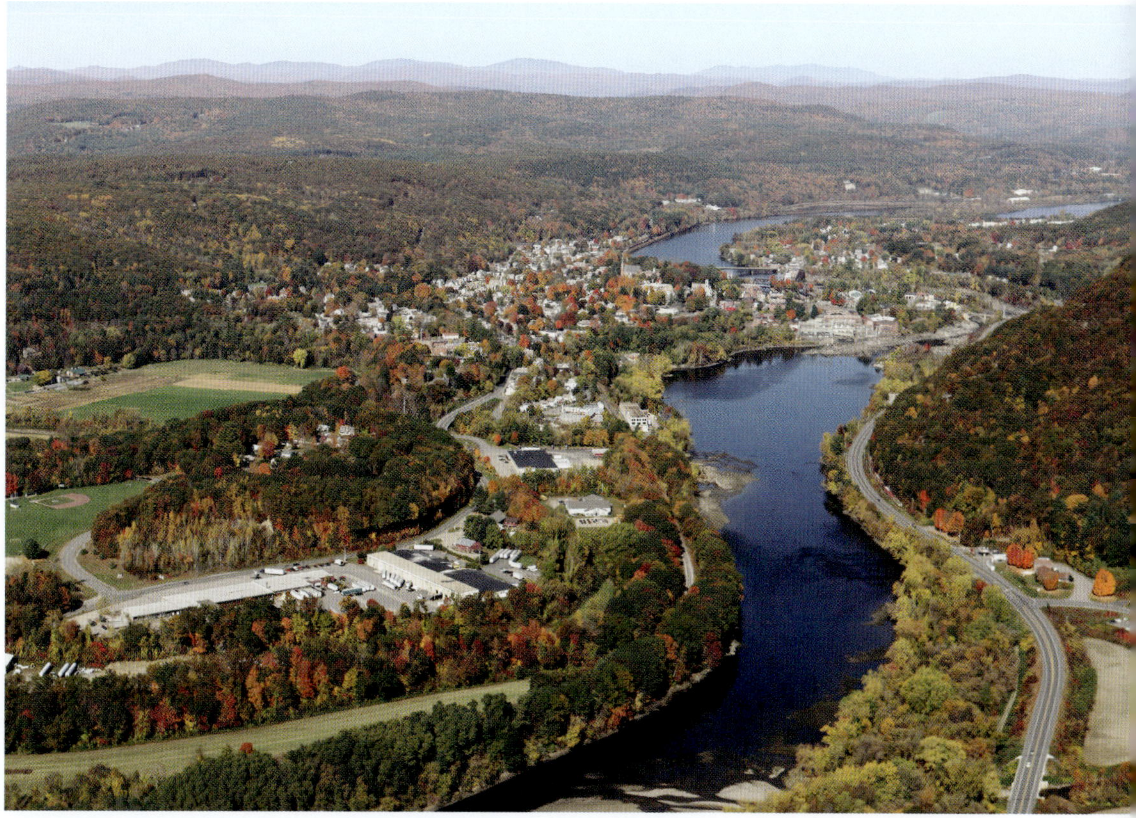

(above) Approaching Bellows Falls, Vermont, with Mount Kilburn towering above the New Hampshire side of the river.

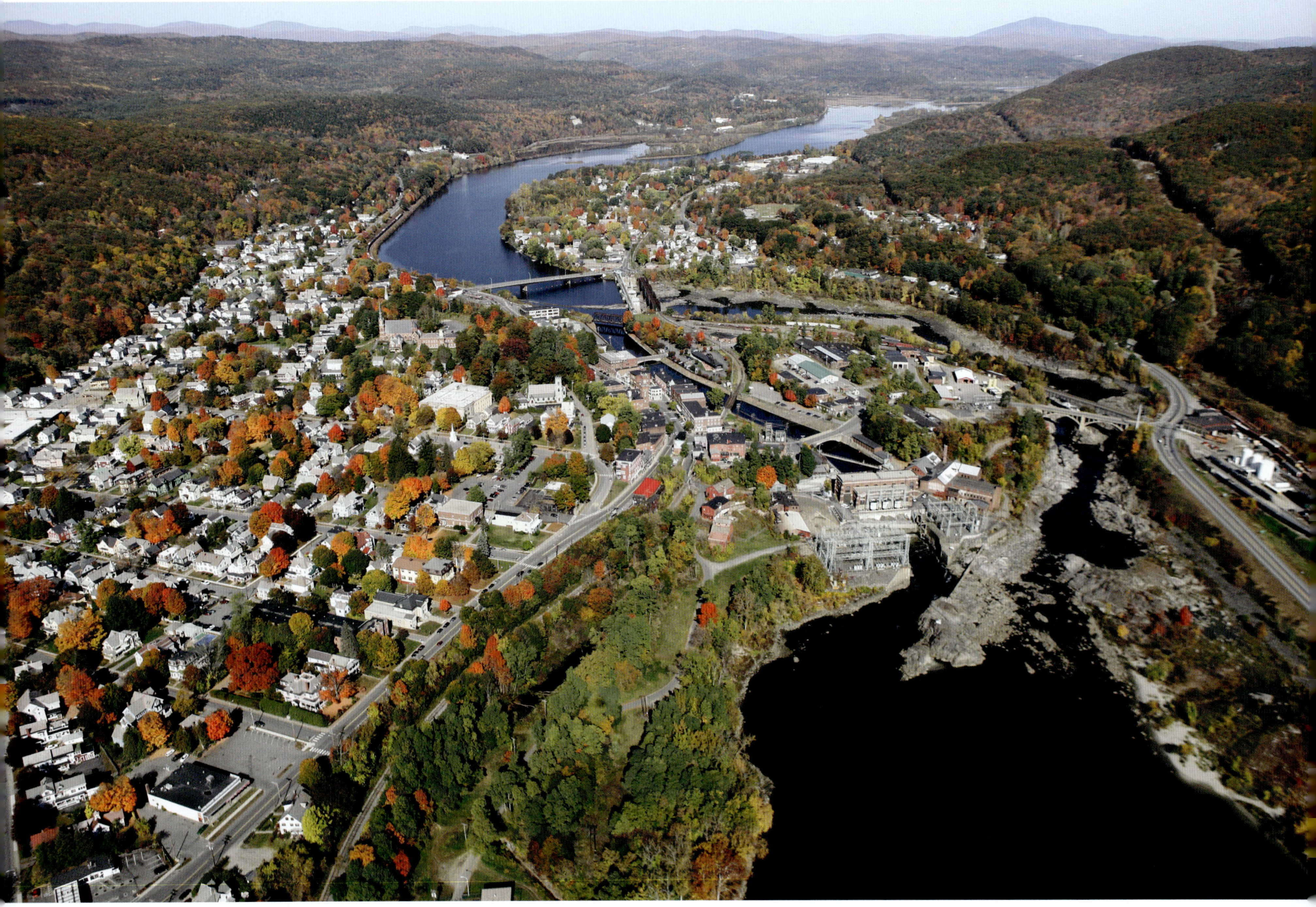

BELLOWS FALLS, VT

Bellows Falls, with its rocky gorge and 54-foot drop, is one of the best examples of technology versus geology at the advent of the industrial revolution. The first bridge ever built on the Connecticut River was constructed here in 1785 joining Bellows Falls and North Walpole. The obvious impediment to river transportation was solved in 1802 by the completion of a canal that bypassed the falls and incorporated eight sets of locks for lifting vessels. By 1849, two railway lines made transporting goods easier than by boat. This allowed the canal to be used instead to power mills and factories that produced paper, textiles, carriages, rifles, furniture, organs, and a variety of other products. Since 1928, a dam and hydroelectric power plant at the end of the canal have been producing energy from the river, one of sixteen such plants on the Connecticut River. The headwaters formed by the dam reach twenty-six miles upstream.

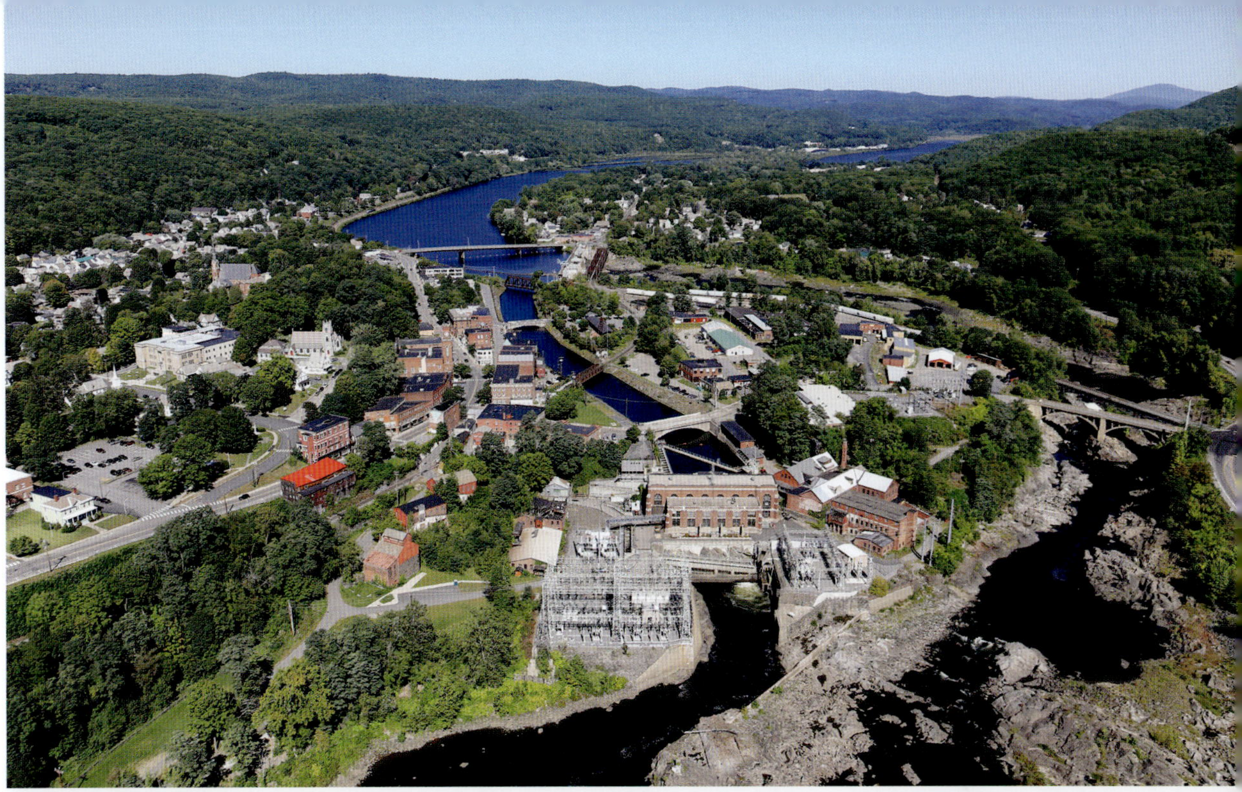

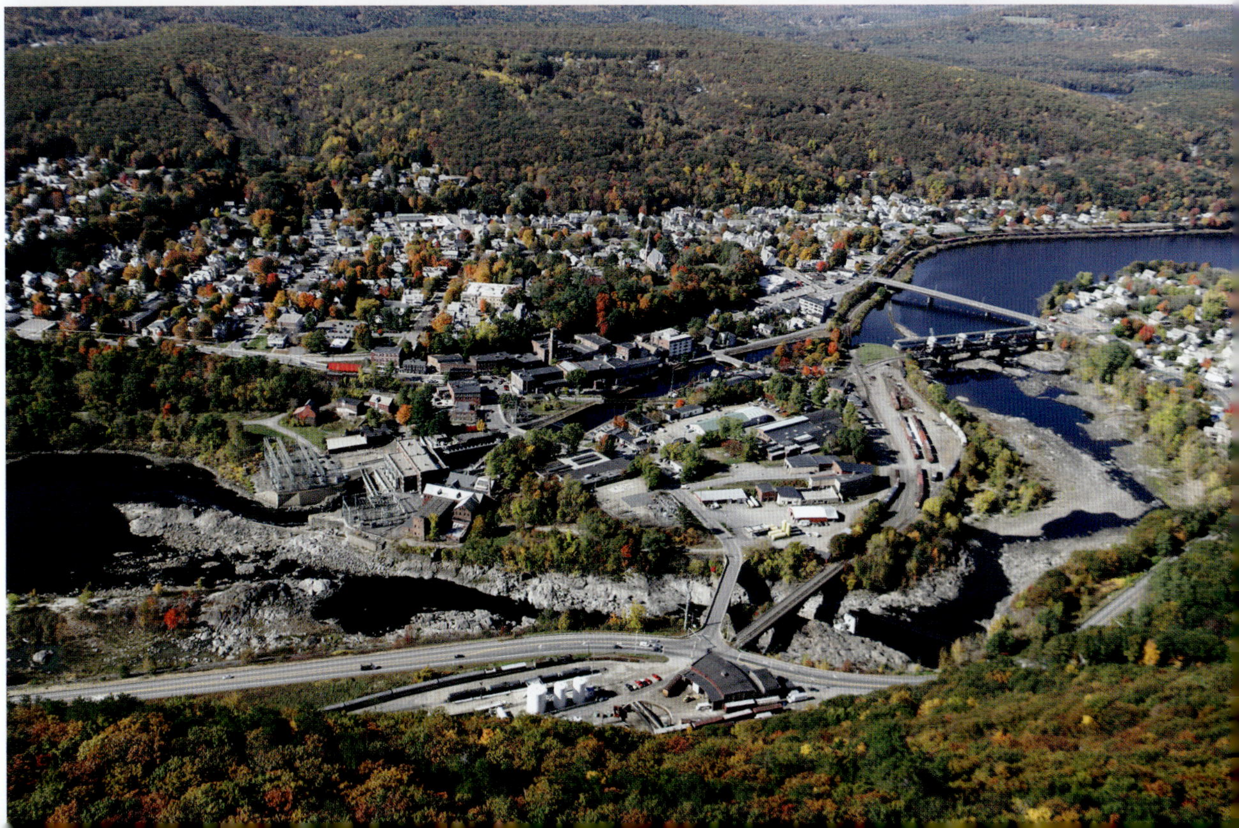

(top right) The hydroelectric plant at the end of the canal has a maximum generating capacity of 49 megawatts

(bottom right) The entire complex seen from above Mount Kilburn reveals the interwoven labyrinth that includes the river, the roads and bridges, and the town nestled just beyond factories behind the canal.

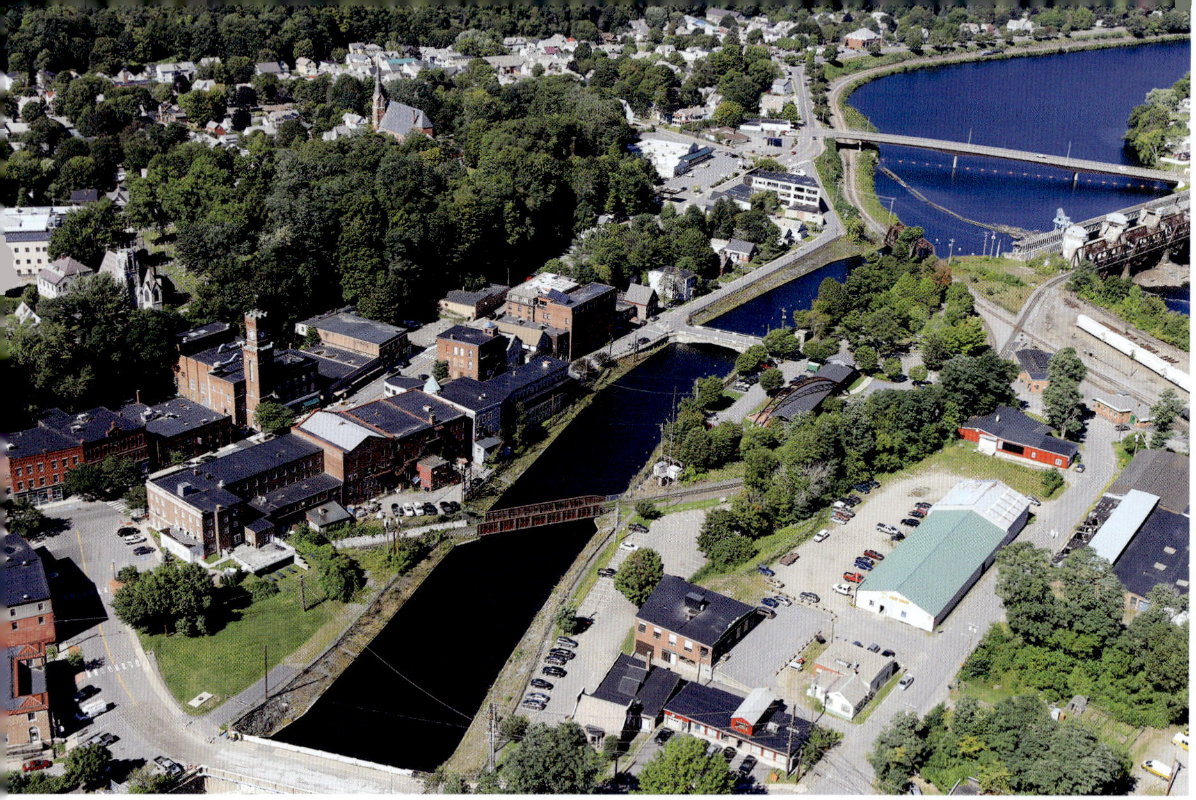

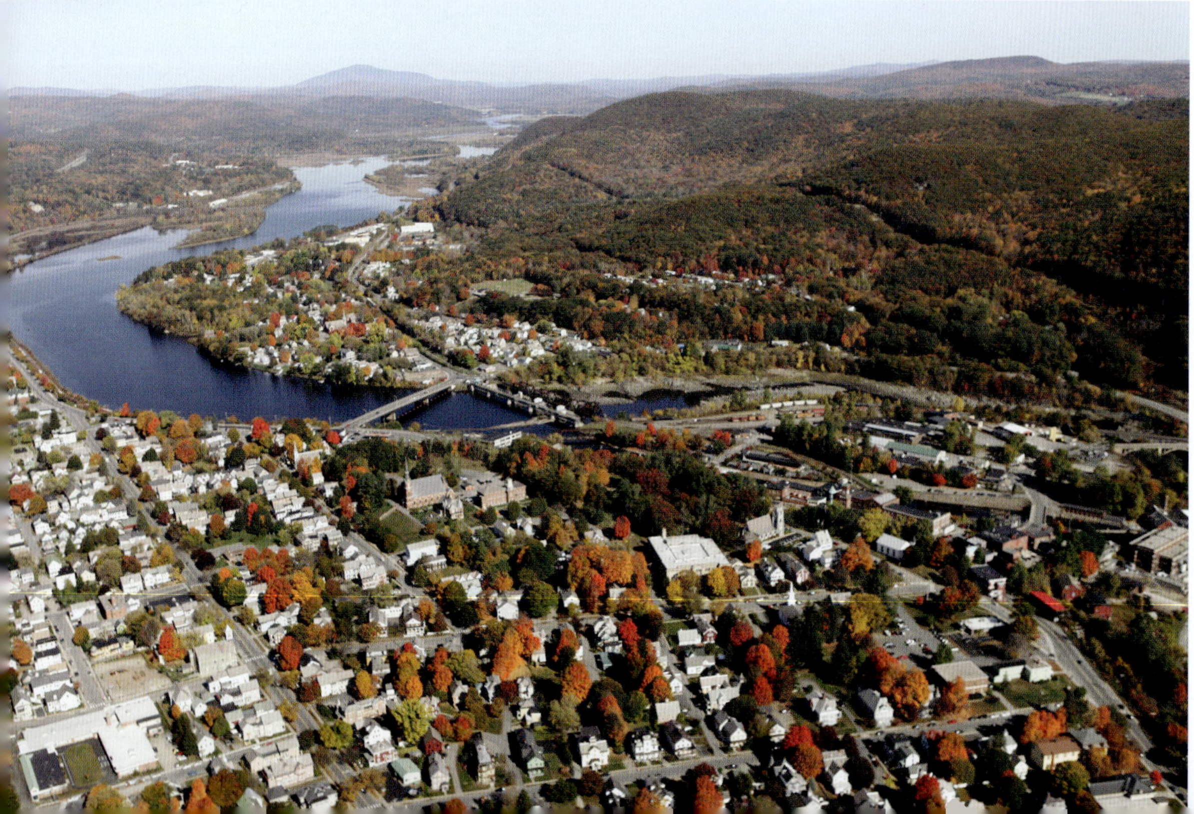

(top left) Old factories and mills line the canal that provided waterpower via the river just above the falls.

(bottom left) Looking upriver toward the headwaters of Bellows Falls Dam, North Walpole juts out beneath Mount Kilburn.

(right) The headwaters of Bellows Falls Dam stretch twenty-six miles up river. The river bends and twists through farmland as it flows south from Charlestown toward Bellows Falls and Walpole

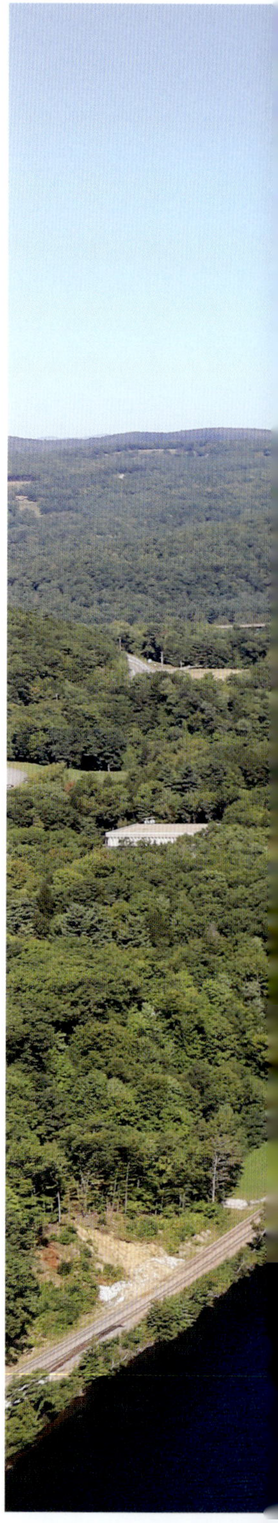

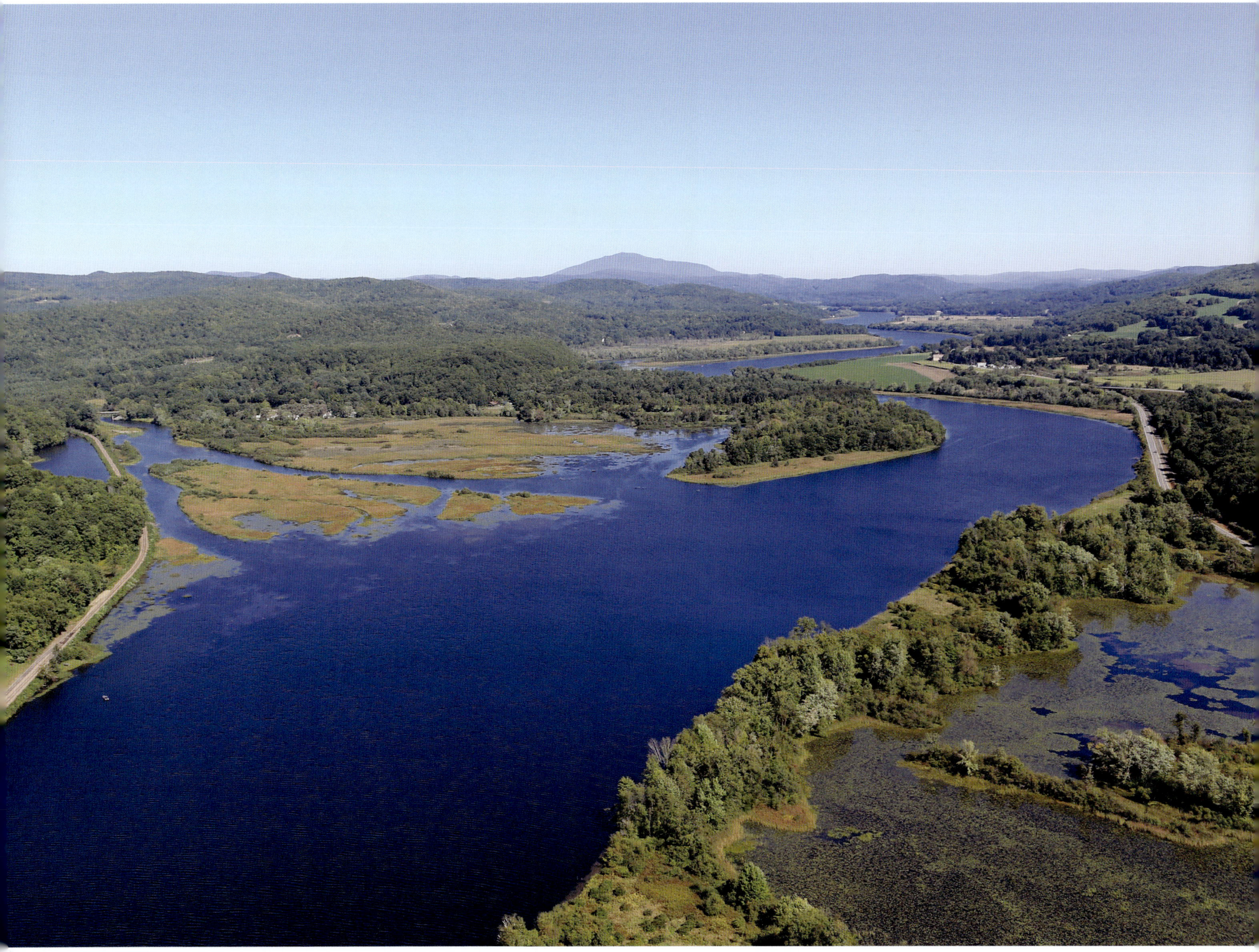

RIVER RESOURCES, WATER, WOOD, SOIL AND STONE

The drained ancient lake bottom, rich with fertile sedimentary soil, became the productive farmland that helped New England prosper.

The varied rock formations, created millions of years ago, shaped the river's course and the landscape around us. Quarrying stone became one of the most important industries along the lower river, peaking between the 1880s to the 1920s.

Waterpower, propelled by the river's never-ending drive towards the sea, turned colonial mill wheels, and later filled canals and powered the industrial revolution. It still generates much of the electricity we depend on in New England today.

The once limitless forests along the course of the river have fed shipyards, sawmills and paper mills, making timber one of the region's most important commodities.

Add to all of this the energy and ingenuity of the people who have come to live and work along the river, from early native inhabitants, to European settlers and immigrants from around the world, and there is a pretty amazing story to tell.

(right, top) Along the course of the Connecticut, numerous dams and canals were built to harness the water-power generated by the river's 2,760 foot drop from the source to the Sound. It powered the industrial revolution. (right, bottom) Stone, like that quarried in Portland, Connecticut (now a recreation center), has been one of the region's most valuable resources.

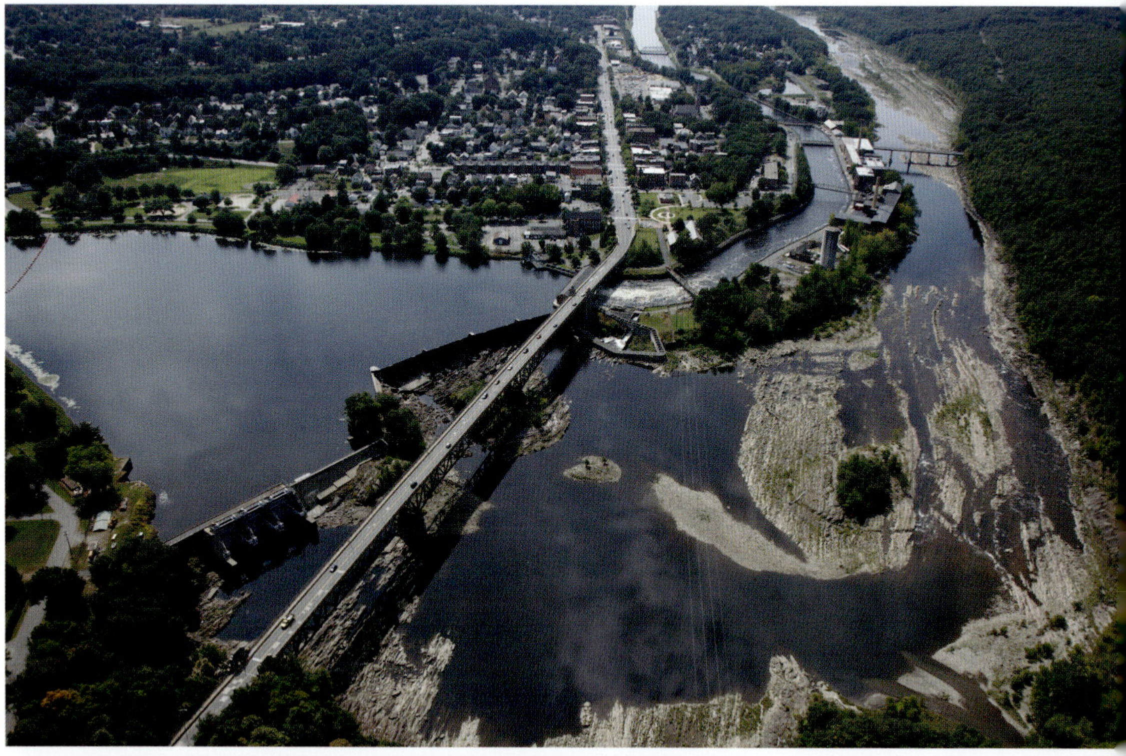

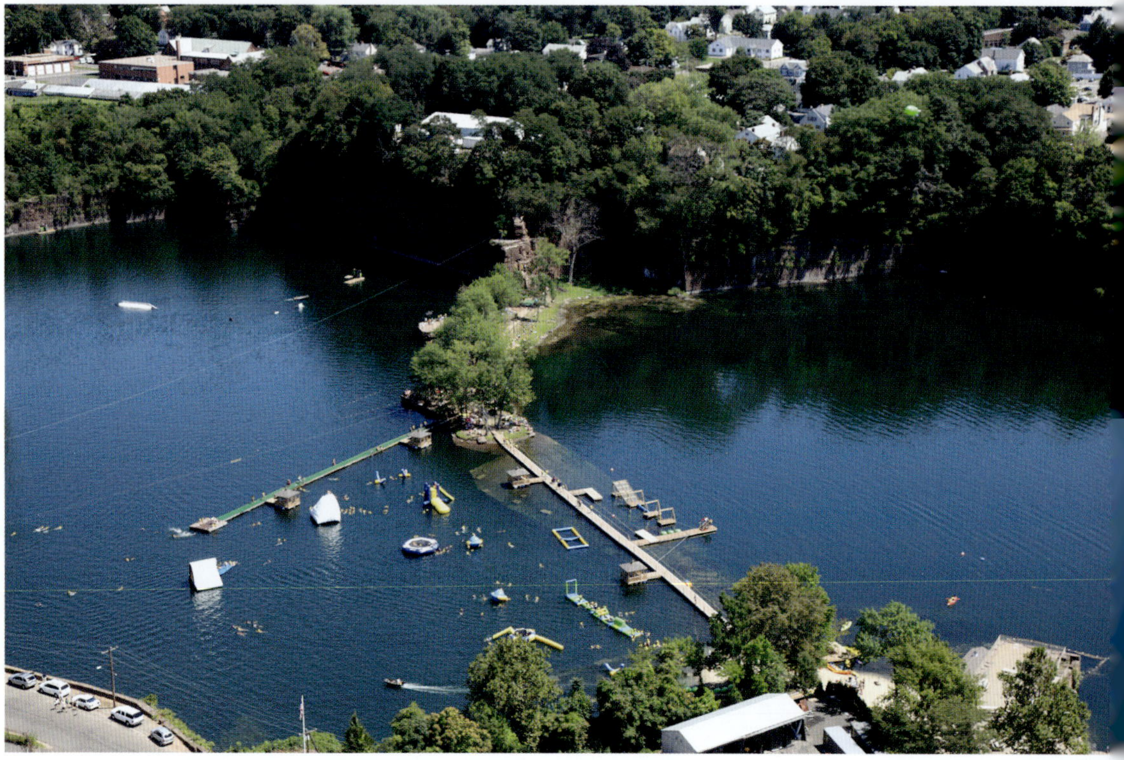

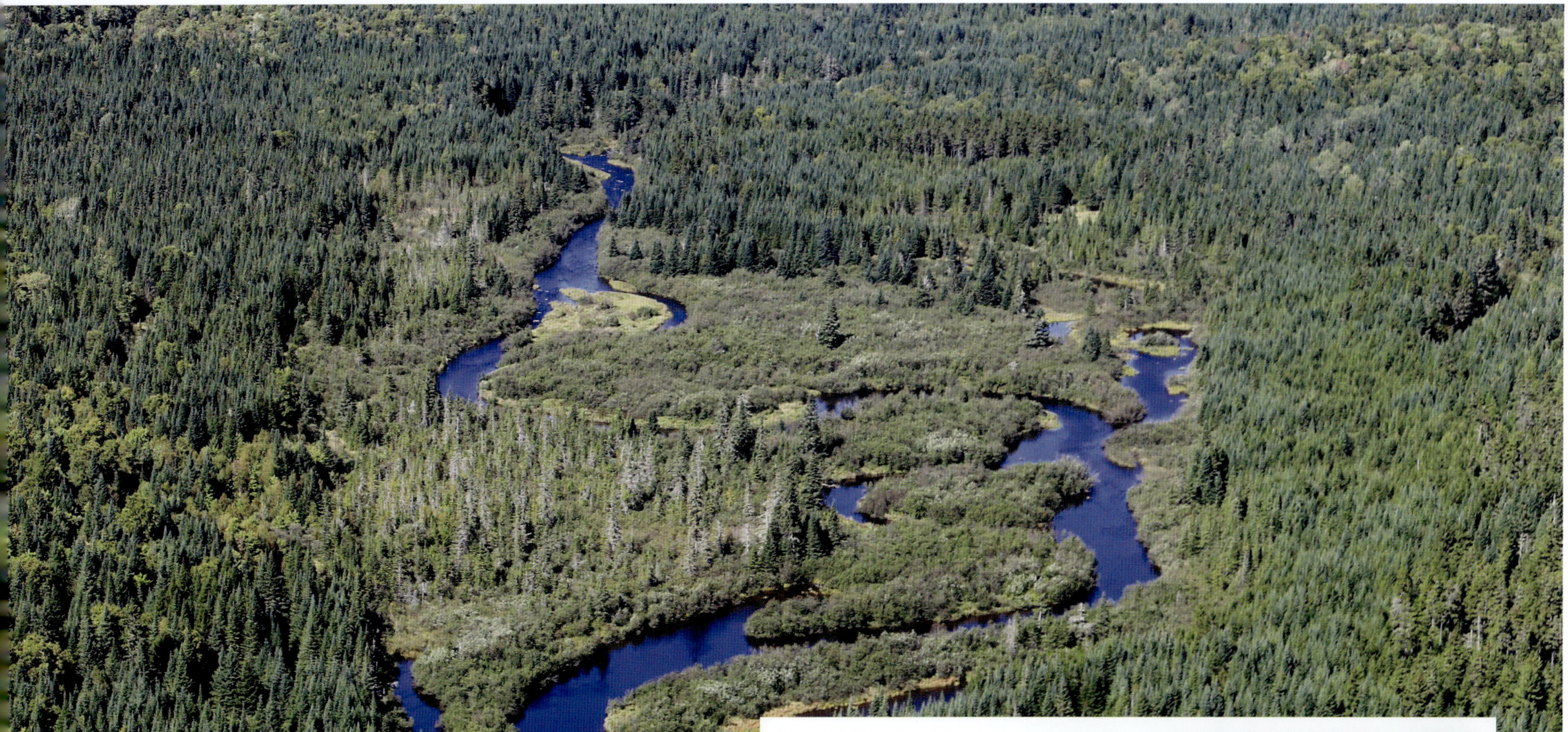

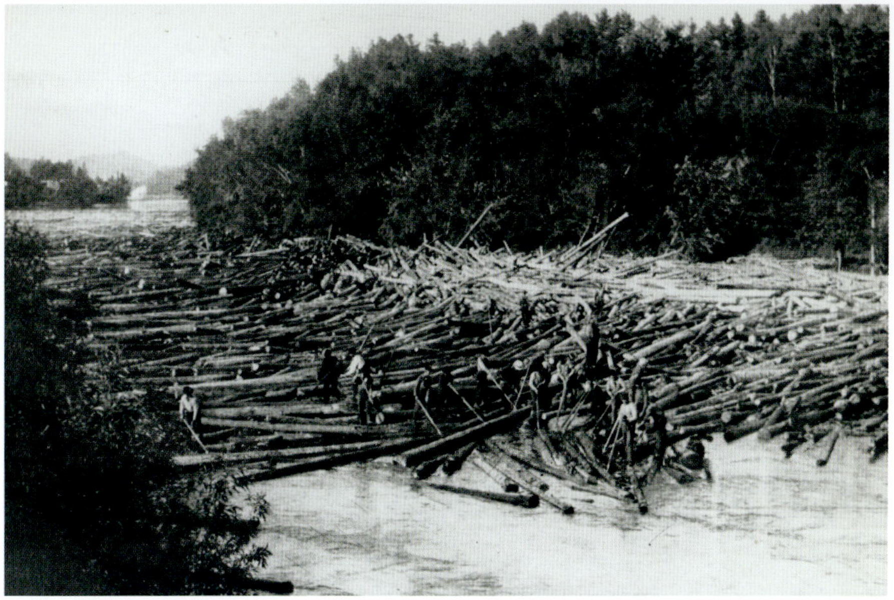

(right) Log drives brought timber from northern forests to supply paper and lumber mills along the river and shipyards near its mouth

THE NEXT HUNDRED MILES

Charlestown to Comerford Dam

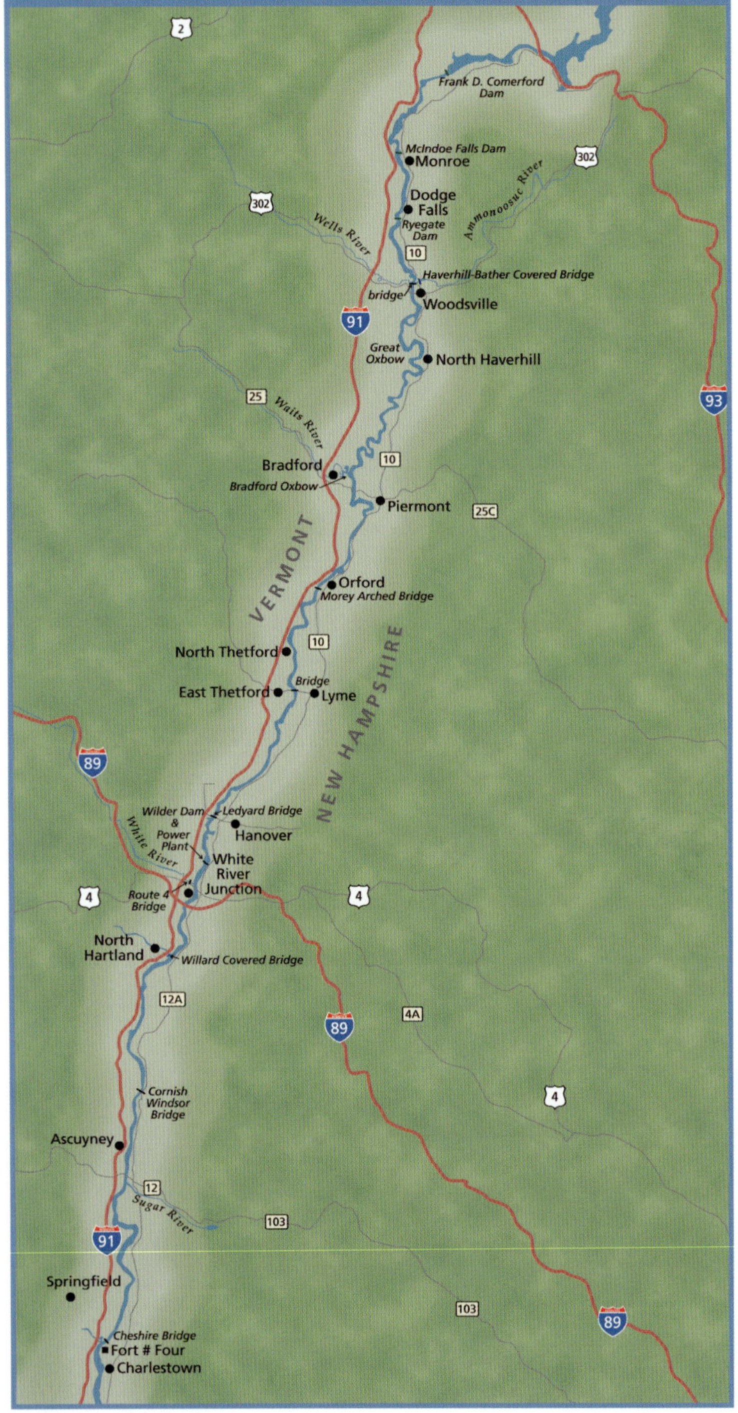

CHARLESTOWN, NH

Colonial outpost, Fort Number Four, was settled in 1740 in a bend in the river where the Black River joins the Connecticut. The fort played a significant role during the French and Indian wars. Most famously, thirty-two defenders withstood a four-day siege by an enemy force comprised of 400 French troops and their Native American allies. Named Charlestown in 1753, the New Hampshire town became known as a center of law, rivaled only by Boston. Today a reproduction of the fort is an important attraction where re-enactments keep this strategic outpost's legacy alive.

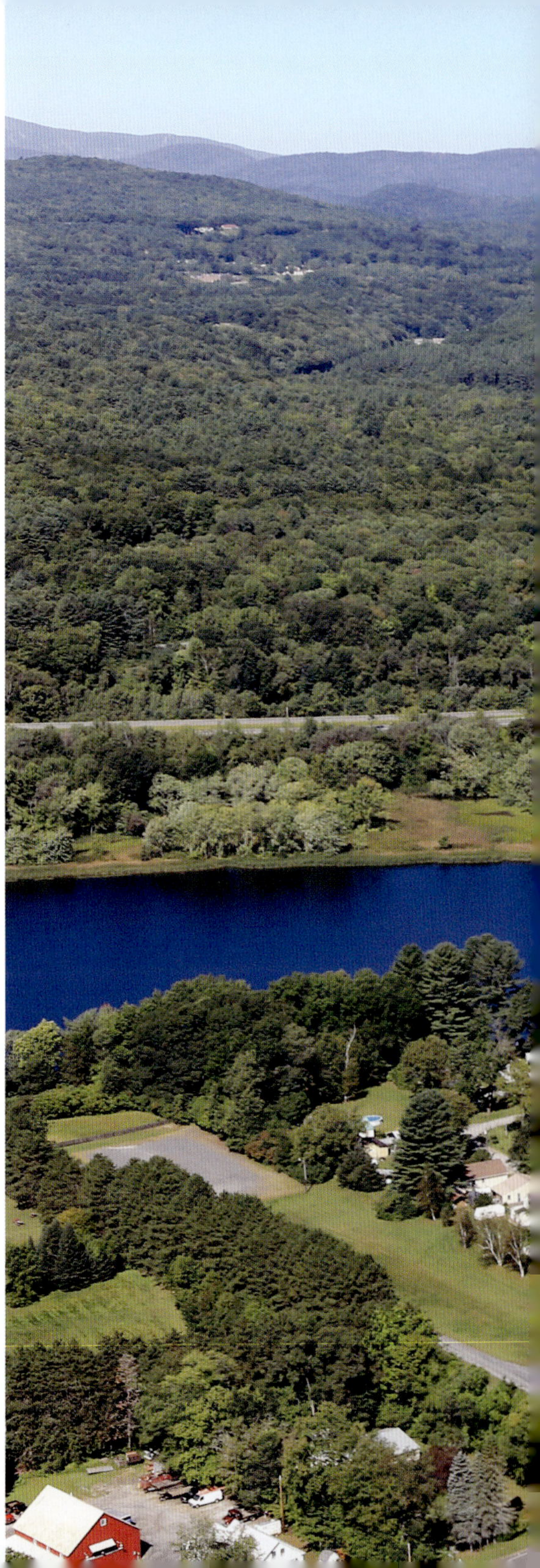

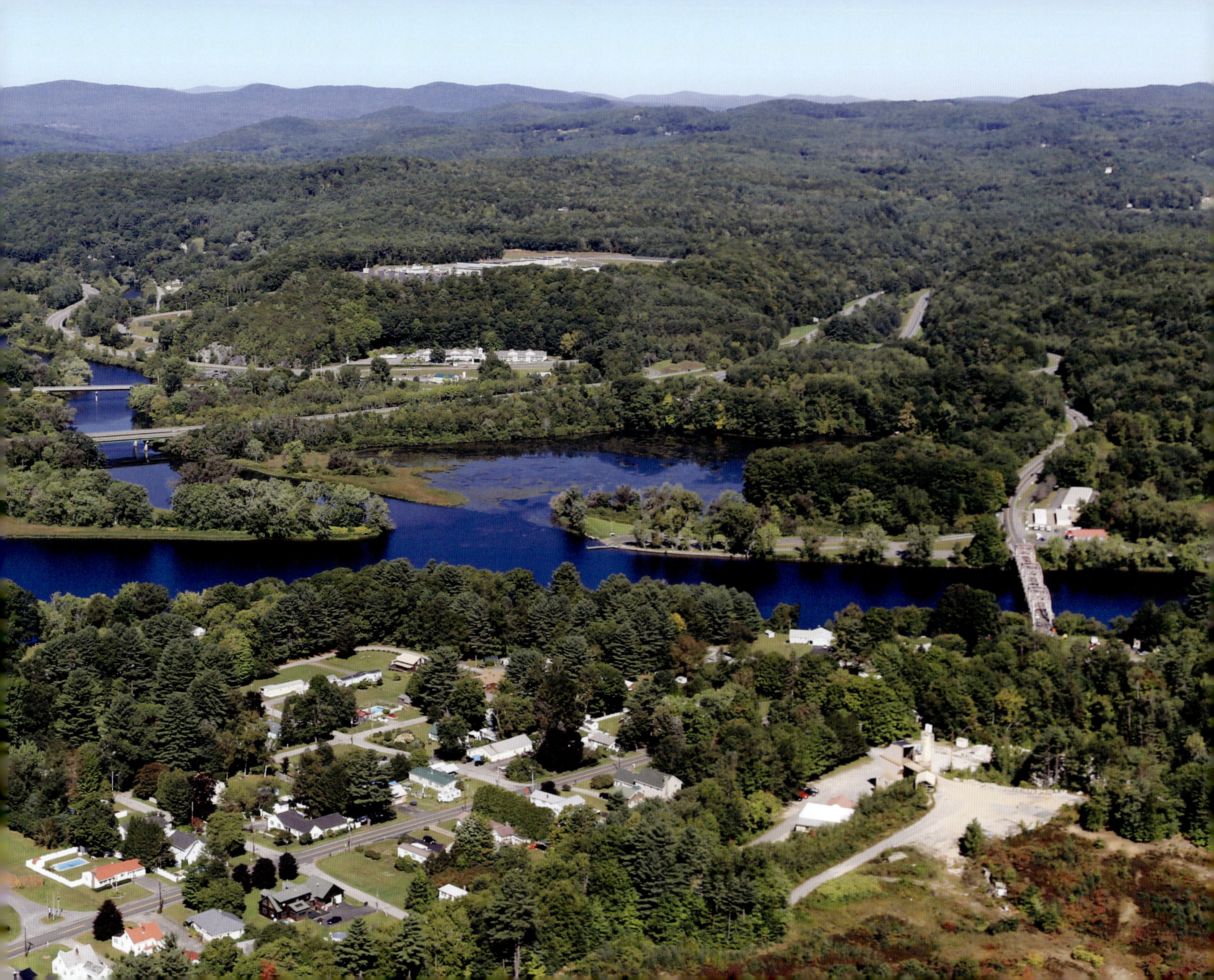

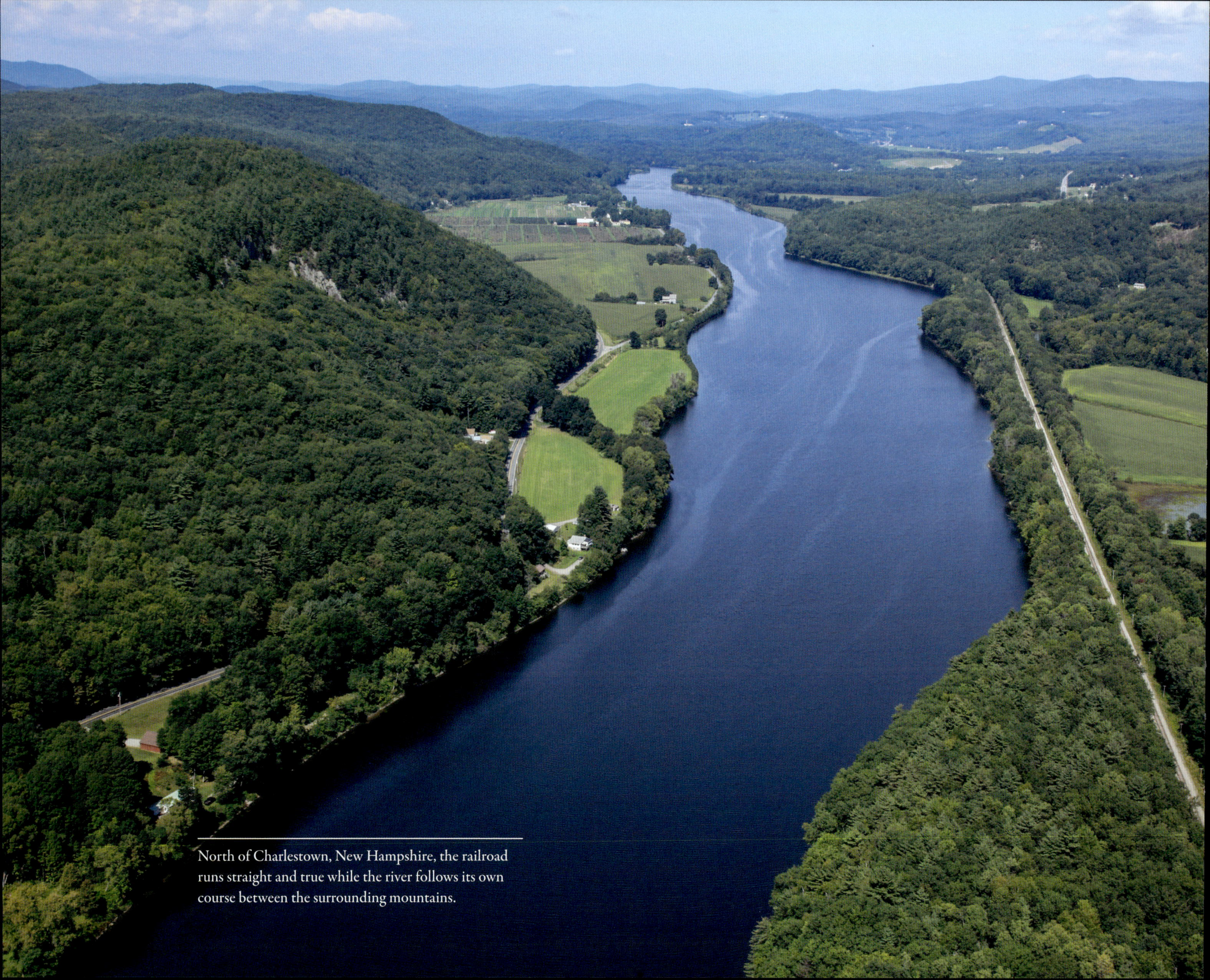

North of Charlestown, New Hampshire, the railroad runs straight and true while the river follows its own course between the surrounding mountains.

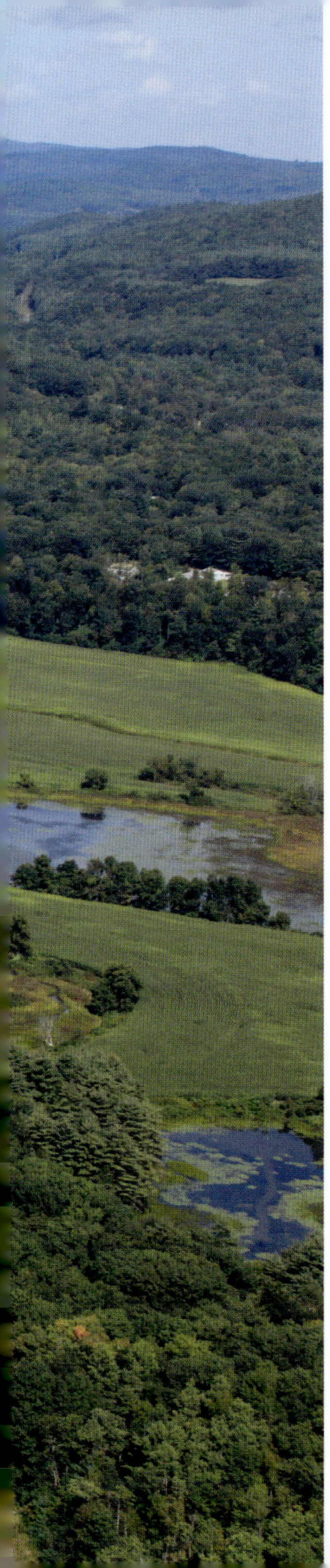

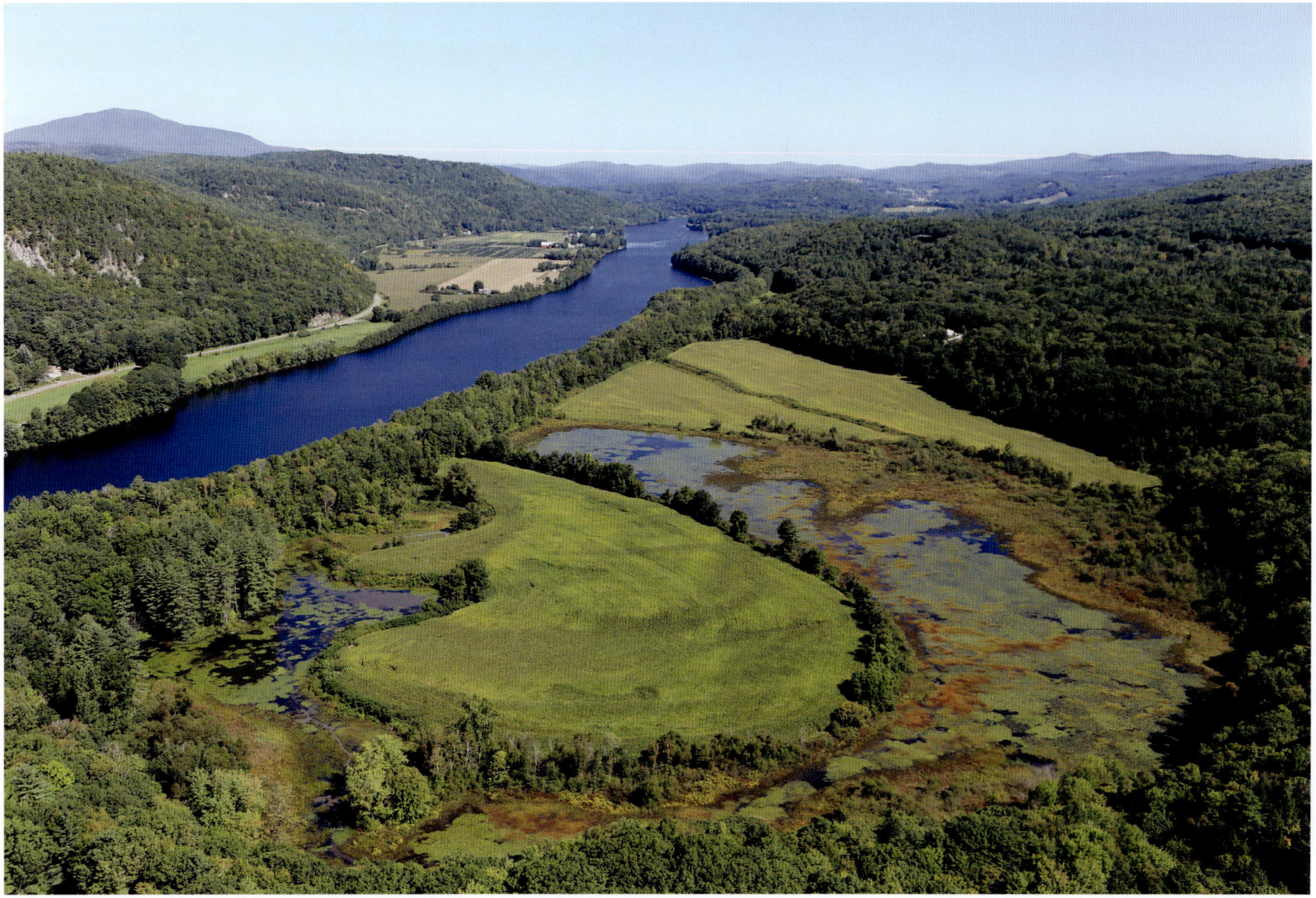

(above) With the 3,130-foot-high peak of Mount Ascutney in the distance, a cut-off oxbow on the New Hampshire side of the river provides an oddly shaped patch of farmland surrounded by marshes that mark what was once part of the river's course.

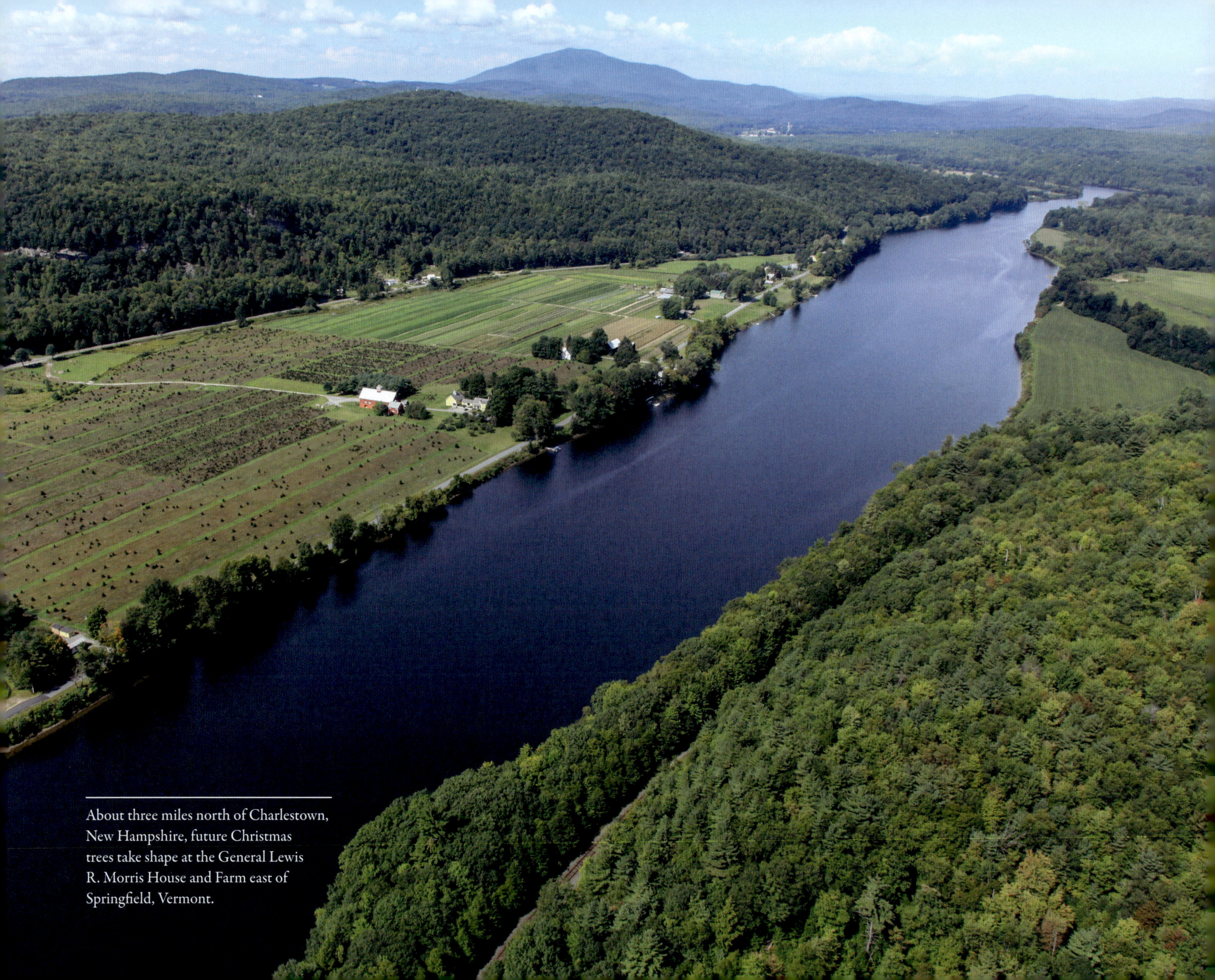

About three miles north of Charlestown, New Hampshire, future Christmas trees take shape at the General Lewis R. Morris House and Farm east of Springfield, Vermont.

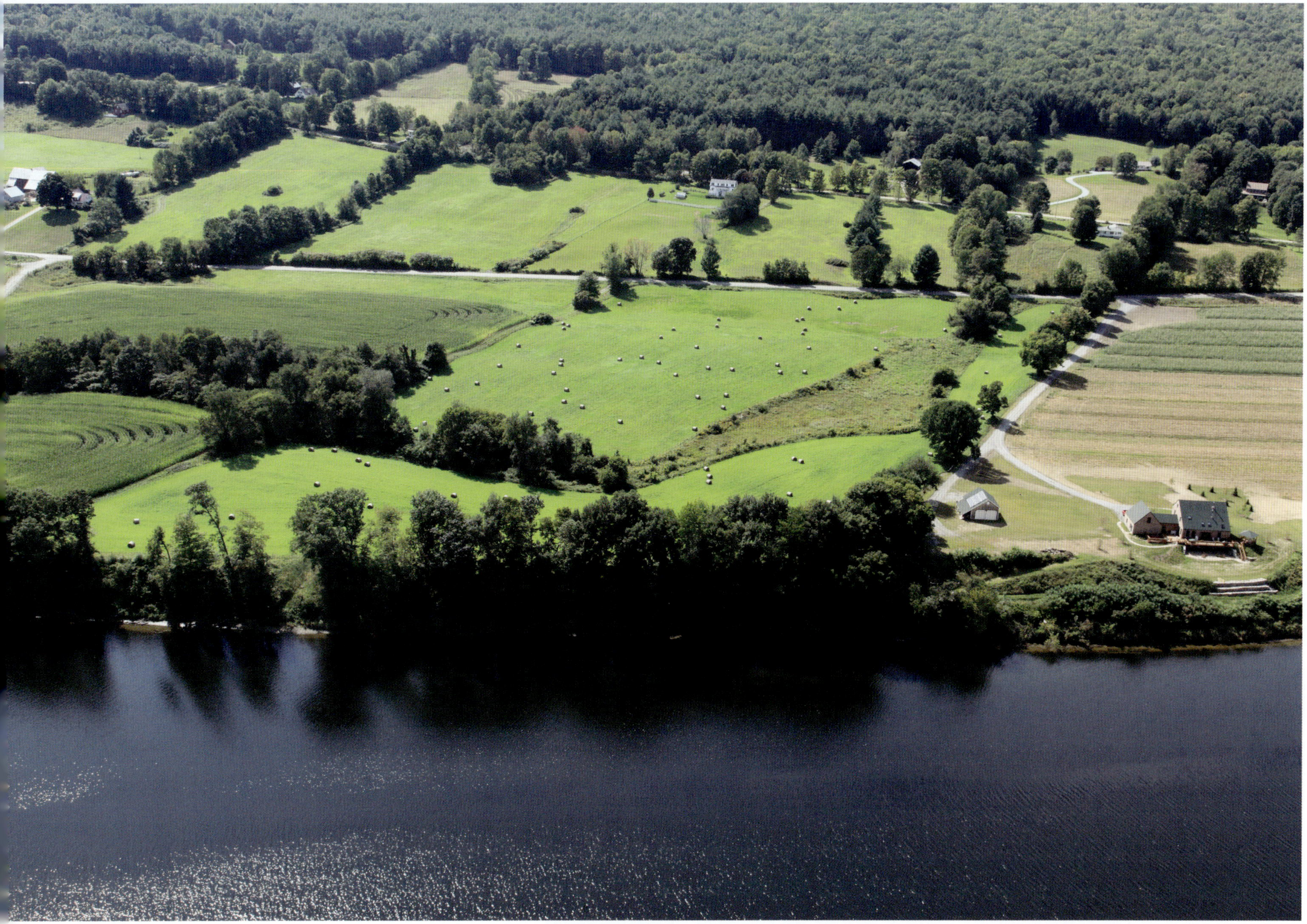

Rolled hay bales dot a pastoral scene along the New Hampshire side of the river.

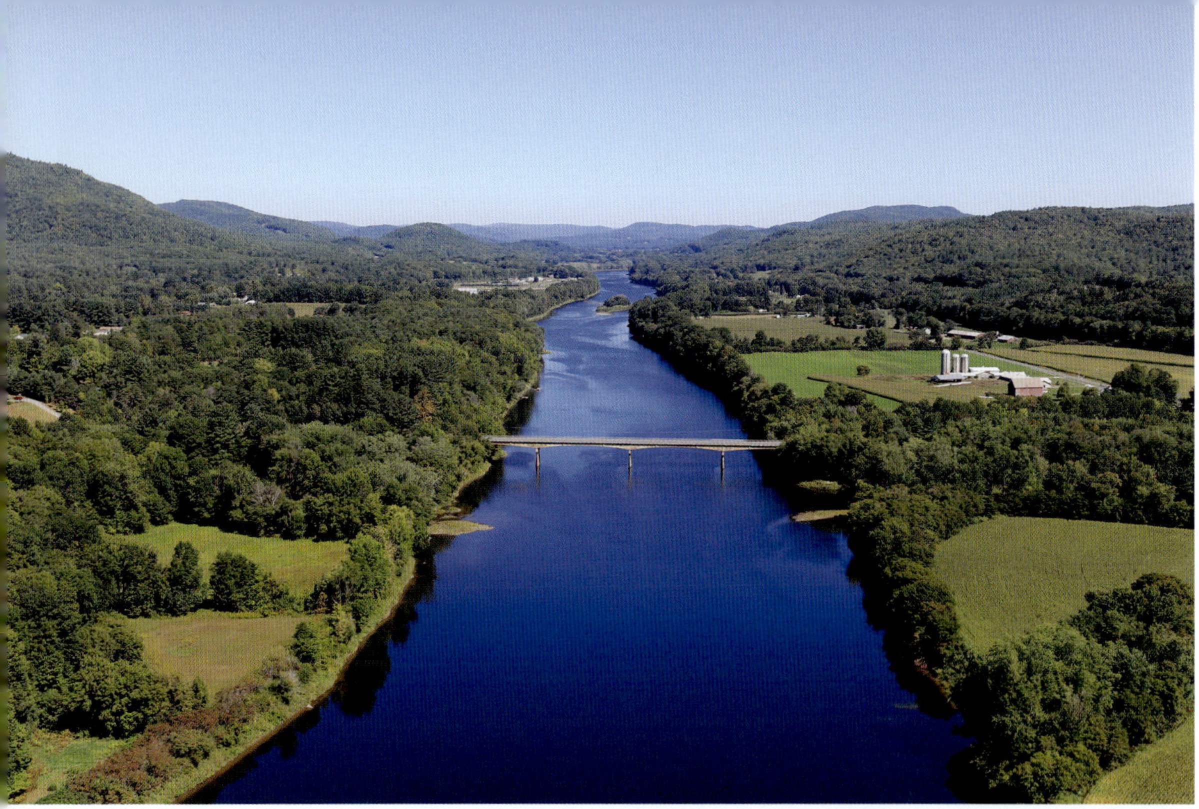

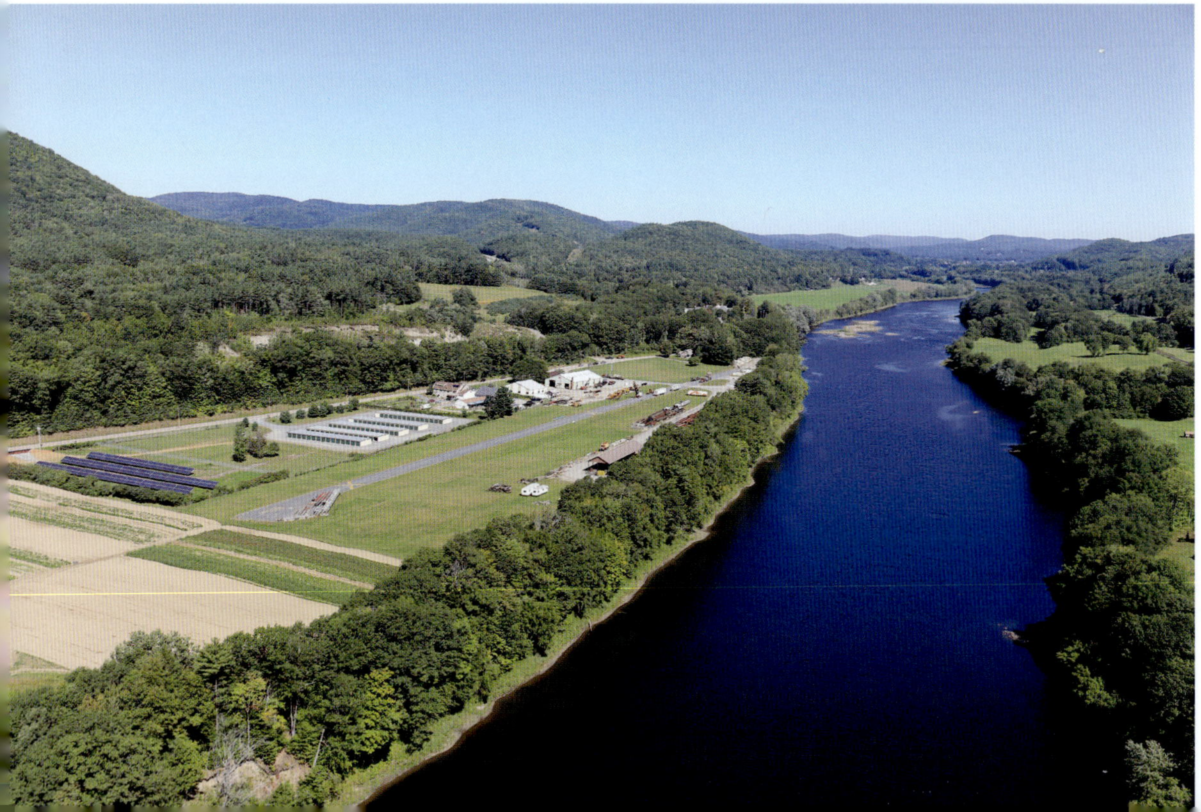

(top left) VT Route 12 crosses the river near Ascutney, Vermont, where the Sugar River joins the Connecticut.

(bottom left) X marks the spot. Tom pointed out that the X's on the runway indicate to pilots that Miller airport is no longer in service.

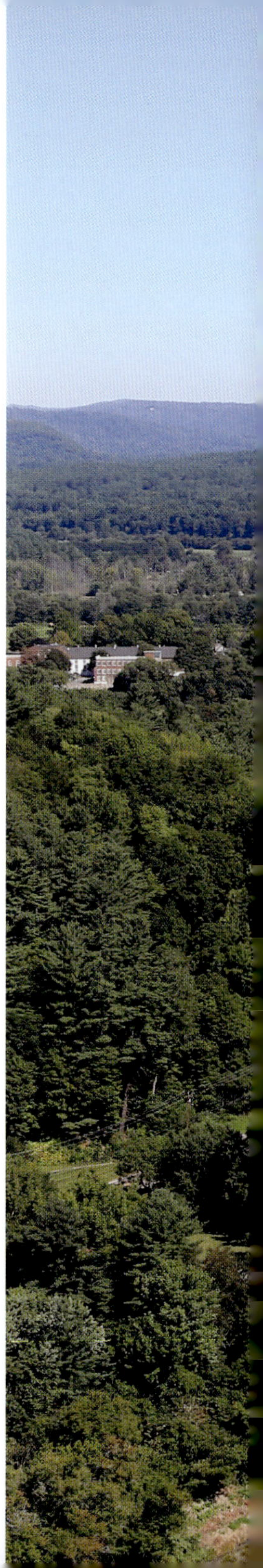

(right) Beyond the railway bridge lies Windsor, Vermont, and the Cornish-Windsor covered bridge.

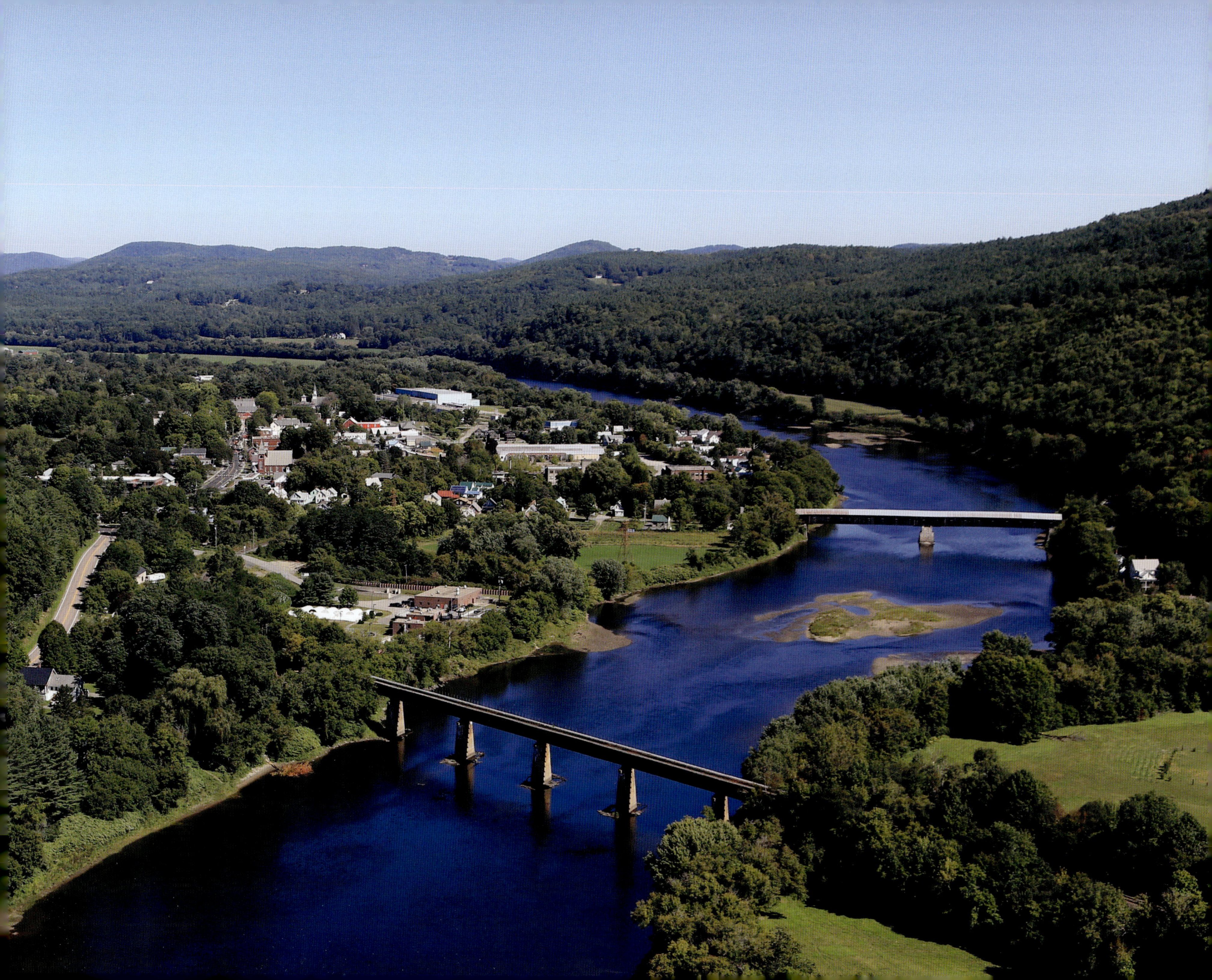

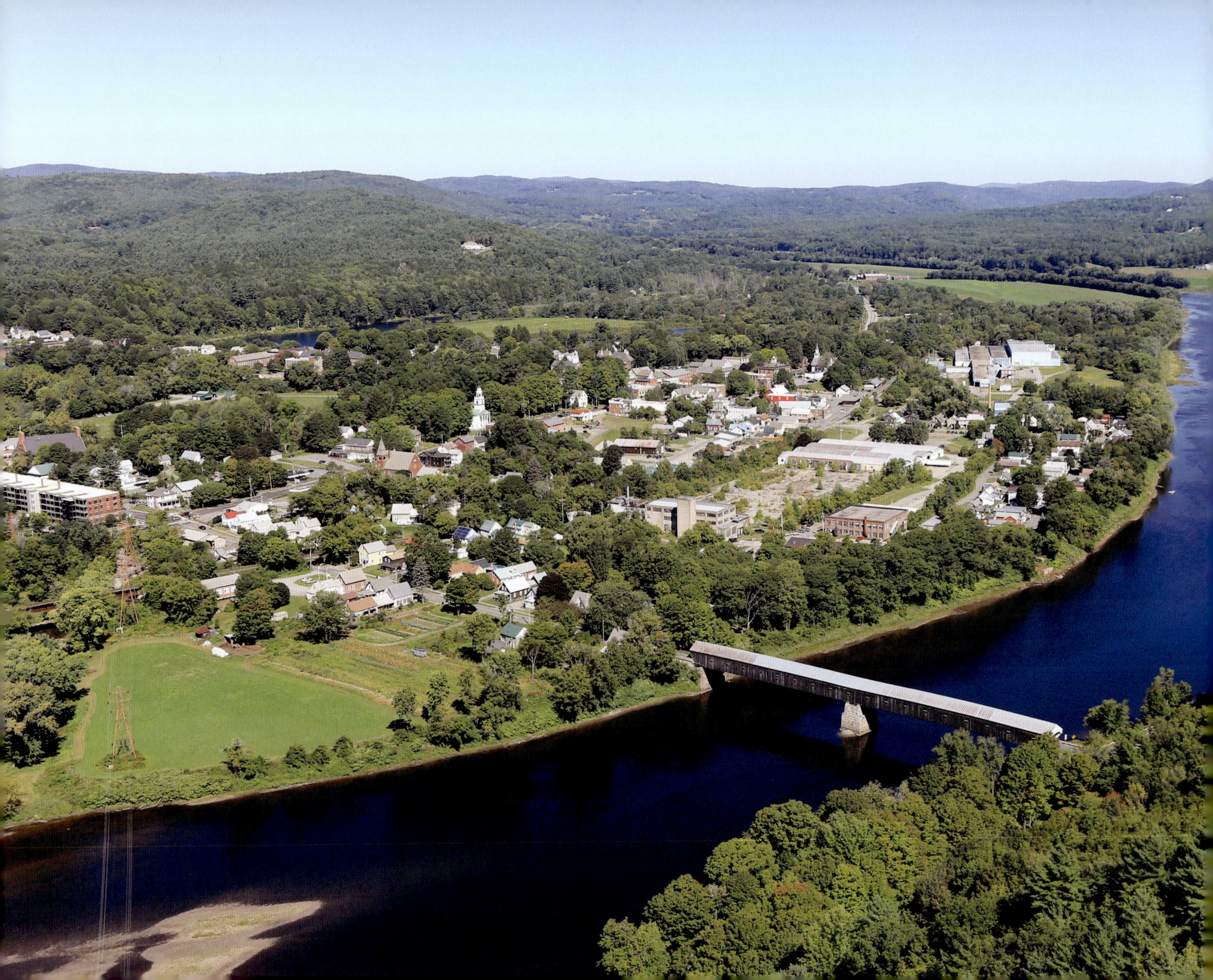

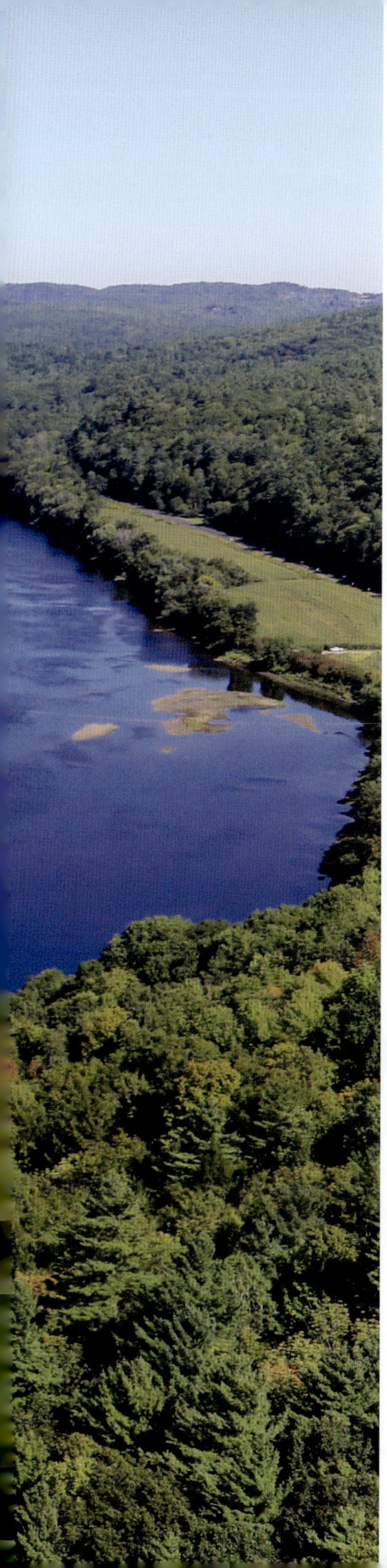

CORNISH-WINDSOR BRIDGE

Completed in 1866, the 450-foot Cornish-Windsor Bridge is the longest covered wooden bridge in the United States. It is the fourth bridge built on this site linking Windsor, Vermont, with Cornish, New Hampshire. The previous three bridges, built in 1796, 1824, and 1849 respectively, were each washed away by floods. The present bridge was completed less than seven months after the previous bridge was destroyed and has survived several floods. It incorporates two spans of diagonal lattice truss construction supported by one central stone block pier. Designed in the age of horse and buggies, the bridge now supports modern two-lane traffic restricted only by a legal load limit of six tons. In 1970 it was designated a National Historic Civil Engineering Landmark and is on the National Register of Historic Places.

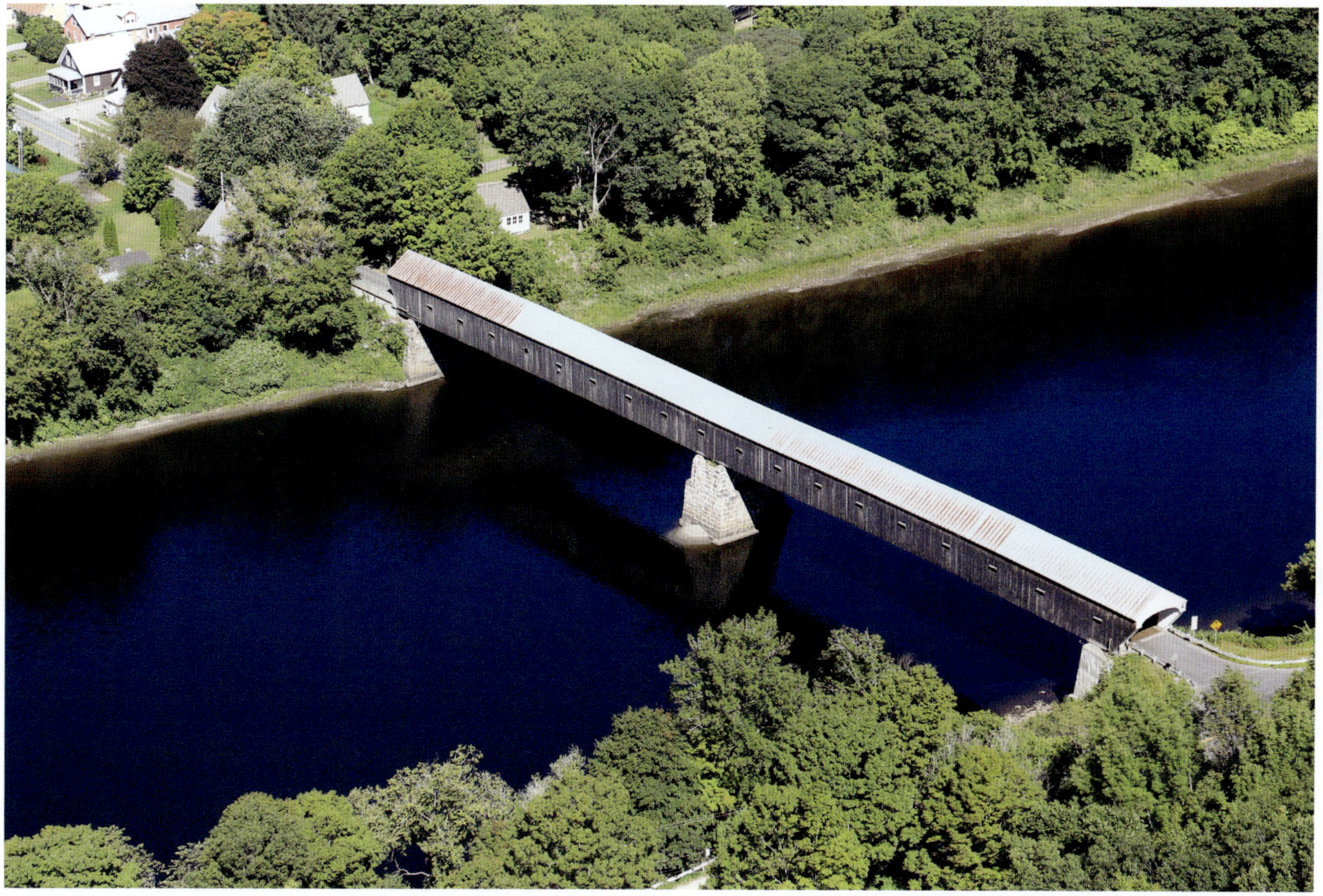

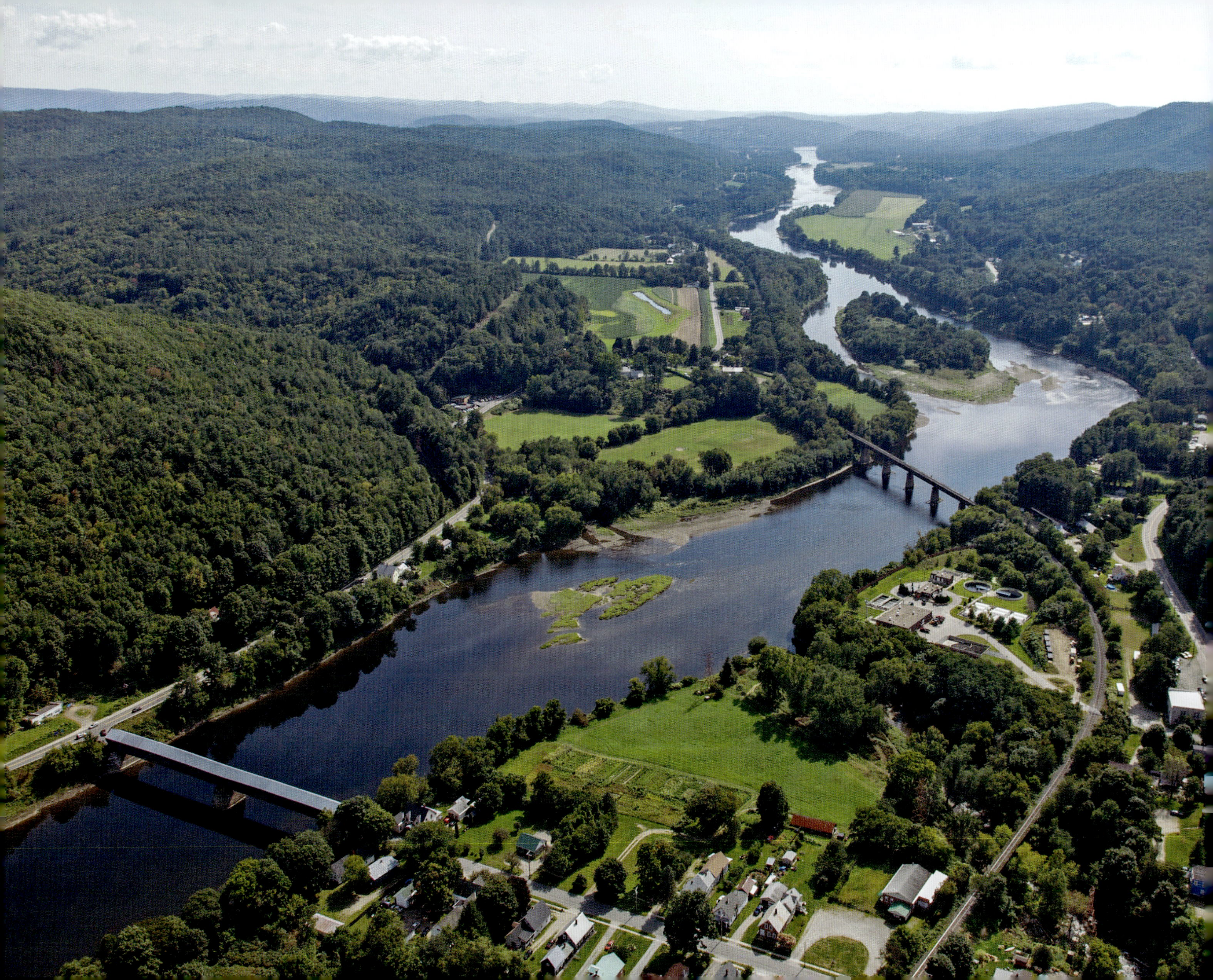

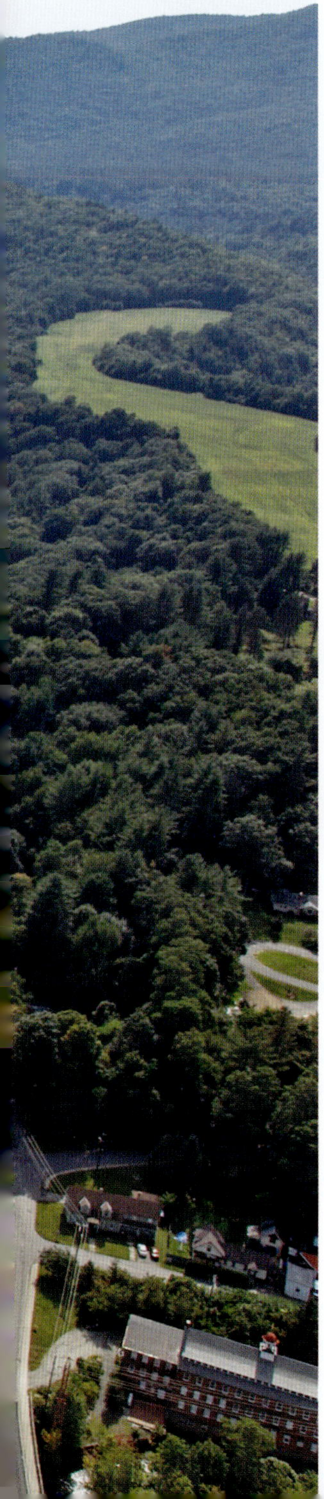

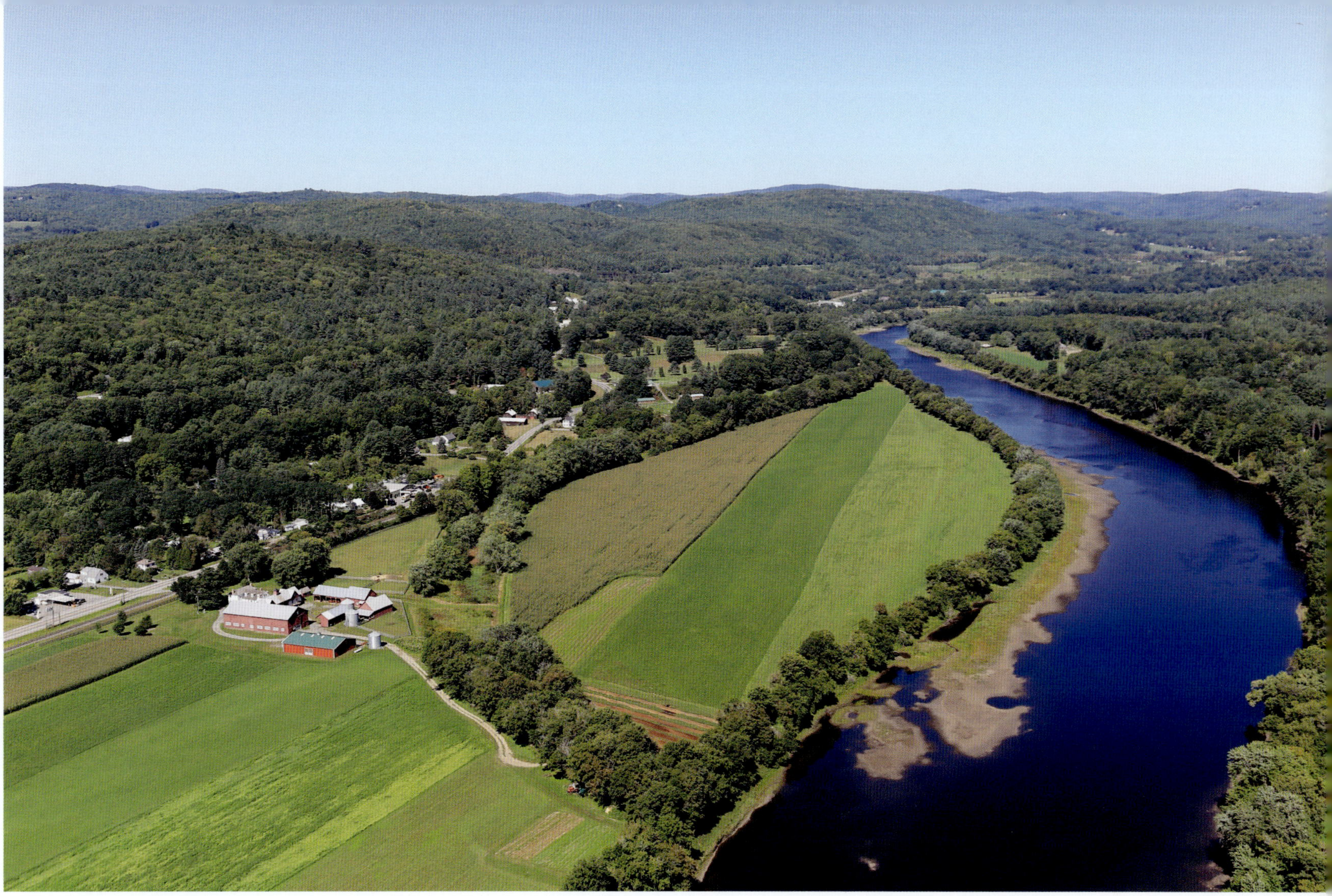

(left) Looking south down the course of the river with Vermont on the right and New Hampshire on the left. Nestled in the river valley, this classic scene appears to have it all, including the vintage covered bridge, a classic stone and steel railway viaduct, wooded foothills, and the river itself winding south toward the distant sea. Still, the cultivated and fertilized fields in the distance and the sewage treatment plant next to the railway bridge remind us that every community along the river's course has a cumulative effect on downstream ecosystems.

(above) Just north of Windsor, this arc of trees inland of the striped rows of crops may outline an earlier branch of the river that flowed behind an almond-shaped island.

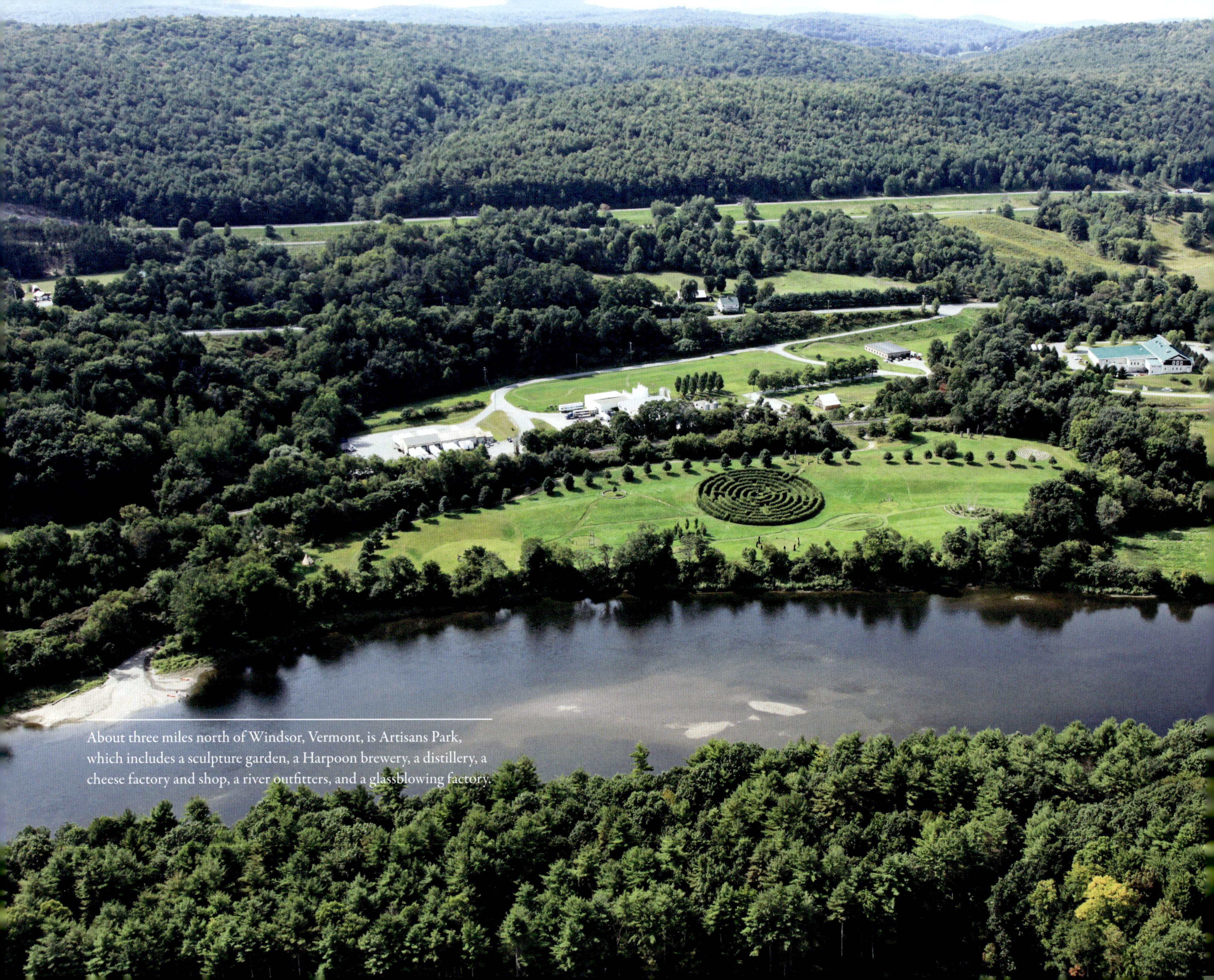

About three miles north of Windsor, Vermont, is Artisans Park, which includes a sculpture garden, a Harpoon brewery, a distillery, a cheese factory and shop, a river outfitters, and a glassblowing factory.

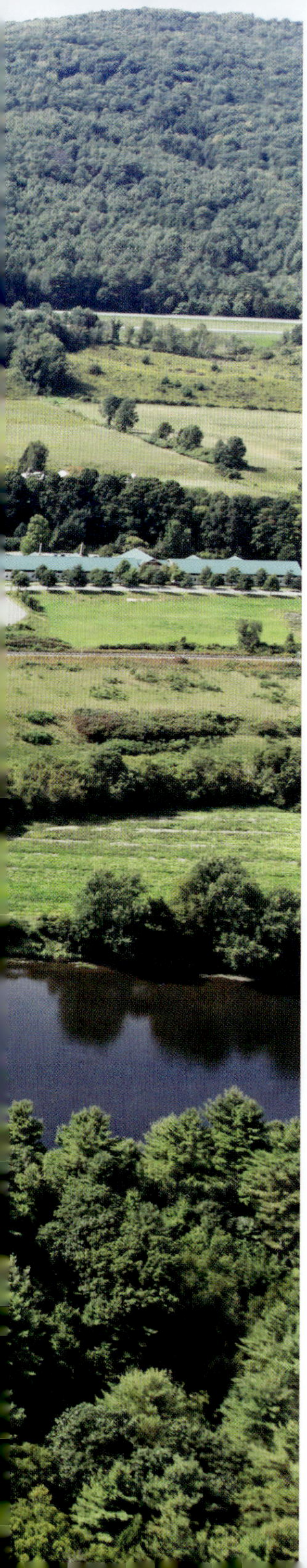

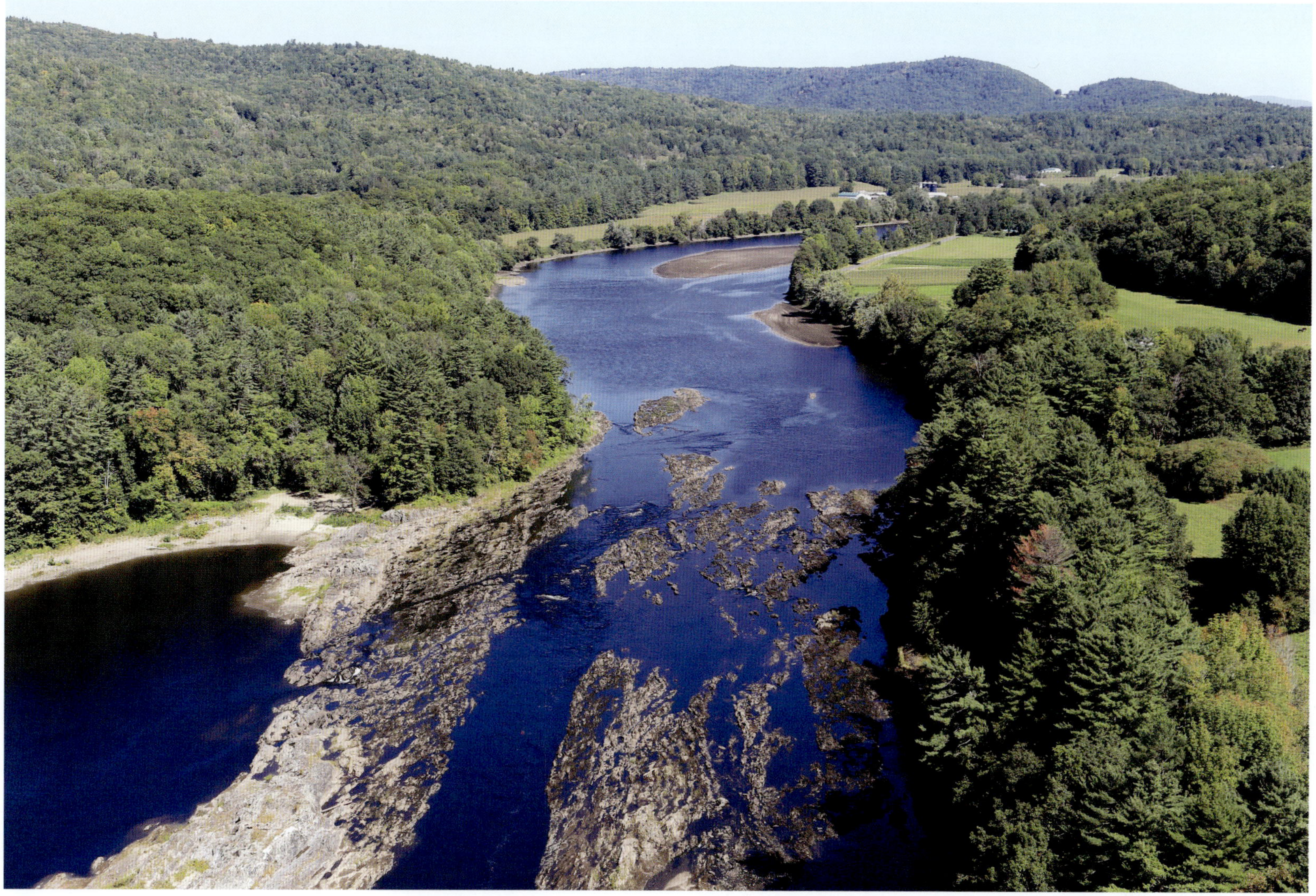

HALF WAY POINT

Congratulations, this unspoiled stretch of river between Hartland and North Hartland, Vermont marks the halfway point between Long Island Sound and the Connecticut River's source near the Canadian border. Ledge Island and Sumner Falls provide a favorite pullout and play area for white water enthusiasts. The rapids can be portaged or run by the more experienced.

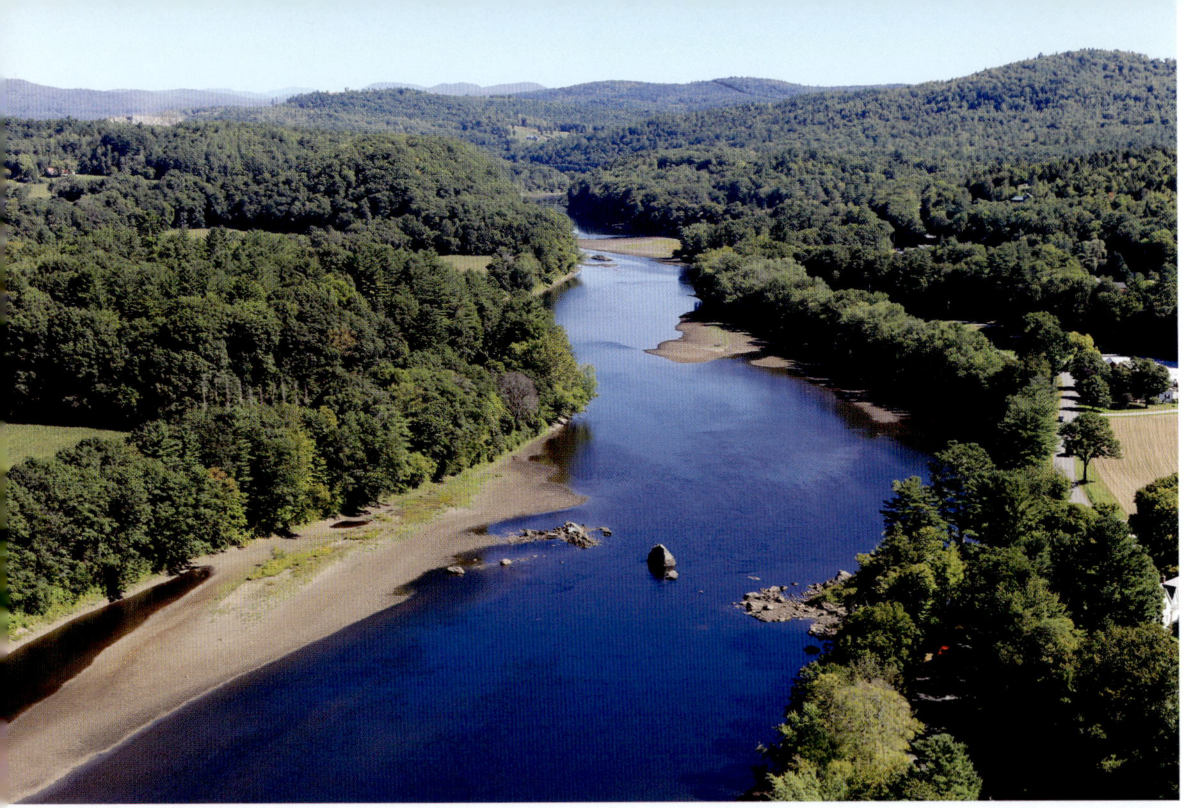

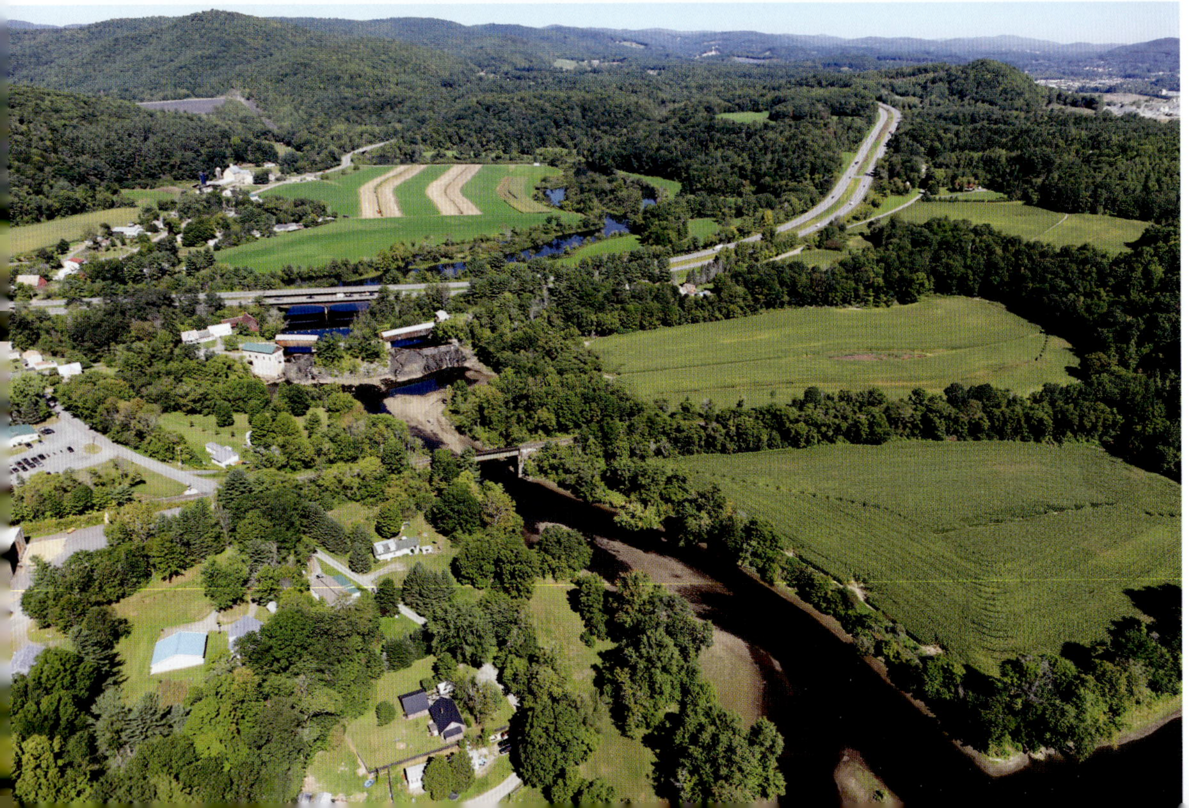

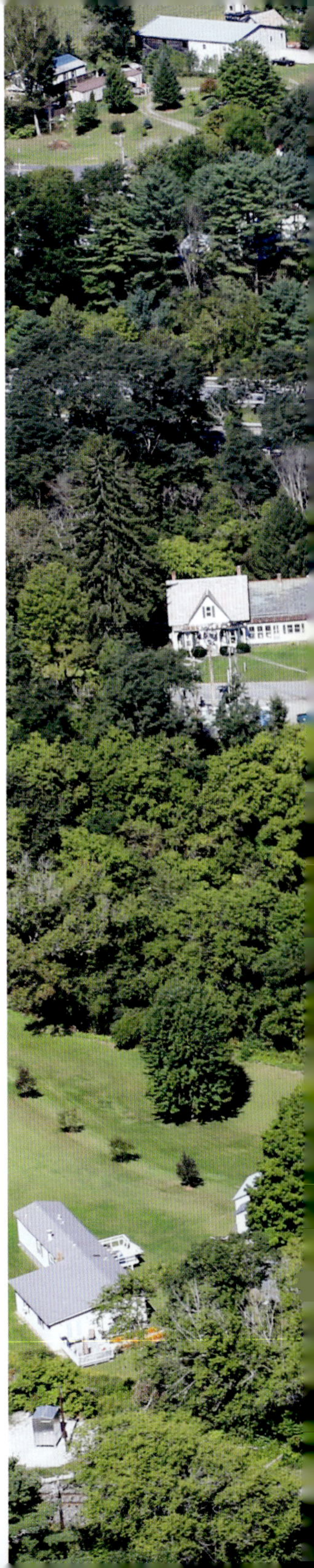

(top left) Remnants of another long lost bridge at North Hartland, Vermont

(bottom left and right) Motorists speeding past North Hartland, Vermont, on Interstate 91 may not notice the two picturesque covered bridges, each spanning small dams where the Ottaquechee River joins the Connecticut. Willard Covered Bridge, the eastern of the two (on the left), was built in 1870. There is also a small hydro-mill attached to the eastern-most dam.

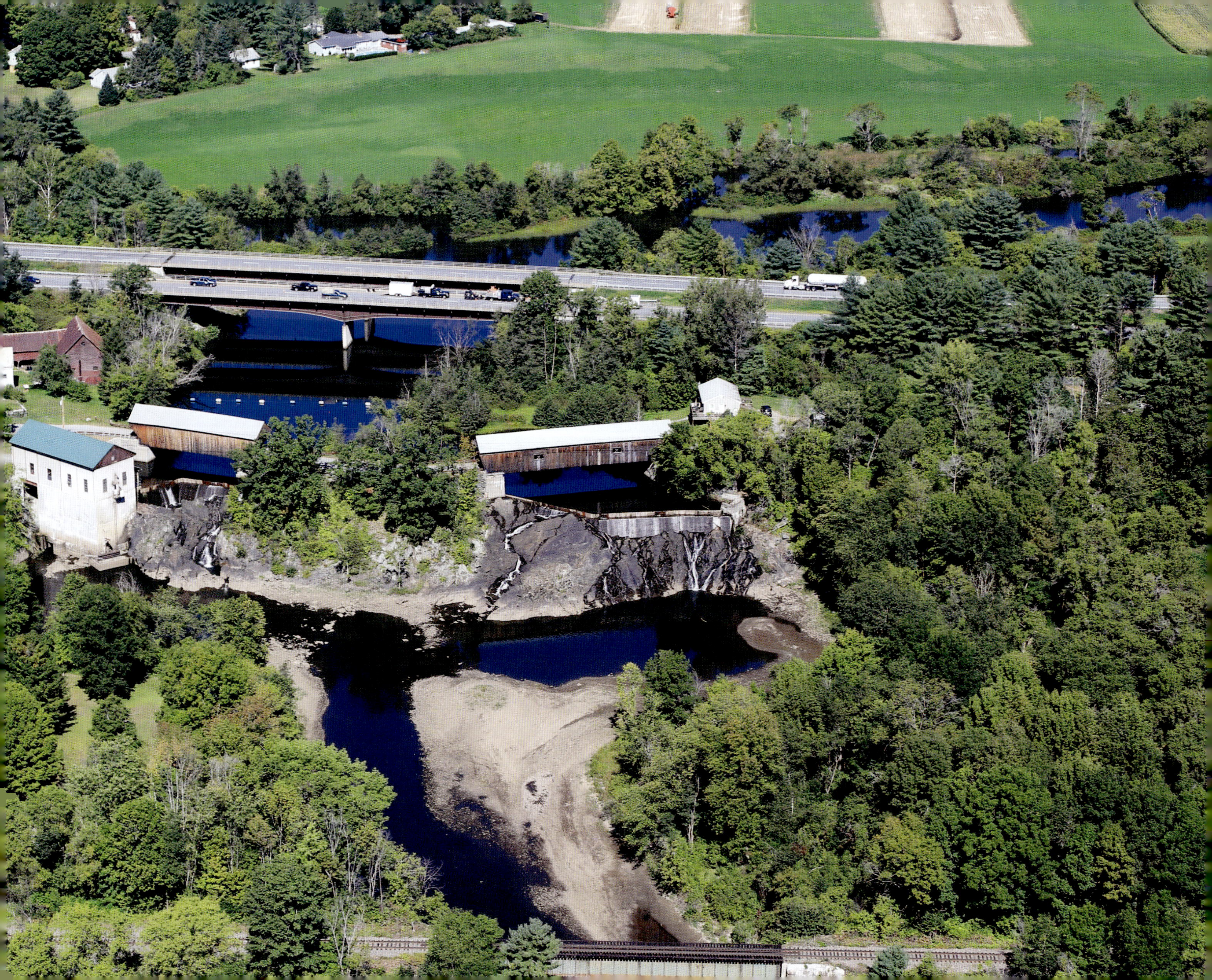

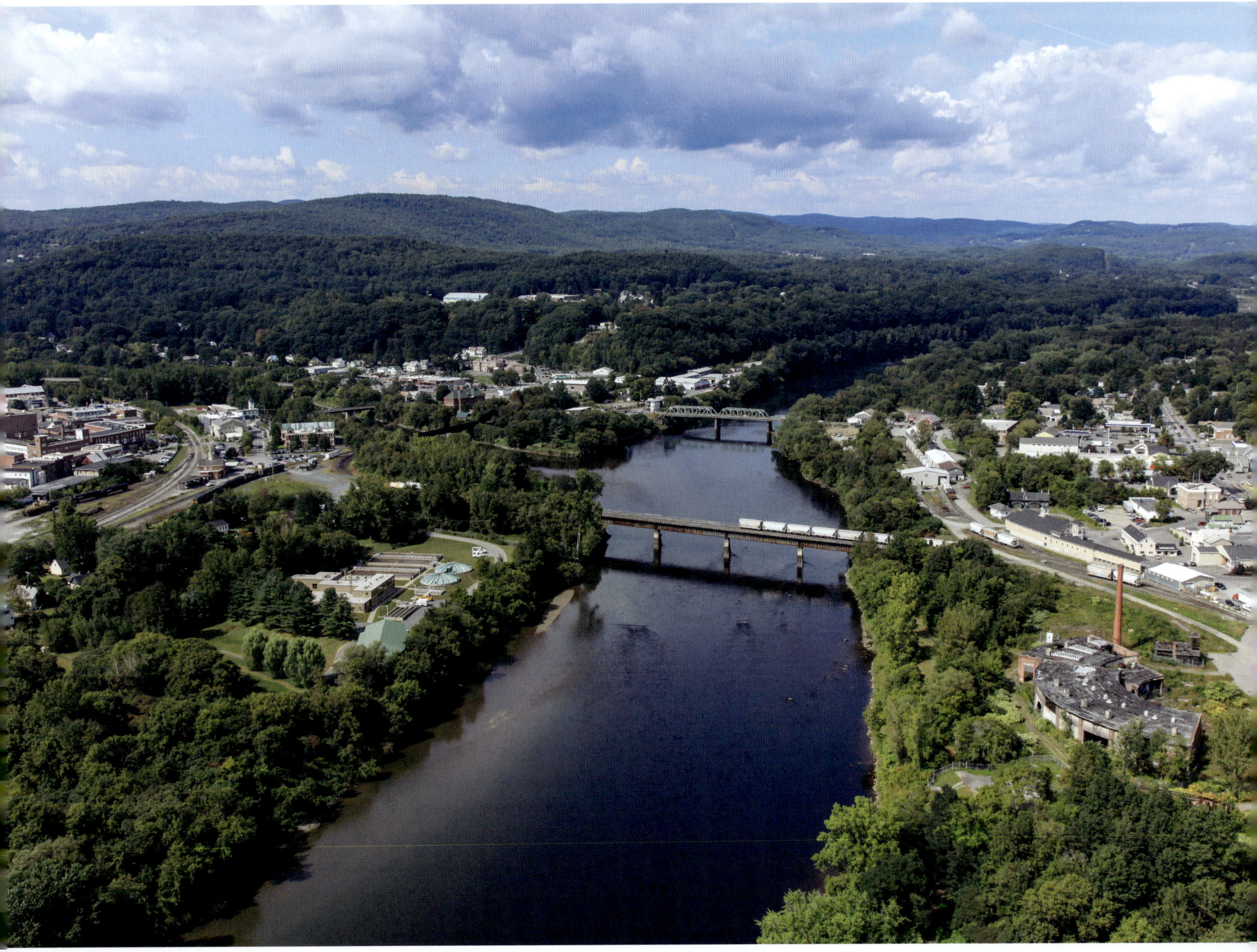

WHITE RIVER JUNCTION, VT

Located where the White River flows into the Connecticut, White River Junction became an important transportation hub in the 1800s. It began with the first bridge built here in 1803. In 1810, a canal was built about three and a half miles farther up the Connecticut River to allow boats to bypass the forty-foot drop at Olcott Falls. By the late 1840s, railroads reached the town and by 1863, five lines ran through this growing community making it the most important railroad junction in the state. At its height, the junction served fifty passenger trains a day.

(left) Looking north, with White River Junction, Vermont on the left and West Lebanon, New Hampshire, on the right. The White River joins the Connecticut between the railway bridge in the foreground and the Maple Street, Route 4, bridge with its twin trusses just up river. Note the old roundhouse in the foreground, an artifact of the days when this was one of the most important rail line junctions in the region.

(right) Just north of White River Junction, Olcott Falls once dropped 40 feet along a 650-foot stretch of river preventing water transportation. In 1810 a canal was built on the New Hampshire side to bypass the falls. A cribwork dam was built here in 1882 and a concrete dam was built just downstream in 1927. In 1950, the present Wilder Dam and power plant were built beneath the two older dams, flooding them, and the falls, with its backwater that now stretches up river. Wilder Station provides an output capacity of 42 megawatts.

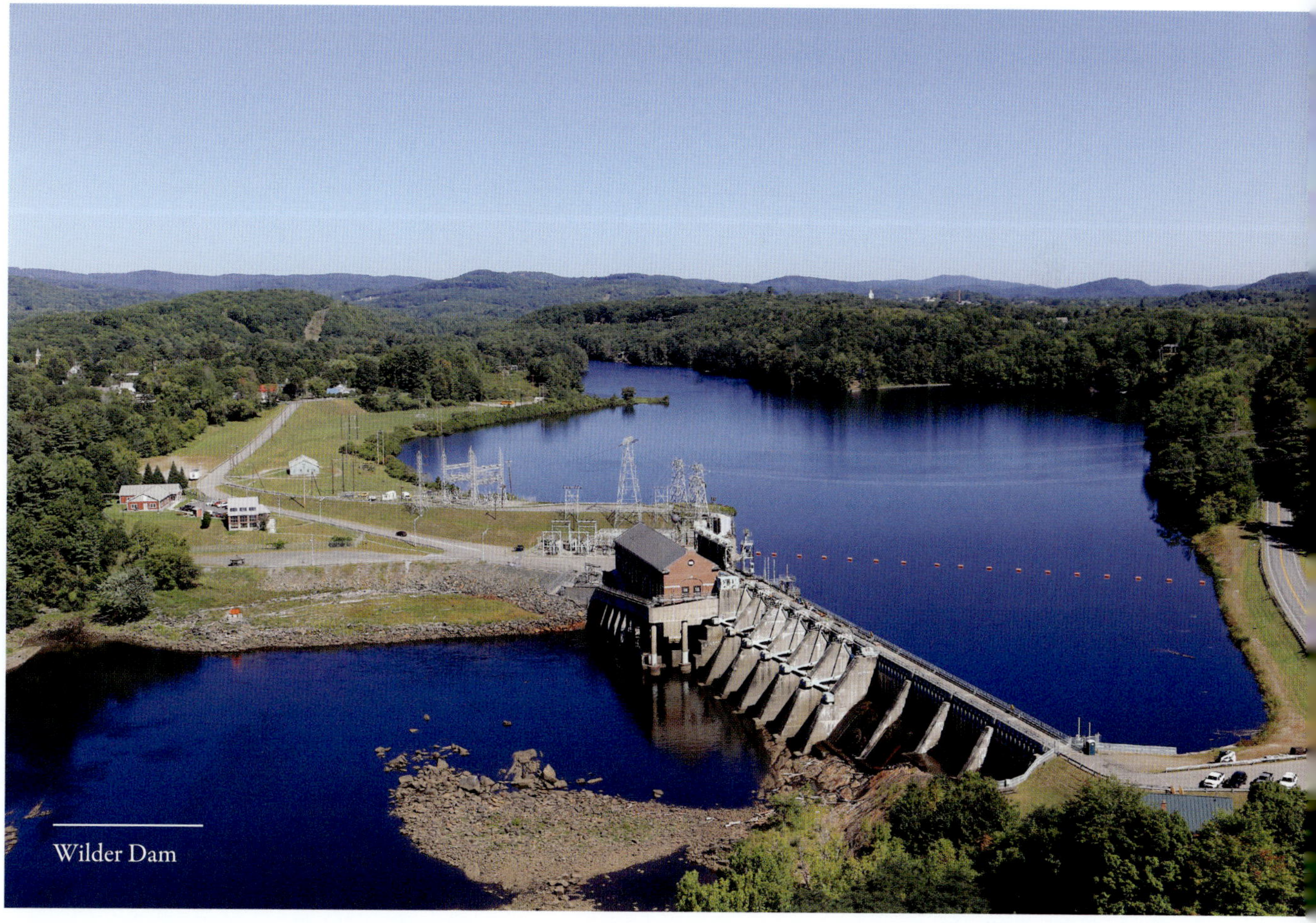

Wilder Dam

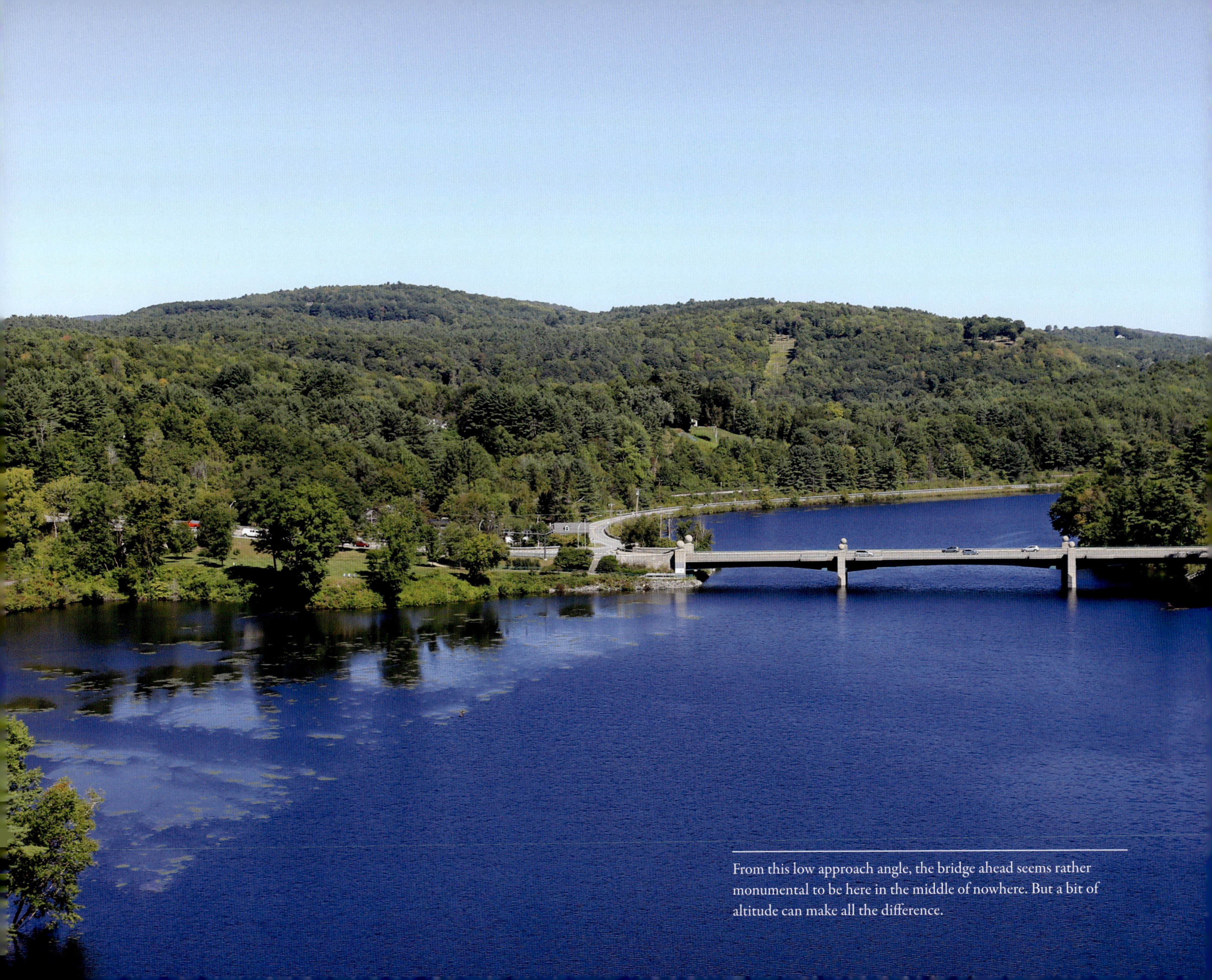

From this low approach angle, the bridge ahead seems rather monumental to be here in the middle of nowhere. But a bit of altitude can make all the difference.

THE LEDYARD BRIDGE

The Ledyard Bridge leads from Vermont to Hanover, New Hampshire, and Dartmouth College founded in 1769. Dartmouth is one of only nine colonial collages established before the Revolution. One of the more quirky traditions perpetuated here by daring Ivy League students is the Ledyard Bridge Challenge in which individuals or groups climb down to the river bank on the Dartmouth side, remove their clothes, swim across the river and return by "streaking" back across the bridge, attempting to get back into their clothes before being caught by the Hanover Police.

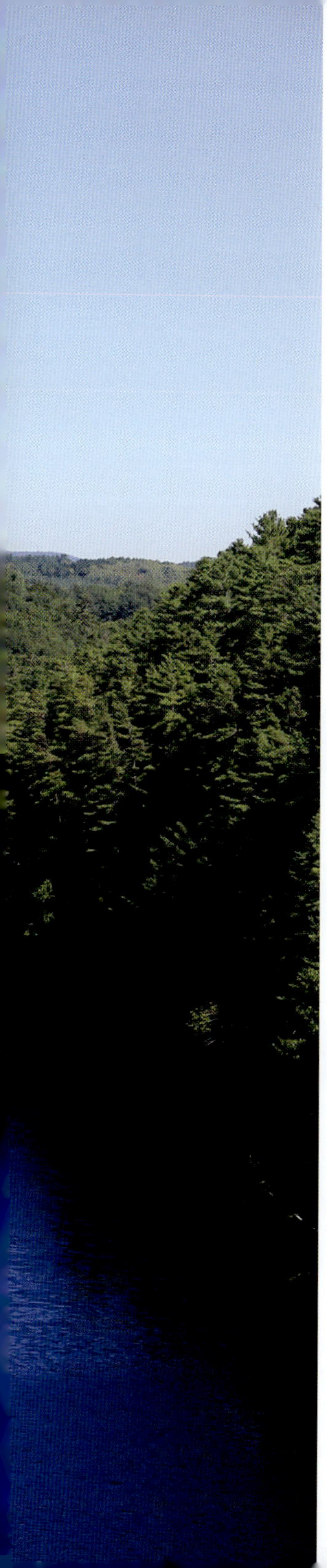

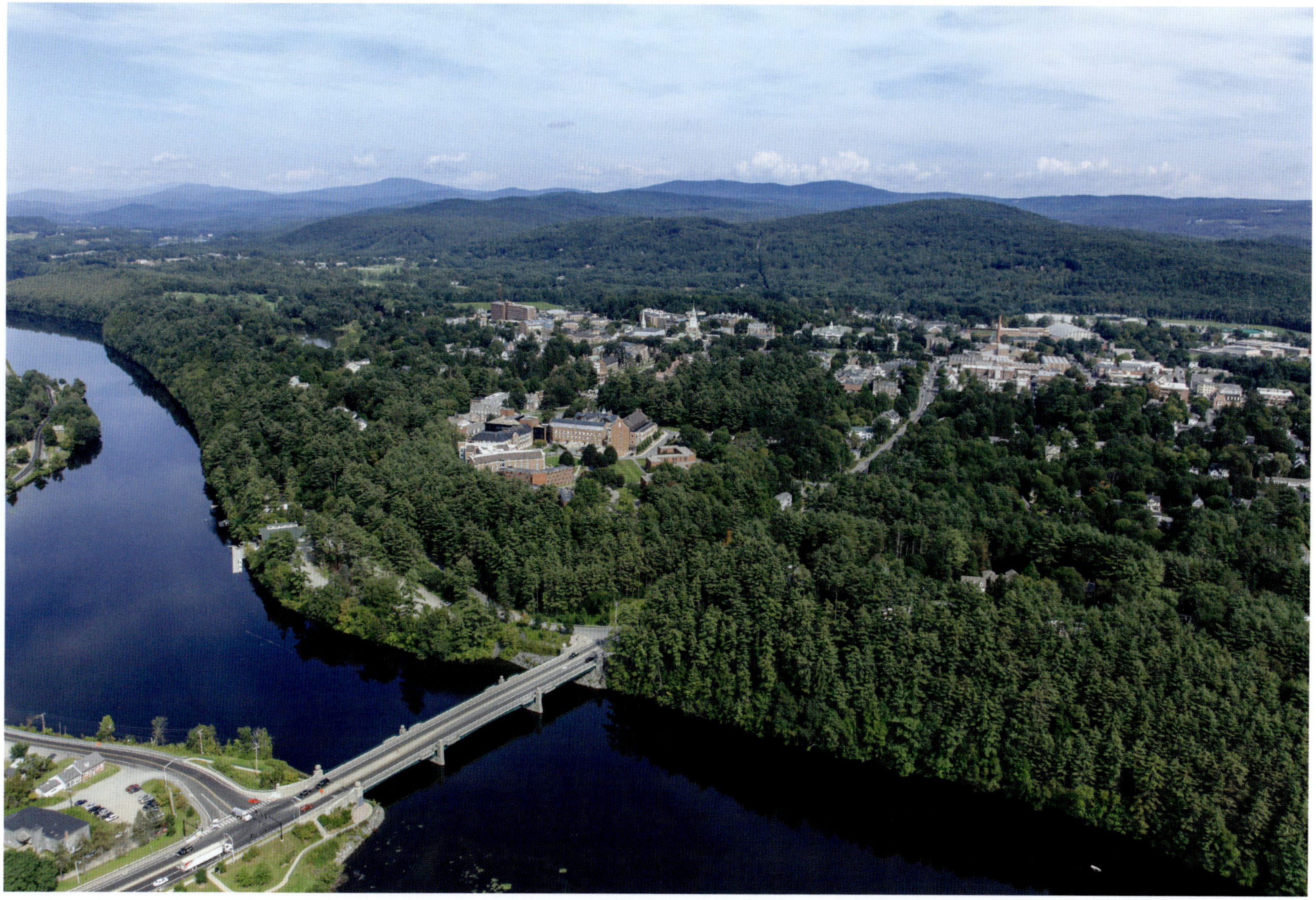

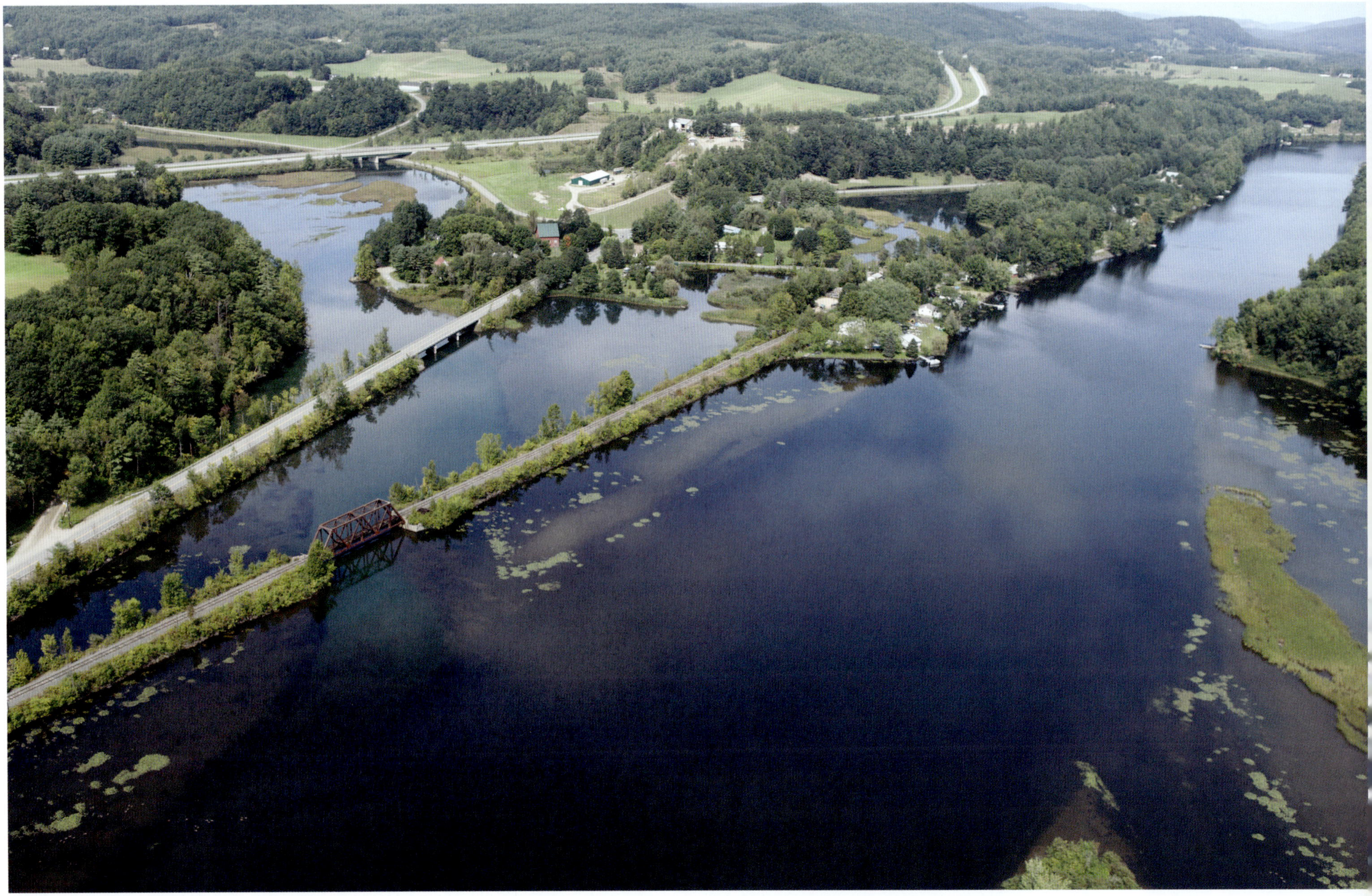

(above) About five miles north of Hanover where the Ompompanoosuc River joins the Connecticut, there is an interesting confluence between the railway line, US 5, VT Route 132, and Interstate 91. Note also the interface between the visible river bottom and the reflected sky and clouds.

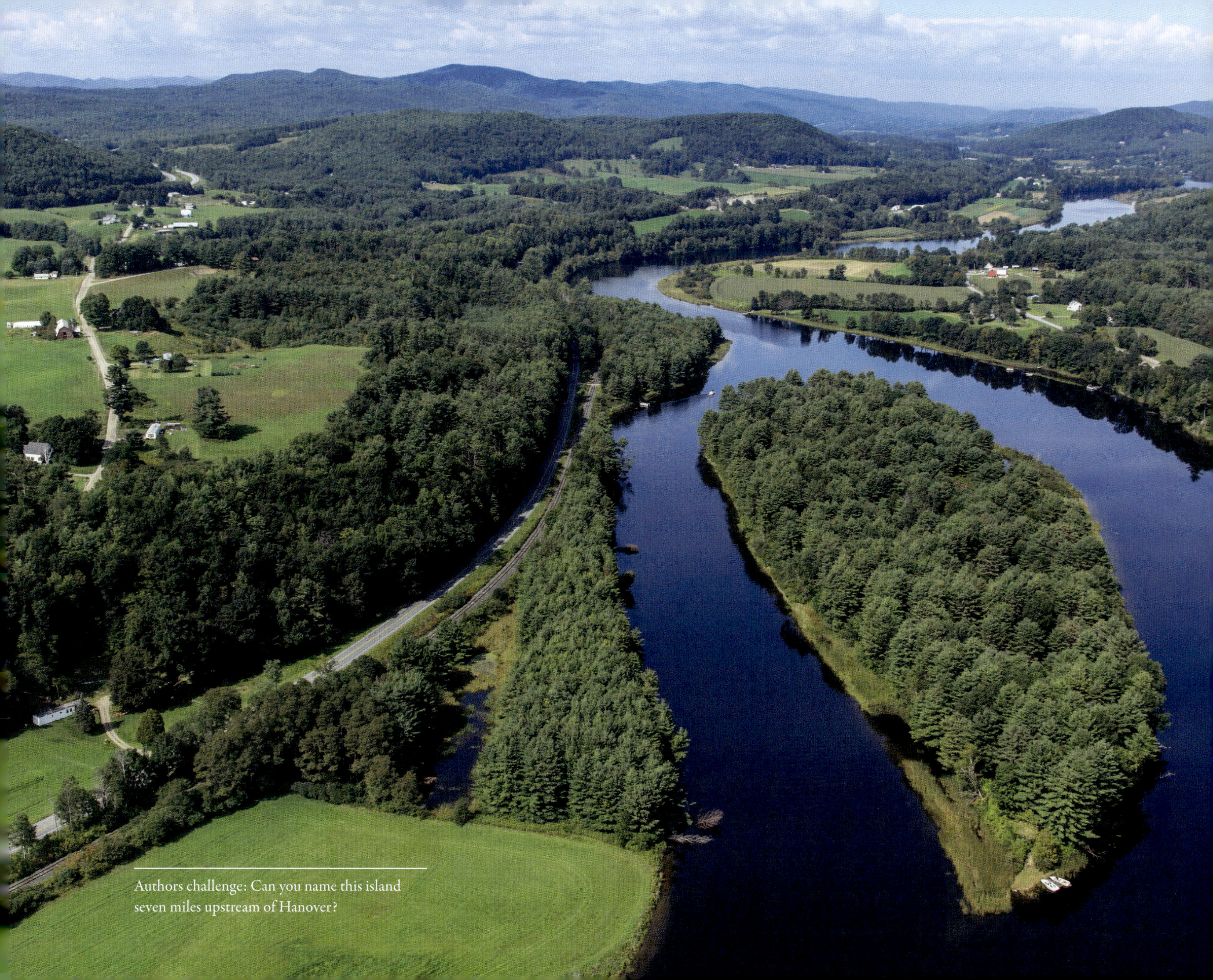

Authors challenge: Can you name this island seven miles upstream of Hanover?

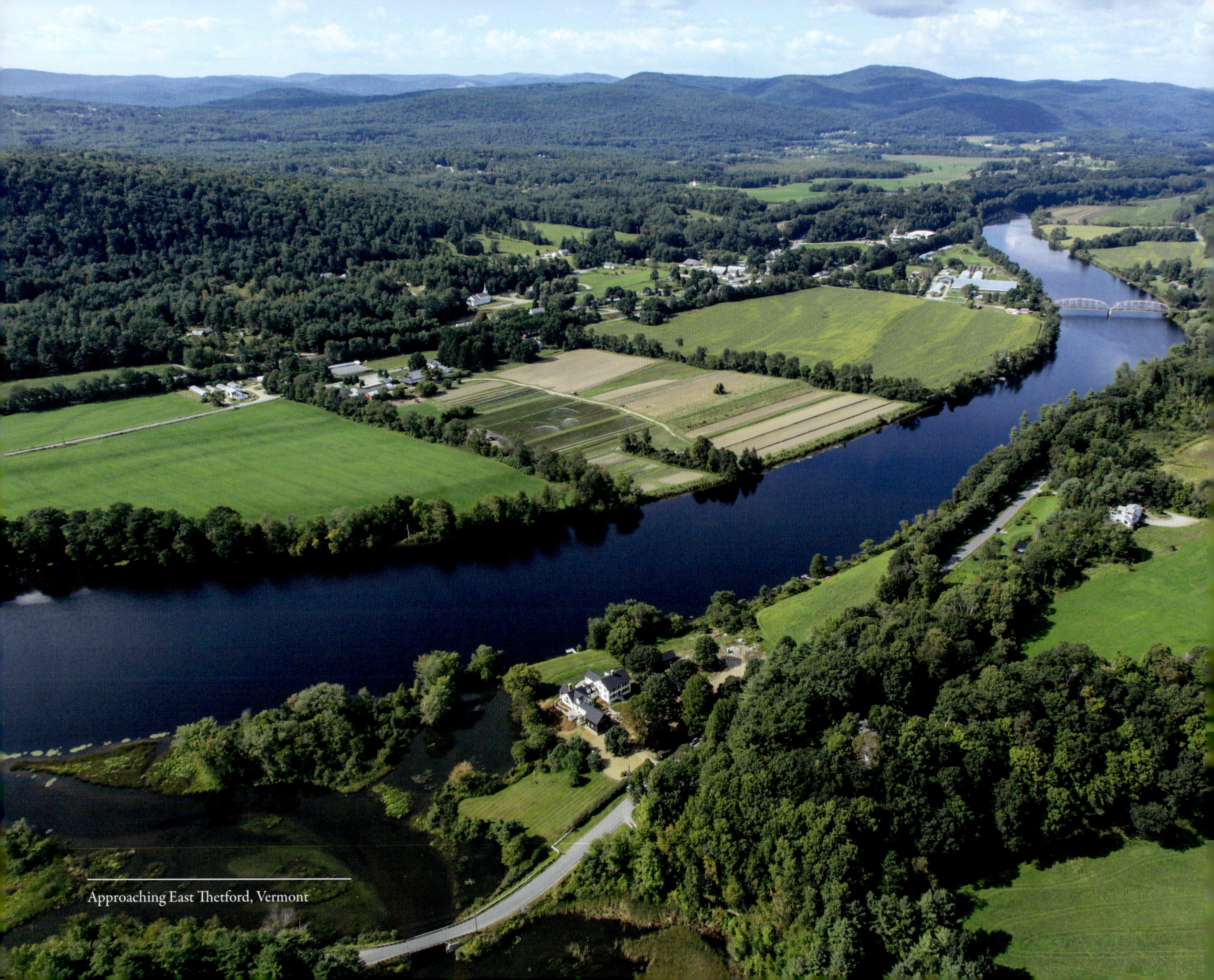

Approaching East Thetford, Vermont

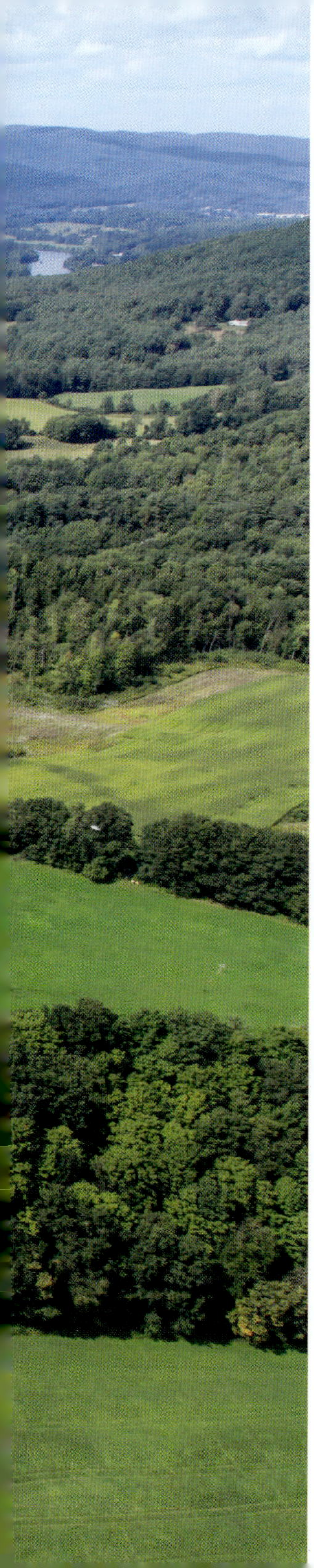

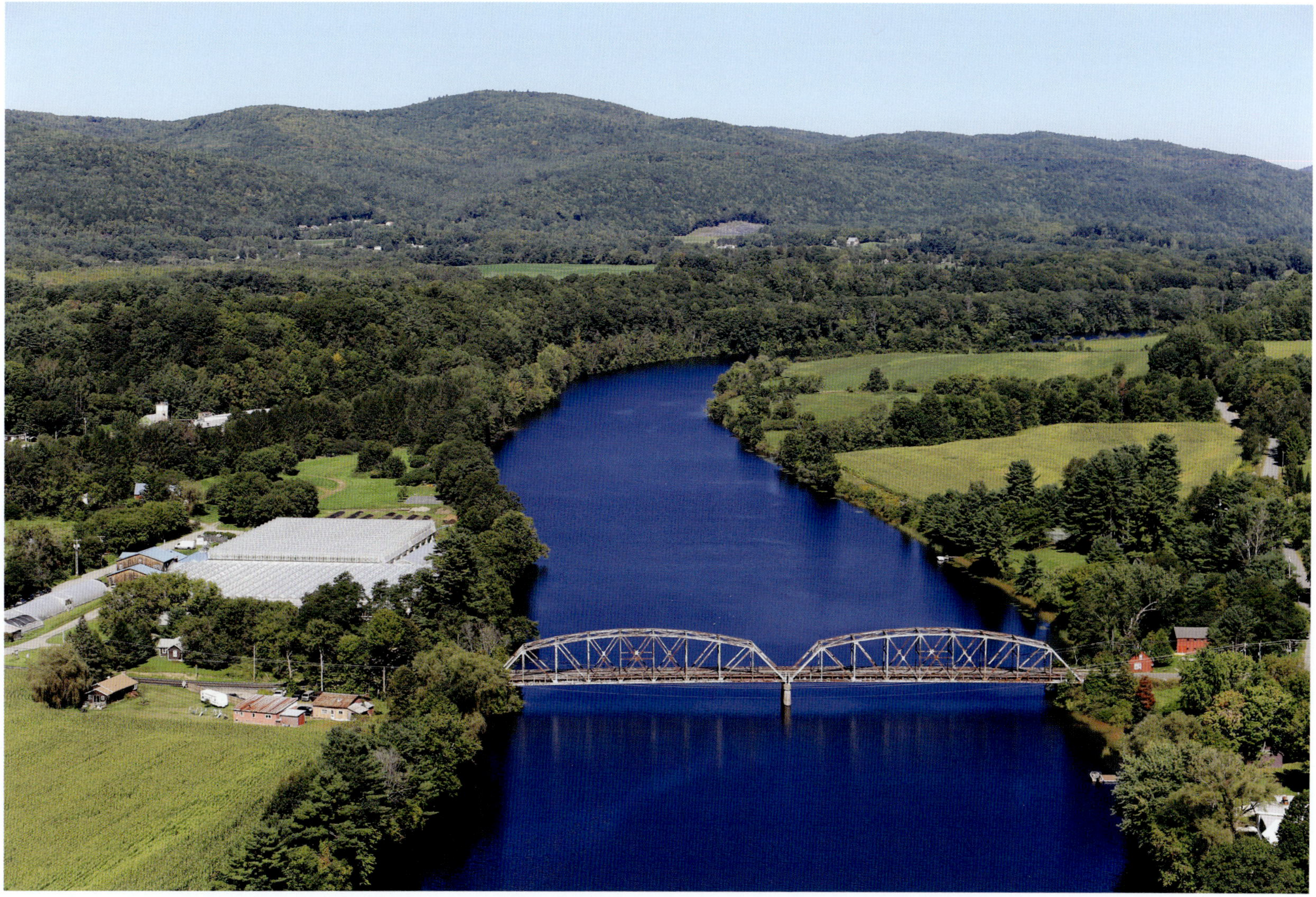

(above) The double span bridge that connects East Thetford, Vermont, with Lyme, New Hampshire, via Route 113. The massive greenhouse array is part of Long Wind Farm. Thetford, with its historic center located three miles to the west, received a royal charter in 1761 and was settled three years later. The Campfire Girls were founded nearby in 1910 and soon became a national organization.

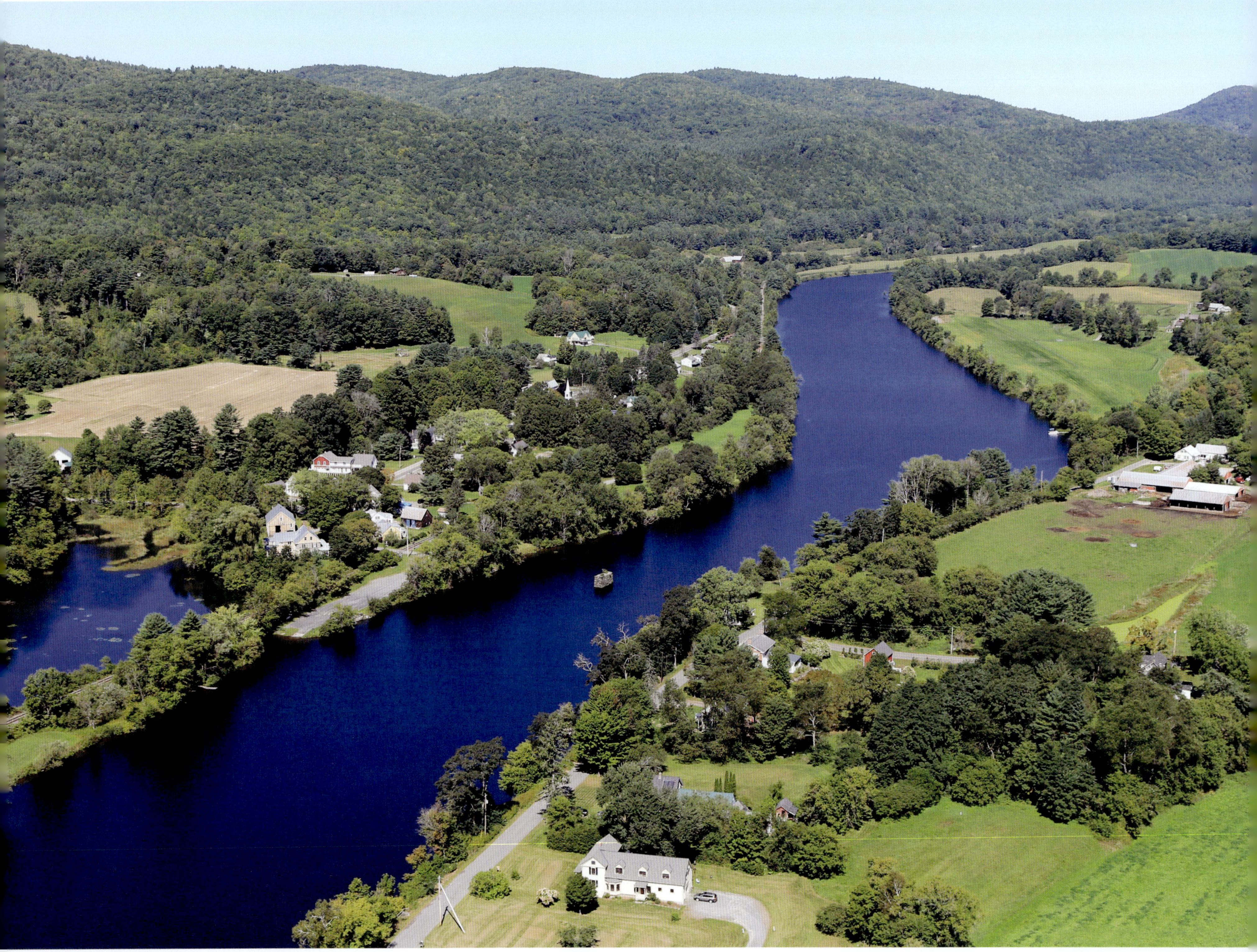

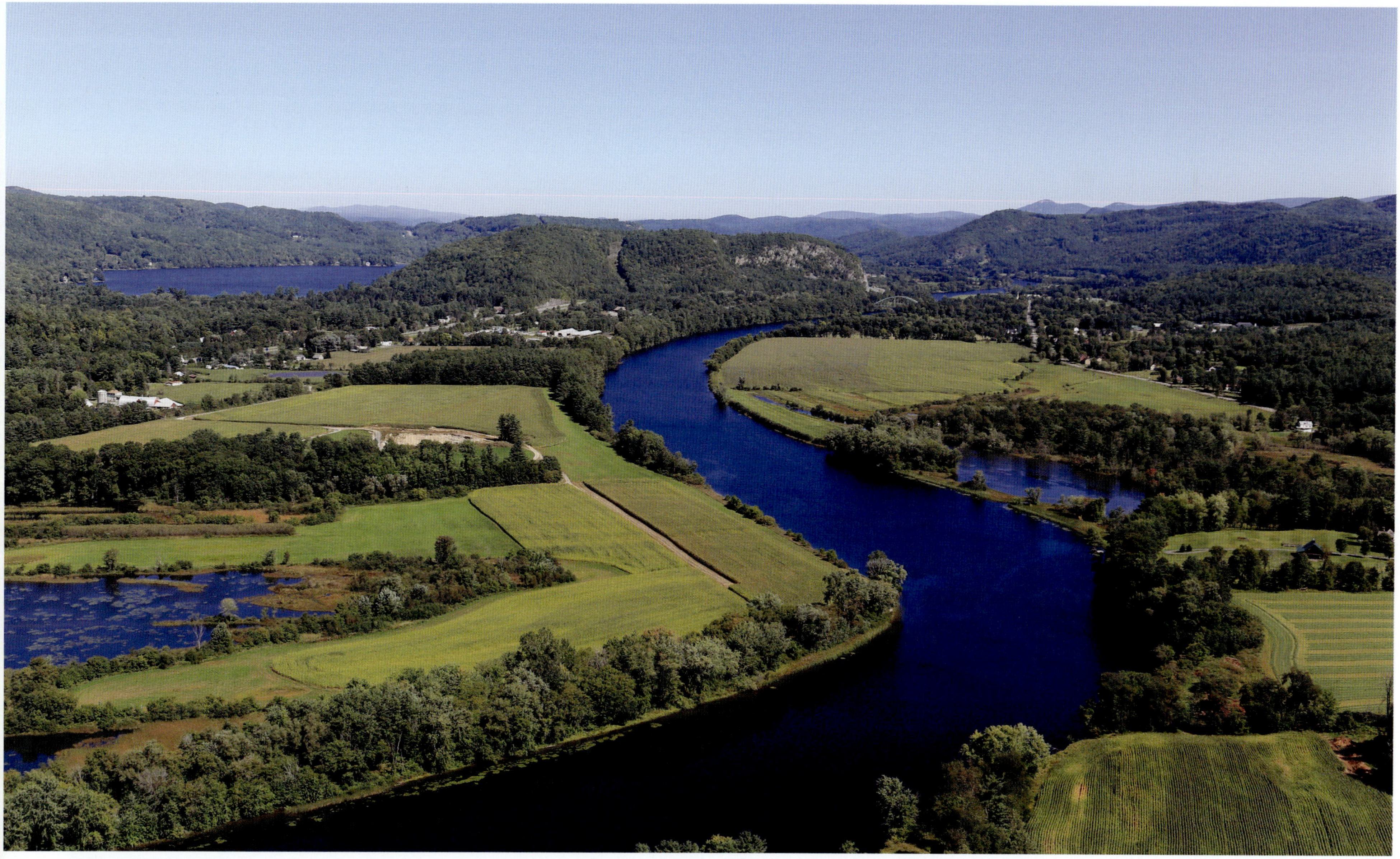

(left) All that remains of the bridge that once spanned the river at North Thetford is a single pylon with a shrub growing on top. On the Vermont side a road that now leads nowhere is still called Bridge Street. On the New Hampshire side its counterpart is called North Thetford Road recalling a time when the little town was only 300 feet across the water. Today the closest bridge is the twin span bridge at East Thetford, two miles to the south.

(above) Approaching Orford, New Hampshire, with Fairlee, Vermont, and Lake Morey on the west side of the river.

ORFORD, NH

Incorporated in 1761, Orford was named in honor of England's first prime minister, Robert Walpole, the first Earl of Orford. It was one of the original numbered colonial fort towns strategically located along the river. The 432-foot arched bridge that connects Orford to Fairlee, Vermont, was completed in 1938, replacing an earlier wooden bridge weakened by flooding. It is named for native son and lifelong resident Samuel Morey, a pioneer in the development of steam propulsion for marine use and the first to demonstrate the paddle wheel. The town prospered through agriculture as well as a number of mills and factories. When author Washington Irving visited Orford in 1832 he proclaimed, "In all my travels in this country and in Europe, I have seen no village more beautiful than this. It is a charming place—nature has done her utmost here." He was right.

Tom's original photos of this village, with its ached bridge and looming palisades across the river, so impressed me that I took my family there to experience it with our own feet on the ground. We were not disappointed. This image—with the quintessential New England town, the arched bridge, and the river and road pointing the way farther north—remains one of my personal favorites.

(right facing page) One of the most distinctive features of the town are the seven "ridge houses" built between 1773 and 1839 on a hill above the main street. They have been called the finest group of Federal-style homes in the United States.

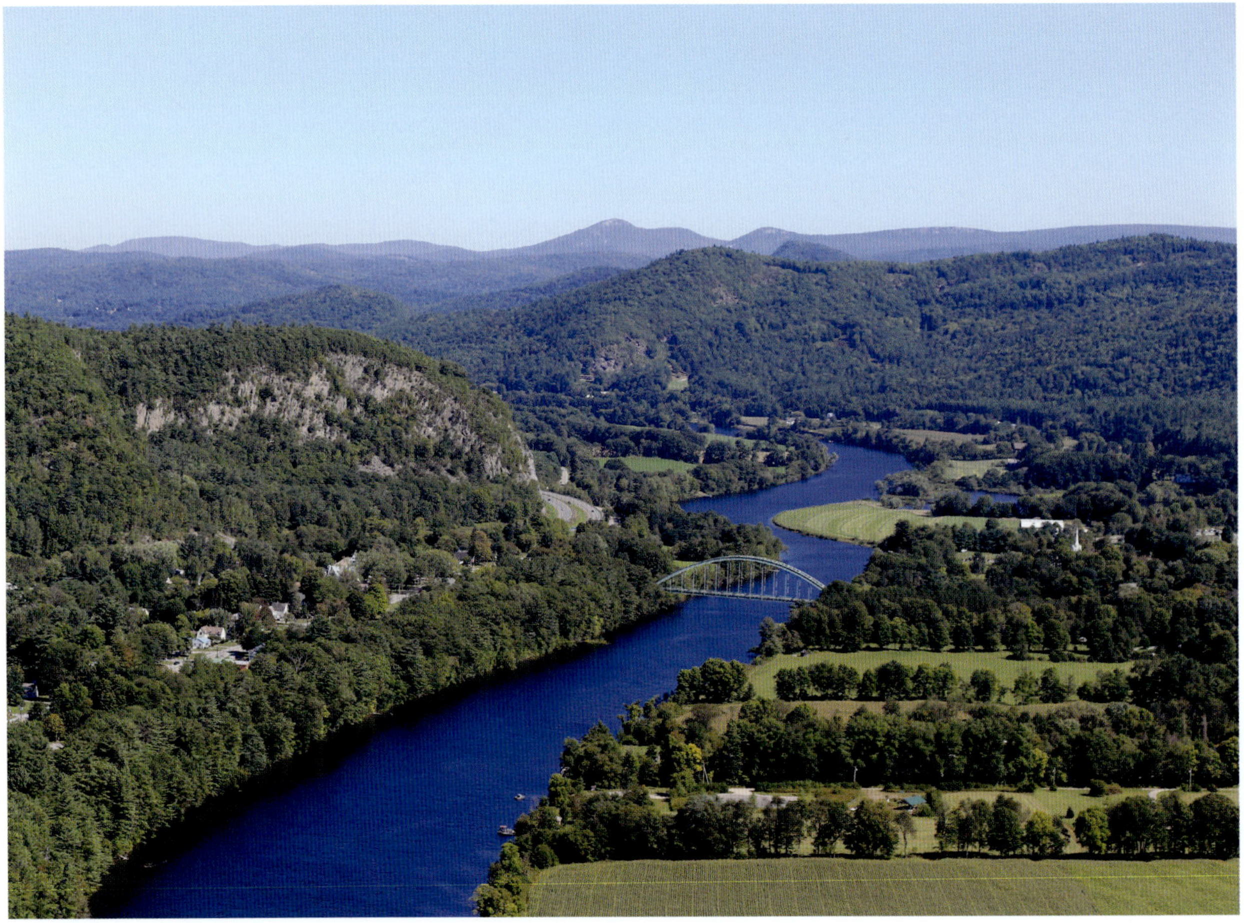

The majestic Morey arched bridge spans the river here beneath the imposing escarpment aptly named The Palisades.

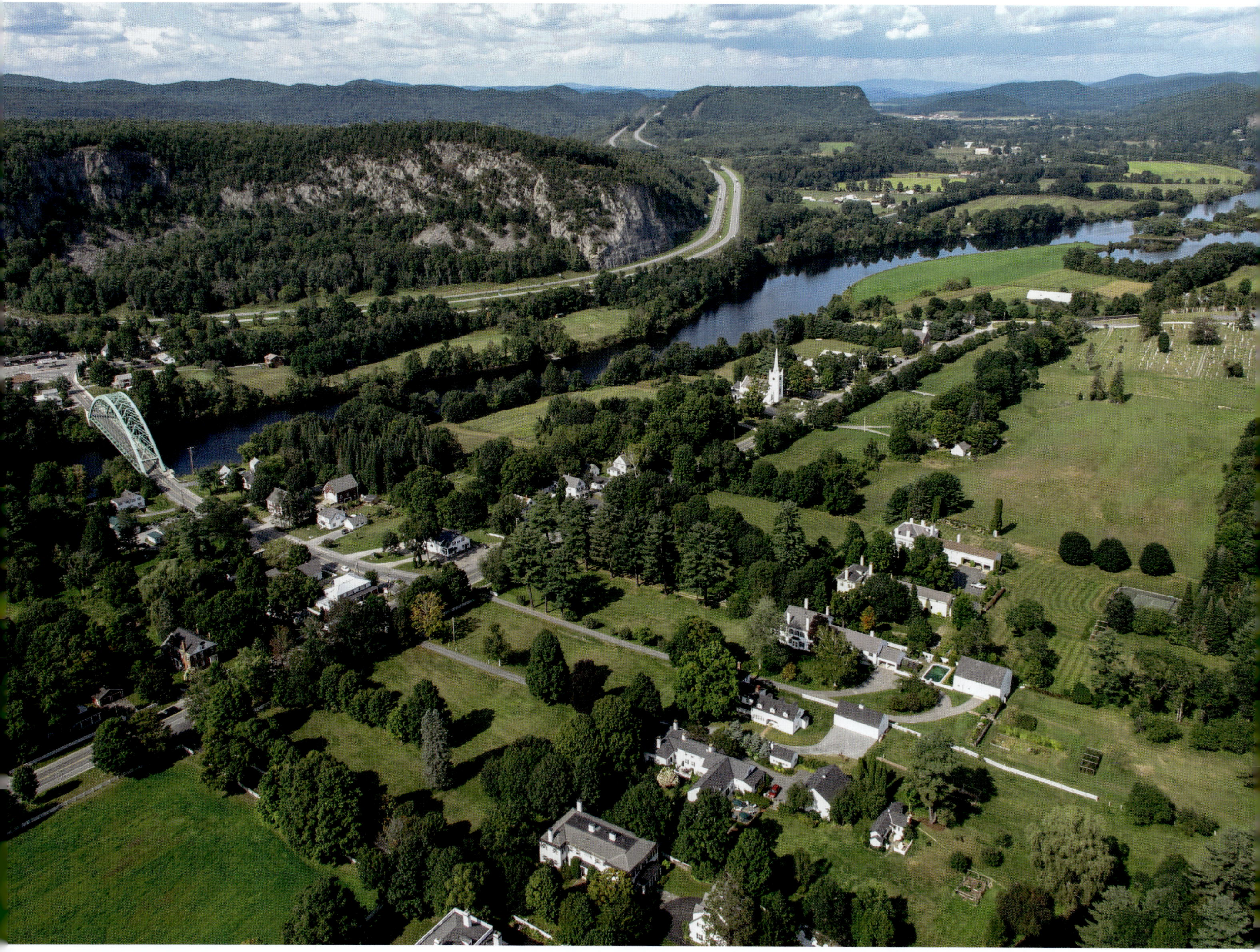

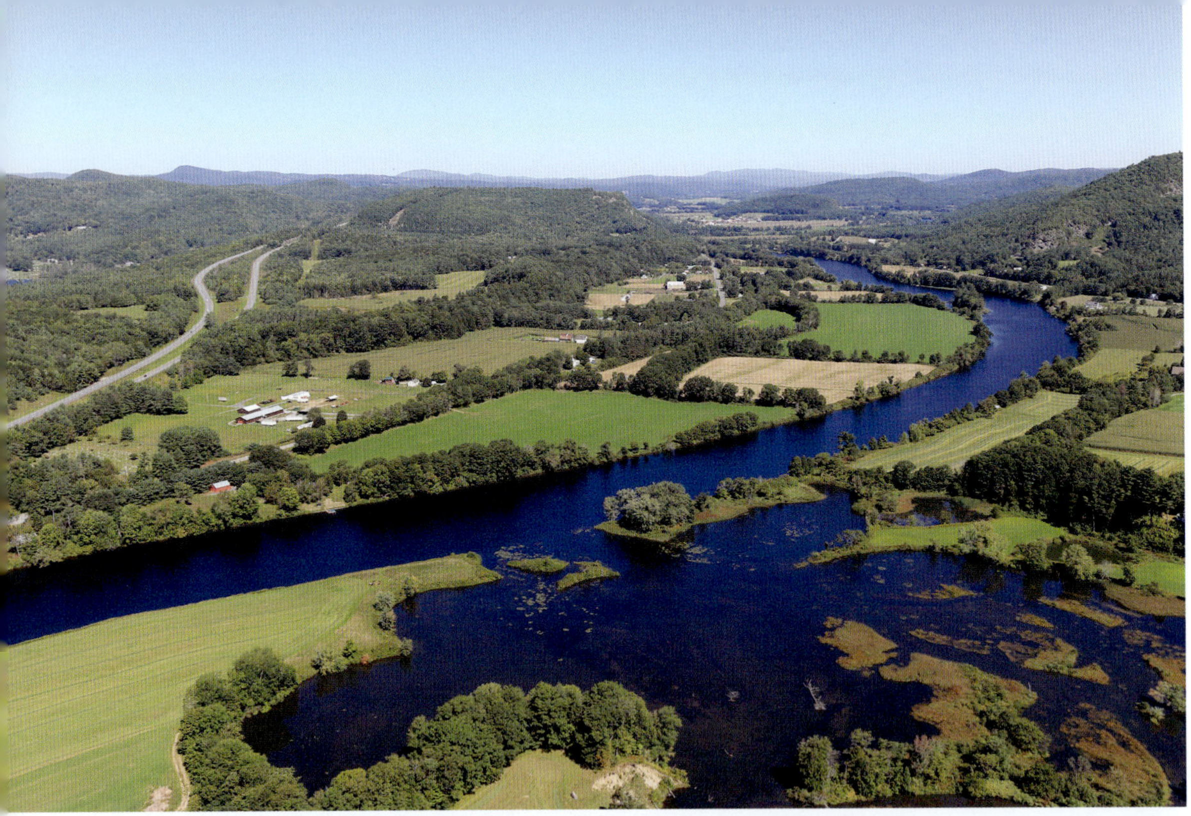

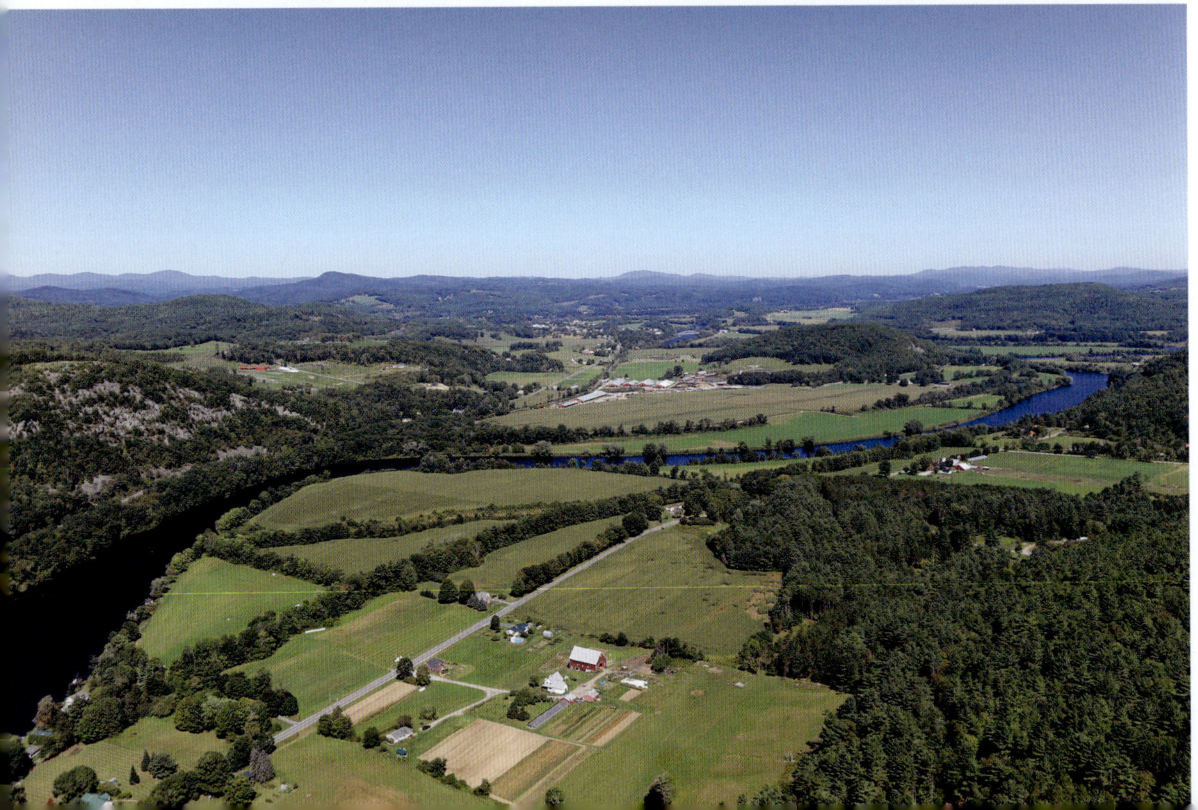

(top left) A set of mini-oxbows have been formed just north of Orford where the Jacobs Brook River enters the Connecticut.

(bottom left) Just above Orford, the river's course is deflected by a major rock face.

(right) Looking back down the river along the impressive rock face north of Orford

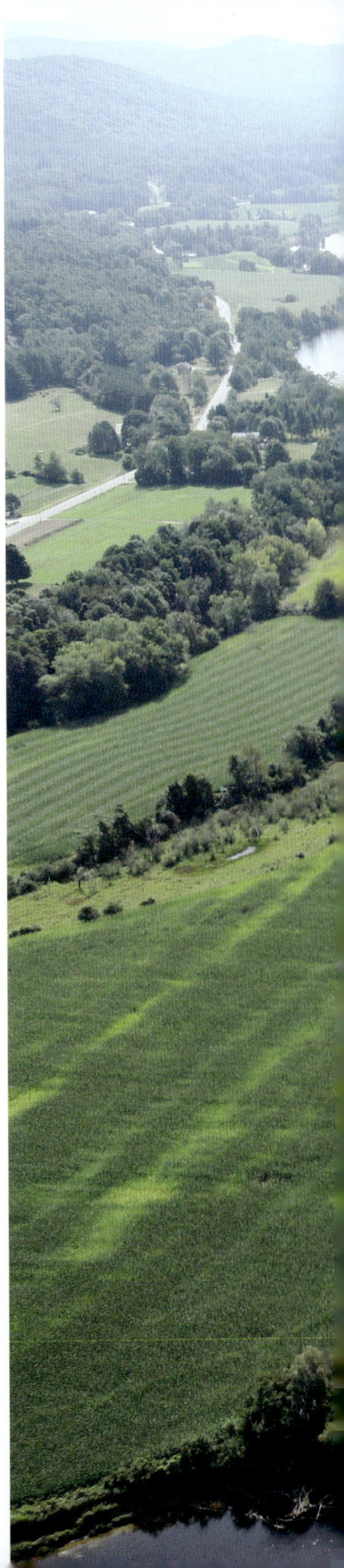

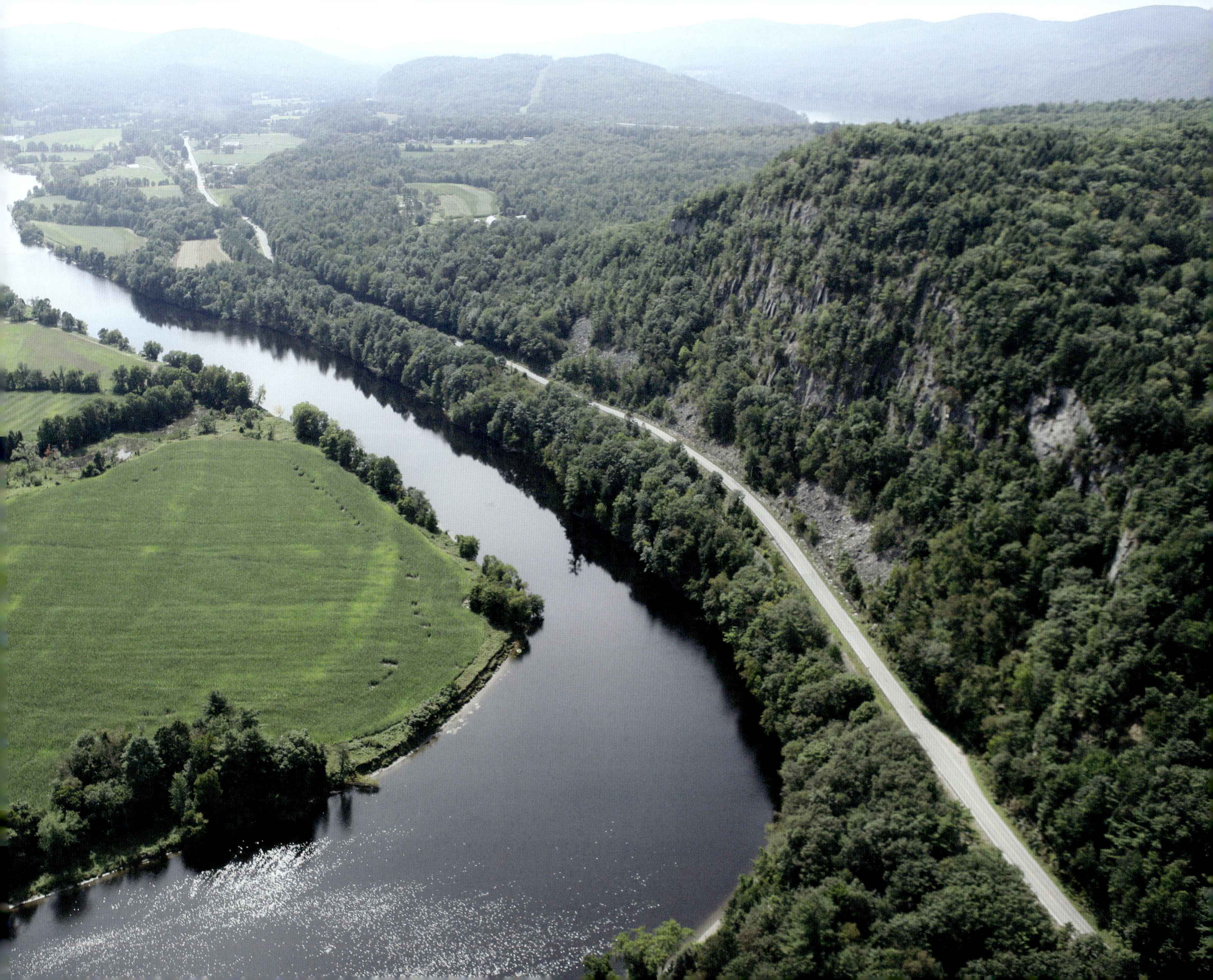

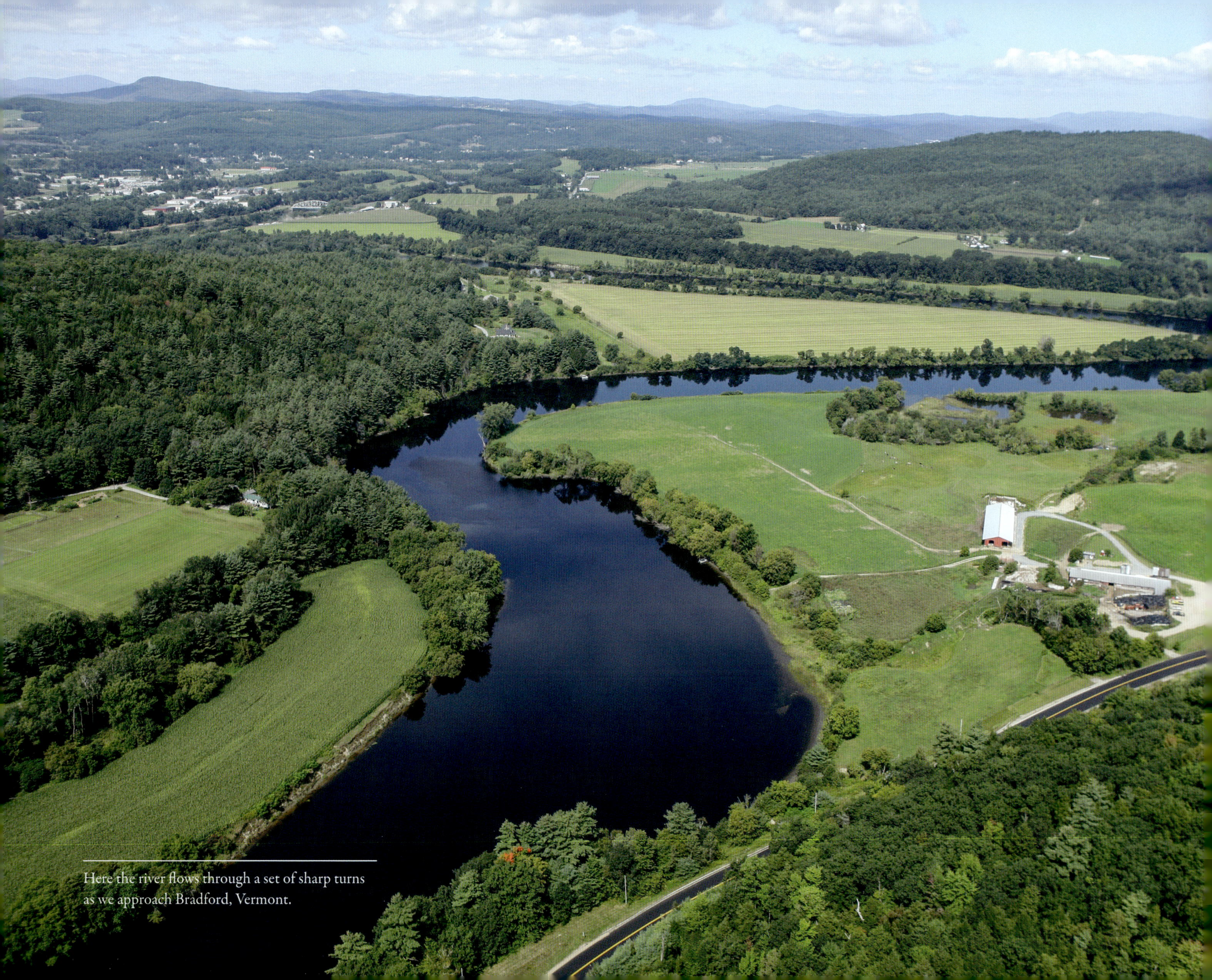

Here the river flows through a set of sharp turns as we approach Bradford, Vermont.

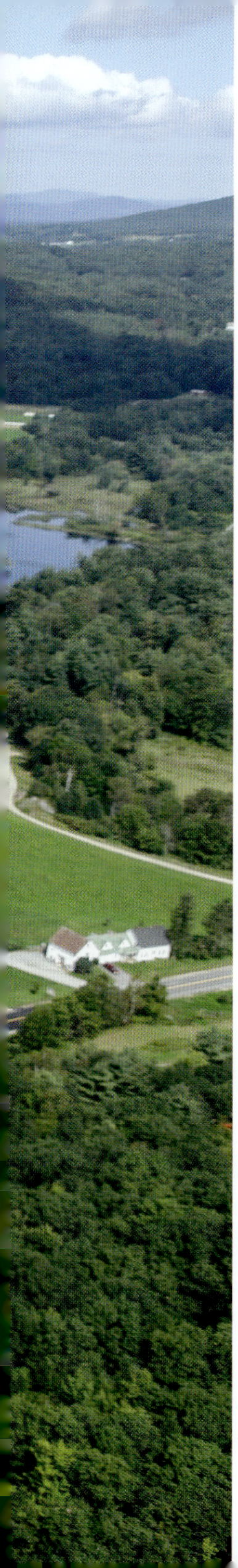

(top right) Note the kayakers off the end of the point as mechanized harvesting takes place nearby. It's a day off on the water for some, just another day in the fields for others.

(bottom right) Around another sharp bend lies Bradford, Vermont, long an industrial and commercial hub. Established in 1770 as part of the province of New York, it was named Mooretown after New York's royal governor, Sir Henry Moore. A few years after the Revolution it became part of Vermont and was renamed Bradford. Note the arched pattern of trees on the riverbank that outline part of a former oxbow.

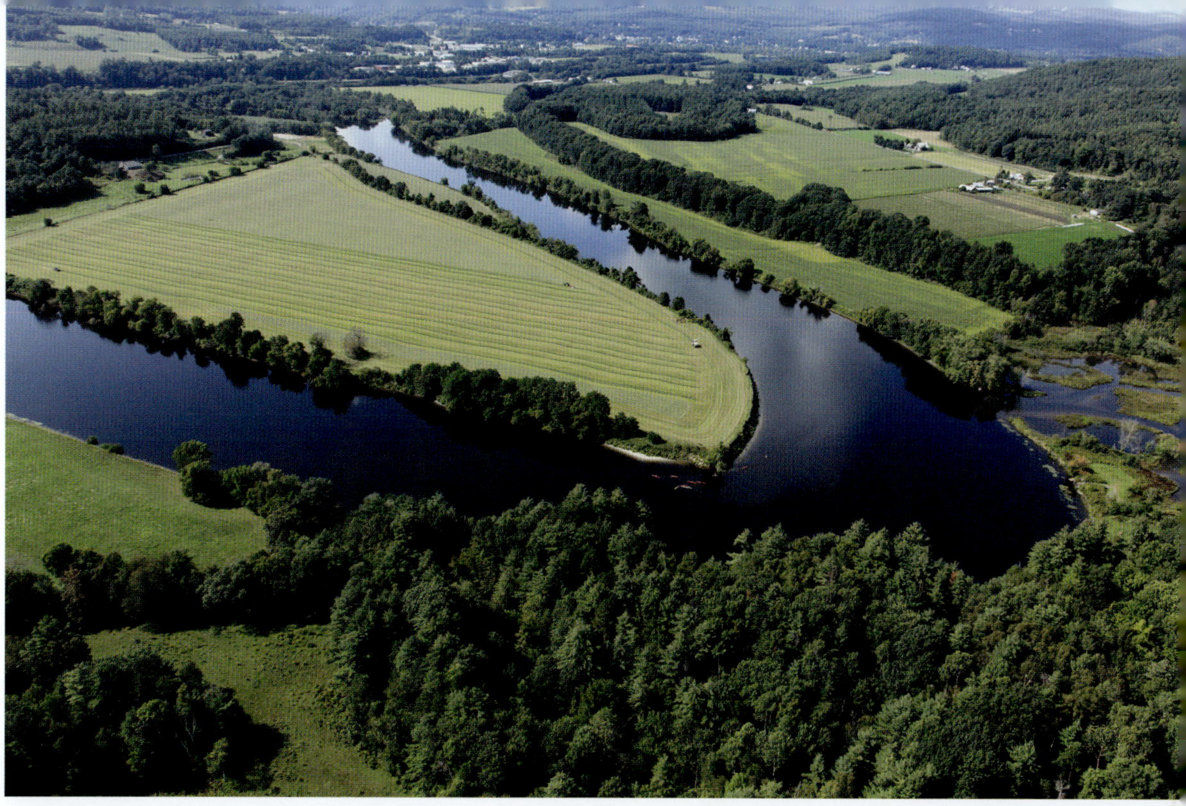

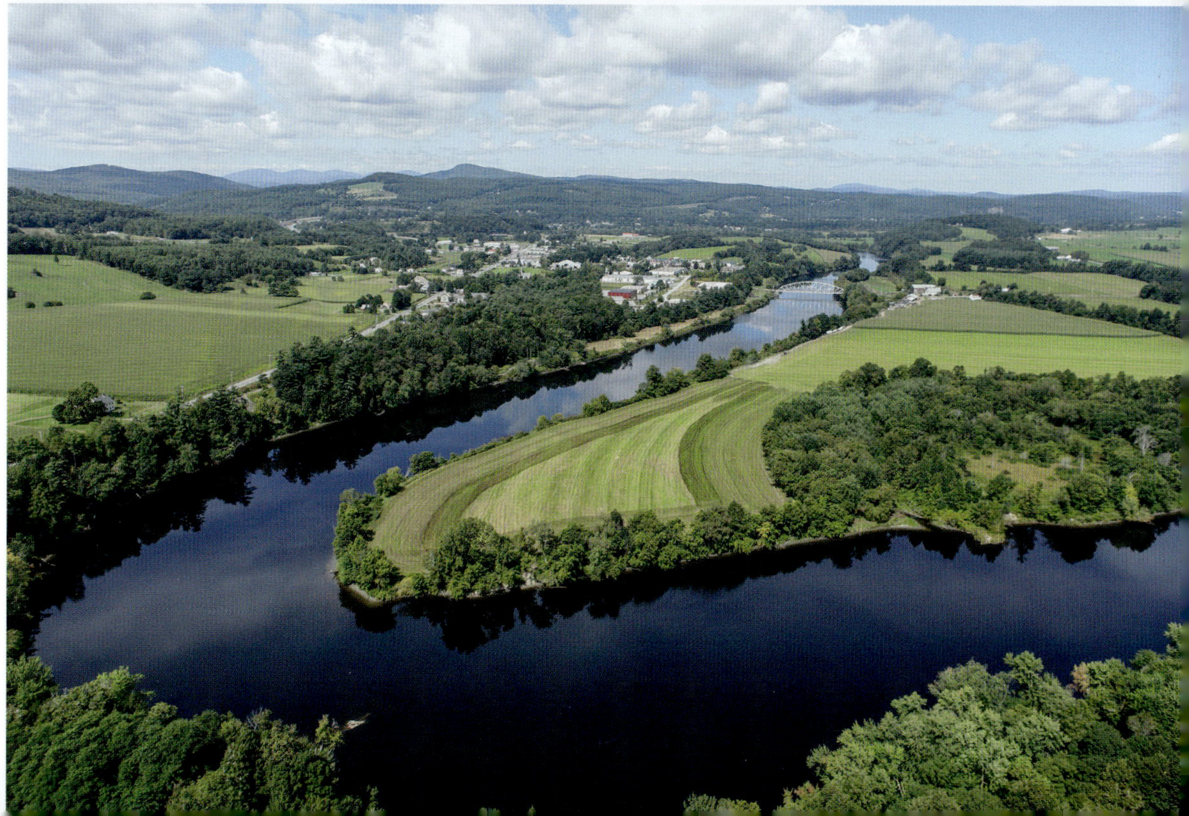

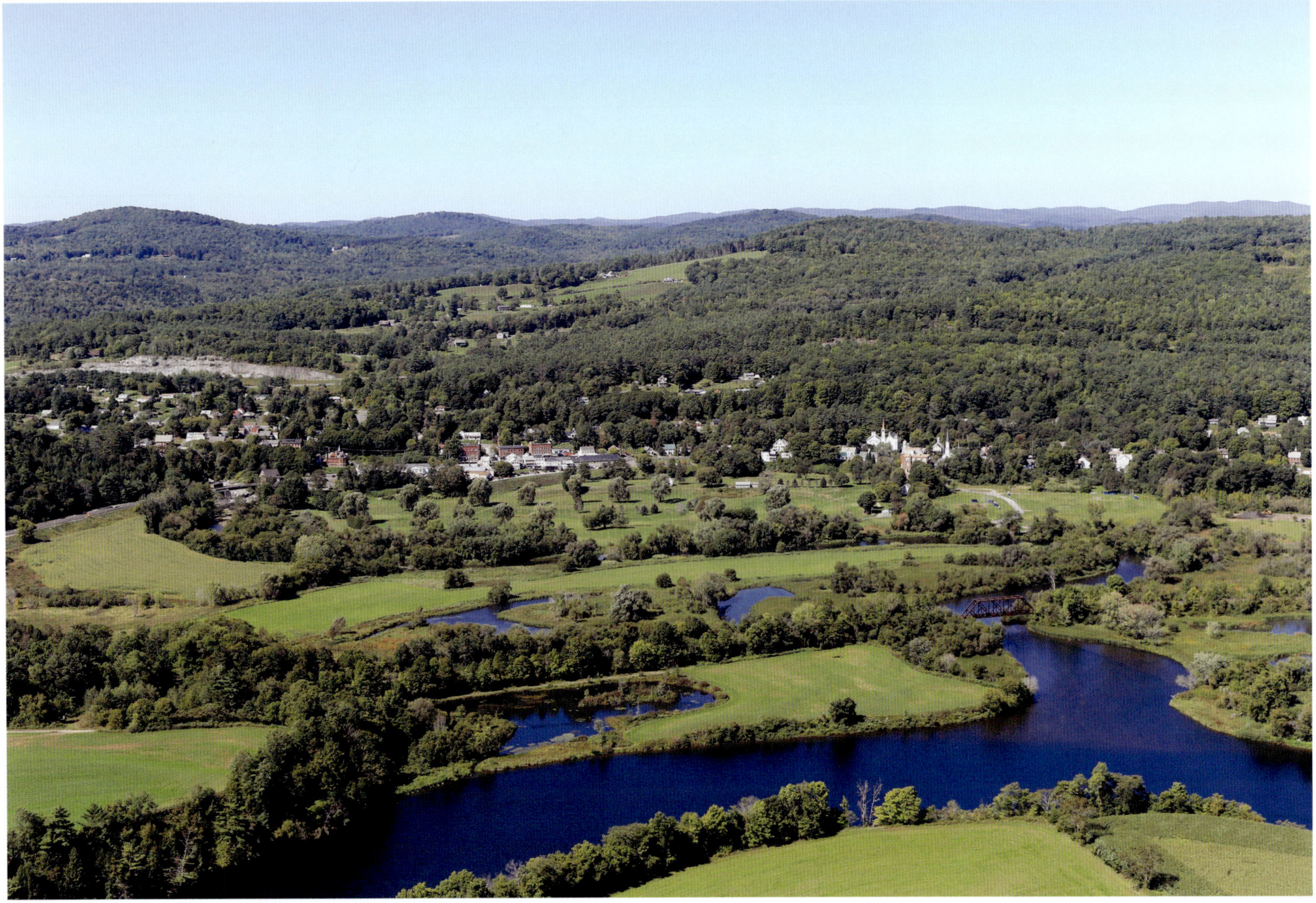

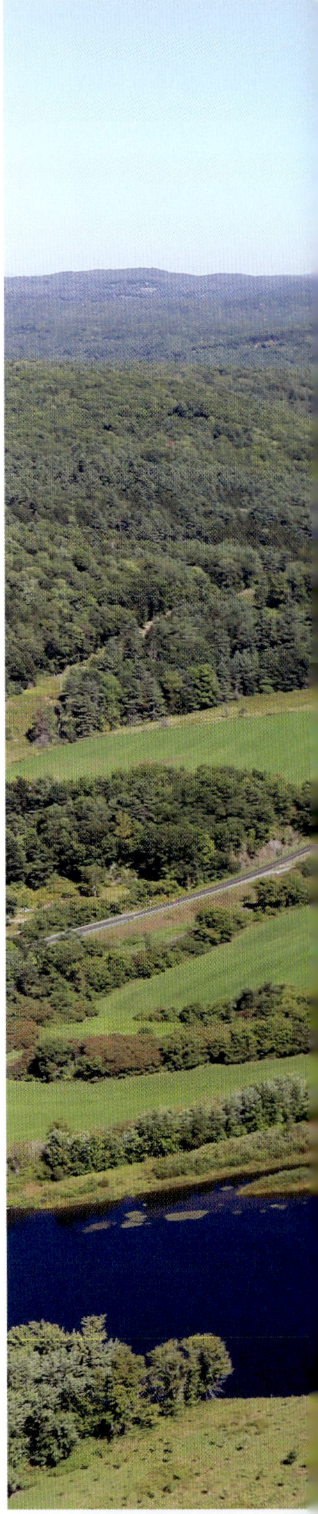

(above) At Bradford, Waits River, named after one of the Rogers Rangers, flows through town into the Connecticut River. The Rangers were made up of provincial soldiers from New Hampshire attached to the British army during the French and Indian Wars.

(right) The river twists and turns near the base of the Bradford Oxbow. Photographer Tom Walsh says: "This is another one of my favorite shots. I love how the river undulates like a snake in this area and I was trying to capture that feeling."

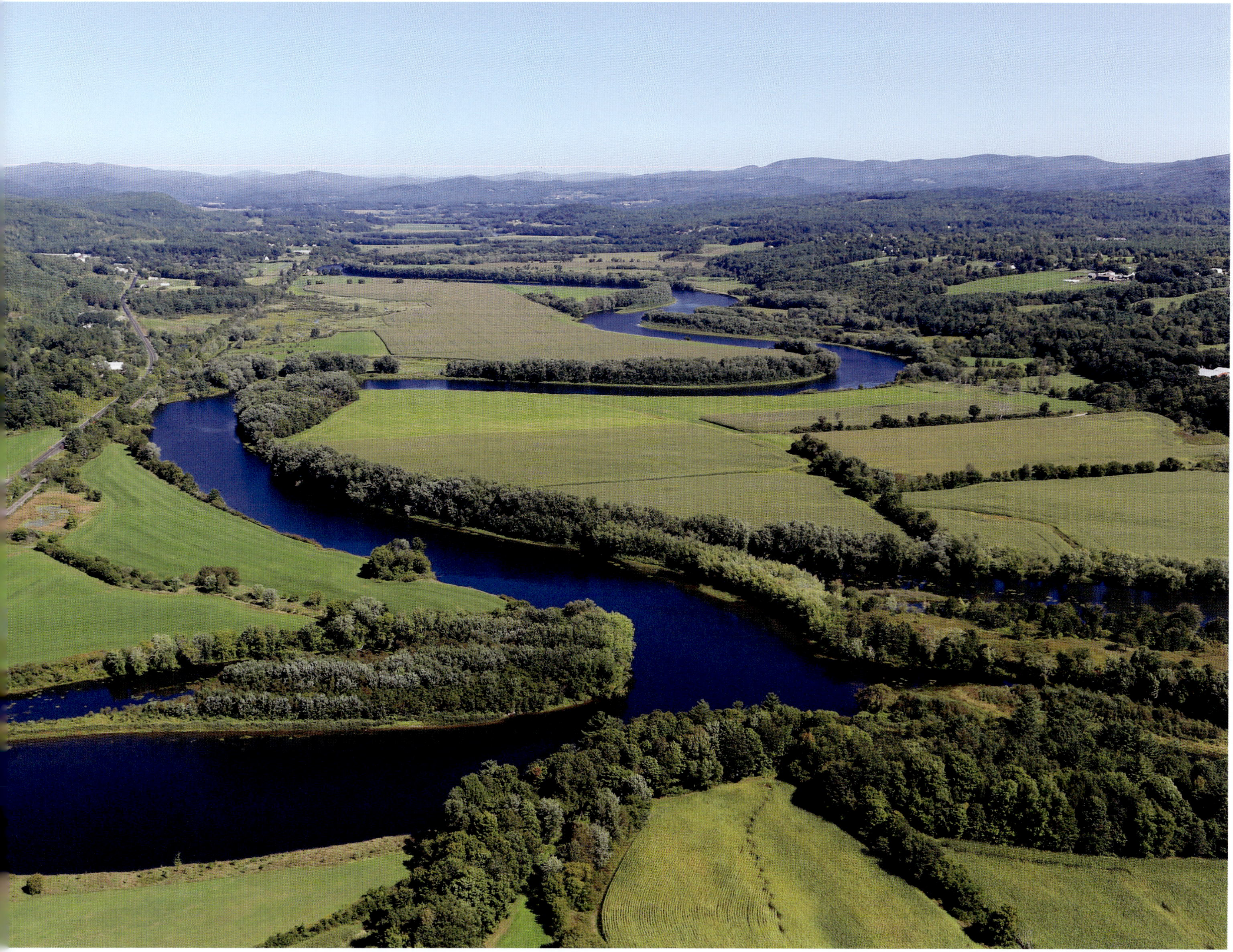

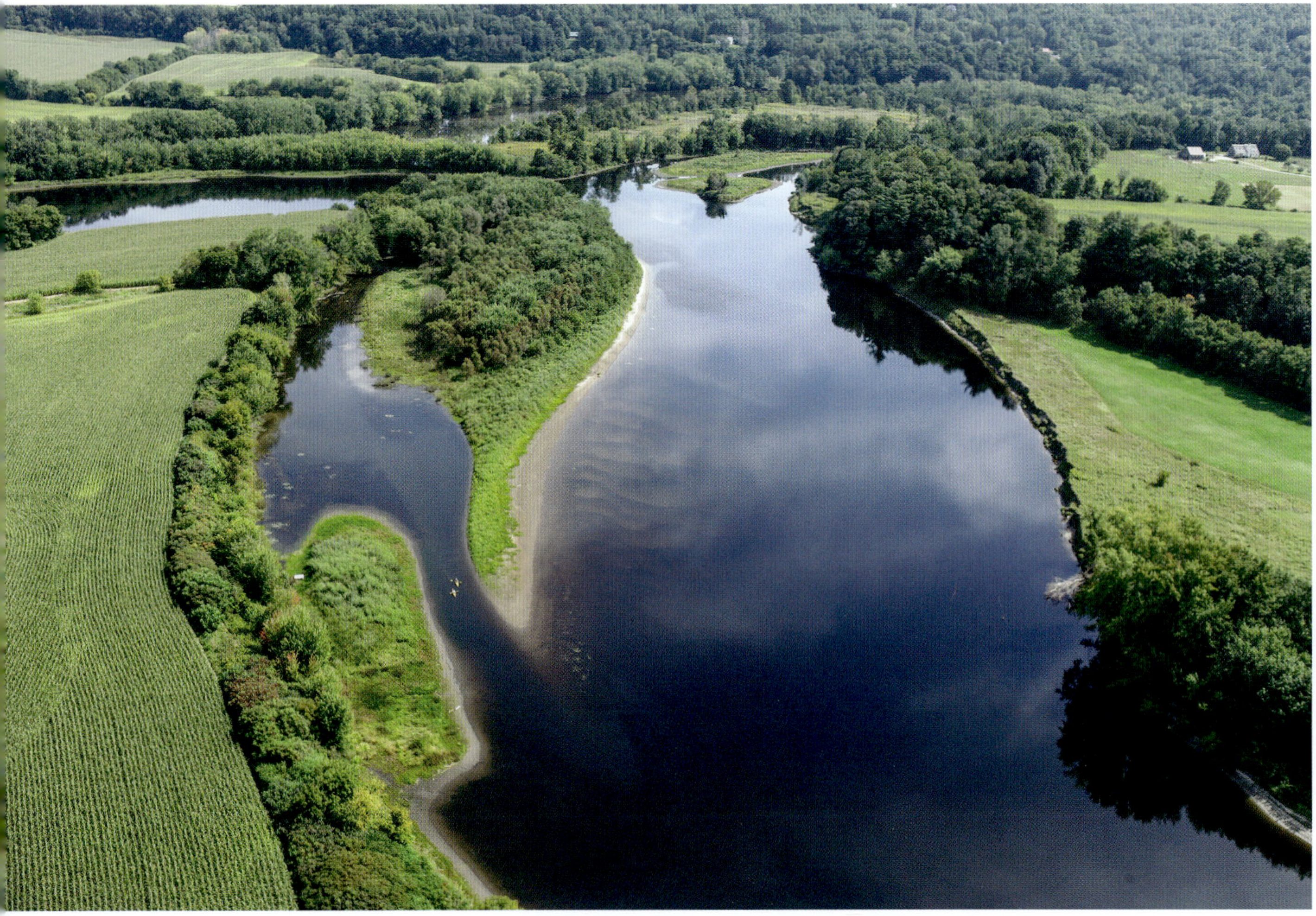

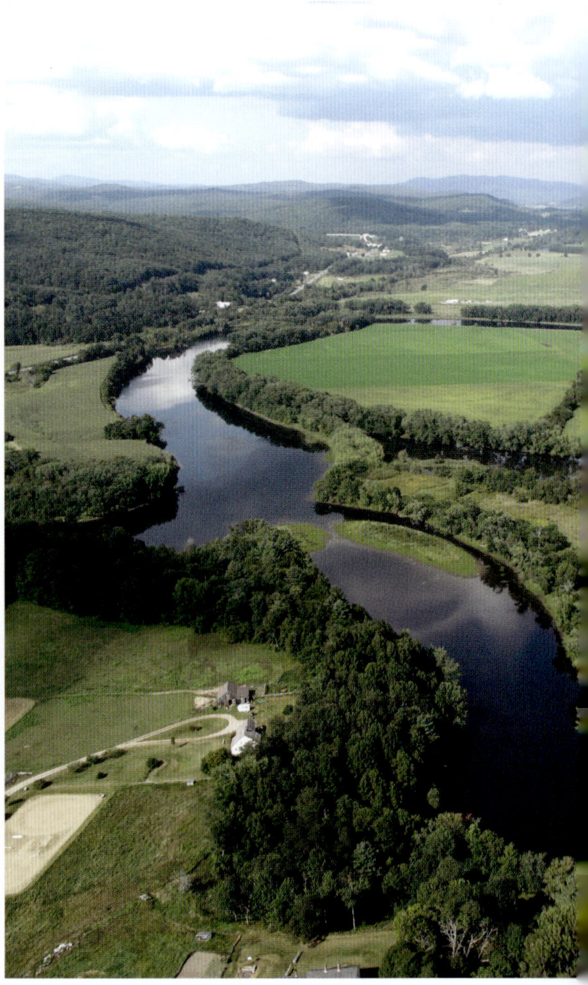

A pair of kayakers explore a cove created at the entry of the still-evolving oxbow near Bradford.

The magnificent Bradford oxbow within the fertile river valley ascending to the north.

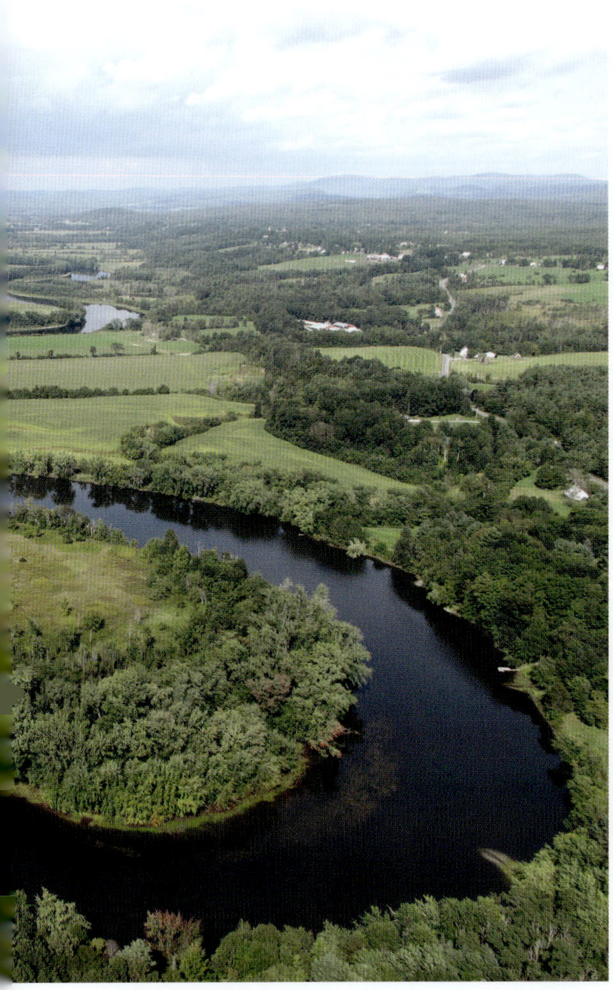

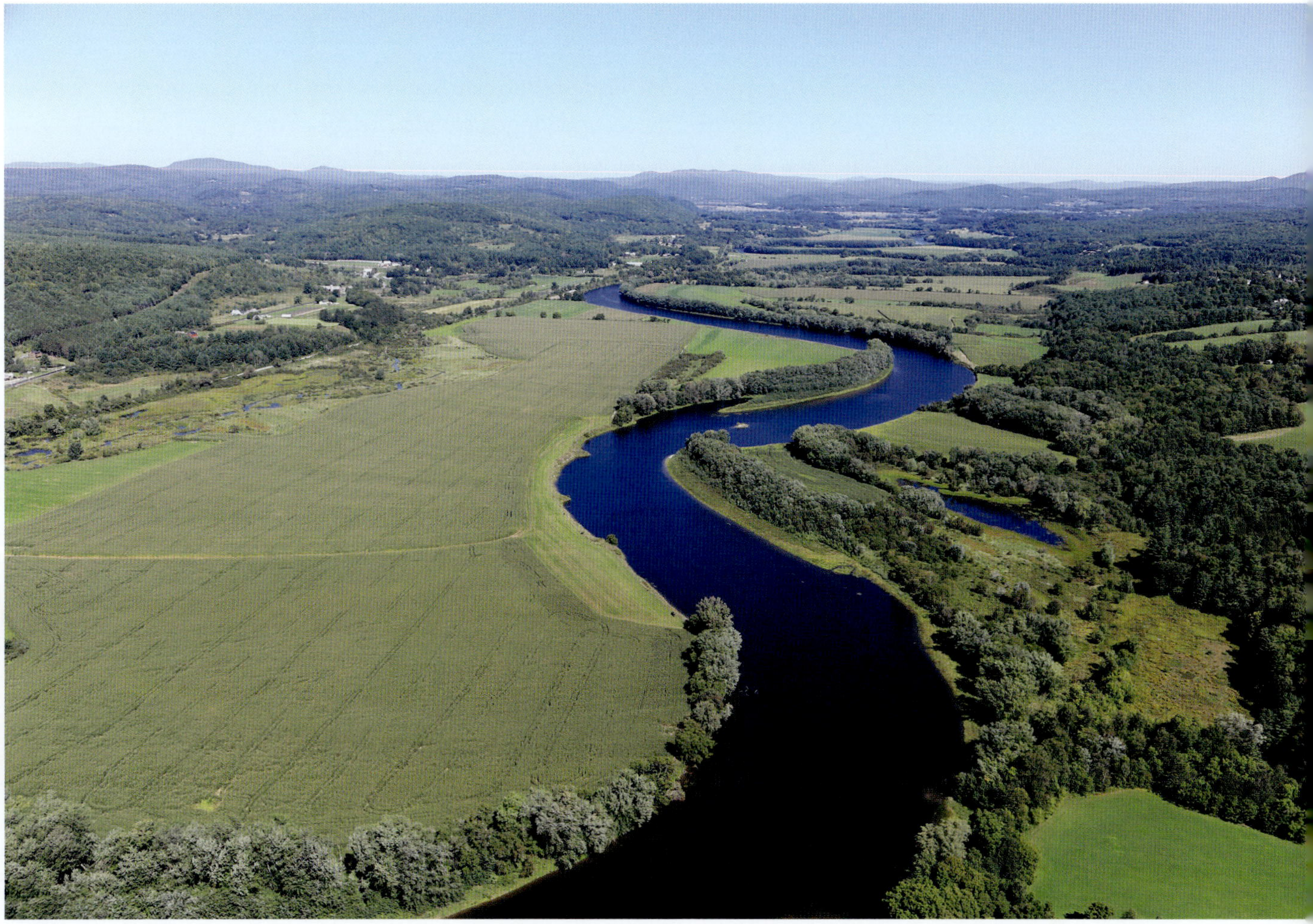

Some interesting patterns formed by trees hugging the river's course just upriver of the Bradford Oxbow.

BEDELL BRIDGE

Near Haverhill, New Hampshire, a lone bridge abutment stands in the middle of the river with a small tree growing from its top. The historic two-span Bedell Bridge, the second longest wooden bridge in the country, crossed the river here between Newbury, Vermont, and Haverhill, New Hampshire. Built in 1866, it was at last brought down by high winds 1979. It was in fact, the fifth bridge built at this location. All four of its predecessors had also been destroyed by flood, storm, or high winds. The road that once led from Haverhill to the bridge now leads to a turnaround and a boat ramp with a sign for Bedell Bridge State Park. On the other side it is the same story, a road to nowhere that once joined communities on either side of the river. There are no plans for a sixth bridge here!

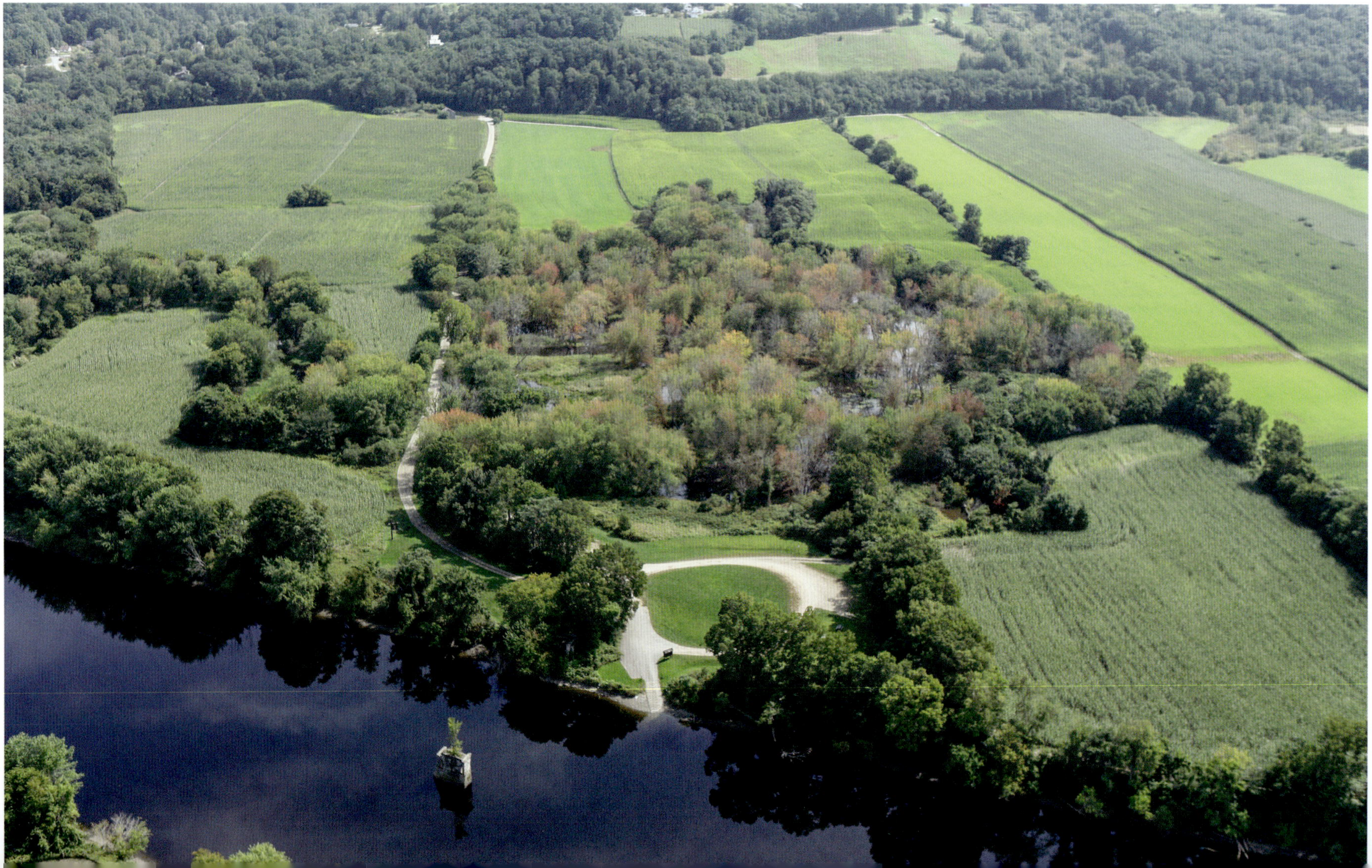

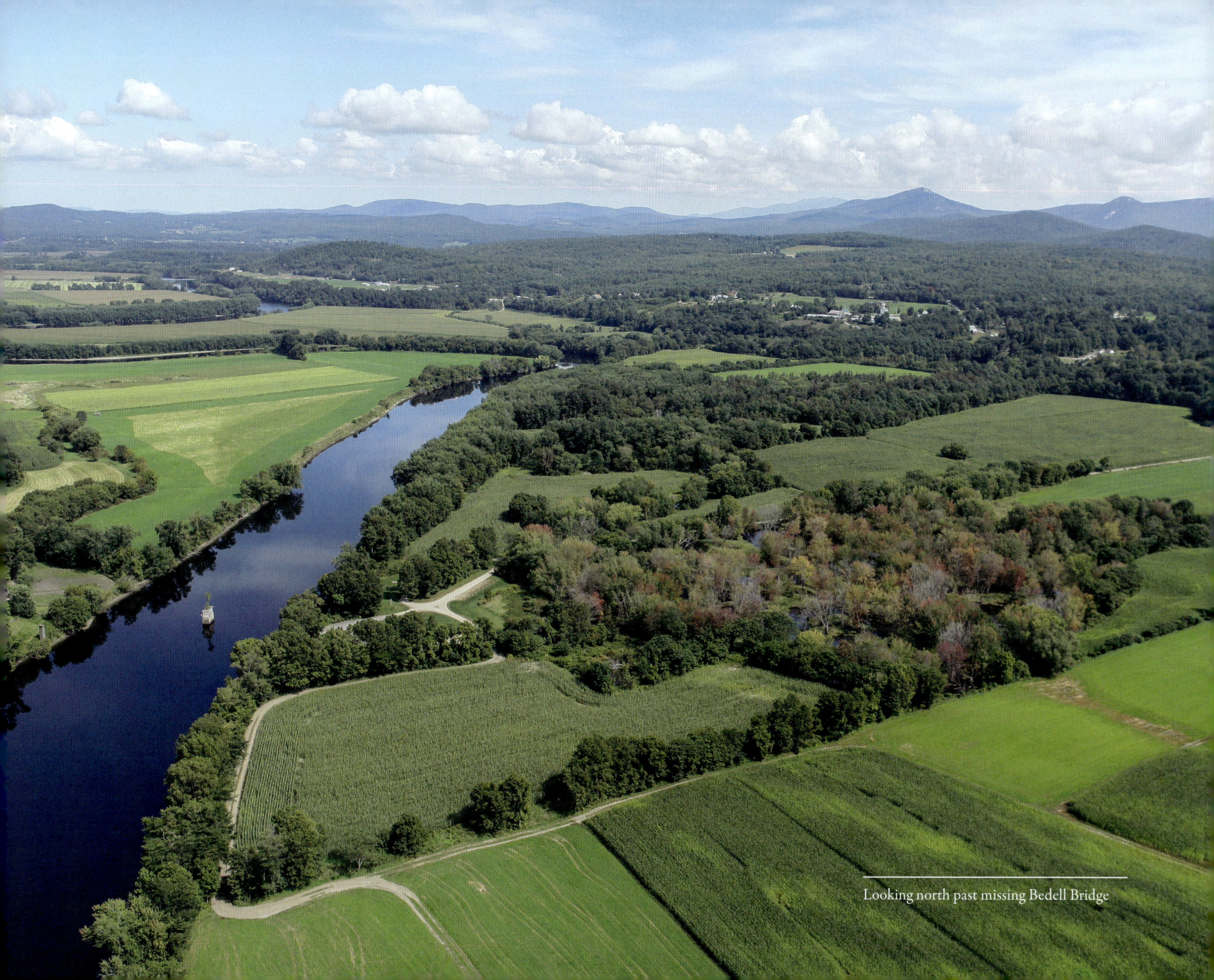

Looking north past missing Bedell Bridge

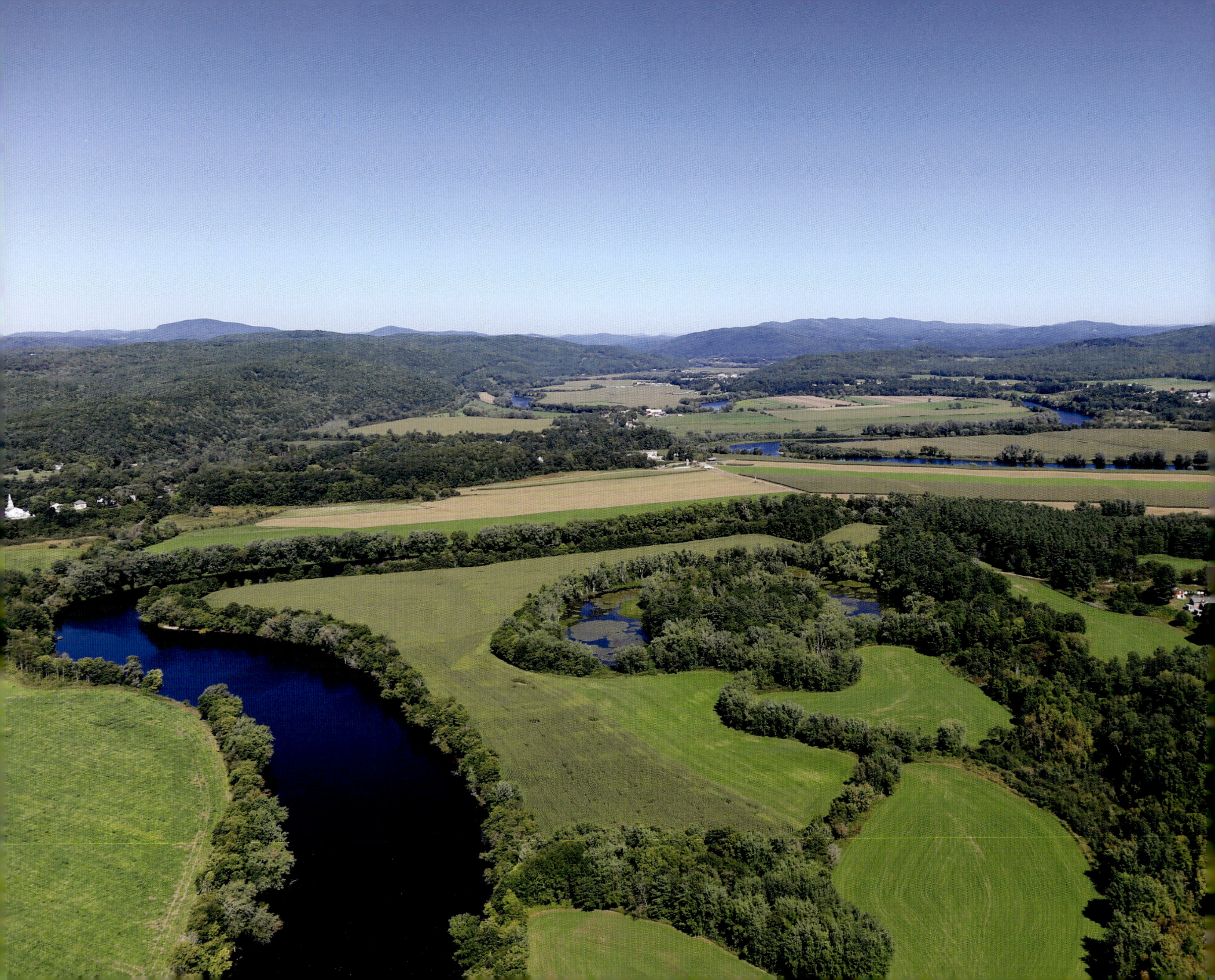

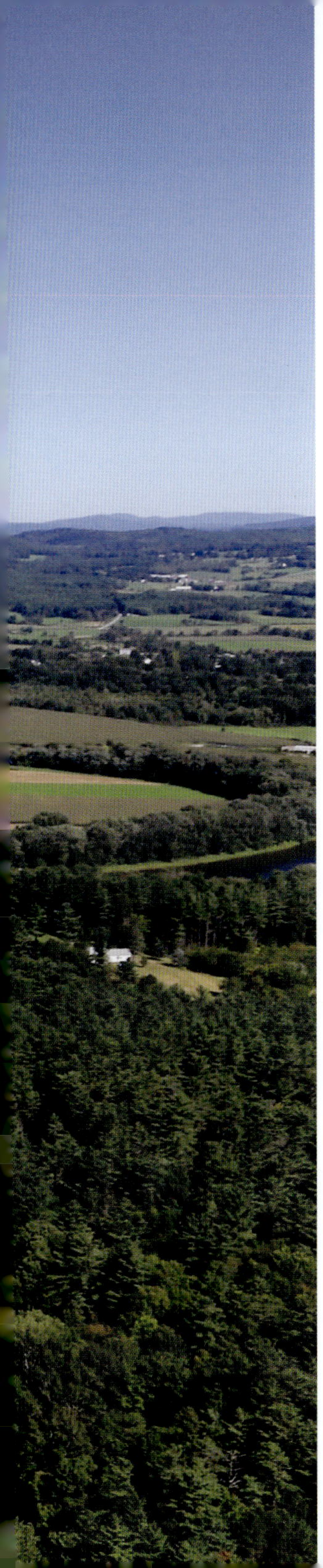

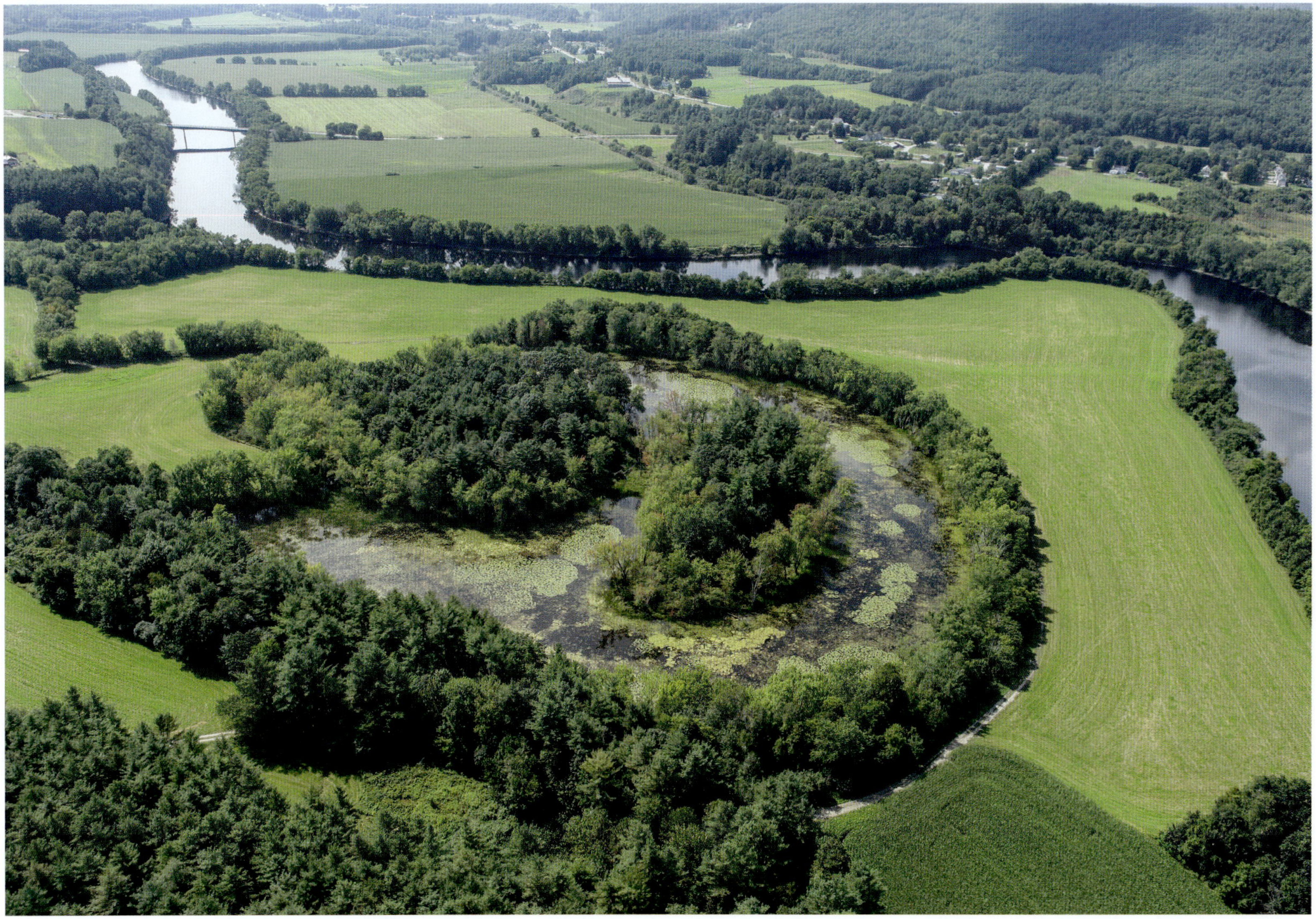

(left) A bypassed oxbow within a bend in the river near Newbury, Vermont, where the church steeple on the left is the tallest structure in town.

(above) Looking south over the isolated Newbury Oxbow, the thicket of trees at its core has become an island within an island. It is surrounded by the marshy remnants of the former oxbow, the trees that once lined its flowing course, well-tended farmland, and the new course of the river that flows southward, oblivious of its distant landlocked ancestor.

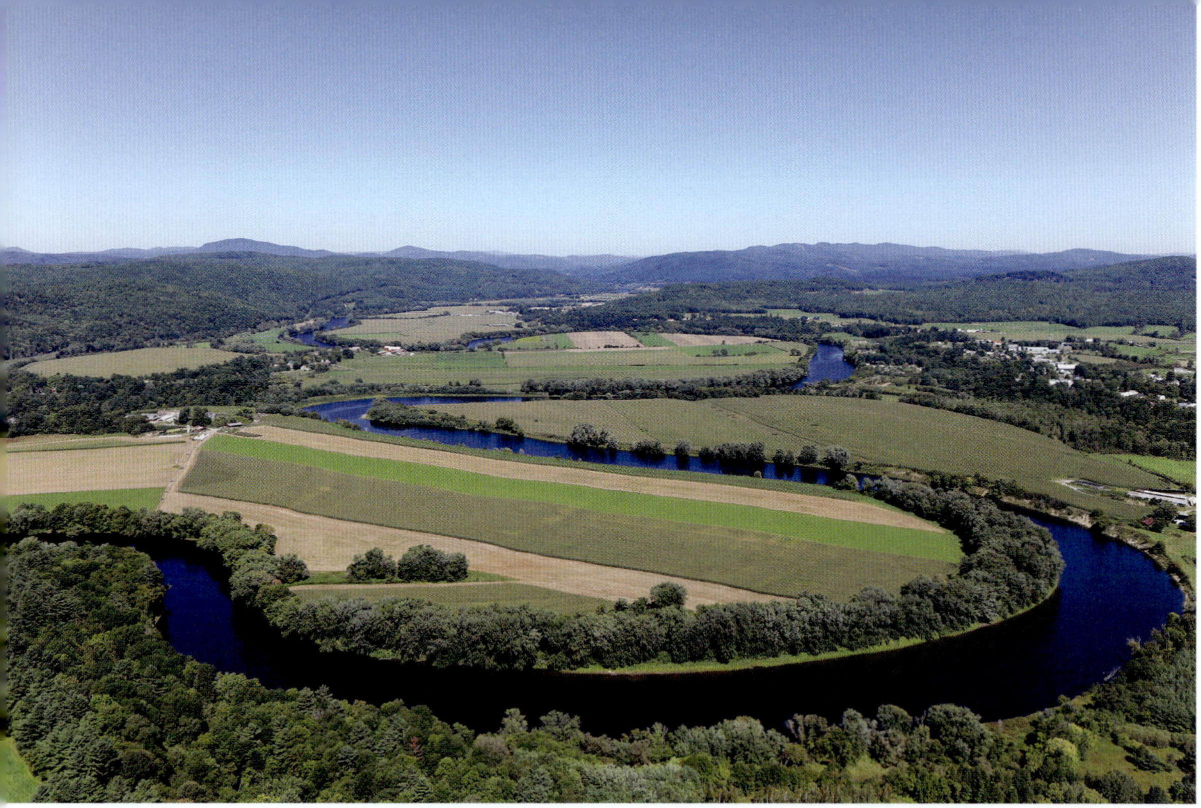

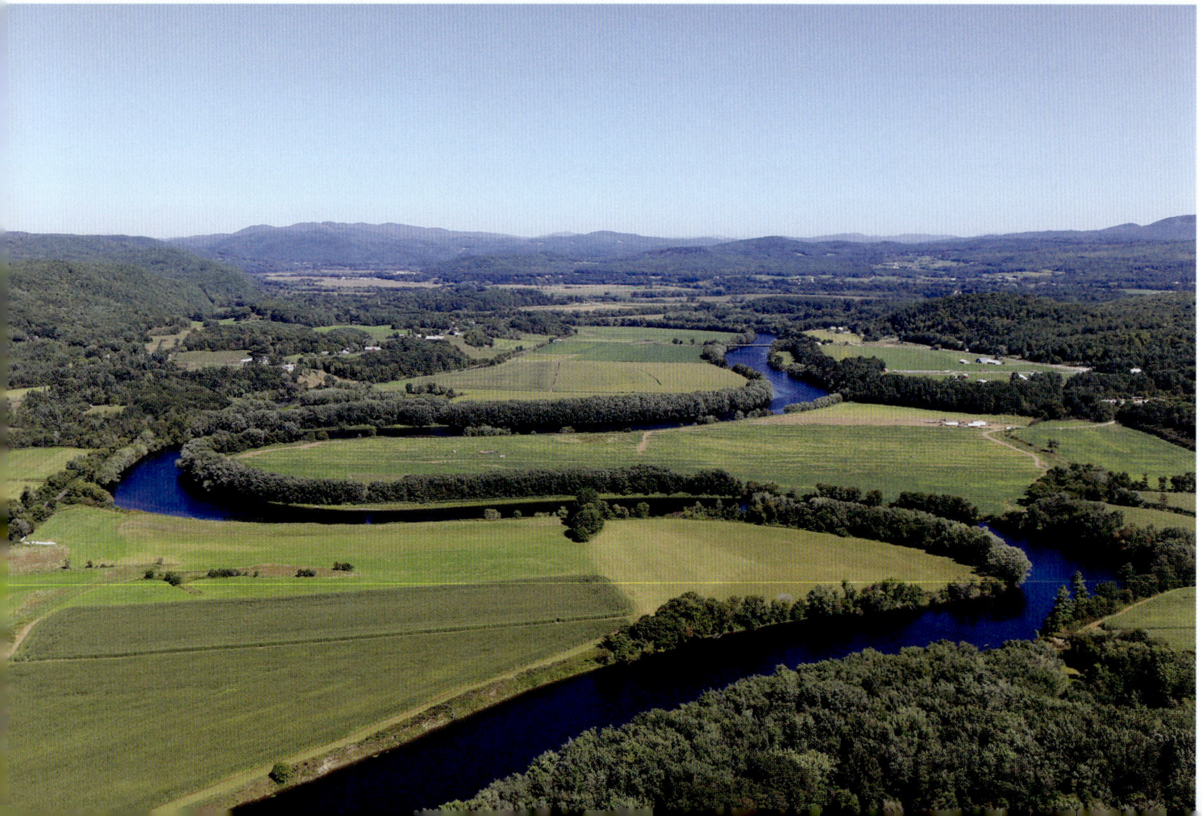

(top and bottom left) More twists and turns, farms, forests, and mountains on the way north

(right) North Haverhill, New Hampshire, lies along Route 10 next to a great bend in the river that doubles back on itself. Is this perhaps another grand oxbow in the making?

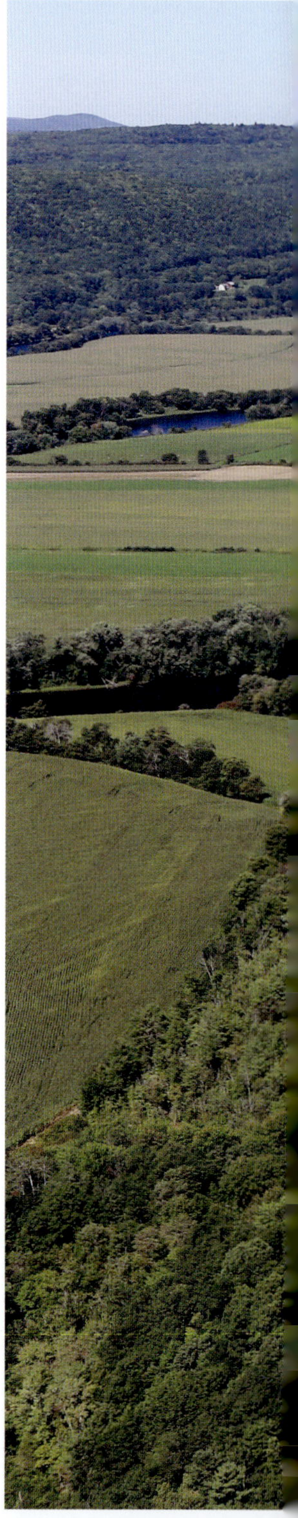

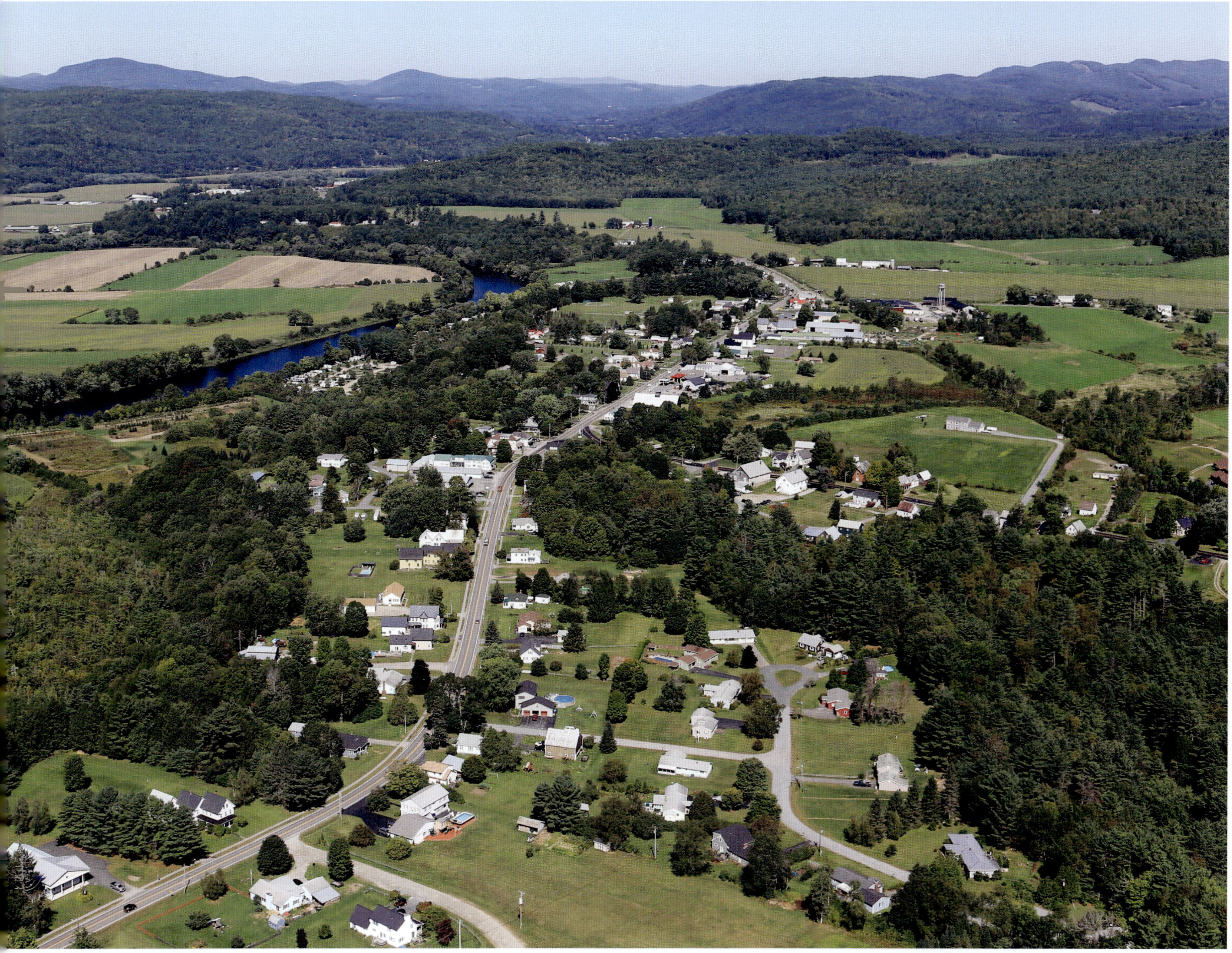

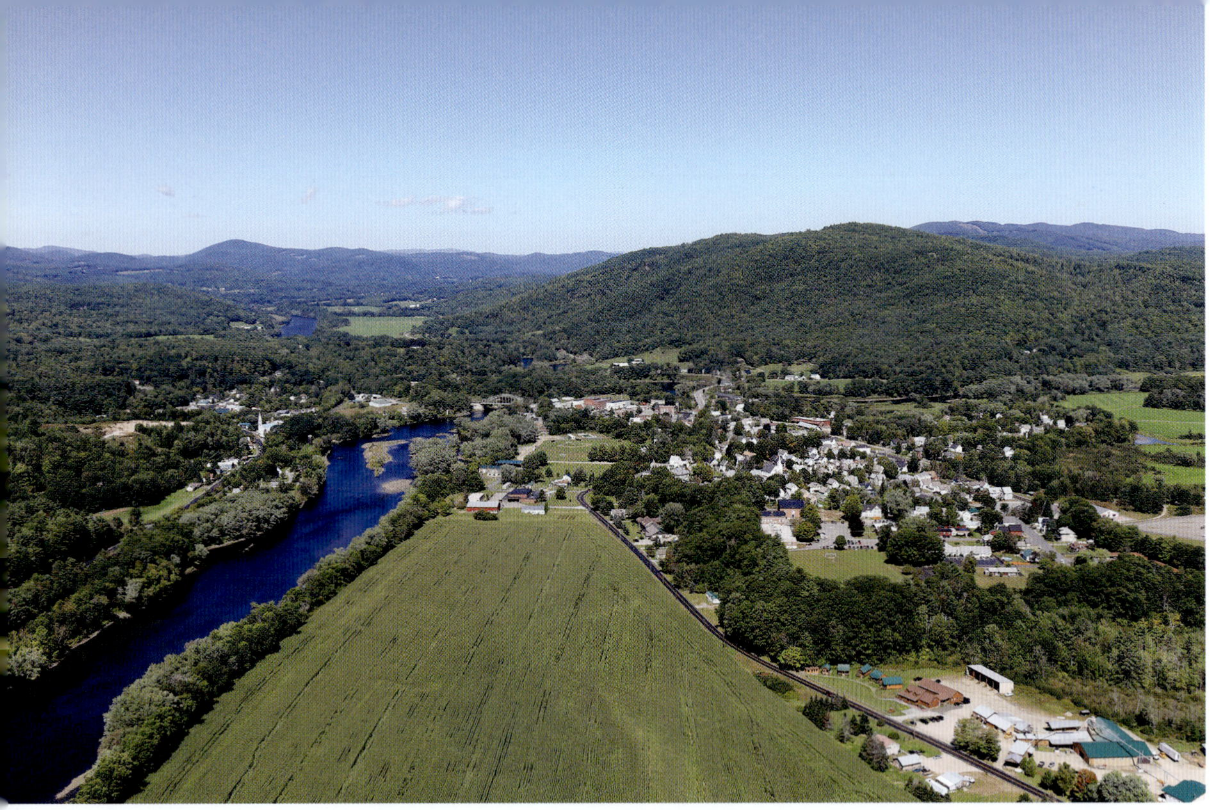

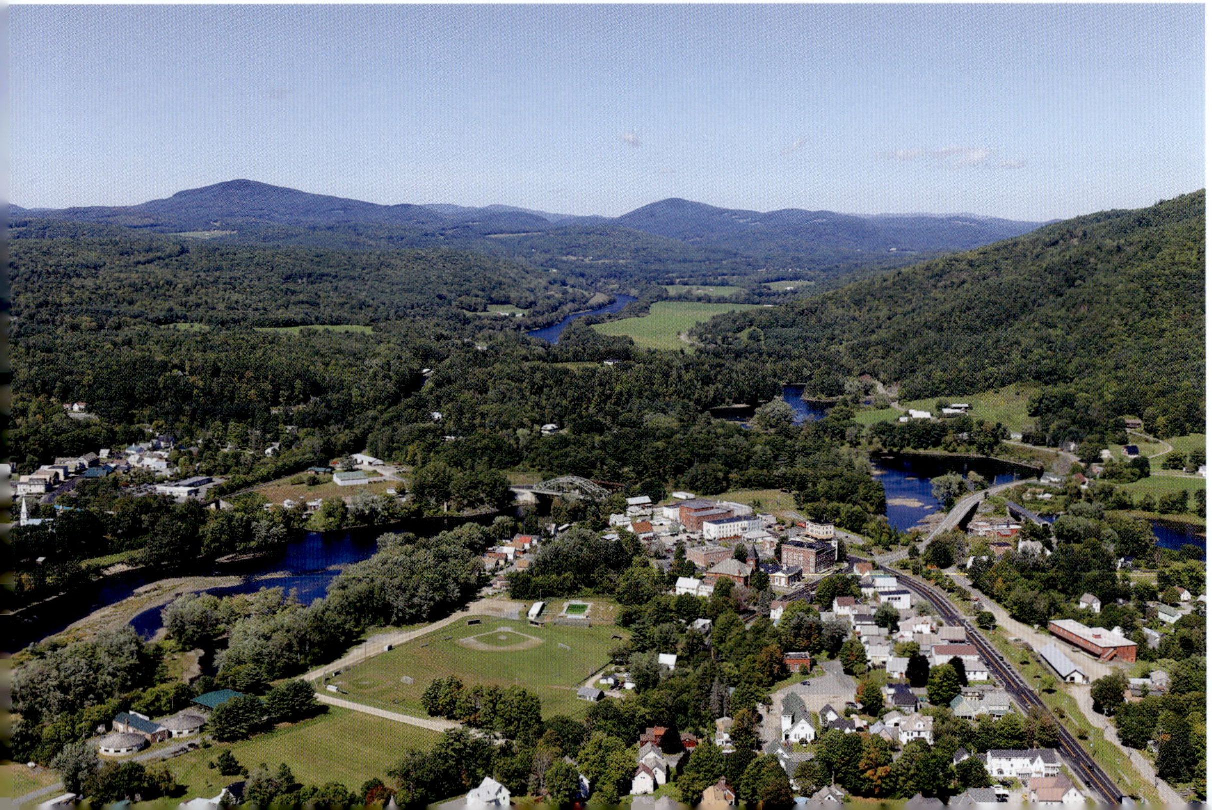

(top left) Approaching Woodsville, New Hampshire, on the east bank, with Wells River, Vermont on the west

(bottom left) Woodsville in the foreground with Wells River just across the Connecticut River

(right) Looking west over the Haverhill-Bather covered bridge which spans the Ammonoosuc River as it flows into the Connecticut River. Built in 1829, it is the oldest remaining covered bridge in the United States. Its crossing is now bypassed by a modern bridge that carries State Route 135. In the distance, the arched span connects Woodsville, New Hampshire with Wells River, Vermont.

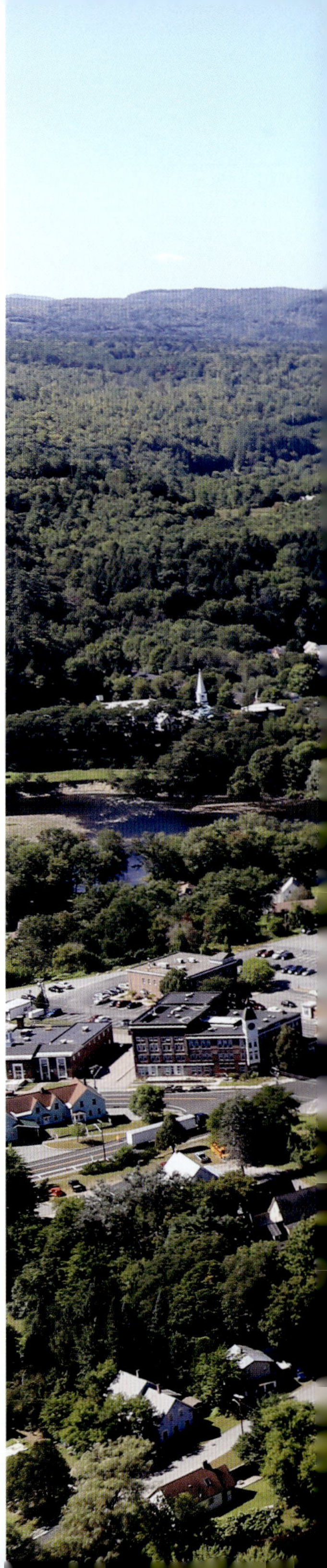

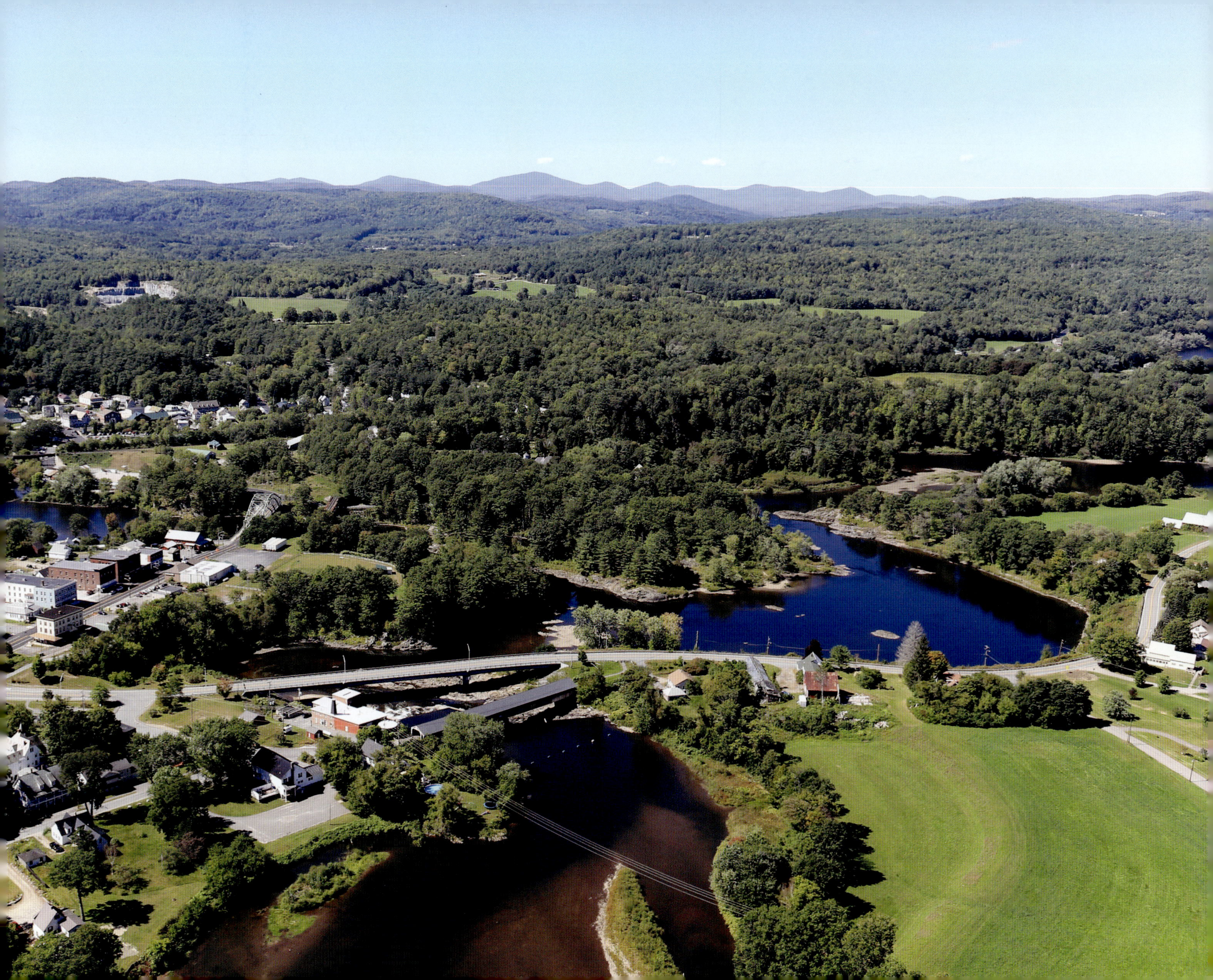

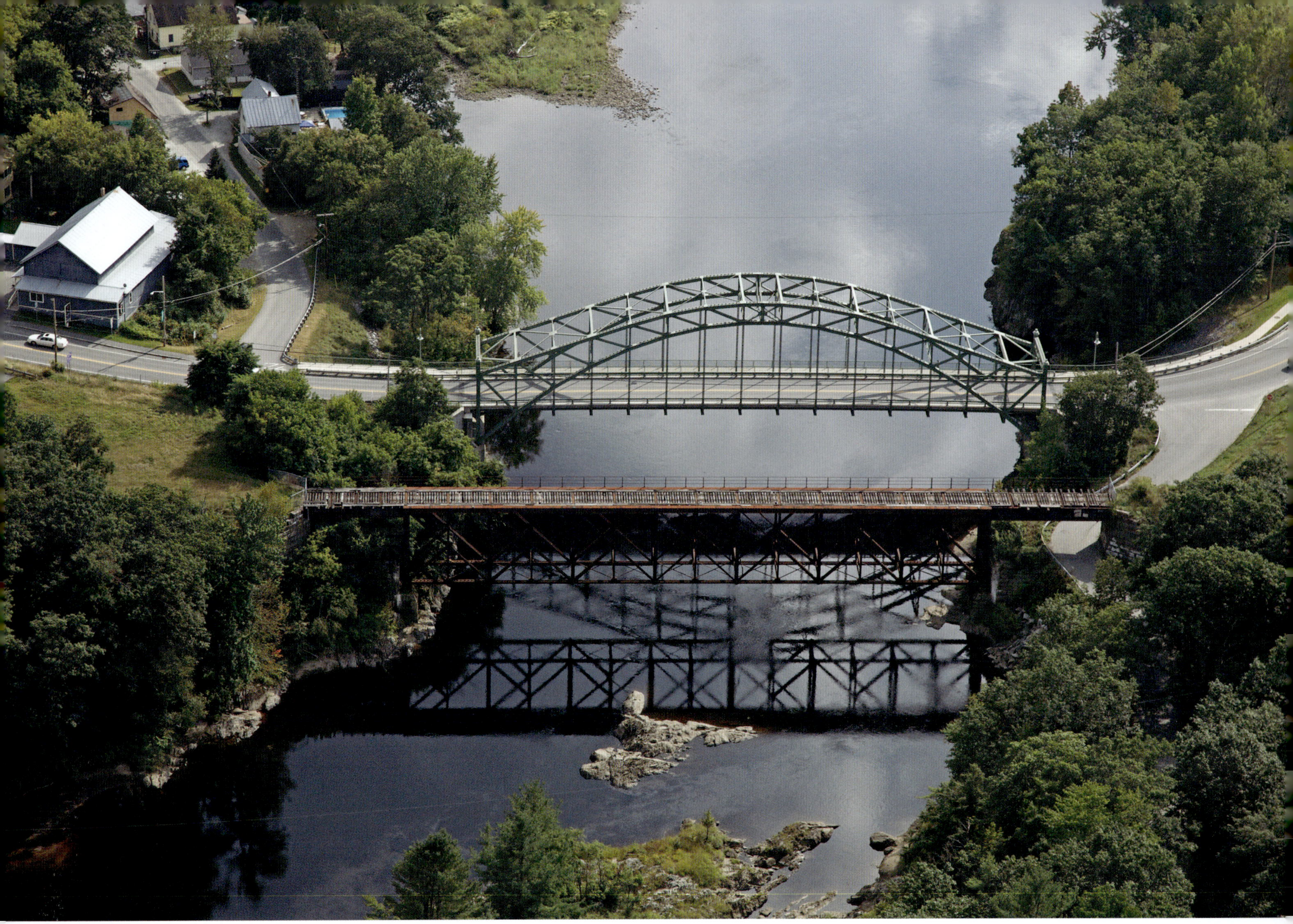

WOODSVILLE, NH

Woodsville, New Hampshire, where the Ammonoosuc River flows in from the east and the Wells River flows in from the west, has a long history associated with sawmills, log drives, and the railroad. A boom was hauled across the Connecticut River to Wells River to hold timber coming down from the north for sorting. Some of the logs would be sent to the town's mills while the rest were released to flow downriver. In 1853, Woodsville became an important center for the Boston, Concord & Montreal Railroad, launching the town's prosperity. A two-level bridge joined the town with Wells River featuring a toll road on the bottom and railroad track on top.

Wells River, Vermont became a center for trade due to its location at the northernmost point of practical navigation along the Connecticut River. Pole-propelled canal boats carried lumber and other products down the river and returned with staples such as rum, molasses, salt, and iron. In 1848, the Connecticut & Passumpsic Rivers Railroad reached Wells River. Soon connected to Woodville by the two-level railway and toll bridge the two towns became formidable regional transportation hubs strengthened by the arrival of Montpelier & Wells Railroad in 1873.

(left) Looking south, the arched bridge connects Woodsville on the left to Wells River on the right. The two-level steel bridge in the foreground was closed in 2001. It was built in 1903 to replace the earlier wooden double-deck bridge that was built here in 1853, which replaced an earlier 1805 bridge. Both bridges originally incorporated a roadway on the lower level and train tracks above.

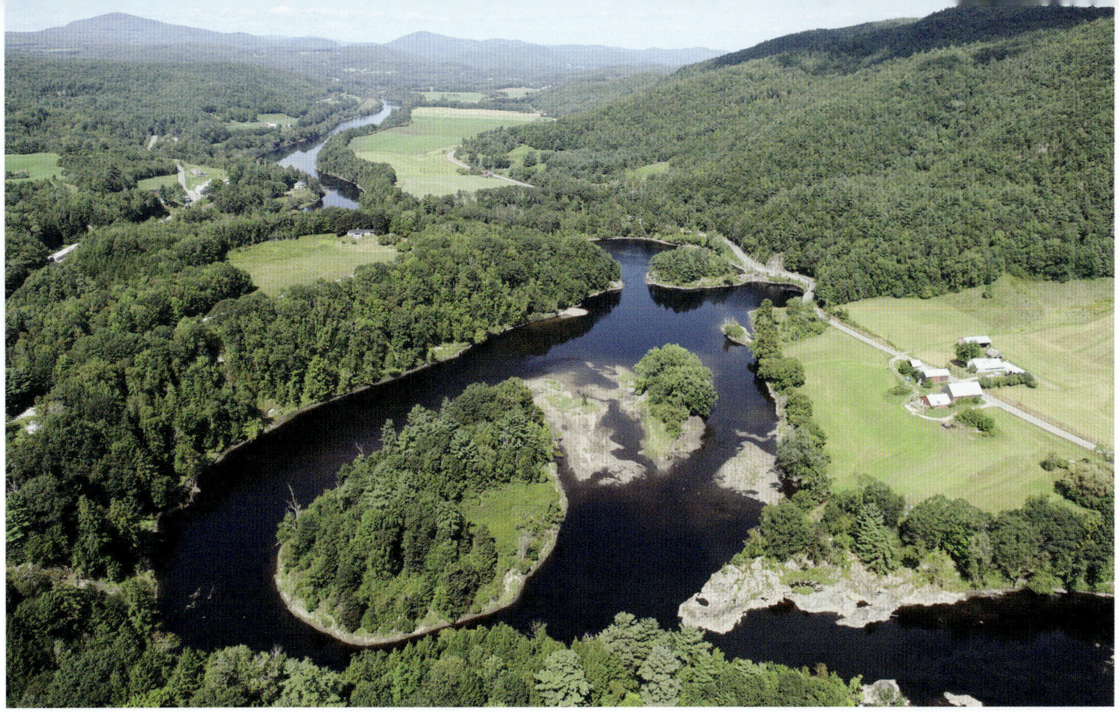

(above) Just above Woodsville the river flows down from the north and around this oxbow before passing between the two towns.

(below) Looking downriver, about a mile north of Woodsville, what at first appear to be three insignificant islands are in fact sunken wooden barges piled with stones and overgrown with vegetation. This image was headed to the discard pile until we noticed this little secret of the river.

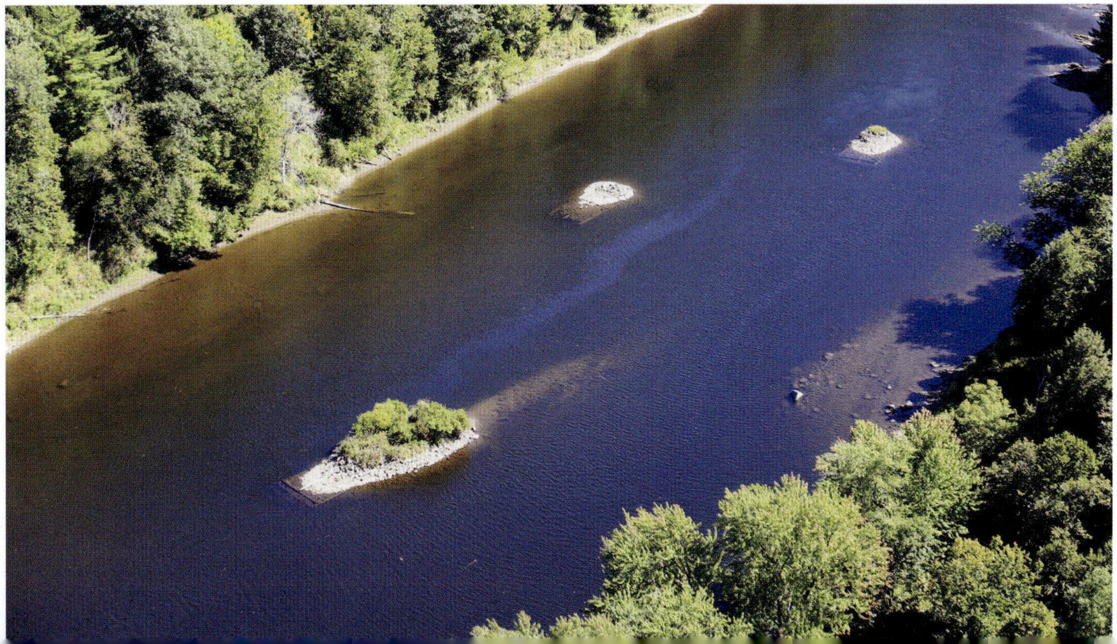

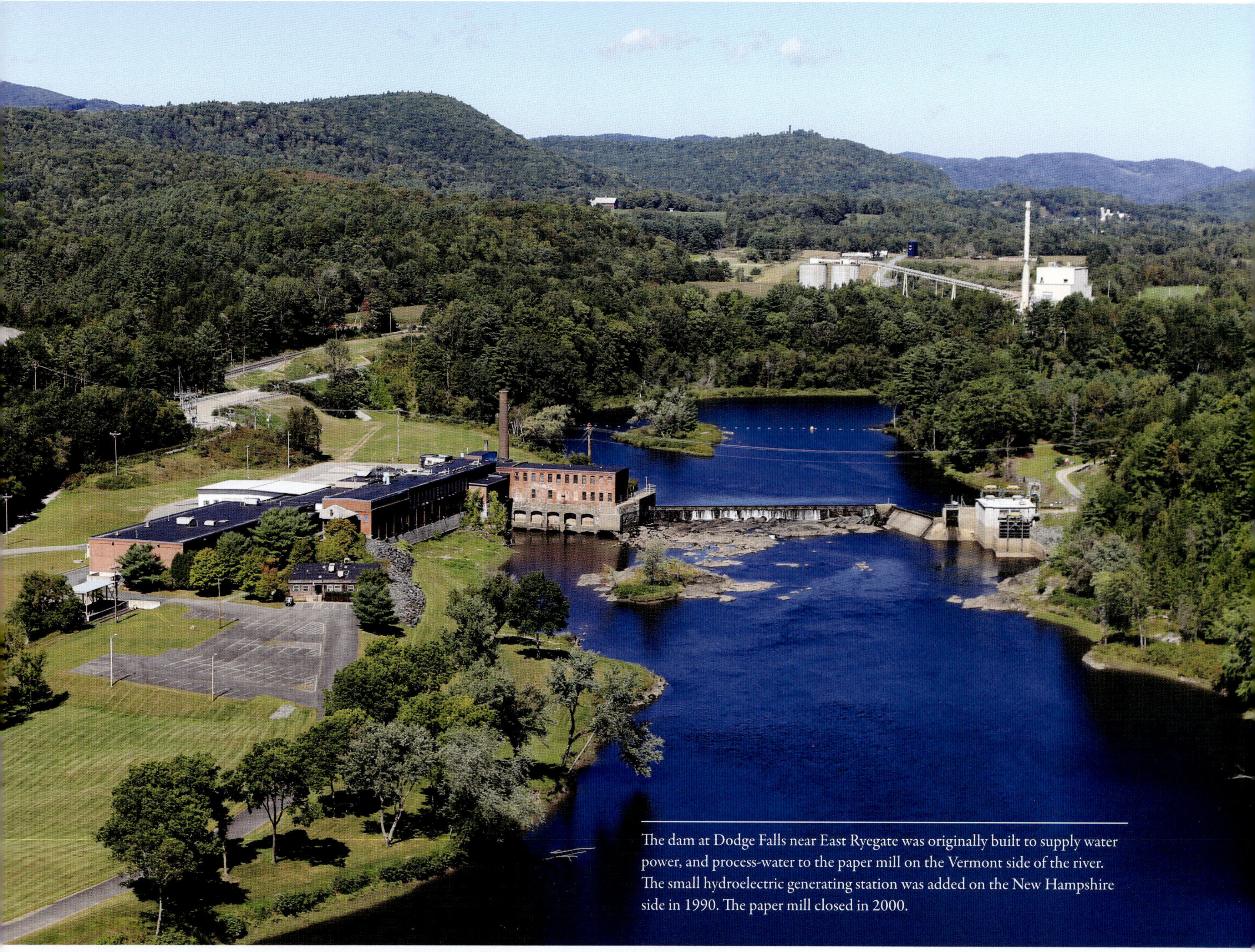

The dam at Dodge Falls near East Ryegate was originally built to supply water power, and process-water to the paper mill on the Vermont side of the river. The small hydroelectric generating station was added on the New Hampshire side in 1990. The paper mill closed in 2000.

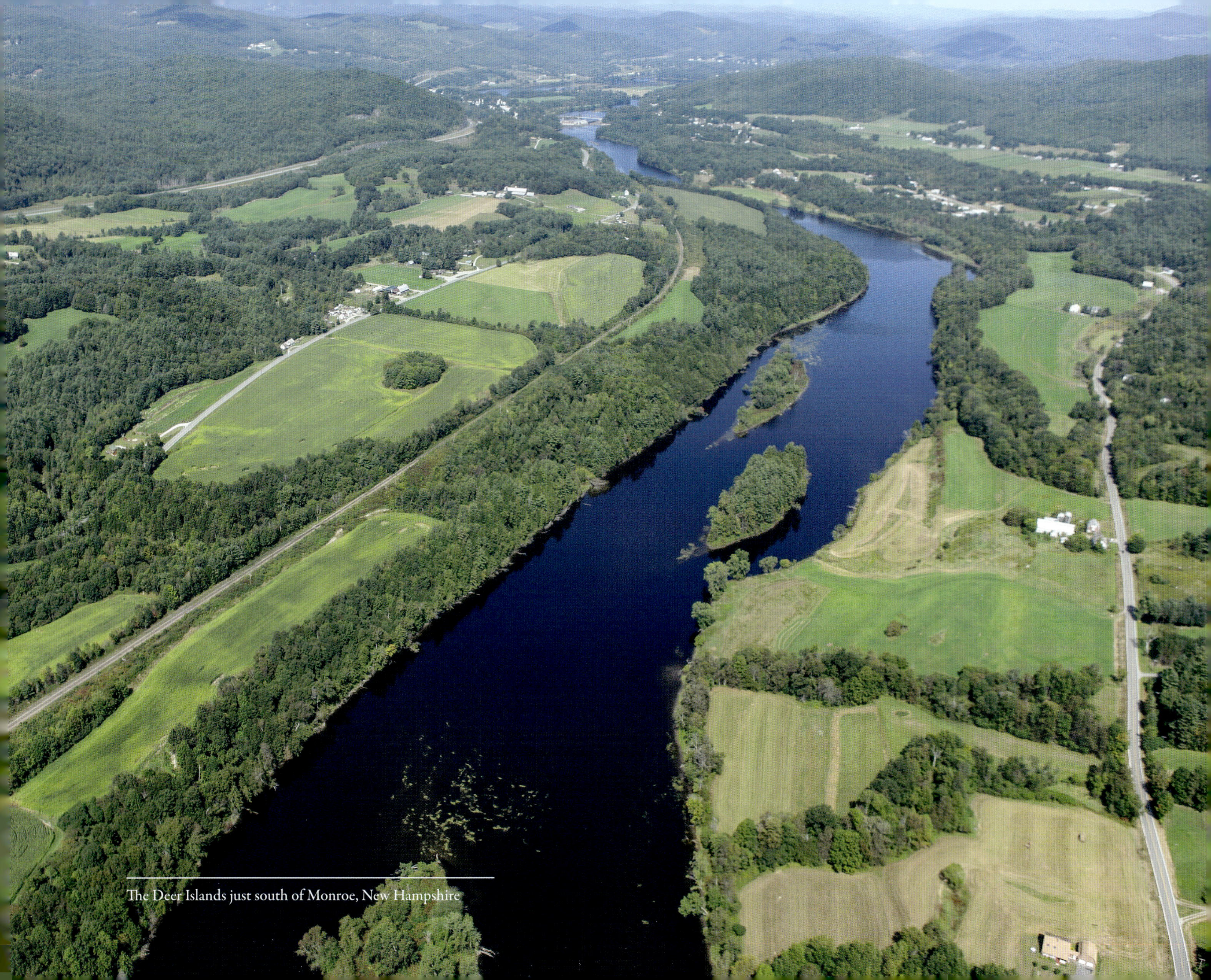

The Deer Islands just south of Monroe, New Hampshire

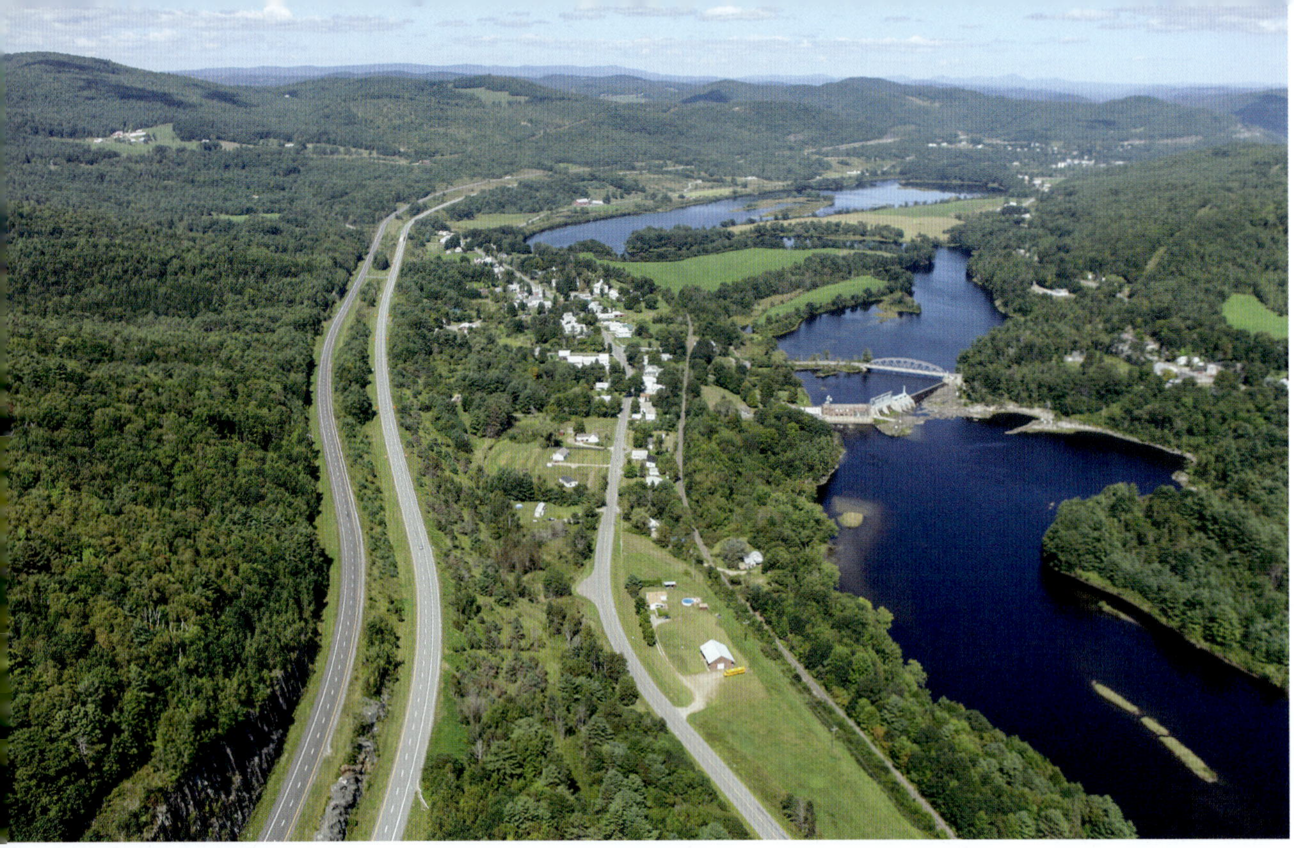

McINDOE FALLS DAM

McIndoe Falls Dam spans the river between the towns of Barnet, Vermont, and Monroe, New Hampshire. Completed in 1931, it is the southern-most of the three dams and power stations that were built along what were once known as the "15 Mile Falls," a stretch of the Connecticut where the river drops 350 feet. As early as 1900, the potential for waterpower along this stretch was recognized and plans were laid for the series of dams and power plants to tap it. The other two are the Comerford and Moore dams.

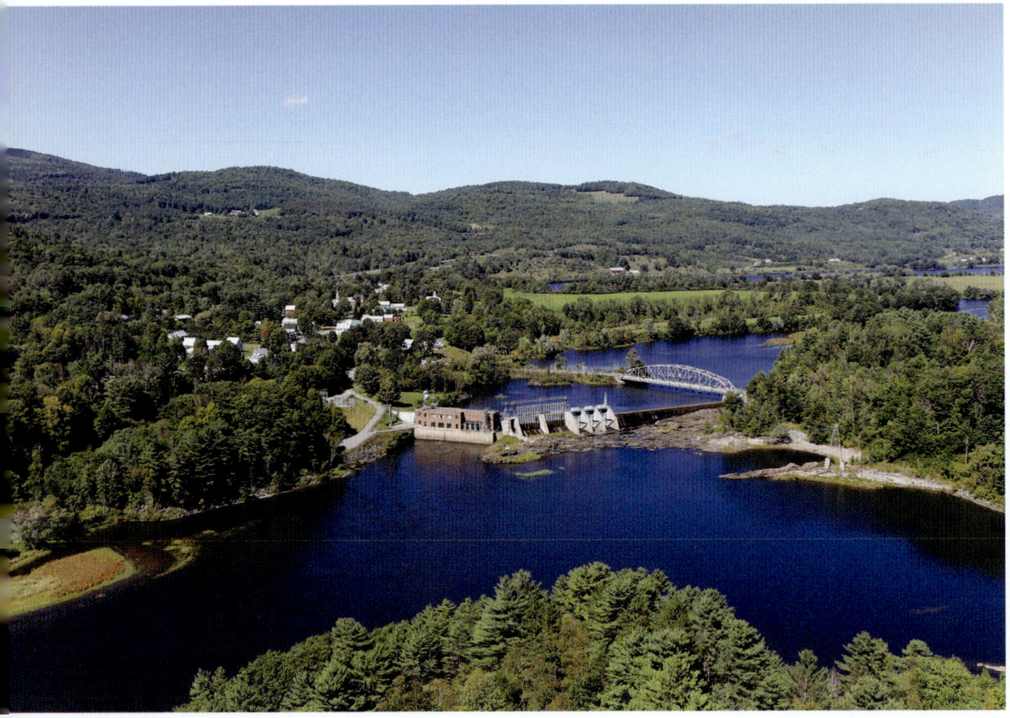

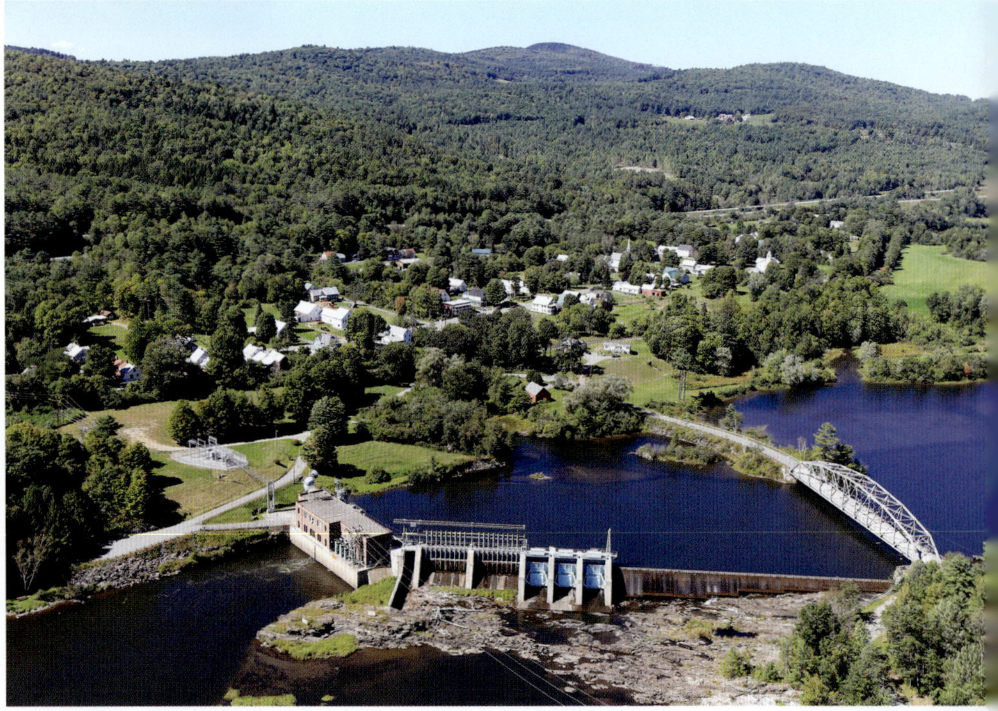

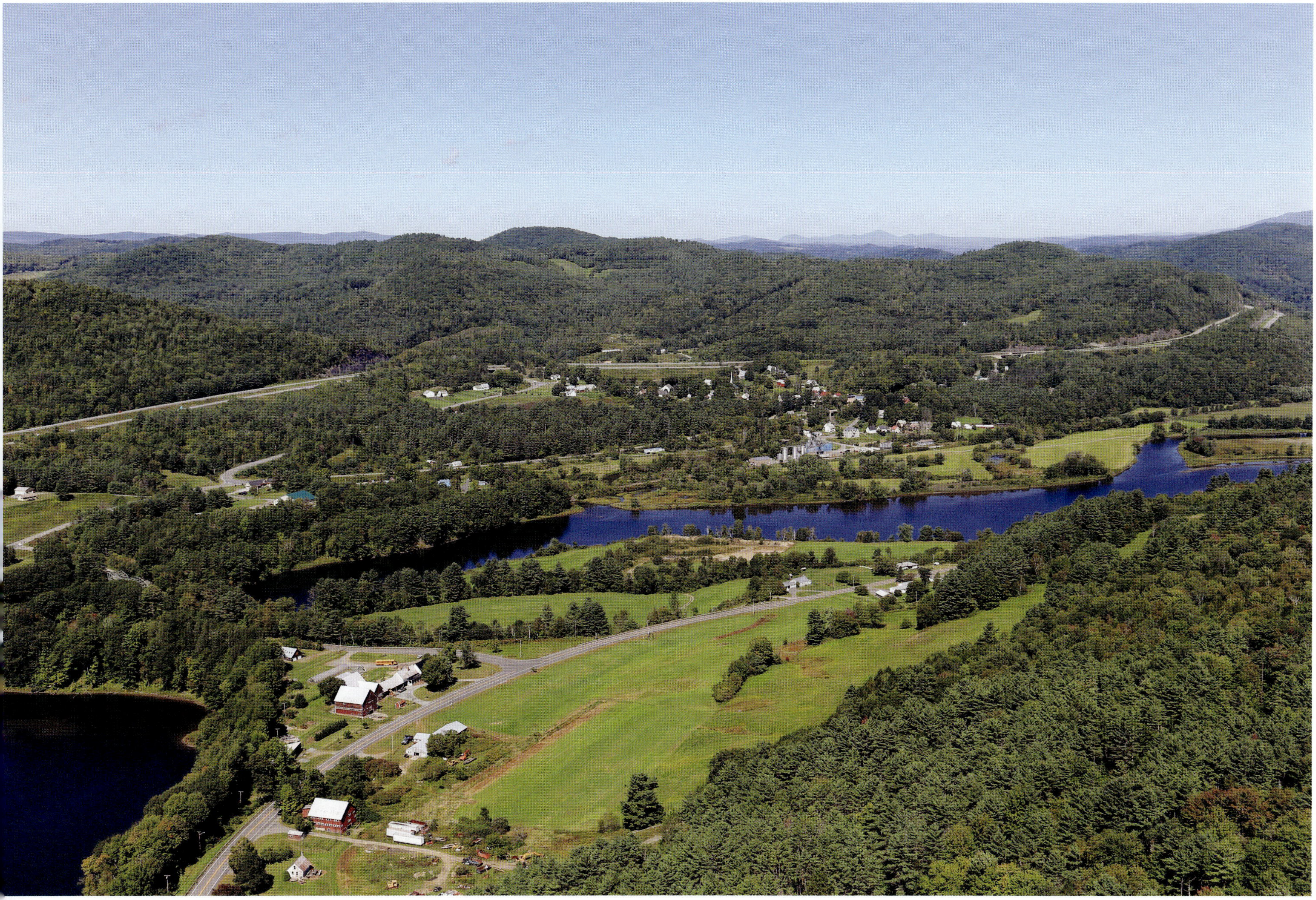

The town of Barnet, Vermont, lies just above the river at the northern end of the McIndoes Reservoir.

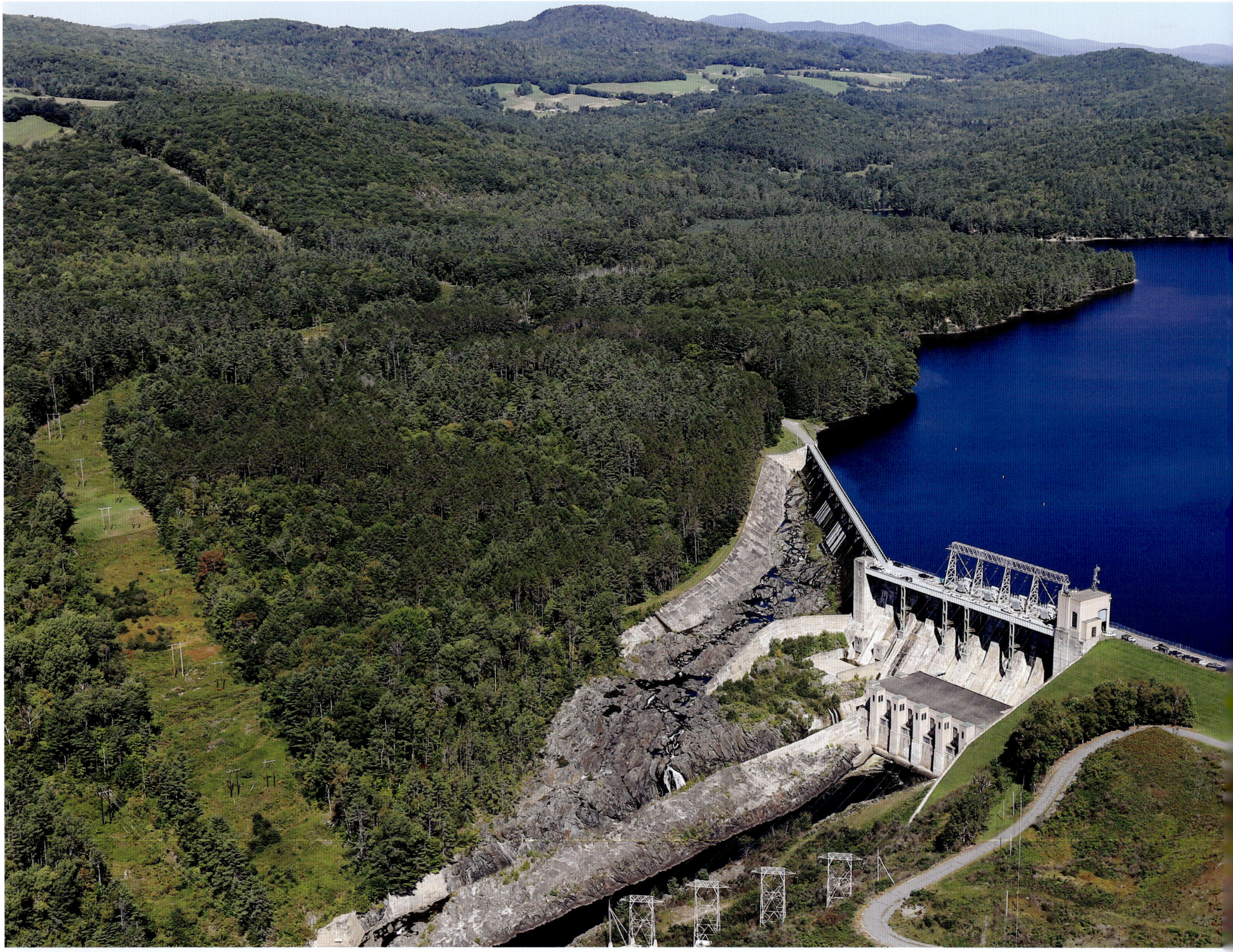

THE GREAT NORTH WOODS

This region includes the four Connecticut Lakes near the Canadian border and stretches south about 130 miles to where the Passumpsic River joins the Connecticut just below the Comerford Dam. On the Vermont side of the river this region has also been known as the Northeast Kingdom. In the northern parts of New Hampshire, which juts up above the 45th parallel between Canada and Maine, national and state border disputes, and even the declaration of an independent northern republic, were not settled until 1840. Dominated by spruce and fir forests this less populated region launched the great log drives that fed paper and timber mills hundreds of miles downstream.

THE LAST HUNDRED MILES

Comerford Dam to Source

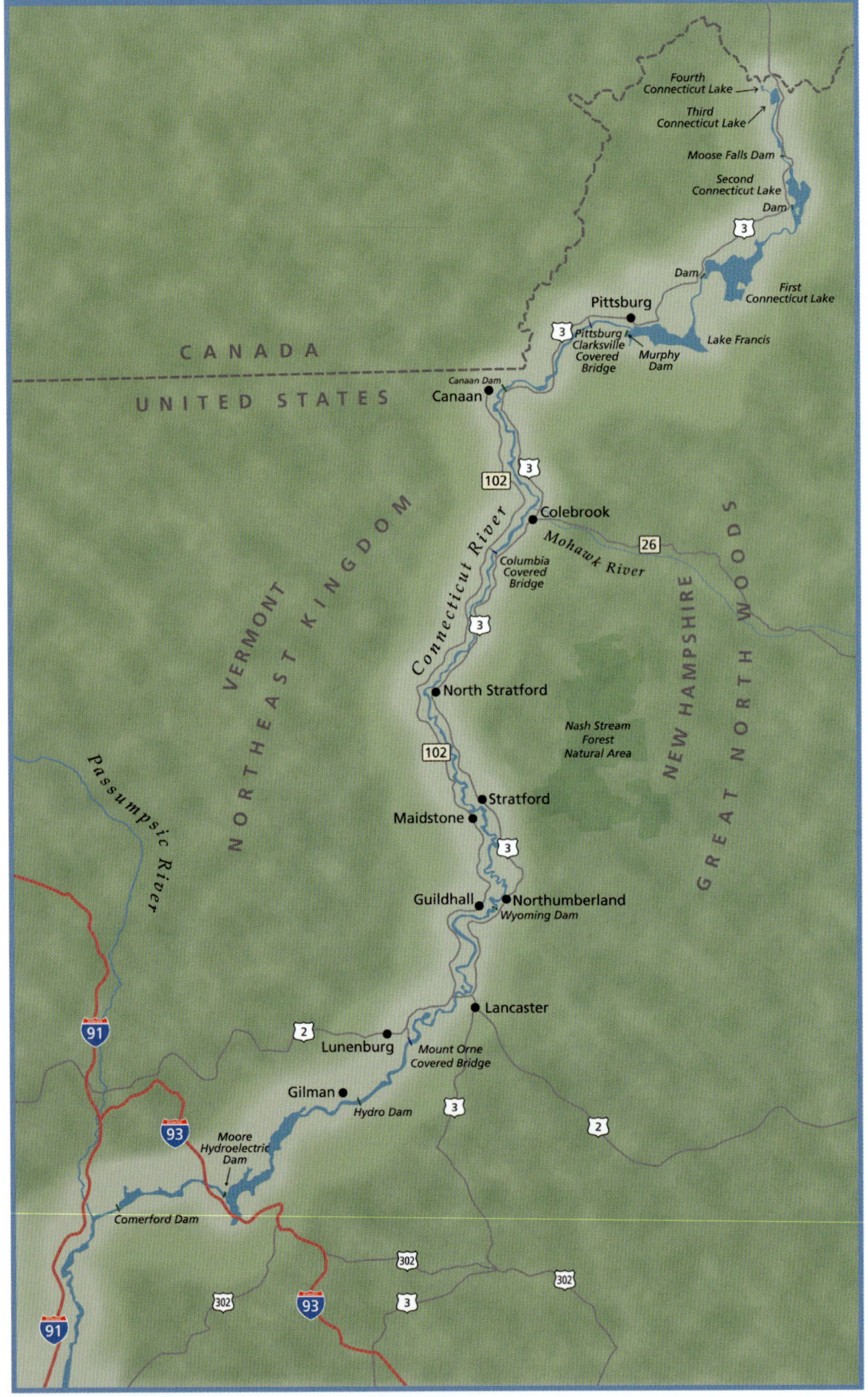

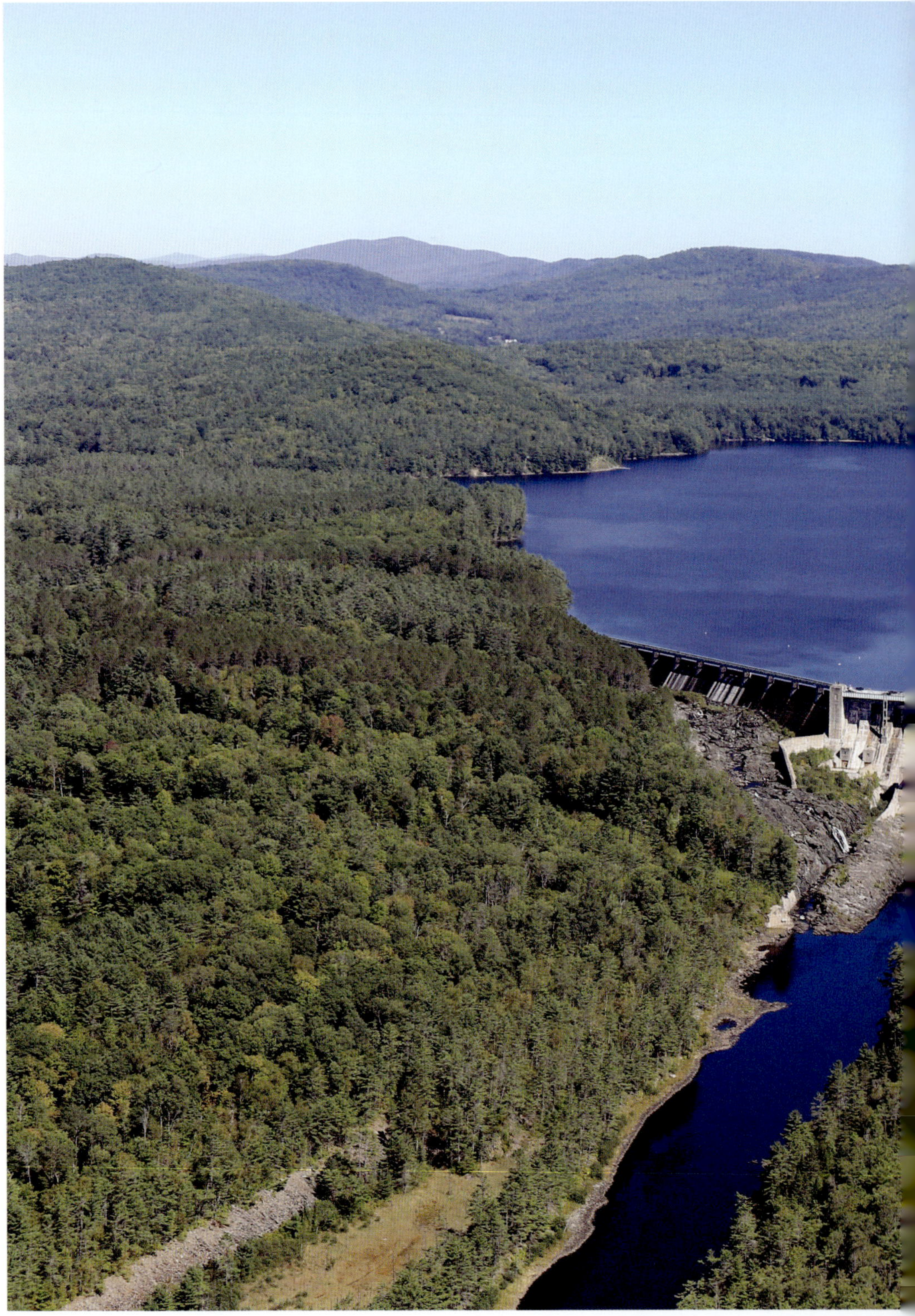

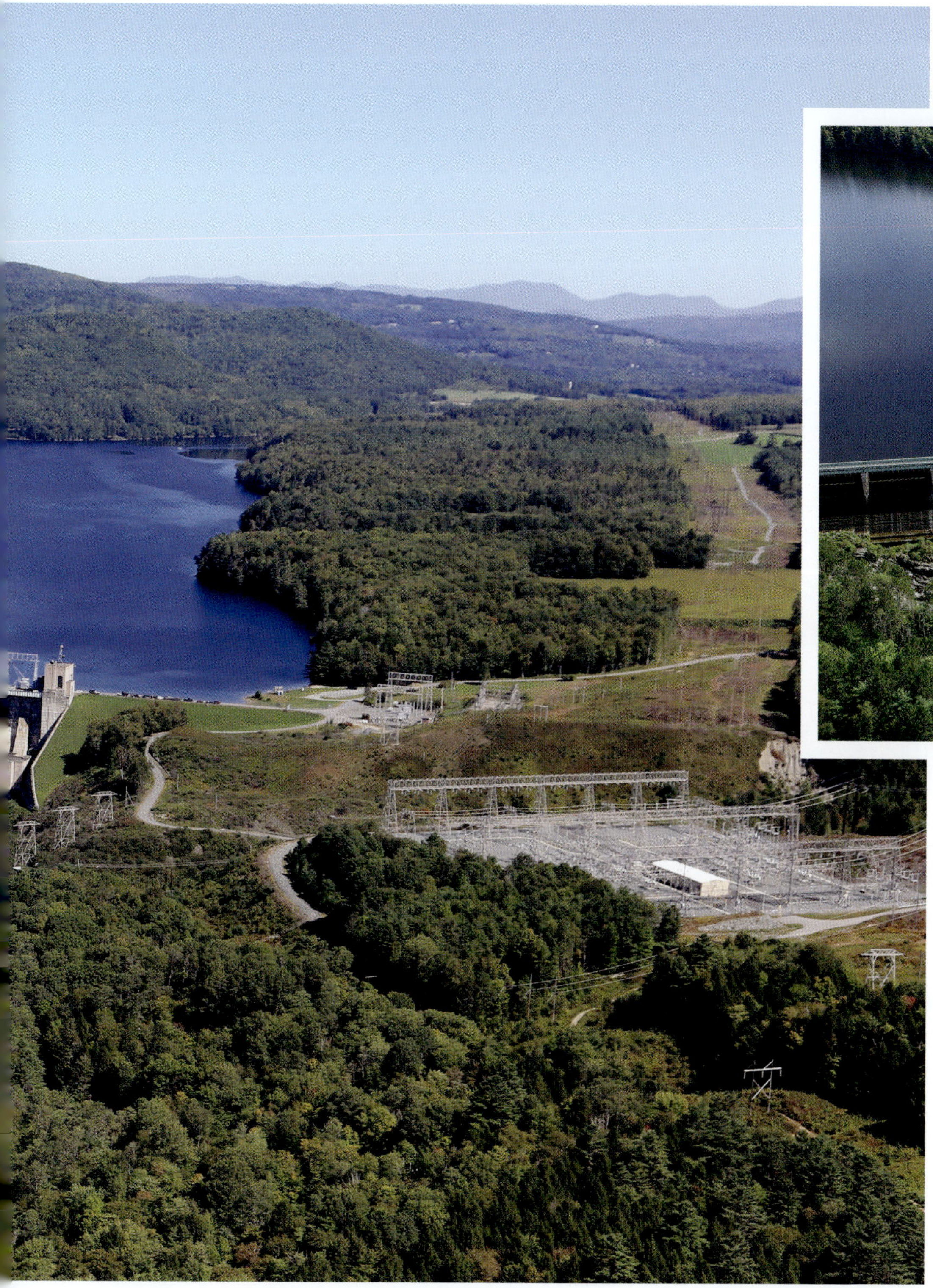

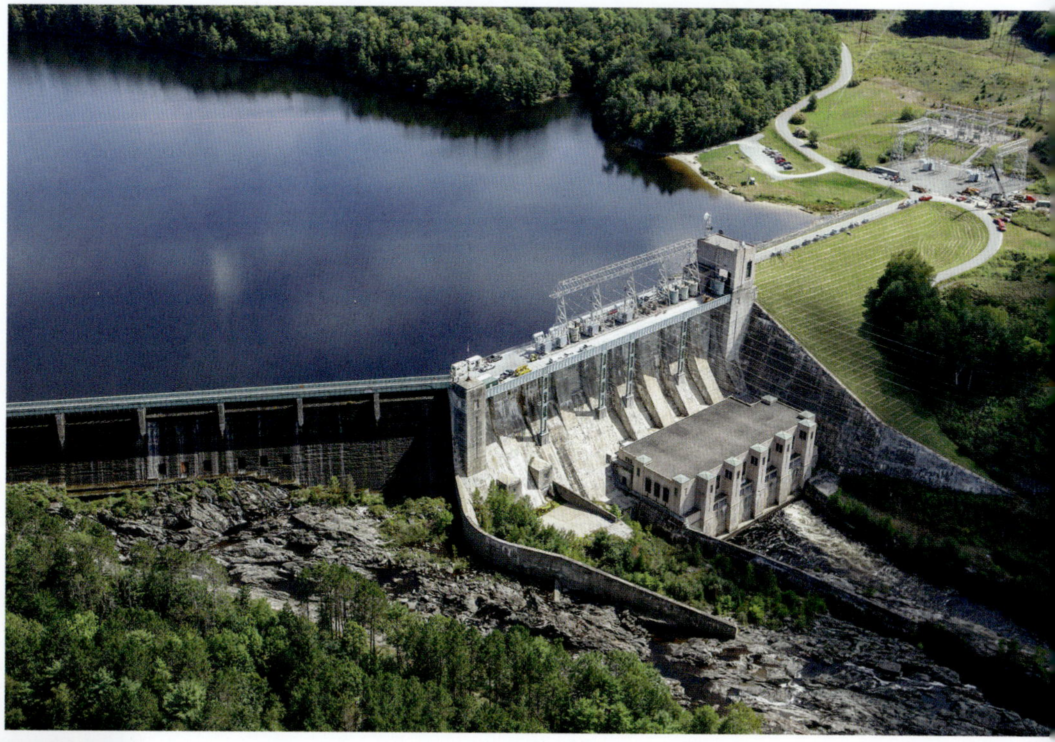

Frank D. Comerford Dam with its 164-megawatt power station was built in 1930. It is the middle of the three dams and power stations built along the 15 Mile Falls. Its backwaters stretch all the way to the base of the Moore Dam more than seven miles upstream.

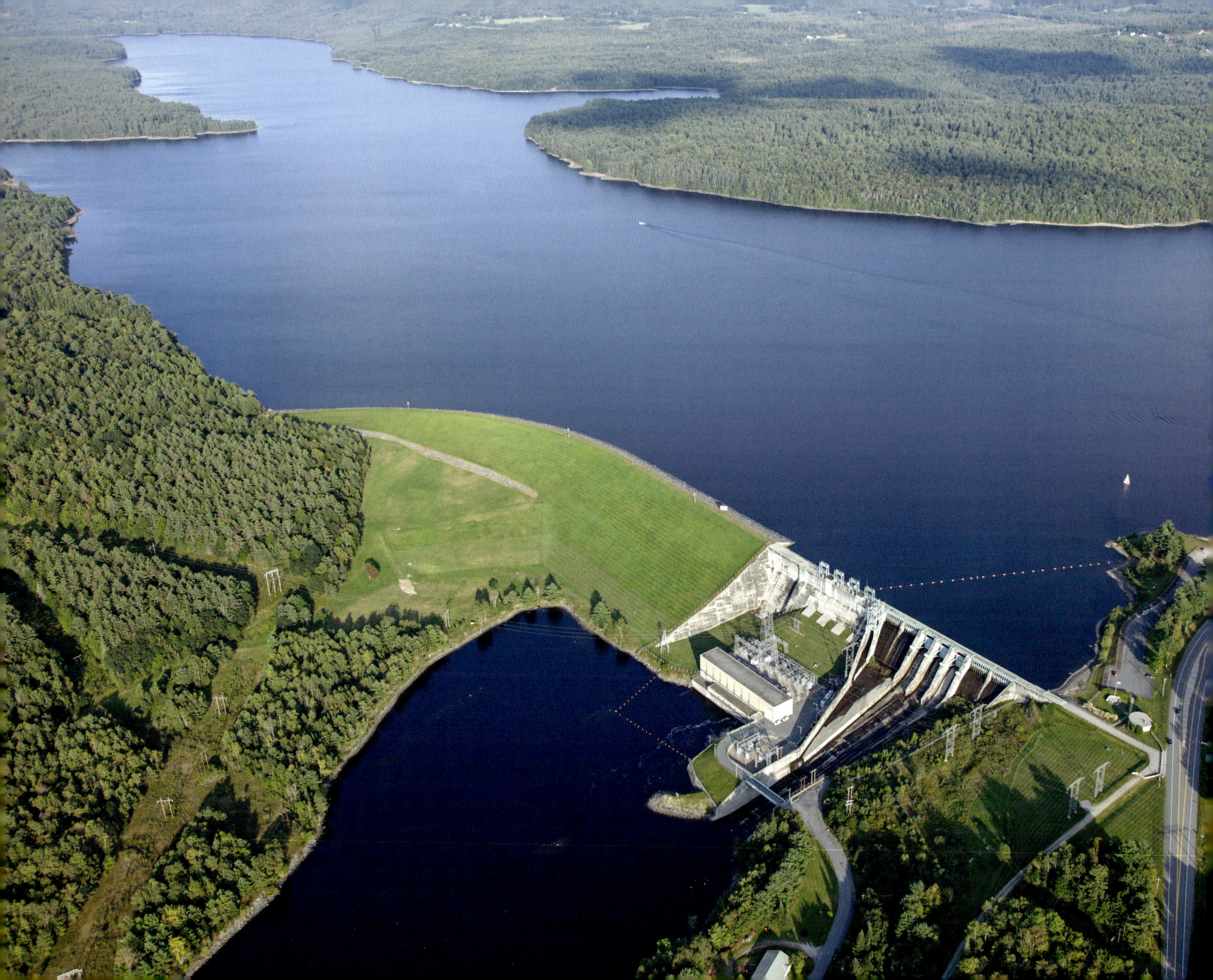

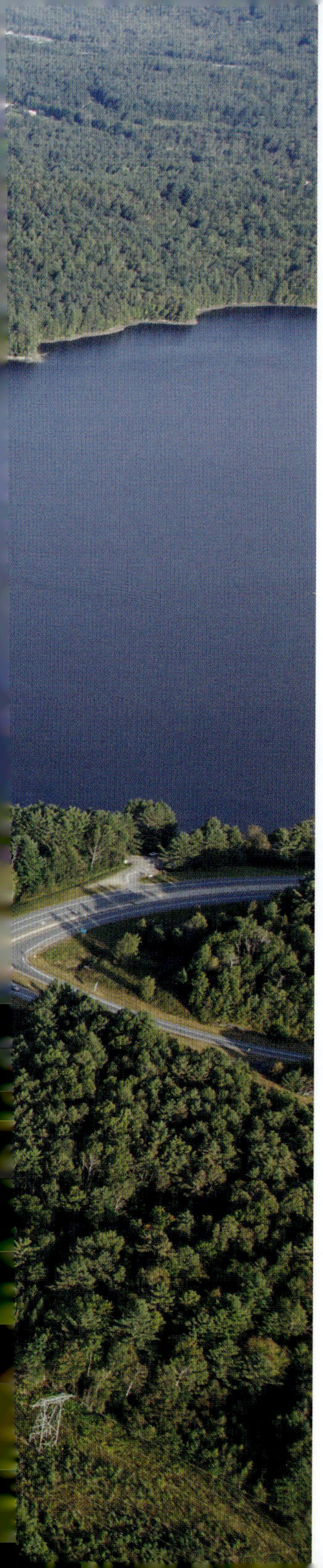

(left) The Moore Hydro Dam was completed in 1956 as the northern-most of the three dams and power stations build along the 15 Mile Falls. The Moore Reservoir comprises the fourth largest lake in New Hampshire and its creation swallowed up three small towns and 3,000 acres of farmland. It is the most productive of the sixteen hydroelectric plants on the river.

(top right) At the eastern end of the Moore Reservoir is an interesting stone shape on a rocky spit of land. Is it a stone wall, or a foundation built before the reservoir flooded three towns and hundreds of acres of farmland?

(bottom right) A fjord-like enclave in the headwaters of the Moore Reservoir

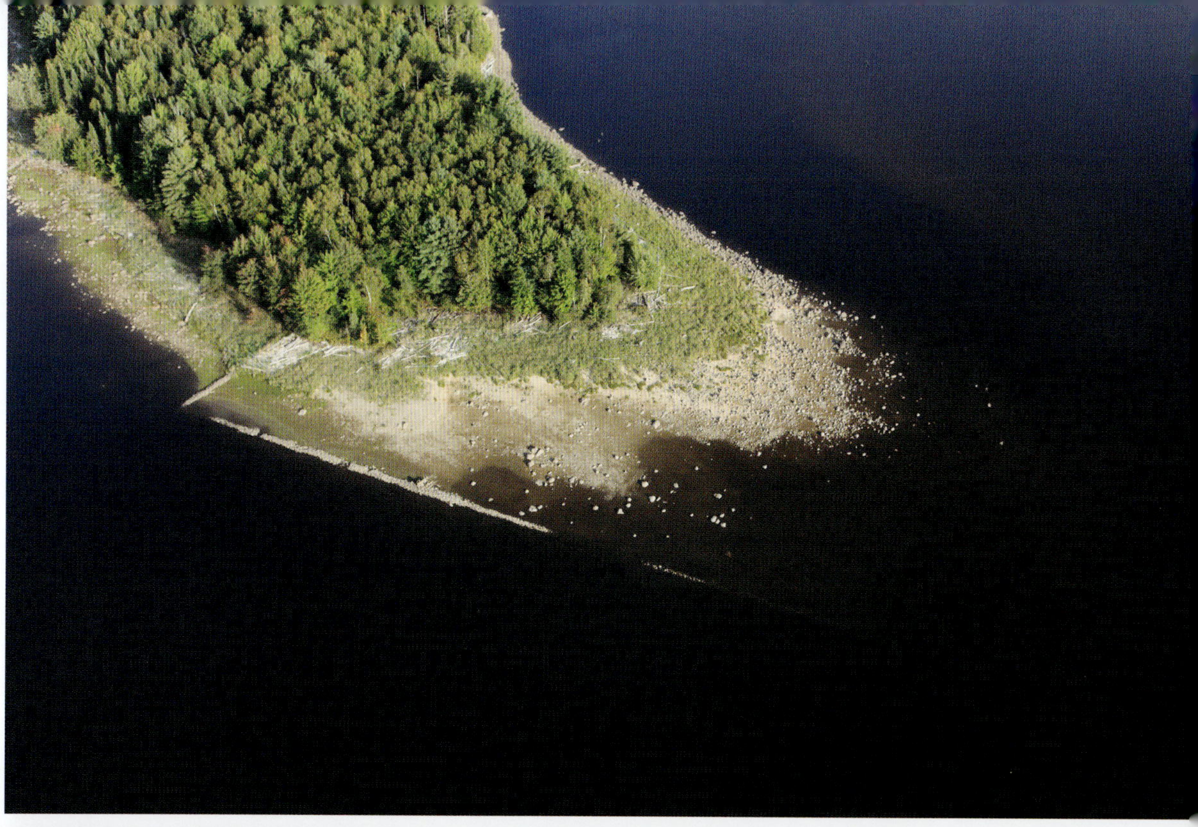

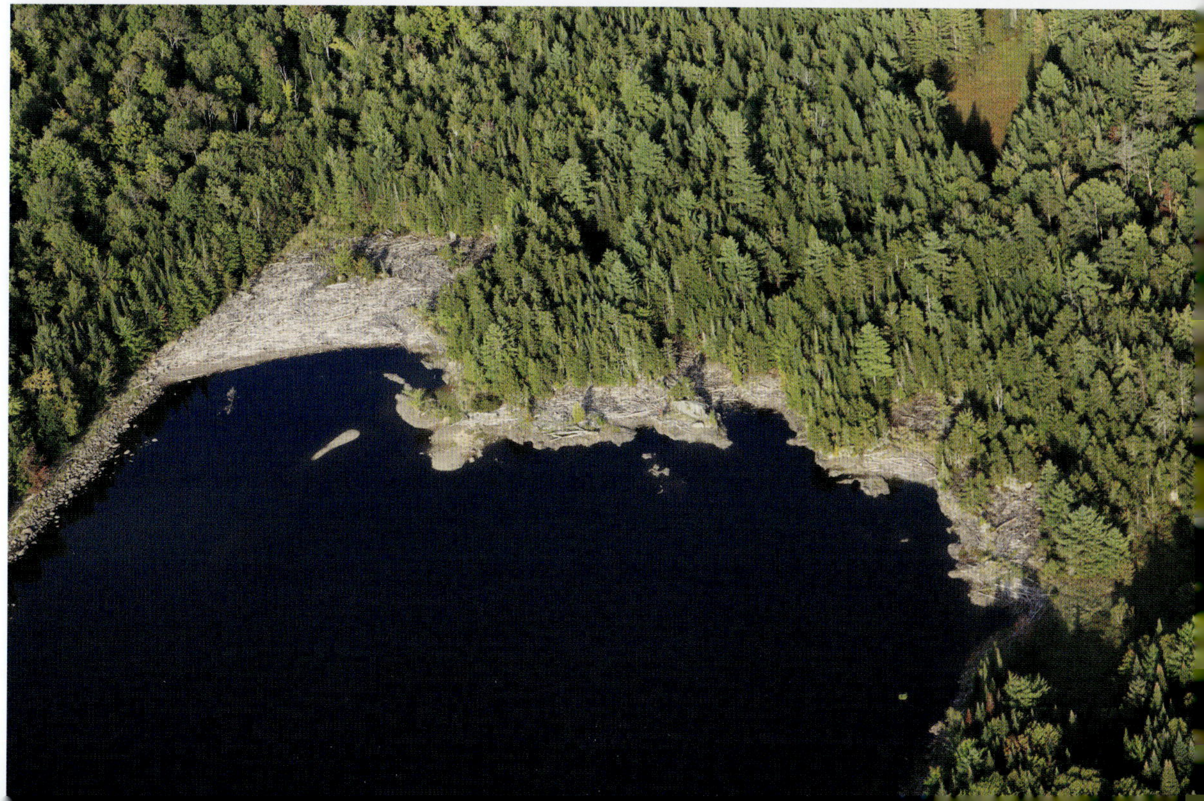

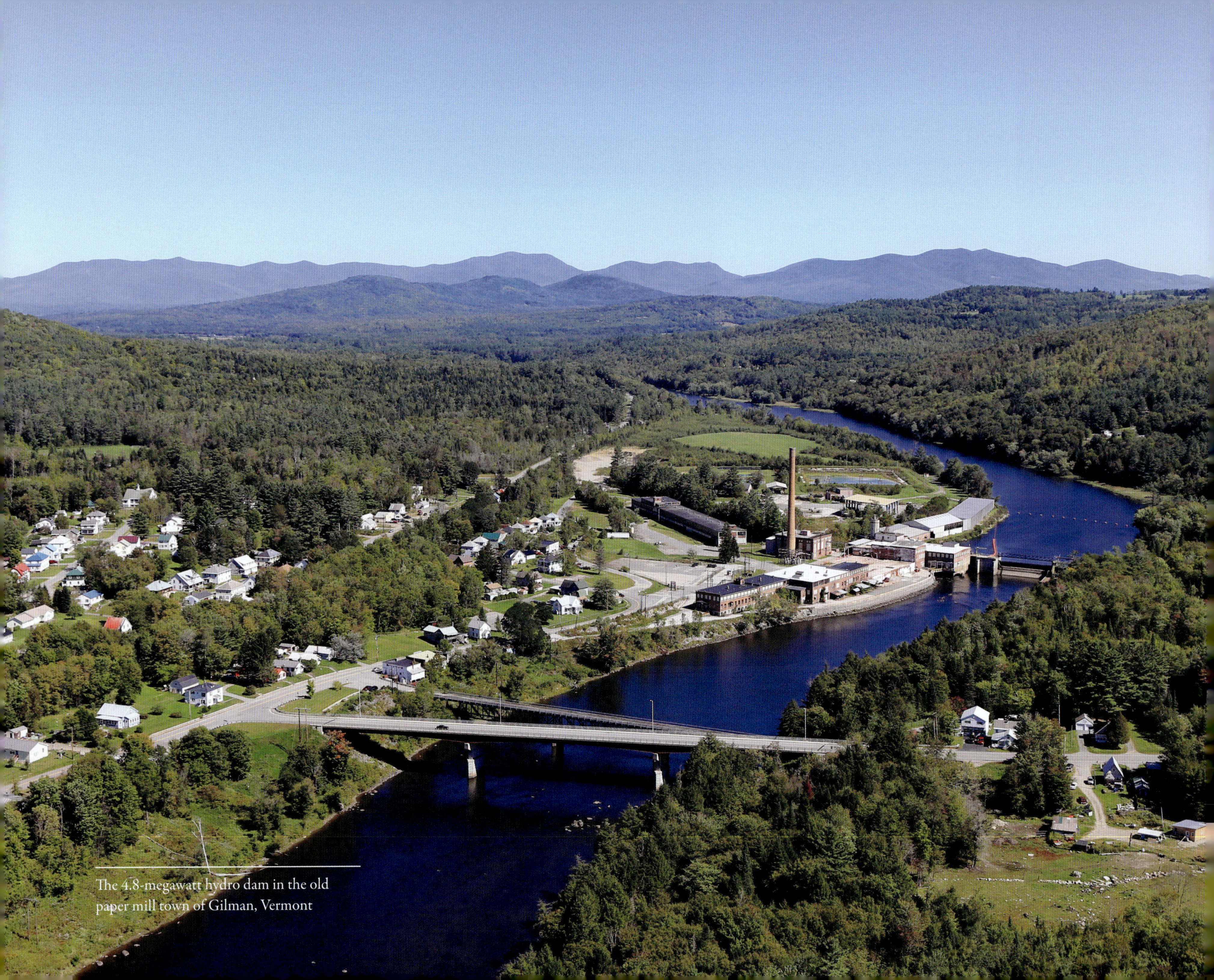

The 4.8-megawatt hydro dam in the old paper mill town of Gilman, Vermont

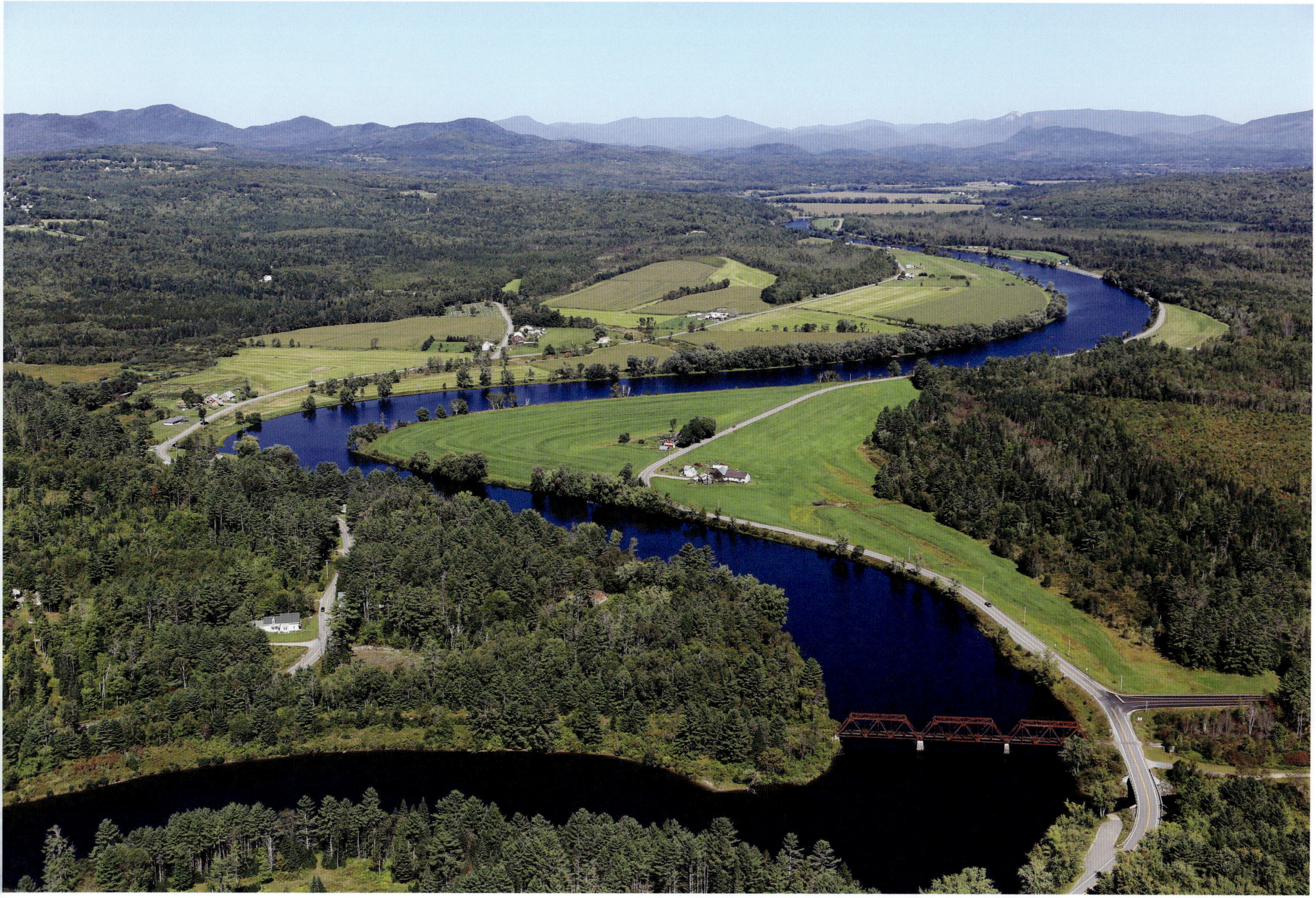

Old triple-span railway bridge near South Lunenburg, Vermont

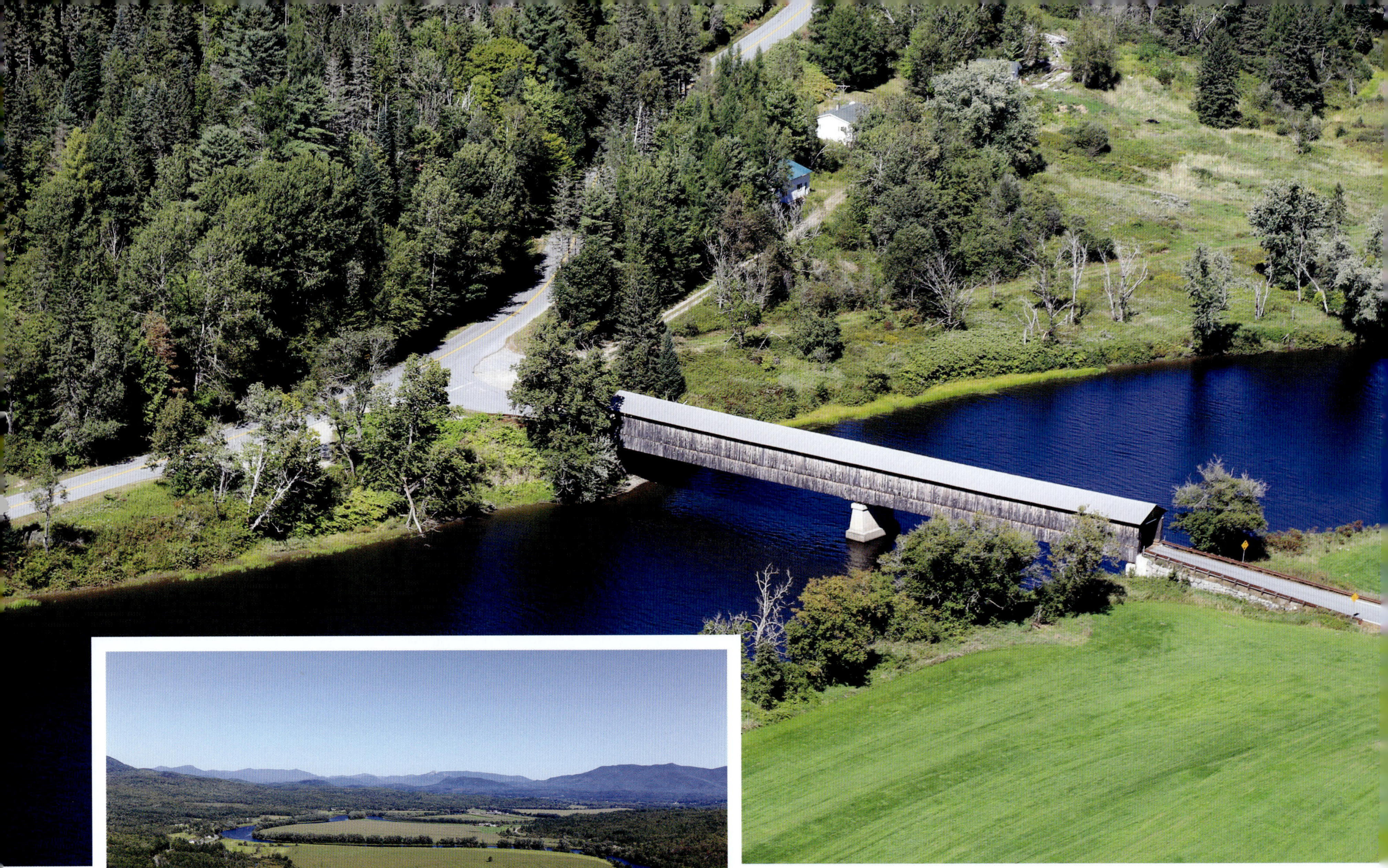

The Mount Orne Covered Bridge, built in 1911, connects Lunenburg, Vermont, with Lancaster, New Hampshire, just below a great S-curve in the river overlooked by Colby Mountain.

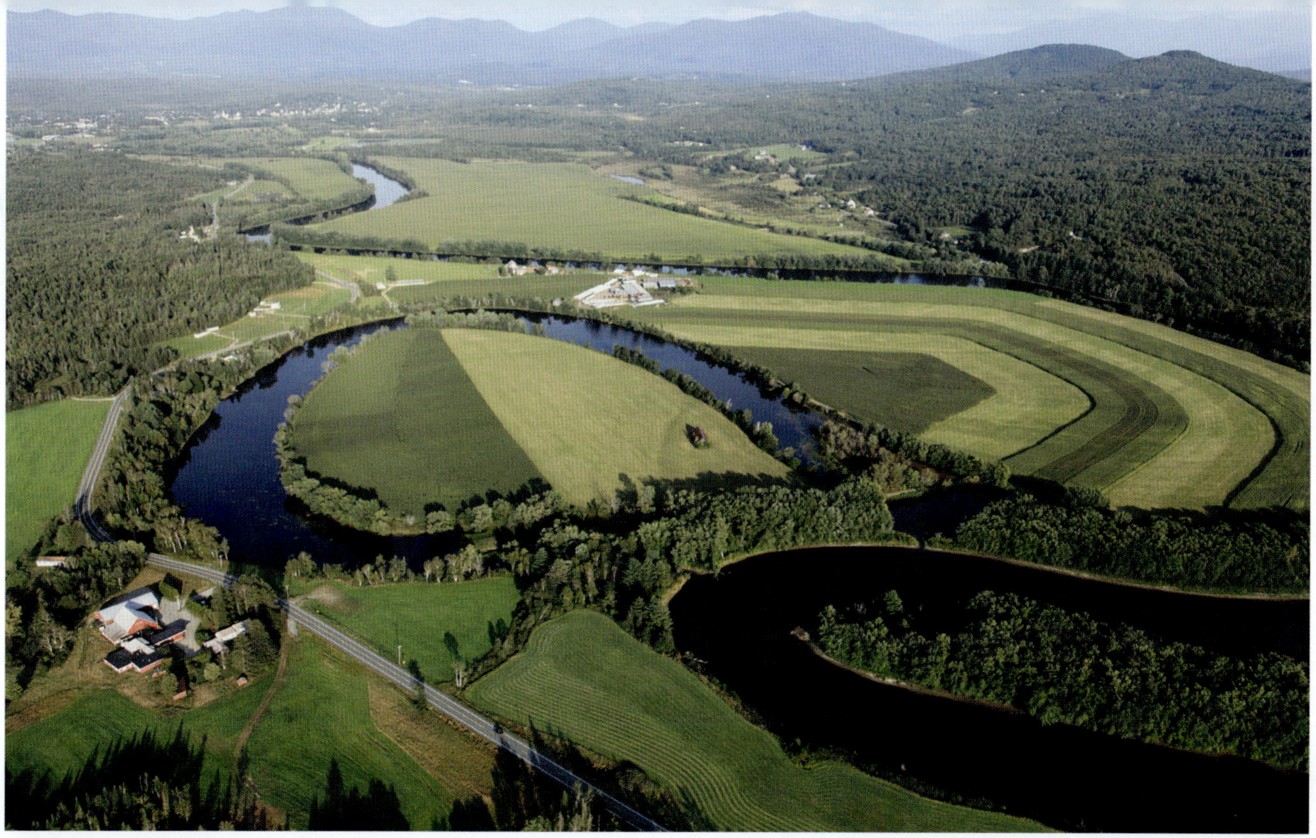

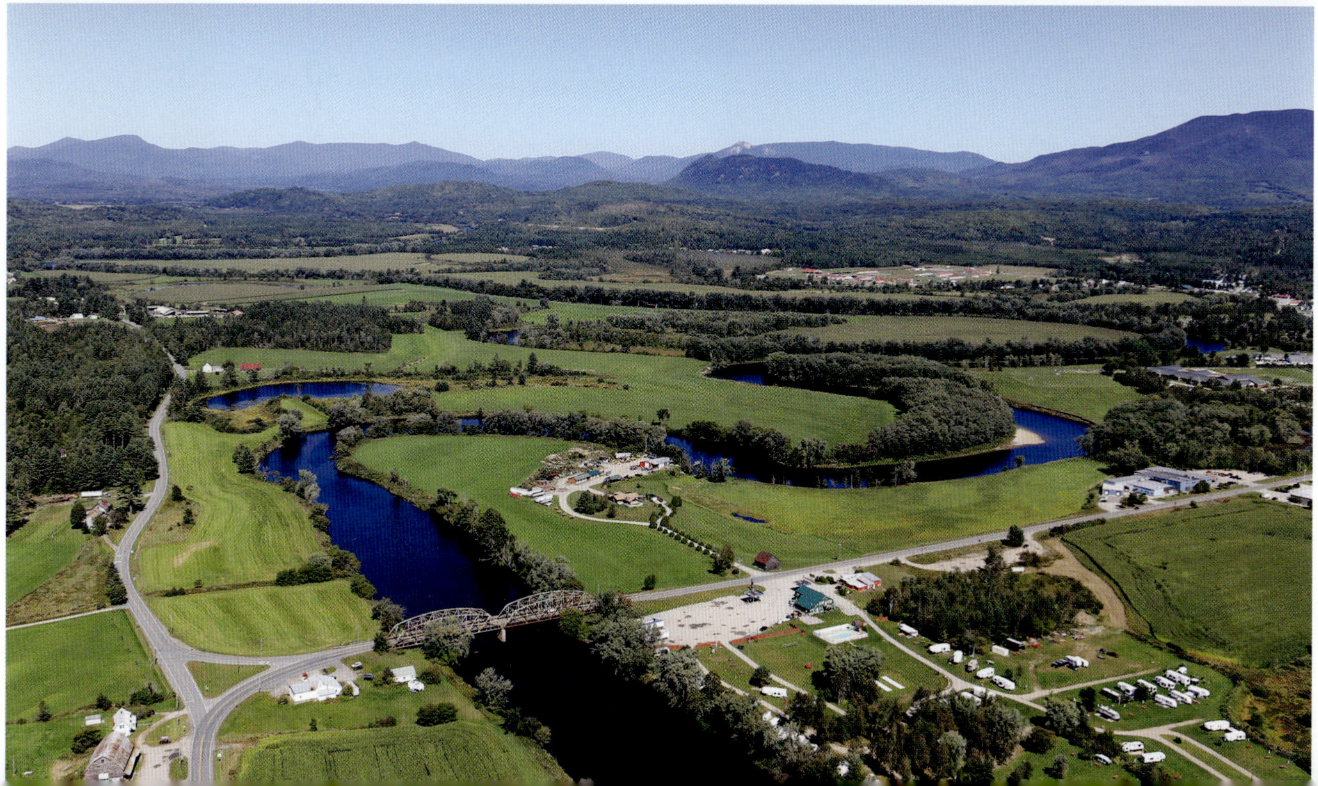

(top left) An interesting set of oxbows with patterned crops between Lunenburg and Lancaster.

(bottom left) Double span bridge crossing the river to Lancaster, New Hampshire

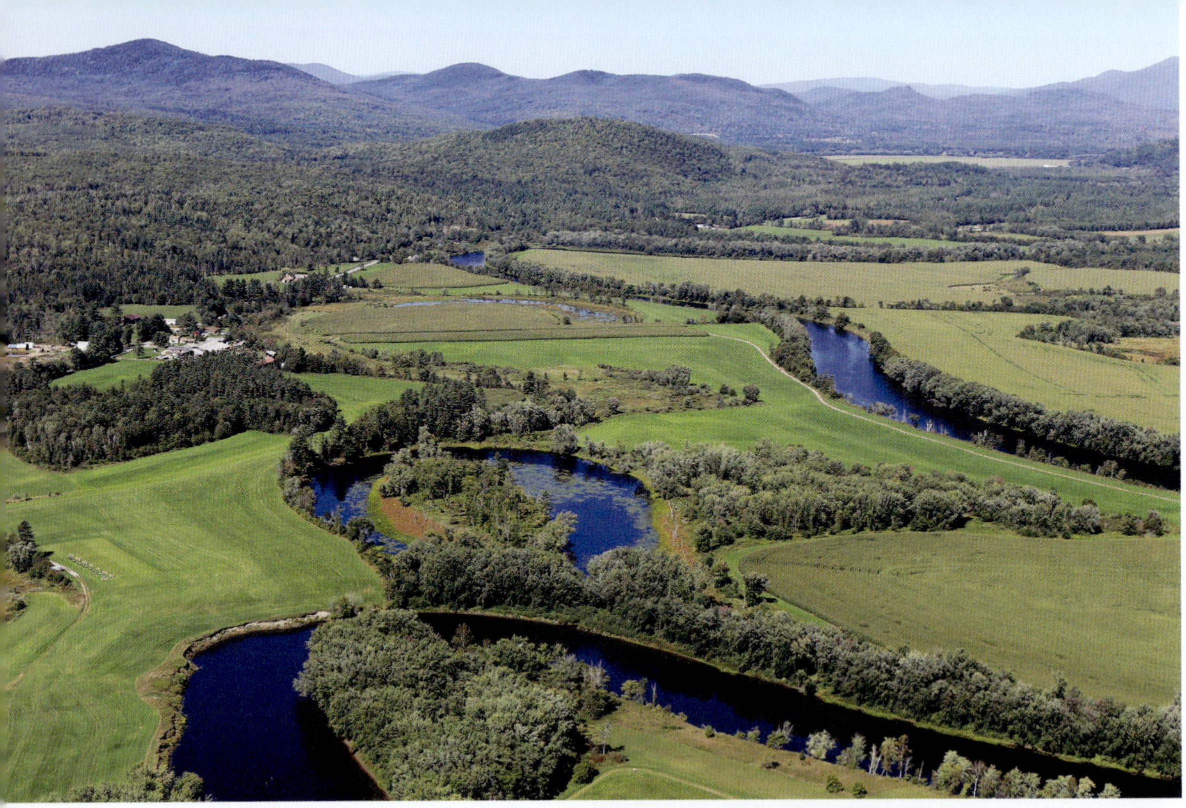

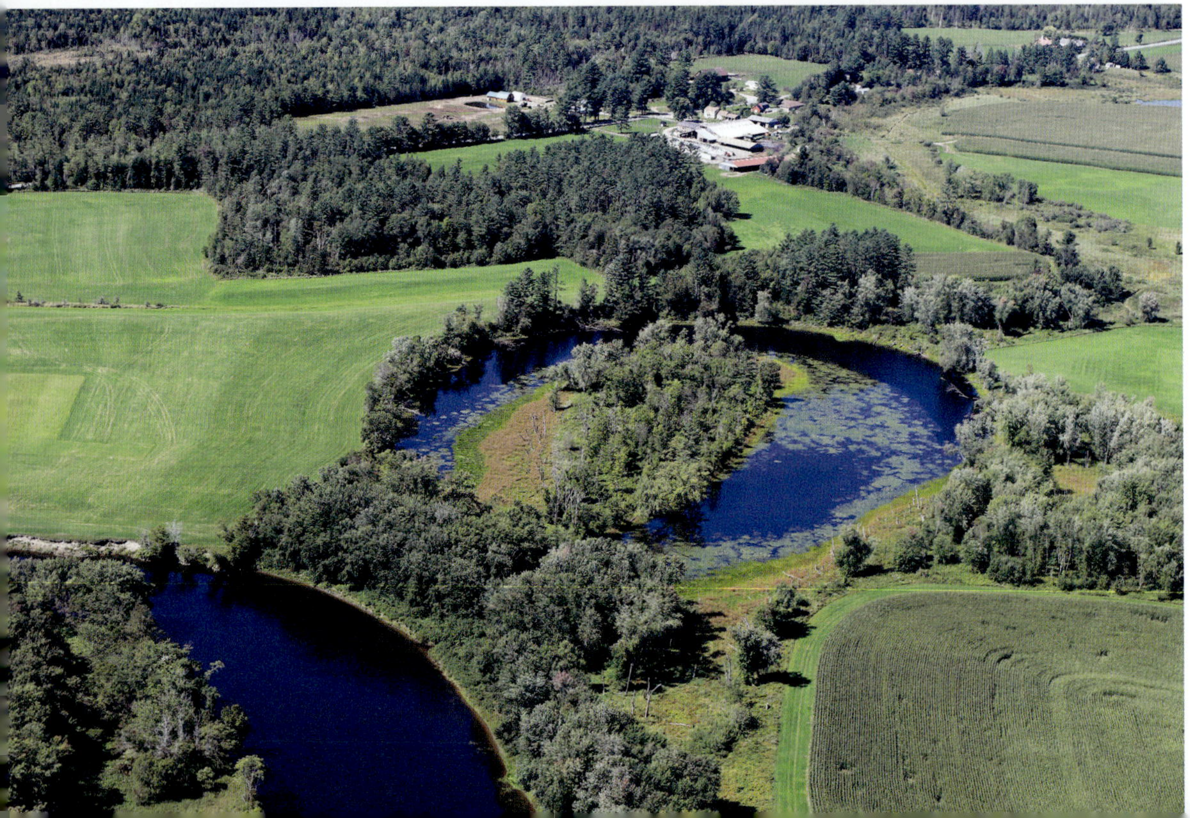

(top and bottom left) A cut-off oxbow on the Vermont side of the river just across from Lancaster

(right) Cumulus clouds and the late afternoon light cast an ominous glow over the Lancaster oxbow and the fairgrounds with Hutchins Mountain, New Hampshire in the distance to the northeast.

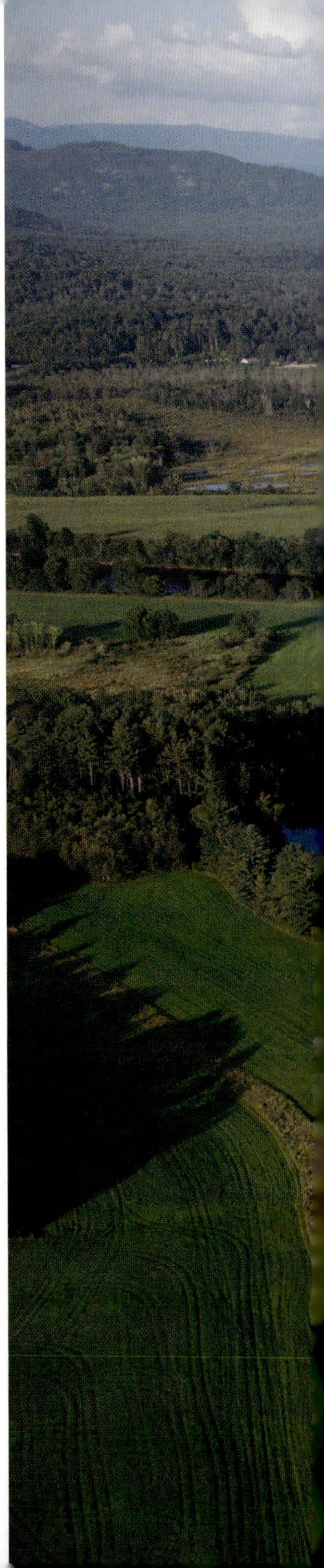

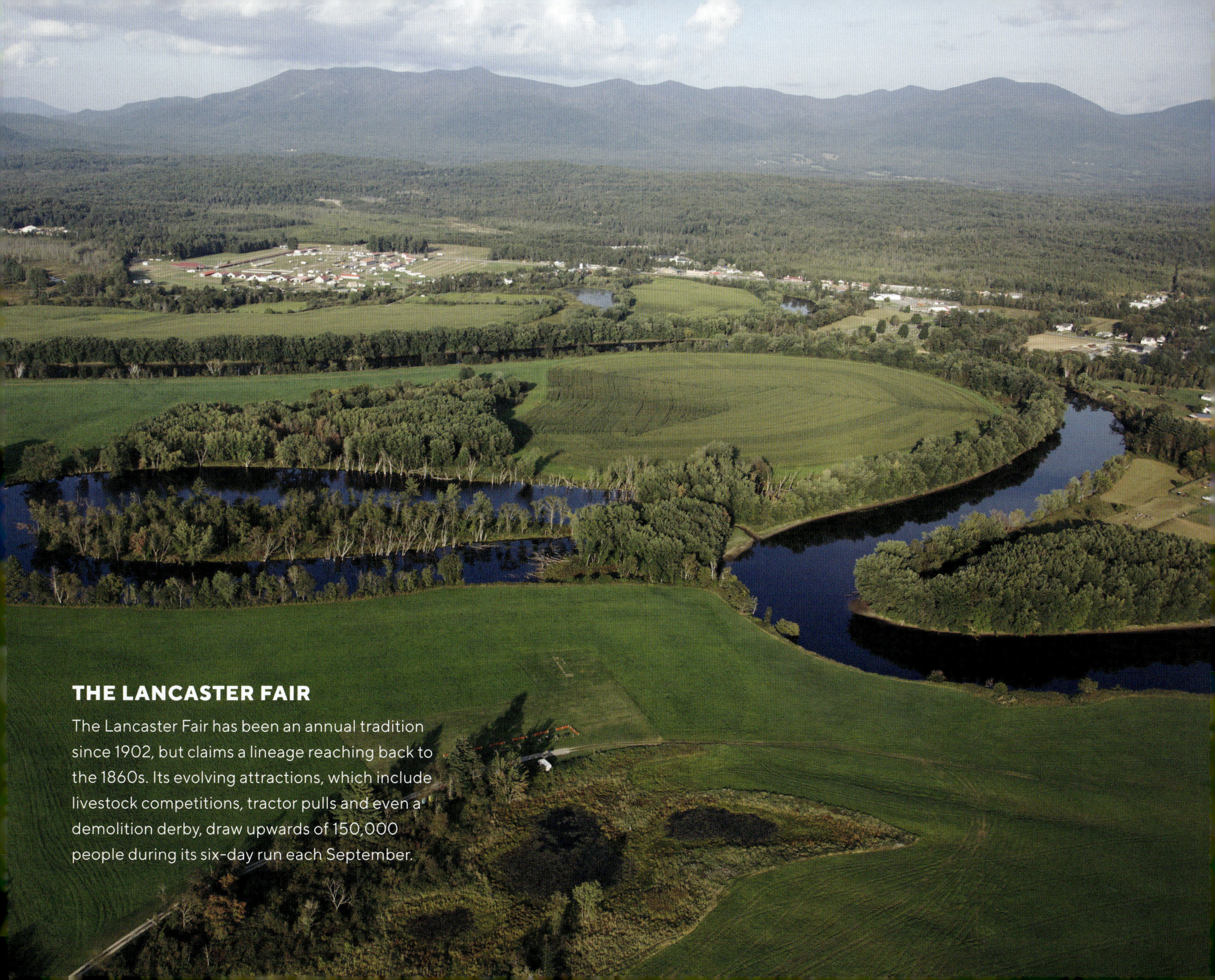

THE LANCASTER FAIR

The Lancaster Fair has been an annual tradition since 1902, but claims a lineage reaching back to the 1860s. Its evolving attractions, which include livestock competitions, tractor pulls and even a demolition derby, draw upwards of 150,000 people during its six-day run each September.

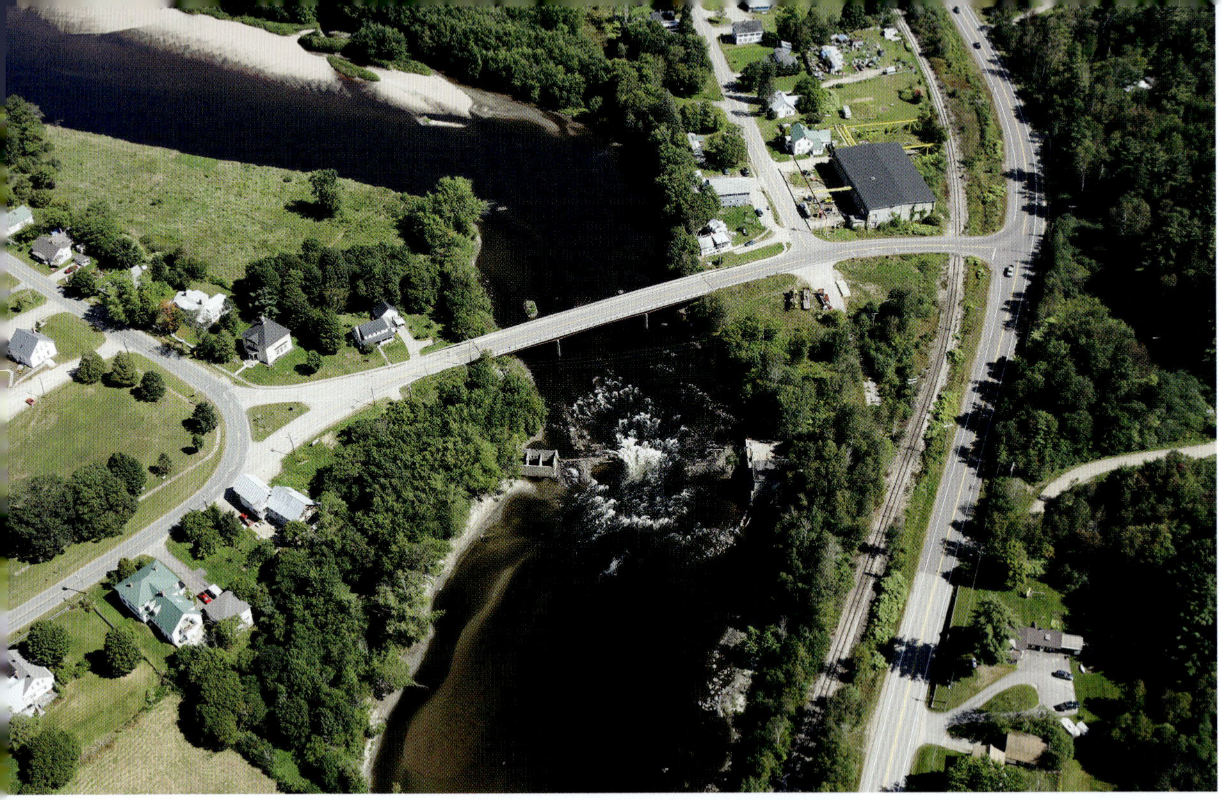

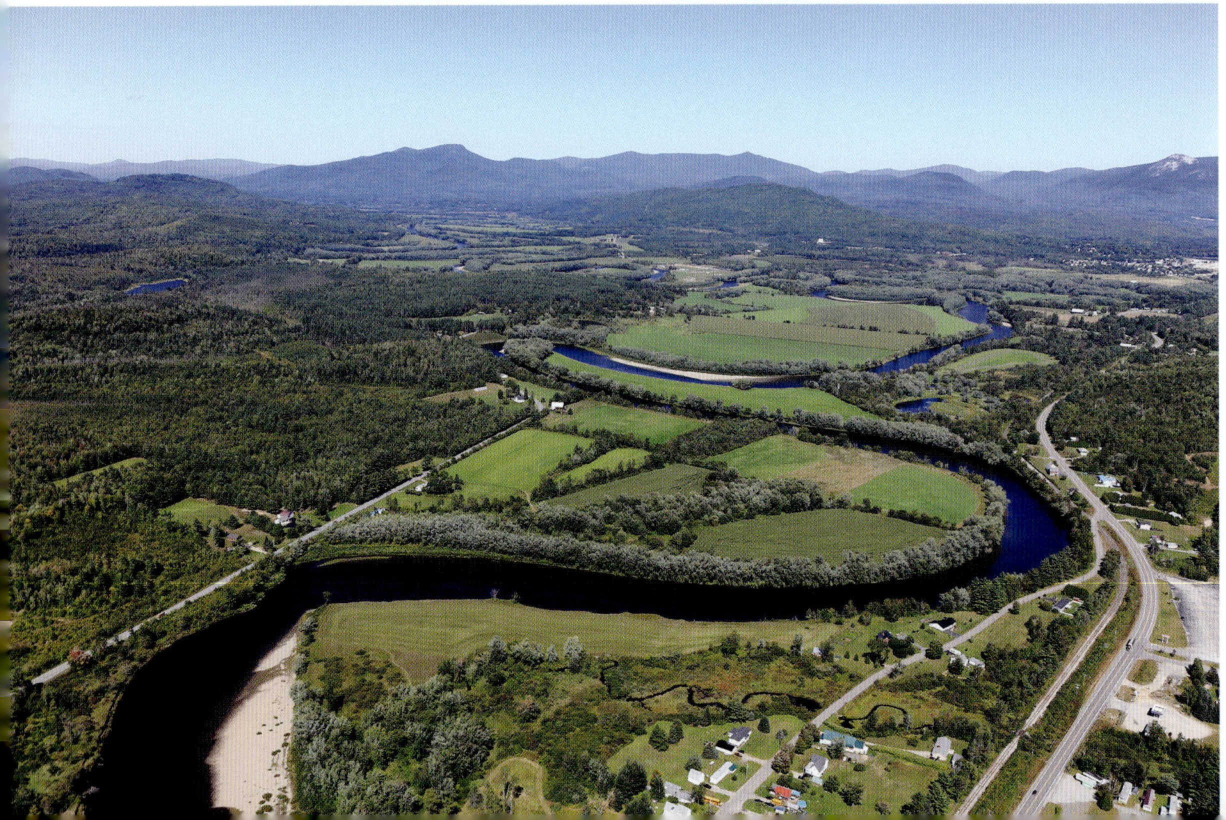

(top left) The breached Wyoming Dam at Guildhall, Vermont, is listed as a major hazard to boaters, kayakers, and canoers. Despite the available portage around the failed dam many boaters have had to be rescued from the smashed concrete and rebar after thinking they could run the whitewater here.

(bottom left) Near Northumberland, New Hampshire. Note the quillwork patterns within the bend in the river, and the winding creek in the foreground, looking like a miniature version of the Connecticut itself.

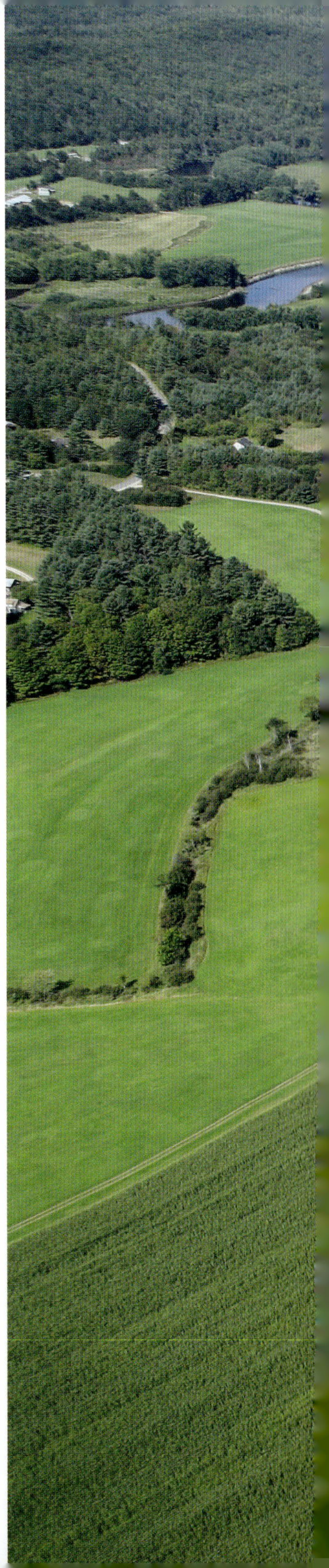

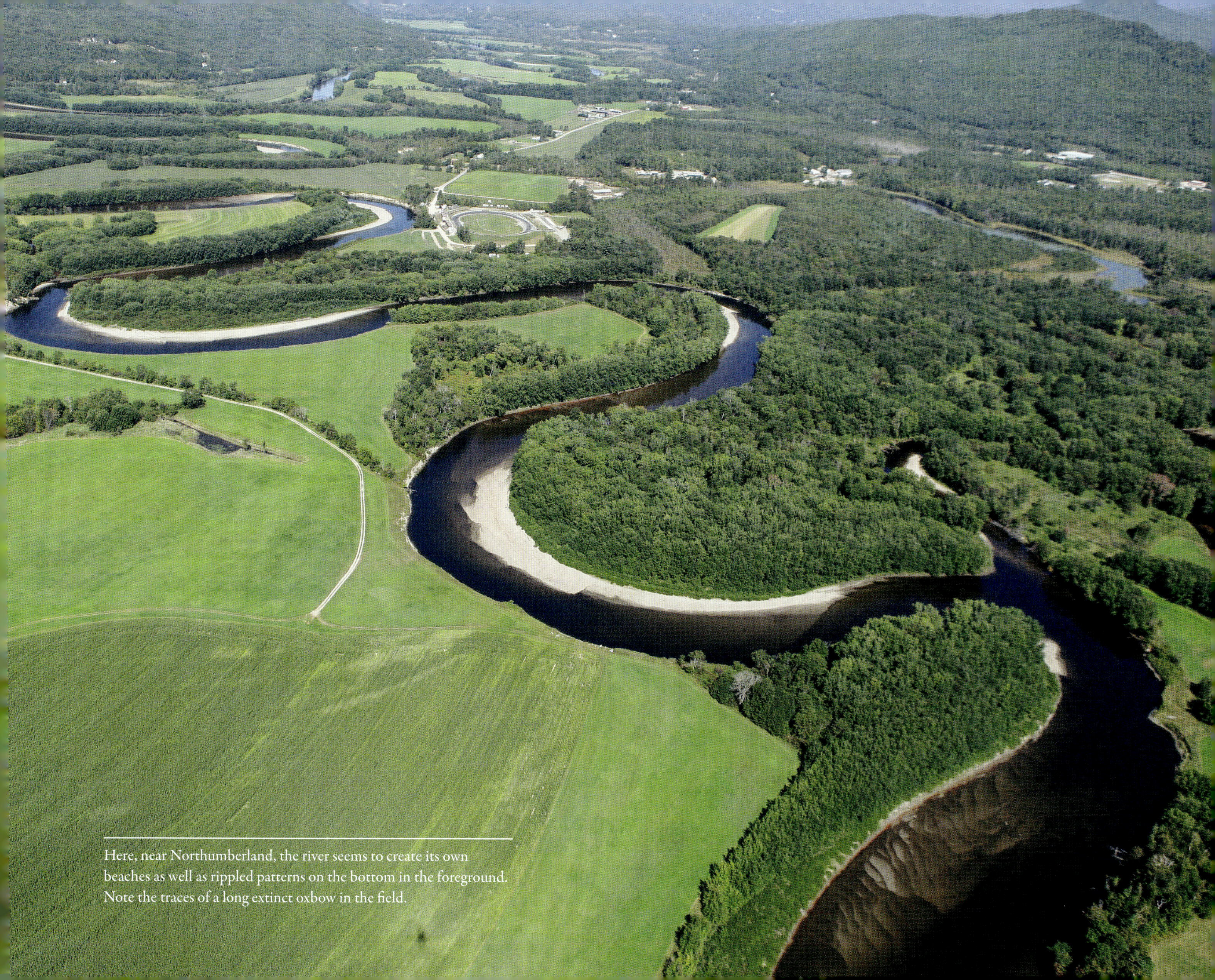

Here, near Northumberland, the river seems to create its own beaches as well as rippled patterns on the bottom in the foreground. Note the traces of a long extinct oxbow in the field.

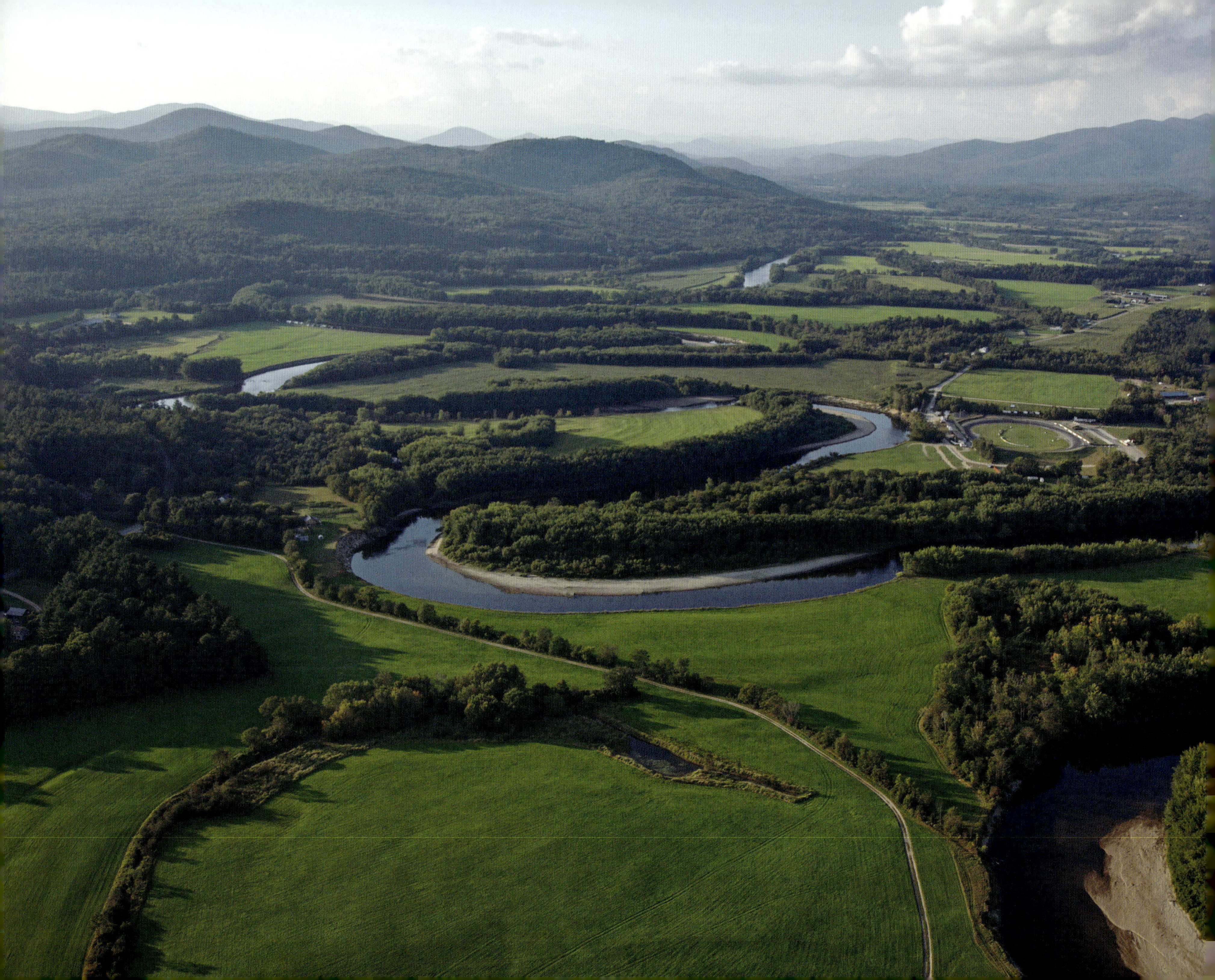

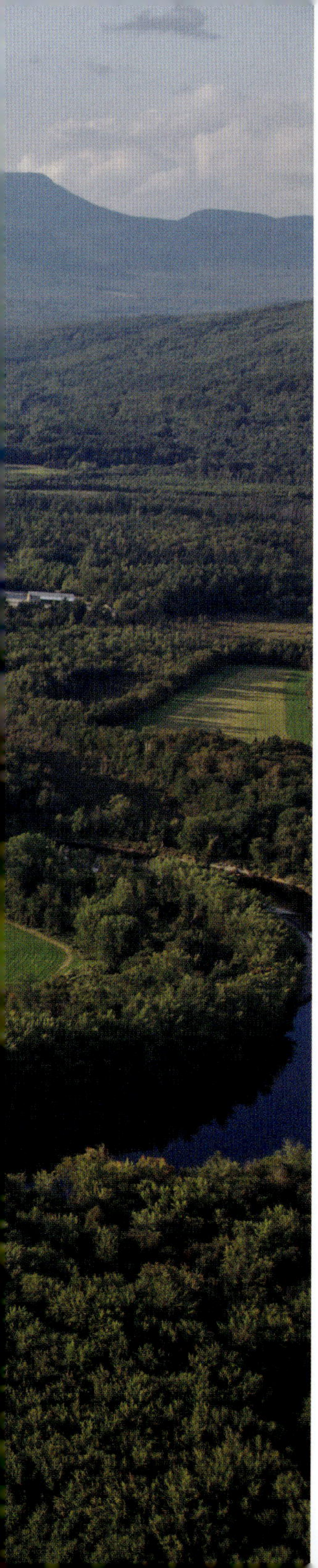

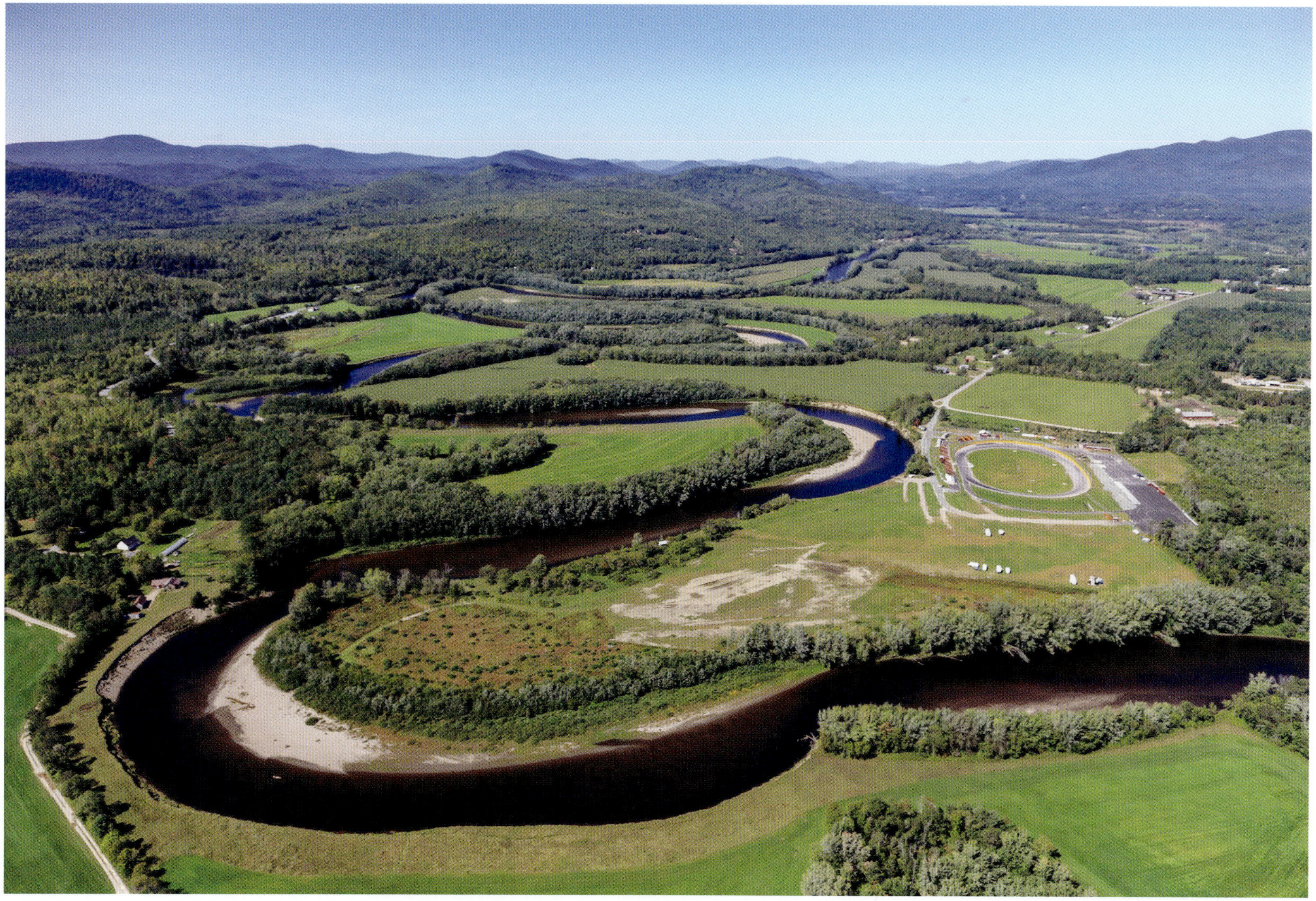

(left and above) Riverside Speedway, a quarter-mile asphalt racetrack, is an unexpected sight amidst the natural beauty near Groveton, New Hampshire.

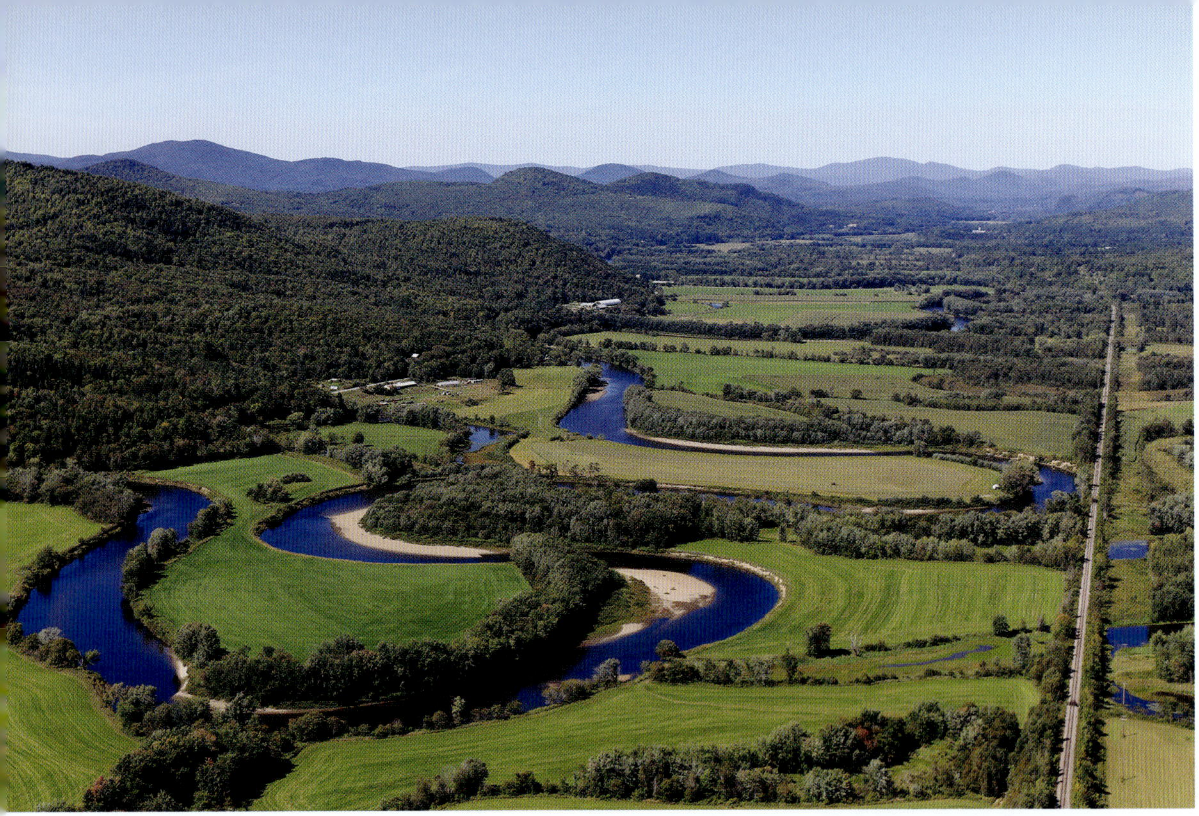

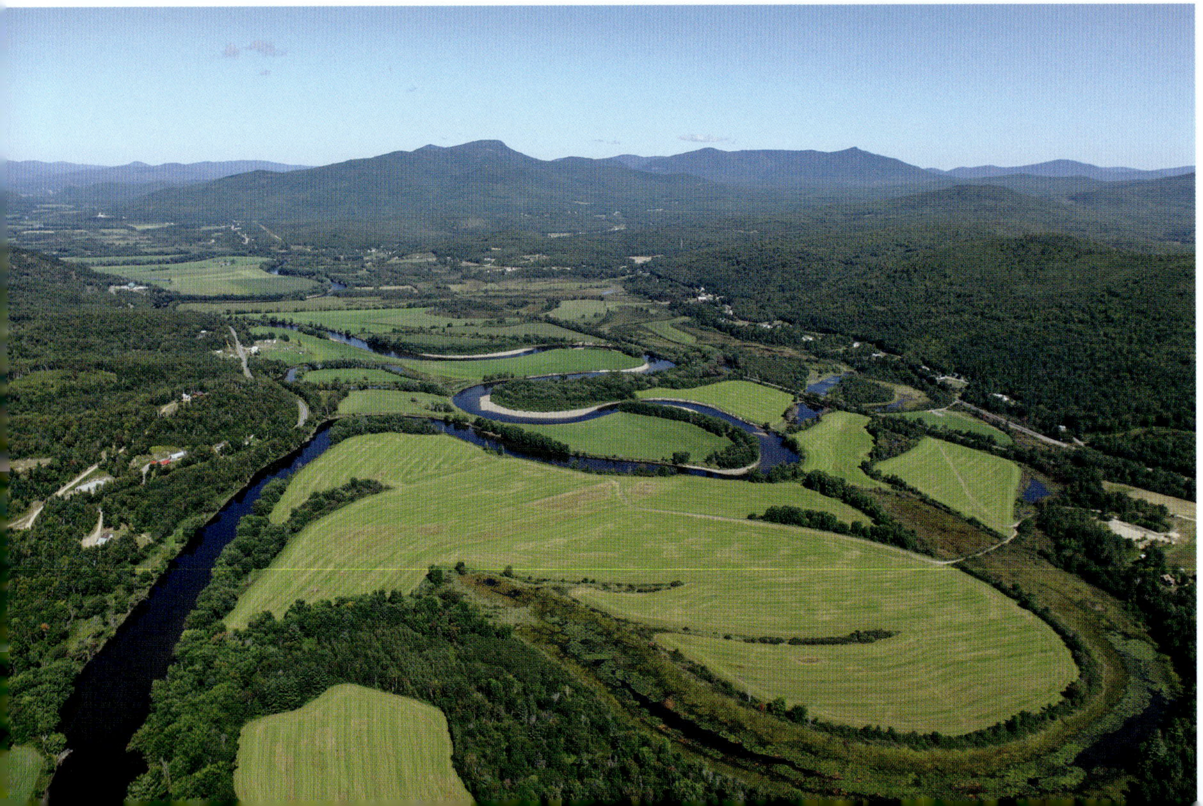

(top left) The railroad runs straight up the valley toward Stratford as the river twists and turns on its way south.

(bottom left) A mixture of active and extinct oxbows show how the river bounced between sets of mountains on either side south of Stratford, New Hampshire.

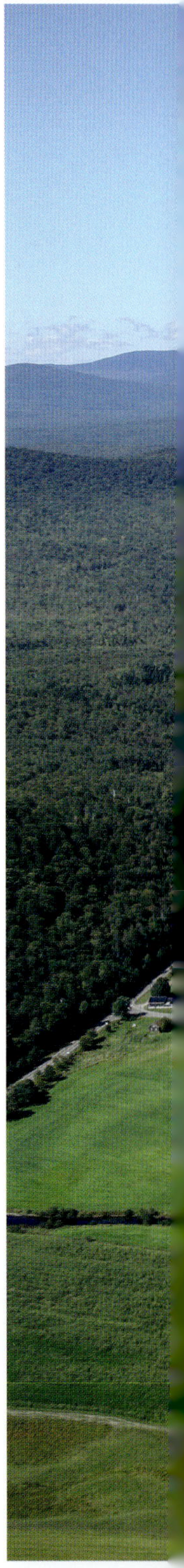

(right) The river, the railway, and several roads all seem to converge here where a steel truss bridge connects Stratford, New Hampshire, with Maidstone, Vermont. Settled in 1773, Stratford thrived on agriculture, logging, and small mills, as did so many other towns along the river.

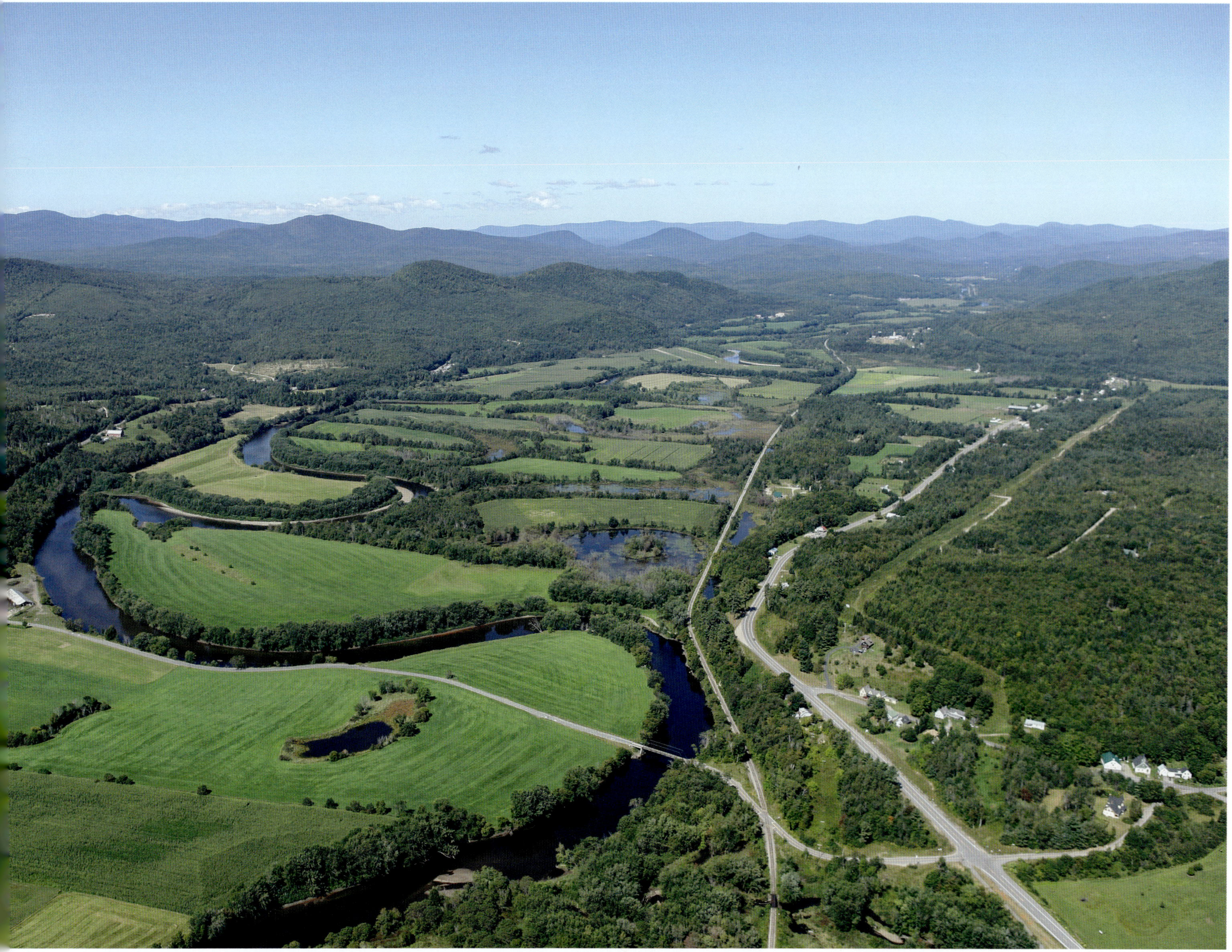

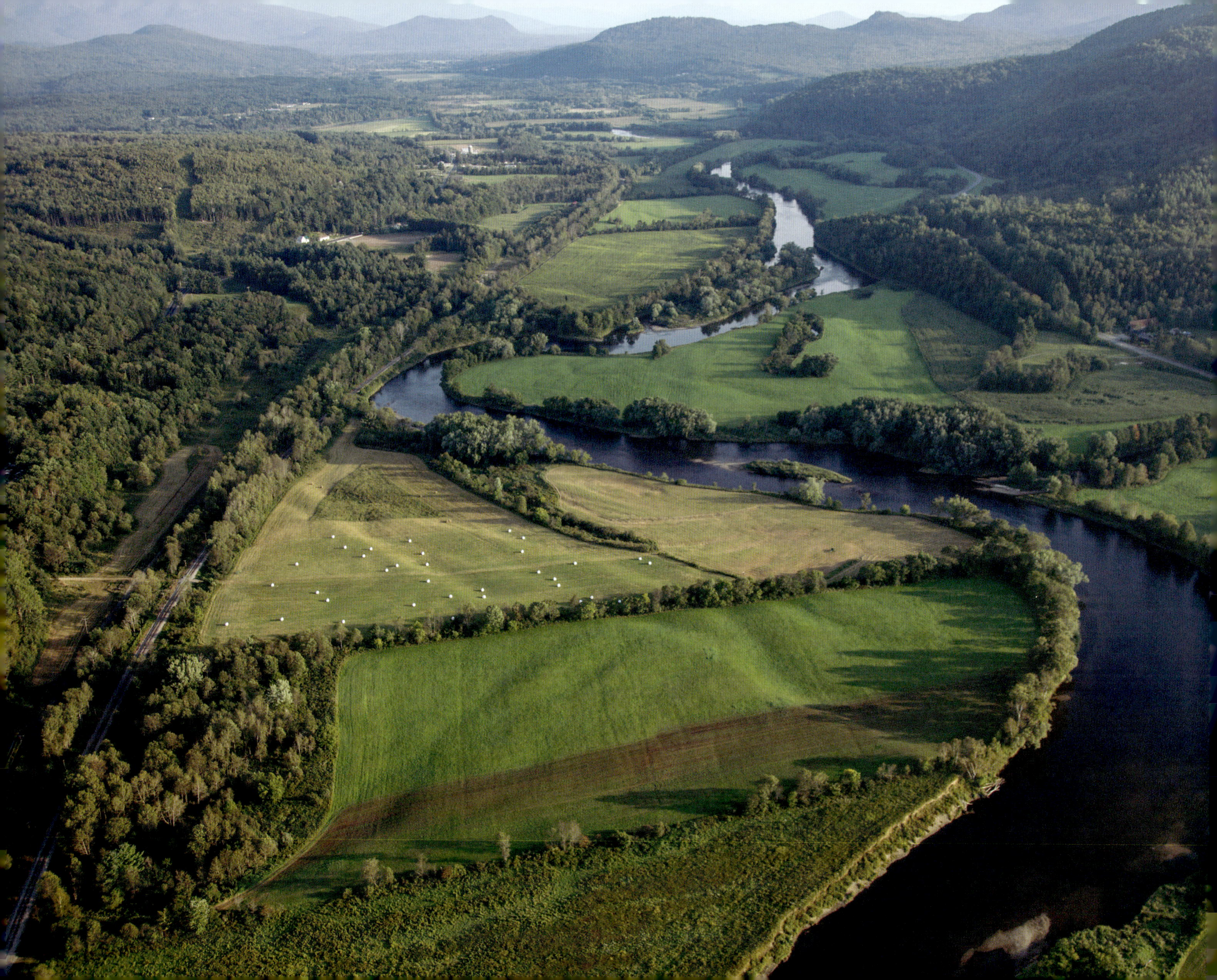

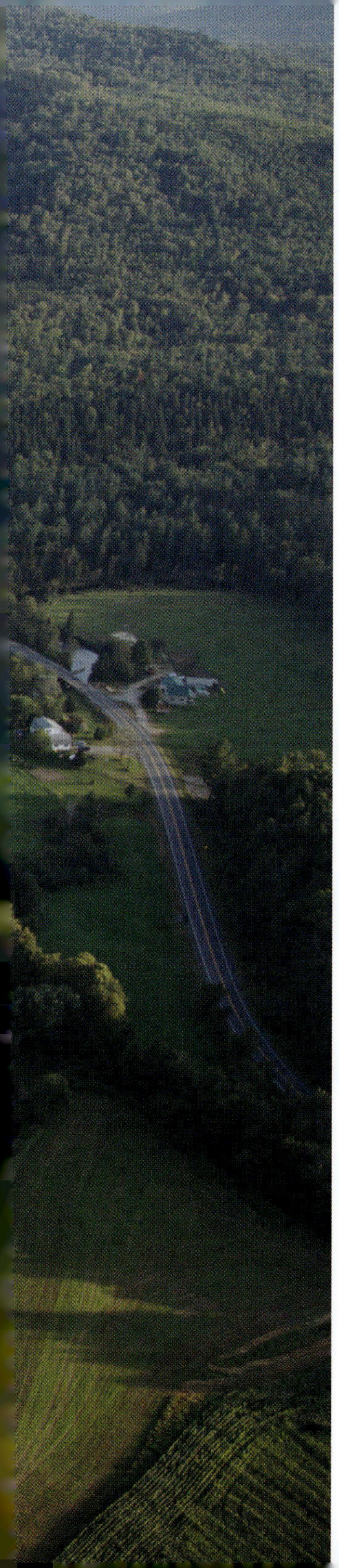

(left) In this photograph, our cover shot, we are looking south as the river descends between cultivated fields and mountains north of Stratford, New Hampshire.

(top right) Approaching North Stratford, settled in a major bend in the river

(bottom right) North Stratford looking east from the Vermont side of the river

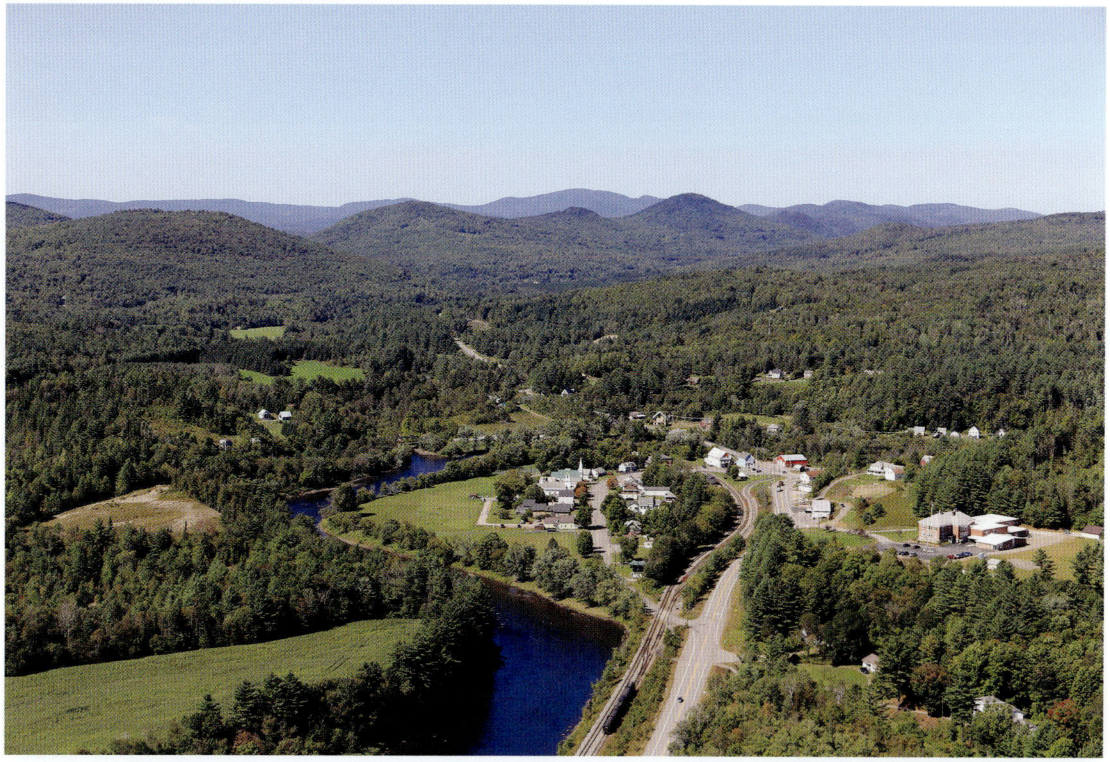

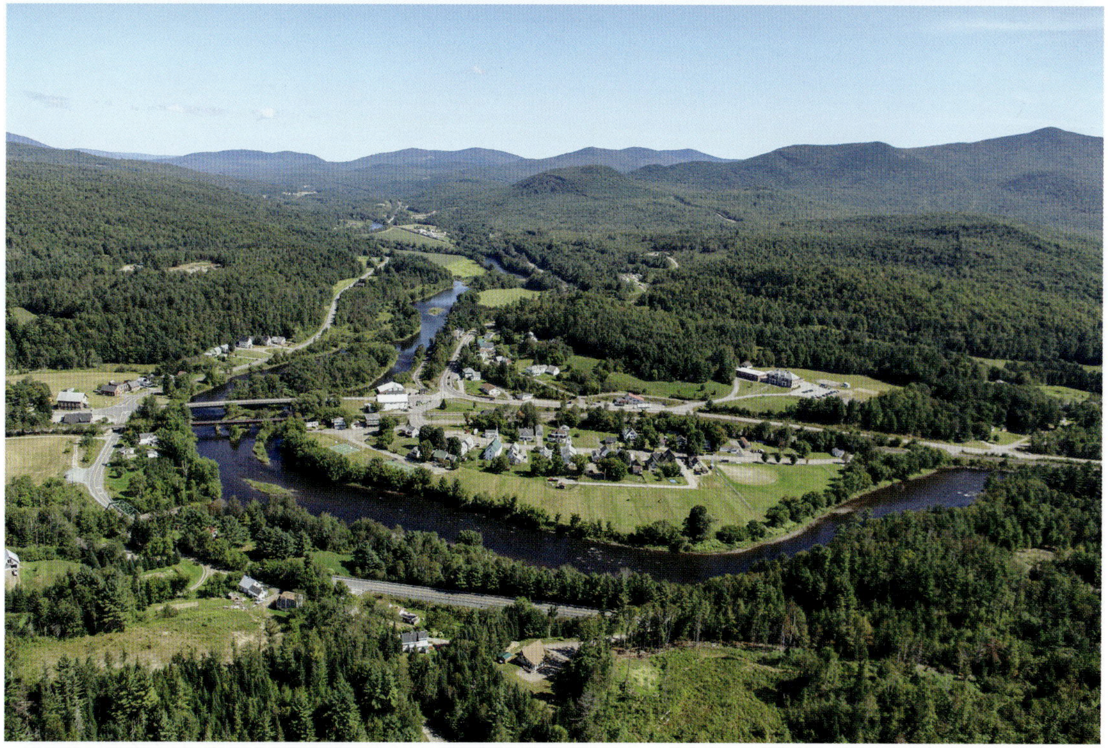

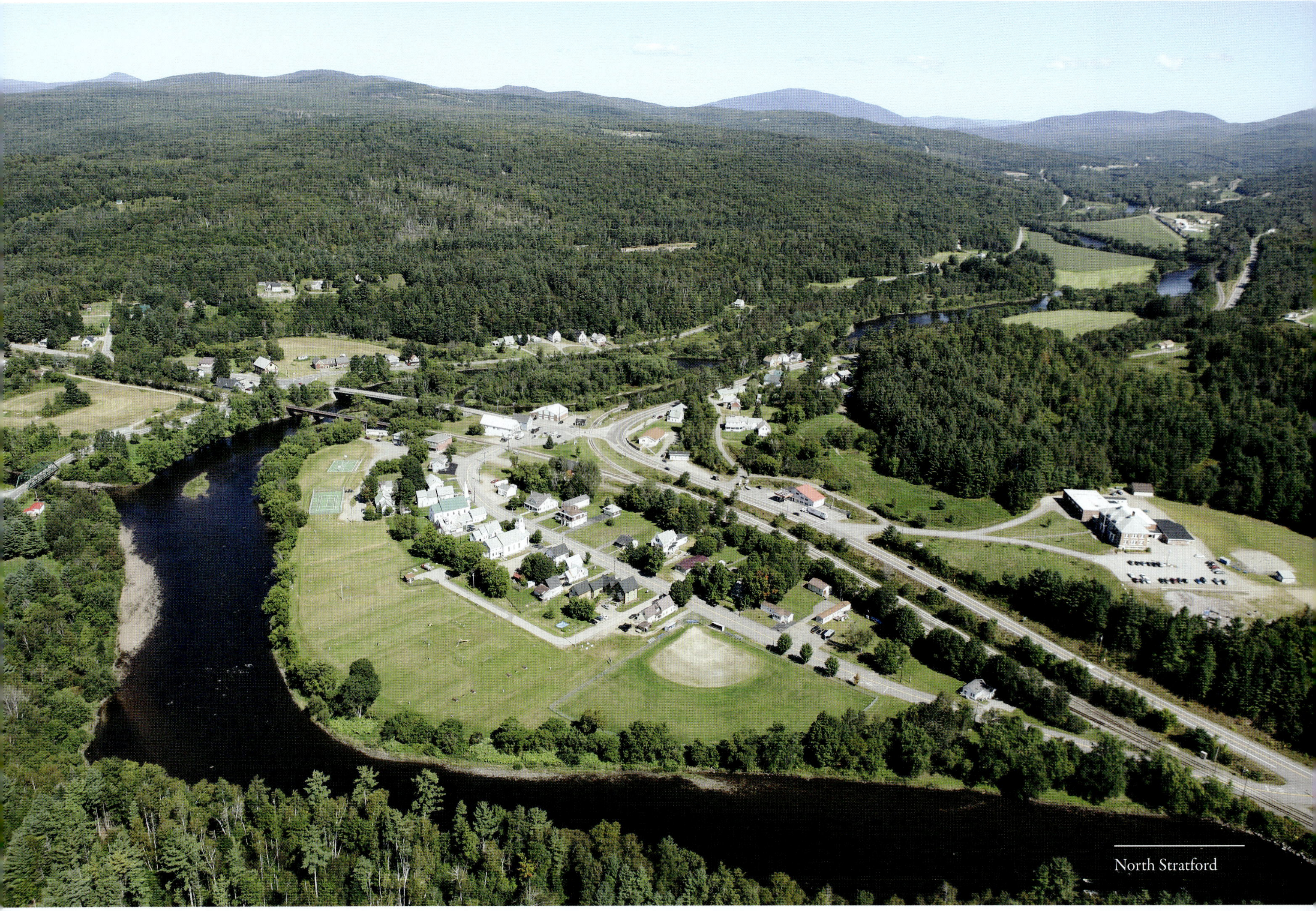
North Stratford

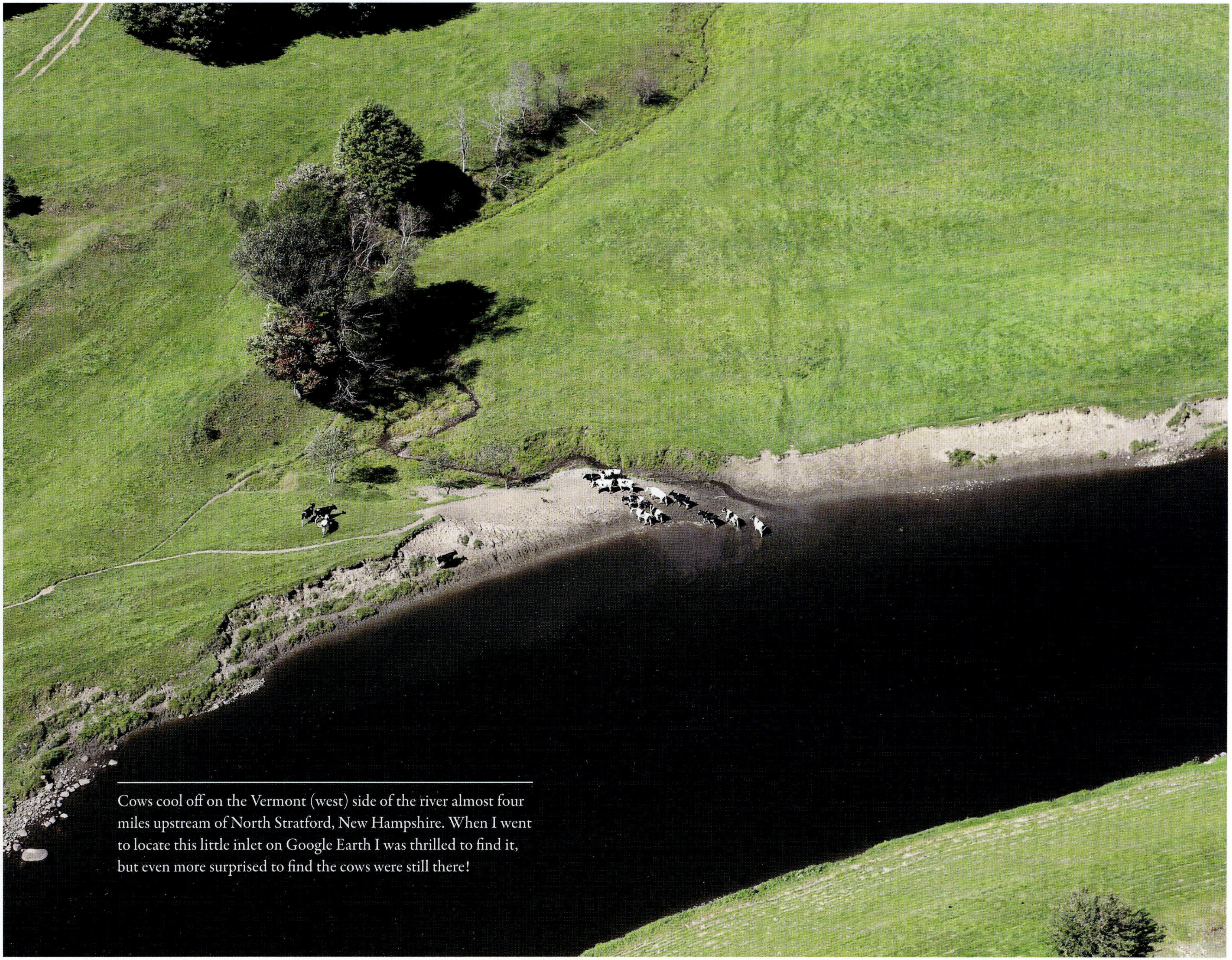

Cows cool off on the Vermont (west) side of the river almost four miles upstream of North Stratford, New Hampshire. When I went to locate this little inlet on Google Earth I was thrilled to find it, but even more surprised to find the cows were still there!

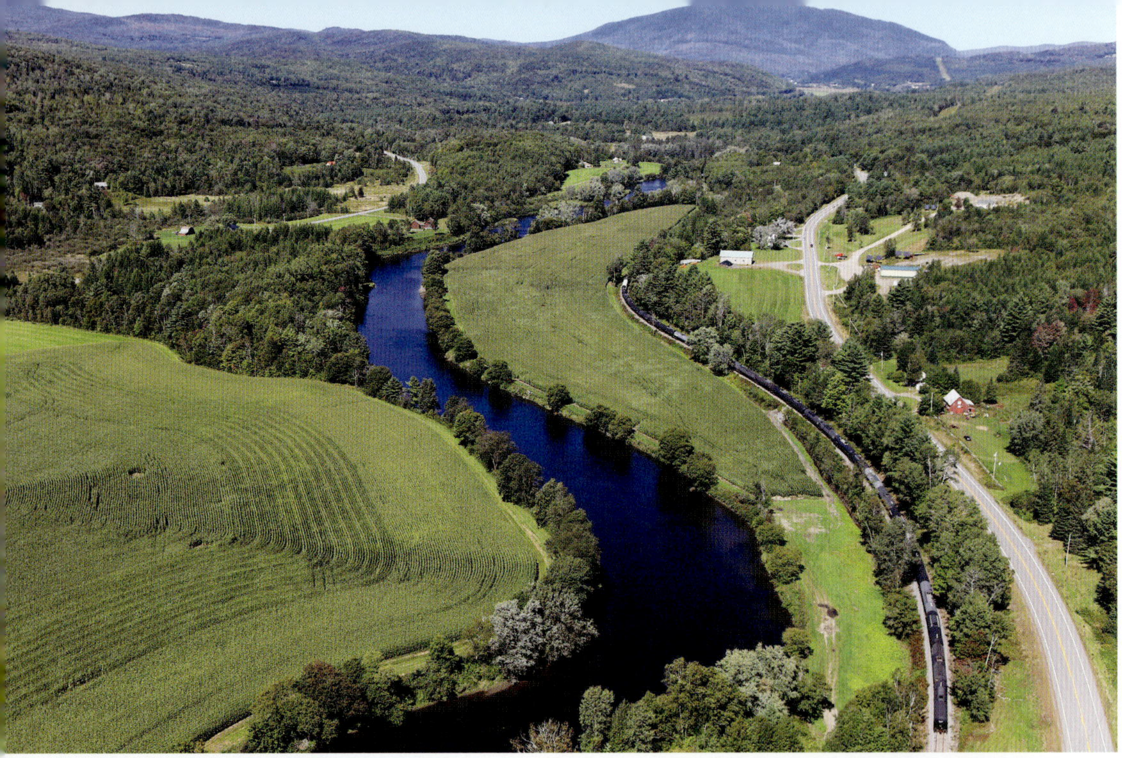

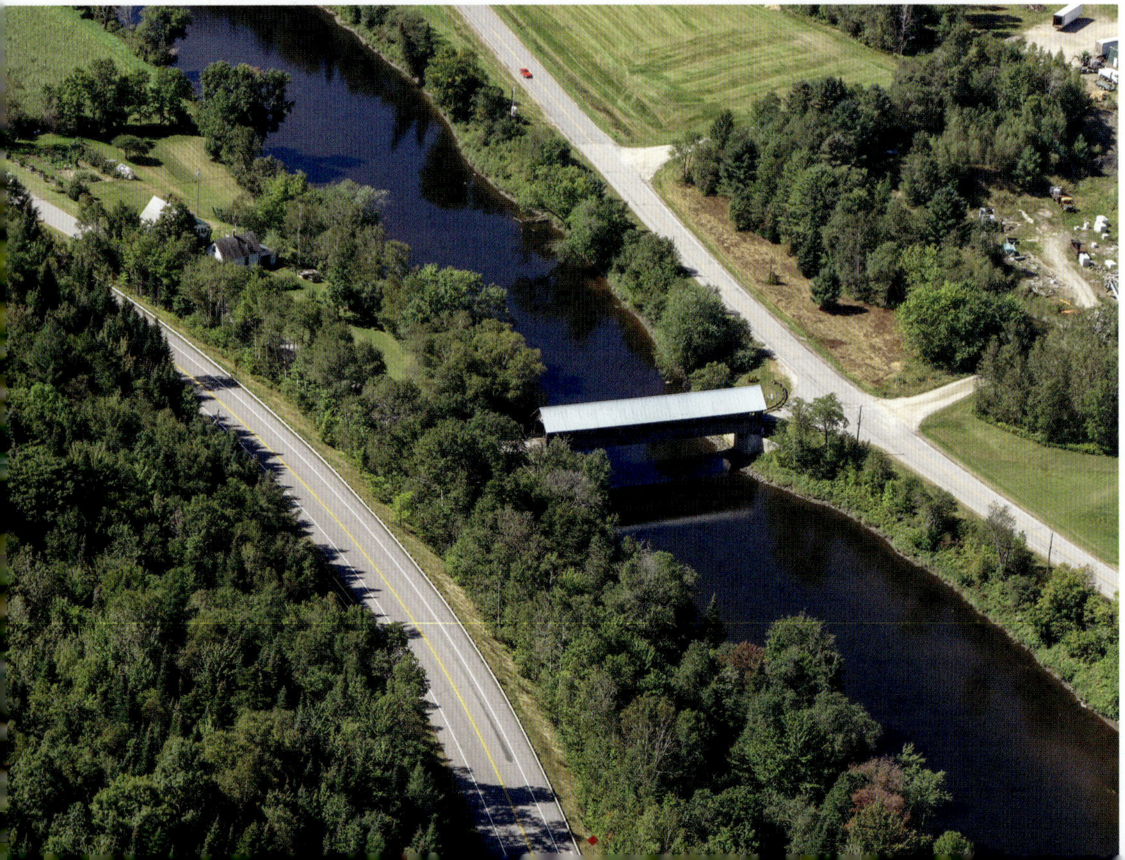

(top left) Four miles above North Stratford, the road, the train, the trees, and the crops all follow the contours of the river.

(bottom left) Looking downriver over the Columbia Covered Bridge. Built in 1912, to replace its predecessor destroyed by fire the year before. This was one of the last of its type built on the river.

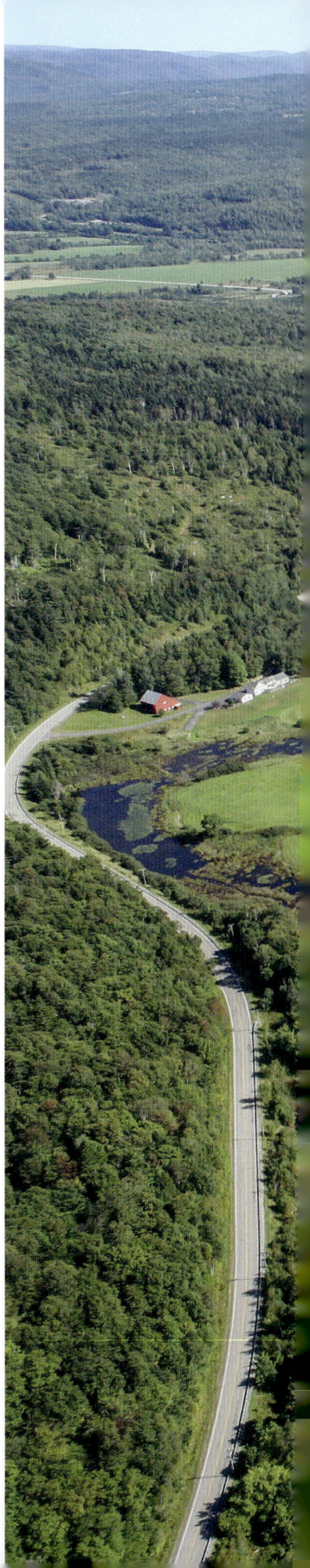

(right) Several extinct oxbows mark the approach to Colebrook, New Hampshire, from the south. The long strip of grass paralleling the local road on the right is the small airstrip Tom has landed on during photographic expeditions for this book.

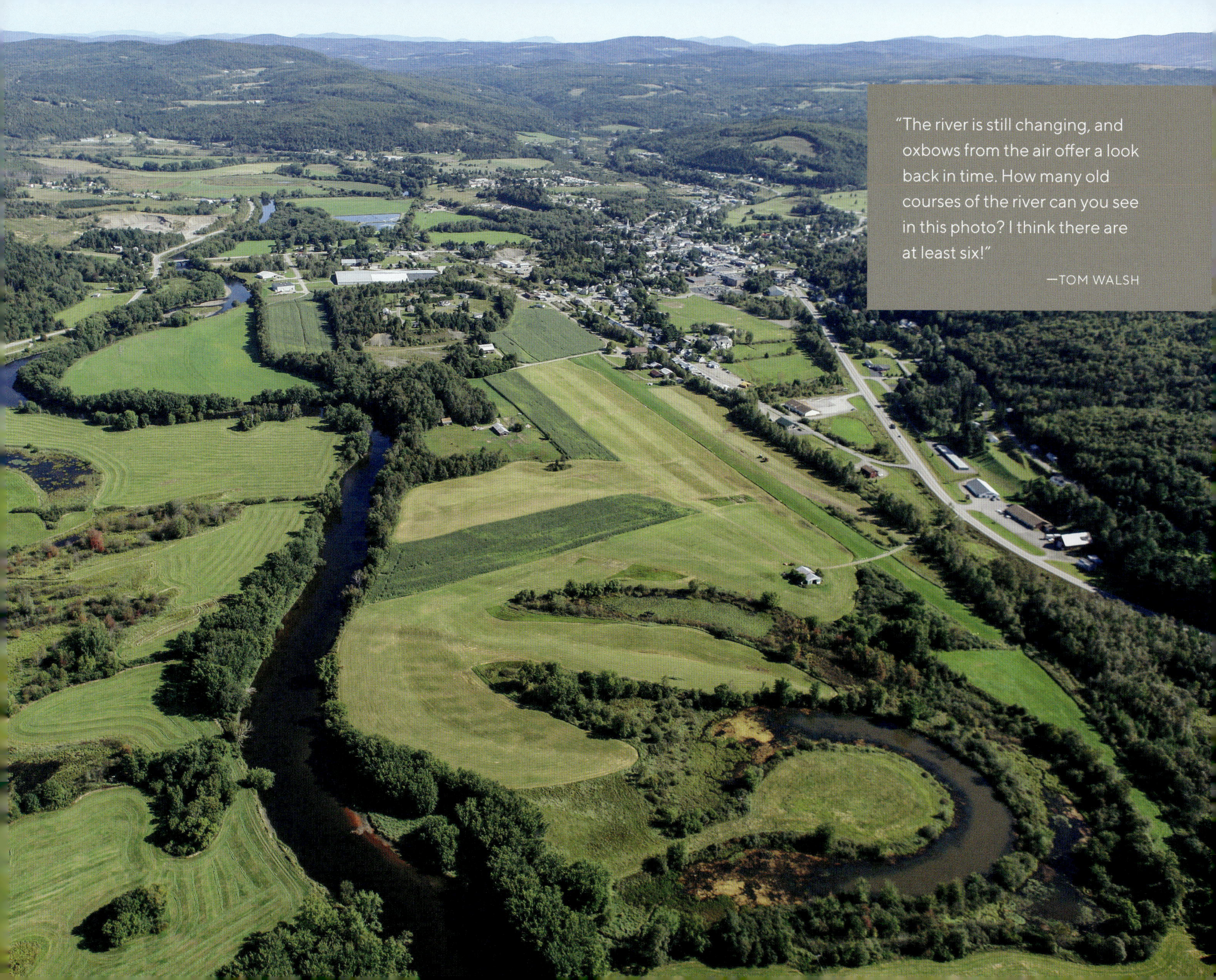

"The river is still changing, and oxbows from the air offer a look back in time. How many old courses of the river can you see in this photo? I think there are at least six!"

—TOM WALSH

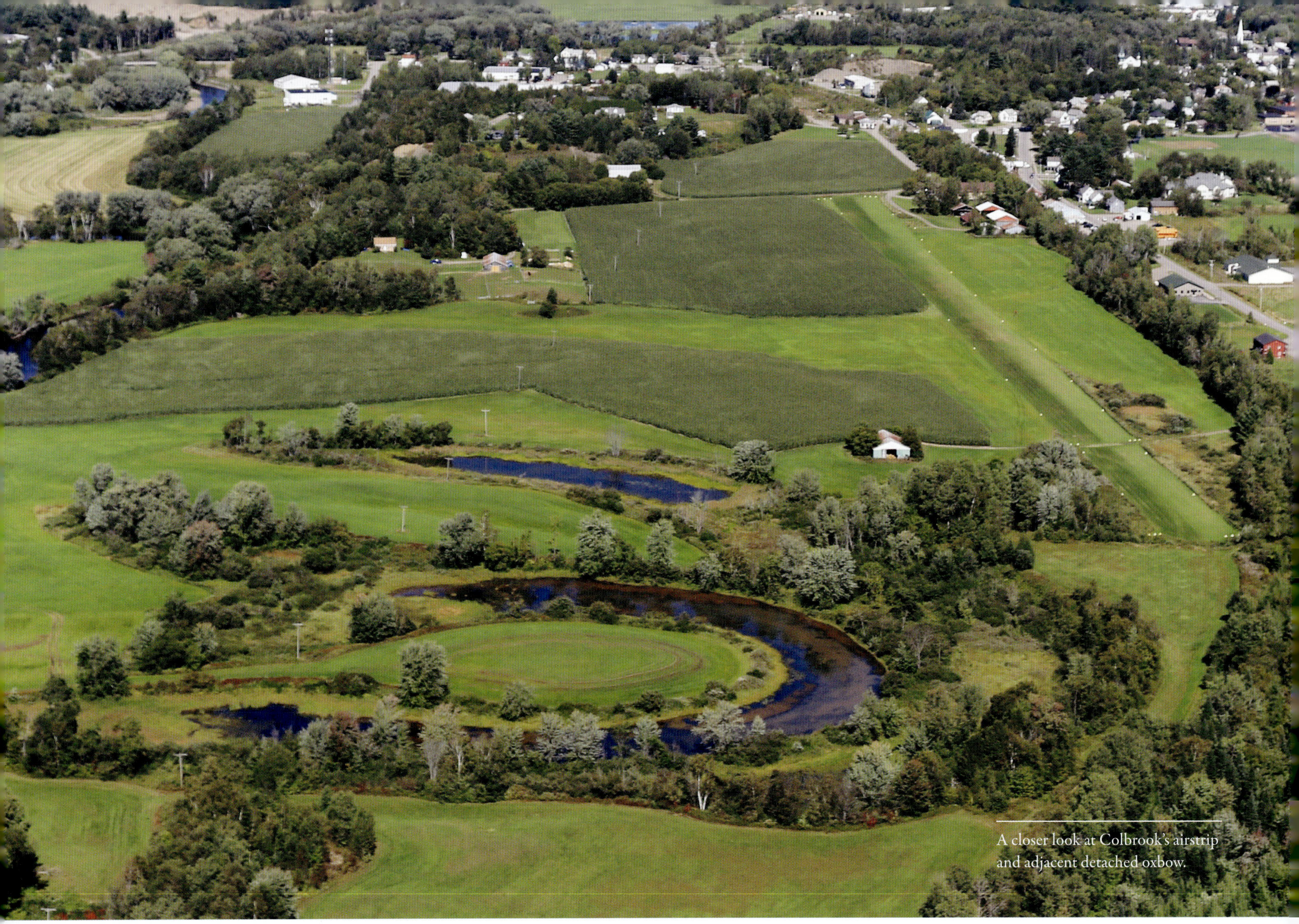

A closer look at Colbrook's airstrip and adjacent detached oxbow.

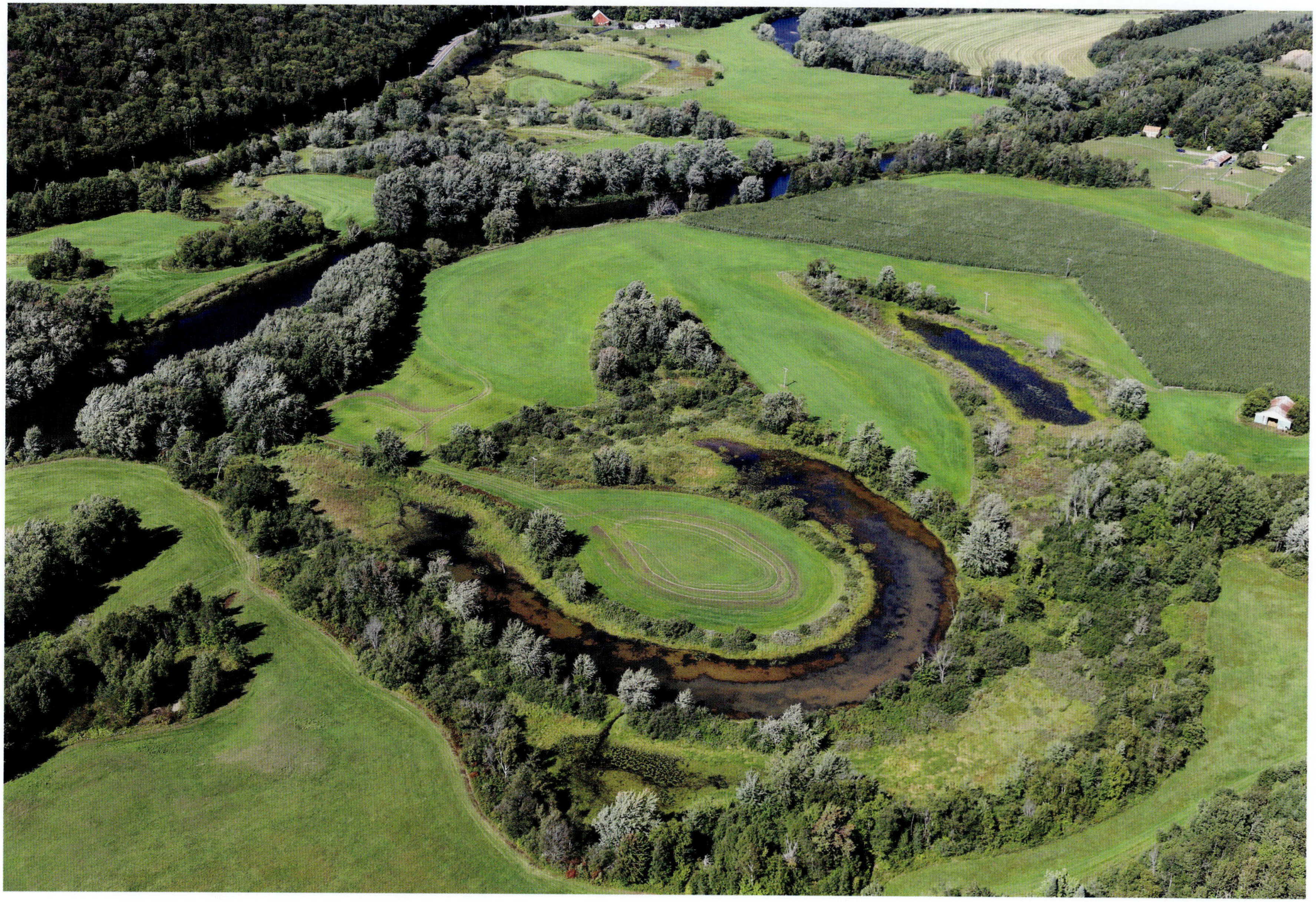

Note the interesting sets of tracks leading into the neck and around the center of this fading oxbow.

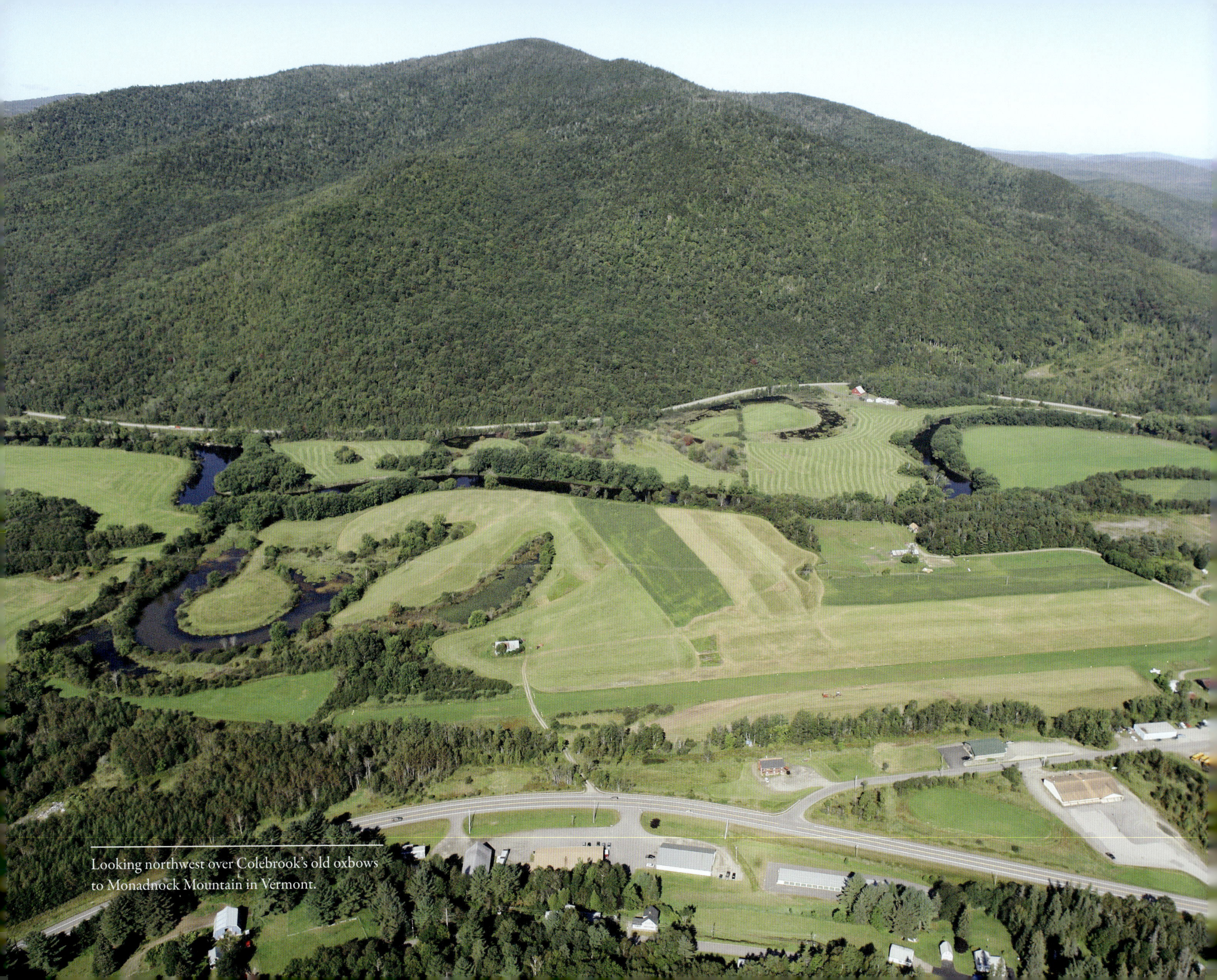

Looking northwest over Colebrook's old oxbows to Monadnock Mountain in Vermont.

COLEBROOK, NH

Colebrook, New Hampshire is located where the Mohawk River meets the Connecticut. Although it was established in 1770, settlement did not really take hold until after the Revolution. The town featured a sawmill, a gristmill, brick production, and a woolen mill. Later, shoes, carriages, and other manufactured goods were produced. Log drives on the river helped make Colebrook an important lumber center. By the 1870s it was also known as the potato capital of New Hampshire. Dairy farming and cheese making also became prominent here. The arrival of the railroad enhanced the transportation of both people and products and by the mid-1800s Colebrook had already become a tourism and resort destination featuring several large hotels and even a Victorian-era golf course!

(below) The Mohawk River can just be seen winding around a sharp bend near the church steeple in the center of town. Then it turns again to flow past the two water-treatment ponds before joining the Connecticut River, which flows through the line of trees adjacent to the gravel pits.

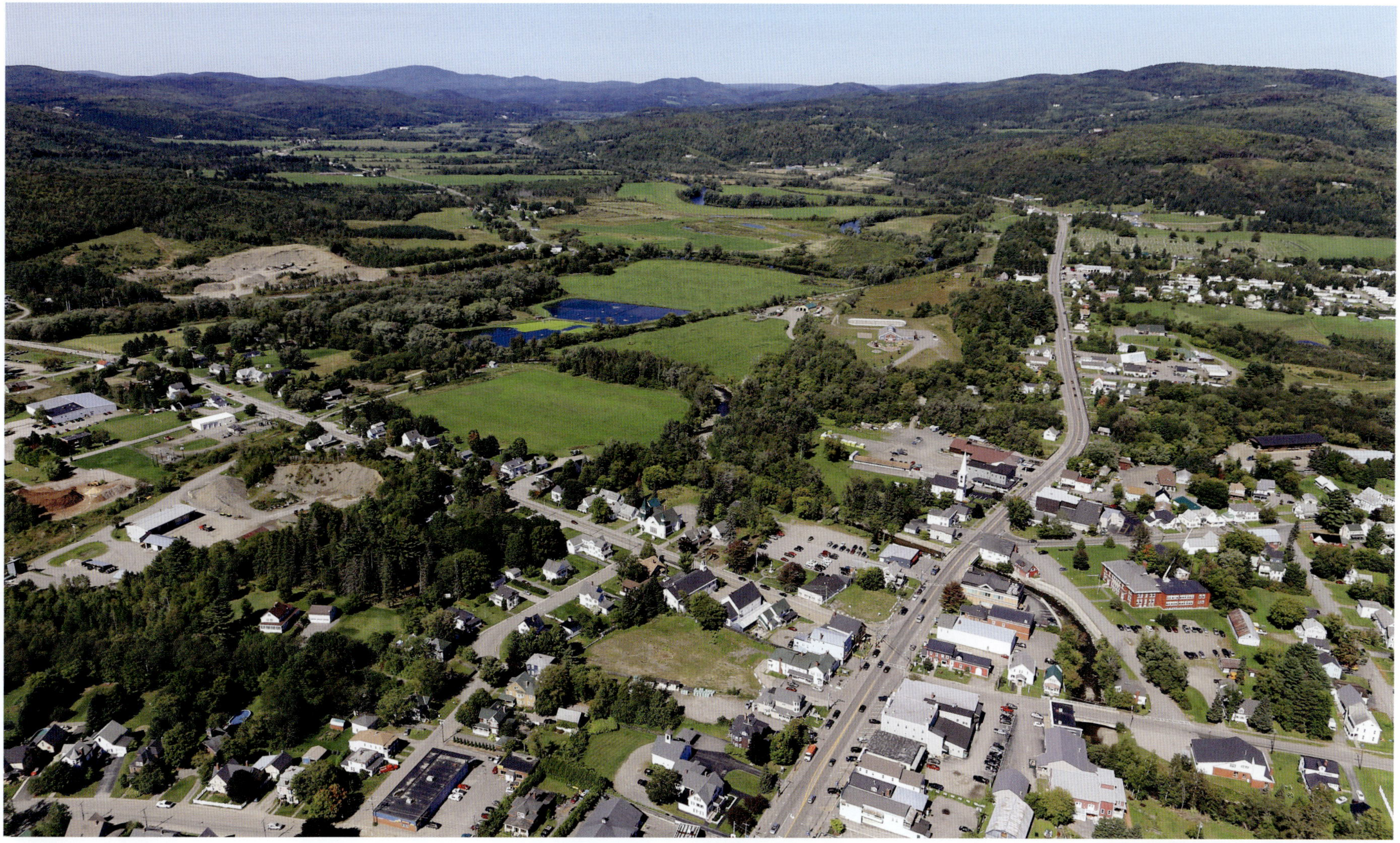

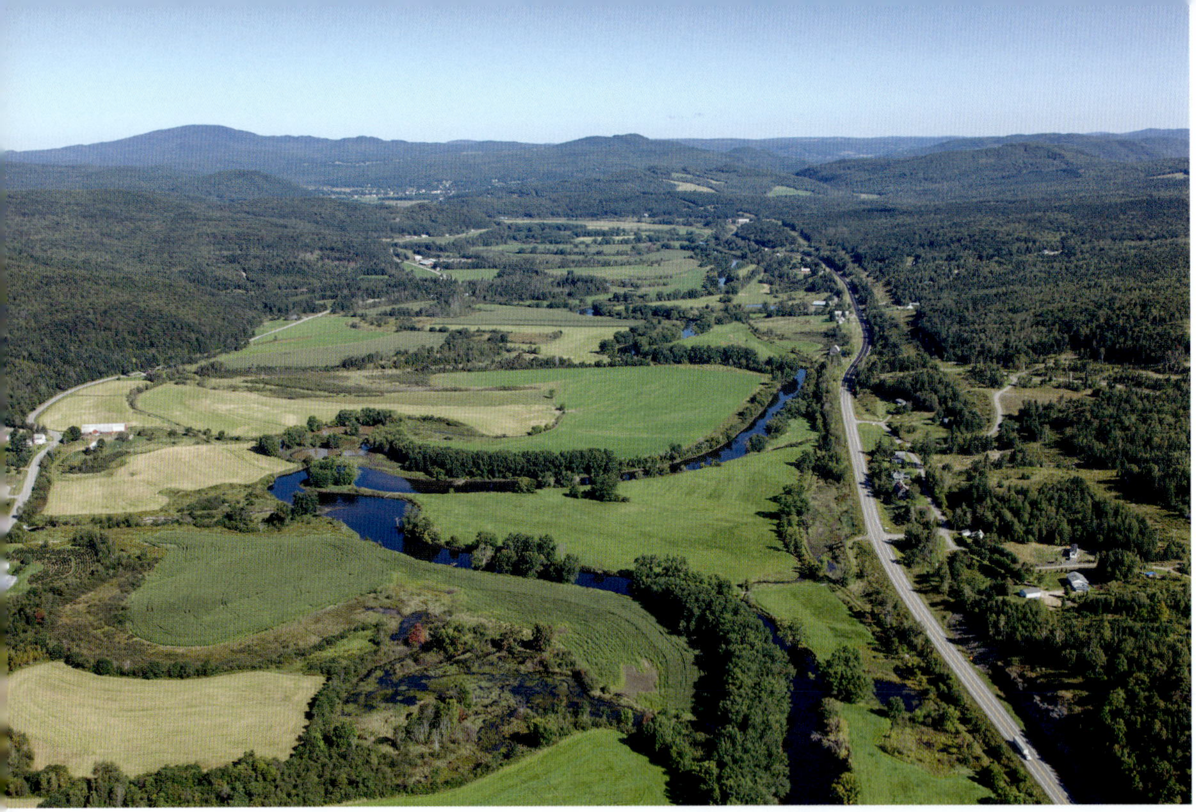

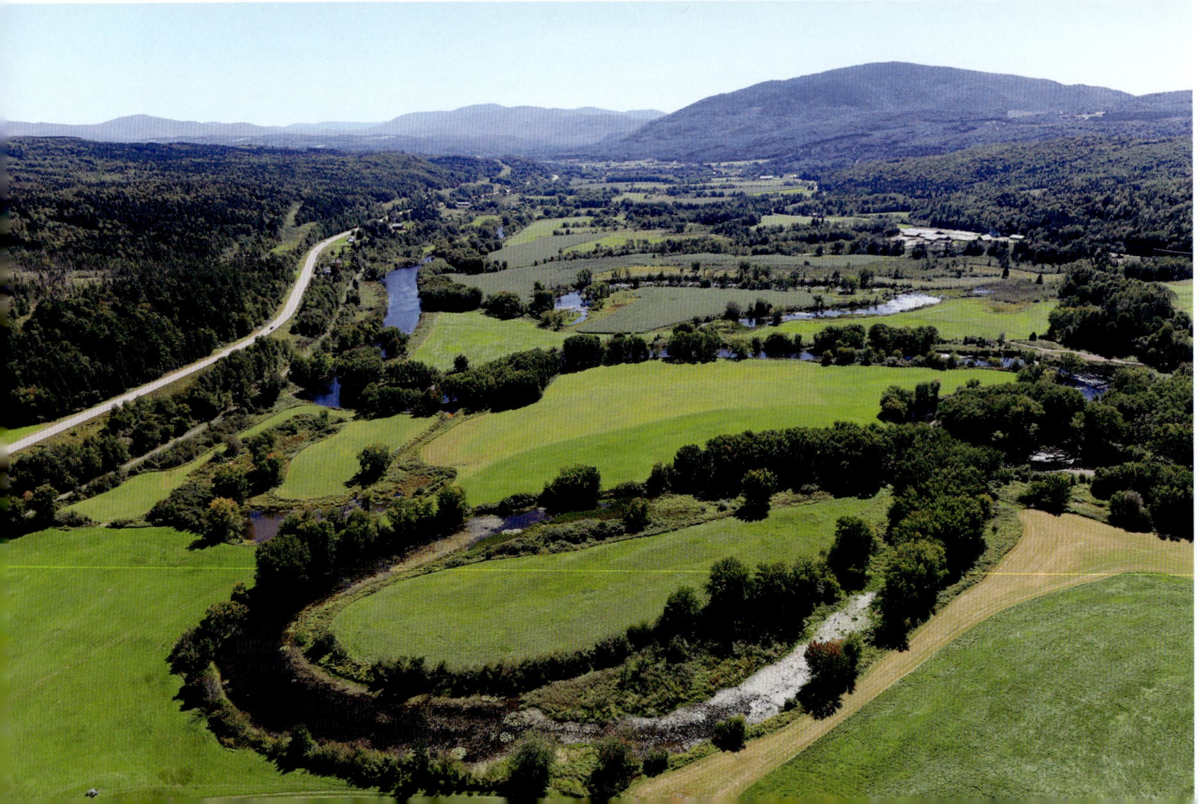

(top left) About three miles north of Colebrook with NH Route 3 on the right, note the deceased oxbow in the foreground and the tiny active one in the center with the small clump of trees at its eye.

(bottom left) Looking south over a classic cut off oxbow about two miles below West Stewartstown, New Hampshire, and Canaan, Vermont.

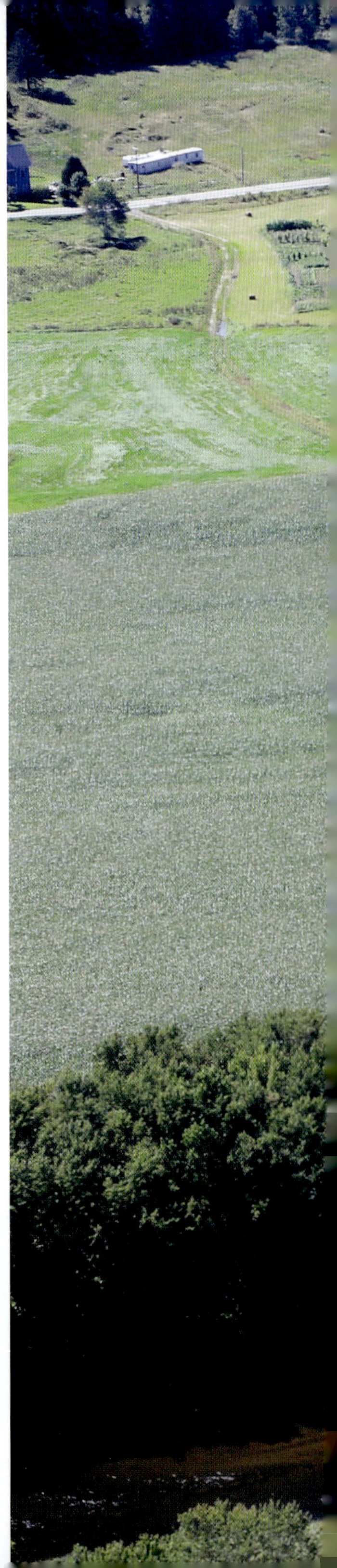

(right) Kayakers take a break on a sandbar about a mile south of Canaan, Vermont, and West Stewartstown, New Hampshire.

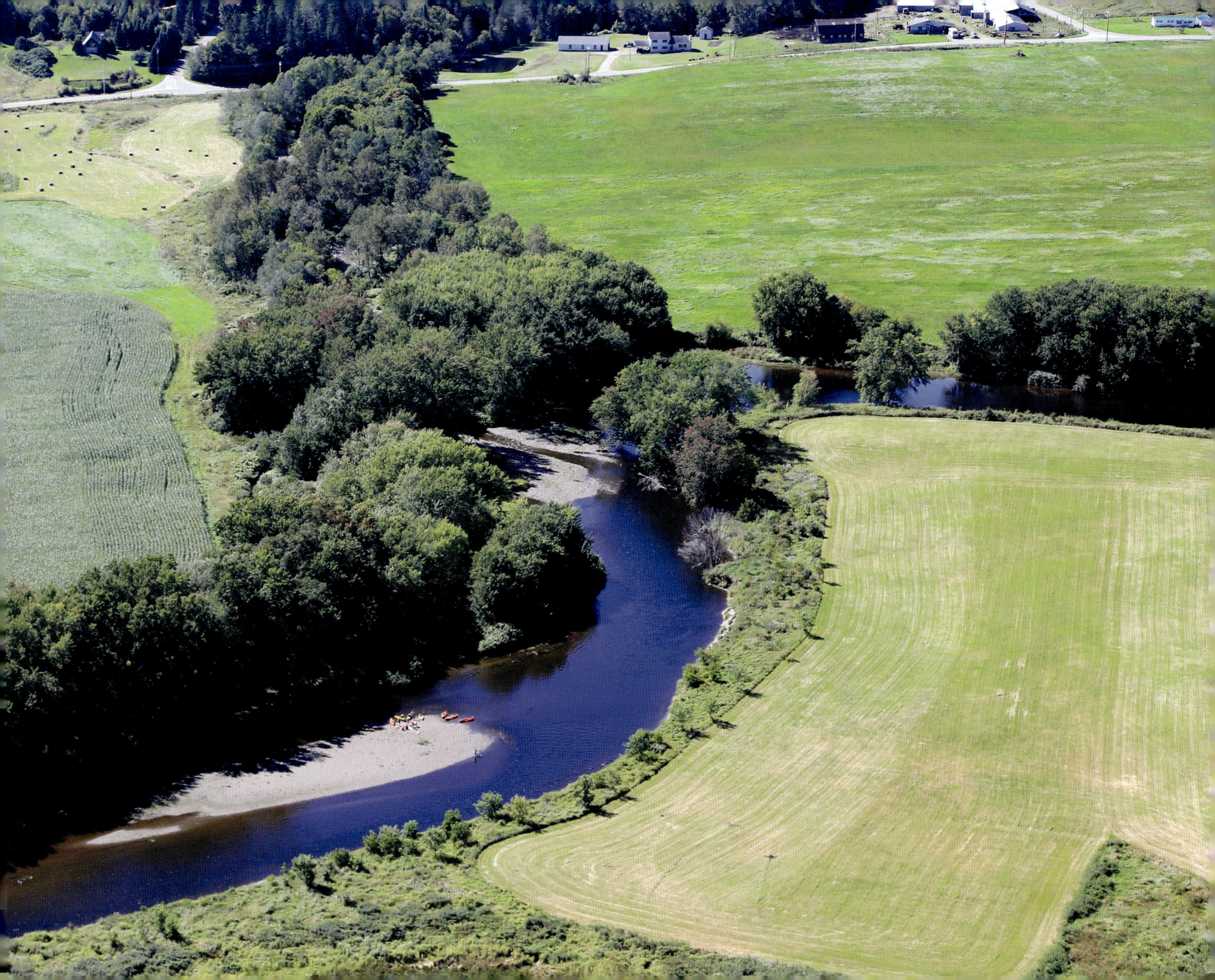

CANAAN, VT

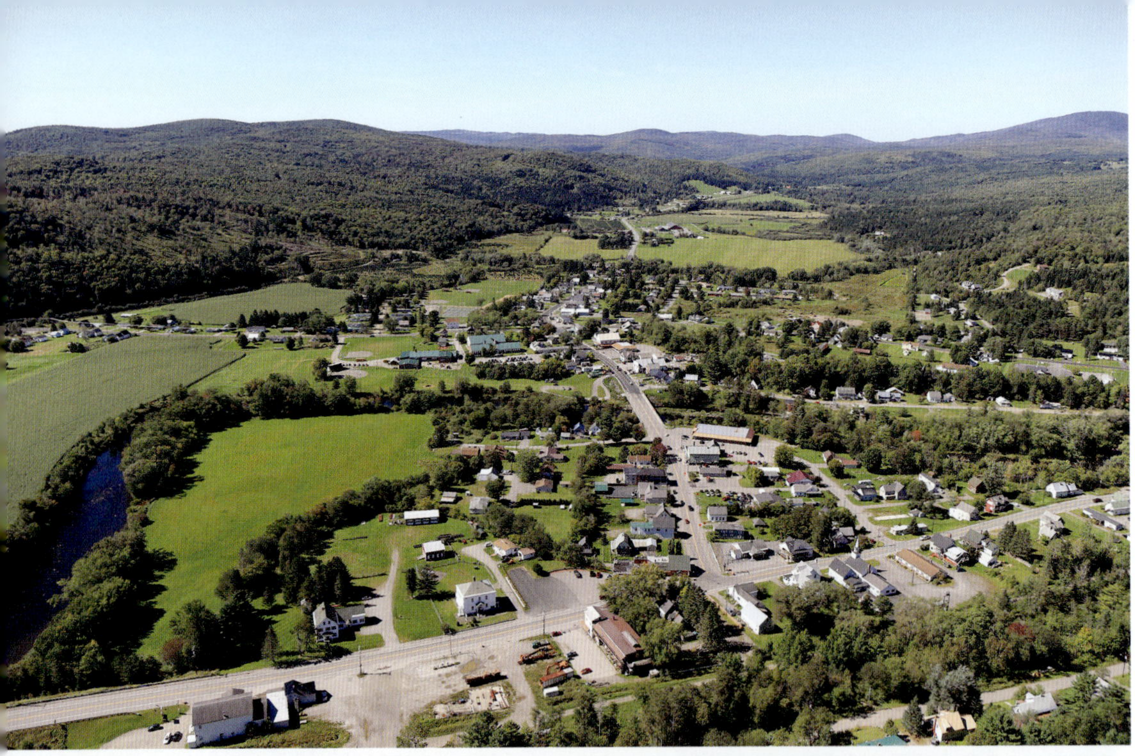

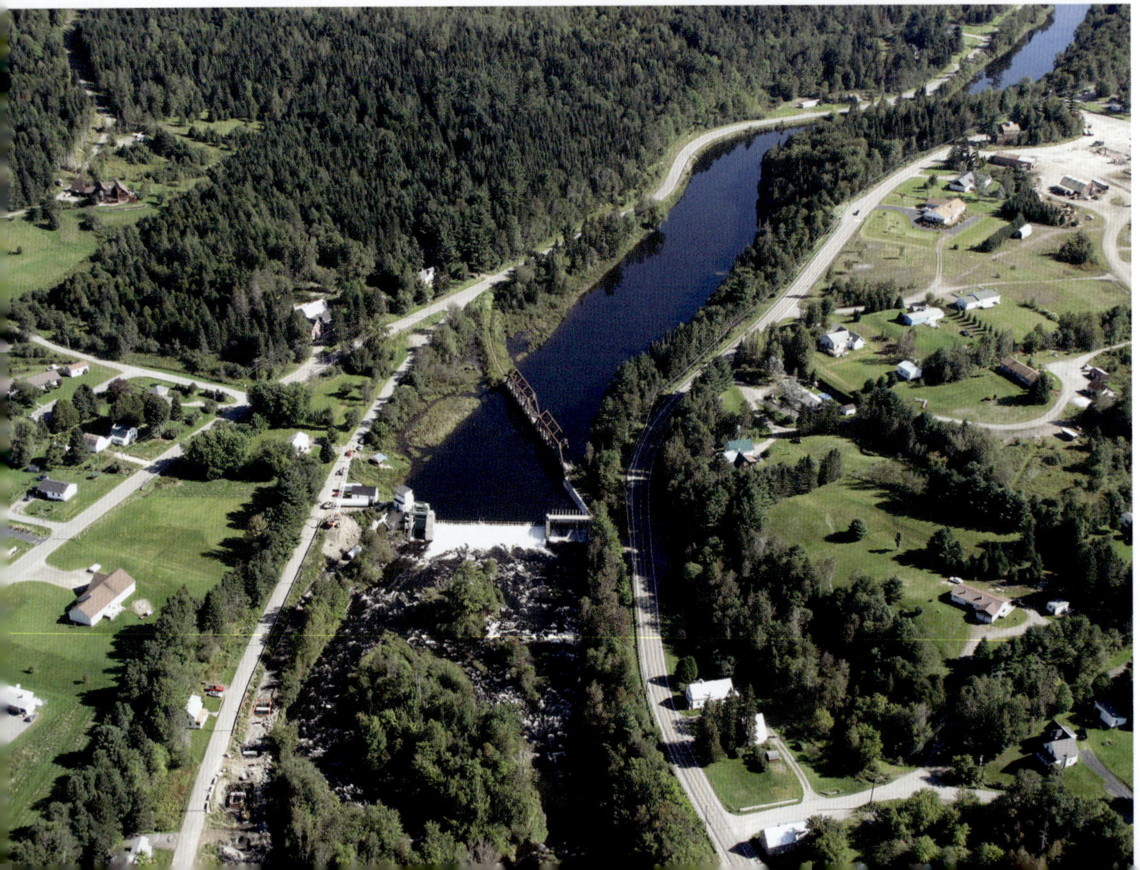

(top left) Canaan, Vermont, looking to the west

(bottom left) The Connecticut River pours over the Canaan hydro dam between Canaan, Vermont, and West Stewartstown, New Hampshire.

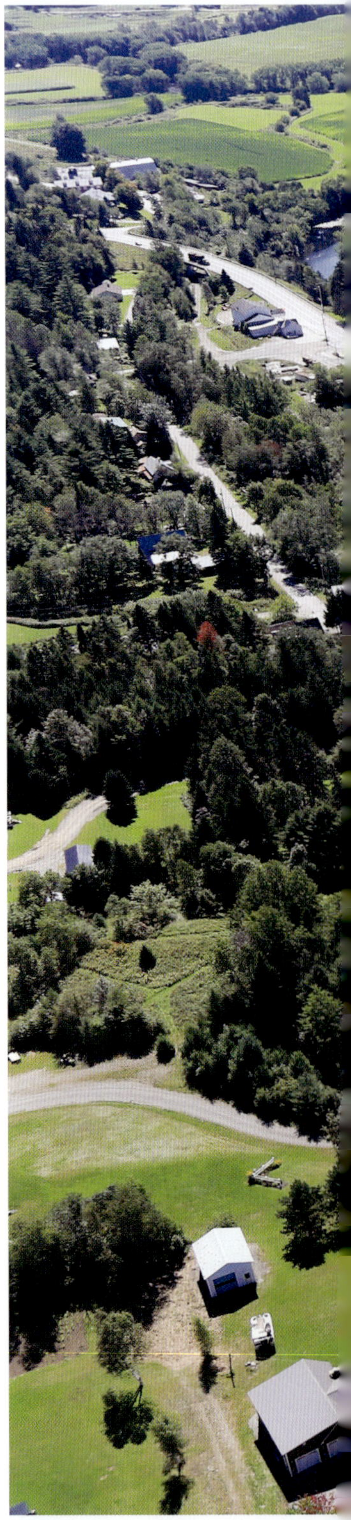

(right) Looking south over the Canaan hydroelectric dam

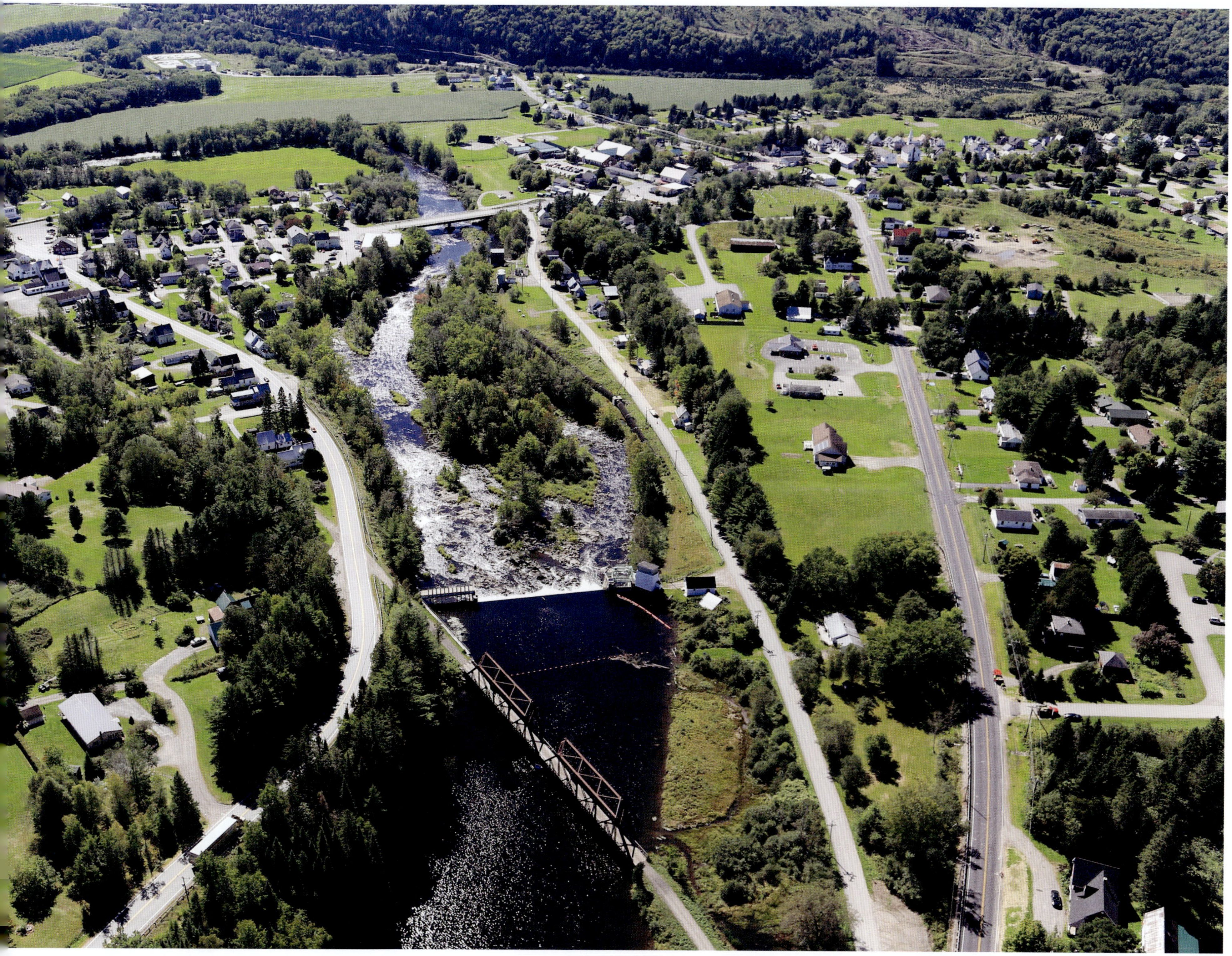

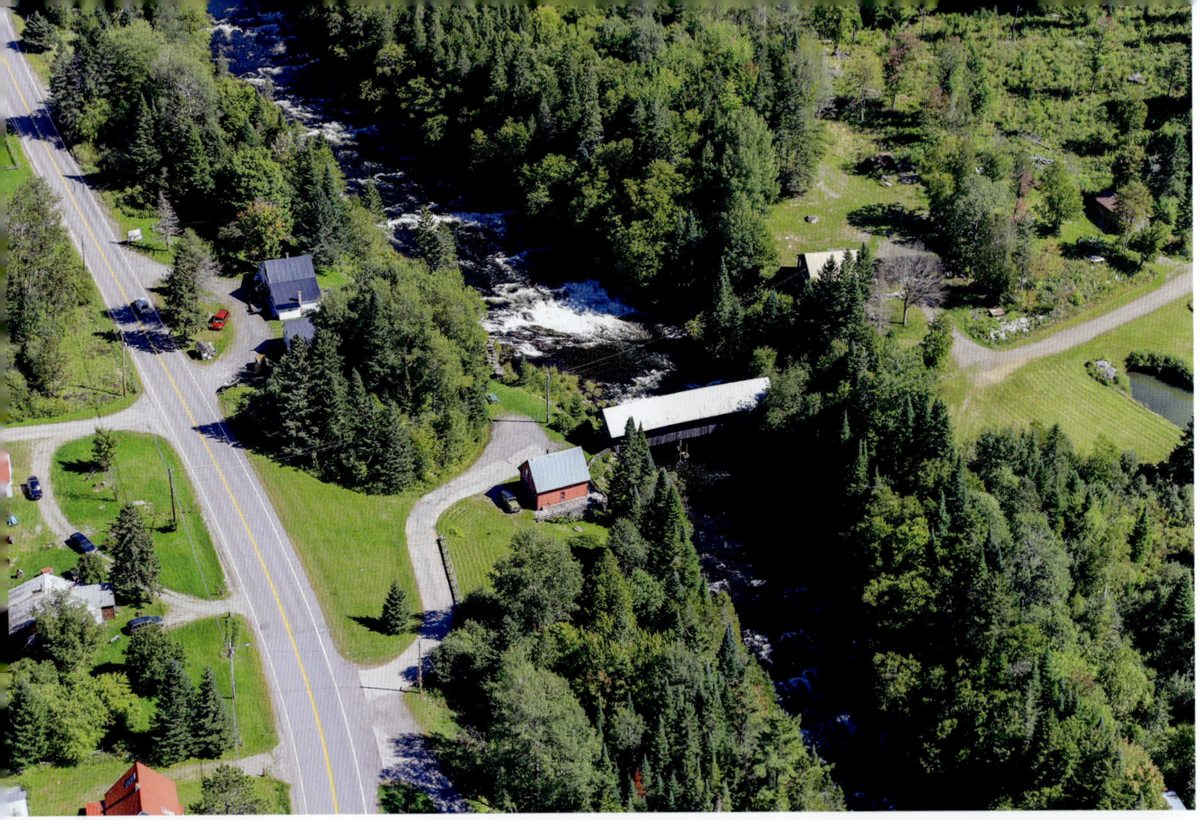

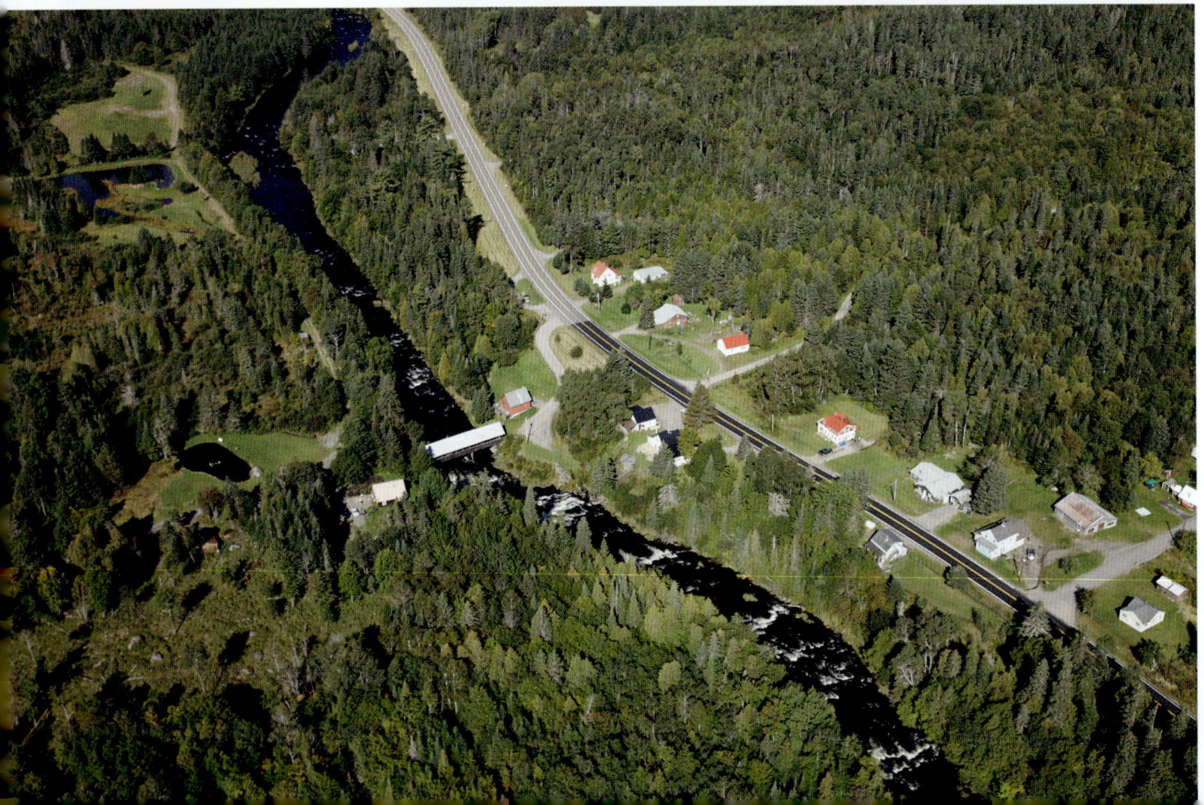

(top left) Looking north over the Pittsburg-Clarksville covered bridge. Originally built in 1876, it is locally known as the Bacon Road Bridge and is the northernmost covered bridge on the Connecticut River. The river is only about eighty-feet wide at this point.

(bottom left) The river looking downstream as it flows under the Bacon Road Bridge. It is here that the Connecticut River truly begins to run free.

(right) Looking north again from the Bacon Road Bridge to the town of Pittsburg, New Hampshire, which lies just below the Murphy Dam and Lake Francis. This 100-foot high dam was built in 1940 to help regulate the river's flow after the devastating flood of 1936.

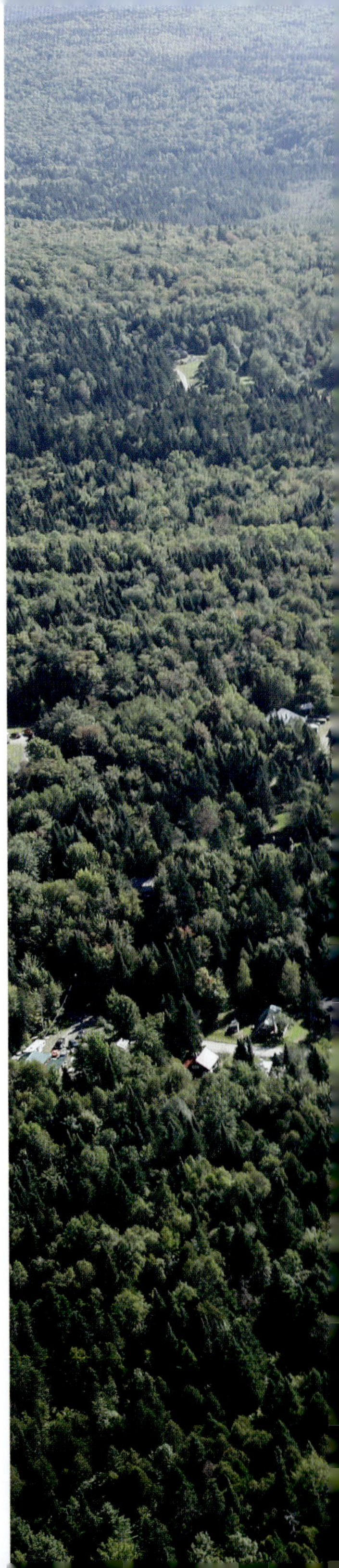

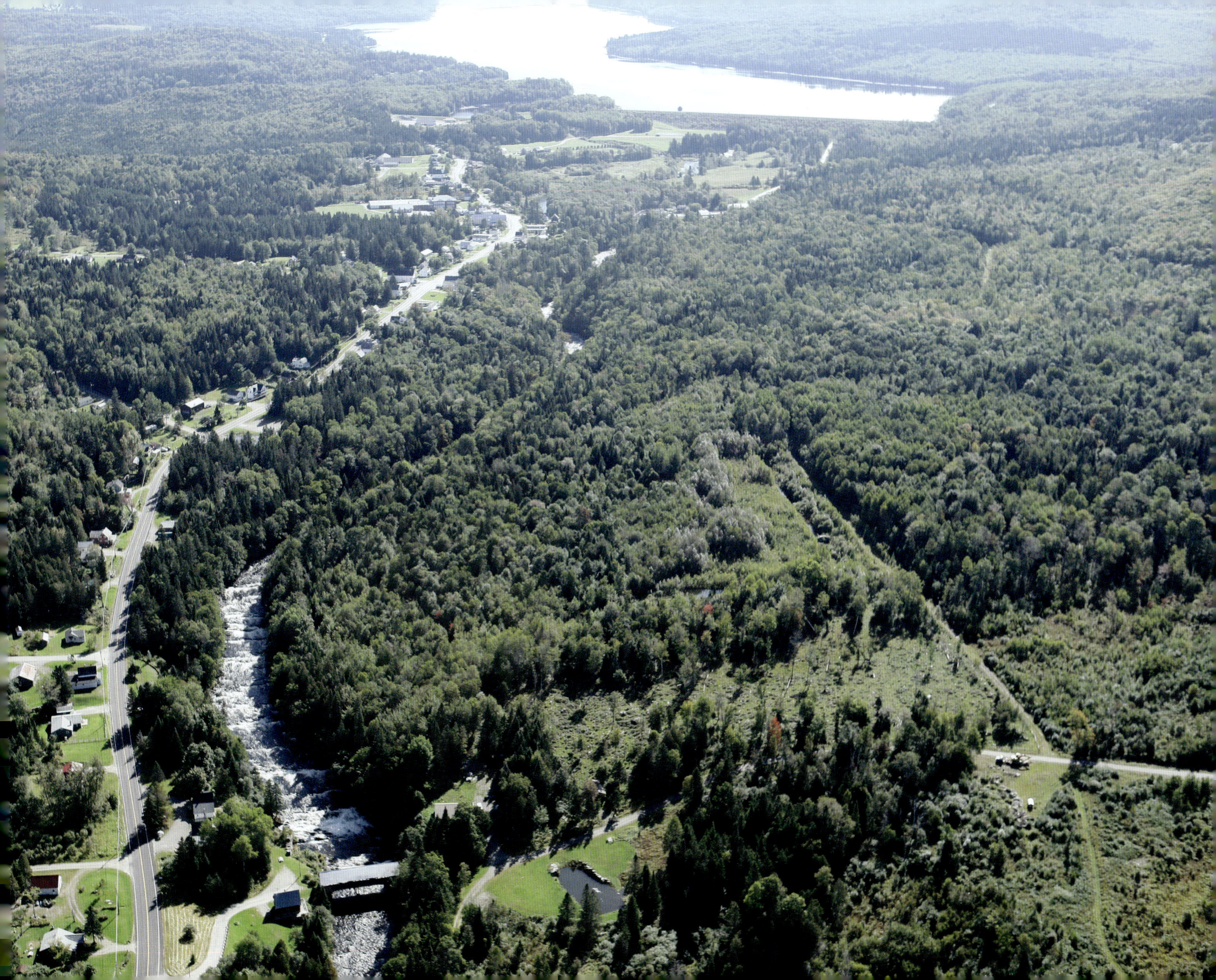

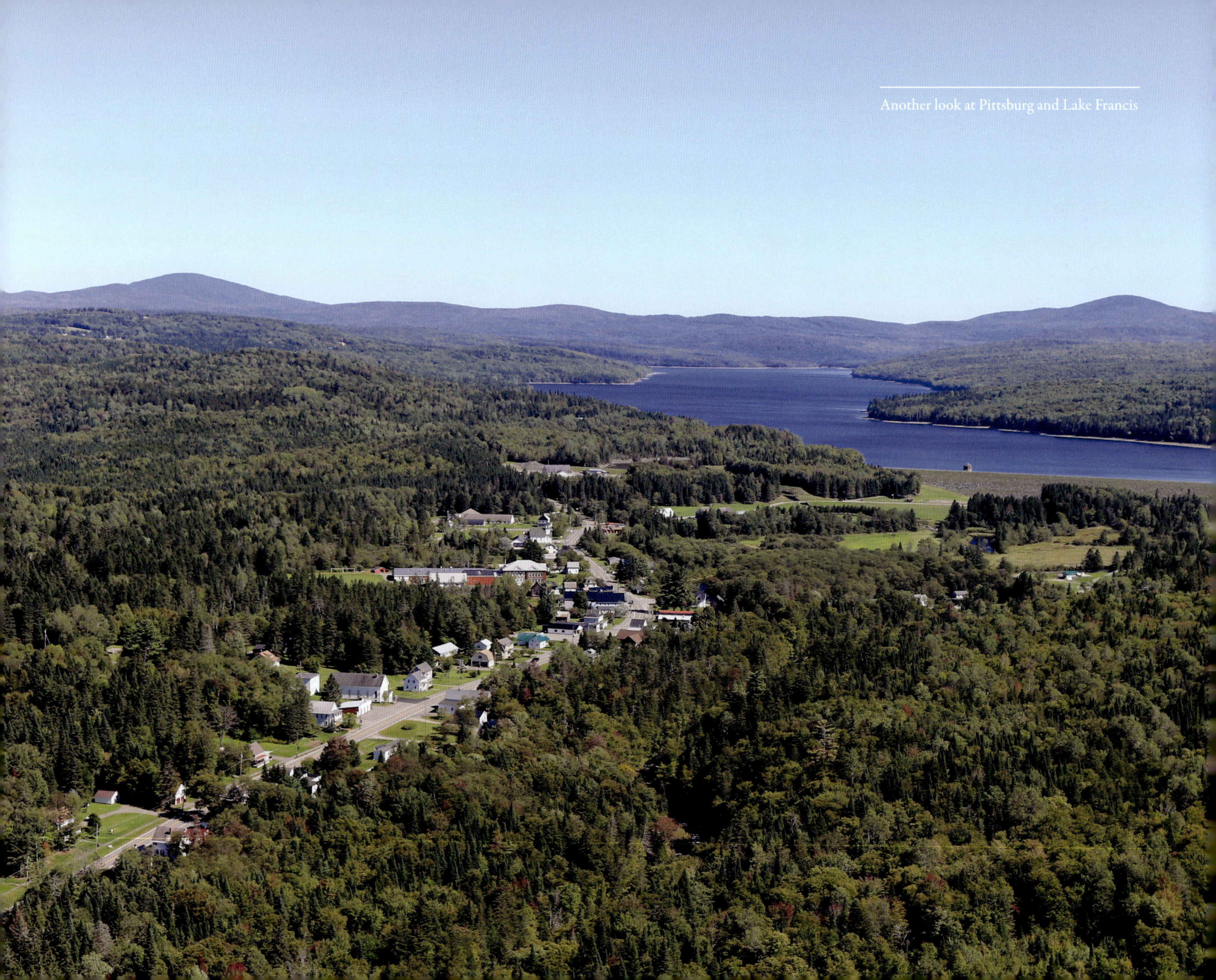

Another look at Pittsburg and Lake Francis

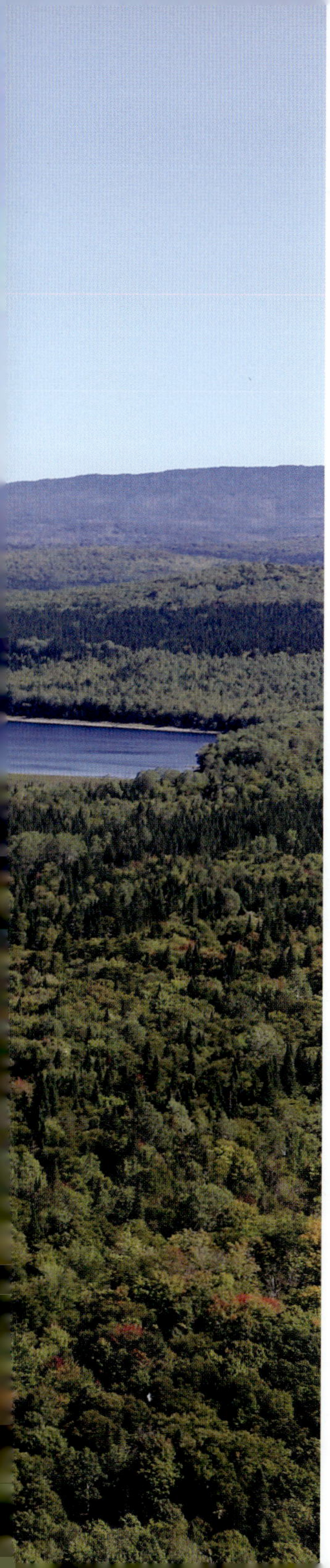

PITTSBURG, NH

Pittsburg is the most northerly town both on the Connecticut River and in the state of New Hampshire. It serves as a gateway to this remote region of lakes and mountains protruding above the 45th parallel between Canada and Maine. Even after the Revolution this area was disputed territory, at one point declaring itself an independent republic before becoming part of New Hampshire in 1840. With a permanent population of fewer than 900, Pittsburg proudly boasts that it has more moose than people. It does. It is also a mecca for hikers, hunters, anglers, snow mobile and ATV enthusiasts, and tourists. Its lodges, inns, cabins, and campgrounds provide a perfect base of operations for those wishing to explore and experience the great and untamed North.

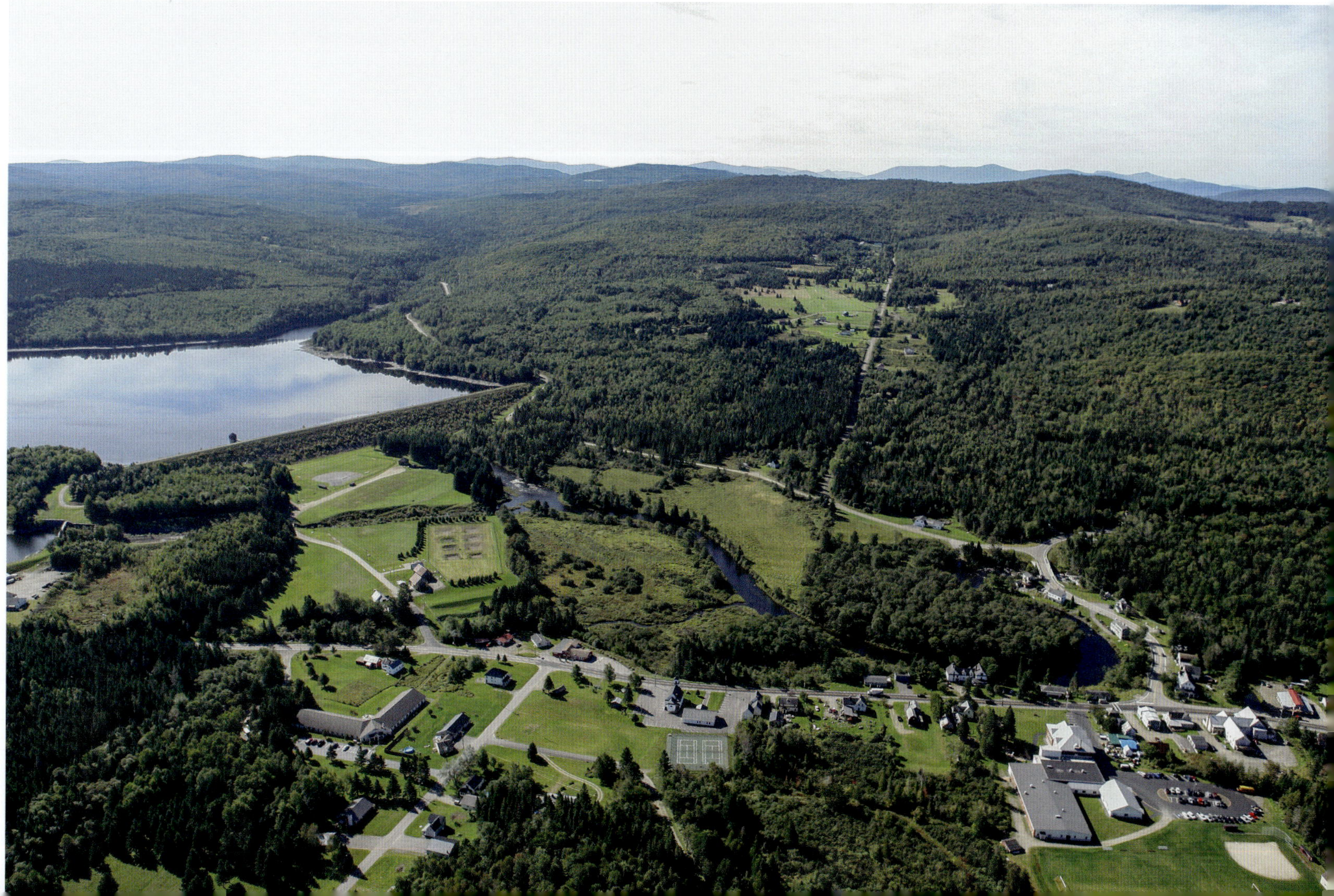

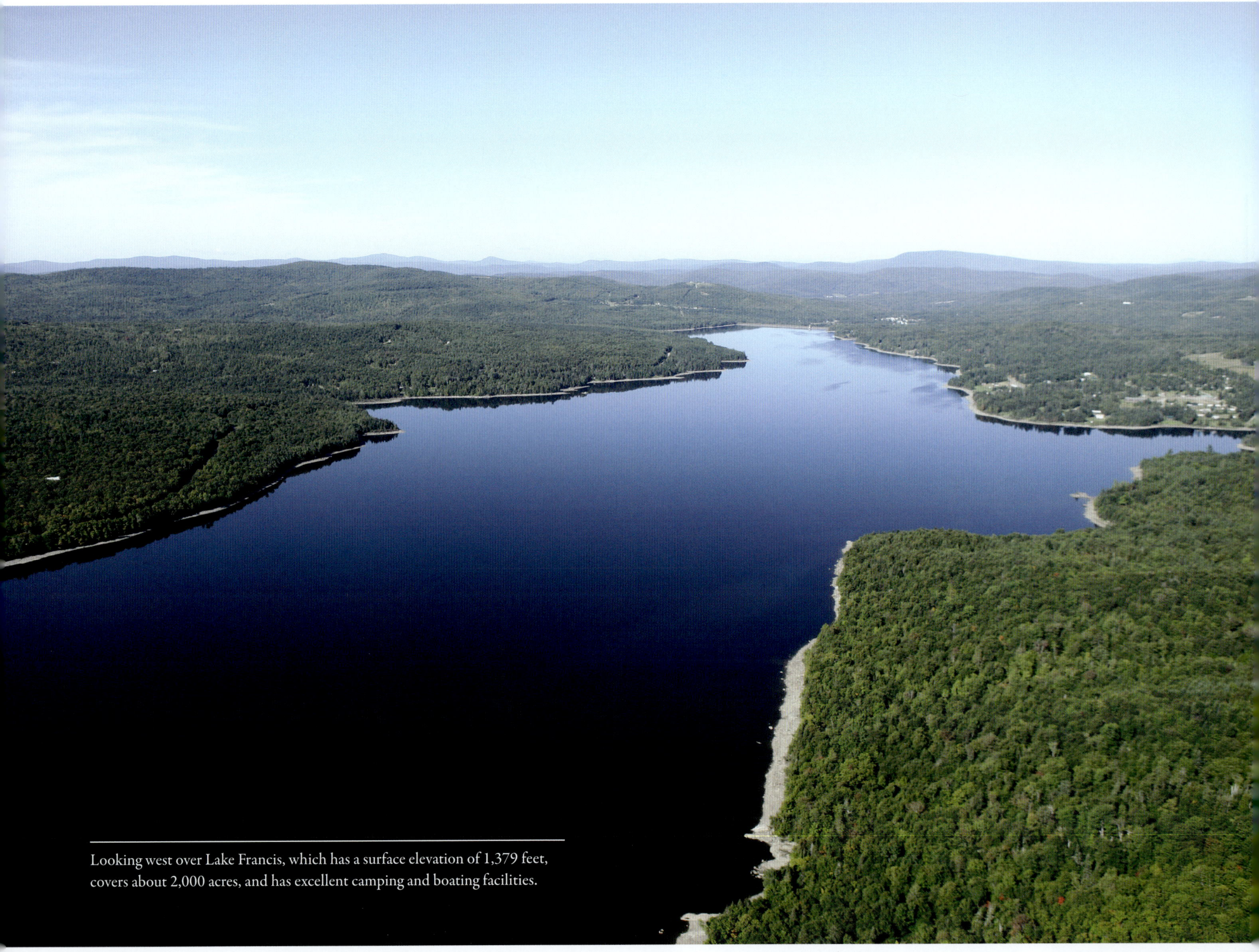

Looking west over Lake Francis, which has a surface elevation of 1,379 feet, covers about 2,000 acres, and has excellent camping and boating facilities.

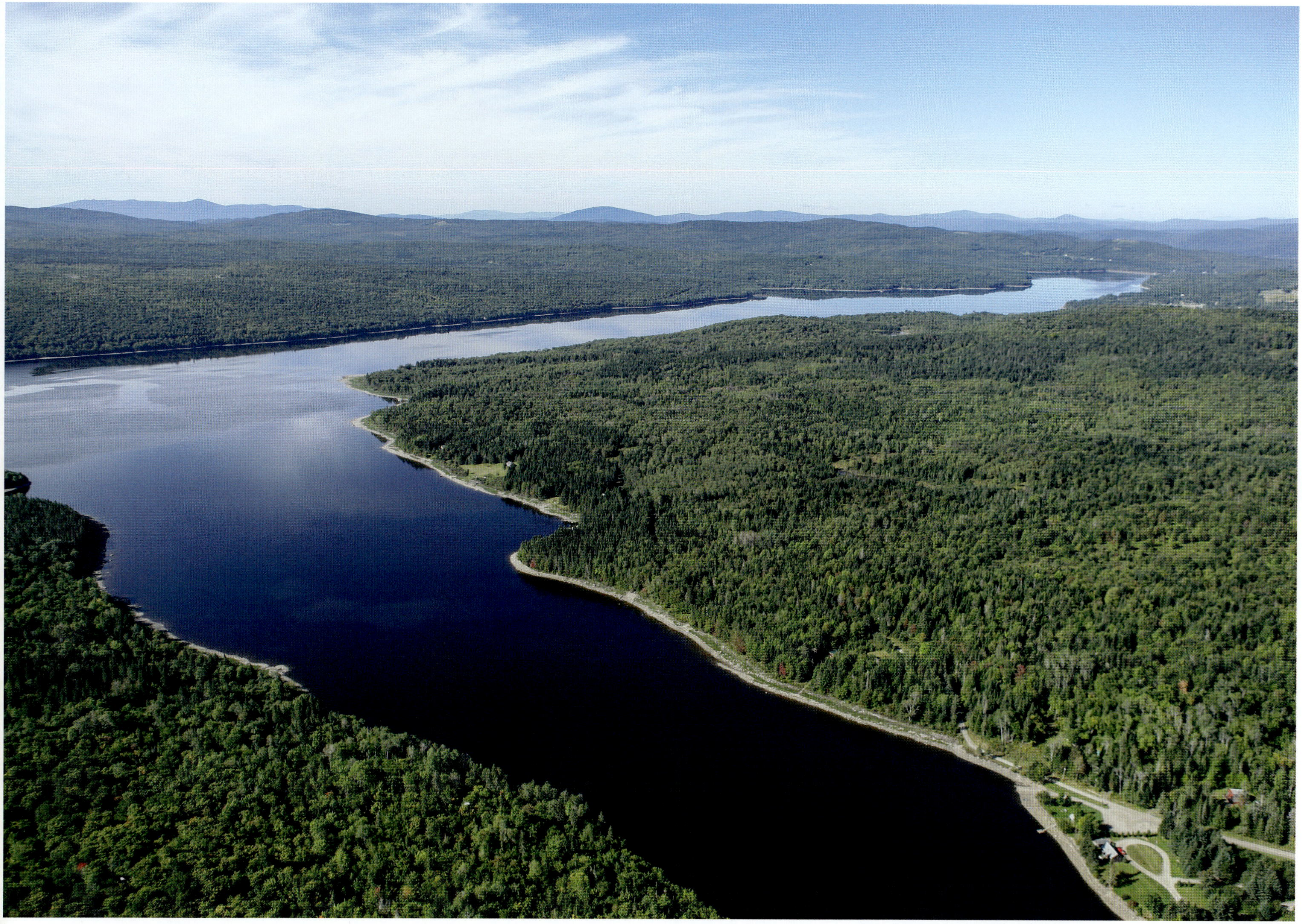

Looking south from the northern end of Lake Frances

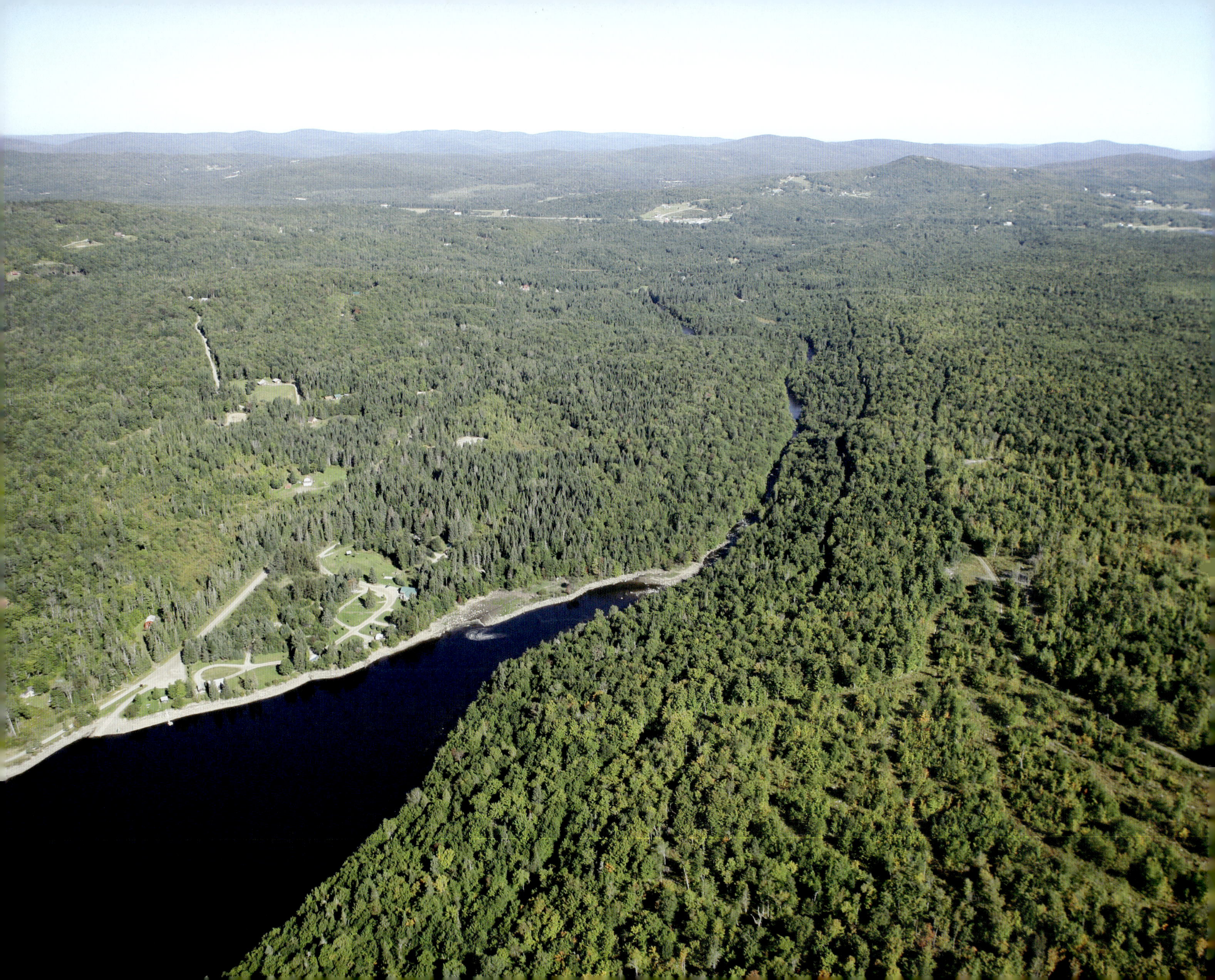

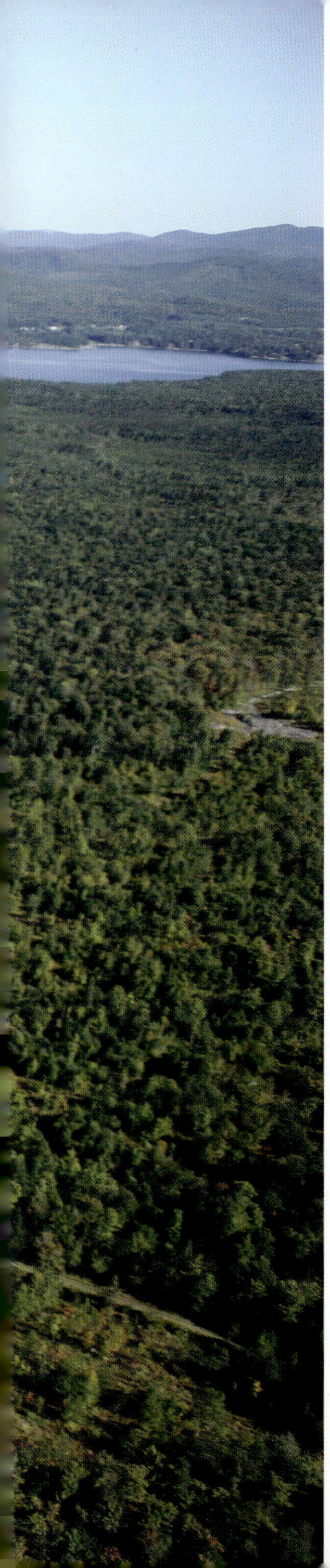

(left) Here, at the northern end of Lake Francis, the river winds down from the First Connecticut Lake, which lies just over two miles to the north as the crow flies. This stretch is not navigable but is cherished by anglers who can pull trophy-winning trout and salmon from the river here.

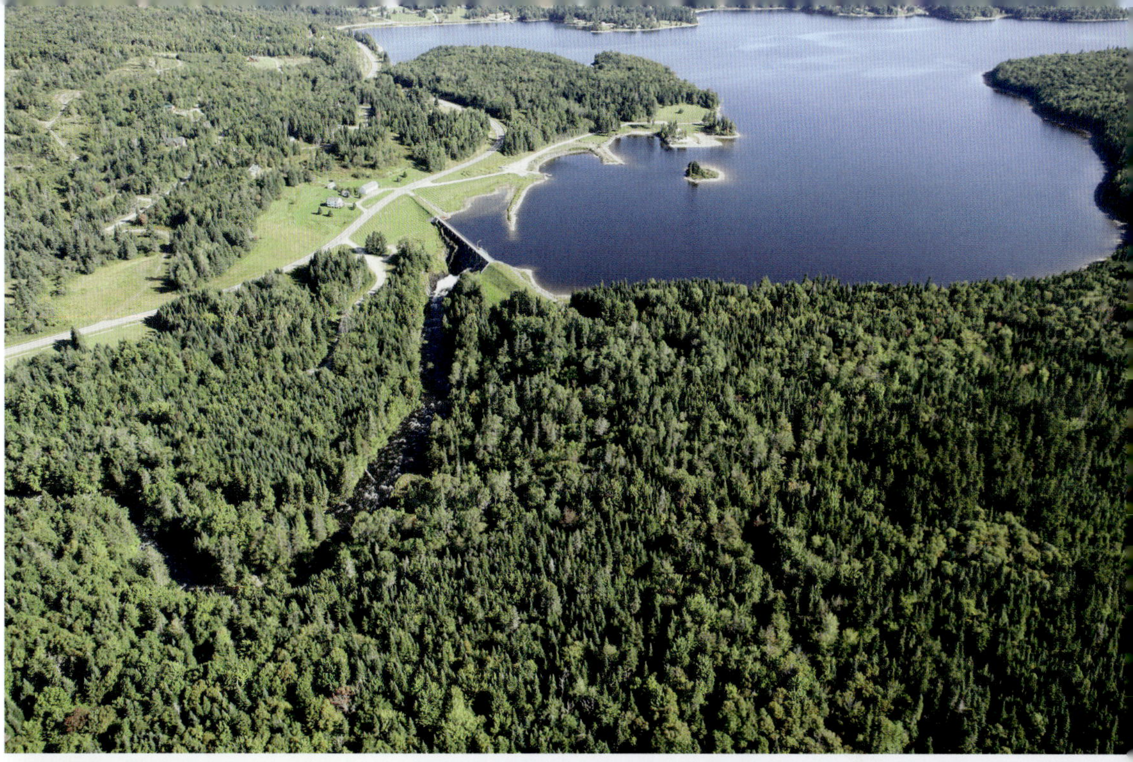

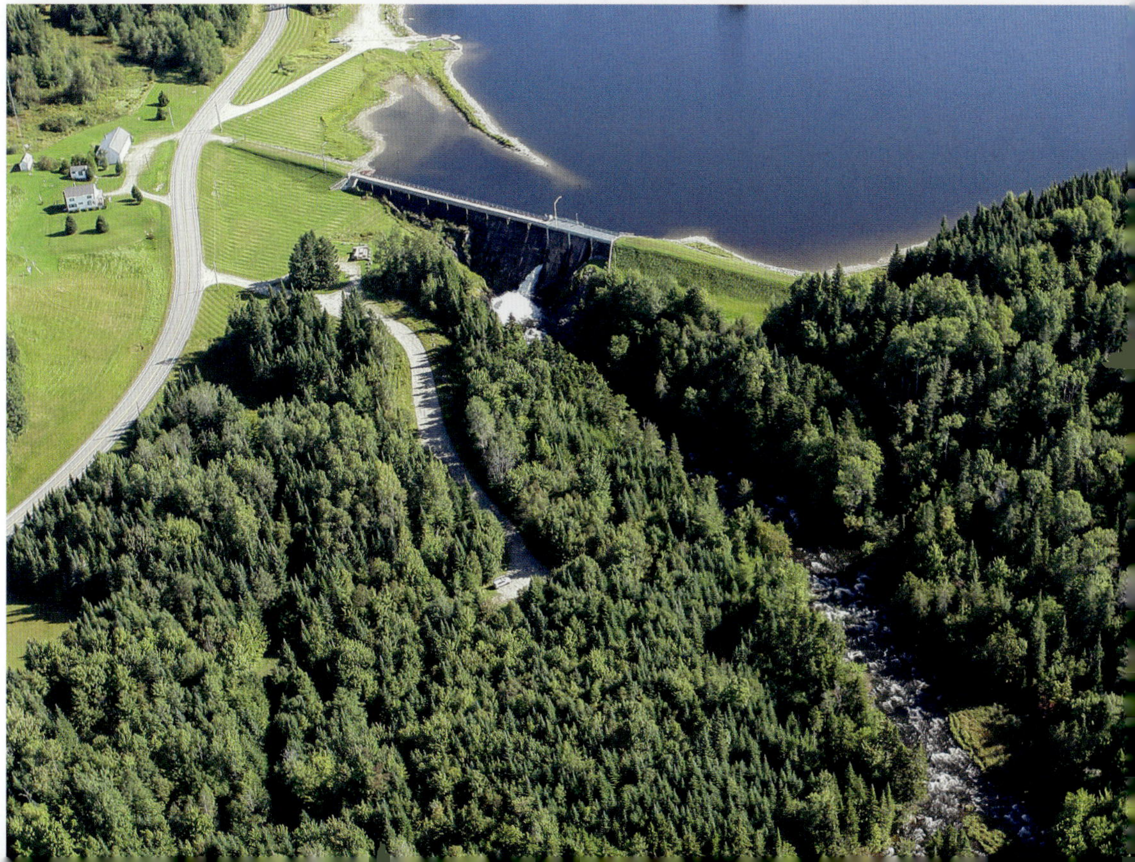

(top right) From the dam at the western end of the First Connecticut Lake, the water that will eventually become New England's largest river squeezes through a spillway before flowing down to Lake Francis. Covering about 3,000 feet, it is the largest of the four Connecticut Lakes. It sits at 1,638 feet above sea level and its depths can reach 160 feet. The dam is a "tailwater dam" meaning its discharge comes from deep in the lake, keeping the river cool even in the summer and providing an excellent trout habitat.

(bottom right) Detail of river flowing through spillway at the First Connecticut Lake Dam

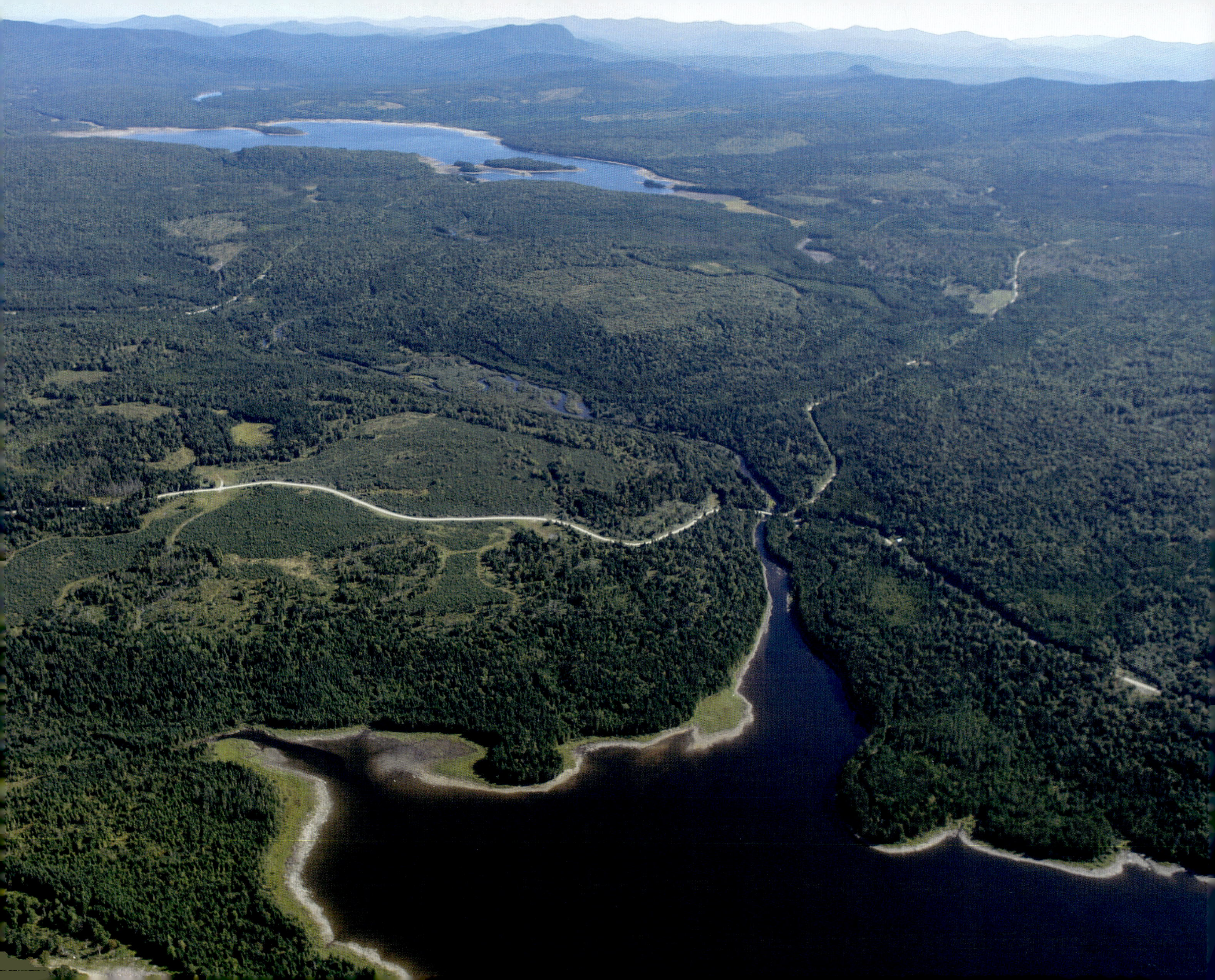

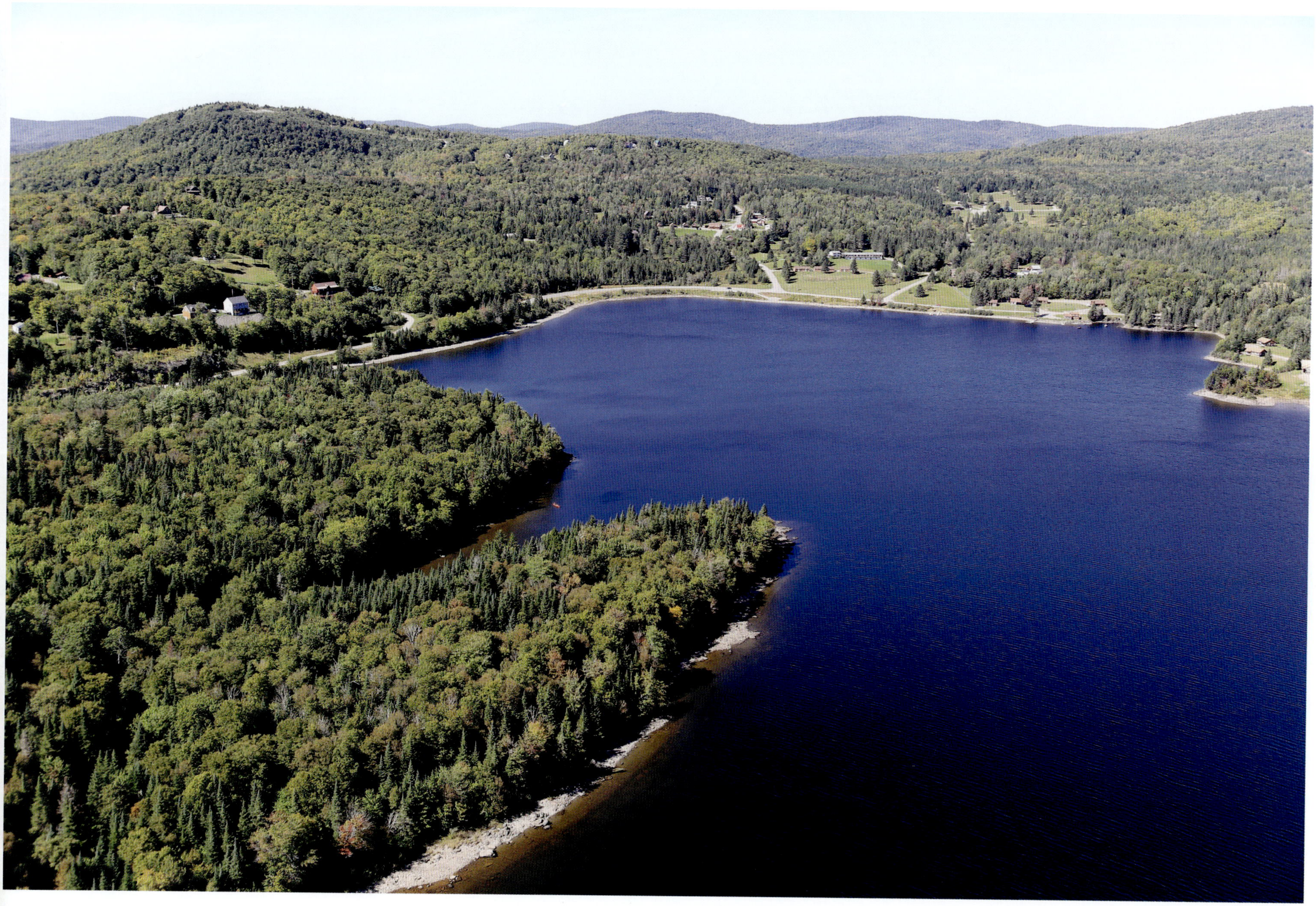

(left) Looking north over the First Connecticut Lake and the river's course flowing down from the Second Lake
(above) Cabins, lodges, and homes dot the northwestern shore of the First Connecticut.

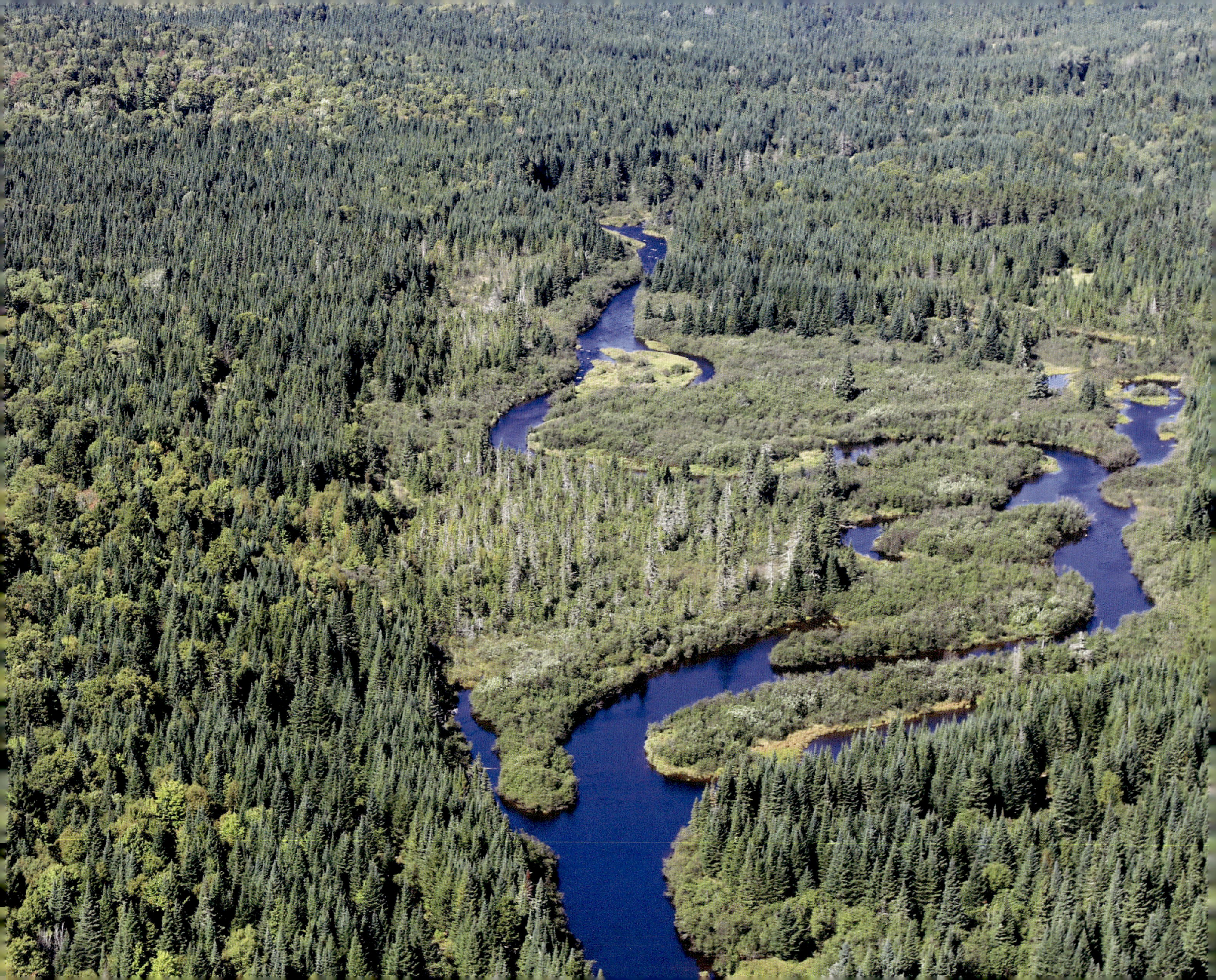

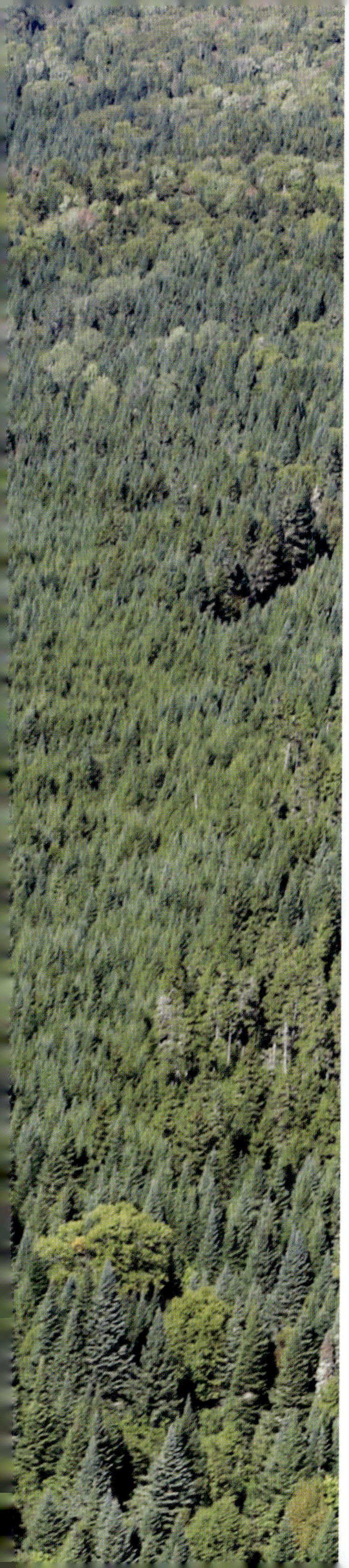

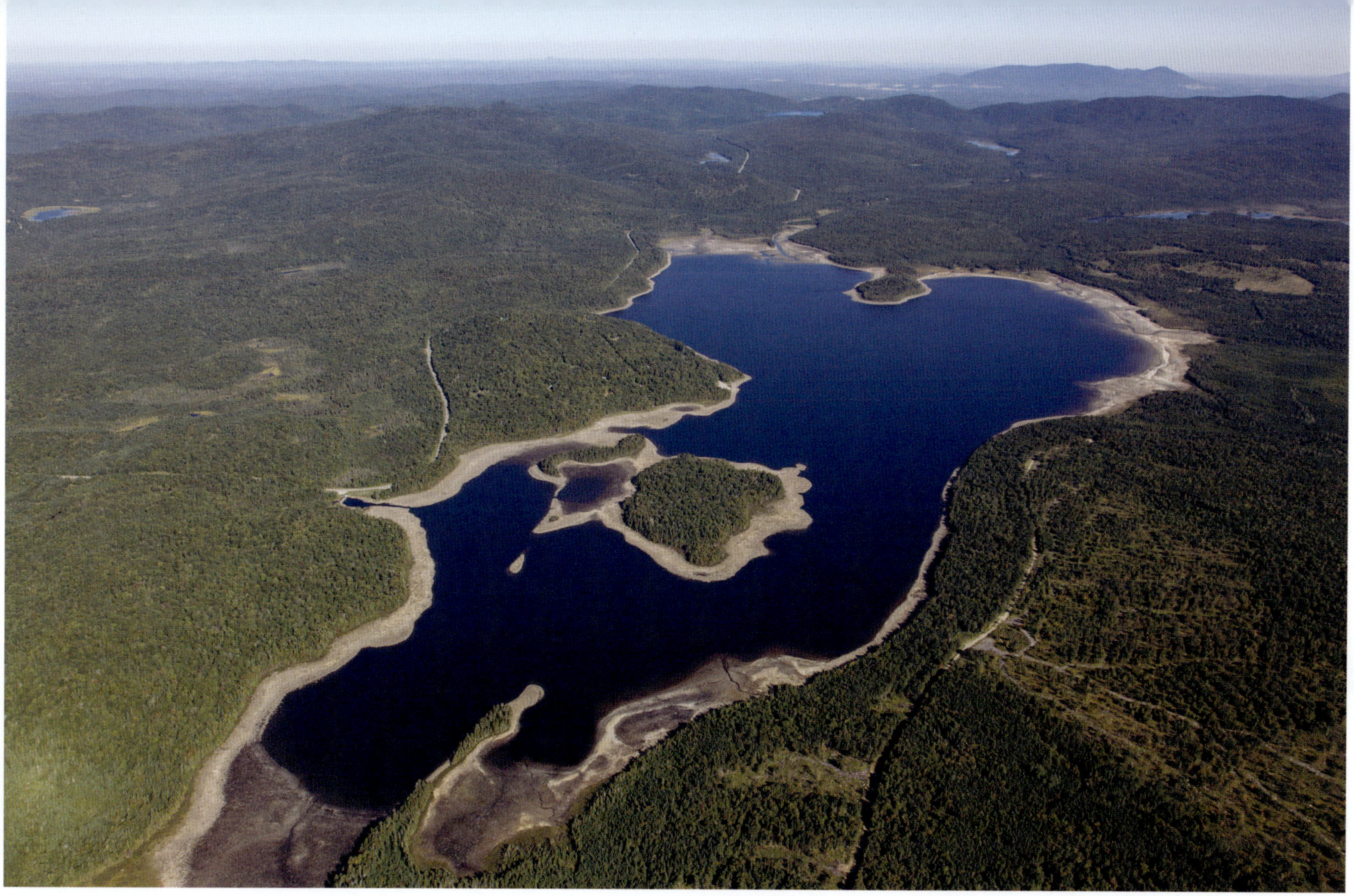

(left) Looking north, the river winds its way down through woodlands and wetlands from the Second Connecticut to the First Connecticut Lake. The river drops 200 feet between the two lakes!

(above) The Second Connecticut Lake with the mountains and valleys of Canada in the distance comprises about 1,200 acres at an elevation of 1,800 feet above sea level. It has a maximum depth of sixty feet and supports land-locked salmon and trout. From the small dam on the western side of the lake, the river makes its way down to the First Connecticut Lake. At the northern end of the Second Connecticut Lake the river enters from the Third Connecticut Lake, which lies four and three quarter miles to the north. Along this stretch of river, Moose Falls Dam creates a small pond and wetlands. This is, in fact, moose country.

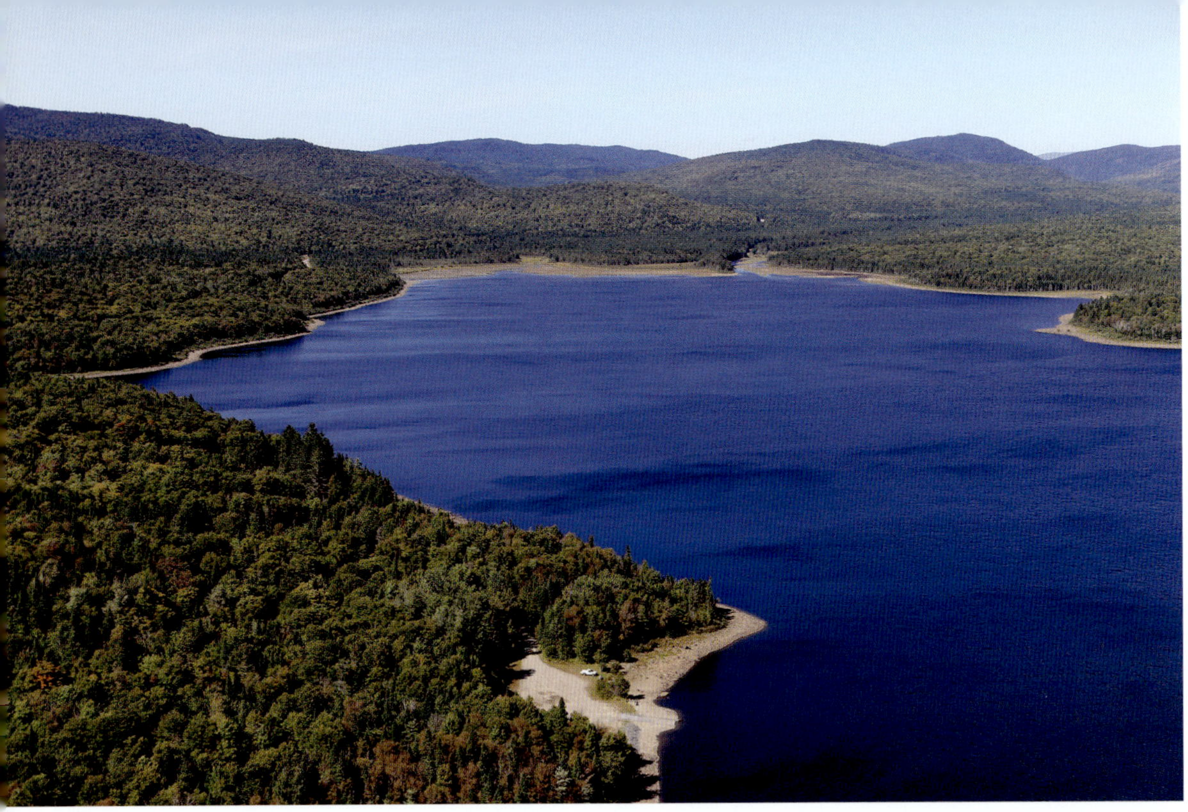

(left) Another view of the Second Connecticut Lake

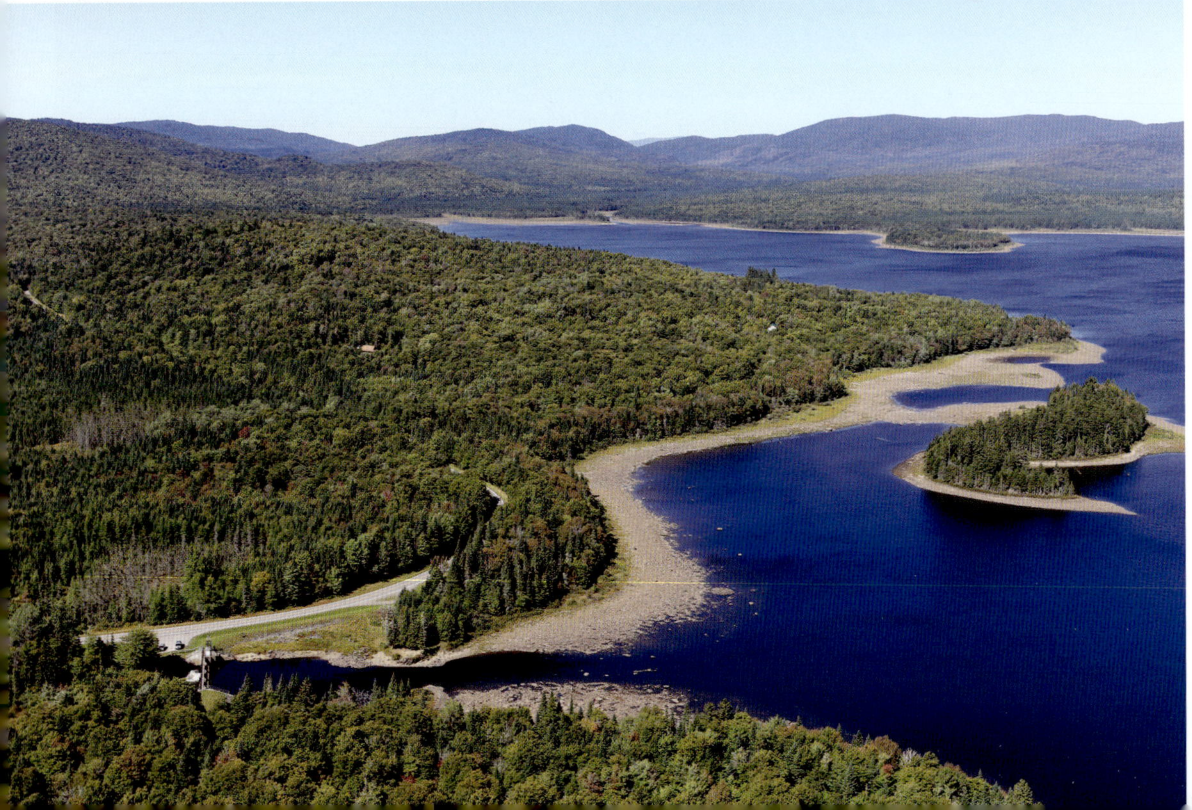

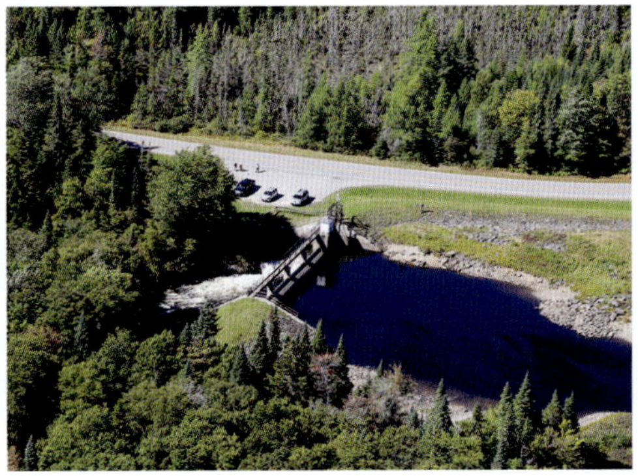

(left and above) The small dam in the western end of the Second Connecticut Lake from which the river begins its journey down to the First Connecticut Lake

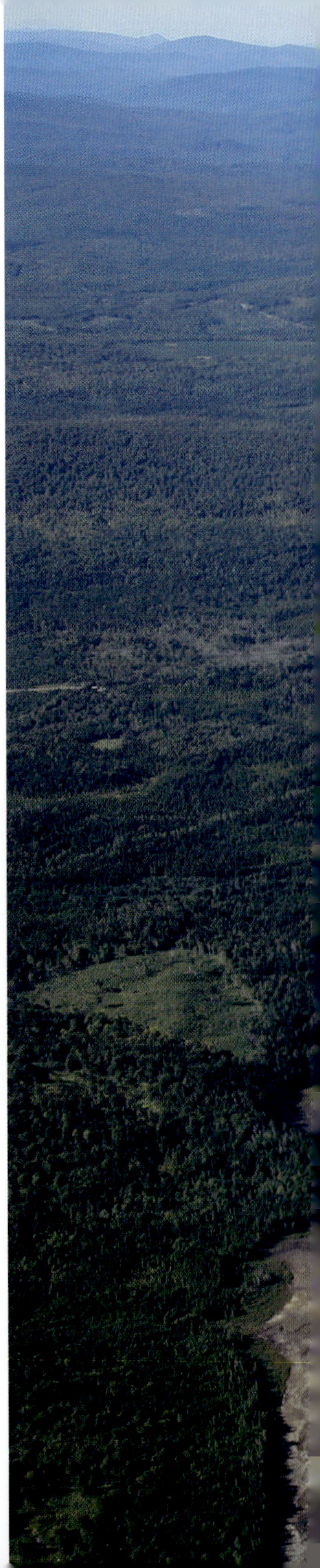

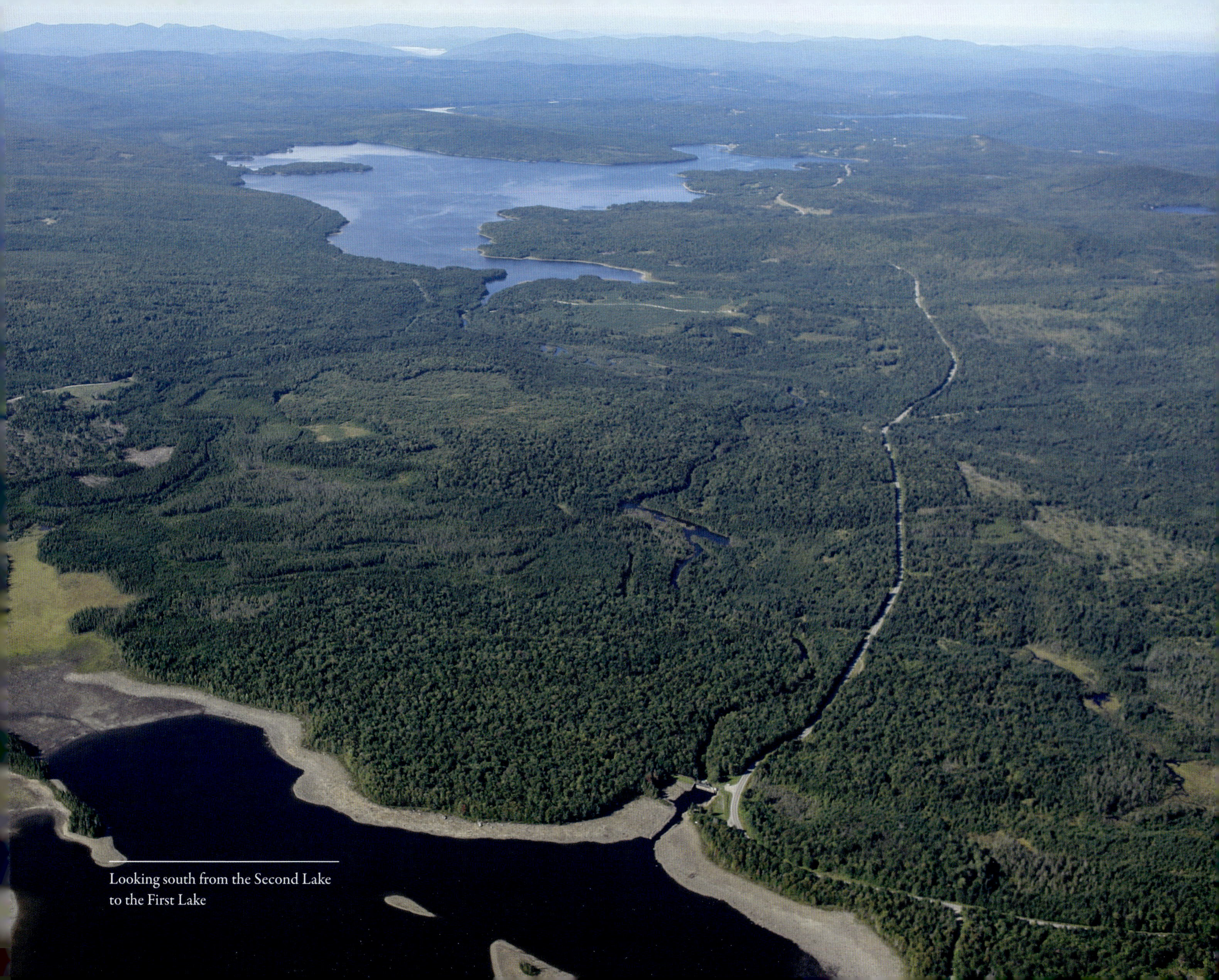

Looking south from the Second Lake to the First Lake

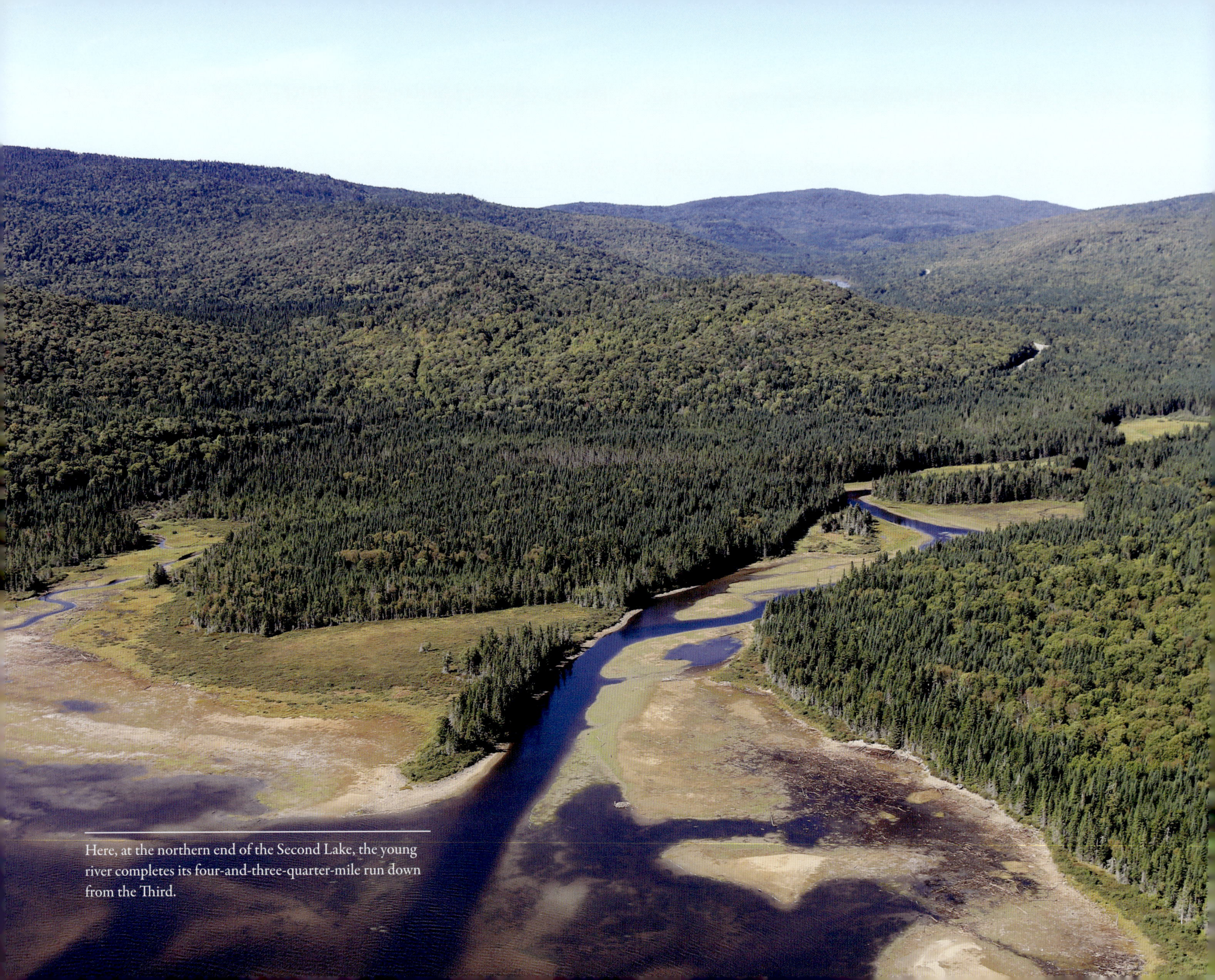

Here, at the northern end of the Second Lake, the young river completes its four-and-three-quarter-mile run down from the Third.

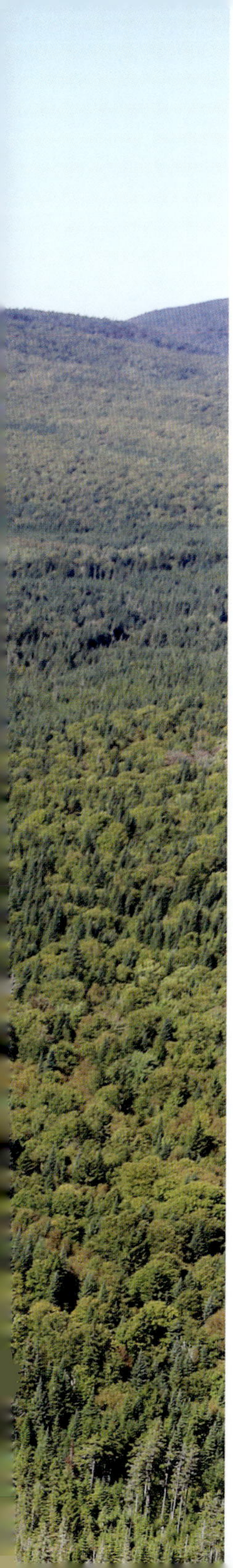

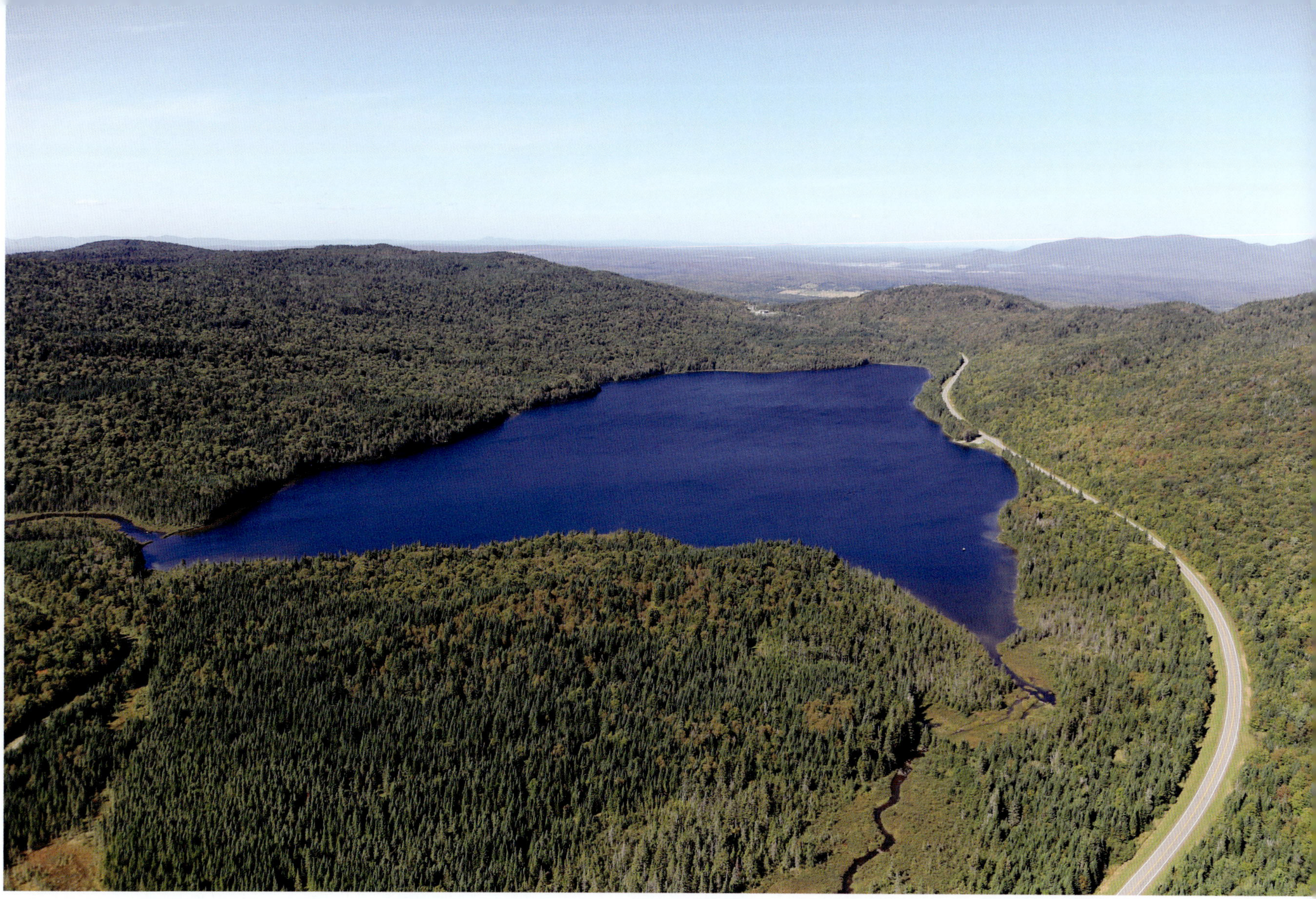

The Third Connecticut Lake is located one mile south of the United States and Canadian border. Our neighbor to the north can be seen here just over the ridge. The Third Connecticut sits at an elevation of 2,118 feet, covers 231 acres, and has a maximum depth of 110 feet with a forty-two-foot average. Surrounded by mountains, forests, and an uninhabited shore, this pristine body of water is home to rainbow, brook, and lake trout as well as landlocked salmon. The brook that will eventually become the Connecticut River can be seen here flowing down from the Third Lake alongside US 3. After crossing the border into Canada at the ridge, this local road becomes Provincial Highway 257 and leads to the town of Chartierville, Quebec, three miles to the north.

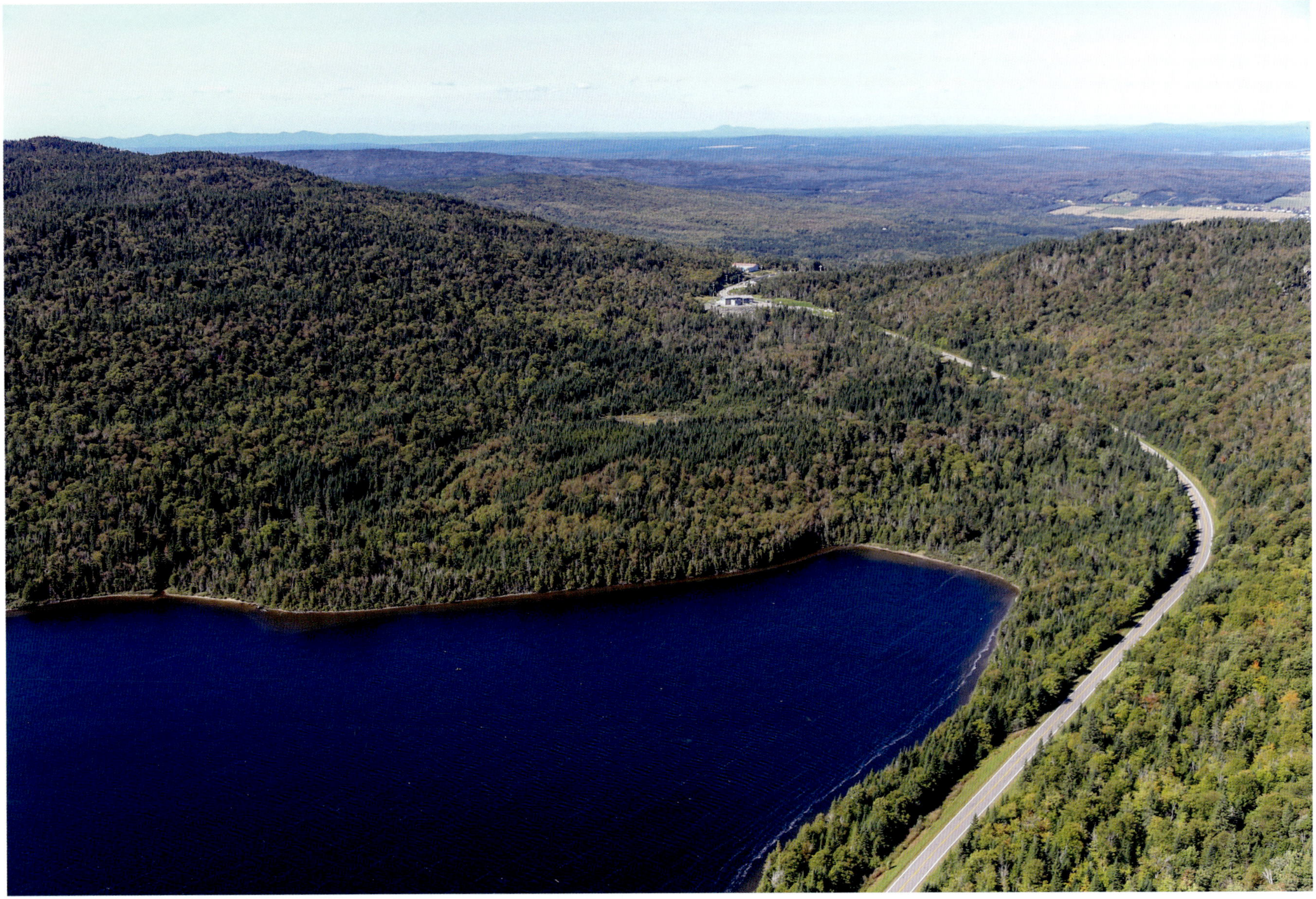

(above) We are almost there. The building on the ridge where US Route 3 crosses over into Canada is the U.S. Customs station. The Fourth Connecticut Lake, the source of the river, lies on the hillside to the left.

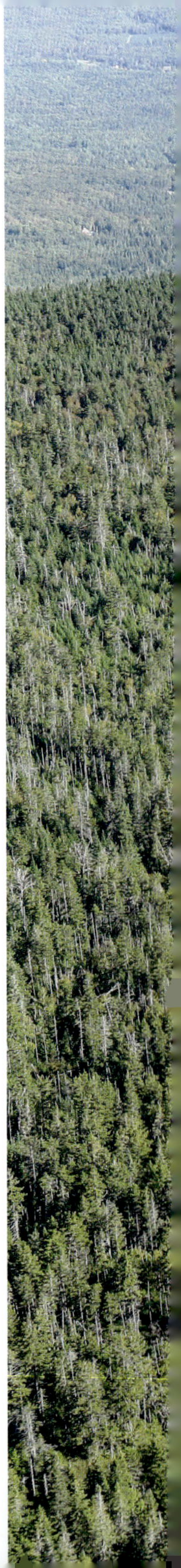

(right) Here, with Canada just over the ridge, the great river begins its 410-mile journey to the sea in a diminutive pond, optimistically named the Fourth Connecticut Lake.

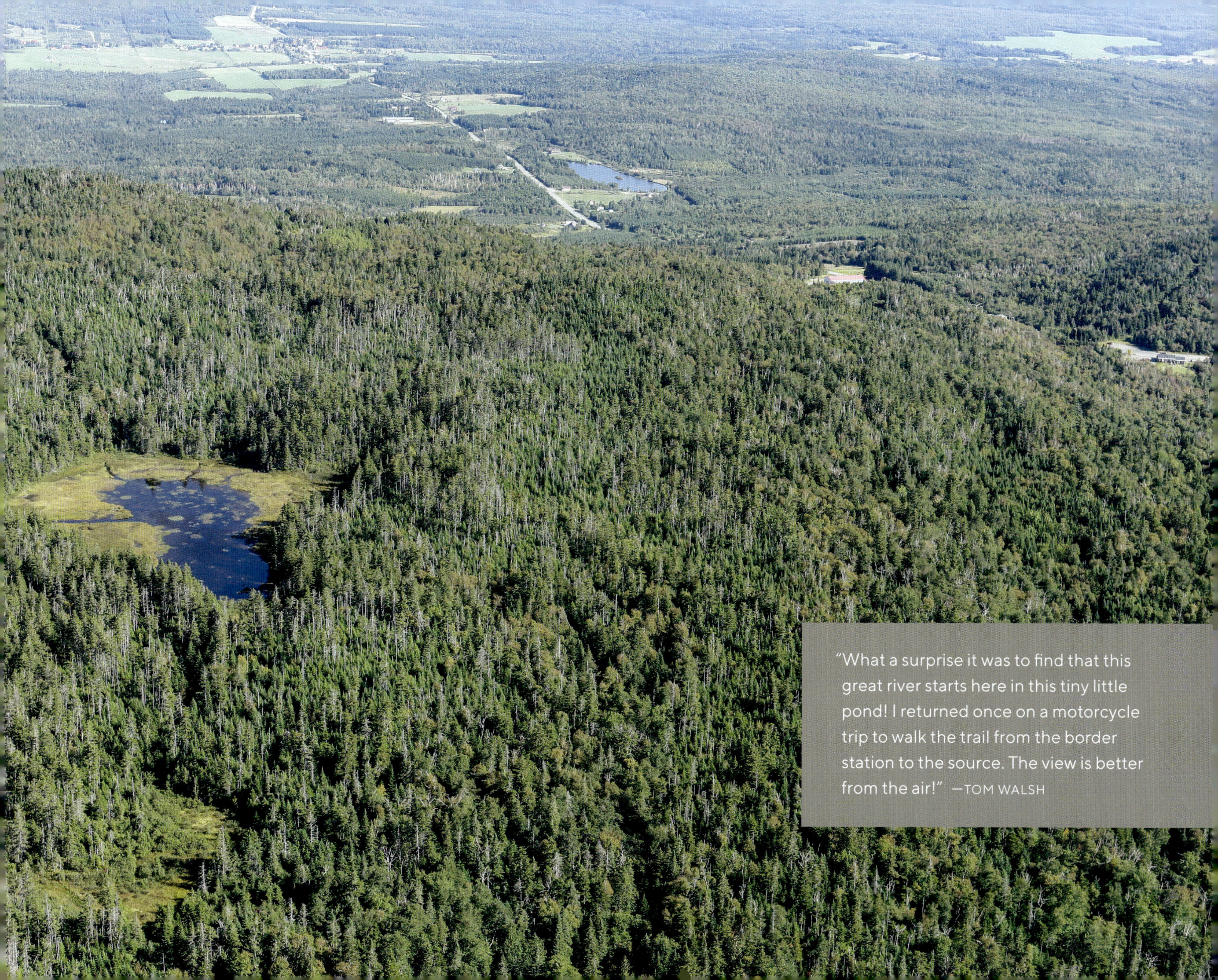

"What a surprise it was to find that this great river starts here in this tiny little pond! I returned once on a motorcycle trip to walk the trail from the border station to the source. The view is better from the air!" —TOM WALSH

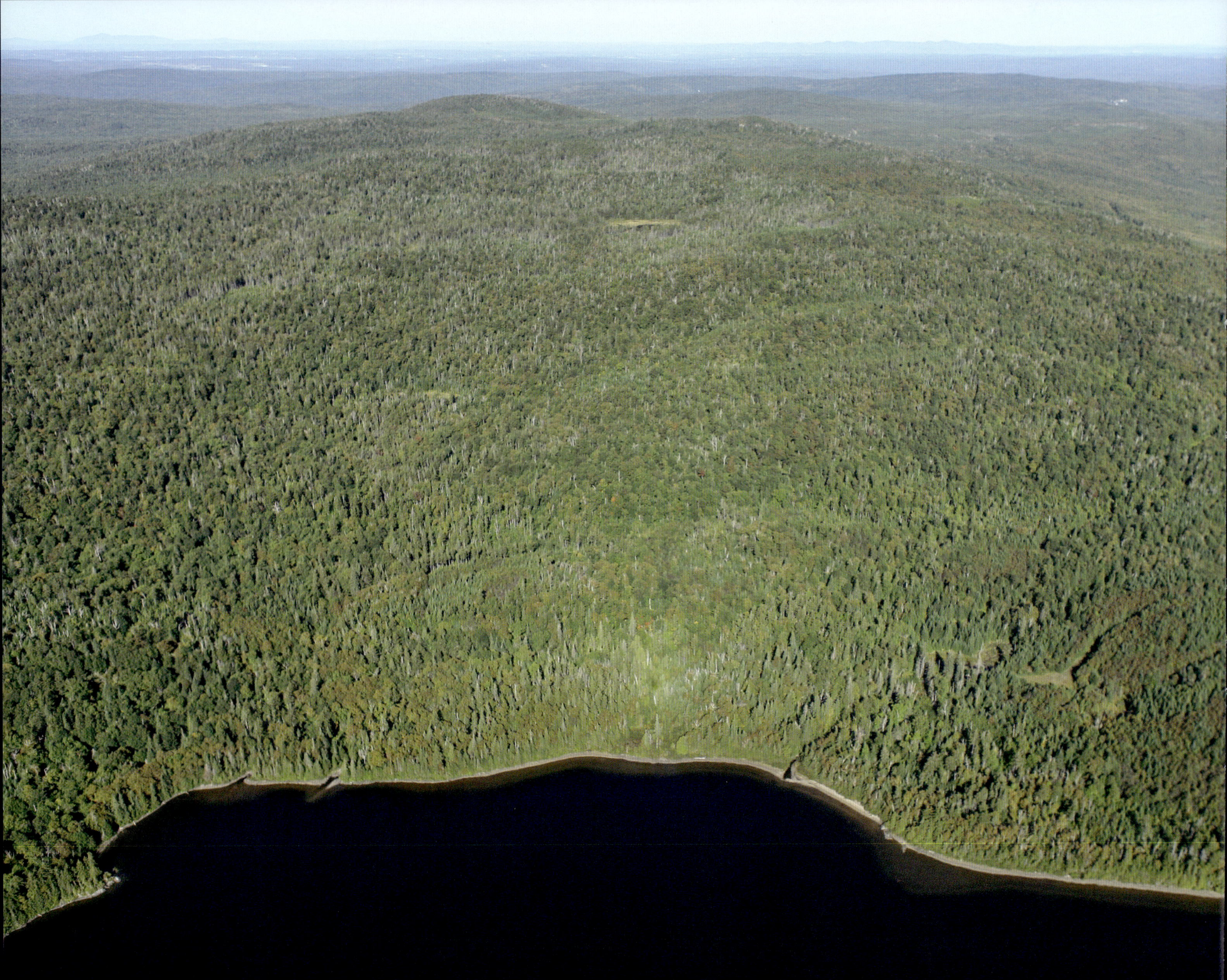

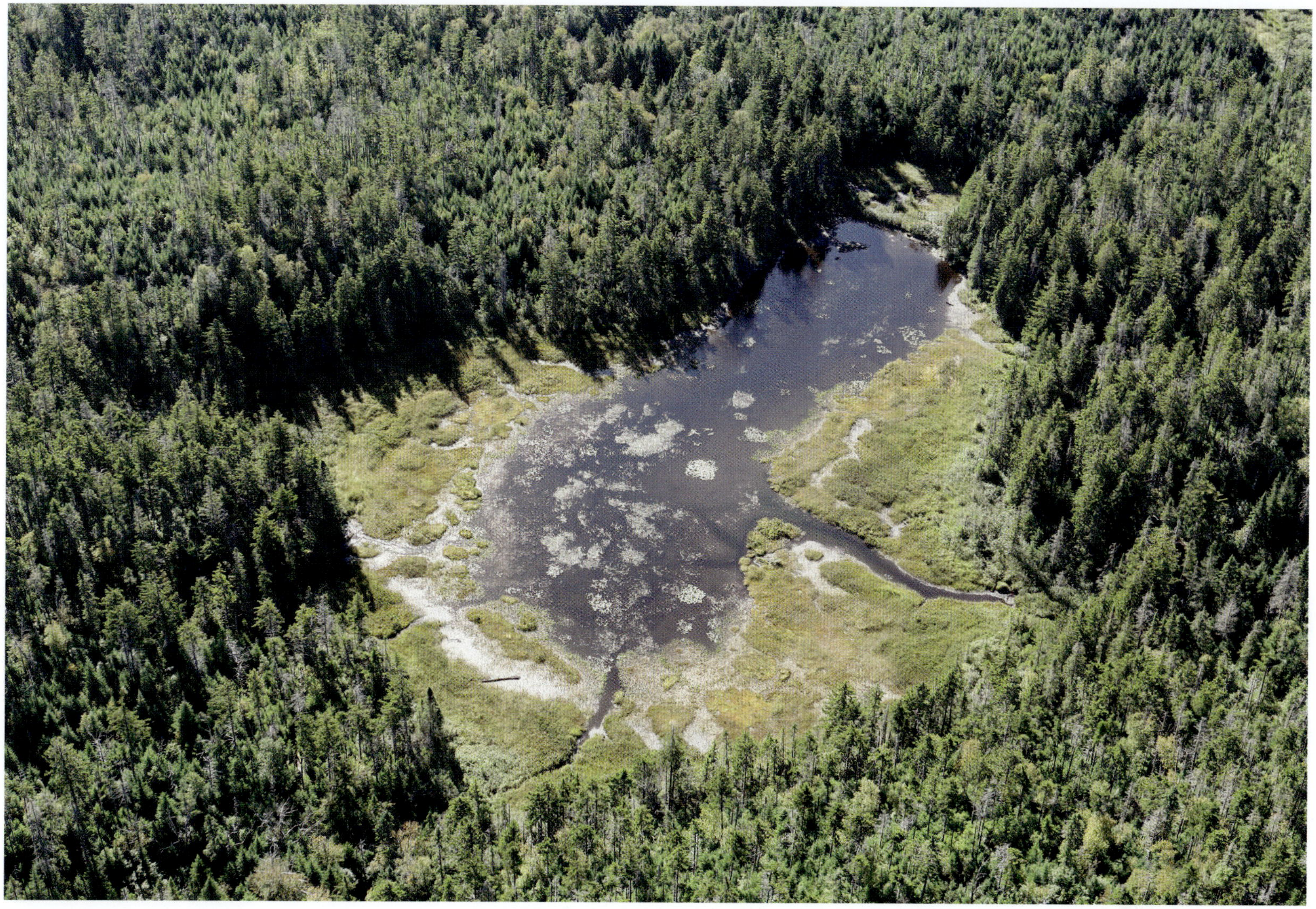

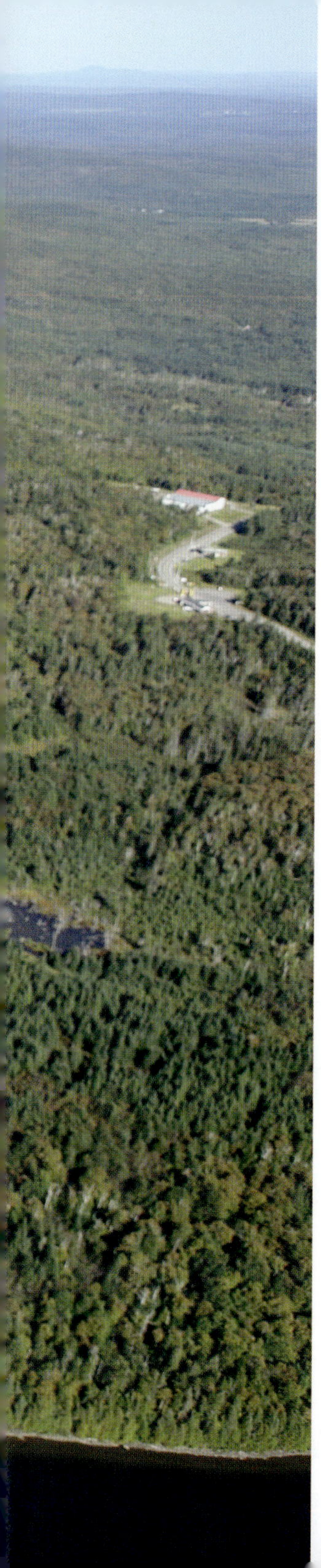

(above) Owned by the New Hampshire Nature Conservancy, the remote Fourth Connecticut Lake covers 78,400 square feet, is 528 feet long, and sits 2,760 feet above sea level. It features a floating bog and numerous insectivorous plants . . . that's right, insect-eating plants! For the ambitious trekker, the lake is accessible by 3,800 feet of trail starting at the U.S. Border Patrol station. Don't count on cell phone coverage. Welcome to the Source!

(left) The Fourth Lake sits on top of the hill in the center, with the boarder crossing station on the lower right, and Canada beyond.

ONE LAST LOOK

From the source of the Connecticut River looking back toward the Third Connecticut Lake and the river's long eventful journey to sea.

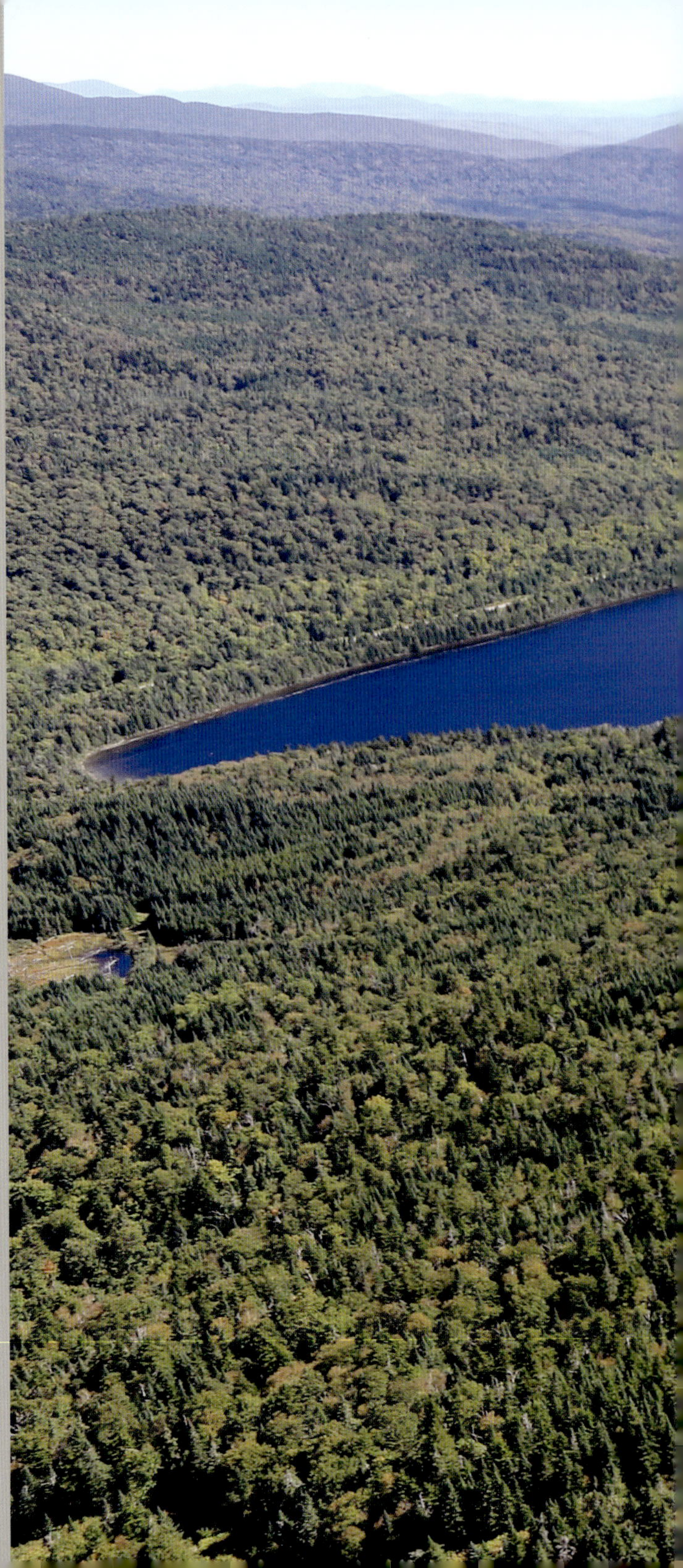

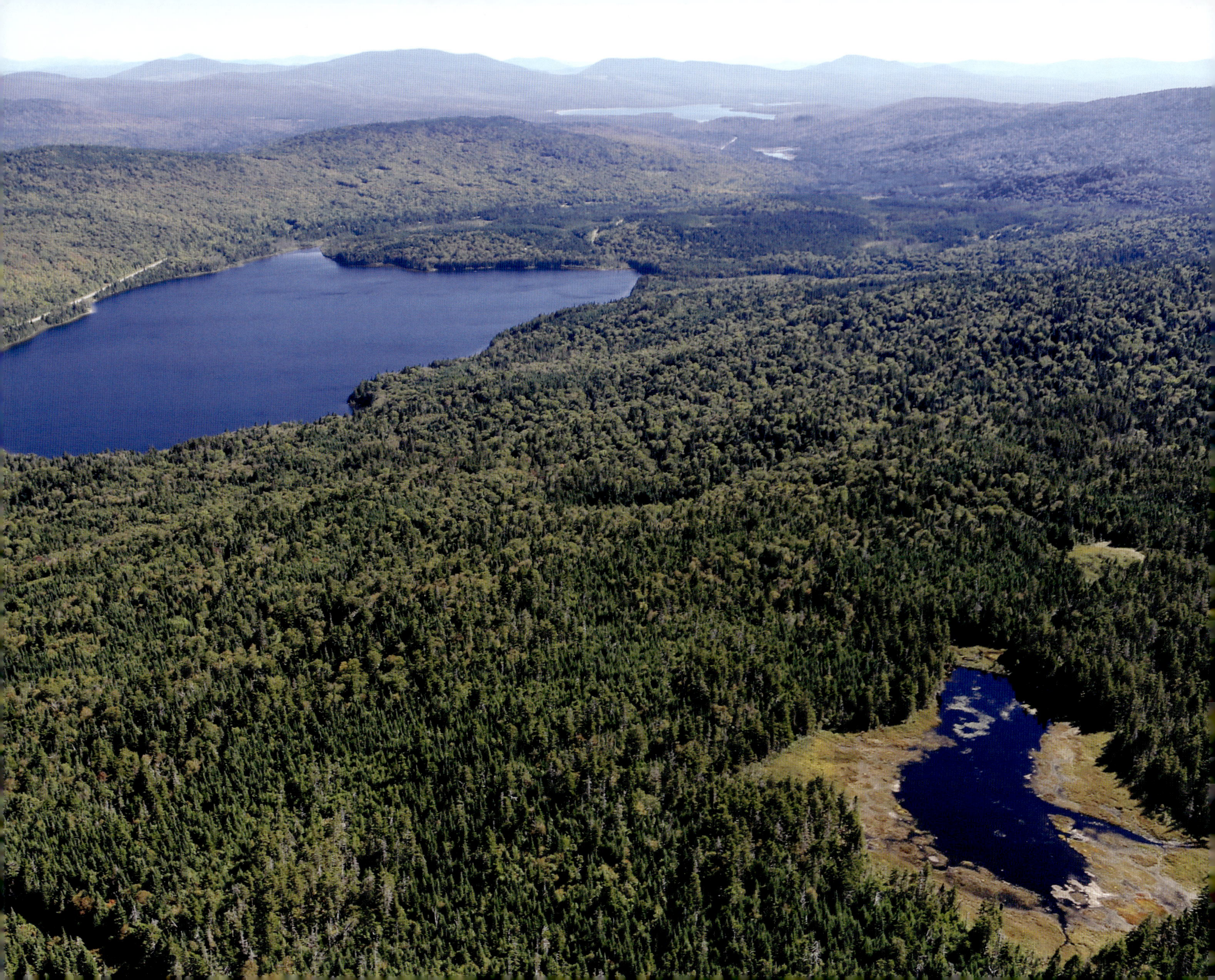

ACKNOWLEDGMENTS

Aside from Tom and his camera in the air and me and my computer, mostly on the ground, several other people have helped make this publication possible. We want to thank Bob VanKeirsbilck of Long Cat Graphics who created the maps for this book, as he has for many of my other projects. His tenacity in researching roads and geographic features helped put our words and images in perspective over the 410-mile course of the river. Amy Trout, curator at the Connecticut River Museum, was pivotal in helping Tom and I create the original exhibit there, and a lot of her research supported this book as well. She also graciously agreed to vet the text just to make sure the river is still on course, while the River Museum has supported our use of work we did for the original exhibit. Also indispensible to the original project was CRM volunteer, Warner Lord, who painstakingly used Google Earth to identify images from Tom's earlier flights that did not have embedded GPS locations. He then created descriptive notes on many of the images. This was a big help to me while writing this script. I followed his lead by personally finding the location of every single image we considered (about 600) on Google Earth. It was tedious work but extremely valuable in identifying nearby towns, roads and rivers, etc.

My wife Jeni not only labored with the unenviable task of pre-proofing the work of a dyslexic writer, but she did a lot of fact checking and discovered many off-the-beaten-path stories including my favorite, the Ledyard Bridge Challenge (find it on page 151). Former State Senator Con O'Leary, a trustee at the New England Air Museum also gave me some pretty interesting back-stories and leads to follow which added color and flavor to the project.

Three other invaluable resources were the books, *Thar She Goes, Shipbuilding on the Connecticut River* by former CT State Historian Ellsworth Grant, *The Connecticut River Boating Guide* published by the Connecticut River Watershed Counsel, and *The Connecticut River, a Photographic Journey* by Al Broden. I highly recommend these publications to anyone wanting to know more about the river, its resources and its history.

We want to thank Elizabeth Norman, managing editor of Connecticut Explored, and Connecticut State Historian Walter Woodward for generously helping to vet the text while adding some tidbits of their own here and there.

We, of course, want to thank Amy Lyons, and her team at Globe Pequot Press, for taking this project on. Her perseverance, prodding and patience, cheerleading and professionalism over the span of nearly two years are evident and well rewarded within these pages.

We also want to thank all of the local towns and historical societies whose websites I tapped into for specific information and statistics. Reading these, and cross referencing them with other information, is a great affirmation of how proud these communities, large and small, are, of their place in the grand story of the Connecticut River

Above all, I want to thank my partner Tom Walsh. His passion for sharing his lofty perspective, his generosity of spirit and friendship, have made this project an incredible journey for me, as I am sure it will for you. Tom, I look forward to many more shared adventures both in print and in the air!

—Jerry Roberts

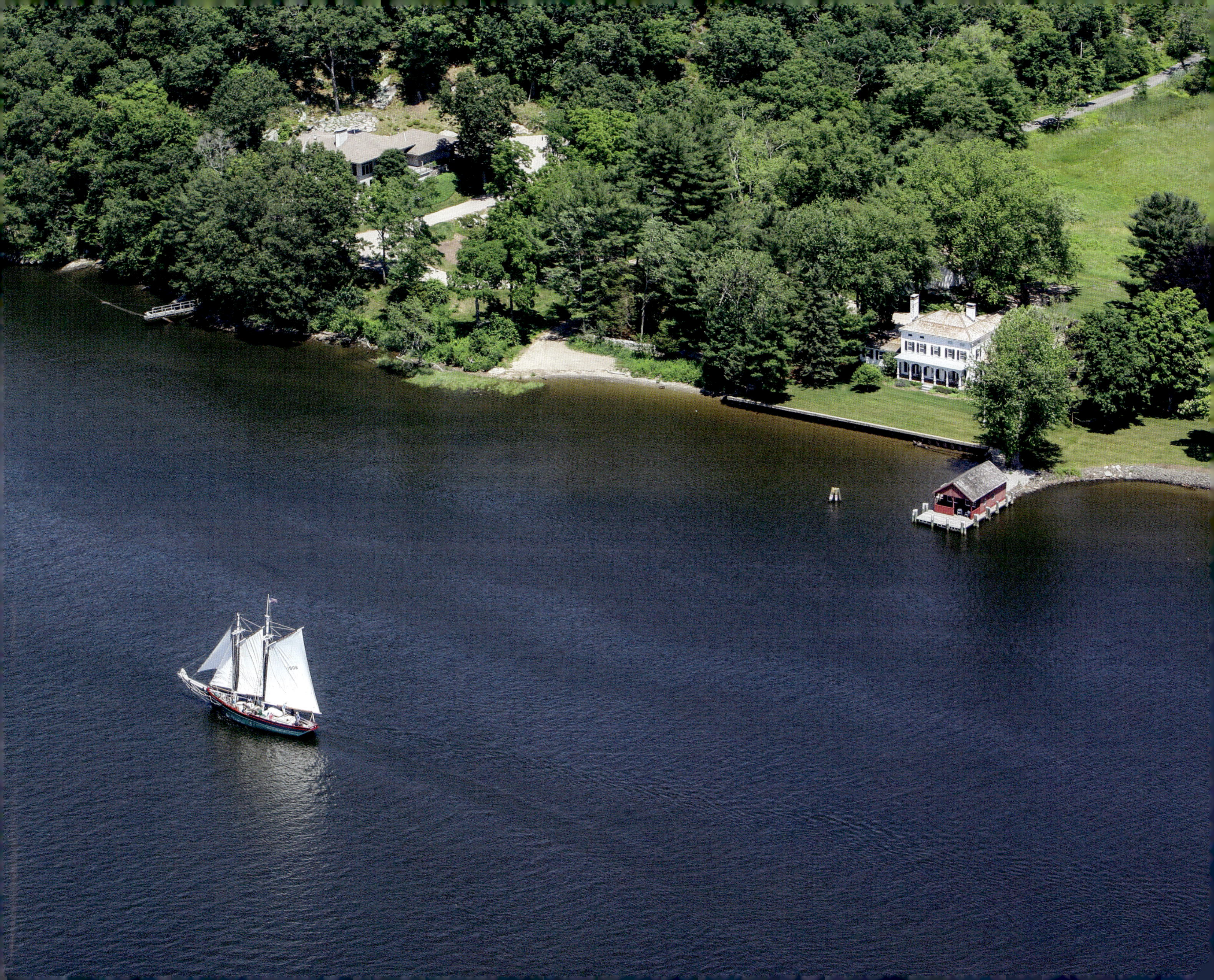

ABOUT THE AUTHOR & PHOTOGRAPHER

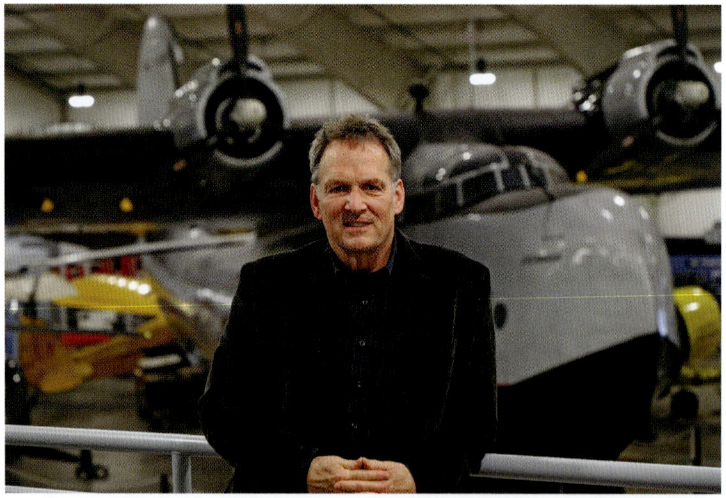

JERRY ROBERTS is a career historian, writer and museum professional. He is currently executive director of the New England Air Museum at Bradley International Airport in Windsor Locks, Connecticut. He and his family live on a hill overlooking the Connecticut River, across from Selden Island, about 400 miles downstream from its source.

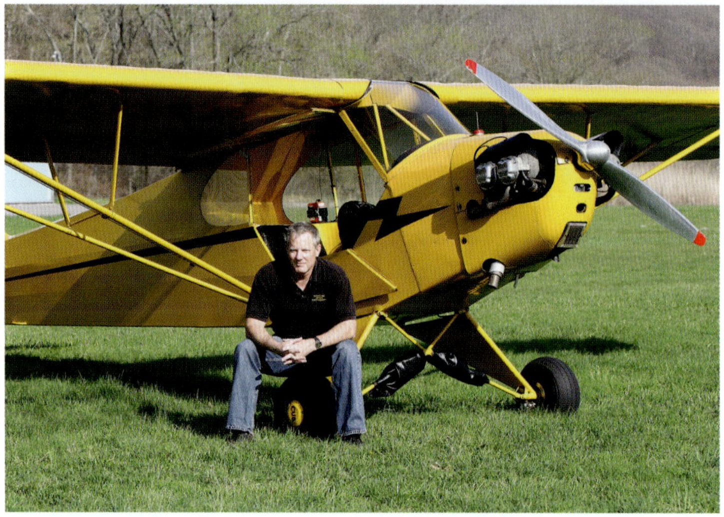

TOM WALSH is a former US Marine Corps fighter pilot who is now a senior international Captain for a major US airline. Through his company, Shoreline Aerial Photography, he has photographed thousands of sites all over the US. He and his wife raised their two children just a few miles from the Connecticut River. He now lives in both Connecticut and Florida.